Leone Levi

History of British Commerce and of the Economic Progress of the British Nation 1763-1870

Leone Levi

History of British Commerce and of the Economic Progress of the British Nation 1763-1870

ISBN/EAN: 9783742826596

Manufactured in Europe, USA, Canada, Australia, Japa

Cover: Foto ©ninafisch / pixelio.de

Manufactured and distributed by brebook publishing software (www.brebook.com)

Leone Levi

History of British Commerce and of the Economic Progress of the British Nation 1763-1870

HISTORY

OF

BRITISH COMMERCE

AND OF THE

ECONOMIC PROGRESS OF THE BRITISH NATION

1763–1870

BY LEONE LEVI, F.S.A., F.S.S

OF LINCOLN'S INN, BARRISTER-AT-LAW; PROFESSOR OF THE PRINCIPLES AND PRACTICE OF COMMERCE AND COMMERCIAL LAW IN KING'S COLLEGE, LONDON; DOCTOR OF POLITICAL ECONOMY IN THE UNIVERSITY OF TÜBINGEN; ETC.

LONDON

JOHN MURRAY, ALBEMARLE STREET

1872

TO THE

BARONESS BURDETT COUTTS.

MADAM,

Among those who first contributed to raise British Commerce to the position it has since acquired, was one whose name your Ladyship so worthily upholds.

Of representatives of old British Merchants and Bankers there are but few remaining; and I value the honour of dedicating this work to you, especially since your munificence has given to the acquisition of wealth a high moral import, and to British philanthropy increasing renown and lustre.

Your Ladyship's humble servant,

LEONE LEVI.

10 FARRARS BUILDING, TEMPLE:
February 1872.

PREFACE.

No history of British Commerce for the last one hundred years has as yet appeared, though the facts connected with it are replete with interest and instruction. The large quarto volumes of Macpherson and Anderson are chronological records of commercial transactions, rather than histories, and they end just when commerce began to expand into any real importance. Tooke's 'History of Prices,' valuable as it is, is intended mainly to illustrate the effects of the circulation on prices. And though every history of Great Britain gives so far a history of British commerce, the inventions and discoveries which have so largely promoted productive industry, the political and economic events which have aided or hindered commerce and navigation, free trade with its attendant blessings, those commercial and monetary crises which have so shaken public confidence, the introduction of railways, steam packets, and telegraphs, which have imparted fresh life to international intercourse, and the discovery of gold in California and Australia, have histories of their own, as well as a place in the history of Great Britain. Scarcely any of the reforms, moreover, which have completely altered the aspect of national industries, have been introduced without much misgiving and great opposition. In most cases, errors and prejudices had to be encountered, and many difficulties more or less formidable to be surmounted. A record of the arguments by which such victories have been gained, and of the work done by those noble champions of progress to whose labour, skill, and wisdom the nation is indebted, must prove for ever valuable.

Though dealing directly with British commerce, occasional glances are taken of the state of commerce in foreign countries, especially at the commencement and end of the period embraced by our history. Economic laws are not limited in their operation to time or place, nor are the conquests of science the exclusive property of any single state. We can advantageously, therefore, study the lessons of experience of this and other nations; and should the following pages ever meet the eye of foreign statesmen or finance ministers, they will see in them that Britain has attained her present elevated position, not by restricting and entangling trade and industry, not by thwarting the laws of nature, but by removing every barrier, and by opening every avenue to the legitimate exercise of personal energies. Nay more, they will see that, for the last fifty years, the principal efforts of the British Legislature have been directed to giving the greatest possible freedom to commerce, and to ensuring the greatest possible safety in mercantile transactions.

Ample are the materials at hand for a history of British commerce. The reports of parliamentary committees and royal commissions, always full and exhaustive; Hansard's 'Debates,' re-echoing the state of public opinion, at the commencement and end of every agitation; the works already quoted, and many more of a sectional character, yet of wide reach and solid value; the 'Economist,' rich in economic facts, and the reports of Secretaries of embassies and of British consuls in foreign ports—these and many other important works, to which I am greatly indebted, have furnished the threads which I have attempted to weave together.

A history of British commerce in so limited a compass can offer little more than the main outlines of a vast subject. The monograph of special trades could only be given here and there. The revolution which has taken place in the value of many commodities has been simply hinted at, and but little room was left for any pictorial representation of the wonders of British commerce among civilised and uncivilised states. Every effort has, however, been made to attain accuracy in data and soundness in the conclusions drawn. In most cases the authorities quoted are given, and these are generally the highest and most trustworthy extant. As an account of one of the most important interests in the empire, as a repertory of facts for the financier and economist, as a manual for the British trader all the world over, and as a class book for students of political and commercial economics, I trust the 'History of British Commerce' may prove of practical utility.

LEONE LEVI.

FARRAR'S BUILDING, TEMPLE:
January 1872.

CONTENTS.

PART I.

1763—1792.

FROM THE END OF THE SEVEN YEARS' WAR TO THE FRENCH REVOLUTION.

PART II.

1792—1820.

FROM THE FRENCH REVOLUTION TO THE RESUMPTION OF CASH PAYMENTS.

PART III.

1820—1842.

FROM MR. HUSKISSON'S GOVERNMENT REFORMS TO SIR ROBERT PEEL'S ADMINISTRATION.

PART IV.

1842—1857.

FROM SIR ROBERT PEEL'S ADMINISTRATION TO THE COMMERCIAL CRISIS OF 1857.

PART V.

1860—1870.

FROM THE CONCLUSION OF THE TREATY OF COMMERCE WITH FRANCE TO THE STATE OF COMMERCE IN 1870.

APPENDIX.

PART I.

1763–1792.

FROM THE END OF THE SEVEN YEARS' WAR

TO THE

FRENCH REVOLUTION.

SUMMARY.

1763–1792.

From the end of the Seven Years' War to the French Revolution we have thirty years, which may be designated the seed-time of British commercial prosperity. During this period the commerce of the country remained within a very limited compass, and productive industry was only establishing the basis for its future development; yet it is to the manner in which the ground was prepared, and to the richness and fruitfulness of the seed itself, that we must ascribe many of the subsequent triumphs of British enterprise, and, above all, the power to resist and overcome the discouraging influences of revolution and war. One grave error was committed. It was the persistence in—or rather the extension of—the mercantile system, with all its restrictions and prohibitions, which fettered trade and took it out of its natural course. But Adam Smith arose, and with him came a more certain and safer guidance to the real sources of the Wealth of Nations.

HISTORY

OF

BRITISH COMMERCE.

CHAPTER I.

THE FOUNDATIONS OF BRITISH PRODUCTIVE INDUSTRY.

1763–1776.

The War and its Results.—State of England.—The Cotton Machinery.—Opposition to Machinery.—State of the Woollen Manufacture.—The Silk Manufacture and French Competition.—The Linen Industry.—Iron and Coal.—The Earthenware Industry.—The Steam Engine.—Progress of Chemical Science.—The Society of Arts, and Royal Academy.—Foundation of the Royal Exchange and Gresham College.

ABOUT one hundred years ago, England concluded another of those wars which she waged so frequently, in days now happily gone by, and which, too often, left behind only mingled feelings of gratification and disappointment. Glory, 'the fair child of peril,' is but a phantom which vanishes at the touch; 'like glowworms, afar off shine bright, but, looked too near, have neither heat nor light.' Miserable is that nation which is deceived by its attractions. British influence and power seemed, indeed, safely established over the whole of North America; France was dislodged from Canada, Spain was shorn of her best colonies. The British colonists were masters of their position. But, however great its achievements, however dazzling its exploits, whatever lustre it may throw on national arms, war always imposes burdens and sacrifices which curb the industries of a nation, and destroy the very vitals of a state. And we need not be surprised if, with increasing taxes and an accumulating debt,[1] one is apt speedily to forget the joys

The war and its results.

[1] The cost of the Seven Years' War, 1756–1763, to the United Kingdom is estimated at 82,623,738*l.* The public debt of Great Britain and Ireland, which in

of victory or the gains of conquest. Nor were the economical results of the war promising or satisfactory. A boundless field was, certainly, open for purposes of colonisation and investment. The vast prairies of America offered scope enough for the surplus energies and active forces of a country whose boundaries nature had permanently fixed, and whose resources were but imperfectly known or developed; and many there were ready to neglect their possessions at home for a portion of wilderness beyond the Atlantic. But England was not overcrowded with people;[2] she had not much capital to spare for investment in regions so distant; and, whatever might be the prospect of future and permanent advantage, it was more than counterbalanced by the difficulty and expense of defending the extensive territories now added to the Empire.[3]

State of England.

Though, politically, England had by this time, and especially after the success of the Seven Years' War, become a first power in Europe, economically she had as yet acquired no absolute supremacy. Her industries had accomplished none of their prodigies. Manchester was not glorying in her tall and ever-smoking chimneys. An inland town of no pretensions for beauty, and at some distance from the sea, she consumed but small quantities of cotton to work into fustians, vermilions, and dimities. To London her manufacturers went for the raw material from Cyprus and Smyrna, and thither they returned their goods for exportation. Liverpool[4] had scarcely any of her glorious docks; the stately barks from America had not yet found their way to her harbour. She had but an insignificant

1756 was 74,575,025*l*., rose in 1763 to 132,716,049*l*. See Return of Net Public Income and Expenditure from 1688 to 1869 (House of Commons Paper, 366 of 1869, Part II. pp. 708, 802.

[2] In 1750, as computed from the registers of baptisms, burials, and marriages, the population of England was stated as 6,517,000. In 1763 the population would probably have reached 7 000,000.—Preface to Census Enumeration, Abstract, for 1841.

[3] The acquisitions included Canada West, Dominica, Grenada, St. Vincent, and Tobago.

[4] In 1773 the population of Liverpool was ascertained to be 34,000. She possessed only three floating docks, a tolerably-sized basin, and three graving docks. The gross receipt of customs in 1775 was 274,000*l*.; and in 1775 eighty-one ships of 9,200 tons were cleared from Liverpool for the African or Slave Trade. In 1775 there was only one letter-carrier for all Liverpool, and the mail-bags were carried in and out of the town on horseback.

trade, and a large portion of it consisted in the wretched traffic of slaves from Africa to the West Indies. Alas! that it was so profitable a trade. Leeds and Bradford were not very conspicuous; and even London, the only place of real importance in the kingdom, which then monopolised almost the whole of the foreign trade of the country,[3] had not a tithe of the shipping and commerce which now enrich the banks of the Thames. In size she was little more than what was left by the Romans—'the city within the walls.' Her population was probably half a million only. There was then but one bridge connecting London and Southwark. The Bank of England was but a small building flanked by a church. The Royal Exchange was one rebuilt after the destruction of that built by Sir Thomas Gresham, which was again destroyed by fire in 1838. Lloyd's was still a coffee-house at the corner of Abchurch Lane. There was no Stock Exchange, and not a single dock. The port was blocked up by a fleet of merchantmen, and the quays heaped with bales, boxes, bags, and barrels in the greatest possible confusion. Scarcely one, indeed, of the great institutions and buildings which constitute modern London was in existence one hundred years ago. What England possessed then, as she does now, was a geographical situation the most favourable for purposes of maritime commerce, in close proximity to the continent of Europe, and bordering on the ocean, the great open highway to America; mineral riches of enormous value; and, above all, a people of sturdy race, the Anglo-Saxon, distinguished for innate sentiment of independence and right, energy of character and aptitude for work, capacity for material conquests, and courage and tact as colonisers and discoverers. With advantages such as these, how can we wonder that England succeeded in overcoming all difficulties; and that, with a rapidity almost unexampled in history, she acquired for herself a position of the highest eminence in commerce and navigation?

[3] London was early a large emporium of trade. William Fitz-Stephens, giving an account of it in the time of Henry II., said:—

> Arabia's gold, Sabæa' spice and incense;
> Scythia's keen weapons, and the oil of palm
> From Babylon's deep soil; Nile's precious gems,
> China's bright shining silks, and Gallic wines,
> Norway's warm peltry, and the Russian sables,
> All here abound.

Of all British industries, the cotton[6] had hitherto probably been the least conspicuous. Suddenly, however, a change, wonderful in its character and effects, was accomplished in it, the result of the big thoughts and extraordinary ingenuity of a few mechanicians, the far-famed Lewis Paul, Lawrence Earnshaw, Hargreaves, Arkwright, and Crompton. How much each of these individually contributed towards the full development of the cotton machinery it would be difficult to say. 'The law of continuity, or rather of gradual progress,' said Lord Brougham, 'governs all human approaches towards perfection. The limited nature of man's faculties precludes the possibility of his ever reaching at once the utmost excellence of which they are capable. Survey the whole circle of the sciences, and trace the history of our progress in each, you will find this to be the universal rule.'[7] Think not that Black and Priestley, Bacon and Adam Smith, Cuvier and Watt, were respectively the unaided discoverers of the theory of latent heat and aeriform fluids, of the inductive system and economic science, of fossil osteology and the power of steam. Even Newton, though far in advance

The cotton machinery.

[6] Cotton is certainly not a new article. All warm climates within a limited zone, especially countries in the vicinities of the sea, and with a soil dry and sandy, produce cotton. From time immemorial cotton has been grown in Hindustan, China, Persia, Egypt, Candia, and Sicily, and, when South America was discovered, the natives were found growing cotton. The Patagonians bound their hair with cotton threads, and in Mexico the people wore cotton clothing of remarkable beauty. Yet, as it has been well said, cotton could only become an article of trade to those countries which were able by their industries to manufacture it into a beautiful and durable material at moderate prices. In ancient times, probably as early as the eighth century, India furnished Europe with her muslin, so called from Musul in Mesopotamia. The Assyrians brought cotton manufactures into Europe, together with their silks from China, their carpets from India, and their spices from the East. But, with all this, up to and during the Middle Ages, cotton never seemed to have constituted the ordinary clothing of the people. In England the consumption of cotton was confined to very small quantities, principally used for candle-wicks, and nearly the whole of the cotton imported came from the Continent. Though as far back as 1328 the Flemings, settling in Manchester, laid the basis of the British woollen manufacture in what was called 'Manchester Cotton,' it was not till the middle of the seventeenth century that cotton, wool, fustians, dimities, and other articles began to be exported from this country to the Continent. As late as the accession of George III. no fabric consisting entirely of cotton was made, and it was only by the operation of those wonderful inventions which suddenly performed so great a revolution, that cotton acquired the present prominent position.

[7] Brougham's address on the opening of the Newton Monument at Grantham, 1847.

of all others in mathematical and experimental science, was preceded by Cavalleri, Roberval, Fermat, and Shooten, who came as near as possible to the discovery of the differential calculus. But be it as it may, whatever be the share respectively taken by the great builders of the cotton manufacture, it is to the inventors of the spinning-jenny and the carding-machine, to the makers of the water-frame and the mule, that we are indebted for the fact that cotton-spinning ceased to be a domestic manufacture, and became almost entirely the product of machinery. To them it *is* that we owe the factory system with its attendant advantages—economy of power, division of labour, and concentration of skill and superintendence; and to them, too, we are beholden for that extraordinary change in the fortunes of Lancashire, which, as by magic, thenceforth threw aside her agricultural garb and almost pastoral simplicity to assume the more active and stirring occupations of industry and manufactures.

Opposition to machines.

The principal actors in this great revolution were humble operatives, working alone without status or patronage, scarcely conscious themselves of the value of a work which would place their names in the very forefront of the industrial progress of Britain. Alas! that they should have been so ill-requited for the magnificent boon they were conferring on the nation and on the world. But it has always been so with the pioneers of progress, the glorious martyrs of science. As soon as it became known that a machine was invented which would work more expeditiously, and produce goods more economically, than any human hands could ever achieve, extreme jealousy was excited among the workers against such an innovation. The house of Kay was entered into, and every machine it contained was knocked to pieces. The Blackburn spinners and weavers were not content till they destroyed the Jenny and all its belongings, and drove Hargreaves himself from his home. Arkwright was compelled to resort to all manner of stratagems to evade pursuit. And poor Crompton, more than once, was compelled to take his mule to pieces, and hide its various parts in a garret. But should we be surprised at the inability of working-men one hundred years ago to apprehend the value of machinery, when so many of much higher grade in society are utterly ignorant on the subject this very day? It all arises, however, from want of thought. The weavers of the last century, and those who obstruct the introduction of machinery at the present time, do not fully realise, that whatever superiority we possess over other animals, arises precisely from this, that we are able to economise human labour by the use of mechanical contrivances. We could not live without using tools or implements of some sort; for, after all, we have fewer natural means of appropriating to our own wants objects which nature offers to us than other animals possess. Thankful we should be if, by artificial helps quite as powerful as any animal power, we can grind our corn by water, wind, or steam; we can carry our loads not by hands, but by carts and waggons, by horse-power or railway. And who can see those stupendous pieces of mechanism which are used in the spinning of yarn or the weaving of lace, without being astonished at their extreme beauty and nicety of contrivance? Little, indeed, did the Blackburn spinners think, when they were enraged at the appearance of such inventions, that instead of curtailing employment, machinery would multiply it a thousandfold, and that, instead of reducing the amount of wages, it would produce so great an improvement in the economic condition of the labouring classes.

Unfortunately for other industries, their progress was hindered by prejudices or fettered by legislative restrictions.

State of the woollen manufacture.

The woollen was an old English industry, though greatly advanced by the Flemish, when they took refuge in this country in the fourteenth century. Long had Norwich been known for her baize, Sudbury for her serges, Colchester for her broad-cloth, Gloucester for her cloth, and Kendal for her coarse cloth. Even London and York continued for a considerable time to be important centres of the woollen industry. But the increasing prices of provisions, high rates of wages, difficulty of obtaining commodious streams for the scouring and fulling of cloth, and the restrictions imposed by the municipalities, drove the woollen manufacture away to the villages and townships of Yorkshire. And there it remained in a dull and unsatisfactory condition, the manufacturers always dreading the contact of French competition, yet utterly unable to overcome it. They knew that the success of the French was mainly owing to their ability to use a mixture of native and foreign wool, and to their better method of spinning; but instead of striving to acquire these advantages for themselves, they unfortunately neglected every means of improvement, and took an unworthy refuge in protection and restriction. And well, indeed, they might dread the danger of competition. From the time of Elizabeth scarcely any alteration or improvement had been made in the processes of manufacture, either of woollen or worsted, beyond the variation of colour or pattern to suit the fashion of the day. It was only when the mechanical inventions applied to the spinning and carding of cotton were found applicable, with some modifications, to the woollen and worsted manufactures, that these began to undergo a complete transformation.

Nor was it any better with the silk manufacture. There, too, French competition was a constant source of anxiety, and the weavers lost no opportunity of protesting against such interference. In 1763 the discontent assumed a serious aspect, and the journeymen gave themselves to riot and demonstrations. At Spitalfields they destroyed the looms, cut large quantities of rich silk, and carried about the effigies of their masters to hurl upon them their wrath and vengeance. At Dublin, the silk weavers expressed their sense of the importation of a quantity of French silk by assembling in great numbers, and destroying the mercers' looms. But, really, it was not easy for the Government to decide what was wanted. Whilst the weavers prayed for an immediate remedy for their distress, by the imposition of further and more effectual restrictions, the silk throwsters were as convinced that the quantity of raw silk on hand was not sufficient to answer the demand of the trade; and the mercers affirmed that, in truth, there was no want of employment, but that there was not a sufficient number of skilful and intelligent men to execute the work. For the moment the legislature succeeded in evading the question, but two years after, in 1765, another demonstration having been organised by the journeymen silk weavers, and a large procession having marched with drum and

The silk manufacture and French competition.

colours to Parliament, followed by their wives and children, Parliament had to yield to absolute force, and passed two acts, one[8] reducing the duties on the raw material, and another[9] prohibiting the importation of foreign silk. It was deemed a great concession to allow Italian organzine to come in for warp, but the importation was allowed on condition that it be entered only at the London Custom House. How unfortunate was it that the legislature was not sufficiently enlightened on the bearing of commercial legislation. By it both manufacturers and labourers were encouraged to make demands which were utterly irreconcilable with economic laws. Witness the act passed in 1773 to secure the weavers against the supposed extortions of their masters, by empowering the magistrates of the city of London to settle the wages of journeymen silk weavers.[10] Witness the renewal, year after year, of the prohibition of foreign manufactures, and the laws passed against combinations amongst workmen. How could manufactures prosper with a legislation so restrictive and meddling?

England seems never to have looked with favour on the linen industry. The English Linen Company was established in 1764, but its operations were exceedingly small. No better evidence, indeed, could be afforded of the weak and almost exotic character of the linen manufacture than the fact that, whilst the exports were forced by a bounty of three-halfpence per yard offered on all linen exported, petitions were constantly coming in from different parts of the country, some asking for additional duties on foreign linen, and some for a reduction of the same, the exclusionists, however, always gaining their point. Ireland and Scotland were important centres for the linen manufacture, and from this period date their Linen Halls and British Linen Company.[11]

The linen industry.

In the iron industry not much progress had yet been made. Some time had elapsed since Lord Dudley substituted coal for charcoal in smelting, though, owing to the want of adaptation of the furnaces, the Coalbrook Dale Iron-works were really the first that employed it with any success.

Iron and coal.

[8] 5 Geo. III. c. 29. [9] 5 Geo. III. c. 48. [10] 13 Geo. III. c. 68.

[11] The British Linen Company was formed in 1746, for the purpose of encouraging the linen manufacture in Scotland, but gradually became a banking company.

So the introduction of the new blowing apparatus, and the reverberatory or air furnace, by which pig iron could be made malleable without blasting, were great improvements. But as yet, with a scanty supply of air, and with little density, the produce of the best firms did not exceed ten or twelve tons weekly, and the average annual make of each furnace was less than 500 tons. When, however, it was shown that by the process of puddling and rolling, invented by Mr. Henry Cort in 1784, coals could be used instead of dear charcoal, and the slow operation of the hammer could be altogether superseded, so as to enable the workers to produce a much greater quantity than could be made under the hammer, and of a far superior quality, the ironmasters became alive to their own interests, and felt that with the requisite capital this discovery might be made immensely profitable. And what was the result? In South Staffordshire, in 1768, there was not a single furnace making charcoal iron, and only nine where pit coal was used, producing fifteen tons each per week; while in all other parts of England there were twenty-four charcoal furnaces and forty-four pit-coal furnaces. In very few years these multiplied enormously, production increased apace, and an immense industry sprang up as by magic in hardware and locks, japanned goods and ironmongery. Yet the inventor of this puddling and rolling derived little or no advantage for himself, and his family only wrung from the government a small pittance as a recognition of the enormous value of his discovery. Of coal the production was as yet comparatively insignificant, and the Durham and Northumberland coalfields yielded about a fourth of the whole produce of the kingdom. In 1770 the vends of the northern ports amounted to 1,551,000, and the whole kingdom would yield 6,205,000 tons.[13]

Other branches of industry received at this time a wonderful impulse. This was the era of Wedgwood, and the time when the earthenware manufacture began to attract great interest. Though possessing all the materials for the fabric of earthenware, England had hitherto depended almost entirely on the importation of a red lustrous pottery from France, Germany, and Italy. By successive improvements,

The earthenware industry.

[13] See Report of the Coal Commission, 1871, and more especially Mr. Robert Hunt's Report.

such as the substitution of salt for lead ore, the reproduction of a certain red ware from Japan, and the substitution of stone for iron, considerable advance had been made in the manufacture; but it was not till Josiah Wedgwood, with his skilful hand and artistic eye, began to work in Staffordshire, that the industry attained any importance. 'Up to that time,' said his talented biographer, 'there had been nothing worthy of the name of decorative art; of colour, proportion, or form. A mixture of different coloured clays, of rude outlines scratched in by a nail, a blue or brown edge line, or a paste-like medallion luted to the surfaces, were the highest efforts of ornamental art. After all that had been done for the improvement of the different bodies, they were at best flimsy and indifferently glazed, the hue of the white ware was bad, and the forms and their adjuncts were ill-proportioned, often angular, and almost always without those flowing outlines that, whilst severely true to geometrical principles, show the utmost grace, delicacy, and beauty. Wedgwood, true to the inductive spirit of the age then opening to his generation, and those which would follow, took up his art as a science, and based its improvement upon principles.'[10]

The steam-engine.

But with all these mechanical and artistic improvements, little real progress would have been made had it not been for the greatest of all discoveries, the discovery of steam as a new motive power. Animal forces had been found utterly insufficient. It was very well for the Laplanders to yoke their reindeer, the Esquimaux their dogs, and the Arabs their dromedaries or camels; but we well know that animals are at best limited in number, that they require constant replenishing and food, that they are uncertain from sickness and casualties, and that they are unequal and quickly worn out. Water, again, which is capable of such a momentum when producing a cataract, or when moving in rapid streams; and wind, whispering in zephyrs, or murmuring in the breeze, and rushing with the impetuosity of the gale, had been, and might be, effectively used for many purposes, but neither could be controlled at pleasure and so rendered subservient to human want everywhere and under every circumstance. Steam was

[10] The Life of Josiah Wedgwood, by Eliza Meteyard, vol. i. p. 167.

found to be at once the most potent and the most pliable of motors, and was destined thenceforth to work miracles in our behalf. The history of this great discovery may be quickly told. Many had been the attempts to use steam as a motive power. As far back as 1543, Blasco de Garay exhibited in the harbour of Barcelona a steamboat of his own invention. In later times De Caus used steam for raising water. Worcester performed the same operation on a greater scale. Papin used the condensation of steam; and through that the atmospheric pressure, as well as the direct expansive force, and worked the engine by a piston. Savery condensed by refrigeration, instead of by the mere absence of fire, but did not use the atmosphere. Newcomen used the jet for condensing and the atmosphere for pressure, though he did not use the direct force of steam. Desaguliers introduced the safety valve; Beighton and Smeaton further improved the mechanism;[14] but the desired object was not yet accomplished, there being a great loss of steam, only about one-fourth of what was admitted into the cylinder being actually available as a motive power. On January 5, 1769, however, Watt's patent 'for a method of lessening the consumption of steam and fuel in fire-engines' was published, and what a change was produced from that day! 'To recount the achievements of the steam-engine,' said Arago, 'is to go over the greater part of what adorns and interests civilization and science. By its aid we penetrate into the bowels of the earth, excavate vast mines, and extract from the virgin soil inexhaustible mineral treasures. Combining delicacy with power, it twists with equal success the huge ropes of the gigantic cable, by which the man-of-war rides at anchor in the midst of the raging ocean, and the microscopic filaments of the aerial gauze and lace, of which fashionable dresses are principally formed. The great mechanical powers, formerly sought for in mountainous districts, or at the foot of rapid cascades, are thereby obtained in the midst of towns, on any floor of a house; whilst the extent of such power may be governed at the will of the mechanician. To it we owe that the different branches of each manufacture may be carried on in the same space, under the same roof. Installed in ships, it exercises a power a hundredfold greater

[14] See Brougham's Life of Watt.

than that of the triple and quadruple ranks of rovers of former days; and, by the help of a few bushels of coals, we can vanquish the elements and play with calm and contrary winds or storms. And whilst drawing in its train thousands of travellers, it runs on railways with greater speed than the swiftest race-horse!"[1] How can we estimate sufficiently services so rare and so great?

This period was also the starting-point of chemical discoveries. Hitherto chemical science could scarcely be said to have existed. A few facts had been observed, but no attempts had been made to account for them. There were but few chemists. The names of Becker and Stahl were almost unknown, and little progress had really been made in elevating chemistry to the rank of an experimental science. The founder of this structure was Dr. Black, the instructor of Watt, who enriched the world with his experiments on the air, and on latent and fixed heat. Then came Cavendish, with his researches on the composition of water and on the force of attraction. Priestley, too, gave forth his discovery of oxygen, and Lavoisier generalised and systematised the whole of chemical science. The philosophy of meteorology also attracted attention. In 1773, the council of the Royal Society resolved to make daily observations at their house with the barometer, thermometer, hygrometer, and wind gauge; and they entrusted the guidance of these observations to the Hon. Henry Cavendish. In 1780 the Royal Society left their secluded quarters in Crane Court, and went to Somerset House.

Progress of chemical science.

And the Arts kept pace with Science. As early as 1721 a proposal was made to establish a society to be called the 'Chamber of Arts,' for the preservation and improvement of useful knowledge and mechanical arts, inventions, and manufactures. In 1748 Benjamin Franklin published his proposal for the advancement of useful knowledge among the British plantations in America, by the formation of a society to be called the American Philosophical Society. In 1753, the still existing and flourishing 'Society for the Encouragement of Art, Manufactures, and Commerce' was first established, the original address signifying the intention of the society to 'bestow rewards from time to time for such productions, inventions, or

The Society of Arts and Royal Academy.

[1] Historical Eloge of James Watt, by M. Arago.

improvements as shall tend to the employing of the poor, the increase of trade, and the riches and honours of the kingdom.' And this period was distinguished by the formation of Academies of Fine Arts in different countries. Of these that of St. Petersburg took the lead, the Empress Catherine having, in 1765, endowed it with a considerable revenue. The Venetian Senate followed by founding one in 1766, which took the name of 'Reale Academia delle Belle Arti.' A year after, the Elector Carl Theodor founded one in Dusseldorf; and, in 1768, the Royal Academy of Arts in London was established, with Sir Joshua Reynolds as president. In the same year, the Academy of San Carlo was established in Valencia by Charles III. One was established at Brussels in 1770. The Empress Maria Theresa founded one at Milan in 1775; the Landgraf Frederick II. established one at Cassel in the same year, and, four years later, another in Augsburg. Surely, then, this was a time of decided progress in everything that could stimulate and improve the productive industry both of this and of other countries.

Foundation of the Royal Exchange and Gresham College.

Alas! that in the very midst of all this progress a piece of absolute Vandalism should have been perpetrated in the city of London. In 1768, Gresham College, including the old mansion of Sir Thomas Gresham and all its buildings, was sold to the Government to form a site for the Excise Office, for the miserable compensation of five hundred pounds a year. Sir Thomas Gresham was a great and an enlightened citizen. Largely engaged in financial and commercial operations, frequently charged by Edward VI. and Queen Elizabeth with the negotiation of foreign loans, and even called to act as ambassador to the court of Spain and the Duchess of Parma, Sir Thomas had learned to regard trade more as a science than as a craft. He saw the need of an Exchange to serve as a shelter to the merchants, who then met twice a day in the open street, and made over certain property to the city for the purpose. But he was not content with this. He was anxious for the cultivation of the mind. He saw the advantage of education, and he bequeathed his splendid mansion in Bishopsgate Street for the purpose of a college, appropriating the revenue of the Royal Exchange building for its endowment. By his will, executed in 1575, he granted this property in one moiety to the mayor and commonalty and citizens of London, and one moiety to the Mercers' Company, in trust that with the revenue of the same the corporation of the city should provide for the endowment of four lectureships in the same college, viz. on Divinity, Astronomy, Music, and Geometry; and the Mercers' Company should also establish three lectureships, viz. Law, Physic, and Rhetoric. Sir Thomas evidently intended that the college should serve as a technical university for the mercantile classes, and he took every step to secure the utility and renown of such an institution.

Sale of Gresham College.

And for a time all went well. The professors were men of great distinction. The college, so nobly provided for, in the very heart of the city, did really become the seat of learning and liberal arts, and the resort of the most enlightened among the mercantile classes. It was there that the Royal Society had its rise, and for a lengthened period it possessed a large library and an excellent museum. But, unfortunately, a temporary diminution of income in consequence of the fire induced the corporation of the city and the Mercers' Company, in an evil moment, to commit the sacrilegious act of selling the edifice to the Government.[16] Another small building was afterwards erected in Gresham Street, where lectures are still delivered; but the spirit is gone, and the trustees have allowed the college and lectures to fall far short of the original design. Can it be that whilst all educational institutions are acquiring new life and usefulness, this noble legacy of one of our merchant princes is to remain almost useless and purposeless? Would it not be worthy of an effort to rescue it from the slumber and ruin into which it has fallen? Let Gresham College be adapted to the exigencies of the age in which we live, and we shall show by our deeds that we value the munificent and princely endowments of one of our great and philanthropic citizens.

[16] In 1858, Gresham House was purchased from the Government by the Gresham House Estate Company, limited, for upwards of 100,000*l.*, and mercantile offices have been built on the ground, the present rental of which amounts to about 20,000*l.* per annum. Thus property, which was sold in 1768 for a rental representing a capital of about 10,000*l.*, was disposed of in 1852 for more than 100,000*l.*, and now with new buildings erected on it represents a capital of 400,000*l.*,—a wonderful illustration of the increasing value of land in the city of London.

CHAPTER II.

DEVELOPMENT OF NATIONAL RESOURCES.

1763–1776.

Canal Navigation.—State of the Roads.—Postal Organisation.—Progress of Towns.—State of Ireland.—Corn Laws.—The High Price of Corn.—Interference with Trade and Industry.—Adam Smith and the Progress of Political Economy.—What is the true Source of Wealth?—Statistics and Political Economy.

FOR the increase of the productive power of a state, nothing is more important than the extension of the means of communication. It was fortunate, therefore, that side by side with the great discoveries which we have already noted, attention was given in England to the improvement of roads, the formation of canals, the extension of harbours, and, above all, to the economic laws which regulate national and international intercourse. The Duke of Bridgewater had a rich coal mine at Worsley, only a few miles distant from Manchester, the place of consumption; yet the produce of the one was quite unavailable to the other, in consequence of the high cost of land carriage,[1] which amounted to about forty shillings per ton. How to connect Worsley with Manchester was a great problem. It was proposed to render Worsley brook navigable, but that was almost impossible. A canal between the two places was suggested, with better hopes of success. The necessary powers were obtained, and with the assistance of Brindley, the great engineer, the duke succeeded in constructing the canal, first from Worsley to Stafford, and afterwards over the Mersey and Irwell by an aqueduct. To the proposal of introducing this new method of inland navigation, all manner of objections

Canal navigation.

[1] Before the opening of the canal, 12s. the ton was paid from Liverpool to Manchester by the river navigation, and 40s. the ton by land carriage. The Duke's charge on his canal was limited by statute to 6s. See an able article on Aqueducts and Canals in the 73rd vol. of the Quarterly Review, 1844.

were urged—precisely the same as those which, at a later time, were made against railways. Extend canal navigation, and you diminish the breed of horses, injure the coasting trade, and weaken the navy. To undertake such a work you will require to sink large sums of money, to destroy great quantities of land capable of producing corn and cattle, whilst the natural navigation of rivers will be neglected. The objectors did not understand that, by opening up the country, and by procuring outlets to our mineral resources, and inlets for foreign produce, fresh life would be given to established industries, new branches of internal trade would be opened, and the external would be largely promoted. But the error was speedily perceived, and the objectors were silenced. From 1760 to 1773, many were the acts[1] passed for widening and improving roads and making of canals. Then it was that Lynne was joined to Northampton, the Shannon to Dublin, and the Forth to the Clyde. Then, too, by a grand system of canals, the ports of Liverpool, Hull, Bristol, and London were joined together. And we have it on the testimony of a committee of the House of Commons on the State of the Poor in Ireland in 1830, 'that the effect of opening lines of inland navigation, when formed upon scientific principles, and executed with due economy, has been, on the concurrence of all testimony, the extension of improved agriculture, the equalisation of prices of fuel and provisions in different districts, the diminishing the danger of scarcity in both of these necessaries of life, and advancing the general improvement of the condition of the people, by the creation of a new, vigorous, and continued demand for labour.'

State of the roads.

But still more illustrative of the hindrances which then existed to commerce and industry, was the singular deficiency in the means of personal communication. The time was not quite gone when, as in the days of Milton, a traveller

> O'er bog or steep, through straight, rough, dense, or rare,
> With head, hands, wings, or feet, pursued his way,
> And swam, or sunk, or waded, or crept, or fled.

It was only in 1763, after the Peace of Paris, that turnpike roads were extended to all parts of the kingdom. In 1766, Lord

[1] In the first fourteen sessions of the reign of George III., 452 acts were passed for repairing the highways of different districts.

Eldon took four days to perform a journey from Newcastle to London in a fly. From London to Liverpool a flying machine was started three times a week, and it performed the journey in forty-eight hours. The London and Liverpool diligence gave the passengers a rest of ten hours the second night. From Liverpool to Manchester the coach started at six o'clock, the passengers lunched at Warrington, and arrived in time for dinner. From Liverpool to Glasgow two days and a half were required, and from Edinburgh to London there was only one stage coach, which set out once a month, and took twelve to fourteen days to perform the journey. In Lancashire the roads were most deficient. When, in 1770, Arthur Young entered into his journey of inspection, he found it almost impossible to go from Preston to Wigan without personal danger. And the result of all this was the greatest possible inequality in the distribution of produce, and a corresponding variety in prices; so that, whilst London was often suffering from want of food, farmers, in certain localities, were not able to get more than five farthings the pound for good mutton. A long time had yet to elapse before the railway was to traverse the length and breadth of the land; but means were speedily taken for providing better modes of communication than as yet existed.

Postal organisation.

The postal organisation also was most imperfect. The rates of postage were high, and the facilities miserably small. In 1763 the Post Office establishment was of very insignificant proportions. The secretary had only two supernumerary clerks assigned to him. Before 1764,[9] members of both Houses of Parliament were able to frank their letters by merely writing their names upon the covers, and parcels of such franks were obtained from members for their friends, which were put aside for use like the stamped envelopes sold by the post office at the present day. The packet establishment consisted of four Harwich packet boats for the German mail; six Dover boats for Calais, Ostend, and Flushing; and five Falmouth boats for the mail to North America and the West Indies, which cost the office 10,000*l.* per annum. With

[9] In 1763 the act 4 Geo. III. c. 24 restricted the privilege to certain official persons; and, by the 4 Geo. III. c. 25, a district penny post was established for distances not exceeding one post stage.

the lengthy passages then made, the speed of sailing ships being at least one-third less than at the present time, and without steam vessels, by which all the correspondence is now carried, letters must have borne a far back date when they reached our merchants and bankers.[4] By this time, the merchant marine of Great Britain had become somewhat considerable, especially in relation to other countries; but the majority of ships were of very small size. It was only in 1770, or soon after, that copper was substituted for wood for the sheathing of ships' bottoms; and need we say that a ship of a hundred years ago would exhibit a wondertul contrast to the graceful clipper, the steamer, or the iron vessel of the present day. And when the large, heavy, and ill-shaped barques arrived, there was no dock where they might safely load or unload.

Of the facilities of banking which we now possess, there were scarcely any at that time. The Bank of England,[5] founded in 1694, was in the enjoyment of perfect monopoly as a joint

[4] The *inland* rates of postage were much altered. In 1763 they were the same as those fixed by a statute of Queen Anne in 1710 (9 Anne c. 10). In 1765 they were fixed at 1*d*. for every single letter for not more than one whole post stage; 2*d*. for every double letter; 3*d*. for every treble; and 4*d*. for every ounce; and 2*d*. more for every additional post stage. In 1764 the rates were again modified, and a penny post was allowed for letters delivered within ten English miles from the general letter office in the metropolis. A single letter from France to London cost 10*d*.; double 1*s*. 8*d*.; treble 2*s*. 6*d*. A single letter from Spain 1*s*. 6*d*.; double 3*s*.; a single letter from Italy, 1*s*. 8*d*. The packets were regular, but the service was very infrequent. To and from India and China there was no regular mail. The letters were despatched by merchant ships as opportunities occurred. The ships of the East India Company in 1763–4 were of about 500 tons each, and they employed about eighteen months for the double voyage to India and China and back. The 'Egmont' sailed to St. Helena and China on January 1, 1763, and arrived back on July 19, 1764; the 'Neptune' left for the East and China on January 2, 1763, and returned August 4, 1764; the 'Glatton' left March 1, 1763, and came back November 5, 1764. The rates of insurance also were double the present rates. From London to Naples 30*s*.; to Cadiz 21*s*.; to Bilboa 25*s*.; to Carthagena 30*s*.; to New York 42*s*.; to the East Indies and back 7 guineas.

[5] The Bank of England was established in 1694 with a capital of 1,200,000*l*. lent to the state with a charter under the 5 & 6 Will. III. c. 20. In 1697 the charter was continued till 1710, under the 8 & 9 Will. III. c. 20, the capital being increased by 1,000,000*l*. In 1708 the charter was renewed by 7 Anne c. 7 till 1732, and in 1713 by 12 Anne c. 11 till 1742, the capital of the Bank having been increased to 9,000,000*l*. In that year the charter was again continued till 1764 by 15 Geo. II. c. 13, and at the latter period the capital of the Bank was 10,780,000*l*.; from which time it underwent no change till 1782, when it was increased to 11,642,000*l*., and again in 1816 to 14,553,000*l*.

stock bank over the whole of England. Its charter was renewed in 1764[*] for twenty-one years, and again in 1781, on both occasions on condition of its making some advances to the state. Since 1759 the Bank issued notes for 15*l.* and 10*l.*, but there were no notes of 5*l.*, which were not issued till 1793. The private banks were all banks of issue as well as banks of deposit; and the clearing house system was already so far in operation; but there were but few cheques in circulation, and the number of persons having banking accounts was miserably small. In Scotland, too, the Bank of Scotland, established in 1695, was in operation, as well as the Royal Bank of Scotland and the British Linen Company. But the Bank of Ireland was not established till 1783. Our refined and complicated system of credit, consisting really in a kind of ledger currency, and a simple method of transferring credits in bankers' books, was altogether unknown.

Progress of towns.

Gradually, however, a rapid and wonderful change was produced in commerce and industry by the expansion of some of our leading commercial and manufacturing towns. Liverpool derived enormous benefit from the extension of manufactures in Lancashire, from the rapid increase of population and wealth in the American colonies, from the new acquisitions of England in Canada, and the extended cultivation of the West Indies. Birmingham felt all the advantage of the opening of the Birmingham, Staffordshire, and Worcestershire Canals, which enabled her to receive all her supplies of coal and materials for manufacture and building at prices much under the usual carriage rates. The Soho factory was by this time built, and Watt was producing his wonderful engines with increasing success. Manchester, though not much of a corporation, was being surrounded by a cluster of manufacturing towns, all busy and thriving. Bristol, for a long time without a rival, was carrying on a considerable foreign trade, and enjoying all the benefits of the confluence of many rivers; whilst Glasgow greatly extended her relations with the West Indies.

One portion of the United Kingdom was not in a position to derive any benefit from all these improvements, and that

[*] 4 Geo. III. c. 25.

was Ireland, then, as on many subsequent occasions, in a turbulent and discontented spirit. Nor was she altogether unjust in her complaints, since she was really suffering from the iniquitous commercial policy pursued against her. By the old navigation laws,[1] no productions of Europe and Ireland included were allowed to be exported to the colonies unless shipped from England and Wales, the only relaxation from this prohibition of all direct trade with the colonies being the permission to export to them white or grey linen cloth. By a later statute no colonial merchandise could be landed in Ireland unless first landed in England, and no manufacture of wool was to be exported from Ireland to any place except England.[2] She could import no East India produce except through England; and even if under the reign of George I. some slight freedom was granted, care was taken that it should not interfere in any way with the substantial monopoly of England. A committee of the House of Commons sat in 1778, to find means to allay the discontent. But whilst the English merchants exhibited an unworthy spirit of exclusiveness, and the Dublin merchants were loud in their condemnation of the anti-commercial policy of England, dictated by the unjust, illiberal, and impolitic opposition of self-interested people, no arrangement was possible.

State of Ireland.

In truth, however, this was only a part of a totally defective commercial legislation. Most backward of all were the laws affecting the corn trade, both inland and foreign. In olden times, when the population of England was small, and the wealth at her disposal not very great, England was usually an exporter, and not an importer of grain. But by this time a different phenomenon was observable. For a series of years, from 1763, the prices of grain and other provisions ruled very high, so much so, that food riots took place in different parts of the country, and it became necessary, by royal proclamation, to allow the free import of salt beef, salt pork, and butter from Ireland, to suspend the exportation of corn, and to prohibit the distillation of wheat. Not content, however, with these simple and

Corn Laws.

[1] 15 Car. II. c. 7. [2] 22 & 23 Car. II. c. 26.

natural measures, rewards were offered for the discovery of any unlawful combinations, and, what was still worse, the laws of Edward VI.[9] and Elizabeth against forestallers and engrossers were enforced, and an embargo was laid on all vessels laden with wheat and flour in any of the ports of Great Britain. The apology for the laws of forestalling and engrossing was, that such practices diminished the competition which ought to exist between the different persons having the same merchandise for sale. The forestaller, it was said, buys all up with an intention to sell with more profit, as he has, by that means, taken other competitors out of the way, and appears with a single interest on one side of the contract, in the face of many competitors on the other. This person is punished by the state because he prevents the price of the merchandise from becoming justly proportioned to the real value. He has robbed the public and enriched himself, and in the punishment he makes restitution. It was not then understood, that by withdrawing from the market an article, which is becoming scarce, a greater equality of supply, and consequently lower prices are, in fact, secured, than if people were allowed to bask in abundance for a time to be suddenly thrown into a state of complete starvation. It was not till 1772[10] that the laws against forestalling and regrating were repealed after abundant experience of their injurious tendency.

The high price of corn.

What was the cause of the high price of corn was not well understood at the time. Some ascribed it to the large increase of population, others to the great number of horses kept; some sought for the reason in the increasing use of tea and milk, others in the vast quantities of land turned into dairies, and the incorporation of farms, whilst many had a suspicion that it was owing to the fall in the value of silver. But, in truth, the seasons had proved most unfavourable for many years through the greater part of Europe, whilst the disorders in Poland increased the scarcity in all the countries usually supplied from that market. Unfortunately, no means yet existed for obtaining the average price of grain in England. It was only in 1770,[11] that the first

[9] 5 & 6 Edw. VI. c. 14. [10] 12 Geo. III. c. 71. [11] 10 Geo. III. c. 39.

act was passed for obtaining returns of such average prices. And in 1773[18] the first comprehensive corn law was enacted, which allowed the importation of wheat at a duty of 6d. per quarter when the price reached 48s., and the exportation of the same when the price fell to 44s.; the preamble of the act throwing much stress evidently on the influence of the corn laws on the advancement of tillage and navigation.

The *beau ideal* of Government at that time seems to have been to exercise a certain paternal superintendence over the transactions of society, to endeavour to repair by artificial means the shortcomings of private industry, and even to hamper or interfere if need be with the management of business, with a view to the advancement of certain interests which were deemed deserving of public support. Fortunately the advocates of such measures did not always succeed. For a considerable time a tax was levied on all stuff made of cotton, or of cotton and linen mixed; but complaints were made against such a tax. The Manchester manufacturers and Glasgow operative weavers strongly urged the repeal of all duties on manufactures, and called upon Parliament, as Heaven's trustees for the nation, not to strangle an infant industry. The petition was successful, and the duties were repealed. Would that the woollen manufacture had been left as free from legislative interference as the cotton has been. The cotton manufacture was not born under an atmosphere of protection, was never the petted child of government or parliament, and yet grew and prospered most vigorously. The woollen, the object of so much care, was for years weak and slow in its progress. Nothing could have been more suicidal than the action of the woollen manufacturers. They were not content to shut out all woollen goods from the British market. They went much farther. The long-stapled or English combing wool being superior for some manufacturing purposes to that of any other country, the most severe laws were passed, prohibiting the exportation of English wool. Nay, more. An act was passed, in 1788,[19] prohibiting the exportation of live sheep, imposing all kinds of restrictions on the carriage of wool from one part of the country to the other, and even prohibiting sheep-shearing within five miles of the sea. This was,

Interference with trade and industry.

[18] 13 Geo. III. c. 43. [19] 28 Geo. III. c. 38.

indeed, carrying the protection policy to its legitimate results; but what were the consequences? Trade and industry were hampered and misdirected; the interest of the consumer was disregarded, in the vain hope of favouring the producer; and even the processes of agriculture were unduly interfered with. So that blunder was heaped upon blunder, producing in the end nothing but disappointment and loss. To some extent the policy of obtaining, free of duty, the raw materials of industry was acknowledged and acted upon. Indigo, cochineal, and logwood, necessaries for dyers, were allowed to come in free, and the duties on oak and bark were lowered. But the prohibition of foreign goods was very general, and bounties were freely given to encourage the exportation of British manufactures. These were the times when apprenticeship was everywhere prescribed, when workmen were kept by force in the country, and when the combination laws were in full operation.

Adam Smith and the progress of political economy.

Much need, indeed, there was of a master mind to seize the real bearing of such legislation, and to enlighten both manufacturers and workmen on the result of their clamour. And happy was it that just at that moment a work was published entitled 'An Enquiry into the Nature and Causes of the Wealth of Nations,' which removed much error, revealed much truth, and reduced many scattered and disconnected ideas into a homogeneous and compendious system. To understand what Adam Smith has accomplished we must briefly trace the history of political economy at least in its main features.[14] Adam Smith was not the first inquirer into the causes of wealth. Doubtless in every age, in one way or another, nations have endeavoured to ameliorate their physical or material condition, but they appear to have been wonderfully ignorant of the means for attaining the object. The Greeks, though not indifferent to riches, indulged far too much in idleness, and were, moreover, for ever looking for help from the state. In their opinion the government was bound to feed them, and the problem with their statesmen was, how they could best enrich the people with the property of the state, then regarded as common property? The Romans never thought of the advantage of promoting national wealth. For

[14] Blanqui, Histoire de l'Économie politique en Europe: Paris, 1837-8.

a long time they gave themselves wholly to wars and conquests; and, when Augustus introduced order and civilisation into the empire, all that the people sought was an abundant distribution of food. The Roman statesmen did not descend into the study of industrial details. They did not understand their importance.

After the fall of the Roman Empire, and during the disorder caused by the irruption of hordes of barbarians, no attempt was made to create or preserve wealth; but as the Italian cities, the birthplace of modern society, rose to power and affluence solely by their commerce and industry, the importance of manufacture and foreign trade began to dawn in the mind of thinkers and writers on economic questions; and the idea was suggested that these were the only real source of wealth. But in what manner commerce and manufacture contributed to the production and distribution of wealth, was a mystery not yet fathomed. Was it because they led to the importation of gold and silver? If so, the truest policy would be by all means to promote the exports of merchandise, and to hinder as much as possible the exports of the precious metals. The French economists, or the Physiocrates as they were called, started the suggestion, that trade cannot of itself be productive of wealth, since it only promotes the transport or distribution of the products of the earth. According to them agriculture is the only source of wealth. But if so, how did it happen that foreign trade appeared to be the means of creating much wealth, whilst agriculture seemed scarcely able to lift people up from a state of poverty? Then the doctrine of the balance of trade was suggested. The advocates of this theory did not contend, that wealth consisted exclusively in gold and silver, but that wealth depended on the profitable exchange of native for foreign products, on our ability to sell goods for more than they cost, and in the excess of gold and silver obtained by the transaction. In truth, at the time when Adam Smith wrote his famous work, the most erroneous conceptions existed as regards the relative functions of agriculture, commerce, and the precious metals on the production of wealth.

What is the true source of wealth?

Nor was there any complete treatise on the subject. In Italy several works had been published on several branches of economic science. Davanzati and Scaruffi wrote some able works on money, in consequence of the frequent alterations and falsifications of the coinage resorted to by the petty sovereigns who reigned in the different states. Bandini and Broggia advocated freedom as the basis of public prosperity and condemned monopolies. Galiani, Beccaria, and Verri contributed valuable works on value, capital, and labour. With them free trade in corn was a primary condition of national prosperity, and they boldly condemned the usury laws. The French economists wrote much; Quesnay,[15] Mirabeau, De la Rivière, Dupont de Nemours, Turgot, and many others were the forerunners of Adam Smith. Yet none of them constructed like him what we may call the science of political economy.

Works on political economy.

Happily, too, the Wealth of Nations recognised, though not as fully as more modern economists, the value of statistics in economic inquiries. 'The method I take,' said Sir William Petty, 'is not yet very usual, for instead of using only comparative and superlative words and intellectual arguments, I have taken the course as a specimen of political arithmetic I have long aimed at, to express myself in terms of number, weight, or measure; to use only argument of sense, and to consider only such causes as have visible foundations in nature, leaving thus what depends upon the unstable minds, opinions, appetites, and passions of particular men, to the consideration of others.' Statistics were thus early recognised as a means of verifying the conclusions and deductions of political economy. It is by the use of statistics that political economy has acquired the character of a fixed science; and by it, that it has ceased to be tentative, and has become to a large extent an inductive or experimental science. Adam Smith availed himself largely of statistics, and hence the solidity and permanent utility of his works. And what has the Wealth of Nations taught? It established, in a most distinct manner, that labour is the only true source of wealth; it destroyed the theory that wealth consisted in the abundance of gold and silver; it abolished the theory of the mercantile system; and laid down sound principles for the economic policy of the country.

Statistics and political economy.

[15] See Quesnay's Tableau économique, Paris: 1758; Physiocratie, ou Constitution naturelle du Gouvernement: publié par Dupont: Yverdun, Paris, 1768; and Mauvillon, Physiokratische Briefe an Dohm: Braunschweig, 1780.

CHAPTER III.

STATE OF TRADE AFTER THE SEVEN YEARS' WAR.

1763–1776.

Extent of British Commerce.—Trade of the Hanse Towns.—Trade of Prussia.—Trade of Russia, Sweden, and Denmark.—Trade of Spain and Portugal.—Trade of France.—Trade of the East Indies.—Trade of the West Indies.—The Slave Trade.—Customs Duties.—Navigation Laws.—The Board of Trade and its Functions.

Extent of British commerce.

Accustomed, as we now are, to dimensions so extended, and to amounts of enormous magnitude, it needs an effort of the imagination to realise the narrow limits and meagre proportions of the commerce of England one hundred years ago. In truth, England had then but little to give to foreign nations, and consequently her means of obtaining foreign products were just as circumscribed. If the 3,000,000 lbs. of tea then imported have swollen to 140,000,000 lbs., and the 4,000,000 lbs. of cotton into 1,000,000,000 and upwards, it is because British industry has succeeded in giving a wonderful development to national resources. Thirty millions is the official annual value of all the imports and exports in 1763; but that included some 2,500,000*l.* of trade with Ireland, which is now part of the inland trade. And such as it was, constant fears were entertained of its working, from the singular attention paid to the balance of trade. The navigation of British ports was then equally contracted, and though British seamen had already acquired a great reputation for bravery and daring, as well as for a spirit of discovery and indefatigable industry, the British had not yet quite supplanted the Dutch and other maritime nations as the common carriers of the world's traffic.

Trade of the Hanse Towns.

But small as it was, the trade of England was fast excelling that of other countries. This was a time of transition. Ancient commerce, with all its adventures and romance, had passed away. A new era had begun; new nations were taking the place of the old, and England certainly among them assumed the foremost rank. Look at the condition of the Hanse Towns. At one time the League was supreme in Europe, and in London itself it enjoyed a considerable monopoly, under the name of the Steel Yard Company.[1] But its privileges had long since been repealed, and by this time the League had practically ceased to exist; yet Hamburg was then, as now, a port of considerable traffic, and the mercantile spirit and high character of the members of that league were still in her merchants. Nor was it in vain that that League had existed. Traces of its wholesome action were still visible in the great marts of Northern Europe. And to it we owe the abolition of the right of wreck, the safety of locomotion by land and by sea, a better administration of justice, the abolition of the *droit d'Aubain*,[2] and the upholding of the rights of neutrals. Would that, in its efforts to secure the protection and development of its own trade, the League had not ignored the rights of other nations, and had better apprehended the economic value of an open and free competition. In 1763, Hamburg was suffering from a commercial crisis, attributed to the failure of many merchants and bankers in Amsterdam.

In the North of Europe trade was struggling for existence, and the different states seemed scarcely able to master its difficulties. Prussia was just then rising to importance under the energetic rule of Frederick II., but his policy was not well calculated to further industry. With monopolies of every description, and with prohibitions and prohibitory duties of the most oppressive character, Prussian trade could not well prosper. The financial policy of Frederick II. was most objectionable. He confided the administration of the finances to Helvetius, a Frenchman, who went to Berlin with a regiment of excise and customhouse officers. Under him there were four heads of departments, and they

Trade of Prussia.

[1] The Steelyard, or Staelhof, consisted of certain tenements conveyed by the king to the Hanse merchants in 1475.

[2] The *droit d'Aubain* was the right of the sovereign to succeed to the estate of a foreign subject when he died intestate. The Assemblée constituante of France abolished it in 1790; but it continued to exist in several countries of Europe for some time, and was only abolished in relation to different countries by special treaty.

employed a large number of *visitateurs, controlleurs, jaugueurs, plombeurs*, and *commis—rats de cave*, or cellar rats, detested by the people. No one was exempted from their control. These cellar rats, as Carlyle calls them, had liberty to enter into all houses, at any hour of the day or of the night, to search for contraband. All foreign merchandise was prohibited, or charged with oppressive duties. The administration of tobacco was farmed out to a Frenchman for 1,000,000 dollars, and in 1768 the sovereign took for himself the monopoly of the sale of coffee; while he gave to a society the exclusive right of selling timber, both for burning and construction.[1]

Trade of Russia, Sweden, and Denmark.

Russia, under the enlightened and liberal policy of Catherine II., was pursuing the sound and safe path of renouncing all monopolies. In 1766, Sir George Macartney concluded a treaty of commerce between England and Russia, which led to a considerable extension of transactions between the two countries. Sweden was suffering from the insatiable ambition of Charles XII.; and Denmark, by a strange infatuation, was just trying the effect of the mercantile system. Intent upon introducing manufactures and restoring the balance of trade, she neglected agriculture, and at great expense brought to her shores foreign manufacturers and Protestant refugees. But unsupported by native skill, and with no natural advantages, the artificial impulse given by the state led to no practical result, and a reaction became inevitable, which rendered Denmark more than ever dependent on foreign merchandise.

Trade of Spain.

Spain was by this time fully disabused of her foolish notion, that the treasures of America would for ever continue to pour into the country, whether she laboured for them or not. Constantly engaged in wars, without skill or prescience in politics, Spain had by this time sunk very low as a commercial nation, and notwithstanding all her prohibitions and restrictions, French and English traders were fast ousting the Spaniards of all their trading with the American Continent. In vain did Spain endeavour to counteract British influence in the West Indies by opening that trade to all her own subjects.

[1] Carlyle's Life of Frederick II., vol. vi. p 308–373.

In vain, for the same object, did she issue ordinances prohibiting the importation into Spain of cotton velvets and other cotton fabrics. Spanish manufactures now and then obtained fresh life and vigour, but the effort was in the end transient and unsuccessful. With a despotic government and the Inquisition in full exercise of absolute power over persons and property, no security whatever was afforded in Spain for trade, and loud complaints reached this country of the oppressive laws and customs which pressed hard upon British traders.

Portugal was wistfully looking back to the days of her prosperity, and, under the administration of an able but sadly mistaken minister, the Marquis de Plombal, she was trying to retrieve her reversed fortunes by a singular method. Justly conceiving that the real causes of the decadence of his country were to be found in the ignorance, idleness, bigotry, and pride of the people, he, unfortunately, strove to eradicate such evils by taking in his own hands the guidance of all the economies of the state. Conceiving that too large a portion of land was employed in the culture of the vine, and too little in grain, he compelled a change of cultivation—caused the vine to be uprooted, and corn to be planted in its stead. The Portuguese were not able to spin silk like the Italians, and to remedy this he sent for Italian spinners, and compelled the Portuguese to get lessons from them. New towns were desirable, and he drew men and women away from their homes to plant them. The prices of provisions and merchandise were fixed by law. A general system of monopoly was established. Companies were chartered with many privileges. To the Oporto Company the exclusive right was granted to buy all the wine produced at home at the lowest price, and this in total disregard of the rights of foreign traders. But measures of such a character could not fail to produce utter disappointment, and, what was worse, had the effect of causing much difficulty in the relations of Portugal with foreign countries. British merchants were indignant at such proceedings. Was this the reciprocity which they were led to expect when England acceded to the Methuen treaty, by which she bound herself to admit Portu-

Trade of Portugal.

guese wines at lower duties than those of other nations? An open rupture under such circumstances seemed imminent.

Our commerce with France was very small. There was no treaty between the two countries, and when, some years earlier, France made overtures for a liberal convention, England, determined to maintain a system of prohibitory duties, refused to accede to it. Internally, also, the state of France was unsatisfactory. The Peace of Paris had been received with great disappointment by the people, and had produced considerable discontent. Allowing that its conditions were the necessary and natural results of a defeat, the people complained bitterly of the cession of Canada, the commercial importance of which seemed to have been disregarded, whilst the islands of the West Indies ceded to England were considered of far greater value than had been represented. French finances were in great disorder. The National Debt had largely increased, and at a time when the people were suffering from bad harvests, it was a grievous complaint that persons of the highest influence were buying up all the available grain, sent it to Jersey and Guernsey, and thence imported it afresh into France at an enormous profit. When, in 1769, Terray was appointed controller of finance, bad faith and insecurity were visible in all the operations of the state. He arbitrarily reduced the interest and annuities belonging to the public creditor, on the plea that the debt had been contracted on too onerous conditions. And in 1771 he completed his unscrupulous administration by seizing and appropriating the capital deposited with the *fermiers généraux*, thus causing the bankruptcy of many bankers. Happily, at that very moment, Turgot was preparing himself to inaugurate a great reform. Originally of a Scottish family, Turgot first studied at the seminary of St. Sulpice, and obtained the degree of bachelor of theology; but the direction of his studies was changed when he became acquainted with Quesnay, who had just published his *Tableau économique*, and with Vincent de Gournay, the author of the axiom, *Laissez faire, laissez passer*. On a tour with the latter in the provinces, Turgot saw everywhere the bitter fruits of monopoly; and as he witnessed a bad harvest bringing out all the evils of seclusion, he could not resist the

Trade of France.

conviction that nothing but freedom could ameliorate the condition of the people. When he became intendant, he set himself to carry into effect the views which he had published in his *Réflexions sur la Formation et la Distribution des Richesses.* And when in 1774, on the accession of Louis XVI., Turgot became comptroller of finance, he rendered his administration illustrious by the removal of a large number of taxes, the establishment of external free trade in corn, and by great improvements in the financial condition of the country. But Turgot remained in power only two years, and the policy of peace and retrenchment in France fell with him.

With more distant countries the trade was at that time pretty much in the hands of chartered companies. The trade with Turkey was monopolised by the Turkey Company. The trade with Africa was in the hands of the African Company. The South Sea Company was still in existence; and also the Hudson's Bay Company and the Sierra Leone Company. Greatest of all companies, however, was the East India Company; and it was in 1763 that, after the memorable battle of Plassy, Lord Clive extorted from the Mogul, for a small annual rent, a formal grant of the administration of the provinces of Bengal, Behar, and Orissa. A transaction of such importance could not fail to excite the greatest interest, and at home not only did it raise the value of East India Stock from 260*l.* to 1,000*l.*, but also opened the eyes of the legislature to the necessity of imposing some check or control on the action of the merchant politicians. Accordingly, a committee of the House of Commons was appointed in 1766 to inquire into the state of the company's affairs, its charters, transactions, and treaties with the princes of India, as well as its revenues and expenditure. And the result of such inquiries was the passing of two acts, one[3] forbidding the company to declare any dividend above ten per cent. per annum, and another[4] prescribing that no proprietor of that or of any other company shall be entitled to vote, who had not possessed his or her share for six months, or who had acquired it by legacy, marriage, or custom of the City of London, and that a declaration of dividend should not

Trade with the East Indies.

[3] 7 Geo. III. c. 48. [4] 7 Geo. III. c. 49.

be made more frequently than on each half year. Then too, for the first time, a burden was imposed on the company of paying 400,000*l.* a year to the public, in consideration of its territorial acquisitions, and with a view to promote its trade the duty of one shilling per lb. on tea was abolished. Looking back at the progress of the East India Company, a company of merchants, it is surprising how, little by little, by its influence over the many reigning princes of India, and by its adroitness and power, it succeeded in becoming a state within a state; and how having ceased, in great measure, to be the representative of peaceful trade, it acquired the character of conqueror and ruler.

Trade with the West Indies.

With the West India colonies the trade was of considerable importance, those colonies being then almost the sole sources of our sugar supplies. But they were after all but little developed, and their prosperity proceeded from a condition of labour and a policy of protection not likely to be of permanent duration. Not long before a pamphlet appeared showing that Tobago was not then settled, that St. Lucia was lost, that St. Vincent and Dominica were in the hands of the French; that Antigua, Nevis, St. Christopher, and Montserrat, as well as Bermuda, Anguilla, and Spanish Town, were all capable of great improvements; whilst of the Bahamas only four were inhabited by the English. It was long indeed before the West Indies became of importance to the kingdom. Yet it was to foster these colonies that an act was passed for securing and encouraging the trade of the sugar colonies by providing that no sugar, rum, or molasses of the plantations of foreign nations should be imported into Britain or Ireland, or any of the king's dominions in America, under forfeiture of the cargo, ship, and furniture; which act was renewed in 1761.

The slave trade.

What disgraced the trade of the West Indies at this period was the slave trade, then a crime of long standing, which the Portuguese have the discredit of initiating, the Spaniards of following, and the English of improving upon.[a]

[a] In 1443 the Portuguese, while engaged in their discoveries, having kidnapped some Moors along the coast of Africa, Prince Henry ordered that they be returned to their own country; but the officers obliged the friends of the captives to redeem them, and they received in exchange ten negro slaves and some gold. A new

After the War of the Succession, in 1713, England gave a monopoly of this infamous trade to the South Sea Company. Then the African Company claimed the exclusive right of prosecuting the trade; and London, Liverpool, and Bristol vied with each other in advancing it. But the conveyance of negroes from Africa to the West Indies could never be a legitimate traffic. The whole process for obtaining and conveying them was criminal and outrageous. By wars got up in the interior of Africa with the sole view of obtaining prisoners, by piratical expeditions undertaken for the very purpose of making slaves, by kidnapping, subterfuges, and artifices, poor Africans in the prime of life were inveigled to the coasts. On the rivers Senegal and Gambia, on the Windward Coast, and on the Gold Coast, European merchants, principally English, a scandal to their pretended civilisation, and a disgrace to the religion they professed, had ships fitted for the reception of such slaves. Two and two they were chained and stowed on board, and with a cold-heartedness and barbarity which, at last, roused the indignation of the world, they, or such of them, at least, as survived the transit, were carried thence to work on the plantations in the West Indies. A committee of the House of Lords was appointed in 1772 to inquire into the whole subject of slavery and the slave trade; but though the report and evidence made considerable impression, exhibiting as they did facts of appalling magnitude, and the guilty connivance of men in high

article was thus offered to the avidity of the Portuguese, and very speedily all prejudices vanished. A charter was given to some merchants at Lagos for the purpose of trading with the Moors of the African coast, and a few vessels arrived at the island of Nar. But, instead of trading with the Moors, they made a hostile attack on them, and brought off 155 captives. A fort was afterwards built on the island of Arguin, and there they imported manufactured goods which they exchanged for negro slaves. In 1508 the Spaniards having found in Hispaniola that the Indian natives were not able to work mines and fields, brought thither negroes from Africa from the Portuguese settlement on the Guinea Coast. In 1562 three English ships were fitted out for Guinea, and took thence negroes for Hispaniola. In 1689 a convention was concluded between England and Spain for supplying the Spanish West Indies with negro slaves from the island of Jamaica. In 1713 England secured, by treaty, the right of introducing negroes into Spanish America at the rate of 4,800 per annum for thirty years. From 1752 to 1762, 71,000 negroes were imported into Jamaica, and sold at 30*l.* each. In 1766 the governor of Senegambia reported that, in the previous fifty years, 70,000 of its inhabitants had been shipped.

position in the colonies, the time had not yet come for legislative action to arrest the great evil; and many years had still to pass ere the friends of humanity were allowed to utter their complaints against so nefarious a trade. The Society of Friends, in 1754, was the first to pass a resolution against the monstrous trade. In 1772 the important dictum was pronounced by the English court of law, 'that when a slave puts his foot on English ground he is free;' and it was in 1785 that Clarkson's essay on the slavery and commerce of the human species—particularly the African—first appeared, and two years after the first meeting was held of the committee of a society for the abolition of the slave trade, composed of such men as Granville Sharp, Samuel Hoare, and Thomas Clarkson, backed in and out of the House by Wilberforce and William Pitt. The seal of the society was a negro in chains kneeling, and in a supplicating manner lifting up his hands to heaven. Its motto was, 'Am I not a man and a brother?'

A great hindrance to the foreign trade of England was the existence of a cumbrous tariff. The customs were originally granted by Parliament to the sovereign on wool and leather exported. A tonnage duty on wine and a poundage on other goods imported followed; and from that time a complete tariff of duty was imposed, embracing a most extensive number of articles, levied in the most confusing manner, as old subsidies and new subsidies, one-third subsidies and two-third subsidies, petty customs and additional duties, certain to create immense embarrassment to importers and exporters. The excise duties also were very general. Scarcely an article of home production escaped its checks and interference. And if we add the burden of the most restrictive navigation law ever invented, and the danger of capture which existed, even in time of peace, from either belligerents or pirates, it will be seen that the trade of England was by no means in a satisfactory condition.

Customs duties.

A board of trade had long before been established, first by Charles I. in 1636, and afterwards by Cromwell, to meet and consider by what means the traffic and navigation of the Republic might be best promoted and regulated, and he appointed to it his son with many lords of his council, and

The Board of Trade in 1655.

about twenty merchants of London, York, Newcastle, Yarmouth, Dover, and other places. In 1660 Charles II. established a council of trade for exercising a control and superintendence over the whole commerce of the nation, and also a council of foreign plantation, both of which were, in 1672, united. In 1782, however, the board was abolished, in consequence of an attack made upon it by Lord Shelburne and Mr. Burke,* and the business of the office was managed by a committee of the privy council, whose duty was to examine the custom house account of all goods and merchandise exported and imported to and from the several ports in the kingdom as well as foreign ports, in order to inform the government of the advantage and disadvantage of the trade of the nation with other kingdoms and states in regard to the balance of trade; and also to encourage our plantations abroad by endeavouring to promote their trade, and by discovering and encouraging such branches as were most conducive to their respective interests, as well as to those of this kingdom at large. In 1786, by an order in council, the board of trade, as at present constituted, was formed; but the board, for a considerable time, possessed neither sufficient economic knowledge to guide wisely the economic policy of the kingdom, nor sufficient power to influence much its legislation.

Functions of the Board of Trade.

The functions of the Board of Trade are at present of the most varied character. It has to advise the colonial secretary on matters affecting the commerce of the colonies; and the Treasury on questions affecting the customs and excise. It has to communicate with the foreign secretary on commercial treaties; to report on every local bill; to superintend the statistics of trade, navigation, and railways; and to attend to the department of science and art, and the registration of designs. In 1864 a committee of the House of Commons made some recommendations for facilitating the arrangements between the Foreign Office and the Board of Trade, in reference to the trade with foreign nations.

* A proposal was also made in the year 1780, by Mr. Burke, to abolish the Mint, and place the coinage entirely in the hands of the Bank of England; but the provisions for carrying out these objects were eventually omitted from the bill for economic reforms brought in that year.

CHAPTER IV.

THE AMERICAN REVOLUTION AND WAR.

1764–1782.

The Colonial System.—Dissatisfaction of the American Colonists.—Taxing the Colonies.—Opposition to the Tax.—Alarm in England.—Fresh Agitation in America.—New Legislation.—Repressive Measures.—Formation of the United States.—France and the American War.—Holland and Neutral Rights.—Russia and the Armed Neutrality.—War with Holland.

The colonial system.

Had the colonial policy of England been congenial to the feelings, and advantageous to the interests of the American colonists, the further acquisitions on that continent might have had the effect of increasing their spirit of patriotism, and drawing closer the ties which bound them to the mother country. But it was otherwise. A colony was then considered in the light of a patrimony of the mother country. Spain, Portugal, France, Holland, England, each and all, adopted a colonial policy which seemed entirely to ignore the duties of the mother country towards the colonists, and to regard only their duties towards herself. The mother country alone had the right of disposing of their productions. Mexico was bound to send all her silver to Spain. Brazil could dispose of her gold nowhere but in Portugal. The sugars of St. Domingo and Martinique had no other market but France. The tobacco of Virginia and Maryland could be sold only in England. Nor were the colonists more free in purchasing than in selling. They were not allowed to carry on any direct trade with other countries. By the navigation laws none but natural born or naturalised British subjects were allowed to trade in the British possessions, and American colonists could carry on no trade whatever except in British ships. They were even prohibited from erecting any mill or engine for rolling iron, lest it should injure the iron industry of the mother country. A policy like this could not fail to irritate the feelings of the colonists, and render them peevish and discontented. 'Why,' said a New York paper, 'should a people, of whom one-half were of foreign ancestry, be cut off from all the world but England? Why must the children of Holland be debarred from the ports of the Netherlands? Why must their ships seek the produce of Europe, and, by a later law, the produce of Asia, in English harbours alone? Why are negro slaves the only considerable object of foreign commerce, which England does not compel to be first landed on her shores?'

Dissatisfaction of the American colonists.

The American colonists had long felt the wrong and injury of such a policy, and little was wanting to animate them to resent the affront; if need be, to assert their independence. So long as France shared with England the empire of North America, and Spain was possessed of Florida, the British colonists were almost compelled to cling close to the mother country for support and protection. As soon as they became free from all apprehensions, they began to realise their inherent strength, and became restive and impatient at every token of colonial dependence. 'Colonies,' said Turgot, 'are like fruits which cling to the tree only till they ripen: as soon as America can take care of herself she will do what Carthage did.' And it was not long before an occasion presented itself for the full manifestation of her altered tone and bearing towards England.

Taxing the colonies.

The first budget of a new ministry is always a trying one, though in years when retrenchments and reductions of taxes may be safely introduced, no difficulty need be apprehended. By a singular fatality, however, the British Government, soon after the war, sought to inaugurate a great novelty in the imposition of taxes, well calculated to test rather sharply the disposition of the American colonists. With the national expenditure greatly increased, and with the national debt pressing heavily on the resources of the country, the government thought it not unreasonable that the colonies, for whose protection a great expenditure had been incurred, should bear some part, at least, of the annual burdens. For their maintenance Britain had made enormous sacrifices.

In the shape of compensations and rewards large sums had been paid for their civil government. And it was not deemed very unjust if, in consideration of such sacrifices, they were called upon to give some help in relieving the exigencies of the state. A precedent of taxing the colonies appeared to exist in the Navigation Act,[1] which permitted certain produce of the plantations in America, Asia, and Africa to be carried to any other of the plantations free of customs duty, either of export or import. In 1672[2] certain rates of export duties had been imposed; and protective duties were levied in the sugar colonies in 1733;[3] but the produce of such duties was exceedingly small, and was kept apart from the imperial revenue. Sir Robert Walpole had long before suggested the propriety of taxing the colonies, but he shrunk from the responsibility of such a measure. Grenville deemed the proposition both excellent and practicable; and in committee on ways and means, on March 10, 1764, he introduced resolutions for levying certain duties in the American plantations, which passed without opposition.[4] Another resolution was also passed the same evening, towards the close of the sitting, to the effect that towards defraying the expenses of the colonies it might be proper to charge certain stamp duties in them; but this part of the budget was postponed till the following year. Accordingly, a bill was brought in to impose certain taxes on articles imported into the American colonies which readily passed into law;[5] and the occasion was also seized for restricting and, if possible, putting an end to the clandestine trade carried on between the British and Spanish West Indies, by appointing the officers of the ships stationed on the coast revenue officers.

Opposition to the tax.

No one in this country imagined that the American colonists would offer any effectual opposition, not to say resistance, to such measures; but such confidence arose from an utter misapprehension of their present atti-

[1] 12 Car. II. [2] 25 Car. II. c. 7. [3] 6 Geo. II. c. 13.

[4] The expense of the military service in the colonies amounted to nearly 500,000*l*., and the tax was expected to produce 150,000*l*.

[5] 4 Geo. III. c. 15. The produce of these duties somewhat exceeded 6,000*l*. a year.

tude. The colonists, who were extensive carriers of merchandise for their own consumption, and that of the West Indies, were not prepared especially for the latter unwonted hindrance, and remonstrated in no measured terms on the subject with the British Government. Moreover, whilst they did not deny the right of Britain to tax them, they were prepared to resist an impost to which they had not hitherto been subjected. Finding, however, that a deaf ear was turned to their entreaties, and having failed in all their efforts to get the taxes repealed, they met in Congress for the first time in October, 1765, with delegates from only ten colonies, and agreed that the people were not and never could be represented in the House of Commons of Great Britain; that taxes never had been and never could be constitutionally imposed in the colonies but by their respective legislation; that all supplies to the crown are free gifts; that for the people of Great Britain to grant the property of the colonists was neither reasonable nor consistent with the spirit of the British constitution; and that, as a measure of retaliation, they would make the utmost effort to become thenceforth independent of British goods and manufactures. Independent of England! How could they be? Had not colonial manufactures and industry been effectively discouraged? Were not the colonists entirely dependent on the mother country for almost every article of clothing and food? Well might England attach but little weight to such resolutions of the colonists, and have indulged in the belief that the mother country should always be able and have a right to count upon the patriotism and devotion of her subjects wherever situated. A moderate amount of grumbling might have been expected, but no one ever imagined that the British Government should be thereby deterred from carrying out its designs for the good of the empire. Unmoved, therefore, by remonstrances or protests, the British legislature proceeded in the following year to impose stamp duties on numerous instruments and contracts in the American colonies.* But, after all, a serious blunder this indeed proved to be, for, no sooner did the news of the passing of such an act reach the colonies,

* 5 Geo. III. c. 12. The only receipts into the exchequer arising from the Stamp Act were 3,000*l*. in 1767, and 1,000*l*. in 1768.

than meeting upon meeting was held, and the determination was come to that all orders for British goods should at once be countermanded, and everything done to inflict the greatest possible injury on the mother country.

Alarm in England. Repeal of taxes.

Little had the British Government realised the enormous mischief which was about to result from the measures they had thus at an evil moment introduced, but serious consequences speedily ensued from them on commerce and industry. The general suspension of orders from America produced great alarm among the merchants and manufacturers of Bristol, Liverpool, Leeds, and Manchester; and the anxiety felt was intensified by the fact that upwards of 4,000,000*l.* due by America to this country was placed in great jeopardy. Hence complaints from all quarters and petitions poured in upon Parliament and the king, earnestly praying for immediate relief. The people were in great agitation; a committee of the House of Commons was sitting, before whom Benjamin Franklin was examined, and all eyes were turned to Pitt as the only man who could extricate the country from its great difficulty. But Pitt could not be prevailed upon to take office; and as the Grenville ministry could no longer be maintained, the Marquis of Rockingham became first lord of the treasury. There was no withstanding the absolute necessity for retracting the mischievous policy, and the new government boldly met the difficulty by 'introducing a bill to repeal the stamp act, which passed into law.'[1] Would that this had been done with good grace and in a manner calculated to win back the heart of the disaffected; but as if the Government and Parliament were intent upon encouraging a rebel spirit, another act was passed at the same time, declaring the American colonists subordinate to and dependent upon the Crown and Parliament of Great Britain.[2] The discussion of these measures in both Houses of Parliament was, throughout, serious and animated. Had the state the right of taxing the colonies? Was it prudent, was it wise to give way to clamour and revolution? Mr. Pitt opposed the policy of the government. 'Taxation,' he said, 'is no part of the governing or legislative power. The distinction between legislation and

[1] 6 Geo. III. c. 11. [2] 6 Geo. III. c. 12.

taxation is essential to liberty. The Crown and the Peer have equally legislative powers with the Commons. If taxation be a part of simple legislation, the Crown and the Peer have rights in taxation the same as yourselves, rights which they will claim whenever the principle can be supported by might. There is an idea in some that the colonies are virtually represented in the House. I would fain know by whom an American is represented here? Is he represented by a borough? The idea of a virtual representation in this House is the most contemptible idea that ever entered into the head of men; it does not deserve a serious refutation.' Lord Camden in the same strain said, 'Taxation and representation are inseparable. The position is founded on the laws of nature; nay more, it is itself an eternal law of nature. There is not a blade of grass growing in the most obscure part of the kingdom which is not, which was not ever represented since the constitution began; there is not a blade of grass which, when taxed, was not taxed by the consent of the proprietor.' These utterances of the wisest men of the day ought to have deterred the legislature from rushing again into the blunder of levying taxes on people living thousands of miles apart, whose wants were scarcely known, whose opinions and feelings could ill be appreciated or understood. Yet, notwithstanding all such warnings, in the following years* new duties were imposed on the American colonies, some of them on articles the produce of the United Kingdom; and besides this, to the amazement of the colonists, a board of customs was established in Boston.

Fresh agitation in America.

Can we wonder at the consequences of these fresh provocations? Where was the wisdom, where the prudence of the British legislature at such a juncture? The passing of such an act aroused, among the colonists, a spirit of rebellion more determined than ever. A mass meeting was held at Boston, and quite unanimous were the resolutions to defeat the act by abstaining from the use of any of the commodities so taxed, and encouraging, by every means, the manufactures of British America. At Massachusetts a similar meeting was held at which, besides agreeing to the refusal

* 6 Geo. III. c. 52 and 7 Geo. III. c. 46.

to use such superfluities, as they were called, a circular was sent to all the colonies for the purpose of seeking to establish a greater accord among themselves. Everywhere the greatest commotion and strongest feeling were excited; and an open rebellion was evidently ready to burst out, when two other circumstances contributed greatly to fill up the measure of national indignation. The first was the appearance of a British frigate with a regiment of troops, sent over to assist the civil magistrate and the customs authorities in the execution of their duties: the second, the seizure, by that frigate, of a sloop laden with wine belonging to a Boston representative, a seizure which was followed by a riot, when the sloop was forcibly discharged in defiance of the collector of customs.

Difficult, indeed, was the position of the British Government in such circumstances. Doubtless it was incumbent on the executive to see that the law should be upheld so long as it was in force, and that rebellion should, under any circumstances, be quelled. More unlawful are the means used, more resolute must be the steps for the repression of rebellion; and we cannot wonder if, in repealing some of the duties imposed in previous years, care was taken to state that it was not as a concession to the rebellious acts of the colonists. But it seems that the measure was very partial in its operation, and that the duties repealed were only those levied upon articles of the produce and manufacture of Great Britain, which in their nature tended to the prejudice and discouragement of British trade.[10] Lord North especially was very decided in his opposition to concessions. 'What is to be done?' he said. 'Shall we, while they now deny our legal power to tax them, acquiesce in the argument of illegality and give up that power? Shall we betray out of compliment to them, and through a wish of rendering more than justice to America, resign the controlling supremacy of England? God forbid! The properest time to exert our right of taxation is when the right is refused. The properest time for making resistance is when we are attacked. To temporise is to yield, and the authority of the mother country, now unsupported, is in reality relinquished

New legislation.

[10] 10 Geo. III. c. 17.

for ever.' Accordingly, the duty on tea was left untouched, avowedly as an assertion of the supremacy of the British Parliament in the legislative and revenue concerns of the colonies; and this alone was a sufficient obstacle to the removal of the asperity between the colonies and the mother country. Whilst matters remained in a condition so unsatisfactory, three large ships, laden with tea, belonging to the East India Company, appeared in the Boston harbour. It was not usual for the East India Company to export tea direct to the British colonies of America; and under other circumstances the colonists would have rejoiced at this commencement of independent dealings with other states; but now it was different. In order to deprive the British Government of every particle of revenue from such a source, the Bostonians would not allow any portion of such tea to be landed, and by night a number of men entered the ships in disguise, discharged the vessels, and threw the valuable cargoes into the sea, thus rendering the adventure a complete failure to the East India Company.

Repressive measures.

It was by this time evident that a strong policy, either of defence or of conciliation, was needed towards the rebellious colonists; and therefore the British Government and Legislature gave themselves in earnest to the task of checking such outrages. For that purpose, in 1775, committees of both Houses of Parliament were formed, and all letters patent, charters, and commissions in force were ransacked and passed under review. A proposal was made to revive some acts of Henry VIII. and Edward III., whereby a special commission might be issued for trying the offenders in Britain. But this method was deemed impracticable and insufficient. A still more stringent course was thought necessary, and acts were passed suspending the landing, discharging, lading, and shipping of goods and merchandise in Boston, as well as for the better administration of justice, and the suppression of riots and tumults in the province of Massachusetts Bay. Nay more, as if threats and restrictions could remove discontent and rebellion, another act was passed restraining the commerce of the revolted provinces, and prohibiting them from carrying on any fishery on the banks of Newfoundland.[11]

[11] 15 Geo. III. c. 10.

We know the result. A complete and irreparable rupture ensued, and the 4th of July, 1776,[18] became the ever memorable day when the United States of America declared themselves to be a free, independent, and sovereign state, with full power to levy war, conclude peace, contract alliances, establish commerce, and do all other acts and things which independent states may of right do. And from that day vain were the efforts of Britain to prevent the consummation of the dreaded separation between herself and the American colonies. It was hard to part with colonies so flourishing. It seemed cruel, after having been tantalised with exercising supreme and unlimited power over nearly the whole continent of America, to have to resign the reins of the best portion of it, not to an enemy after a fair trial of strength, but to the colonists themselves who had been spoiled by over-kindness.[19] Surely such an issue was never contemplated when Mr. Grenville made the modest request that the Americans should be made to pay, at least, a small portion of the heavy expenses incurred for their protection. But matters had advanced too far. The die was cast. In vain did the British Government try to withdraw from the hostile attitude it had hitherto assumed. In vain an act was passed to repeal the tea duties, and to re-

Formation of the United States.

[18] Twelve states originally joined in declaring the Republic. These were the New England colonies, originated by the Puritans, viz. New Hampshire, comprising Vermont, Massachusetts, Connecticut, and Rhode Island; the state of New York, called New Netherlands, colonised by the Dutch; New Jersey, originally part of New Netherlands; Pennsylvania, founded by Penn; Delaware, originally occupied by the Swedes, next by the Dutch; Maryland, founded by Sir George Calvert; Virginia, founded by Raleigh; Carolina, North and South, a charter of which was granted by Charles II. to a number of proprietors; Georgia, owing its name to George II., founded by James Oglethorpe, M.P. In 1765 their population was about 2,000,000 European and about 500,000 of other nationalities. —Mahon's History of England, vol. viii. p. 97.

[19] George III. held that the acknowledgment of the independence of America would place this country in a state of inferiority, and be tantamount to its ruin as a great and powerful state. Lord Chatham was of the same opinion. Lord Shelburne said that when America became independent the sun of England would set. Mr. Pitt said, 'The era of England's glory is past; she is now under the awful and mortifying necessity of employing a language corresponding with her new position. The visions of her power and preeminence are passed away.' Coxe, describing the effect of the treaty of 1783, said, 'The Bourbon courts exulted in the success of their machinations, and confidently anticipated the speedy downfall of the British power.' The court of Vienna prophesied that England would ultimately sink in the unequal contest with the House of Bourbon.

nounce to a great extent the right of taxing the colonies in any form. The United States became conscious of their own strength and resources; they were alive to the noble destinies which awaited them; and resolved that force, and force alone, should decide the contest.[14]

Would that better counsel and greater magnanimity had obtained in the British cabinet even at this last moment, and that making virtue of hard necessity it had accepted with good grace the inevitable consequences of separation. Any sacrifice short of actual war would have been better. But probably thoughts of moderation and peace would have prevailed, even at the last hour, had not old animosities against foreign powers entered as an additional element of discord. The United States, anxious to secure the good will and official recognition of other civilised states, sent Dr. Franklin and others as plenipotentiaries to the several courts of Europe. What tempting offers were made by them to France especially is not well known; but it was not long ere it became manifest that considerable assistance reached the colonies in the shape of money and ammunition. England, suspicious of such conduct, sent a formal note to the French Government accusing it of favouring the revolt of the Anglo-Americans; but the French Government denied having given any such assistance, and for a time nothing transpired proving the fact of any actual agreement. As the war, however, progressed between England and America, and every chance of reconciliation ended, France felt no longer any hesitation to follow her natural impulses; and on February 7, 1778, she concluded two treaties with the American Republic, one of friendship and commerce, and another of eventual defensive alliance. Nor did France keep the transaction any longer secret. Boldly she communicated these treaties to Britain, and she justified her course by maintaining the right of France to recognise a state which had for some time asserted and achieved her independence, formed a regular government, and acted as a sovereign state. In her own judgment France was authorised by the law of nations to regard the Ameri-

France and the American War.

[14] On November 15, 1777, the thirteen colonies agreed to certain articles of confederation and perpetual union, and the confederation was afterwards replaced by the constitutional act agreed to in Congress on September 27, 1787.

can Republic as a *de facto* independent state; and she asserted, that by forming a treaty with that republic she had violated no treaty, nor interfered with the sovereign right of any state. France herself, it was said, had reason to complain of the interruption of her trade with that republic by British cruisers. Counter demands were advanced, and, after an angry correspondence, a declaration of war was made by both sides, followed by the recall of the respective ambassadors, the seizure of ships, and an embargo on British vessels in French ports.[18] But the 'beginning of strife is like the letting out of water.'

Holland and neutral rights.

Soon after the rupture with France the relations with Holland became disturbed. A nation, so essentially commercial and maritime as Holland, was too ready to seize the opportunity of carrying on a trade with the American colonies, from which she was hitherto shut out by the British navigation laws. And there was good reason for suspecting that the Dutch countenanced the Americans in many ways, and that at the very time when Britain was doing her utmost to compel her American colonies to return to their allegiance, the Dutch were frustrating her efforts by providing them with both arms and ammunition. It was hinted also that a treaty of commerce had been secretly negotiated between America and Holland, and Britain was convinced that Holland did not observe in the war a strict neutrality. On the demand of the British Government, the States General of Holland issued a decree prohibiting the export of articles of war to the American colonies without a licence from the admiralty; but the Dutch continued their trade notwithstanding, and St. Eustace became the entrepôt whence the American rebels were easily supplied. In vain did the British cruisers make constant seizure of Dutch ships; in vain did they exercise increased vigilance. A contraband trade was pursued without diminution, and the British Government, seeing no way but compulsion, appealing to the treaties of 1678

[18] The order for reprisals on the part of France bears date July 16, 1778. In a subsequent order of April 5, 1779, the commencement of hostilities is directed to be reckoned retrospectively from June 17, 1778. The effect of war on the shipping trade may be judged from the fact, that the rate of insurance between London and New York, which in time of peace was two guineas, rose in 1778 to 21l. per cent., on condition of returning five guineas if the ship sailed with convoy and arrived. From Jamaica to London even 30 guineas was charged.

and 1716, whereby both countries agreed to assist each other in case of need, asked Holland to come to her aid in her war against America. Holland was deeply interested in the maintenance of her neutrality. She had been warned by France, that, should she join England, Dutch vessels would cease to be protected, as heretofore, by the rules she had established, that free ships should make free goods, and that neutral ships might carry on their trading between the ports of any enemy, except with blockaded ports, and she hesitated in giving any answer to the British demand. On both sides was Holland hard pressed, and either course seemed fatal to her commercial interests.

Pending such negotiations, Britain felt it necessary to sound the Empress of Russia as to her intentions on the war. At first the Empress made an offer of an armed mediation, on condition that she should be left free to prosecute her designs on Turkey. But eventually she retracted from the overture. It so happened too that, at this moment, two Russian ships were seized by Spanish cruisers, on the pretext that they were intended to provision Gibraltar; and though Russia had purposed taking steps against Spain, and demanding immediate satisfaction, she preferred taking the opportunity for asserting and defending the right of neutral trading. Hence the famous declaration of armed neutrality issued by the Empress on February 26, 1780, which was communicated to the courts of London, Versailles, and Madrid. The principles contended for by that declaration were: 1st, That neutral vessels should freely trade from port to port on the coasts of the nations at war; 2nd, That goods belonging to the subjects of belligerent powers should be free in neutral ships, excepting contraband of war; 3rd, That the Empress would consider as contraband only such goods as were so indicated in the 10th and 11th articles of her treaty of commerce with Britain; and 4th, That by a blockaded port should be understood a place the entrance of which is opposed by the attacking fleet. And to this declaration the Northern powers gave in their adhesion. Denmark and Sweden were the first to enter into a convention to maintain a joint fleet for their mutual defence, and both of them declared the Baltic *mare clausum*. In a short time the United States, Prussia,

Russia and the armed neutrality.

Denmark, Sweden, Austria, Portugal, and the Two Sicilies also joined in the armed neutrality.

War with Holland.

As for Holland, nothing could have been more propitious to her interest than the league thus established between the Northern powers; and when, at last, her secret treaty with America was published, and Britain entered into open hostilities against her, she too was glad to accede to the declaration.[16] Thus the range of hostilities continued to widen, and from a small difference with her own colony, England saw herself in open war with France, Spain, Holland, and the United States of America. Six years of calamitous war failed, however, to force the American colonies to return to their allegiance with the mother country; and, after a wasteful expenditure of lives and resources,[17] Britain was obliged to bow to necessity; and the treaty of Versailles, concluded in 1783, put an end to all differences, and admitted the United States of America to all the rights of an independent sovereign state.

[16] War was declared against Holland, December 20, 1780.

[17] The total cost of the American war was estimated to be 97,599,496*l*. The public debt of the United Kingdom rose from 132,716,049*l*. in 1763 to 245,580,470*l*. in 1783. The American war of independence lasted seven years, and was closed by the treaty of peace signed at Paris on November 30, 1782.

CHAPTER V.

MR. PITT'S PEACE ADMINISTRATION.

1783–1792.

Mr. Pitt.—Increase of Taxation.—Consolidation of Customs Duties.—Benefits of International Exchanges.—Relations between France and England.—Proposal of France for Mutual Freedom of Trade.—Negotiations for a Treaty of Commerce.—More Treaties of Commerce.—Trade with the United States.—Relations of the West Indies to the United States.—Mr. Pitt's Motion on the Slave Trade.—Affairs of the East India Company.—State of the Country.

UNDER a system of government purely representative like that of the United Kingdom, it is not the sovereign but the first minister of the crown who stamps the administration with the mark of his character and genius. The sovereign is, indeed, the corner-stone on which all the institutions of the country are securely fixed; but the minister is the builder who shapes and constructs the national edifice. The responsible adviser of the sovereign, and yet the representative of the people, it is the prime minister who truly holds the reins of the state; and though each branch of the administration is presided over by a minister immediately responsible for the duties connected with it, the management of the state is primarily entrusted to the head of the cabinet, and to him all the ministers are responsible. Seldom, however, has the administration been so personified in its prime minister as during the eventful government of Mr. Pitt. Just twenty-one years old when he made his first speech in Parliament, and only twenty-three when, in 1783, he was appointed first lord of the treasury and chancellor of the exchequer, young, eloquent, and energetic, a minister of great talent, a man of commanding influence, for upwards of seventeen years he held absolute sway over the destinies of his country. Mr. Pitt.

For many years, either from incompetency of the finance

minister, or from insuperable difficulties, no attempt was made to maintain equilibrium between revenue and expenditure, whilst the taxes were, in many instances, oppressive, and the customs and excise duties were evaded by an organised system of smuggling. Laws against smuggling there were in abundance, but, hazardous as it was, the temptation to it was great, and that could be diminished only by the lowering of the taxes. Tea[1] was a favourite article with the smuggler, so long as the duty was nearly 120 per cent. *ad valorem*; and the result was, that scarcely a third of the quantity consumed was imported in an open and lawful manner —a state of things as injurious to the revenue as it was unjust to the fair dealer. Mr. Pitt was wise, therefore, in reducing the duty to 12½ per cent., though the treasury could ill spare even a temporary loss of revenue. Convinced, however, as he was, that the resources of the people admitted an additional weight of taxation, Mr. Pitt did not hesitate in imposing tax upon tax, in the selection of which he seemed to pay but little regard either to the incidence of taxation or to its influence on the industries of the people. We may well imagine that no small amount of grumbling was occasioned as he levied taxes on bricks and tiles, on houses and windows, on male and female servants, on horses and coaches.

Increase of taxation.

One essential benefit conferred by Mr. Pitt in connection with taxation, was the consolidation of the customs duties,[2] by abolishing all existing imposts and substituting for them one single duty upon each article equivalent to the aggregate of the various duties by which it had previously been loaded. The difficulty of this reform may be conceived from the fact, that the resolutions submitted to the House of Commons for the purpose amounted to upwards of three thousand

Consolidation of customs duties.

[1] In 1689 an excise duty was laid on tea of 5s. per lb.; it was afterwards reduced to 4s. per lb., with a customs duty of 11 per cent. In 1745 the excise duty was reduced to 1s. per lb. and 25 per cent. *ad valorem*; but in 1759 the duty was raised, and from that date to 1781 it ranged from 65 to 120 per cent. *ad valorem*.

[2] The first attempt to consolidate the customs duties was made in 1660, under the act 12 Ch. II. c. 4; but the duties were greatly complicated when the consolidation of customs duties was recommended by the commissioners of public accounts in their thirteenth report, dated March 18, 1785; and the recommendations were carried into effect by Mr. Pitt under the Consolidation Act, 27 Geo. III. c. 13.

in number. But such a consolidation was beneficial not to the public only, but the revenue itself gained immensely from the simplicity thus introduced, and it had the effect of reducing somewhat the cost of collecting the customs duties, which was then as high as 6*l.* 7*s.* per cent. on the gross, and 8*l.* 9*s.* 10*d.* per cent. on the net revenue. The public, however, paid much more than appeared in the public accounts, from the multiplicity of fees charged by the various officers, in part sanctioned by law, but chiefly claimed on the ground of ancient usage. And it was the more vexatious, since the fees charged differed much in every port, constituting another source of uncertainty. The warehousing system not being then in existence, the watching and guarding of custom house officers must itself have been annoying to the last degree, and must have hindered trade in a manner of which we have no idea at the present time.

More interesting, however, than taxes and consolidation acts is the treaty of commerce with France, which Mr. Pitt was fortunate in concluding. The commercial relations between England and France commenced very early. As far back as the time of Charlemagne, a convention was concluded between the two countries with a view of exempting travelling pilgrims to Rome from the payment of customs duties upon the fine works in gold and silver which they were in the habit of carrying with them. In 1303 a treaty of commerce was established, by which liberty was granted to merchants on both sides to trade freely in all kinds of merchandise on paying duties. In 1467, under the reign of James III., a treaty provided that it should be lawful for all Scottish merchants to navigate and trade to Rochelle, Bordeaux, and other parts of France. In 1513 a treaty of peace was concluded by which all imposts or tolls laid on merchants or others of either country within the previous forty-seven years were abolished. And many were the conventions entered into for the purpose of fostering relations of trade between the two states, but wars and contentions suspended or broke them all. In a treaty concluded with Henry IV. it was stipulated that, in the ports of London for England and of Rouen for France, all controversies between merchants should be referred to the merchants of each nation,

Relations between France and England.

who should be called 'conservators of commerce.' But, as in other cases, it was successively confirmed or abrogated, as war or peace reigned. In 1678 all trade with France was absolutely prohibited, and it was not resumed till the conclusion of the treaty of Utrecht, which provided for mutual rights and privileges in courts of justice, commerce, and taxes, and the repeal of all prohibitory tariffs on both sides. But again France and England were at war, and all commercial relations were suspended.

Nor was it from political causes only that the relations of commerce between England and France were thus precarious and spasmodic. Economic blunders were a prominent cause of mutual estrangement. Unfortunately the two nations, though placed in such proximity to one another, with produce and manufactures in many respects so different, yet both eminent in art, civilisation, and science, regarded each other not as friends and allies, but as competitors and rivals. How illiberal, how repulsive to natural law does it seem that England and France should have so long considered each other as natural enemies, and that they should have sacrificed their best interests to petty jealousies and diplomatic quarrels! How sad that two countries which, by the diversity of their products and manufactures, seem destined by nature to be helpful to one another in supplying their deficiencies, should have been so completely alienated as to be driven to seek, thousands of miles distant, for those very commodities which they might have had so near at hand. The principle of free trade, indeed, is of universal application. Let each of us seek from the other what we cannot produce ourselves; let each of us husband and foster to the highest possible degree and excellence such articles as are natural and indigenous to our soil and industry, and we shall best fulfil the gracious designs of Providence. Follow its dictates and the sum total of human labour will be greater, the labourers will receive a greater reward, and the resources of the world will be rendered available for the immediate necessities of each country. Frustrate them, and we shall only reap disappointment and loss. Mr. Pitt well understood the benefit of a free exchange between the different countries of the world; and he sought to secure for both countries the benefit of their respective resources. He well knew, that whilst British industry was directed to the production of comfortable clothing, or of articles which diffuse substantial comforts, or the means of enjoyment, among the great body of the people, the French provided articles of finery, taste, and luxury, and he wished to promote a free interchange between them.

As soon as the treaty of Versailles was concluded, in 1783, France came forward with a noble proposal, that the two countries should, in conjunction with the other powers, abolish all exclusive trading. But England was not prepared for such a liberal measure, and the British Government declined giving an answer without knowing the mind of Russia on the subject. An excellent opportunity for inaugurating a new era of commercial freedom was thus lost; and consequently the French Government, which had just dissolved the old East India Company, gave a charter to a new company, with exclusive right of trading to all countries beyond the Cape of Good Hope. The restrictive tariff of England was then an object of just complaint on the part of France. Soon after the war quite a rage existed in France for foreign goods, and more especially for British. But the French Government considered it unreasonable to open the French market to British goods whilst the British market was almost entirely closed to French goods, and a decree was issued that, unless a liberal system were universally and reciprocally established, France would be compelled to prohibit the importation of foreign goods.

Proposals of France for mutual freedom.

At this juncture it was that negotiations for a treaty of commerce were set on foot between the two countries. The treaty of peace with France, concluded in 1783, anticipated the necessity of revising the subsisting treaties of commerce, and provided that immediately after the exchange of ratifications the two high contracting parties should name commissioners to treat concerning new arrangements of commerce between the two nations, on the basis of reciprocity and mutual convenience, such arrangements to be settled within two years from the conclusion of the treaty. Mr. Pitt acted upon this, and appointed Mr. Eden, a political opponent, to represent England. France also appointed M. de Rayneval a commissioner to negotiate the treaty, and they gave them-

Negotiations for a treaty of commerce.

selves in earnest to the work. It was a difficult task to perform, but Mr. Eden obtained all the requisite information from the merchants and manufacturers of this country, whom he examined at the privy council. Negotiations were then commenced, and, on April 17, Mr. Eden sent a project of a commercial treaty, completed and settled, which met with the approbation of Mr. Pitt. But the British Government did not deem the proposal sufficiently advantageous, and it had to be abandoned. A new mode of negotiation was then adopted. Instead of making any alteration in the suggested treaty, the British Government sent a 'declaration' to the French, and that was replied to by a counter-declaration, a method which occasioned much correspondence. For a time, indeed, doubts were entertained in this country as to the sincerity of the French Government, but demands were made which could not meet with acceptance, and Mr. Eden himself wrote that he could not propose the free importation of English cotton into France so long as French silks were excluded from England. The negotiations thus advanced very slowly for many months, but the treaty was at last concluded on September 26, 1786, the principal provisions of which were:—That the wines of France should pay no higher duties in Great Britain than those paid by the wines of Portugal; that the duty on French vinegar in Britain should be reduced from 67*l.* 5*s.* 3*d.* to 32*l.* 18*s.* 10*d.* per tun; that the duty on brandy should be reduced from 9*s.* 6*d.* to 7*s.* per gallon; that the duties on hardware, cutlery, cabinetware, turnery, steel, copper, &c., should not exceed 10 per cent. in either country; that the duties on cotton manufactures and woollen manufactures should not exceed 12 per cent. in both countries, excepting those mixed with silks, which were prohibited on both sides; and that porcelain, earthenware, and pottery should pay 12 per cent. *ad valorem.* The conditions were in truth exceedingly liberal, and would bear a favourable comparison with any former or subsequent treaty between Britain and France. But the treaty met with a cold, if not a hostile, reception both in England and in France, each country thinking itself to have been outdone by the other. Whilst in the House of Commons Mr. Pitt had to face an organised opposition led by Mr. Fox, the resolutions having been carried only by a majority of 248 to 118, in France the government of Louis XVI. lost not a little in public favour from the supposed one-sidedness of the treaty in favour of England.

However it be, the conclusion of this treaty between France and England gave considerable stimulus to the conclusion of similar treaties between other countries. One was concluded between France and Russia. The United States entered into a treaty of commerce with Prussia; Russia concluded one with Austria; and, under the combined influence of peace, and better commercial relations, international trading increased considerably. The foreign trade of Great Britain was in a prosperous condition during this period. The value of imports rose from 13,000,000*l.* in 1783 to nearly 20,000,000*l.* in 1792, the value of exports from 14,000,000*l.* to 25,000,000*l.*

More treaties of commerce.

The extension of the trade with the United States of America was, indeed, remarkable. Not a few there were in this country who had entertained the greatest fear that with the loss of the American colonies England would lose the whole of the large and growing trade carried on with the Western continent. But how contrary was the result! Before the American war, from 1766 to 1775, our exports to the American colonies amounted on an average to about 2,000,000*l.* in official value. During the war the trade was, of course, all but suspended; but from 1784 to 1792 the average annual exports amounted to upwards of 3,000,000*l.* in value. From the first the progress of the new Republic has been rapid and extraordinary. The population increased in an unprecedented manner. Immense tracts of land were brought under cultivation. In 1778 cotton was successfully planted in Georgia, with seed brought over from the Bahamas, and Carolina soon followed the example. The shipping of the States increased apace. The United States Bank was established in 1791 with a capital of 10,000,000*l.* The resources of the country were developed in a manner altogether different from the time when the different states were colonies of Great Britain. Unfortunately, the government strove to promote native manufactures by a protective policy; and this is the only department in which the Americans utterly failed to achieve any distinction. George Washington, it is true, recommended to Congress, in 1789, the extension of native manu-

Trade with the United States.

facture; but he did not urge high protective duties. 'Our commercial policy,' he said, 'should hold an equal and impartial hand; neither seeking nor granting exclusive favours and preferences, consulting the natural course of things, diffusing and diversifying, by gentle means, the streams of commerce, but forcing nothing.' And Franklin urged the same course: 'Perhaps, in general,' he said, 'it would be better if government meddled no further with trade than to protect it, and let it take its course. Most of the statutes or acts, edicts, or arrests, and placards of parliament, princes, and states, for regulating, directing, or restraining of trade, have, we think, been either political blunders or jobs obtained by artful men for private advantage under the pretence of public good. When Colbert assembled some of the wise old merchants of France, and desired their advice and opinion how he could best serve and promote commerce, their answer, after consultation, was in three words only, *Laissez-nous faire*. It is said by a very solid writer of the same nation, that he is well advanced in the science of politics who knows the full force of the maxim, *Pas trop gouverner*; which, perhaps, would be of more use when applied to trade than in any other public concern. It were therefore to be wished that commerce were as free between all the nations of the world as it is between the several counties of England; so would all, by mutual communications, obtain more enjoyment. Those counties do not ruin each other by trade, neither would the nations.'

Relations of the United States with the West India colonies.

Upon the conclusion of the war in 1783, Mr. Pitt, desirous to deal liberally with the United States respecting their intercourse with the British colonies, introduced a bill in parliament, by which vessels belonging to citizens of the United States would be admitted into the ports of the West India islands, with goods or merchandise of American growth or produce, and would be permitted to export to the United States any merchandise or goods whatever. But a violent opposition was made to this bill by the British shipping interest, headed by Lord Sheffield, and the bill was laid aside. Soon after, on the fall of Mr. Pitt's administration, an order in council was issued, totally excluding American vessels from the British West Indies, and some of the staple productions of the United States were not permitted to be carried there even in British bottoms. In vain the West India planters protested against any restriction being imposed on their trade with the United States of America. Even in 1788 an act was passed, permitting the importation of American produce into the West Indies in British vessels only. Can we wonder that, with such illiberal measures on the part of England, the United States were induced to adopt a policy of retaliation?

Public opinion in the matter of the slave trade, between Africa and the West Indies especially, had by this time made considerable progress. The committee which first met in a private dwelling with no other force at their command than that of the principle of right, acting from no other motive than that of pure and expanded benevolence, and with scarcely any of those means of diffusing information which are within our reach at the present day, had already so far indoctrinated the minds of men of eminence as to the rectitude and soundness of their views, as to induce a statesman like William Pitt to advocate them side by side with a philanthropist like Wilberforce in the senate-house of England. The first effective measure adopted was the appointment of a committee of the council of trade in 1788 'to inquire into the state of that part of Africa whence the slaves are brought, the manner of obtaining them, the transportation and sale of them, and the effects of the slave trade upon the colonies and the general commerce of the kingdom.' The second was the presentation, by the hands of Wilberforce to the House of Commons, of a petition, which however, owing to the indisposition of that distinguished leader of the agitation, was presented by Mr. Pitt. Need we say how Mr. Pitt supplied the want, how he performed his task. Lord Brougham characterised his oration, for so it was, as combining with the most impassioned declamation the deepest pathos, the most lively imagination, and the closest reasoning. 'Sir,' he said, 'I trust we shall no longer continue this commerce to the destruction of every improvement on that wide continent, and shall not consider ourselves as conferring too great a boon in restoring its inhabitants to the rank of human beings. I trust we shall not think our-

Mr. Pitt's action on the slave trade.

selves too liberal if, by abolishing the slave trade, we give them the same common chance of civilisation with other parts of the world; and that we shall now allow to Africa the prospect of attaining to the same blessings which we ourselves, through the favourable dispensations of Divine Providence, have been permitted, at a much more early period, to enjoy. If we listen to the voice of reason and duty, and pursue, this night, the line of conduct which they prescribe, some of us may live to see a reverse of that picture from which we now turn our eyes with shame and regret. We may live to behold the natives of Africa engaged in the calm occupations of industry, in the pursuit of a just and legitimate commerce. We may behold the beams of science and philosophy breaking in upon their land, which at some happy period in still later times may blaze with full lustre, and joining their influence to that of pure religion, may illuminate and invigorate the most distant extremities of that immense continent. Then may we hope that even Africa, though last of all the quarters of the globe, shall enjoy at length, in the evening of her days, those blessings which have descended so plentifully upon us in a much earlier period of the world. Then, also, will Europe, participating in her improvement and prosperity, receive an ample recompense for the tardy kindness, if kindness it can be called, of no longer hindering that continent from extricating herself out of the darkness which, in other more fortunate regions, has been so much more speedily dispelled.' This was a magnificent address worthy of Mr. Pitt; but how is it, asked Lord Brougham, that when it came to the votes, he suffered everyone of his colleagues, nay of his mere underlings in office, to vote against the resolution, if they thought fit? Many years had to pass before the enormity and wickedness of that human traffic were fully realised, and before deliberate action was taken for its extinction. It is not indeed to the well-prepared oration of even so distinguished a man as Mr. Pitt that we owe the final triumph of the great cause, but to the ever active, ever plodding, ever loving work of such men as Wilberforce and Clarkson, and especially to the untiring efforts, the fervent, impassioned, and heartrending pleadings, in and out of parliament, of the great Brougham, whose memory will ever live in the hearts of the British people. On April 9, 1791, Wilberforce introduced his bill to prevent the further importation of slaves into the British colonies in the West Indies, but it was lost by 88 to 163. On April 2, 1792, he again moved that it is the opinion of this House that the African slave trade ought to be abolished; and upon this two divisions took place, the first as to gradual or immediate abolition, 193 being for the former and 125 for the latter; the second as to gradual or none, in which 193 voted for the gradual and 85 for no abolition at all. It was only in 1806 that a resolution, moved by Mr. Fox, for the total abolition of the slave trade was carried in the House of Commons; and, on Lord Granville's motion in the Lords, in the following year, the general abolition passed, making the slave trade illegal after January 1, 1808.[3]

Affairs of the East India Company.

The affairs of the East India Company, in whose hands the entire trade with Asia practically remained, continued to attract immense attention during this period. Not content with having imposed on the East India Company the burden of paying a large sum annually to the state, an attempt was made to take from its hand the absolute control of its vast possessions. The administration of Warren Hastings having been particularly distinguished for wars and conquests, great was the regret and moral indignation felt in this country at the atrocities committed in India under the shield of the British name; and so strong, indeed, was the feeling that such policy ill represented the dignity and honour of England, that many efforts were made to abolish the court of directors altogether, and to vest the government of India in the hands of commissioners appointed by Parliament. In November, 1783, Mr. Fox, one of the secretaries of state, introduced a bill into parliament for the purpose of vesting the affairs of the company in seven principal directors or commissioners, with whom should rest the appointment of all its officers and servants, the rights of peace and war, and the entire disposal of the revenue. To such a measure the company of course offered an uncompromising opposition. But Mr. Fox introduced another bill, still more

[3] 47 Geo. III. sess. 1, c. 36.

decisive, for preventing arbitrary and despotic proceedings in the administration of the territorial possessions, for prohibiting the company from making war unless for self-defence, and from acquiring or exchanging territories, and for otherwise restraining the free action of the company. The principal question involved in these bills was, What right has the state to interfere with a chartered company? Can it touch the statutes of the Bank of England, of the universities, or of any corporation? The East India Company did its utmost to resist such an interference of the state, and Mr. Pitt joined in opposing it. After much discussion the bill passed in the House of Commons, but it was rejected in the Lords. The subject, however, was of too great importance to rest as it was; and, in the following year, one of the first measures introduced by Mr. Pitt was a bill for the better regulation and management of the affairs of the East India Company and of the British possessions in India, and for establishing a court of judicature for the more speedy and effectual trial of persons accused of offences committed in the East Indies, which became law. And it was then that the board of control was established, or a board of commissioners, consisting of six members of the privy council, with instructions to check, superintend, and control all acts, operations, and concerns which in anywise relate to the civil or military government or revenues of the territories and possessions of the East India Company. The preamble of the act having formally declared that to pursue schemes of conquest and extension of dominion in India was repugnant to the wish, the honour, and policy of the nation, it was expressly enacted that the governor-general should be prohibited from commencing hostilities or entering into any treaty for making war against any of the princes of the country, unless such princes shall have begun hostilities or made preparations for hostilities against the company or any prince or state dependent upon or under the guarantee of the company.[1]

Other branches of trade were more or less prosperous during this period. And yet the state of the country was not so satisfactory as it might seem. The harvest

State of the country.

[1] 24 Geo. III. sess. 2, c. 25.

for several years after the conclusion of peace proved deficient. There were riots in 1780, when the mob attacked the Bank, though happily not till the directors obtained sufficient force to secure its safety. The finances were in a precarious condition. It was at best a period of transition, with high taxes and with only a prospective vista of increasing prosperity. But there were men in the country who, whilst building colossal fortunes for themselves, were carrying the trade and fair name of England all over the world. London had her Coutts, Hoares, Barclays, Barings, Goldsmids, and Rothschilds; Liverpool had her Heywoods and Cunliffes; Manchester her Peels and Potters; Leeds her Gotts and Marshalls; Glasgow her Tennants, Monteiths, and Dales; Birmingham her Boulton and Watts; Bristol her Miles:—men distinguished for their judicious management of business, eminently shrewd in observation, famous for their charitable dispositions, and the founders of many of our noblest works of benevolence; plain-spoken, it may be, and possessing little refinement in taste, yet endowed with enviable good sense, and, above all, exemplary for their commercial integrity.

PART II.

1792–1820.

FROM THE FRENCH REVOLUTION

TO THE

RESUMPTION OF CASH PAYMENTS.

SUMMARY.

1792–1820.

The French Revolution and war retarded for more than a quarter of a century the natural growth of the goodly seed of mechanical discovery, and other means of improvement, which was sown under happier auspices. This was a time when the finances of the country were tried and stretched to an enormous extent; when the currency was placed in a most abnormal condition; and when international law was cited in defence of maritime rights, the exercise of which was disastrous to trade and navigation. But a war of such vast dimensions, and so long protracted, greatly exhausted the resources of the nation, and paralysed the principal branches of industry. As soon, therefore, as peace was restored, and trade was able to resume its course, it became a necessity to set the house in order, and first of all to put an end to the circulation of a practically inconvertible currency by the resumption of cash payments.

CHAPTER I.

THE FRENCH REVOLUTION AND ITS EFFECTS ON BANKING AND CURRENCY.

1788–1800.

State of France.—England and the French Revolution.—Effect of the Revolution on the Money Market.—Commercial Crisis.—Government Assistance.—Bad Harvests.—State of the Bank of England.—Failure of Country Banks.—Uneasiness of the Bank of England.—Suspension of Cash Payments.—The Bill of Indemnity.—Want of Currencies.

It would have been well had Europe been allowed to enjoy a longer respite from the turmoils of wars, and had England been permitted without disturbance to reap the benefits of the improvements introduced in her manufacturing industry. But France willed it otherwise. The grievous famine of 1788 had completely subverted the economic policy of M. Necker, in itself not the most sound. After it came the profuse and wasteful administration of Calonne, who threw the finances of the country into still more helpless disorder; and then, with the assembling of the States General, were enacted those troublous scenes which rendered France a lesson and a warning to all nations. The first measures of the States General were indeed highly commendable. They opened the Indian trade to the whole nation, abolished the pernicious and partial tax upon salt and the heavy duty upon tobacco, substituting for these a light impost upon property and annuities, duties upon patents, and stamp duties. They restored the property of the Protestants, which had been confiscated upon the revocation of the Edict of Nantes, relieved the Jews from the special burdens imposed upon them, and threw the courts of justice open to the whole people. These were substantial reforms, and of enduring benefit. But very soon the revolution put an end to the calm and dignified demeanour of that legislative assembly. And when, in order to remedy the shattered state of

State of France.

the finances, the States General, rather than listen to Necker's advice to contract new loans, resolved to issue assignats, or states notes, on the guarantee of the crown and church property, they entered into that fatal course which could not fail to end in a complete and irretrievable bankruptcy. With the politics of the French Revolution we have nothing to do. But politics and commerce are intimately connected, and a revolution which plunged France, and nearly the whole of Europe, into an ocean of trouble and suffering, and which, for a period extending over nearly a quarter of a century, filled the land with blood, destroyed every political landmark, and threw a nation, ever foremost in civilisation and science, at the mercy of the wildest passions, could not fail to exercise the most calamitous influence on commerce and industry. And it was long, very long, before Europe was enabled to build the waste places, and restore to life and vigour those springs of activity which throughout the sanguinary contest were very nigh exhausted.

England and the French Revolution.

The French Revolution would not have been nearly so injurious had England maintained a perfect neutrality, and avoided the danger of plunging herself and the rest of Europe into the horrors of a European war. She knew how destructive such a course would prove to her commerce and industry; she knew how much she would have to contend with, by entering into an open conflict with a powerful nation, and at a time when passions were so excited, and when public law was manifestly ignored, or left in abeyance. But there were powerful influences at work, which fed an unrelenting animosity between the two countries, and which, at last, rendered all attempts at remaining passive altogether hopeless. How far Mr. Pitt was responsible for the policy pursued towards France at this critical period, we cannot say. Perhaps a necessity from without and from within determined the action of the British Government far more than any personal inclination, or even the indiscreet advice of enthusiastic royalists. However it be, when the National Convention went the length of reversing all social institutions, dethroning and executing the monarch, and even menacing England herself with her turbulent and incendiary acts, Mr. Pitt suddenly interrupted all negotiations with M. Chauvelin, the French minister in this country and upon that a declaration of war[1] was made by France on February 1, 1793, which placed the commerce and industry of France and England, and indeed of the whole civilised world, in terrible jeopardy.[2]

Effect of the Revolution on the money market.

Clearly to understand what influence was exercised by the French Revolution and war on commerce and industry, it will be well to keep distinct its principal events as they affected banking and the currencies, home and foreign trade, and the finances of the country. The money market is extremely sensitive. Most buoyant in times of prosperity, suddenly it may change into a state of panic at the approach of the least symptom of disaster; and we may well imagine that, when the price of consols fell from 97½ in March 1792 to 70½ in February 1793, it was not long ere capital and credit took wings and fled, leaving the poor merchants to scramble as they might through difficulties of their own creation. The moment the fatal war began, commercial bankruptcies, which hitherto had been rare and of small importance, became very numerous.[3] Many of them, indeed, were not the immediate consequence of the French Revolution, and in several cases were in no wise concerned with the French trade, still we may well imagine that, directly or indirectly, every branch of industry suffered from that catastrophe.

Commercial crisis.

In commerce, whenever the horizon becomes clouded, and confidence begins to shake, the first to

[1] The French declaration of war specifically lays down the following grounds of complaint:

1. That the court of St. James has attempted to impede the different purchases of corn, arms, and other commodities ordered in England either by French citizens or the agents of the republic.

2. That it has caused to be stopped several boats and ships loaded with grain for France contrary to the treaty of 1786, while exportation to other foreign countries was freed.

3. That, in order still more effectively to obstruct the commercial operations of the republic in England, it obtained an act of Parliament prohibiting the circulation of assignats.

4. That, in violation of the 4th article of the treaty of 1786, it obtained another act, in the month of January last, which subjects all French citizens residing in or coming into England to forms the most inquisitorial, vexatious, and dangerous.

[2] On the part of the United Kingdom an order in council was issued on February 4, 1793, laying an embargo on all French ships in British ports, and on February 11, another order for general reprisals against France.

[3] The number of commissions of bankruptcy was, in 1792, 931; and, in 1793 1956, including 26 commissions against bankers.

succumb are always those who have transgressed the strict boundaries of prudence, or embarked in hazardous and speculative adventures. But there were causes at work which could not fail to produce great disasters at a juncture like this. The prices of colonial produce had been unusually high from apprehended scarcity. A considerable laxity in operations of credit had for some time caused anxiety. A very irregular practice existed in country merchants acting as bankers, and circulating paper or notes payable to bearer on demand, with the option to pay them in the country or in London.[4] In a variety of ways the commercial community was ill-prepared for the sudden reverses caused by war, and a crisis became inevitable. Then the prices of nearly every article fell immensely; goods became unsaleable; credit was suspended, and over one hundred issuers of the optional notes failed, which caused the withdrawal of the paper circulation, more than ever required by the mercantile community. No charge could be made against the Bank of England for any undue curtailment of its accommodation.[5] Notwithstanding a heavy drain upon its treasure, occasioned by a great demand from the country, the Bank circulation continued high, and its discounts were on a large scale. What was to be done? Under circumstances so urgent Mr. Pitt attended a meeting held at the Mansion House with the principal merchants and traders, and shortly after, on his motion, a committee of the House of Commons was appointed to inquire into the state of commercial credit. Without loss of time the report was laid before the House, and the result was to show that the crisis was indeed extensive; that, commencing with those who had issued circulating paper without sufficient capital, the ruin had involved other houses who possessed funds ample ultimately to discharge their obligations, but who could not convert such funds at the time; that the sudden discredit of paper had created a deficiency of circulating medium, and consequently great inconvenience in business; that the fear of unusual requirements had induced bankers to keep a large sum of money out of circulation, and materially to restrict their advances; that goods could not be sold, and orders were not

[4] Out of 279 country bankers issuing notes 204 issued optional notes.

[5] The amount of banknotes in circulation on February 26, 1793, was 11,426,381*l.*; and, on August 26, 10,338,214*l.*

forthcoming; that matters were every day assuming a more serious aspect; that great distress existed in Scotland, especially in Glasgow and Paisley; that a large number of failures had already taken place; that workmen were out of employment; and that the only remedy for the evil lay in an advance of exchequer bills to fill the void in the currency.[*]

On the presentation of this report Mr. Pitt hastened to carry out its recommendations, and on April 30 he moved in the House of Commons, 'that his majesty be enabled to direct exchequer bills to the amount of 5,000,000*l.* to be issued to commissioners, to be by them advanced, under certain regulations and restrictions, for the assistance or accommodation of such persons as shall be desirous of receiving the same, on due security being given for the repayment of the sums so advanced within a time to be limited.' To this course, however, Mr. Fox objected, and with much reason. In a speech of great force he observed, that the recommendations of the commissioners were of a most anomalous nature, and fraught with great danger. He questioned the propriety of issuing such a sum because, if it proved insufficient, at what point were we to stop? He urged that, by entering into such an undertaking, Parliament and Government were placing themselves in a new character; that, besides the legislative and executive, they were now assuming the commercial. And he asked, why not leave such a business in the hands of the Bank of England? If the Bank was not prepared to assist the merchants, and saw

Government assistance.

[*] The committee recommended that 'power be given to issue such bills to an amount not exceeding 5,000,000*l.*, in sums of 100*l.*, 50*l.*, and 20*l.*, to bear an interest of two and a half per cent. per day, and to be payable one-fourth on August 31 next, one-fourth in November, one-fourth in February 1794, and one-fourth in May; that power be given to the commissioners to advance such exchequer bills to the persons applying for the same, in equal proportions of bills payable at the different periods before mentioned, on the security of goods to be deposited in the custody of officers to be named by the commissioners in London, Bristol, Hull, Liverpool, Leith, or Glasgow, or on such personal securities of a given number of persons as shall be satisfactory to the commissioners, such security to be given in a form to be prescribed for the purpose, and to be made binding on the persons giving the same to the amount for which each person shall respectively make himself security. That these advances in no case be more than 50*l.* per cent. on the value of the securities, and less at the discretion of the commissioners, and that they be made on condition that the sums so advanced shall be repaid with interest at the rate of five per cent. per annum, fifteen days before the date when the respective exchequer bills shall fall due, or earlier, at the option of the parties.'

reasons for not doing so, why should the Government do it? Yet, notwithstanding all these objections, Mr. Fox declared that he wanted nerve to give the measure a decided opposition; and the resolution having passed, commissioners were appointed to grant such advances.[7] The result of the measure seemed certainly satisfactory; so far at least, that the timely intervention stemmed the current of commercial discredit, and trade revived. Soon afterwards the bullion in the Bank increased, the exchanges once more turned in favour of this country, and again credit improved. But if trade was curtailed and losses had been incurred; if the ordinary avenues of wealth were closed, and politics still sent forth notes of war and discord, the real evils were not likely to be cured by the issue of exchequer bills. Very soon fresh emergencies would doubtless arise, that would again expose the frail condition of many of the houses whose fall was for a time prevented.

Bad harvests.

And nothing could be more effective for that purpose than a succession of bad harvests. The year 1792 was most remarkable for an extremely wet summer, by which the wheat crop was greatly injured, and it became necessary to issue an order in council prohibiting the exportation of grain till the following summer. In 1793 spring corn was very deficient. In 1794 great damage was caused by a very hot summer and drought; and, in 1795, there was a very severe winter, a spring and summer cold and stormy, and likewise a very deficient harvest, to meet the exigencies of which not only bounties were granted for any wheat and flour imported, but the members of both Houses of Parliament entered into the fruitless engagement, to reduce the consumption of wheat in their families by at least one-third of the quantity consumed in ordinary times, and to recommend the practice in their several neighbourhoods. But the effect of this deficiency on the commerce and finances of the country was very serious. Such a succession of bad crops necessarily gave rise to a very

[7] The names of the commissioners were, Lord Sheffield, Sir Grey Cooper, Sir John Sinclair, Messrs. William Pomteney, Richard Maidman Trench Chiswell, John William Anderson, Robert Smith, Samuel Bosanquet, Thomas Boddington, William Manning, John Whitmore, Francis Baring, Edward Foster, William Raikes, Robert Darell, Robert Barclay, Charles Grant, Gilbert Innes, Jeremiah Harman, and James Drogden.

large importation of corn, and with it the obligation of heavy payments to foreign countries.[1] Besides this, large quantities of naval stores had to be bought at exorbitant prices for the war. A considerable amount was required to be sent abroad as subsidies, and for the payment of troops, all of which caused great demands on the Bank of England, and imposed a corresponding caution in its accommodation and discount.

Towards the close of the year 1795, the Bank caused a notice to be put on its door, to the effect that, in future, whenever bills were sent for discount to a larger amount than it was resolved on to discount on the day, a *pro rata* proportion of the bills in each parcel, as were not otherwise objectionable, would be returned to the person sending them, without regard to the respectability of the party sending in the bills, or the quality of the bills themselves. Such an announcement, coupled with an actual restriction of the issue to the extent of 3,000,000*l.*,[2] threw the mercantile world into a state of great alarm; and a meeting was held at the London Tavern on April 2, 1796, complaining of the insufficiency of the circulating medium for the trade of the metropolis, which was attributed to the increase of commerce and the diminution of mercantile discount resolved on by the Bank. As the year advanced matters became worse and worse. Time after time the fear of a French invasion became very prevalent, and as an immediate attack on Ireland was apprehended, the farmers were panic stricken and brought their produce to market. But, instead of keeping the notes of the country banks on hand as their wont was, they sent them in at once for payment.

State of the Bank of England.

This unusual and sudden demand for cash had a most serious effect. Several banks at Newcastle were thereby reduced to the necessity of suspending their specie payment. Others availed themselves of all the means in their power for procuring a supply of cash from the metropolis. And as the news of the run on the Newcastle banks spread over the whole country, applications for assistance poured in

Failure of country banks.

[1] In 1793 there were imported 1,086,781 qrs. of corn and grain; in 1794 1,066,000 qrs.; in 1795, 464,000 qrs.; and, in 1796, 1,570,000 qrs.

[2] In the week ended February 28, 1795, the amount of banknotes in circulation was 14,017,850*l.*; in the week ended November 28, 11,503,100*l.*; and, August 27 1796, 9,427,510*l.*

to the Bank of England from all parts. With the increase of the alarm hoarding became general, the circulation became more restricted, and the position of the Bank was seriously compromised. Meanwhile, money grew extremely dear. The 3 per cent. consols fell below 50.[10] Exchequer bills, bearing 3½d. per day, were sold at 3l. and 3l. 10s. per cent., and even 5l. per cent. discount. And mercantile bills, when they could be negotiated at all, were subject to a heavy commission, so as to evade the operation of the usury laws. What materially aggravated the difficulties of the Bank were the constant demands made by the Government for advances. At one time[11] the Bank of England was prohibited from making such advances without the permission of Parliament; but as it had been the custom of the Bank to make such advances, an act was passed in 1793[12] authorising the Bank to accommodate the Government when necessary, and the Government was not slow in taking advantage of such powers to a large extent.

Uneasiness of the Bank of England.

The Bank could ill afford, however, to grant such accommodation, and, as early as January 15, 1795, the directors passed a resolution not to allow the sum so advanced to exceed 500,000l. Again and again did the Bank reiterate such a declaration, and when in August an application came from Mr. Pitt for a further accommodation of 2,500,000l., the directors only consented to grant the amount on the assurance that he would see that the conditions imposed by the Bank should be punctually complied with. Pressed by these varied exigencies, and finding themselves at last reduced to great straits, the directors of the Bank—having on Saturday, February 25, only 1,272,000l. of cash and bullion in their coffers to meet all their liabilities, and with every prospect of a still greater run on the following Monday—sought the intervention of Government to aid them in taking some vigorous

[10] When the Netherlands were given up to France on June 1, 1797, consols fell to 47½; and, on the receipt of the news of the battle of the Nile, August 1, 1798, consols again fell to 47¼, the lowest price ever reached.

[11] In the Bank Charter Act, 5 & 6 Will. and Mary, heavy penalties are imposed on the Bank directors if they purchase, on account of the corporation, any crown lands, or if they advance or lend to the sovereign any sum by way of loan or anticipation on any part or branch of the public revenue, other than such on which a credit of loan shall have been granted by Parliament.

[12] 13 Geo. III. c. 29, s. 41.

measures. Numerous interviews took place between the Bank directors and Mr. Pitt, and the result was, that on Sunday, February 26, 1797, a special privy council was held, when it was decided that, upon the representation of the chancellor of the exchequer of the effect of the unusual demand for specie in the metropolis, it was indispensably necessary for the public service that the directors of the Bank of England should forbear issuing any cash in payment. A minute to that effect was thereupon made, and a copy of it was sent to the Bank directors, with instructions to conform themselves thereto.[18]

Suspension of cash payments.

Accordingly, on the Monday morning following, the order in council was issued by the directors, together with a notice of their own, in which they stated that the general concerns of the Bank were in the most affluent and flourishing condition, and were such as to preclude any doubt as to security of its notes. We may well imagine what surprise and alarm were produced by such an announcement. Not a few demanded bullion in a rather vociferous manner, and for a time it was quite impossible to foresee the effect of the bold and unprecedented policy. Happily, however, any inconvenience which might have been produced by it was of short duration, thanks to the good sense and practical wisdom displayed on so great an emergency. The merchants well knew that political reasons, greater far than commercial or monetary

[18] The following is the text of the minute of council :—"At the council chamber Whitehall, February 26th, 1797. By the lords of her majesty's most honourable privy council. Present: Lord Chancellor, Lord President, Duke of Portland, Marquis Cornwallis, Earl Spencer, Earl of Liverpool, Lord Grenville, Mr. Chancellor of the Exchequer:

'"Upon the representation of the chancellor of the exchequer stating that, from the result of the information which he has received, and of the inquiries which it has been his duty to make, respecting the effect of the unusual demands for specie that have been made upon the metropolis, in consequence of ill-founded or exaggerated alarms in different parts of the country, it appears that, unless some measure is immediately taken, there may be reason to apprehend a want of a sufficient supply of cash to answer the exigencies of the public service, it is the unanimous opinion of the board, that it is indispensably necessary for the public service that the directors of the Bank of England should forbear issuing any cash in payment until the sense of Parliament can be taken on that subject, and the proper measures adopted thereupon, for maintaining the means of circulation, and supporting the public and commercial credit of the kingdom at this important conjuncture. And it is ordered, that a copy of this minute be transmitted to the directors of the Bank of England; and they are hereby required, on the grounds of the exigency of the case, to conform thereto, until the sense of Parliament can be taken as aforesaid. (Signed) "W. FAWKENER."'

difficulties, had dictated the suspension of cash payments, and they resolved to support the Government. A meeting was therefore held at the Mansion House under the presidency of the Lord Mayor, and unanimous resolutions were passed to the effect, that the parties present would engage to receive bank-notes in all payments to be made to them, and to use their utmost endeavours to make all their own payments in the same medium.[14] In a few days these resolutions were signed by above three hundred merchants and bankers.

Parliament being then sitting, Mr. Pitt lost no time, on the same Monday, to bring the matter before the House, and he gave notice that, on the following day, the Government would move for the appointment of committees of both Houses, to examine the outstanding demands on the Bank. When that motion was made, exception was taken to the summary measure of the Government by Mr. Fox and other members in the Commons, and by the Marquis of Lansdowne in the Lords; but the committees were appointed. Soon after, however, another committee was appointed in the House of Commons, on the motion of Mr. Fox, to inquire into the causes which produced the orders in council, and on the motion of the Marquis of Lansdowne in the Lords. On March 9 a bill of indemnity was brought in, but the discussion was put off till the reports of the committee were presented; and the reports did not disappoint public expectation. The situation of the Bank was represented as most favourable,[15] the Bank having a large capital and abounding resources, but many causes had concurred in bringing about the eventful crisis. Since the war commenced, a complete change had been made in the course of

The Bill of Indemnity.

14 'Mansion House, Feb. 27th, 1797.

'At a meeting of merchants, bankers, &c., held here this day, to consider of the steps which it may be proper to take to prevent embarrassment to public credit, from the effects of any ill-founded or exaggerated alarms, and to support it with the utmost exertions at the present important conjuncture—

The Lord Mayor in the chair—

Resolved, unanimously, "that we, the undersigned, being highly sensible how necessary the preservation of public credit is at this time, do most readily hereby declare that we will not refuse to receive banknotes in payment of any sum of money to be paid to us; and we will use our utmost endeavours to make all our payments in the same manner. (Signed) "Brook Watson."'

15 The total amount of demand on the Bank on February 25 was 13,770,390*l.*, and the total amount of assets, exclusive of 11,686,000*l.* due from Government, was 17,597,280*l.*, leaving a surplus of 3,826,890*l.*, besides the Government debt.

trade. The remittance of money from various parts could only be effected in a circuitous manner, in consequence of interruptions in the means of direct communication, and the state of the countries from which the remittances were due. The increased rates of freight and insurance, the advanced price of labour and of all necessaries of life, the expenses of the war, the operations of the Government with the Bank, each and all had contributed in creating an increased want of circulating medium, just at a time when, in consequence of the alarm, the security of banknotes had become doubtful. Neither the committee of the House of Commons, nor that of the House of Lords, attempted to speculate how far these circumstances were aggravated by the policy of the Bank, or otherwise. They contented themselves in giving the fullest information they could elicit on the subject. Nothing more, in fact, was wanting. Enough had been stated to restore full confidence; and the Government and the Bank, with the full concurrence of the mercantile community, gave themselves to introduce measures calculated to remove or alleviate any inconvenience which might result from the suspension of cash payment. The circulation of notes of *5l.* was commenced, and of notes under *5l.* was sanctioned.[16] As a substitute for guineas[17] a certain quantity of dollars was issued, with a miniature impression of the British stamp.[18] A copper penny was first put in circulation, and the Bank was not only indemnified for the illegality of the suspension, but formally forbidden to give cash in payments, except in stated cases, and up to a limited amount.[19] As for the mercantile classes,

[16] The amount of banknotes under *5l.* on August 26, 1797, was 934,000*l.* in a total circulation of 10,568,000*l.*; but in 1811, and several successive years, the notes under *5l.* constituted more than one-half of the whole circulation.

[17] A 20*s.* piece in gold was first issued by Charles II. at the Restoration, and was subsequently called a guinea. But though issued at 20*s.*, in the reign of Queen Anne it rose in current value to 30*s.*, and its value was not finally fixed at 21*s.* until, on the advice of Sir Isaac Newton, a proclamation was issued in the reign of George I., and a new indenture made, dated May 6, 1718, in which the coin was designated a guinea, or twenty-one shilling piece, and was ordered to pass for 21*s.* sterling.

[18] In 1797 Spanish dollars were issued, countermarked upon the neck of the bust with the king's head; but the number of counterfeits which immediately appeared in circulation rendered it necessary to withdraw them: and, in 1804, dollars, restamped at Birmingham with the effigy of the king, were substituted for them.—*First Report of the Deputy-Master of the Mint*, p. 7 (1871).

[19] 37 Geo. III. cc. 28, 32, 40. 45.

they were never really grieved at such a strange issue; and, when confidence was restored, they indulged in the hope that the Bank of England, thereafter free from the incubus of a metallic currency, would be better able to act liberally in its accommodation.

Sadly disappointed indeed they were when they found that, with or without the obligation to pay gold, the Bank of England wisely decided upon continuing the same cautious management, and on imposing the same effective checks on its issues as heretofore. Again, therefore, they met to complain that the accommodation afforded by the Bank in the discounting of bills and notes was inadequate to the extended commerce of the country;[30] that, without an extension of the circulating medium of the kingdom by discount of mercantile bills and notes, the general commerce of the country would be exposed to the most serious immediate and alarming evils; that the recent mark of confidence reposed in the Bank of England by the respectable association for receiving their notes, notwithstanding the order in council of February 26, had given the merchants and traders a fair claim to reasonable and necessary accommodation; that the capital employed in the export and import trade of Great Britain had amounted, on an average of the last six years, to forty-five millions per annum; that there were always two months' supply of merchandise in the custody of the merchants and traders; and that a discount accommodation to such proportion, backed by such security, might be afforded without risk. These resolutions were communicated to the Bank directors; but they answered that they were unprepared to adopt any fixed plan, or to pledge themselves to advance any specific sum; and that, whilst willing to be as helpful to trade as possible, their transactions with the Government were far too involved to allow them to be liberal towards the merchants. By degrees, however, confidence was restored, and with it the want of currency ceased to be a subject of public grievance.

Want of currency.

[30] The annual average amount of commercial paper under discount at the Bank was, in 1797, 5,350,000*l*.; 1798, 4,490,600*l*.; 1799, 5,403,900*l*. On the week ended February 25, 1797, the amount of Bank of England notes in circulation was further reduced to 8,640,250*l*.; but in May it had increased to 10,892,870*l*.; and, in the week ended February 23, 1798, to 13,003,780*l*.

CHAPTER II.

THE WAR AND THE FOREIGN TRADE AND NAVIGATION.

1793–1800.

Effects of War on Commerce.—Infringement of the Treaty of 1786.—Retaliatory Measures between France and England.—Complaints of Neutral States.—Protests of the United States.—Trade with the United States.—The Dutch and Neutral Trading.—Commerce with Russia.—Trade with Italy.—Fluctuation of Prices.—Progress of Science in France.—Advance of Science and Literature in England.

THE business of the world can be carried on safely and advantageously only in time of peace. Commerce is the handmaid of peace. With the introduction of war, public attention is at once diverted from industrial to military pursuits, the principal marts of merchandise become the scenes of warfare and bloodshed, the sea ceases to be the highway of peaceful industry, the finances of the nation are paralysed, and capital and industry take wing to happier regions. Nothing can be more fallacious than that war can, under any circumstances, be permanently favourable to commerce. It may create an extraordinary demand of certain articles for military and naval purposes, and certain industries may be temporarily benefited. But that produces only a passing gleam of commercial activity. The ultimate results are generally the destruction of property, the impoverishment of the masses, and the overturning of settled industries.

Effects of war on commerce.

As we enter upon the war of the French Revolution it is grievous to find all the circumstances incident to war immensely aggravated by the practice of warfare introduced by the belligerent parties almost in utter defiance of international law. Long before war was declared between France and England complaints were made on both sides of the infringement of the treaty of 1786. On the part of this country, it became almost a necessity to prohibit the circulation of assignats as well as the exports of arms,

Infringement of the treaty of 1786.

ammunition, and naval stores; and with straitened resources at home there was some justification for the prohibition of the export of grain and flour. On the part of France she was not likely to encourage any longer the importation of British goods. It became, in fact, too evident that the altered state of relations and the new exigencies were quite irreconcilable with the policy of freedom which that treaty of commerce had established.

Retaliatory measures between France and England.

Unfortunately France associated these acts with the unfriendly position which England had assumed, and considered them as so many provocatives of hostility. As soon, therefore, as war was openly declared, the Convention passed a decree authorising the French navy to seize and carry into the ports of the republic all neutral vessels laden with merchandise. And, forthwith, orders in council were issued in this country laying an embargo on all French ships, and granting general reprisals against France. As the animosity increased between the two countries the French began to regard all foreigners, and especially the English, with peculiar suspicion, if not hatred. In August the Convention declared that all foreigners, natives of countries at war with France, should be subject to arrest, that their effects should be put under seal, and that all English, Scotch, Irish, and Hanoverians, subjects to the king of England, should be arrested and their property confiscated. Not content with this, a decree was also issued, prohibiting, throughout the territories of France, the use of English merchandise, and ordering all persons directly or indirectly importing, introducing, selling, purchasing, or permitting the introduction of them, to be imprisoned in irons for twenty years. If it was not in the power of England to retaliate in measures of this nature she did not hesitate to destroy the French trade to the very utmost by hindering, by every means in her power, the entry of provisions and merchandise into France. But she did this and more. By a system of treaties and alliances, as well as by agreements of subsidies, she raised all Europe against her. The treaties concluded with the principal powers provided that the ports of such countries should be shut against French vessels; that the exportation of warlike and naval stores, as well as of wheat and other provisions, should be prohibited; and that all such nations should unite in their effort to prevent neutral powers from affording any protection, direct or indirect, to the property and commerce of France. Need we comment on measures like these? The utter disregard of neutral rights shown by the first decree of the Convention; the mad hatred of France against British subjects and British goods, as if that would in the least affect the policy of England; and, finally, the British effort to raise up a European conflagration, one and all are acts of barbarism utterly unworthy of civilised states.

The evil of such measures was, that they inflicted even greater injury on states which had nothing whatever to do with the war than on France herself. A few countries which stood in danger of being subjugated by France applauded any effort that might have a tendency to keep her in check. But neutral powers, the Northern especially, loudly resented this interference with their trade and navigation, and positively asserted their determination to insist on their rights. Entirely dependent for their trade on a free navigation, and accustomed to carry on their trade between the belligerent powers, and to supply the contending nations with their produce, Sweden and Norway saw, very speedily, that the pretensions of France and England would, if not resisted, altogether destroy their commerce; and therefore, in 1794, they entered into a convention for the defence of their mutual rights.

Complaints of neutral states.

But another power, still more formidable, the United States of America, was interested in securing the freedom of her ships in European waters. At first, when both French and British cruisers were instructed to take enemy's property found in neutral vessels, an exception was made in favour of American ships; but the privilege was not long maintained, and consequently the remonstrances of the United States Government were not very measured. When, however, the British cruisers went so far as to impress or to wrest,[1] by

Protest of the United States.

[1] The power of impressing men for the sea service was long held by England as a prerogative of the Crown, though it was submitted to with great reluctance. The practice was deduced from the maxim that private mischief had better be submitted to than public detriment and inconvenience should ensue. The prerogative, however, could at most extend within British soil and British territory, and it is quite clear that when a British cruiser entered an American vessel in order to take therefrom supposed British subjects, he far exceeded the limits of such prerogative

force, British mariners out of American ships, the Americans were not disposed to condone the offence, and, both against England and France, the cabinet of Washington thundered its protests. Anxious to bring about a collision between England and the United States, France, in answer to such protests, made a show of recognising neutral rights by offering to relax her navigation law in favour of neutral countries, and by opening the ports of her colonies to every neutral flag, concessions which she might well make at a time when she was shut out from all her colonies. But soon after the issue of a decree to that effect, she ordered her ships of war and privateers to seize and carry into the ports of the republic any merchant vessel wholly or in part laden with provisions, being neutral property, bound to an enemy's port, or having on board merchandise belonging to an enemy. Nor did England remain behind France in restricting still further neutral trading. Little caring for the interests of neutrals, she issued instructions to British cruisers, authorising them to stop all vessels laden wholly or in part with corn, bound to any port of France, or any port occupied by French armies, making provision, however, for indemnifying the owners and releasing the crews.

Yet, notwithstanding these difficulties, our commerce with the United States was increasing at a rapid pace. In 1793 the imports from the States amounted to 903,000*l.*, and the exports to 3,513,000*l.* In 1798, our imports thence amounted to 1,800,000*l.*, and our exports to 7,000,000*l.* The United States benefited immensely by the war, and it was then that their maritime resources were materially developed. With a large number of merchant ships, and in an excellent position for carrying on maritime operations with distant regions, the United States could, in many cases, oust Britain from her accustomed traffic. A great part of West India produce was carried to America for the purpose of being reshipped for Europe in neutral bottoms. American produce was in great demand for the armies and navies of the belligerent powers; and, better than all, the productive power of the United States was growing apace. We have mentioned already that cotton had been successfully introduced into Georgia and South Carolina; but hitherto the operation of separating cotton from the seed was

Trade with the United States.

excessively slow. In 1793, however, Whitney invented a machine for the purpose, which did for the planters of the American states what the genius of Arkwright and Watt did for the cotton manufacturers of England. Previous to 1790 the United States did not export a single pound of cotton: Whitney's invention came into operation in 1793, and, in 1794, 1,600,000 lbs. were exported. In 1791 they grew $\frac{1}{313}$th of the produce offered to the markets of the world. In 1861 they exported upwards of one thousand million pounds of cotton; another instance of the power of machinery. For many years England was most anxious to conclude a treaty of commerce with the United States; yet the treaty, which was concluded by Lord Grenville and Mr. Jay on November 19, 1794, was not accepted by the House of Representatives of the United States till April 30, 1796, and was not sanctioned in this country till 1797.

The Dutch and neutral trading.

Our trade with Holland had been for some time considerable, and in 1793 and 1794 our exports thither amounted to upwards of 1,600,000*l.*, but the operations of the French in that territory put an end to nearly the whole trade; and in 1795 our exports barely amounted to 100,000*l.* When Holland was invaded by France, England extended to her all the restrictions imposed against France. On February 9, instructions were given to the commanders of our ships of war and privateers, to bring into the ports of the United Kingdom all Dutch vessels bound to and from any port of Holland. And on September 15 an order in council was issued for general reprisals against the Dutch.[1] But the Dutch were not free to act as they pleased, and it was only under the dictates of their invaders, the French, that they issued a proclamation prohibiting the importation into the United Provinces of any British produce and manufacture.

The commercial treaty concluded with Russia in 1766 having been allowed to expire in 1793, a new commercial treaty was concluded, the preamble of which set forth the desire of the King of Great Britain and the Emperor of Russia thereby to

[1] An order in council for granting general reprisals against Spain was made on November 9, 1796.

promote the commercial prosperity of their subjects. Yet by a strange inconsistency, soon after its renewal, the Russian Government issued a ukase prohibiting the importation into Russia of a large number of articles, principally of British manufacture.

Commerce with Russia.

With the Italian States the trade was greatly disturbed. On August 29, 1798, an order in council was issued declaring the coasts and port of Genoa, and those of the territories of the Pope, as in a state of hostility with Britain. On April 26, 1799, an embargo was laid on all ships bound to the territories of the Grand Duke of Tuscany; and on August 17, 1803, letters of marque and reprisals were issued against the Ligurian and Italian republics. As for Venice, she whose power and industry were supreme in the Middle Ages—Venice, once the queen of the Adriatic, the home of mariners, and the great entrepôt of Eastern produce long before the English and the Dutch were heard of on the vast ocean—she of whose dockyards Dante said,

Trade with Italy.

One here a vessel builds, another there
Caulks that which many voyages had made;
One strikes the prow, one hammers at the poop;
One mends a main, and one a mizen sail;
One shapes an oar, another twists a rope;
So, not by fire beneath, but art divine,
Boiled up thick pitch throughout the gloomy vale,
Whose viscous spatterings all the margin line—

Venice, by the treaty of Campo Formio in 1797, ceased to be a republic, and for ever to have even an independent existence. Everywhere, by land and by sea, there were confusion and reverses, and commerce and navigation had either to relinquish their peaceful mission altogether, or to encounter dangers and risks baffling all calculations.

The necessary sequence of all these external and internal troubles was an extreme fluctuation of prices, and a trade most uncertain and speculative. At the commencement of the war a considerable fall of prices took place, caused in a great measure by the monetary crisis which set in with force, and a low range continued throughout 1794. Gradually, however, the loss of the vintage in France, the extraordinary compe-

Fluctuation of prices.

tition in the purchase of naval stores for the belligerent powers, the prospect of war, first with one and then with another of the great producing countries, the close of the ports, and the long-continued deficiency of the crops in this country, caused prices to run up to an extraordinary height in 1795 and 1796, so high indeed, as to cause a reduction of consumption and a consequent reaction. The following are specimens of fluctuations, taken from Mr. Tooke's History of Prices:[3]

	1793–4	1795–6	1796–7	1798–9
Ashes, per cwt. . .	34s. to 31s.	60s. to 70s.	39s. to 55s.	46s. to 52s.
Flax ,, ton . .	58l. ,, 57l.	64l. ,, 67l.	44l. ,, 48l.	67l. ,, 64l.
Hemp ,, ,, . .	32l. ,, 22l.	58l. ,, 59l.	32l. ,, 34l.	34l. ,, 37l.
Iron, foreign, per ton .	17l. ,, —	23l. 5s. ,, —	— ,, 19l. 15s.	20l. ,, 21l. 10s.
Linseed, per qr. . .	34s. ,, 40s.	60s. ,, 63s.	30s. ,, 34s.	— ,, —
Oil, Gallipoli, per ton .	42l. ,, 46l.	70l. ,, 71l.	60l. ,, 63l.	66l. ,, 68l.
Rice, per cwt. . .	15s. ,, 16s.	41s. ,, 43s.	14s. ,, 16s.	16s. ,, 17s.
Tallow, per cwt. . .	36s. ,, 39s.	78s. ,, 80s.	46s. ,, 47s.	54s. ,, 57s.
Timber, per load . .	43s. ,, —	90s. ,, —	60s. ,, 65s.	78s. ,, 80s.
Coffee, Jam., per cwt. .	77s. ,, 86s.	116s. ,, 185s.	132s. ,, 145s.	165s. ,, 196s.
Sugar, Muscov. ,, .	52s. ,, 56s.	61s. ,, 75s.	53s. ,, 74s.	62s. ,, 87s.
Indigo, E. I. sup. ,, .	7s. 6d. ,, 9s. 6d.	8s. 6d. ,, 11s.	6s. ,, 10s.	11s. ,, 12s. 6d.
Pepper, black, per lb. .	16d. ,, —	13½d. ,, —	14½d. ,, —	22d. ,, —
Tobacco, per lb. . .	3d. ,, 6d.	6½d. ,, 9d.	6d. ,, 16d.	11½d. ,, 16d.

As for grain, the average prices were as follows:—

	1793		1794		1795		1796		1797		1798		1799		1800	
	s.	d.	s.	d.	s.	d.	s.	d.	s.	d.	s.	d.	s.	d.	s.	d.
Wheat	49	3	52	3	75	2	78	7	53	9	51	10	69	0	113	10
Oats	20	6	21	3	24	5	21	10	16	8	19	5	27	6	39	4
Barley	31	1	31	9	37	5	36	4	27	2	29	0	36	2	59	10

Such prices as wheat at 113*s*. per qr., sugar at 62*s*. to 87*s*. per cwt., and coffee at 165*s*. to 196*s*. per cwt., must have put provisions far beyond the power of the masses of the people; but we must remember that the risks of navigation were great, and that to the famine prices everywhere prevalent there were to be added extraordinary high rates of freight and very high rates of insurance.

Progress of science in France.

One happy feature amidst all this change, destruction, and poverty, was the steady advance of science and discoveries. Scarcely in any period has there been greater mental activity, both in France and England, than during the first years of the French revolution; and it must be allowed that if that event has overturned many old institutions, it has also

[3] Vol. I. p. 188–190, and vol. II. Table of Prices.

been the parent of not a few important reforms, and the herald of many novel and beneficent principles for which Europe and the world will be ever grateful. Some of the noblest principles of the civil code were established in the very midst of the revolution. We should never forget that, as by an ovation, France then proclaimed the abolition of slavery, not only in France but in all the French colonies; and that it was then that liberty of conscience, equality before the law, the participation of every citizen in the government of the state, the opening of the public service to merit, the incompatibility of the legislative with the executive functions, the freedom of the press and of meeting, the institution of the trial by jury, the publicity of debates, the abolition of torture, the free exercise of professions and trades, and open and free instruction to all classes, were one and all proclaimed. Certainly these are precious conquests which marked the close of the eighteenth century, and we must hail them as the inauguration of an entirely new system of politics, economics, and legislation.

Advance of science and literature in England.

In England it was the same. 'The reign of George III.,' said Lord Brougham, 'may in some important respects be justly regarded as the Augustan age of modern history. The greatest statesmen, the most consummate captains, the most finished orators, the first historians, all flourished during this period. Though it could show no poet like Dante, Milton, Tasso, or Dryden, no dramatist like Shakspeare or Corneille, no philosopher to equal Bacon, Newton, or Locke, it nevertheless in some branches, and these not the least important, of natural sciences, very far surpassed the achievements of former days, while of political science, the most important of all, it first laid the foundations and then reared the superstructure.' In March, 1799, the Royal Institution of Great Britain was formed for diffusing the knowledge and facilitating the general introduction of useful mechanical inventions and improvements, and for teaching, by courses of philosophical lectures and experiments, the application of science to the common purposes of life. And it was a happy idea to produce, in a great historical engraving beautifully executed, the most authentic portraits of upwards of fifty eminent men of science, supposed to have met together in the upper library of that institution, just before the close of last century.[4] The sight of such an engraving is well fitted to inspire us with the sentiment of Longfellow's beautiful stanza:—

> Lives of great men all remind us,
> We can make our lives sublime;
> And, departing, leave behind us
> Footprints on the sands of time.

There, in the central group, we have the great Watt demonstrating the advantage of his improved engine to his friends Rennie, Telford, Mylne, Jessop, Chapman, Murdock, Rumford, Huddart, Boulton, Brunel, Watson, Bentham, and Maudslay, all eminent engineers and architects, constructors of navigable canals and bridges, to whom we owe such works as the Thames Tunnel and Menai Bridge, and one of whom, Murdock, was the first to apply the light of coal gas to general purposes. At the opposite side of the table, and looking towards the great engineer, is Dalton, the propounder of the atomic theory, surrounded by a group of eminent chemical philosophers, such as Davy, Hatchett, Wollaston, Henry, Allen, Howard, and Smith, the father of English geology; and, sitting in front of them, is the illustrious Cavendish. The group on the right represents Crompton, the inventor of the spinning mule; Charles Tennant, the well-known chemist and bleacher of Glasgow; Cartwright, the inventor of the power-loom; and Ronalds, who first passed an electric message through a space of eight miles made in trenches dug in his garden at Hammersmith. These are listening to Charles Earl Stanhope describing his printing press and his process of stereotype printing. Behind his lordship is Bramah, the inventor of the hydraulic press, speaking to Trevethick, the inventor of the first high-pressure steam-engine, and of the first successful railway locomotive. Near Earl Stanhope is Nasmyth, the Scottish Claude, and a man of science. Next to him are Miller of Dalswinton, and Symington, who invented and built the first practical steamboat. Close to Symington is Thomson, the distinguished professor of chemistry at Glasgow, who first intro-

[4] The engraving was published in 1862 by Messrs. William Walker and Son, London, with Memoirs of the distinguished men, and an Introduction by Robert Hunt, F.R.S.

duced to the notice of the world Dalton's views of the theory of definite proportions, which had been privately communicated to him. Troughton, the astronomical instrument maker; Donkin, the inventor of a machine for making paper, as well as of the polygonal printing machine; and Congreve, the constructor of missiles, complete this division of the picture. The group on the left represents Herschel, the great astronomer and philosopher, conversing with his friend Maskelyne; behind whom are Baily, Frodsham, Leslie, Playfair, Rutherford, and Dollond. Dr. Young is near them, celebrated for his universal acquirements; Brown, the distinguished botanist; Gilbert and Banks, the presidents of the Royal Society; Kater, too, eminent for the part he took in the trigonometrical survey of India, and for the construction of standard weights and measures; and near to Sir William Herschel and Sir Joseph Banks, sitting in front, is Jenner, the discoverer of vaccination. Can we wonder that, with such a host of eminent men, the progress of the nineteenth century has been rapid and enduring? Of them may be said, what Lord Jeffrey said of Playfair and his friends:—'Theirs was the understanding, at once penetrating and vigilant, but more distinguished perhaps for the caution and sureness of its march than for the brilliancy and rapidity of its movements, and guided and adorned through all its progress by the most genuine enthusiasm for all that is grand, and the justest taste for all that is beautiful. Great men they were—men whose instinct it was to work for the world. Some of them wealthy, some of them poor, with visions perchance of wealth to come, but still working for the world's welfare as the only path by which to ensure their own. These belonged to that race of pathfinders that were ever setting copies for the English nation to work by. To them most assuredly is due a great share of the more recent development of national energy. They are not dead. They live in the gratitude not only of this country but of the world.'

CHAPTER III.

BRITISH AND FRENCH FINANCES DURING THE WAR OF THE FRENCH REVOLUTION.

1793–1800.

Financial Exigencies.—Hoarding of Treasure.—Early Modes of borrowing Money.—Commencement of the National Debt.—Debt at the Revolution in 1688.—The National Debt from Queen Anne to George III.—Perplexity at the Growth of the Debt.—The Sinking Fund.—Loans contracted by Mr. Pitt.—The Loyalty Loan.—The Income Tax.—Review of Mr. Pitt's Financial Policy.—State of Finances in France.—Issue of Assignats.—Issue of Territorial Mandates.

To realise what war produces we must turn our attention to the finances of the nation during this eventful period. It is easy to declare war, but we cannot raise and maintain large armies, build, equip, and put in commission huge ships of the line, and secure the aid of needy allies and mercenary troops, without incurring a heavy expenditure. No greater evidence in truth could we possess of the wonderful power wielded by Mr. Pitt at this momentous crisis, than the hold he obtained on the leading capitalists, with whom, after all, it rested to supply the necessary funds. Often he must have been at a loss how to solve the difficult dilemma of loans and taxes, and it must have been an irksome task to him to have to knock so frequently at the door, either of the Bank of England or of the few bankers and money dealers who had then the monopoly of capital. We know that where there is no competition a contract is always made at great disadvantage, and we may well fancy how ill Mr. Pitt fared when he had to recur to the same parties, who formed one united band, for the negotiation of his successive loans. Nor could there be any disguising of the pressing necessity. The revenue of the country was very far

Financial exigencies.

behind the annual expenditure.[1] Fresh taxes could not be raised. If the war is to be continued, it must be with borrowed money; and we need not be surprised if we find Mr. Pitt consenting to any terms in order to obtain the wherewithal to pay for the armies and navies, and to meet the many other exigencies of war. The wonder is whence the money came from. Had the millions, yearly expended, been accumulated from the labour of former years? Did they represent the actual saving of the nation? We fear they did so only to a limited extent. It was not the past earnings that were used. It was the future earnings that were mortgaged, and for these the credit of the capitalists became pledged. It should be remembered also that England was then probably the safest state in Europe, and that foreign capitalists invested their funds more readily in British than in any other securities. In so far then as the amount expended really represented the earnings of previous labour, it was not of England alone but of the whole of Europe, ay of America also, whence came large amounts.[2] Only England became indebted for it all, and she is still bearing the burden on her shoulders.

Hoarding of treasures.

The story of the national debt[3] is an interesting one, and before we enter into the immense additions made to it in consequence of the French Revolution and war, it may be well to trace in a few words the progress of the debt from the beginning. The resources of national credit were not known among the ancients, consequently, in time of peace, they used to amass stores of wealth to meet the contingencies of war. Cyrus, it is said, accumulated a considerable treasure, and the treasure of Ptolemæus Philadelphus was estimated at 74,000 talents. Alexander found at Ecbatana 38,000 talents. Tiberius had amassed vast amounts of sesterces, which Caligula wasted in one year. Cæsar seized a treasure at the battle of Pharsalia, and in later times Charles V., Henry IV.,

[1] The total net income of Great Britain from customs, excise, stamps, taxes, post office, and other receipts, in 1793, was 18,131,342*l*., and at about that limit it continued till 1799, when it increased to 31,783,084*l*. The total expenditure meanwhile increased from 25,118,154*l*. in 1793, to 86,163,816*l*. in 1799.

[2] The amount of foreign property in the British funds on November 24, 1810, was 14,360,991*l*. Stocks, and 5,760*l*. Terminable Annuities.

[3] See Return of Income and Expenditure, 1688–1869 (366 of 1869); History of the National Debt, by J. J. Grellier, London, 1810.

Popes Paul and Sixtus V., and the Swiss Cantons each amassed treasures for their wars. Napoleon, too, made use of a treasure found in the crypt of the Tuileries for the battles of 1813 and 1814, and large sums were understood to be buried in the fortress of St. Petersburg previous to the Crimean war. But whatever may have been done in the direction of hoarding in ancient times, the practice had long been abandoned, especially since the introduction of the mode of obtaining money by public loans.

The earliest traces of a state borrowing money for national purposes may be found in the history of Venice. In 1170, the finances of the republic being in disorder, in consequence of a disastrous conflict with the Mussulmans and a war with Frederick Barbarossa, the great council raised a forced loan, for the interest of which the public revenues were pledged. In England the early sovereigns, experiencing great difficulty in raising the necessary income, not only anticipated the revenue by tallies,[4] but frequently resorted to borrowing money sometimes from the clergy, often from the Jews[5] and foreigners, and occasionally by the sudden levying of forced loans. As a security for the repayment of a loan of 200,000*l.* granted to her by the citizens of London, Queen Mary, in 1558, mortgaged land; and King Charles, in 1625, sent the Duke of Buckingham to Holland to borrow 300,000*l.* on the pledge of

Early modes of borrowing money.

[4] The word 'tallies,' derived from the French, signifies cutting. The tallies were pieces of wood cut in a peculiar manner of correspondency: for example, a stick or rod of hazel, or some other wood, well dried and seasoned, was cut square and uniform at each end and in the shaft. The sum of money which it bore was cut in notches in the wood by the Cutter of the tallies, and likewise written upon two sides of it by the Writer of the tallies. The tally was cleft in the middle by the deputychamberlains with a knife and mallet, through the shaft and the notches, whereby it made two halves, each half having a superscription and a half part of the notch or notches. A notch of such a largeness signified m. l.; a notch of another largeness c. l., &c. It being thus divided or cleft, one part of it was called a tally, the other a counter tally. And when these two parts came afterwards to be joined, if they were genuine, they fitted so exactly that they appeared evidently to be parts the one of the other.—Madox, *History of the Exchequer*, fol. ed. p. 709.

[5] King Henry the Third borrowed of Richard, Earl of Cornwall, 5,000 marks sterling, and for securing the payment thereof assigned and set over all his Jews of England to the said Earl, and bound them to pay the Earl 3,000 marks, which they owed to the King, at certain terms or days, under pain of forfeiting 500*l.* for every default of payment, and gave the Earl power to distrain them by their chattal and bodies for the same.—Madox, from Roll of 39th Henry III., anno 1253.

the crown jewels. Privy seals and letters patent were also used as securities for loans; but in all cases loans were contracted by the sovereign upon his own authority and upon the security of his own property or revenue. In process of time, however, and during the reign of Henry VI., the burden of the debt was shifted from the king's shoulders to those of the nation, but even then, and for a long time after, the expedients used by the state in raising funds were in marked contrast with those afforded by modern practice.

At the period of the Revolution in 1688, the whole amount outstanding on tallies of loan, excluding the bankers' debt, contracted in consequence of the shutting of the exchequer in 1672, was 84,886*l.*, which was issued in anticipation of the duties on French linen. This amount constituted the whole of the public debt at that time, though there were arrears due to the army and navy amounting to 300,000*l.* But the war expenditure necessitated the raising of large sums by loan in addition to increased taxation.[6] At first such sums were raised in the ordinary mode by tallies of loan charged on and in anticipation of various duties. In consequence, however, of the large amount required, the several funds proved wholly insufficient to meet the charges upon them, and the tallies fell to a heavy discount. It then became necessary to raise money by loan in other ways, and the first operation was made in 1692 by the commencement of the system of government life annuities[7] and tontines,[8] followed soon after by long

Debt at the Revolution of 1688.

[6] The war in Ireland, and against France, 1688 to 1697, entailed an expenditure of 32,643,000*l.*

[7] Under the 4th W. & M. c. 3, 1,000,000*l.* was authorised to be raised, for which the contributors were to receive 10*l.* per cent. per annum for seven years, and afterwards 7*l.* per cent. on the lives of their nominees, with benefit of survivorship till the number was reduced to seven. In 1694, life annuities were granted for one, two, or three lives at the option of the purchasers. (See a Paper on the Financial Statistics of British Government Life Annuities, by Frederick Hendriks, Esq., 'Journal of the Statistical Society,' vol. xix. 325.)

[8] A tontine or annuity, with benefit of survivorship among the subscribers or nominees, was first proposed by Tonti, a Neapolitan, in 1653. The first time a tontine was tried in England was in 1692, in the reign of William III., under 4 W. & M. c. 3, for 1,000,000*l.*, in shares of 100*l.* each. There were 1,002 nominees. The age of the oldest male life nominated was 46, and female life 51. The tontine annuity expired on the 5th July, 1783, by the death of the last nominee. The second tontine was in 1766, but it almost wholly failed. The third and last

annuities. But the sums so obtained were far from sufficient. At a time when few opportunities were offered for investment, and when commercial adventures were exceedingly dangerous and speculative, money-holders were easily persuaded that they could do no better than lend to the state at a high rate of interest, and once the idea was suggested of a great national bank, with the exclusive monopoly of banking as a compensation for such a favour, the Bank of England was forthwith incorporated in 1694, and 1,200,000*l.* was advanced by it to the state at 8 per cent. A few years after another 2,000,000*l.* was obtained on like terms from the East India Company, and thus the foundations were laid of our present national debt.

The National Debt from Queen Anne to George III.

At the accession of Queen Anne in 1701, the funded debt of the nation was 3,200,000*l.*; but her reign was signalised by the war with France to humble the Bourbons and to deprive Philip of the crown of Spain; a war which lasted ten years, during which the finances continued in a wretched condition. Though heavy war taxes were raised, by the conclusion of Queen Anne's reign in 1713 the debt rose to 26,000,000*l.*[9] Public credit was then extremely depressed, and the securities of the state were at a discount of 40 to 50 per cent. in the market. Under these circumstances the Government allowed the Bank to purchase exchequer tallies and other securities to the amount of 1,000,000*l.*, and upon condition of withdrawing them from circulation to add them to the capital as so much money lent to the Government. The reign of George I. was one of uninterrupted peace; yet a considerable sum was obtained from the South Sea Company; and, at the conclusion of his reign in 1727, the debt had risen to 53,000,000*l.*, with an annual interest of 2,200,000*l.* Some time afterwards the Spanish war[10] took place, which caused another large increase of debt, so that, in

English tontine was created in 1789, under 29 Geo. III. c. 41, when it was proposed to raise 1,002,500*l.* in sums of 100*l.* 5*s.* each. The total amount raised was 1,002,140*l.*, but the contractors not being able to complete the subscriptions on these terms, the several contributors were allowed in the following year, under the act 30 Geo. III. c. 45, the alternative of a long annuity.

[9] The war of the Spanish Succession, 1702–1713, cost this country 50,684,000*l.*

[10] The war with Spain, 1718–1721, cost 4,547,000*l.*; and, in 1739–1748, 43,655,000*l.*

1749, it amounted to 76,000,000*l.* After it occurred the Seven Years' War, and the debt increased to 135,700,000*l.* No change was made in the public debt from 1763 to the commencement of the American war in 1776; but by the end of it, when the finances were somewhat organised in 1786, the nation found itself burdened with the heavy sum of 260,000,000*l.*, from which sum it rose to 269,000,000*l.* on January 5, 1793.

Perplexity as the growth of the debt.

This increased legacy of debt which the American war left behind, pressed hard on the mind of the country and staggered the best politician; the more so at a time when the moral sense of the nation was more alive to the duty of paying, not only the interest but the entire capital of the debt than it has ever since been. Not a few indeed prognosticated a national bankruptcy; all dreaded the consequences of such a grievous burden on the industries of the nation. And there were not wanting physicians ready with their remedies.[11] Dr. Price came forward with his appeal to the public, and with his plan for redeeming the public debt. Another writer published his 'thoughts on paying the debt by a lottery, the prizes to arise out of a diminution of the annual interest.' Another wrote 'on the dangerous situation of England. Another published a pamphlet entitled

[11] Numerous were the writers on the national debt. They included the Earl of Stair, Earl Stanhope, Lord Newhaven, Lord Dundonald, Pulteney, Lord Bath, the Bishop of Cloyn, Baron Gilbert, Sir Matthew Decker, Sir John Dalrymple, Sir John Barnard, Edmund Burke, Samuel Johnson, Daniel Defoe, Mr. Eden, Sir John Sinclair, Dr. Price, Henry Hartley, Arthur Young, Dr. Shebbeare, &c. &c. The following works may be consulted:—The National Debt no National Grievance, 1768; A Scheme to pay off the National Debt by a Repeal of the Marriage Act, 1767; An Appeal to the Public on the National Debt, by Robert Price, D.D., F.R.S., 1772; A candid Inquiry into the present ruined State of the French Monarchy, 1770; A Scheme to pay the National Debt in 80 Years without an additional Tax, 1778; The Debt compared with the Revenue, and Impossibility of War without Economy, 1781; Old Funds sufficient for a New Loan, and Proposal to lower the Interest of Money and tax the Funds, 1781; Means to raise the Supply within the Year, 1780; Plans for redeeming the Public Debt, by R. Price, D.D., 1783; Thoughts on paying the Debt by a Lottery, the Prizes to arise out of a Diminution of the Annual Interest, 1784; A Plan for consolidating into one Rate the Land and other Taxes, 1784; Plan for future National Defence, by the Duke of Richmond, 1785; Dangerous Situation of England, and Address to the Landed, Trading, and Funded Interests, 1786; National Debt productive of National Prosperity, 1787; Efficacy of a Sinking Fund considered, 1786; National Debt discussed, towards a radical and speedy Payment, 1786; Renovation: a new Mode of Representation and Raising Supplies; Machiavel's Infallible Means to pay off our Debt, 1788.

'Machiavel's Infallible Means to pay off the Debt.' And since experience had proved that the old plan of imposing certain duties and appropriating the produce to the payment of interest, and eventually to the cancelling of the debt itself, had not worked well, the only plan which appeared feasible was the renewal of the sinking fund, which had been tried before and had really worked with some success. The scheme was first suggested by Earl Stanhope in 1716 under the administration of Walpole, when the sum of 32,000*l.*, saved in the interest on the capital due to the Bank of England and the South Sea Company, was left to increase at compound interest.[13] By 1727 the fund thus created paid off all the redeemable debt not subscribed into the South Sea stock; and, on that year, a reduction having been effected in the interest of the debt, that saving was also allowed to swell the sinking fund, so that the amount increased to 1,000,000*l.* per annum. So far, indeed, the scheme seemed to be working satisfactorily, and an address of congratulation, full of the brightest anticipations, was presented to the king on the subject. The nation was fully impressed with the value of the sinking fund, and so certain was it of the wonderful effect it would produce on the crippled state of British finances, that any sacrifice would have been cheerfully made rather than interfere with its working. But, alas! in an evil hour the spell was broken, and 200,000*l.* were drawn out of the fund for the service of the year; a precedent which was afterwards followed on other emergencies.

The sinking fund.

Confidence in the wonder-working sinking fund was in truth already rudely shaken when, on the suggestion of Dr. Price, Mr. Pitt in 1786 nominated a committee of the House of Commons to inquire into the ordinary income and expenditure of the country. The report of that committee being to the effect that so long as the country was in peace a surplus of about 1,000,000*l.* a year might be realised, Mr. Pitt[14] proposed

[13] 3 Geo. I. c. 7.

[14] Mr. Marsh, in his work on the Origin of the French War, said: 'Pitt's favourite object was a diminution of the national debt, the abolition of taxes, the promotion of commerce and of general welfare throughout the kingdom; the attainment of which would of necessity be impeded by the expense of a foreign war.' And in the same spirit Mr. G. C. Lewis, on his Administration of Mr. Pitt, said: 'We have reason to know that he, an early disciple of Adam Smith, contemplated, in

that all the branches of the revenue should be united under the name of the Consolidated Fund, and one million, taken from that fund, should be vested annually in the hands of the commissioners for the redemption of the national debt, to be applied in purchasing capital in such stocks as they should judge expedient at market prices. And that to this fund should be added the interest of the debt redeemed, and any annuities fallen in by the failure of lives, or by the expiry of the terms for which they were granted, as well as that any life annuities unclaimed for three years, should be considered as expired, and added to the sinking fund. Further, that when this fund amounted to four millions, the interest of the redeemed debt and the annuities fallen in should no longer be applied to it, but should remain at the disposal of Parliament. The scheme sounded well, and we do not wonder that many were allured with the idea of a sinking fund. Fancy having within reach the means by which we can accumulate a vast treasure with the smallest amount of trouble and sacrifice. Why, it sounds like the alchemist's creed, the ability of transmuting plain iron and other metals into gold and silver. Is it really true that a penny annually laid out at compound interest will, in years, become a great mountain of gold? Yes, on condition that you continue to pay that penny and the accumulating interest from year to year, century after century. But who can guarantee the continuance of that payment, or the power to resist the temptation of using the growing amount when required? Alas, alas! it was a mere illusion. If I have to repay 100*l*., is it not precisely the same whether I lay by any portion of that sum year by year, and let it grow, whilst I pay interest to the lender for the whole; or I pay to the lender that portion from year to year, and thus diminish the liability, till the debt is entirely extinguished? But what if, whilst the amount laid by grows at the rate of 3 per cent., I am borrowing money for the purpose of continuing the payment, at the rate of 5 per cent. or more? Am I not in this case actually losing instead of gaining? In the former case the idea is nothing more than a simple delusion; and in the

1792, a larger measure of free trade than the national debt accumulated during the subsequent war now permitted; we mean an abolition of all customs' duties, and a limitation of public income to internal taxation.'

latter it is worse—the operation is certain to produce a clearly appreciable loss. Mr. Pitt had, however, evidently full faith in the efficacy of the fund to remedy the great evil of an exorbitant debt, and the speech with which he introduced the scheme to the House of Commons glowed with enthusiasm. 'To behold this country,' he said, 'emerging from a most unfortunate war, which added such an accumulation to sums before immense that it was the belief of surrounding nations, and of many among ourselves, that our power must fail us, and we should not be able to bear up under it; to behold this nation, instead of despairing at its alarming condition, looking its situation boldly in the face, and establishing upon a spirited and a permanent plan the means of relieving itself from all incumbrances, must give such an idea of our resources and of our spirit of exertion as will astonish the nations around us, and enable us to regain that pre-eminence to which we are on many accounts so justly entitled.' The bill was well received in the House of Commons. Mr. Fox agreed on the necessity of establishing a sinking fund, with the proviso that such a fund should not be inalienable in time of war, and after a lengthened discussion the measure was carried.[14] Whatever may be the fallacy involved in the sinking fund, there is no doubt that its great advocate believed in its efficacy, and long he con-

[14] The new sinking fund was established under the act 26 Geo. III. c. 31. In 1792, under 32 Geo. III. c. 12, the sum of 400,000*l.* was authorised to be paid out of the supplies of the year in the same manner as under the previous act; and 1*l.* per cent. of capital created by any new loan to be carried to the sinking fund. In 1793, under 30 Geo. III. c. 22, further sums were carried to the same fund, and so by successive acts till 1802. In the latter year, however, the 42 Geo. III. c. 71, which united the two sinking funds of 1786 and 1792, modified the acts. A new plan of sinking fund was proposed in 1807 by Lord Henry Petty, and adopted under the act 47 Geo. III. c. 55; but the system was complex, and was not followed up. In 1813, Mr. Vansittart's modification of a sinking fund was proposed and begun under the act 53 Geo. III. c. 35. But on June 8, 1819, the House of Commons resolved, that to provide for the exigencies of the public service, to make such progressive reductions of the national debt as may adequately support public credit, and to afford to the country a prospect of future relief from a part of its present burdens, it is absolutely necessary that there should be a clear surplus of the income of the country above the expenditure of not less than 5,000,000*l.* sterling. In 1822 the committee of public accounts recommended that the annual sinking fund loans be discontinued, and that the whole of the redeemed capital stock of funded debt remaining in the names of the commissioners for the reduction of the national debt be cancelled. In 1823 the 4 Geo. IV. c. 19 carried that into effect; and, in 1828, an entire change was made in the existing system.

tinued to cherish his opinion of its beneficial effect. Almost at the eve of the French Revolution, on January 31, 1792, the king, on the opening of the session, said, 'I entertain the pleasing hope that the reductions which may be found practicable in the establishments, and the continued increase of the revenue, will enable you, after making due provision for the several branches of the public service, to enter upon a system of gradually relieving my subjects from some part of the existing taxes, at the same time giving additional efficacy to the plan for the reduction of the national debt, on the success of which our future ease and security essentially depend. With a view to this important object, let me also recommend it to you to turn your attention to the consideration of such measures as the state of the funds and of public credit may render practicable and expedient, towards a reduction in the rate of interest of any of the annuities which are now redeemable.'

The financial measures of Mr. Pitt at the commencement of the war were of a very tentative character. In 1793 he imposed 300,000*l.* of assessed taxes, and somewhat increased the duties on British spirits, contenting himself with a loan of 4,500,000*l.*, the terms of which were, that for every 72*l.* advanced the contributor should be entitled to 100*l.* 3 per cent. stock. In 1794 one million more of taxes was imposed, principally in objectionable excise duties on bricks and tiles, stones and slate, plate and crown glass; and another loan of 11,000,000*l.* became necessary, for which was given for every 100*l.* of cash 100*l.* of 3 per cent. stock, 25*l.* of 4 per cent., and a terminable annuity of 11*s.* 5*d.* lasting for 66½ years. Mr. Pitt admitted that the terms were much more disadvantageous to the public than might have been expected, but having done everything in his power to excite a competition, he had to accept the best terms he could procure. Nor did the amount thus obtained cover the deficiency without the aid of another loan and the funding of some navy and victualling funds. In 1795 the taxes were again increased by 1,600,000*l.*, by the imposition of additional duties on wine, tea, coffee, and fruit, taxes on insurance, and taxes on hair powder; and again two great loans were required, one of 18,000,000*l.*, negotiated at 100*l.* 3 per cent., 33*l.* 6*s.* 8*d.* 4 per cent., and 8*s.* 6*d.* long annuity; and another of 18,000,000*l.*,

Loans contracted by Mr. Pitt.

for which there was given 145*l.* 3 per cent. and 6*s.* 6*d.* long annuity; besides a loan for the Emperor of Germany for 4,600,000*l.*,[13] for the interest of which England became responsible. The year 1796 found the finances of the country in a still worse state, and taxes and loans increased apace. Then it was that the legacy duty was first established, proposed by Mr. Pitt on both real and personal property, but carried only on personal. The wine duty was also increased. A salt duty was imposed, as well as duties on hats, horses, and dogs, the whole addition amounting to 1,600,000*l.*; yet all this was but a trifling sum compared with the wants of the state, and another loan was contracted for 7,500,000*l.* at 145*l.* 3 per cent. and 6*s.* 6*d.* long annuity. This was a year when the political condition of the country gave rise to serious apprehensions. Certain negotiations for peace which were commenced in Paris proved unsuccessful. In Ireland there was great discontent. A mutinous spirit pervaded the navy, and trade was much depressed.

The loyalty loan.

But, with all these discouraging circumstances, the spirit of the nation was not crushed, and the people were determined to support the Government at whatever cost. A large sum being still wanted for the year, and the Bank directors, having apprehended some difficulty in raising it in the ordinary manner, or by competition among the principal bankers, it was proposed to throw the subscription open, and to make an appeal to the public for support.[14] And the success of the new experiment exceeded all expectations. No sooner was it known that 18,000,000*l.* were wanted than subscribers came forward with wonderful alacrity. In its collective capacity the Bank subscribed 1,000,000*l.*; the directors subscribed 400,000*l.* each; and when, on the Monday, the parlour doors of the Bank were opened, an immense crowd assembled of persons anxious to take part in what was considered a

[13] The total amount advanced by way of loan, subsidy, or otherwise, to foreign states from 1792 to 1817 was 57,133,619*l.* The principal recipients were the German States, Portugal, Russia, Spain, Austria, &c.

[14] The system of national loans was introduced in France by Napoleon III., in 1854, when, for a loan of 250,000,000 f., as many as 99,224 subscribers came forward, offering 468,000,000 f. In 1855, for a loan of 500,000,000 f., 180,480 subscribers offered 2,198,000,000 f.; and so for other loans in 1855 and 1859, with the same results.

highly patriotic act. Numbers could not get near the books. Many called on those more fortunate as to locality, to put down their names for them. At about twenty minutes past eleven the subscription was declared to be completely full, and hundreds left disappointed. In 1797, matters did not improve and new taxes were imposed on all branches of the revenue to the extent of 3,400,000*l.* In 1798, a convoy tax on imports and exports was imposed, the assessed taxes were trebled, and voluntary contributions were invited, which produced upwards of 8,000,000*l.* In 1799 more loans were wanted.

The income tax.

Mr. Pitt, however, now began to feel the need of raising a much larger part of the supplies within the year, and having regard to the deficiencies of the taxes previously imposed, he, for the first time, introduced a tax upon incomes of 200*l.* and upwards, with smaller graduated rates on incomes between 60*l.* and 200*l.* He estimated the annual rent of land and houses, tithes and mines, at 45,000,000*l.*, profits of trade and professions at 40,000,000*l.*, and dividends and income from other sources at 17,000,000*l.*—total, 102,000,000*l.*, and a tax of 10 per cent. he calculated would produce 10,000,000*l.* a year.[17] In 1800, notwithstanding the improved condition of politics, 20,500,000*l.* more were obtained, only a small addition having been made in that year to the duties on tea and spirits, yielding an increase of 350,000*l.* Mr. Pitt is praised for having obtained all the supplies he needed, for having secured the confidence and co-operation of all classes, and for having infused into all an intense desire for the maintenance of freedom and independence. But at what cost and sacrifice these objects were secured!

Review of Mr. Pitt's financial policy.

During the American war, not to go further back, several loans were contracted in the 4 per cent. stock, but with annuities and lotteries which made the terms much more onerous. When Mr. Pitt, in 1794, funded a portion of the unfunded debt, he said: 'It was always my idea that a fund, at a high rate of interest, is better to the country than those at low rates; that a 4 per cent. fund is preferable to a 3 per cent., and a 5 per cent. to a 4. The reason is, that in all operations of finance we should always have

[17] In 1798 the produce of the tax was 1,855,996*l.*; in 1799, 6,046,624*l.*

in view a plan of redemption. Gradually to redeem and to extinguish our debt ought ever to be the wise pursuit of government. Every scheme and operation of finance should be directed to that end, and managed with that view.' Very different, however, was Mr. Pitt's practice a few years after. Probably it was a case in which necessity made its own laws. But there is something very fallacious in the manner in which the loans were contracted.[18] It was a mere pretence borrowing at 3 per cent. when, in reality, the nation was paying a considerably higher rate. It was folly to engage to pay only 3 per cent. interest, and make up a further sum by annuities for a number of years, and a certain number of tickets in a lottery. Had this country borrowed at the real value of money, or at the rate at which the public credit of the country could procure it at the time, future finance ministers might easily have reduced the heavy charge for interest when the condition of the country improved. But with a 3 per cent. stock no reduction was possible. From 1793 to 1801 eighteen loans were contracted by Mr. Pitt, and for 202,000,000*l.* received he funded a capital of 314,000,000*l.*[19] What justification could be offered for an extravagance so marked as this? The only one urged is, that the nation was in the position of a spendthrift at the mercy of money lenders and usurers, and that, as long as the demands of the state continued excessively heavy, the accommodation required could only be had on terms correspondingly onerous. That it was not a question of how much the nation was prepared to pay for accommodation, but how much the lender demanded for granting it; and that Mr. Pitt was not the man to give much weight to economy when the safety of the state appeared in question. Mr. Pitt's financial and commercial administration was remarkable, certainly, for directness of aim, boldness of action, and firmness of grasp. Realising to the full as the paramount obligation of a man

[18] See the valuable paper on the loans raised by Mr. Pitt during the first French war, 1793–1801, with some statements in defence of the methods of funding employed, by William Newmarch, Esq., F.R.S.—Journal of the Statistical Society, vol. xviii. p. 104 and 242.

[19] From 1793 to 1816, for 586,158,357*l.* cash actually paid into the exchequer, there was created stock for 881,615,943*l.*, carrying dividends at 3, 4, and 5 per cent. to the amount of 29,405,972*l.*, besides 884,696*l.* terminable annuities.

placed at the helm of the state to secure, above all, its internal and external safety, his whole mind was impressed with the duty of leaving no stone unturned to achieve that end. So long as peace lasted he strained every nerve to bring about an equilibrium in the budget, by equalising the revenue with the expenditure. Immediately the war commenced he threw aside every other consideration, and placed first and foremost the safety of the state. But after all what poor results in an economic aspect have come from an administration otherwise most brilliant. There is but little indeed in Mr. Pitt's career which an economist can regard with gratitude or satisfaction; and, though deserving well for his treaty of commerce with France, and entitled to esteem for his disinterestedness and devotion to the country's good, his name cannot be enrolled in the annals of the nation side by side with those of Peel, Cobden, or Gladstone.

State of finances in France.

But if the financial administration of England was defective at this critical time, infinitely more objectionable was that of France. When the Assemblée constituante was constituted, a financial committee was formed, consisting of economists, philanthropists, and chemists, men of no experience or financial ability, and their first measure was the abolition of a large portion of indirect taxation and the institution of new taxes affecting land and luxuries. But as the expenses of the state increased, and borrowing either at home or abroad was out of the question, the assembly was utterly unable to provide for the wants of the country, always pressing and immediate. Some hopes, at first entertained, that the ecclesiastical property confiscated by the state could easily be sold soon vanished, and when land of the value of 16,000,000 livres was suddenly put up for public sale, it was found that bidders were but few, and that the realisation of any large amount would be utterly hopeless. What was to be done? In order to monetise the extensive property, it was decided to transfer the whole of the land to the municipalities, on their bond for the price, so that the state might use their bonds in payment of its creditors.

These securities, called *assignats*, from representing land which might be transferred, offered several advantages. They gave to the creditors a claim on the municipal bodies; they enabled them, at pleasure, to extinguish the debt by buying up the land, and they might be given in ordinary *Issue of assignats.* payments, for which purpose they were made legal tender. The first issue was for 16,000,000 livres, and bore interest like exchequer bills; shortly after 32,000,000 livres more were issued, and upon the sequestration of the property of wealthy emigrants, several other issues were authorised, until, in January 1796, the assignats in circulation amounted to 2,000,000,000 livres. Such an enormous issue of paper money could not fail to cause a corresponding depreciation of the currency. When the assignats were first issued in 1789, they were worth 96 per cent., and they maintained their value in 1790. But as the amount of issues increased, and the condition of the country became more and more perplexing and perilous, the public ceased to have any confidence in such securities. In 1791 they fell to 71; in 1792, to 70; in 1793, to 51, and even 22; in 1794, they were at 20; and in 1795, one could have purchased one thousand francs worth of them for 15 francs.[20] With the depreciation of the *assignats*, everything rose enormously in value, holders of produce necessarily fixing their prices at the level of the silver currency. Bread, amongst other things, became extremely dear, but the penalty of death was declared against any baker who should refuse to sell at a given price. All this, however, had no effect. In a short time the value of *assignats* was so completely destroyed that it became impossible to use them any longer as a standard of value, and they were taken out of circulation and demonetised.

But the financial experiment did not end with them. No sooner were the *assignats* withdrawn than another kind of paper money, called territorial mandates, was issued. *Issue of territorial mandates.* Again it was officially notified, that such securities would be received in all public treasuries, and that they should be a mortgage on public property. The purchaser was assured that he would always be able to change them for a real estate,

[20] The rate of exchange with Paris at the end of March 1791 was 25. By the end of that year it fell to 19¾, and from that rate it continued to fall to 17 in December 1792. In 1793, commencing with 17, it fell to 12 in April, to 9½ in June, and to 6 in July. In August it was as low as 4¾; thence it rallied a little, but from October 1 there were no more quotations till April 1801.

in the proportion of twenty-five times the value as regards a rural property, and eighteen times the value for a town estate or factory. And contracts in any other money were prohibited. This new financial law was published on March 27, 1796;[21] but in a short time the mandate lost all its value, and no alternative was left but to cause it to be demonetised. But the reason for such extreme discredit was evident. Although the security was perfectly good, being landed property amounting to half the territory of France, yet the tenure of such land afforded no security whatever. Moreover, the amount of *assignats* or mandates bore no proportion to the value of the land, no valuation of the confiscated property having ever been made; and finally, however good the security, it was not realisable in gold or silver, the only currency of practical use in exchange. Eventually, the unfortunate holders of *assignats* and territorial mandates lost a large proportion of the sums invested in them. The *assignats* which had accumulated in the hands of the land proprietors, manufacturers, and others were reduced in amount by a forced loan of 600 million francs in specie, raised from the wealthy classes of the community, in which loan 100 francs of assignats were subscribed as equivalent to 1 franc in specie. This occasioned a reduction of 14,000 millions of assignats, and the remainder were reduced to one-thirtieth part of their nominal value, and were made exchangeable at that rate for territorial mandates. In 1793 Napoleon changed all perpetual and life annuities, old and new, for two-thirds of the amount in notes called *dette publique mobilisée*, and one-third was entered in the *grand livre* under the title of *tiers-consolidée*.[22] The two-thirds, exchangeable only for national property, soon lost all value, and the third became the origin of the present national debt of France.

[21] In 1796, a company was formed in Paris under the name of 'Caisse des Comptes courants,' for carrying on any operations connected with trade and commerce, and in 1798 another company was formed, called the 'Caisse d'escompte du Commerce;' but in consequence of the events of the 18th Brumaire, the Committee of National Safety resolved on forming a state bank, which took the title of the Bank of France, with a proposed capital of 30,000,000 f.

[22] The tiers-consolidée amounted to 40,216,000 f. of interest 5 per cent. Under the first empire 23,091,637 f. interest were added to this, so that at the Restoration in 1815 the interest of the debt in France amounted only to 63,307,637 f. (2,532,000*l.*).

CHAPTER IV.

THE ORDERS IN COUNCIL AND THE BERLIN AND MILAN DECREES.

1807–1812.

Armed Neutrality.—Peace of Amiens.—Renewal of the War.—Maritime International Policy.—The Rule of 1756.—Relaxation of the Rule.—Neutral Trading with Colonies.—Effect of Neutral Trading on British Commerce.—Order in Council of May 1806.—The Berlin Decree.—Orders in Council of January and November, 1807.—The Milan and Fontainebleau Decrees.—British Policy towards Neutrals.—The Evil of the Licensing System.—The United States and the Orders in Council.—Lord Brougham's Motion.—Declaration of the Prince Regent.

Armed neutrality. Peace of Amiens.

THE political horizon was ominously darkening at the commencement of the nineteenth century. Whilst grievously suffering from the high prices of corn and provisions, and oppressed by the burden of a contest already sufficiently prolonged, England was threatened by the renewal of another armed neutrality on the part of the Northern powers—a neutrality based on a new code of maritime law then deemed utterly inconsistent with the rights of this country. The Northern powers wished to proclaim that free ships should make free goods; but England was determined that the trade of the enemy should not be carried on by neutrals. The Northern powers asserted, that only contraband goods should be excluded from the trade of neutrals, and these of certain definite and known articles. England did not wish the enemy to obtain timber, hemp, and other articles, which, though not contraband of war, are still essential for warfare. The Northern powers declared that no blockade should be held valid unless real. England had already assumed the right to treat whole coasts as blockaded, in order to prevent the enemy receiving supplies from any quarter. And when the Northern powers added that a merchant vessel accompanied and protected by a belligerent ship ought to be safe from the right of search, England was not prepared to recognise the authority of such ships, and would place no limits to the action of her cruisers. When therefore Russia, Denmark, and Sweden entered into a convention to enforce the principles of the armed neutrality, and, in pursuance of the same, Russia caused an embargo to be laid on all British vessels in her ports, the British Government, ill-disposed to bear with such provocation, issued a proclamation on January 14, 1801, authorising reprisals, and laying an embargo on all Russian, Swedish, and Danish vessels in British ports. What followed is well known, and with the battle of Copenhagen the Northern confederacy was completely dissolved. By this time Mr. Pitt had given in his resignation, and a change of government took place, which led to a change of policy towards France, and to negotiations which ended with the conclusion of the treaty of Amiens.[1]

Renewal of the war.

But, alas! from whatever cause it was, that peace was of short duration, and more than ever the patriotic spirit of the people was evoked to defend British soil against Britain's inveterate enemies.[2] From class to class the national enthusiasm spread and increased, and even the merchants, setting aside their books and business, issued a declaration, promising in a solemn manner to use every exertion to rouse the spirit and to assist the resources of the kingdom; to be ready with their services of every sort and on every occasion in its defence; and rather to perish altogether than live to see the honour of the British name tarnished, or that sublime inheritance of greatness, glory, and liberty destroyed which descended to them from their forefathers, and which they were determined to transmit to their posterity. Again was Mr. Pitt called to be prime minister, as the only man who could really be trusted in times of so much anxiety and peril. And then it was that that continental system was

[1] Peace was ratified on October 10, 1801; and the treaty of Amiens was concluded March 25, 1802.

[2] On May 16, 1803, an order in council was made issuing letters of marque and reprisals against France, and another laying an embargo on all ships belonging to the French and Batavian republics. Reprisals against Spain were ordered December 19, 1805; against Prussia on May 11, 1806; and against Russia on December 18, 1807.

inaugurated which made of oceans and seas one vast battlefield of strife and bloodshed.

Maritime international policy. The rule of 1756.

Fully to understand the policy of this country as regards these orders in council, we must briefly retrace our steps, by examining the measures taken in previous wars. During the Seven Years' War, which ended in 1763, France, hemmed in on all sides by England, and hindered by the British naval force from carrying on any trade with her West India colonies, adopted the plan of relaxing her colonial monopoly, and allowing neutral ships to carry the produce of those islands to French or foreign ports in Europe. The produce being thus carried really or ostensibly on neutral account, it was assumed that no danger of capture could be incurred. But the prize courts of England condemned such vessels as were captured while engaged in the trade, and the rule was then adopted, called the rule of 1756,[a] that a neutral has no right to deliver a belligerent from the pressure of his enemy's hostilities by trading with his colonies in time of war in a way that was prohibited in time of peace.' As Sir William Scott said, 'The general rule is, that the neutral has a right to carry on, in time of war, his accustomed trade to the utmost extent of which that accustomed trade is capable. Very different is the case of a trade which the neutral has never possessed; which he holds by no title of use and habit in time of peace; and which, in fact, he can obtain in war by no other title than by the success of the one belligerent against the other, and at the expense of that very belligerent under whose success he sets up his title.' During the American war this principle did not come practically into action, because, although then also the French Government opened the ports of her West India islands to the ships of neutral powers, it had the wisdom to do so before hostilities were commenced, and not after.

In accordance with these principles, when the war of the French Revolution commenced, instructions were given, on

[a] The rule of 1756 had been acted upon even by France on previous occasions. See Note 1, On the Practice of the British Prize Courts with regard to the Colonial Trade of the Enemy during the American War, in 6 Rob. Rep. App.; and *Considérations sur l'Admission des Navires neutres aux Colonies françoises de l'Amérique en Tems de Guerre*, p. 18, 1779; and see The Wilhelmina, 4 Rob. Rep. p. 4; and The Immanuel Tudor.—Leading Cases of Mercantile Law, p. 814.

November 6, 1793, to the commanders of British ships of war and privateers, ordering them 'to stop and detain for lawful adjudication all vessels laden with goods the produce of any French colony, or carrying provisions or other supplies for the use of any such colony.' And this order was the more necessary from the fact that American ships were crowding the ports of the French West Indies, where the flag of the United States was made to protect the property of the French planters. Great numbers of ships under American colours were thus taken in the West Indies and condemned, the fraudulent pretences of neutral property in the cargoes being too gross to be misunderstood. Complaints were, however, made of the hardship of this practice on the *bonâ fide* American trader, and in January, 1794, the instructions were so far amended that the direction was to seize 'such vessels as were laden with goods the produce of the French West India islands, *and coming directly from any ports of the said islands to Europe.* This rule continued in force till 1798, when again it was relaxed, by ordering that 'vessels' should be seized 'laden with the produce of any island or settlement of France, Spain, or Holland, and coming directly from any port of the said island or settlement to any port in Europe, not being a port of this kingdom, or of the country to which the vessel, being neutral, should belong.' European neutrals were thus permitted to bring the produce of the hostile colonies from thence to ports of their own countries; and European or American neutral ships might carry such produce direct to England. But when the war was resumed in 1803, the rule of 1798 was again put in force, and instructions were given 'not to seize any neutral vessels which should be found carrying on trade directly between the colonies of the enemy and the neutral country to which the vessel belonged, and laden with property of the inhabitants of such neutral country, provided that such neutral vessel should not be supplying, nor should have on the outward voyage supplied, the enemy with any articles of contraband of war, and should not be trading with any blockaded ports.'

Relaxation of the rule.

By thus allowing, however, neutrals to trade safely to and from neutral ports, means were opened to them to clear out for a neutral port, and under cover of that pretended destination to make a direct voyage from the colony to the parent state, or really to proceed to some neutral country, and thence re-export the cargo in the same or a different bottom to whichever European market, neutral or hostile, they might prefer. The former, or an assumed voyage to the parent state, being the shortest and most convenient method, was chiefly adopted by the Dutch on their homeward voyages, because a pretended destination for Prussian, Swedish, or Danish ports in the North Sea, or the Baltic, was a plausible mask, even in the very closest approach the ship might make to the Dutch coast down to the moment of her slipping into port. The latter method, or the stopping at an intermediate neutral country, was commonly preferred by the Spaniards and French in bringing home their colonial produce, because no pretended neutral destination could be given that would consist with the geographical position and course of a ship coming directly from the West Indies, if met with near the end of her voyage in the latitude of their principal ports. The American flag in particular was a cover that could scarcely ever be adapted to the former method of eluding our hostilities; but it was found peculiarly convenient in the latter. Such is the position of the United States, and such was the effect of the trade winds, that European vessels, homeward bound from the West Indies, could touch at their ports with very little inconvenience or delay; and such was also the case, though in a less degree, with regard to vessels coming from the remotest parts of South America or the East Indies. The passage from the Gulf of Mexico, especially, runs so close along the North American shore, that ships bound from the Havannah, from Vera Cruz, and other great Spanish ports bordering on that gulf to Europe, could touch at certain ports in the United States with scarcely any deviation. On an outward voyage to the East and West Indies, the proper course would be more to the southward than would well consist with touching on North America; yet the deviation for that purpose was not a very formidable inconvenience. From these causes the protection given by the American flag to the intercourse between our European enemies and their colonies was chiefly in the way of a double voyage, in which America was the half-way house or central point of com-

Neutral trading with colonies.

munication. The fabrics and commodities of France, Spain, and Holland were brought under American colours to ports in the United States, and from thence re-exported, under the same flag, for the supply of the hostile colonies. Again, the produce of those colonies was brought in a like manner to the American ports, and thence reshipped to Europe. But the Americans went still farther. The ports of this kingdom, having been constituted by the royal instructions of 1798 legitimate places of destination for neutrals coming with cargoes of produce directly from the hostile colonies, the American merchants made a pretended destination to British ports a convenient cover for a voyage from the hostile colonies to Europe, which their flag could not otherwise give, and thus rivalled the neutrals of the old world in this method of protecting the West India trade of the enemy, while they nearly engrossed the other. As the war advanced, after the peace of Amiens, the neutrals became bolder and more aggressive. American ships were constantly arriving at Dutch and French ports with sugar, coffee, and other productions of the French and Spanish West Indies. And East India goods were imported by them into Spain, Holland, and France.

Effect of neutral trading on British commerce.

By these and other means, Hamburgh, Altona, Emden, Gottenburgh, Copenhagen, Lisbon, and other neutral markets were glutted with the produce of the West Indies and the fabrics of the East, brought from the prosperous colonies of powers hostile to this country. By the rivers and canals of Germany and Flanders these were floated into the warehouses of the enemy, or circulated for the supply of his customers in neutral countries. He rivalled the British planter and merchant throughout the continent of Europe and in all the ports of the Mediterranean, and even supplanted the manufacturers of Manchester, Birmingham, and Yorkshire; and by these means the hostile colonies derived benefit, and not inconvenience, from the enmity of Great Britain. What, moreover, especially injured the commerce of this country was the increase in the cost of importation into this country from the British colonies, from freight, insurance, and other charges which, taken together, were as much as, if not superior to, those to which the enemy was subjected in his covert and circuitous trade. It was a general complaint, therefore, that the enemy carried on colonial commerce under the neutral flag, cheaply as well as safely; that he was enabled not only to elude our hostilities, but to rival our merchants and planters in the European markets; that by the same means the hostile treasuries were filled with a copious stream of revenue; and that by this licentious use of the neutral flag, the enemy was enabled to employ his whole military marine in purposes of offensive war, without being obliged to maintain a squadron or a ship for the defence of their colonial ports. It was moreover contended that since neutral states have no right, but through our own gratuitous concession, to carry on the colonial trade of the enemy, we might, after a reasonable notice, withdraw that ruinous indulgence; that the neutral did not require such privileges; that the comparative cheapness of his navigation gives him, in every open market, a decisive advantage; that in the commerce of other neutral countries he could not fail to supplant the belligerent; and that he obtained an increase of trade by purchasing from one belligerent, and selling to his enemies the merchandise for which, in time of peace, they depended on each other.

Order in council of May 1806.

Such complaints made against neutral states found a powerful echo by the publication of a work entitled 'War in Disguise and the Frauds of the Neutral Flag,' supposed to have been written by Mr. James Stephen, the real author of the orders in council. The British Government did not see its way at once to proceed in the direction of prohibiting to neutral ships the colonial trade, which they had enjoyed for a considerable time; but the first step was taken to paralyse the resources of the enemy, and to restrict the trade of neutrals, by the issue of an order in council in May 1806, declaring that all the coasts, ports, and rivers from the Elbe to Brest should be considered blockaded, though the only portion of those coasts rigorously blockaded was that included between Ostend and the mouth of the Seine, in the ports of which preparations were made for the invasion of England. The northern ports of Germany and Holland were left partly open, and the navigation of the Baltic altogether free.

Napoleon, then in the zenith of his power, saw, in this order in council, a fresh act of wantonness, and he met it by the issue of the Berlin decree of November 21, 1806. In that document, remarkable for its boldness and vigour, Napoleon charged England with having set at nought the dictates of international law, with having made prisoners of war of private individuals, and with having taken the crews out of merchant ships. He charged this country with having captured private property at sea, extended to commercial ports the restrictions of blockade applicable only to fortified places, declared as blockaded places which were not invested by naval forces, and abused the right of blockade in order to benefit her own trade at the expense of the commerce of continental states. He asserted the right of combating the enemy with the same arms used against himself, especially when such enemy ignored all ideas of justice, and every liberal sentiment which civilisation imposes. He announced his resolution to apply to England the same usages which she had established in her maritime legislation. He laid down the principles which France was resolved to act upon until England should recognise that the rights of war are the same on land as on sea, that such rights should not be extended either against private property or against persons not belonging to the military or naval forces, and that the right of blockade should be restricted to fortified places, truly invested by sufficient forces. And upon these premises the decree ordered, 1st, That the British islands should be declared in a state of blockade. 2nd, That all commerce and correspondence with the British islands should be prohibited; and that letters addressed to England or Englishmen, written in the English language, should be detained and taken. 3rd, That every British subject found in a country occupied by French troops, or by those of their allies, should be made a prisoner of war. 4th, That all merchandise and property belonging to British subjects should be deemed a good prize. 5th, That all commerce in English merchandise should be prohibited, and that all merchandise belonging to England or her colonies, and of British manufacture, should be deemed a good prize. And 6th, That no vessel coming direct from England or her colonies be

The Berlin decree.

allowed to enter any French port, or any port subject to French authority; and that every vessel which, by means of a false declaration, should evade such regulations, should at once be captured.

The British Government lost no time in retaliating against France for so bold a course; and, on January 7, 1807, an order in council was issued, which, after reference to the orders issued by France, enjoined that no vessel should be allowed to trade from one enemy's port to another, or from one port to another of a French ally's coast shut against English vessels; and ordered the commanders of the ships of war and privateers to warn every neutral vessel coming from any such port, and destined to another such port, to discontinue her voyage, and that any vessel, after being so warned, which should be found proceeding to another such port should be captured and considered as lawful prize. This order in council having reached Napoleon at Warsaw, he immediately ordered the confiscation of all English merchandise and colonial produce found in the Hanseatic Towns. Bourrienne, Napoleon's commissioner at Hamburg, declared that all who carried on trade with England supported England; that it was to prevent such trading that France took possession of Hamburg; that all English goods should be produced by the Hamburghers for the purpose of being confiscated; and that, in forty-eight hours, domiciliary visits would be paid and military punishments inflicted on the disobedient. But Britain, in return, went a step further, and, by order in council of November 11, 1807, declared all the ports and places of France, and those of her allies, and of all countries where the English flag was excluded, even though they were not at war with Britain, placed under the same restrictions for commerce and navigation as if they were blockaded, and consequently that ships destined to those ports should be liable to the visit of British cruisers at a British station, and there subjected to a tax to be imposed by the British Parliament.

Order in council of January and November, 1807.

Napoleon was at Milan when this order in council was issued, and forthwith, on December 17, the famous decree appeared, by which he imposed on neutrals just the contrary of what was prescribed to them by England, and further declared that every vessel, of whatever nation, that submitted to the order in council of November 11, should by that very act become denationalised, considered as British property, and condemned as a good prize. The decree placed the British islands in a state of blockade, and ordered that every ship, of whatever nation, and with whatever cargo, proceeding from English ports or English colonies to countries occupied by English troops, or going to England, should be a good prize. This England answered by the order in council of April 26, 1809, which revoked the order of 1807 as regards America, but confirmed the blockade of all the ports of France and Holland, their colonies and dependencies. And then France, still further incensed against England, issued the tariff of Trianon, dated August 5, 1810, completed by the decree of St. Cloud of September 12, and of Fontainebleau of October 19, which went the length of ordering the seizure and burning of all British goods found in France, Germany, Holland, Italy, Spain, and in every place occupied by French troops. Strange infatuation! and how many States took part in this mad act of vindictiveness! The princes of the Rhenish Confederation hastened to execute it, some for the purpose of enriching themselves by the wicked deed, some out of hatred towards the English, and some to show their devotion towards their master. From Carlsruhe to Munich, from Cassel to Dresden and Hamburg, everywhere, bonfires were made of English goods. And so exacting were the French that, when Frankfort exhibited the least hesitation in carrying out the decree, French troops were sent to execute the order.

The Milan and Fontainebleau decrees.

By means such as these the commerce of the world was greatly deranged, if not destroyed altogether, and none suffered more from it than England herself. Was it not enough to be effectually shut out from all commerce with French ports, that we should have provoked the closing of neutral ports also? Was it politic, at a time when our relations with the principal powers were in a condition so critical, to alienate from us all the neutral states of Europe? Was it wise to inflict so grievous an injury upon neutral states, as to force them to make common cause with the enemy? It is scarcely possible to describe at what peril the commerce of

British policy towards neutrals.

the world was carried on. The proceedings of the court of admiralty are full of the most romantic incidents. An American ship,[4] with a cargo of tobacco, was sent from America to Vigo, or to a market for sale. At Vigo the tobacco was sold under contract to deliver it at Seville, at the master's risk, and the vessel was going to Seville to deliver the cargo when she was captured. A British vessel[5] was separated from her convoy during a storm, and brought out by a French lugger which came up, and told the master to stay by her till the storm moderated, when they would send a boat on board. The lugger continued alongside, sometimes ahead, and sometimes astern, and sometimes to windward for three or four hours. But a British frigate, coming in sight, gave chase to the lugger and captured her, during which time the ship made her escape, rejoined the convoy, and came into Poole. Ships were taken because they were sailing to false destinations, under false papers, false flags, false certificates of ownership, and false bills of sale. They were seized for running the blockade, and for escaping from blockaded ports. They were arrested for carrying despatches, military men, and contraband of war. In every way, at every point of the ocean, the pursuit was carried on, till the seas were cleared of merchant ships, and the highway of nations, the widest and freest arena for trade, was converted into an amphitheatre for the display of the wildest and worst excesses of human cupidity and passions.

The evil of the licensing system.

But a greater evil than even this extreme derangement of maritime commerce was that which flowed from the system of licences,[6] an evil which undermined the first principles of commercial morality. It was forcibly stated by the Marquis of Lansdowne, that the commerce of the country was one mass of simulation and dissimulation; that our traders crept along the shores of the enemy in darkness and silence waiting for an opportunity of carrying into effect the simula-

[4] The 'Atlas,' 3 Rob. Rep. p. 299.

[5] The 'Edward and Mary,' 3 Rob. Rep. p. 305.

[6] The number of commercial licenses granted for imports and exports was 68 in 1802, 836 in 1803, 1,141 in 1804, 791 in 1805, 1,620 in 1806, 2,606 in 1807, 4,910 in 1808, 15,226 in 1809, 16,356 in 1810, and 7,602 in 1811.

tive means, by which they sought to carry on their business; that such a system led to private violation of morality and honour of the most alarming description; and that, instead of benefiting our commerce, manufactures, and resources, the orders in council diminished our commerce, distressed our manufactures, and lessened our resources. Yet all these warnings and expostulations were unheeded. The national mind was preoccupied by the *one* thought of compelling France and her military leader to a complete submission; and no consideration of a commercial or pecuniary character, no regard to the bearing of her measures upon other countries, were sufficient to induce a reversal of this military and naval policy.

Upwards of fifteen years had elapsed since the first shot was fired between England and France after the great revolution, and yet the two nations were as intent as ever on securing their mutual destruction. England had indeed learnt, by this time, to make light of all such decrees, and she had found by experience that British goods found their way to the Continent in spite of all vindictive measures. But the attitude of the United States became more and more threatening, and the nation saw an absolute necessity for revising the policy of the orders in council. For years past Lord Temple, Lord Castlereagh, Mr. Perceval, Sir John Nichols had brought the subject before the House, and many a long discussion had taken place on the subject. In their opinion this country had, without any alleged provocation from the United States of America, interrupted nearly the whole of their commerce with Europe, and they held that such orders in council were unjust and impolitic, and that the issuing of them, at the time and under the circumstances, was an act of the utmost improvidence and rashness. Yet the nation was disposed to be guided by the government, and when Lord Grenville moved resolutions of similar import, in 1809, he met with no better response. When, however, the United States, after having passed the Non-intercourse Act, proceeded still further in the way of preparation for open hostilities, the merchants began to speak their mind on the subject; and from London, Hull, Bristol, and all the chief ports, petitions came to the legisla-

The orders in council and the United States.

ture praying for the revocation of the obnoxious orders. The merchants of London represented that trade was in a miserable condition, chiefly from the want of the customary intercourse with the Continent of Europe; that employment was very scarce, and the wages of labour very low; that the aspect of affairs threatened additional suffering to those then experienced; that since all the evils then suffered were owing to the continuance of the war, it was all-important to obtain if possible an early restoration of the blessings of peace; that it was not from any dread of the enemy that they made such a request, but from a desire that no opportunity might be lost of entering into negotiations for the purpose; that in their opinion it was a great error to suppose that the policy of the orders in council could in any way be beneficial to trade; but that on the contrary, they regarded with extreme apprehension its effect on our relations with the United States of America. The merchants of Hull complained that the system of license sapped public morals. Those of Bristol represented that they suffered intensely in their general trade; and riots occurred in Lancashire, Yorkshire, and Cheshire.

On April 28, 1812, the House of Commons agreed, without a division, to hear evidence in support of these petitions; and, on June 16, Mr., afterwards Lord, Brougham moved, 'That an humble address be presented to his Royal Highness the Prince Regent, representing to his royal highness that this House has, for some time past, been engaged in an inquiry into the present depressed state of the manufactures and commerce of the country, and the effects of the orders in council issued by his majesty in the years 1807 and 1809; assuring his royal highness that this House will at all times support his royal highness to the utmost of its power, in maintaining those just maritime rights which have essentially contributed to the prosperity and honour of the realm; but beseeching his royal highness that he would be graciously pleased to recall or suspend the said orders, and to adopt such measures as may tend to conciliate neutral powers, without sacrificing the rights and dignity of his majesty's crown.' In the most graphic manner Lord Brougham depicted the distress of the country, showed how erroneous was

Lord Brougham's motion.

the idea that what we lost in the European trade we gained in any other quarter, and warned the country of the certainty of a war with America if the orders were not at once rescinded. 'I know,' he said, 'I shall be asked, whether I would recommend any sacrifice for the mere purpose of conciliating America. I recommend no sacrifice of honour for that or for any purpose; but I will tell you that I think we can well, and safely, for our honour, afford to conciliate America. Never did we stand so high since we were a nation in point of military character. We have it in abundance, and even to spare. This unhappy and seemingly interminable war, lavish as it has been in treasure, still more profuse of blood and barren of real advantage, has at least been equally lavish of glory. Its feats have not merely sustained the warlike fame of the nation, which would have been much; they have done what seemed scarcely possible—they have greatly exalted it. They have covered our arms with immortal renown. Then, I say, use this glory—use this proud height on which we now stand for the purpose of peace and conciliation with America. Let this and its incalculable benefits be the advantage which we reap from the war in Europe, for the fame of that war enables us safely to take it. And who, I demand, give the most disgraceful counsels—they who tell you we are in military character but of yesterday, we yet have a name to win, we stand on doubtful ground, we dare not do as we list for fear of being thought afraid; we cannot, without loss of name, stoop to pacify our American kinsmen? or I, who say we are a great, a proud, a warlike people; we have fought everywhere, and conquered wherever we have fought; our character is eternally fixed—it stands too firm to be shaken; and, on the faith of it, we may do towards America safely for our honour that which we know our interests require? This perpetual jealousy of America! Good God! I cannot, with temper, ask on what it rests? It drives me to a passion to think of it! Jealousy of America! I should as soon think of being jealous of the tradesman who supplies me with necessaries, or the client who entrusts his suits to my patronage. Jealousy of America! whose armies are as yet at the plough, or making, since your policy has willed it, so awkward (though improving) attempts at the loom—whose assembled navies could not lay siege to an English harbour! Jealousy of a power which is necessarily peaceful as well as weak, but which, if it had all the ambition of France, and her armies to back it, and all the navy of England to boot—nay, had it the lust of conquests which marks your enemies and your own army as well as navy to gratify, it is placed at so vast a distance as to be perfectly harmless! And this is the nation of which, for our honour's sake, we are desired to cherish a perpetual jealousy for the ruin of our best interests. I trust, sir, that no such phantom of the brain will scare us from the path of our duty. The advice which I tender is not the same which has at all times been offered to this country. There is one memorable era in our history when other uses were made of our triumphs from those which I recommend. By the treaty of Utrecht, which the reprobation of ages has left inadequately censured, we were content to obtain, as the whole price of Ramillies and Blenheim, an additional share of the accursed slave trade. I give you other counsels. I should have you employ the glory which you have won at Talavera and Corunna in restoring your commerce to its lawful, open, honest course; and rescue it from the mean and hateful channels in which it has lately been confined. And, if any thoughtless boaster, in America or elsewhere, should vaunt that you have yielded through fear, I would not bid him wait until some new achievement of our arms put him to silence, but I would counsel you in silence to disregard him.'

The effect of such an appeal was fatal to the whole system. The government saw that resistance was no longer possible, and on April 21 the Prince Regent made a declaration that the orders in council would be revoked as soon as the Berlin and Milan decrees should be repealed. But it was too late. America had by this time ceased to maintain a neutral attitude. And having made a secret treaty with Napoleon, she issued an embargo on all British vessels in American ports, declared war against England, and proceeded to make an ineffectual attack upon Canada. The political condition of Europe, however, at this stage happily assumed a brighter aspect. The long-desired peace began to dawn on the horizon, and in rapid succession the news came of the battle of Leipzig,

Declaration of the Prince Regent.

the entry of the Allies into Paris, and the abdication of Buonaparte. Negotiations then commenced in earnest, and they issued in the treaty of peace and Congress of Vienna, which once more restored order and symmetry in the political organisation of Europe.[1] On December 24, 1814, a treaty of peace was signed between the United Kingdom and the United States. On June 9, 1815, the principal act of the Congress of Vienna was signed, which established the future political relations of the European States, and laid down the regulations for the free navigation of rivers. And on July 27 of the same year a Treaty of Commerce was concluded between Great Britain and the United States of America.

[1] The total cost of the war with France, from 1793 to 1815 (the war expenditure continued till 1817), was 831,446,449*l*. The national debt, which in 1793 amounted to 247,874,434*l*., rose in 1815 to 861,039,049*l*.

CHAPTER V.

THE FOREIGN EXCHANGES AND THE BULLION COMMITTEE.

1803–1810.

The Foreign Exchanges.—The Par of Exchange.—Exchanges between England and Ireland.—Report of Committee.—State of the Coinage in Ireland.—The Bank of Ireland.—State of Trade in England.—The Crisis of 1810.—Committee on Commercial Credit.—The Bullion Committee.—Report of the Committee.—Mr. Horner's and Mr. Vansittart's Motions.—Effects of the Restriction Act.

OF all economic questions those connected with the foreign exchanges are doubtless the most important to a mercantile nation having dealings with all parts of the world. The main principles by which the exchanges are governed are, indeed, well-defined, and perspicuous; yet the complicated circumstances under which they appear, the conflicting nature of these, and the difficulty of appreciating their proportional influence, contribute to render each occasion of disorder in the exchanges one of perplexity and uncertainty. During the war, and whilst the suspension of cash payments by the Bank of England lasted, the subject became immensely important, and all eyes were directed to them, to see whether they gave any indication that the country was following a dangerous course in her monetary legislation. The foreign exchanges, it should be remembered, are at all times the best exponent of the condition of international transactions. These, as might be imagined, are vast and multifarious, and comprise the imports and exports to and from each country, financial and banking operations, public loans, war expenditure, investments of capital in public and private undertakings, remittances of money, and many other items. Such transactions necessarily produce debts mutually due to or by each country, sometimes of equal amount, and sometimes leaving a balance to be settled, either by the transmission of gold or silver, or by the

The foreign exchanges.

intervention of a third or fourth country. Now, it is according as the payment of these debts, or the settlement of these balances, become more or less onerous, that the exchanges are said to be in favour of or against any country.

The technical term, 'par of exchange,' expresses the amount of money of one country which is equivalent to a fixed amount of money of another country. So long as the amount of debts due by the individuals of one country is the same as the amount of debts due by the individuals of another, and the currencies of both remain intact, the price at which bills on either side will sell in the respective places or countries will correspond to the value of the respective currencies, and the exchanges will be *at par*. Let, however, a balance of payments remain due by either country to the other, and the value of bills in one country will at once be in excess of the value of bills on the other, and the price at which these bills will sell will no longer correspond to the value of the respective currencies, so that the exchange will be below *par* or above *par*. This balance of indebtedness may proceed either from an excess of imports, or from any other cause creating debts in one country in favour of the other. Only it is in the nature of an adverse exchange, when resulting from such causes, to be productive of circumstances having in themselves a corrective influence. As soon, for instance, as a low rate of exchange causes the transmission of bullion to foreign countries, the Bank of England, the great depositary of all the spare bullion of the country, feels the effect of the same in a drain of bullion from its coffers, and, for its own safety, it restricts its accommodation by raising the rate of interest. Speculation is thus arrested. The demand for produce and manufactures lessens, and prices fall to a point sufficiently low to tempt foreign buyers to the market. Orders then coming more plentifully the debts of foreign countries increase, and that produces a gradual equation of indebtedness. In the event of any alteration taking place in the currency of one of two countries, from the wear or debasement of a metallic currency, or from excess of paper currency not convertible into cash on demand, a similar effect on the exchange will appear. A fall having taken place in the intrinsic value of a given

The par of exchange.

portion of one currency, that portion will not longer be equal in value to a given amount of the currency of the other country, and the rate of exchange will be altered. There is no corrective influence, however, operating against this cause of disorder in the exchanges except the restoration of the currencies to their proper metallic standard.

At the commencement of this century, partly from the want of close communication between the two countries, and partly from the difference of currencies, there was an exchange quoted between England and Ireland.[1] For many years the rate was about 9 per cent., and in 1798 it was 9 to 9¾ per cent., but after 1801 the exchanges rose gradually, till in 1803 the rate rose to 14, and even 18 per cent. To what was this to be ascribed? One thing was noted, viz. that whilst the exchange with Belfast, where bills were purchased by guineas, was at 10 per cent., the exchange with Dublin, where bills were purchased by Bank of Ireland and other bank notes, was at 18, or at a rate decidedly against Ireland. It did not appear that the balance of trade was in favour of England and against Ireland. On the contrary, the balance of pecuniary transactions was greatly in favour of Ireland, and, consequently, the real exchange ought to have been under par. In these circumstances a committee of the House of Commons was appointed to inquire into the state of Ireland as to its circulating paper, its specie, and current coin, and the exchange between that part of the United Kingdom and Great Britain. The committee examined many witnesses, and they had no difficulty in divining the cause of the derangement. The Bank of Ireland followed that of England as to the restriction of cash payments in 1797, though without any absolute necessity; and it is to the consequences of that restriction that the committee attributed the unfavourable exchange and all the high and progressive advances of the rate.

Exchanges between England and Ireland.

In the words of the report, 'Such restriction compelled the Bank to refrain from sending into circulation gold, the only common medium between the countries, and it gave occasion to the great issue of paper which followed

Report of the committee.

[1] See Observations on the State of the Currency in Ireland, and upon the Course of Exchange between Dublin and London. By Henry Parnell. London, 1801.

to replace the gold so withdrawn, and removed, at the same time, the best and most effective check against the depreciation of that paper, namely, its convertibility into gold at the will of the holder; it tended to encourage an unlimited and over-abundant issue, by releasing the Bank from performing their engagements, and by taking away from them the former criterion, namely, the diminution of their gold which they were accustomed to look to, for judging when their paper became excessive; it promoted a new and unrestrained trade in paper currency, and excited individuals to speculations which interfered with the steady, natural rates of exchange; while the number of speculators so encouraged contributed to raise the price of bills on England, which, being paid for in depreciated paper, the rate of exchange rose proportionally. Other evil consequences followed, which tended, in a further degree, to assist in depreciating the paper; forgeries were multiplied, particularly of the smaller notes substituted for gold; additional silver currency became necessary, and as it was not supplied by the Mint, its place was filled either by small notes, some as low as 6*d.*, without the checks against forgery attending those of larger value, or by base coin fabricated and forced into circulation.'

State of the coinage in Ireland.

Besides the circumstances thus related by the committee, the silver and current coin of Ireland were in a most unsatisfactory condition. The Bank of Ireland, like the Bank of England, issued a considerable quantity of silver dollars; but they circulated them at the price of 6*s.* Irish, though they contained the same quantity of silver as the English dollar, which passed for 5*s.* The supply of silver consisted of dollars only, without smaller change, and was far short of the quantity supposed to be necessary; while the copper coinage was so defective that there was not a halfpenny in circulation. As for the remedy to this state of things, the committee expressed their opinion that it was indispensably incumbent on the directors of the Bank of Ireland to limit their paper at all times of an unfavourable exchange, during the continuance of the restriction, exactly as they would and must have done if the restriction had not existed. They recommended a diminution of the issue of paper from private bankers and other dealers, by a strict enforcement of the laws respecting the registry of bankers and the full payment of stamp duties; and also the suppression of the issue of silver notes, as soon as a proper and sufficient silver currency was procured. The committee thus placed the restriction of cash payments and the bad state of the currency in the fore-front of the causes of the disordered state of the exchanges between England and Ireland. But there were other causes also in operation. Although the balance of trade was in favour of Ireland, the balance of indebtedness was not, since she had not only to pay a portion of the interest of the national debt, but to remit large sums, amounting to about 2,000,000*l.*, to the nobility and gentry of Ireland who resided in England, the number of whom had greatly increased in consequence of the political insecurity of the country.

Moreover, even as regards the currency, it was not so much the excess of paper currency as the number and description of issuers that engendered discredit. No doubt was ever entertained respecting the solidity of the Bank of Ireland. The bank was opened in 1783 with a capital of 600,000*l.* 4 per cent. stock; but this was increased, and in 1804 it held 1,100,000*l.* of government securities and 400,000*l.* in money. It is true that the amount of notes in circulation was nearly 3,000,000*l.*, whilst before the restriction of the issue of specie it was only from 600,000*l.* to 700,000*l.*; but this arose from the fact, that when gold was taken out of the market the Bank had to supply its place by currency; and the want of such must have been great when we remember that the amount of specie in circulation in Ireland before the restriction was estimated at about 5,000,000*l.* The management of the issue by the Bank of Ireland was probably as good as ever it had been, only the Bank had to contend with adverse influences over which it could have no control.

The Bank of Ireland.

But the interest taken in the state of the exchanges between England and Ireland directed public attention to the effects of the restriction of cash payments in England, especially at a time when in the opinion of many the state of the monetary laws was far from satisfactory. The Cash Restriction Continuance Bill, yearly brought forward, was by no means readily accepted; and it was only in view of the

State of trade in England.

urgent political necessities that the measure was allowed to pass into law. The prices of grain and provisions also began to create considerable suspicion. During the first years of the war, about 1796, when the colonial trade was so much endangered, and the French flag was driven from the ocean, a considerable demand sprang up for colonial produce, principally for Germany, in consequence of which prices rose enormously. But these speculative prices were not maintained, and with a number of bankruptcies in Hamburg, Liverpool, and other centres of trade, a serious fall became inevitable, which wrought consternation among the merchants. In a year or two the state of trade was completely changed. With the return of an excellent harvest in 1803 and 1804, the prices of grain, notwithstanding the increased cost of production, fell considerably, and then the extremely low prices of provisions and colonial articles induced purchasers to come to the market. Still prices continued low, and up to 1805, when the crops proved very deficient, no change of any moment took place. With the orders in council, however, in full operation, with the extreme difficulty of importing colonial and other articles, and with the Baltic shut, all prices, and especially those of hemp, linseed, tallow, and timber rose enormously. Silk also, being very difficult to be had, rose very much in value, whilst the Non-intercourse Act passed by the United States produced a general apprehension that prices would rule very high. What had the issues of the Bank of England to do with such circumstances? Had the rise of prices been caused by an excessive amount of currency, the rise would have been uniform and general. But the greatest difference was observable in the prices of different articles, clearly showing that they were caused by events peculiar to themselves. It is true a certain amount of speculation existed, and a number of companies were started for a variety of objects; but it could not be said that they had involved the country in any extraordinary liabilities. However it be, the excitement, if there was any, did not last very long; the state of trade and the economic condition of the people not warranting the continuance of high prices. In the manufacturing districts orders were exceedingly small, and production was reduced to the minimum; and the labouring classes were suffering from the combination of high prices and want of employment. On February 24, 1808, Mr. Twining moved in the House of Commons, that the House should resolve itself into a committee of the whole House upon the trade and navigation of the country; when he gave a fearful picture of the state of the working classes, and presented a petition from Bolton, signed by upwards of thirty thousand individuals suffering from want of bread. Whilst trade was in such a condition a serious misfortune greatly aggravated public anxiety. In 1809, profiting by the partial opening of the Baltic, extensive operations were carried on in that quarter, and whole fleets, accompanied by our convoys, traded with the Baltic ports. Unfortunately, a convoy having been compelled to stop in Wingo Sound from contrary winds until the middle of June, the French in the meantime seized Stralsund and enforced the continental system. As many as 600 vessels were thus arrested, and the greater part of those which ventured into the Baltic were seized and condemned, causing a loss of several millions of pounds. Thus any attempt to force a trade with blockaded places proved dangerous and often unavailing; commerce with distant countries was uncertain and unsatisfactory; and the accounts from South America, from which the most brilliant results were anticipated, proved particularly distressing to exporters.

As time advanced, the condition of trade did not improve. A commercial report,[1] for August 1810, quoted by Mr. Tooke, gives an interesting detail of the wretched condition of trade at this period. 'The failure of several houses of the very first respectability, both at London and at different provincial towns of Great Britain, have within the last month been unprecedented in number and importance. A West India broker, who had long been considered the first in his line, was, we are told, the prime cause of the stoppage of a banking house whose credit was previously unimpeached. The several banks in the country connected with the London house, of course, shared his fate; and from them the evil spread to merchants, manufacturers, traders, and, in short, to the very servants and dependents of these, numbers of whom are thrown

The crisis of 1810.

[1] Tooke's History of Prices, vol. ii. p. 301.

out of employment and their families deprived of bread. Speculations in Spanish wool, an article which has fallen about 50 per cent., were considered as the origin of those unlooked-for disasters. Five Manchester houses have stopped payment in the city, and, we are sorry to add, have involved numerous industrious persons, both in town and country, in their ruin. The demands upon the five houses are said to amount to two millions; but it is supposed that their real property will ultimately cover all deficiencies. Speculative exports to South America are the rock upon which these houses have split. In consequence of these unexpected events, public credit is at the present moment as low as ever it has been in the memory of man; the fluctuations of prices in the money market is unprecedented, and the depression so considerable that premium is fallen to 2½ per cent. discount. We understand that some respectable merchants have waited upon the Bank directors in order to solicit their aid towards the alleviation of the burden with which our inland commerce is at present borne down. The result of the application is not as yet publicly known; we hope that it will prove favourable. The renewal of our intercourse with the United States of America has in some sorts benefited the manufacturing interest; but this felicitous effect is almost swallowed in the vortex of those calamities which it has been our painful duty to record.'

Committee on commercial credit.

In 1811, a committee of the House of Commons was formed to inquire into the state of commercial credit, and in their report they attributed the disorder rather to temporary than to permanent derangement. They stated that the construction of the West India and London Dock warehouses, and of similar receptacles for merchandise in the principal outports within the last two years, had tended to make Great Britain the emporium of the trade, not only of the Peninsula but of the Brazils, the Spanish settlements in South America, St. Domingo, and the conquered colonies of Guadaloupe, Martinique, and even of countries under the direct influence of the enemy, whose traders had been anxious to avail themselves of the protection of British law and of the honour of British merchants; that from these causes goods had been brought into this country in amount beyond all precedent and calculation; that the power, wealth, and high character of the nation have, in fact, contributed to produce a most alarming evil; and that, as the measures of the enemy have been especially directed to preventing the exportation of the immense quantities of merchandise of all descriptions thus accumulated, the consequences were that the goods became a burden, and the advances to the owners on account, and the payment of freight and insurance, became grievous to such a degree as to threaten the most solid and respectable houses with all the evils of insolvency. Upon the presentation of this report, confirming the complaints made out of doors, the chancellor of the exchequer moved for power to issue 6,000,000*l.* in exchequer bills, to be advanced in the same manner as in 1793, and the measure was adopted.[3] But how could any substantial change in the critical state of trade ever take place, so long as the orders in council continued to trammel every trading operation?

The bullion committee.

It was in the midst of these troubles that two startling phenomena in the form of a great rise in the price of bullion and a most unfavourable state of the foreign exchanges presented themselves, and gave rise to much anxiety. At a time when the conduct of the Bank and the state of the paper currency were closely watched, in connection with the suspension of cash payments, the occurrence of two such phenomena could not fail to attract attention; and they were justly made the subjects of a special inquiry. On February 1, 1810, Mr. Horner moved for several accounts on currency and banking, and on his motion a committee was appointed to inquire into the causes of the high price of gold bullion, and to take into consideration the state of the circulating medium and of the exchanges between Great Britain and foreign parts—a committee which has long been well known as the bullion committee.[4] Certain facts were established beyond doubt by the

[3] 51 Geo. III. c. 15.

[4] The bullion committee consisted of Messrs. Francis Horner (chairman), Right Hon. Spencer Perceval, Right Hon. G. Tierney, Earl Temple, Hon. F. Brand H. Parnell, D. M. Magens, G. Johnstone, D. Giddy, W. Dickenson, Henry Thornton, R. B. Sheridan, Alexander Baring, W. Manning, R. Sharp, G. Grenfell, J. L. Foster, T. Thompson, F. Irving, William Huskisson, and Hon. J. Abercrombie.

committee. First of all the price of gold, which, according to the mint price, is 3*l.* 17*s.* 10½*d.* per ounce of standard fineness, during the years 1806, 1807, and 1808 was as high in the market as 4*l.*, and even 4*l.* 9*s.* to 4*l.* 12*s.* per ounce. The continental exchanges had for some time been very unfavourable to this country; the exchanges on Hamburg and Amsterdam, for instance, being from 16 to 20 per cent. below par, and those on Paris lower still. That this could not proceed from the state of trade was evident from the fact, that the exports greatly exceeded the imports. What then, argued some, could be the reason of it but an excess of currency? Two distinct theories were, however, held in explanation of the fact. One party affirmed that bank notes were depreciated, and that the difference between the market price and the mint price of gold bullion was the measure of that depreciation. Another answered, that it was not banknotes that were depreciated, but specie that had risen. One party maintained, that whilst the extreme limits from which the foreign exchanges could, by the nature of things, fall, in any case, was defined, and easily ascertainable, and was determined by the expense of freight, insurance, and other charges attending the sending of bullion in the state of the exchanges, there was a large excess of depression, which was not attributable to any of these causes. The other party was convinced that the depression of the foreign exchanges was in no way whatever attributable to the depression of the currency, but was entirely caused by the adverse balance of payments to be made by Great Britain, the remittances to the army, the continental measures of Napoleon, and other political circumstances. One party argued, that a diminution of the quantity of banknotes would increase the value of the domestic currency, would cause the foreign exchanges to rise to par, and the market price of gold to fall to the mint price; and that the directors of the Bank of England ought to follow the same rules in fixing the extent of their issues during the restriction of cash payments, as they were obliged to do before it, and to regulate them by the foreign exchanges: enlarging them when the exchanges were favourable and bullion flowing in, and contracting them when the exchanges were adverse. The other party answered, that since the restriction there was no necessity for observing the same rules in issuing notes by discount as before, and to observe the course of foreign exchanges; but that the public demand was the best guide, and that, so long as they followed those rules, there could be no over-issue.

The report of the committee was decidedly favourable to the theory of the bullionists, and upon a review of all the facts and reasonings submitted to their consideration they reported their conclusions:—1st, That there was an excess in the paper circulation of the country, of which the most unequivocal symptom was the very high price of bullion and the low state of the continental exchanges. 2nd, That this excess was to be ascribed to the want of a sufficient check and control of the issues of paper from the Bank of England, and originally to the suspension of cash payments, which removed the natural means of control. 3rd, That no safe, certain, and constantly adequate provision against an excess of paper currency, either occasional or permanent, can be found, except in the convertibility of all such paper into specie. 4th, That the system of the circulating medium of this country ought to be brought back, with as much speed as is compatible with a wise and necessary caution, to the original principle of cash payments at the option of the holder of bank paper. 5th, That no sufficient remedy for the present or security for the future can be pointed out, except the repeal of the law which suspends the cash payments of the Bank of England. And 6th, That early provision ought to be made by Parliament for terminating, at the end of two years, the operation of the several statutes which imposed and continued that restriction.

Report of the committee.

Upon the production of this report to Parliament in April, 1811, Mr. Horner moved a series of resolutions in accordance with its recommendations. But the leading conclusions of the committee were strongly objected to in the House, and, after four nights' debate, the whole of Mr. Horner's resolutions were rejected. The first was thrown out by a majority of 151 against 75. Fourteen others were negatived without a division, and the sixteenth was rejected by a majority of 180 against 45, the majority including, among others, Sir Robert Peel. Mr. Vansittart, however, was not content with his victory over Mr. Horner. He moved other resolutions in direct opposition, and these were agreed to after

Mr. Horner's and Mr. Vansittart's resolutions.

much discussion. The first ten resolutions proposed by Mr. Horner were a mere enunciation of the monetary policy of the country; but the eleventh charged the excess of currency with being the cause of the difference in value between gold and paper; and the thirteenth attributed the fall of the exchanges to the same cause. Mr. Vansittart endeavoured to prove, that a depreciation of the currency and an unfavourable exchange had been experienced more than once even when there was no restriction of cash payments. But what was the use of denying the depreciation of the notes as compared with gold, when, as a matter of fact, a guinea in gold was worth 26*s*. or 27*s*. in paper? It was also quite evident that the issues, though barely proportionate to the wants of trade, were still greatly in excess of the available amount of bullion. All that could be said in excuse was, that at a time when the convertibility of the note into specie was suspended by law, the Bank could no longer regulate its issues by the amount of bullion. The report of the bullion committee was, however, not followed by any legislation, and its publication had only the effect of considerably increasing the alarm already experienced, lest it should lead to a considerable contraction of credit.

Effects of the Restriction Act.

Though the Restriction Act of 1797, and the other measures connected with it, made the acceptance in banknotes obligatory on the public creditor, by placing him in such a situation that if he refused banknotes when tendered to him at the Bank, in payment of his dividend, he could get nothing else, in the settlement of other obligations between individuals the restriction had not the same effect, since banknotes had never been declared legal tender. Their circulation was only secured by the fact that gold was not obtainable, and that great inconvenience must have arisen by a refusal to accept notes. But payment in depreciated notes was the cause of considerable injury to private interests, and matters reached such a point that Lord King in 1811 issued a letter to his tenantry, giving them notice that, in consequence of the depreciated state of the paper currency, he would require payment either in guineas or in banknotes at such a sum as would, at the then market price of gold bullion, purchase gold enough to equalise the value of present and former payments. This letter having attracted great attention, Earl Stanhope brought in a bill for preventing Bank of England notes from being received for any smaller sum than the sums therein specified, and for staying proceedings upon any distress by tender of such notes. It was necessary for the greater currency of notes that proceedings upon any distress should be stayed by tender of the same. But as to any attempt to regulate the value of banknotes in relation to gold, by preventing people from refusing or accepting them for less than the sum therein expressed, it was, on the face of it, a hopeless task. Yet the bill passed both Houses, after lengthened discussion, in which Lord Liverpool, Lord King, and other leading financiers of the day took part and became law.[a]

[a] 51 Geo. III. c. 127.

CHAPTER VI.

RESUMPTION OF CASH PAYMENTS.

1819.

The Bank Restriction Act.—The Question of a Single or a Double Standard.—Authorities in favour of a Double Standard.—Adoption of a Gold Standard.—The Act of 1816.—Sir Robert Peel on a Double Standard.—Gold Coinage.—The Bank of England and Cash Payments.—Parliamentary Inquiry.—Sir Robert Peel's Speech.—The Act of 1819.

The Bank Restriction Act.

With the peace of 1815 we are commencing a new era of progress, which has scarcely ever since been interrupted. Momentous in its consequences to many states, whose limits and relations were then established, and memorable for its declaration of the free navigation of rivers and its condemnation of the slave trade, to England the treaty of Vienna produced no change, excepting the long-expected return to a normal condition, under which her economical resources might be fully developed. Before, however, any measure of trade and finance could receive due consideration, the exceptional condition of the Bank of England, as regards the payment of its notes, demanded legislative action, and to that public attention was first earnestly directed. From year to year the Bank Restriction Act had been renewed, but its operation was to expire on July 5, 1816. The last act on the subject, after reciting in the preamble that it was highly desirable that the Bank should, as soon as possible, resume payment of its notes in cash; and that it was expedient that the provisions of the former acts should be further continued, in order to afford time to the directors of the Bank to make such preparations as to their discretion and experience might appear most expedient for enabling them to resume payments in cash, without public inconvenience, and at the earliest period; and that a time should be fixed at which the said restrictions should cease; enacted that the said restrictions should be continued until July 5, 1818. The transition from a paper medium to a metallic currency was dreaded as a great calamity. With the bankruptcy of many country bankers, and the consequent extinction of their issue, the mercantile community were anxious that no change should be made in the issue of the Bank of England, and would have gladly postponed indefinitely the resumption of cash payments. But the country was not satisfied with protracting any longer the solution of the question, and for several years the state of the coinage and currency became the subject of serious discussion.

The question of a single or a double standard.

The immediate want of a new issue of silver coin, the money in circulation being worn and debased, raised in the first instance the whole question of a single or a double standard. In England the standard had originally been silver. From William I. to the forty-first of Henry III. silver coins were the only legal measure of property. Subsequently, however, gold coins were introduced into circulation; and as trade increased, and the country advanced in wealth, gold began to be preferred to silver. Thus by degrees the two metals acquired alike the character of legal tender, and their relative value was fixed by proclamation. But this method was attended with inconvenience, the mint price being often above or below the market value of either metal. To avoid uncertainty, the value of the guinea was fixed by proclamation in 1717 at 21*s.*, but no proclamation could prevent changes in the relative value of gold and silver any more than in any other commodity. The universal practice, however, of using gold as the only standard of value practically solved the difficulty, and it was when such practice had been sufficiently established, that the legislature gave it so far the force of law as to enact,[1]

[1] In 1773 an act was passed (13 Geo. III. c. 72.) for the better preventing the counterfeiting, clipping, and otherwise diminishing the gold coin in the kingdom as a means for preserving it entire and pure. Any person to whom such coin was tendered was allowed to cut, break, or deface such piece; and if it should appear that it was unlawfully counterfeited or diminished, the person who offered it should bear the loss of the same; if otherwise, the person who cut it should bear the loss or take it at the same rate as it was coined for. In 1774 a great quantity of old silver coin having been imported below the standard weight, an act (14 Geo. III. c. 42, s. 42) was passed prohibiting such importation; no more than 25*l.* was declared to be legal tender in silver coin at any one time for more than according to its value by weight after the rate of 5*s.* 2*d.* for each ounce of silver. Great deficiency being experienced in the gold coin in circulation, a proposal was made to the chancellor of the exchequer, Lord North, 1st, That all the deficient gold coin should be called in and recoined; 2nd, That a compensation should be made to the holders of such deficient gold coin, under certain limits and restrictions; 3rd, That after that operation had been

that no person should be obliged to receive more than 25*l.* in silver money, except by weight at the rate of 5*s.* 2*d.* per ounce. As time advanced, gold became more and more the leading coin of the realm; and with no reason for further hesitancy, the Earl of Liverpool, following the policy initiated by his father, proceeded further in the way of demonetising the silver coin.

The weight of authority was decidedly in favour of a single standard. On this subject Sir William Petty said, 'The money in coin, which is to be the principal measure of property, ought to be made of one metal only.' Mr. Harris, a great writer on financial subjects, said, 'that one only of these metals, that is gold or silver, can be the money or standard measure of commerce in any country, for the standard measure must be invariable and keep the same proportion of value in all its parts. Such is silver with respect to silver and gold to gold. But silver and gold with respect to one another are, like other commodities, variable in their value according as the plenty of either may be increased or diminished, and an ounce of gold that is worth a given quantity of silver to-day, may be worth more or less silver a while hence. It is

Authorities in favour of a single standard.

completed, the currency of the gold coin should in future be regulated by weight as well as by tale (which was conformable to the ancient laws of the kingdom), and that the several pieces should not be legal tender if they were diminished, by wearing or otherwise, below a certain weight, to be determined by proclamation. On January 13, 1776, the king commended the subject to the House in his speech from the throne; and after a debate and a conference between the two Houses on May 13, they agreed in a joint address to recommend that it was proper that all guineas weighing less than 5 dwts. 8 grains, and all half-guineas weighing less than 2 dwts. 16 grains, and all quarter guineas weighing less than 1 dwt. 8 grains, should be called in and recoined according to the established standard of the Mint, both as to weight and fineness; that the said guineas should be called in by degrees, and that the public should bear the loss arising from the deficiency and recoinage of the said guineas, provided such deficiency should not exceed the rates settled by the commission of the treasury, and provided they should be offered in payment of the public revenue, or should be brought to such persons as his majesty should authorise to receive and exchange the same within certain times to be appointed for that purpose. An act was then passed to that effect, and a proclamation was issued accordingly. The Bank of England having consented to receive and exchange the said guineas, 250,000*l.* was granted towards defraying the expense of calling in and recoining the said deficient gold coin. The proclamation was issued on June 24, and commanded that all guineas more deficient in weight than the rates specified by the treasury in 1773, should cease to be current. The principle of weighing the coins having thus been established by statute, provision was made for regulating and ascertaining, according to the established standard of the Mint, the weights to be made use of for that purpose.

therefore impossible that both these metals can be a standard measure of the value of other things at the same time.' In the same view Mr. Locke said, 'that two metals as gold and silver cannot be the measure of commerce both together in any country, because the measure of commerce must be perpetually the same, invariably keeping the same proportion of value in all its parts, but so only one metal does and can do to itself. An ounce of silver is always an equal value to an ounce of silver, and an ounce of gold to an ounce of gold; but gold and silver change their value one to another, and one may as well make a measure, namely, a yard, whose parts lengthen and shrink as a measure of trade of materials that have not always a settled invariable value to one another. One metal, therefore, alone can be the money of account and contract and the measure of commerce in any country.' In similar terms the first Earl of Liverpool, in his celebrated treatise on the Coin of the Realm, published in 1805, distinctly advocated and recommended the adoption of gold as the sole standard of value.[2]

Adoption of a gold standard. The Act of 1816.

Under such circumstances, and in accordance with both the course of legislation already so well established, the practice of merchants, and the opinion of the most experienced financiers, the occasion was taken of the introduction of a new silver coinage for the passing of the famous Act of 1816, which declared that thenceforth gold alone should be the standard of value, and that silver should be legal tender to the extent of 40*s.* only; the regulation for keeping silver coin in the country being the issuing of silver coin at the rate of 66*s.* in the pound instead of 62*s.*, the 4*s.* being a seignorage.[3] By a proclamation dated January 29, 1817, all the silver coin in circulation was ordered to be exchanged throughout Britain, and in a fortnight, 5,124,000*l.* of new silver coins were issued for the purpose.[4]

[2] See Mr. Wellesley Pole's speech in the House of Commons, May 30, 1816.

[3] 56 Geo. III. c. 68.

[4] A commission was appointed in France for the purpose of inquiring into the question of the monetary standard on March 7, 1867. The commissioners were MM. de Parieu, vice-president of the Council of State; Michel Chevalier and Wolowski, members of the Institute; Gouin, vice-president of the Chamber of Deputies; Louvet, deputy; de Lavenay, president of section, Council of State; Andouillé, sub-governor of the Bank of France; Pelouze, president of the coinage

The question of a single or a double standard has, since then, been debated more than once, especially on motions by Mr. Attwood and Mr. Cayley in the House of Commons; but Sir Robert Peel fully adhered to the principle of a single standard. 'I cannot see any advantage,' he said, 'derivable from the institution of a double standard. You cannot make a double standard without first defining the ratio which is to exist between the nominal value of the two metals. To say that every man should pay his debts in silver or gold, whichever he may please, without defining the relative value, would be absurd and impracticable. We might, certainly, have a double standard defining the relative value of gold and silver, and leaving it to the option of a party who had money to pay to make his payments either in gold or silver. But this

Sir Robert Peel on a double standard.

commission and member of the Institute; Dutilleul, director of the general movement of the Funds; and M. de Lalaer, auditor of the Council of State, secretary and reporter; and, on May 24, 1867, they made their report. The history of the question was as follows:—The convention included the monetary unity in the general system of weights and measures, gave the name of *franc* to a piece of 5 grains of silver $\frac{9}{10}$ths fine; established the same title for the gold piece, and left to trade to fix the current value. The Directory was also engaged on the subject, and the Consulat settled it by the Loi Germinal, An. XI. This law, which is still the basis of the French monetary system, constituted the unit under the name of *franc* of 5 grains weight of silver, $\frac{9}{10}$ths fine, and prescribed the coining of pieces of gold of 20 and 40 francs of a certain weight and title; that is, to facilitate commerce, it regulated the rate at which the gold piece should be received in business. According to the basis adopted by the law of An. XI. gold was to silver in the relation of 1 to 15½. But this rate, though fixed by law, could not remain unaltered. Up to 1850 gold was always at a premium, and silver only remained in circulation. After the discovery of the mines in California and Australia, a general substitution of gold to silver took place, and silver was at a premium. Under these circumstances, and in consequence of the monetary convention, concluded on December 23, 1865, between Belgium, France, Switzerland, and Italy, an inquiry into the standard became necessary; and the question was, What is preferable, one standard only, or a double standard? The commissioners, after balancing the reasons in favour of both views, resolved by a majority of 5 to 4 (one having been absent from illness) in favour of the double standard. In 1870 the High Council of Commerce again instituted an inquiry into the same question, the points being, 1st, Would the coinage of a French 25-franc gold piece be useful? 2nd, Would the adoption of a single gold standard be preferable to the existing double or alternate standard of gold and silver; and 3rd, In case of affirmation of the single standard, what measures should be taken with regard to the silver 5-franc pieces, the only subsisting representative of the double standard in the monetary system of France. It is understood that the question of the single gold standard was determined affirmatively. But the report was not authoritatively published when the war with Germany broke out, and the whole question remained as it was.—See Mr. Hendriks' report on the subject in the Journal of the Statistical Society, vol. xxxiii. p. 392.

very option seems defeating the object of a standard, and introducing, unnecessarily, uncertainty into contracts. It appears to me a much less simple course than that of adhering to a single standard, and a course unaccompanied by any advantage countervailing the loss of simplicity. Gold and silver seem to have some necessary connection from being so frequently united in common parlance; but there is no more reason that they should be united in a standard, than that gold and lead, or gold and copper, should be so united. To unite two metals, the value of which is not and cannot be a fixed ratio in a double standard, is to diminish the value and advantage of a standard. The more simple the standard the better—the very name implies unity and simplicity. It is the measure of value, and why not have one measure of value as well as one measure of length and capacity?'

Gold coinage.

Though gold has been for a considerable time practically the only standard in England, the issue of the sovereign is of comparatively recent date. In the time of Henry III. gold pieces of the value of about 10s., coined at Constantinople and known as byzants, circulated in England. Later still Florences, originally struck at Florence, were in circulation, whence the name of 'florin.' In the reign of Edward III. the noble was issued, and in the reign of Edward IV. the angel and rose noble or rial were followed by the double rial or sovereign of Henry VII., which was to pass for 20s., and by the laurel of James I., of which the current value was also to be 20s. The latter coin was adopted by Charles II. at the Restoration, and was subsequently called a guinea. Though the original value of the guinea was 20s., in current value it rose in the reign of Queen Anne to 30s., and its value was not fixed at 21s. until, on the advice of Sir Isaac Newton, then master of the Mint, a proclamation was issued in the reign of George I., and a new indenture made, dated May 6, 1718, in which the coin was designated a guinea or 21s. piece, and was ordered to pass for 21s. sterling.[6] The sovereign was first put into circulation by proclamation on the 1st of July, 1817, and was ordered to be of five pennyweights, three grains, $\frac{2740}{10000}$ the troy weight of standard gold, containing 113·001 grains fine, the same weight as the pound sterling had been since 1717; that being the

[6] See First Annual Report of the Deputy Master of the Mint, 1870.

last of a long series of changes in the weight of a pound, from 407·990 in the reign of Edward III. in 1344, to 160 grains in the reign of Edward VI. in 1547, and 118·651 grains in the reign of Charles II. in 1651. Ever since 1717, however, or for the last 154 years, the weight of the sovereign has undergone no alteration, and a contract to pay one pound sterling has always been understood to mean a contract to pay 113·001 grains of fine gold.*

But the legislation respecting the coinage of the realm did not affect the resumption of cash payments by the Bank, or

* The sovereign was ordered to have, for the obverse impression, the head of his majesty, with the inscription 'Georgius III. D. G. Britanniar. Rex. F. D.,' and the date of the year; and for the reverse the image of St. George, armed, sitting on horseback encountering the dragon with a spear, the said device being placed within the ennobled Garter, bearing the motto, 'Honi soit qui mal y pense,' with a newly invented graining on the edge of the piece. The proclamation of July 1, 1817, ordered the sovereign to be of the weight of five pennyweights, three grains, $\frac{2740}{10000}$ the troy weight of standard gold. The weight of the pound sterling has varied from time to time, as will be seen from the following table from M'Culloch's Dictionary:—

Number of Grains of Fine Gold in 20s., or the Pound sterling.

			Grains
1344	18	Edward III.	407·990
1349	23	"	383·705
1356	30	"	358·125
1401	3	Henry IV.	358·125
1421	9	" V.	322·312
1464	4	Edward IV.	257·850
1465	5	"	238·750
1470	49	Henry VI.	238·750
1482	22	Edward IV.	238·750
1509	1	Henry VIII.	238·750
1527	18	"	210·149
1543	34	"	191·868
1545	36	"	176·000
1546	37	"	160·000
1547	1	Edward VI.	160·000
1549	3	"	155·294
1551	5	"	160·000
1552	6	"	160·000
1553	1	Mary	159·166
1560	2	Elizabeth	160·000
1600	43	"	157·612
1604	2	James I.	141·935
1626	2	Charles I.	128·780
1666	18	" II.	118·651
1717	3	George I.	113·001
1816	56	" III.	113·001

the discontinuance of an inconvertible paper currency. As was expected, as soon as the great exigencies of war ended, the amount of treasure in the Bank increased enormously; and consequently, in January, 1817, the directors offered to pay in cash all the one pound and two pound notes bearing date prior to January, 1816, but no demand was made. In September, also, another notice was issued to the same effect, but with no other result. In 1818, however, an unfavourable state of the exchange, caused mainly by large foreign loans contracted, and a voluntary engagement entered into by the Bank to pay the fractional part of dividends, as well as a certain portion of their notes in cash, effected a considerable drain, and the treasure was greatly reduced. It was under these circumstances that, early in February, 1819, committees of both Houses were appointed to consider the state of the Bank of England with reference to the expediency of the resumption of cash payments. And both committees agreed in reporting that the best mode for restoring a metallic standard would be to permit the Bank to pay its notes in gold bullion at the Mint price instead of gold coin. According to the Lords' committee various advantages attended this plan in preference to a simple resumption, in the first instance, of cash payments by the Bank. It established, equally with cash payment, the principle and the salutary control of a metallic standard, while it afforded the best prospect of avoiding or diminishing many of the inconveniences which many persons apprehended from that measure. It exempted the Bank from the obligation of providing a quantity of gold necessary to replace, in case the public should prefer coin to paper, all the smaller notes to the amount probably of 15 or 16 millions. And it continued to the Bank, and therefore to the nation at large, all the advantages to be derived from the employment of a capital equal to the amount of all the small notes in circulation.

The Bank of England and cash payments.

On May 6, Mr. afterwards Sir Robert Peel presented the report of the committee to the House of Commons, and, on the 24th, he made his famous speech on moving resolutions[7] for the resumption of cash payments by the

Sir Robert Peel's speech. The Act of 1819.

[7] The resolutions, which were carried and formed the basis of the new law, provided, that after February 1 and before October 1, 1820, the Bank of England

Bank. To his mind a return to the old standard of value was absolutely necessary, and every sound writer had come to the same conclusion with Sir Isaac Newton, that a certain weight of gold bullion, with an impression on it denoting it to be of a certain weight and fineness, constitutes the only true, intelligible, and adequate standard of value. Sir Robert Peel proved, by historical facts relating to the reformation of the coinage in the reign of Edward I., Queen Elizabeth, and William III., that the restoration of the value of the currency was always a striking political feature in the history of this country, and concluded with urging the adoption of the sound policy he had indicated in the following terms: 'Let us adhere,' he said, 'to that good faith in time of peace, and towards the public creditor which we practised in war, and towards those foreigners whose country was at war with us. Let us recollect that the fluctuations of price which an inconvertible paper currency occasions are injurious to the labourer, who finds no compensation in the rise of his wages at one time for the evils inflicted by a depression of another. Every consideration of sound policy—every obligation of strict justice—should induce us to restore the ancient and permanent standard of value.' The justness and soundness of these remarks carried conviction in the mind of every one; and though petitions from merchants and bankers continued to be presented, recommending caution, or offering a decided opposition, the bill for the resumption of cash payments met with scarcely any opposition, and became the famous Act of 1819.[a]

should be bound, on any person presenting an amount of their notes not less than of the value of sixty ounces, to pay them on demand at the rate of 4*l.* 1*s.* per ounce in standard gold: that between October 1, 1820, and May 1, 1821, the Bank should pay in a similar manner in gold bullion at the rate of 3*l.* 19*s.* 6*d.* per ounce: that between May 1, 1821, and May 1, 1823, the rate of gold bullion should be 3*l.* 17*s.* 10½*d.* per ounce: that during the first period above-mentioned the Bank should be at liberty to pay in gold bullion at any rate less than 4*l.* 1*s.*, and not less than 3*l.* 19*s.* 6*d.* per ounce; in the second period at any rate less than 3*l.* 19*s.* 6*d.* and not less than 3*l.* 17*s.* 10½*d.*, upon giving three days' notice in the Gazette, and specifying the rate; but that after doing so they should not be at liberty to raise it again; that the payments should be made in bars of ingots of the weight of 60 ounces each, and that the Bank should be able to pay any fractional sum less than 40 oz. above that in the legal silver coin, and the trade in gold bullion was declared to be free and unrestrained.

[a] 59 Geo. III. c. 49.

PART III.

1820–1842.

FROM MR. HUSKISSON'S COMMERCIAL REFORMS

TO

SIR ROBERT PEEL'S ADMINISTRATION.

SUMMARY.

1820–1842.

Rendered wise by war, England set herself in earnest to remove the barriers which hindered her progress, and Huskisson introduced the first measures of commercial freedom. Then the condition of our labourers was improved, and their rights were recognised. The finances were set in order, new means of communication were opened, the field of commerce was enlarged, and the iniquitous slave-trade was prohibited and rendered penal. Two commercial crises interrupted the even course of commercial progress, yet during this period all the relations of trade were enlarged, and commerce increased at a much greater ratio than had hitherto been experienced. From 1820 to 1842 Europe enjoyed more than twenty years of comparative peace, during which a wholesome industrial competition was first initiated. Much, however, remained to be done before all the avenues of wealth were fully opened; and the voice of Cobden was now first heard in the advocacy of practical reform in our economic legislation.

CHAPTER I.

THE PETITION OF THE MERCHANTS.

1820.

State of the Nation.—Low Rates of Wages.—Distress in the Ribbon Trade.—Imports and Exports.—State of Commerce in 1820.—Hostile Foreign Tariffs.—Petitions for Free Trade.—Principles of International Trade.—Erroneous Views of Protectionists.—Prohibitory Policy not beneficial.—Need of an Investigation.—Free Trade essential to remove Hostile Measures Abroad.—Petition of the Edinburgh Chamber of Commerce.—Committee on Foreign Trade.—Mr. Wallace on the Foreign Trade.

IF the coffers of the Bank of England were full to repletion, the private resources of the masses of the people were never more exhausted than in the years immediately preceding the conclusion of the war—ay, and for several years afterwards.[1] With bread at famine prices and trade greatly embarrassed, the poor suffered keenly, and considerable irritation and discontent were apparent throughout the country. Nor did the conclusion of peace produce any decided improvement. As soon as the war ended there was quite a frenzy among traders to plunge into all kinds of operations, in the expectation that there would be an eager demand for British goods especially on the Continent. But this expectation was sadly disappointed. Notwithstanding all the orders in council and all the Berlin and Milan decrees, every market was overstocked with British goods. In truth, the people, everywhere impoverished by the war, could ill afford to buy goods for either comfort or luxury. And with results so

State of the nation.

[1] In 1800 the wages of carpenters, masons, bricklayers paid at the Greenwich Hospital was 18s. per day. The average price of wheat, 113s. 10d. per qr. The price of beef paid at St. Thomas's Hospital at Ladyday, 4s. 4d. the stone. In 1810 the wages of the same class of artisans were 32s., the price of wheat 100s. 5d., the price of meat 5s. 8d. In 1820 the wages were 31s., the price of wheat 67s. 10d., the price of meat 4s. 10d. the stone.

disappointing, production largely diminished, employment became more and more scarce, wages fell lower than before, and the working classes found it harder and harder to live. There is one unalterable law as regards wages. They depend on capital. However fertile the soil, however favourable the position of the country, however great the extent of territory, unless there be sufficient capital on hand to maintain labour, nothing can be done. Unfortunately the capital of the country at that time was greatly reduced. The manufacturers had little to spare. The sales of produce and manufactures caused loss instead of gain. And with a large number of labourers seeking employment, wages were excessively low.

The case of common weavers seemed, indeed, peculiarly hard. They were worse off than any other class of labourers, and year by year they continued to fall. In 1802 they earned 13s. 10d. per week; in 1806 the wages had fallen to 10s. 6d.; in 1808 they were only 6s. 7d.; in 1812, 6s. 4d.; in 1816, 5s. 2d.; and in 1817, only 4s. 3½d. per week. Deduct from this one shilling a week for the expense of the loom, and the poor weaver got only 3s. 3½d. a week to keep himself and his family. How could he live on such a pittance as this, with all the articles of food at extremely high price? The price of corn had, it is true, fluctuated very much. From the close of 1813 to the commencement of 1816 a fall was experienced, which encouraged the landed interest to ask for a new corn law: but from 1816 to 1817 prices rose greatly, both in this country and on the Continent; and though the excellent harvest of 1818 produced a temporary reaction, prices in 1819 soon recovered. The condition of the low-waged classes at this time was, indeed, very pitiable; and in despair they went about destroying machines, breaking down power-looms, smashing stocking-frames, and committing all manner of mischief.

Low rates of wages.

Some branches of trade, such as the ribbon trade of Coventry, were moreover suffering from a change of system. For a long time the custom was for the ribbon manufacturer to provide the silk and the undertaker[1] the looms and machinery, the work being done by himself and his

Distress in the ribbon trade.

[1] The undertaker was the person who received the silk from the master, was responsible for the return of the weight of it, and undertook to get it woven into

family, assisted by apprentices and journeymen. Under this arrangement usually two-thirds of the wages went to the journeymen weavers for their labour, and one-third to the undertaker. So long as the demand was small no inconvenience was felt from this system. In 1812, however, a sudden large demand sprung up for ribbons with large pearl edges tapering out, and a golden age all at once dawned on the distressed weavers. Then labour became more abundant than labourers; the undertakers, pressed for work, had to employ half-pay apprentices, and the manufacturers, who had hitherto paid a uniform rate for the weaving of the silk, began to outbid each other in the labour market. Quarrels commenced, and as the weavers thought themselves aggrieved by this competition, and asked for a uniform advance, the manufacturers published their first list of prices. For three years the demand for that kind of ribbon continued unabated. But with the conclusion of peace the demand suddenly ceased, and with its cessation the trade collapsed, carrying with it failures and panic. A sudden change then occurred in the mode of carrying on the work. The large manufacturers transferred the trade to the London silk warehousemen. Many of them began to use machinery. And what with the bad state of trade, the use of machinery, and the return of many soldiers, causing the labour market to be overstocked, wages fell miserably low, and the Coventry weavers became restless and distressed.

Taken as a whole, the general trade of the country exhibited more than its ordinary oscillations. In 1811 and 1812 the imports were very low, but as better days appeared approaching, prices rose, and a considerable animation followed. No sooner, however, was the horizon once more darkened by the return of Napoleon from Elba, than a heavy fall of prices occurred, and the imports greatly diminished. With the restoration of peace a slight stimulus was given to purchases, but again the bad crops of that season checked it, and a retrograde movement ensued. The exports, too, followed a similar course. Commencing with 23,000,000*l.* as the de-

Imports and exports.

ribbon through the medium of journeymen. As a remuneration for his trouble, and to repay him for the winding, warping, shop-room, and looms, he had a third of the earnings.

clared value of British and Irish produce exported in 1811, the amount rose to 42,000,000*l.* in 1815; but as it was found that the demand was not nearly so great as was expected, the exports in 1819 fell to 33,000,000*l.* There was an increase towards 1820, when the general discredit and fear disappeared; yet the average amount of exports in the decennium from 1811 to 1820 was not greater than in the decennium from 1801 to 1810.

Let us endeavour to form some idea of the trade of the United Kingdoms in 1820, or about fifty years ago, just before free trade measures were initiated. What the real value of imports was we do not know, but the official value of foreign and colonial merchandise imported was given at 32,000,000*l.*, which, with a population of about 21,000,000, would be at the rate of about thirty shillings per head. The exports amounted in real or declared value to 36,000,000*l.*, which came to little more than the same proportion per head. The tonnage of ships entered inwards and outwards was about 4,000,000 tons, and there belonged to the United Kingdom and its dependencies 2,648,000 tons of shipping. In almost every respect the trade of the country was about an eighth or a ninth part of what it is at the present time. And, consequently, the condition of the people and the means of comfort within their reach, were likewise restricted. The consumption of sugar was only 18 lbs. per head, and of tea 1 lb. 4 oz. Wages were low. The savings banks had scarcely any amount belonging to the labouring classes. Altogether, the resources of the nation were greatly restricted and paralyzed.

State of trade in 1820.

Unfortunately for any prospect of improvement in the foreign trade, several countries gave themselves in earnest to alter their tariffs, and more or less adopted a policy of protection. In France the tariff of Colbert[1] had laid down the principle of reducing the duties of exportation on all articles of French produce, diminishing the import duties on articles required for manufactures, and excluding by high duties all foreign goods which competed with French merchandise. But there were no prohibitions in that tariff. These were first enacted three years after the death of Colbert. In

Hostile foreign tariff.

[1] Colbert was Controller-General of Finance to Louis XIV. in 1661.

1786 the treaty concluded with this country introduced a more liberal policy than had hitherto been prevalent; yet France had not attained to any unity in her tariff. She was divided, in this respect, into three divisions. The first comprised the provinces which adopted the tariff of 1664; the second, those which refused to submit themselves to it; and the third those provinces which, when they were united to the crown, made it a condition that their relations with foreign countries should be altogether free. The tariff of 1791 was the first applicable to the whole of France, and its leading characteristics were the abolition of all internal duties, the exclusion by prohibition of certain foreign manufactures, the permission to import other manufactures heretofore prohibited at certain rates of duties, the total exemption from duties of articles of food and raw materials, and a progressive rate of duties on certain kinds of merchandise not exceeding in any case 25 per cent. on manufactures. In 1813, and more especially by another tariff in 1816, very high duties were imposed, and all the prohibitions were maintained, but substantially the tariff of 1791 was confirmed. There was abundant protection, therefore, in favour of French manufactures. Yet with all this France was not very able to supply foreign markets with her produce and manufacture. In 1815 the total value of the imports of France for internal consumption did not exceed 8,000,000*l.*, and her exports amounted only to double that amount. In fact the commercial dealings of France were at that time extremely small in relation especially to her large population and the position she occupied in the centre of Europe.

The experience of France, and of all countries which followed her policy, might, indeed, have deterred England from relying with any confidence on the broken reed of protection; but no intelligent opinion was formed on the subject, and the great works of Adam Smith and other economists had remained sterile of results, when, in 1820, the London merchants entrusted Mr. Baring with the famous petition, embodying a distinct enunciation of free-trade principles, and praying that every restrictive regulation of trade, not imposed on account of the revenue, including all duties of a protective character, might at once be repealed. As this is the first practi-

Petitions for free trade.

cal step in the way of commercial reform, initiated by the mercantile classes, it is well deserving of a conspicuous place in any history of our modern commerce. It is related that when Adam Smith expressed his objections to the laws of forestalling, the great Burke said to him, 'You, Dr. Smith, from your professor's chair, may send forth theories upon freedom of commerce, as if you were lecturing upon pure mathematics; but legislators must proceed by slow degrees, impeded as they are in their course by the friction of interest and the friction of prejudice.' The time had however now arrived when the theories on freedom of commerce, proclaimed by the economists, were urged on the government for adoption by men of mature judgment and of a practical cast of mind, men not usually given to speculative philosophy, but intently anxious to promote their own welfare and that of their country. Nor had London alone the honour of being the pioneer of so great a stride in commercial legislation. The Edinburgh Chamber of Commerce was as explicit and conspicuous in the advocacy of a free commercial policy, and we owe it to these petitions, that the question was removed out of the pale of barren scientific teaching, and became at once the subject-matter of practical legislation. There is something so clear and pointed in the terms of these petitions that we cannot do better than give them almost *in extenso*.

The London merchants started from the first cardinal principles of trade, that foreign commerce is eminently conducive to the wealth and prosperity of the country, by enabling it to import the commodities for the production of which the soil, climate, capital, and industry of other countries are best calculated, and to export in payment those articles for which its own situation is better adapted; that freedom from restraint is calculated to give the utmost extension to foreign trade, and the best direction to the capital and industry of the country; that the maxim of buying in the cheapest market and selling in the dearest, which regulates every merchant in his individual dealings, is strictly applicable as the best rule to the trade of the whole nation; and that a policy founded on these principles would render the commerce of the world an interchange of mutual advantage, and diffuse increased wealth and enjoyments among the inhabitants of each state.

Principles of international trade.

The petitioners complained that the very reverse had been and was more or less adopted and acted upon by the government of this and every other country, each trying to exclude the productions of other countries with the specious and well-meant design of encouraging its own productions; thus inflicting on the bulk of its subjects, who are consumers, the necessity of submitting to privations in the quantity or quality of commodities; and thus rendering, what ought to be the source of mutual benefit and of harmony among states, a constantly recurring occasion of jealousy and hostility. And they expressed their opinion that the prevailing prejudices in favour of the protective or restrictive system might be traced to the erroneous supposition that every importation of foreign commodities occasions a diminution or discouragement of our own productions to the same extent; whereas it might be clearly shown, that although the particular description of production which could not stand against unrestrained foreign competition would be discouraged, yet as no importation could be continued for any length of time without a corresponding exportation, direct or indirect, there would be an encouragement for the purpose of that exportation of some other production for which our situation might be better suited; thus affording, at least, an equal and probably a greater and certainly more beneficial employment to our own capital and labour.

Erroneous views of protectionists.

The London merchants further argued, as respects the numerous protective and prohibitory duties of our commercial code, that, while they were all operating as very heavy taxes on the community at large, very few were of any ultimate benefit to the classes in whose favour they were originally instituted, and none to the extent of the loss occasioned by them to other classes; that among the other evils of the restrictive or protective system, not the least was that the artificial protection of one branch of industry, or source of production, against foreign competition was set up as a ground of claim by other branches for similar protection; so that, if the reasoning upon which these restrictive or prohibitory regulations were founded were followed out consistently, it would not stop short of excluding us from all foreign commerce whatsoever. And that the same train of argument which, with corresponding prohibi-

Protective policy not beneficial to the interests protected.

tions and protective duties, should exclude us from foreign trade, might be brought forward to justify the re-enactment of restrictions upon the interchange of productions (unconnected with public revenue) among the kingdoms composing the union, or among the counties of the same kingdom.

The petitioners further maintained that an investigation of the effect of the restrictive system at that time was peculiarly called for, since it might lead to a strong presumption that the distress which so extensively prevailed was greatly aggravated by that system; and that some relief might be obtained by the earliest practicable removal of such of the restraints as might be shown to be most injurious to the capital and industry of the community, and to be attended with no compensating benefit to the public revenue. They urged that a declaration against the anti-commercial principles of our restrictive system was the more important at that juncture, inasmuch as, in several instances of recent occurrence, the merchants and manufacturers of foreign countries had assailed their respective governments with applications for further protective or prohibitory duties and regulations, urging the example and authority of this country against which they were almost exclusively directed as a sanction for the policy of such measures. And that certainly, if the reasoning upon which our restrictions were defended was worth anything, it would apply in behalf of the regulations of foreign states who insisted upon our superiority of capital and machinery as we did upon their comparative exemption from taxation, and with equal foundation.

Need of an investigation on the effects of the restrictive system.

In the opinion of the London merchants nothing would tend more to counteract the commercial hostility of foreign states than the adoption of a more enlightened and more conciliatory policy on the part of this country. That although, as a matter of mere diplomacy, it might sometimes answer to hold the removal of particular prohibitions, or high duties, as depending upon corresponding concessions by other states in our favour, it does not follow that we should maintain our restrictions in cases where the desired concessions on their part cannot be obtained. Our restrictions would not be the less prejudicial to our capital and industry,

Free trade essential to remove hostile measures abroad.

because other governments persisted in preserving impolitic regulations. That, upon the whole, the most liberal would prove to be the most politic course on such occasions. That, independent of the direct benefit to be derived by this country, on every occasion of such concession or relaxation, a great object would be gained by the recognition of a sound principle or standard, to which all subsequent arrangements might be referred; and by the salutary influence which a promulgation of such views, by the legislature and the nation at large, could not fail to have on the policy of other states. The petitioners then added that whilst declaring their conviction of *the impolicy and injustice* of the restrictive system, and in desiring every practicable relaxation of it, they had in view only such parts of it as were not connected, or were only subordinately so, with the public revenue. As long as the necessity for the present amount of revenue subsisted, the petitioners could not expect so important a branch of it as the customs to be given up, nor to be materially diminished, unless some substitute less objectionable be suggested. *But it was against every restrictive regulation of trade, not essential to the revenue, against all duties merely protective, and partly for that of protection,* that the prayer of the petition was submitted to the wisdom of Parliament.

Petition of the Edinburgh Chamber of Commerce.

The Chamber of Commerce of Edinburgh, in their petition, attributed in a great measure the existing depression to the straitened condition of foreign commerce, the heavy duty on imports tending directly to lessen the demand for the produce of this country. They treated as erroneous the doctrine that wealth is promoted by an excess of exports, but alleged that, on the contrary, the profits of trade are realised by an excess of imports. They conceived that the best way to increase foreign commerce is to encourage the industry of foreign nations by admitting at low duties their produce. They complained that the system of restrictive commerce had been followed by the governments of other nations; and they expressed their opinion that whatever might be the perseverance of other nations in this system, the British Government should begin a more liberal and wise commercial policy without regard to reciprocity of benefit between us and any particular nation. These were noble sentiments, reflecting the highest honour on a city which, though not so conspicuous for trade as London or Liverpool, has nevertheless been always distinguished by its learning and sagacity.

The presentation of these petitions to both Houses of Parliament was attended with the happiest effect, and a committee[1] was appointed to inquire into the means of improving and extending the foreign trade of the country. The session being far advanced, the committee had not sufficient time to exhaust the inquiry. But they conferred a great service by exposing the numerous restrictions which fettered the trade of the country, and their report laid bare important facts for further consideration. The restrictions then in force had been imposed for the improvement of British navigation and the support of the British naval powers; for the purpose of drawing from commerce, in common with other resources, a proportion of the public revenue, and also to afford protection to various branches of domestic industry with a view to securing for them the internal supply of the country and a monopoly of the export trade to the several colonies. Upwards of a thousand laws were moreover in force hindering trade in every direction, and upon a review of all these circumstances the committee had no difficulty in arriving at the conclusion, that by far the most valuable boon that could be conferred on trade was freedom from all these interferences, as unlimited at least as was compatible with what was due to the vested interest, which had grown up under the existing system. This the committee recommended, and they concluded their report with a brilliant passage entirely subversive of the principle of protection and of the grounds on which it had hitherto been defended. 'The time when monopolies could be successfully supported, or would be patiently endured, either as respects subjects against subjects, or particular countries against the rest of the world, seems to have

Committee on the foreign trade of the country.

[1] The committee consisted of Mr. Frederick Robinson, Lord Castlereagh, Mr. Tierney, Mr. Chancellor of the Exchequer, Mr. Baring, Mr. Lamb, Mr. Thomas Wilson, Mr. Irving, Mr. Canning, Mr. Finlay, Mr. Wilmot, Mr. Gladstone, Lord Althorp, Mr. Wallace, Lord Milton, Sir John Newport, Sir N. W. Ridley, Mr. Keith Douglas, Mr. Huskisson, Mr. Sturges Bourne, Mr. Astell, and Mr. Alexander Robertson.

passed away. Commerce, to continue undisturbed and secure, must be, as it was intended to be, a source of reciprocal amity between nations, and an interchange of productions to promote the industry, the wealth, and the happiness of mankind. If it be true that different degrees of advantage will be reaped from it according to the natural and political circumstances, the skill and the industry of different countries, it is true also that whatever be the advantages so acquired, though they may excite emulation and enterprise, they can rouse none of those sentiments of animosity or that spirit of angry retaliation naturally excited by them when attributed to prohibitions and restrictions jealously enacted and severely maintained. They feel that a principle of gradual and prospective approximation to a sounder system as the standard of all future commercial regulations may be wisely and beneficially recommended, no less with a view to the interests of this country than to the situation of surrounding nations. Upon them the policy of Great Britain has rarely been without its influence. The principles recognised and acted upon by her may powerfully operate in aiding the general progress towards the establishment of a liberal and enlightened system of national intercourse throughout the world, as they have too long done in supporting one of a contrary character by furnishing the example and justification of various measures of commercial exclusion and restriction. To measures of this nature her pre-eminence and prosperity have been unjustly ascribed. It is not to prohibitions and protections we are indebted for our commercial greatness and maritime power; these, like every public blessing we enjoy, are the effect of the free principles of the happy constitution under which we live, which by protecting individual liberty and the security of property, by holding out the most splendid rewards to successful industry and merit, has in every path of human exertion excited the efforts, encouraged the genius, and called into action all the powers of an aspiring, enlightened, and enterprising people.'

Mr. Wallace, the chairman of the committee, on June 16, 1820, brought up the report of the committee. He spoke of the evil effects of the navigation law, of the restricted nature of the warehousing system, and of the multiplicity of acts trammelling the action of the merchant; and concluded his remarkable address with these words: 'It had been a reproach to us among foreign nations, that our mercantile system was so full of restrictions against them that they were compelled in self-defence to impose similar restrictions against us. I trust, however, that it will be so no more; and if we should still be compelled to continue any of our present restrictions, either from the pressure of taxation, our compacts with foreign nations, or with our own countrymen, or from any other cause whatsoever, it will be understood that we do so from a principle of justice, that it is a sacrifice to our sense of duty, that it is a matter not of option but of necessity, and not caused by any ideas on our part of promoting our own commercial interests by it; and whatever may be the exclusion or restrictions which foreign states may think it expedient to keep up upon trade, they will no longer have the opportunity of justifying themselves by saying, "Such is the example and such the conduct of England."'

Mr. Wallace on the foreign trade.

CHAPTER II.

MR. HUSKISSON'S COMMERCIAL REFORMS.

1823–1825.

Mr. Huskisson's Policy.—The Navigation Laws.—Trade with Asia, Africa, and America.—European Trade.—Plantation Trade.—Mr. Huskisson's Colonial Policy.—Retaliatory Measures.—Reciprocity Treaties.—Depression of the Silk Manufacture.—Reduction of Duties on Woollen, Iron, and other Manufactures.—Raw Materials.—Timber Duties.—Differential Duties.—Mr. Poulett Thomson's Declarations of Free Trade.—Trade with the East Indies.

MUCH required to be done in order to develope the resources of the country after the severe straining to which they had been subjected, and earnestly did the Government and the nation give themselves to the work before them. Fortunately for the inauguration of the new policy, the president of the Board of Trade under Lord Liverpool's administration was Mr. Huskisson, a man well trained for the onerous duties of his position by his earnest studies in political economy, by his former residence in France during the first years of the turmoil of the Revolution, and by his services in other departments of the state; and now the agreeable task is before us of examining the steps he took for gradually liberating trade from the many trammels by which it was clogged.

Mr. Huskisson's policy.

First and foremost demanding consideration stood the navigation laws, which, although political in their scope and origin, interfered more or less with the whole trade of the country. Even after the political motive had ceased to exist, a narrow commercial jealousy for the Dutch still supported the navigation laws. Our merchants and shipowners, at that time one and the same interest, could not bear to see Dutch ships carrying both British and American produce into the very ports of England. They conceived it a grievance that Dutch ships

The navigation laws.

should be freighted at lower rates than English ships, and they did not admit that the consumer had any right to get the produce of the world brought home as cheap as possible. Therefore, as a check to the growing prosperity of the Dutch, and for the encouragement of British shipping, the legislature enacted that no goods or commodities whatever, produced or manufactured in Asia, Africa, or America, including the British colonies, should be imported into this country or into the colonies except in British ships. But Dutch ships regularly visited France, Germany, and other countries in Europe, to find freights for England; and from this trade also they must be excluded by providing that no goods or manufactures of Europe should be imported into Great Britain or her colonies except in British ships, or in ships of the countries to which such produce belonged. The Dutch often did the people of this country the good service of bringing in fish of their own catch, but to take such fish was to encourage Dutch fisheries. Therefore, no fish should henceforth be imported except those caught by our own fishers. Of course the people—the consumers—suffered by these restrictions, and complained; and a war with the Dutch was the immediate consequence; but that was not worthy of a thought if at any cost British shipping and navigation increased. And thus, for more than one hundred and fifty years, the navigation laws remained in the statute book.

Trade with Asia, Africa, and America.

The moment, however, the committee of the House of Commons began to inquire into the causes of the depression of commerce, the working of the navigation laws became most apparent, and some amendment of them, if not their total repeal, was felt to be absolutely necessary. The navigation laws provided that all goods imported from Asia, Africa, and America[1] should be in British ships, and that the produce of those countries should not be imported in

[1] No goods or commodities whatsoever of the growth, production, or manufacture of Africa, Asia, or America, or of any part thereof, or which are described or laid down in the usual map or cards of those places, (shall) be imported into England, Ireland, Wales, the islands of Guernsey and Jersey, or town of Berwick-upon-Tweed, or any other ship or ships, vessel or vessels whatsoever, but in such as do truly and without fraud belong only to the people of England or Ireland, dominion of Wales, or town of Berwick-upon-Tweed, or of the lands, islands, plantations, or territories in Asia, Africa, or America to his majesty

an unmanufactured state from any parts of Europe. But it had long been found perfectly impossible to maintain these provisions. The first part of this restriction was given up in 1796, when the ships of the United States were permitted to bring the produce of their own country direct to Great Britain.[2] In 1808 the same privilege had to be granted to the inhabitants of the Portuguese possessions in South America or elsewhere.[3] And again, in 1822, Mr. Huskisson extended the exception in favour of countries in America or the West Indies being or having been under the dominion of Spain.[4] The second part, to wit, that the produce of Asia, Africa, and America should be imported only from the place of its production, had to be abandoned first in the case of thrown silk, and afterwards in many other cases. Thus drugs, the produce of America, were allowed to be imported from any British possessions. Cochineal and indigo were permitted to come in British ships from any place.[5] The Russia Company were allowed to import in British shipping from any Russian port, any Persian product.[6] The Turkish Company were allowed to import any goods from any place either in British ships or in ships of countries in amity with us.[7] Mr. Wallace did not make any change on this point; only he narrowed the restriction as to the places whence the produce of Asia, Africa, and America could be brought to a prohibition against importing it from Europe.[8]

The European trade.

As respects the European trade, the navigation law provided that Russian and Turkish produce should be imported only in British ships, or in ships of their respective

belonging, as the proprietors and right owners thereof, and whereof the master and three-fourths at least of the mariners are English (12 Car. II. c. 18, s. 3).

No goods or commodities that are of foreign growth, production, or manufacture, and which are to be brought into England, Ireland, Wales, the islands of Guernsey and Jersey, or town of Berwick-upon-Tweed, in English-built shipping, or other shipping belonging to some of the aforesaid places, and navigated by English mariners as aforesaid, shall be shipped or brought from any other place or places, country or countries, but only from those of the said growth, production, or manufacture, or from those ports where the said goods and commodities can only or are, or usually have been, first shipped for transportation, and from none other places or countries (12 Car. II. c. 18, s. 4).

[2] 37 Geo. III. c. 97.

[3] 51 Geo. III. c. 47.

[4] 3 Geo. IV. c. 43, § 3.

[5] 13 Geo. I. c. 15; 7 Geo. II. c. 18.

[6] 14 Geo. II. c. 36.

[7] 20 Geo. III. c. 45.

[8] 3 Geo. IV. c. 43.

countries.[9] To prevent, however, the Dutch from collecting goods in their ports, and thus competing with British ships in the longer part of the voyage, it was enacted afterwards that no sorts of wines other than Rhenish, no sort of spices, grocery, tobacco, potashes, pitch, tar, salt, resin, timber, or olive oil should be imported from the Netherlands or Germany in any ship whatsoever.[10] The law had been relaxed in various instances, had acted most injuriously, and given rise to many disputes. Therefore, in 1822, it became necessary to allow the importation of the enumerated goods either in ships of the country of which the goods were the produce, or in ships of the country from which the goods were imported. And at the same time the prohibitions against the importation of articles from the Netherlands, Germany, Turkey, and Russia were taken off, whilst tallow and tobacco were added to the list of enumerated articles.[11]

A still greater reform, however, was required in the provisions of the navigation laws affecting the plantation trade.

The plantation trade.

What the spirit and object of the colonial system were may well be gathered from the preamble of the Navigation Act, which said: 'Whereas his majesty's plantations beyond the seas are inhabited and peopled by subjects of this his kingdom of England, and having in view the maintaining a greater correspondence and kindness between them, and

[9] No goods or commodities of the growth, production, or manufacture of Muscovy, or of any of the countries, dominions, or territories to the great duke or emperor of Muscovy or Russia belonging; also no sorts of masts, timber, or boards, no foreign salt, pitch, tar, rosin, hemp or flax, raisins, figs, prunes, olive oil, no sorts of corn or grain, sugar or potashes, wines, vinegar or spirits, called aqua vitæ or brandy-wine, shall be imported into England, Ireland, Wales, or town of Berwick-upon-Tweed, in any ship or ships, vessel or vessels whatsoever, but in such as do truly and without fraud belong to the people thereof, or some of them, as the true owners or proprietors thereof, and whereof the master and three-fourths of the mariners at least are English; and no currants nor commodities of the growth, production, or manufacture of any of the countries, islands, dominions, or territories to the Ottoman or Turkish empire belonging, shall be imported into any of the aforementioned places in any ship or vessel but which is of English build and navigated as aforesaid, and in no other, except only such foreign ships and vessels as are of the build of that country or place of which the said goods are the growth, production, or manufactures respectively, or of such port where the said goods can only be, or most usually are, first shipped for transportation, and whereof the master and three-fourths of the mariners at least are of the said country or place (12 Car. II. c. 18, s. 8).

[10] 13 & 14 Car. II. c. 11, § 23.

[11] 3 Geo. IV. c. 43, § 6.

keeping them in a firmer dependence upon it, and rendering them yet more beneficial and advantageous unto it, in the further employment and increase of English shipping and seamen, vent of English woollen and other manufactures and commodities, rendering the navigation to and from the same more safe and cheap, making the kingdom a staple not only of the commodities of these plantations but also of the commodities of other countries and places for the supplying of them, and it being the usage of other nations to keep their plantation trade to themselves; and further, if colonial commodities should be taken from any part but the plantations, that the trade of them would thereby in a great measure be deserted from hence and carried elsewhere, his majesty's customs and other revenues much lessened, the fair trader prejudiced, and this kingdom not continue a staple of plantation commodities, nor that vent for the future of the victual and other native commodities of the kingdom,' &c. There was no mistaking these words. In the eye of the British legislature, the trade and navigation of the colonies were to be subjected to and made to subserve the interest of the mother country, she in return granting to colonial productions an exclusive or marked preference in her home markets, a facility of meeting in foreign markets a vent for the surplus of their produce beyond her own ample supply, and her needful support and protection against enemies foreign and domestic. Such was the policy of England towards her colonies, and accordingly the act of 1660 established three rules applicable to the plantation trade of singular stringency. They provided, first, that the whole trade of the plantations should be carried on in British ships; secondly, that the principal productions of the plantations should be allowed to be exported only to the mother country, or some other plantation; and, thirdly, by an act of a few years later, that no goods of the produce of Europe should be imported into any of the plantations in Asia, Africa, or America, except such as were *bonâ fide* laden and shipped in England and in English shipping.[19] But some modi-

[19] 'No goods or commodities whatsoever shall be imported into, or exported out of, any lands, islands, plantations, or territories to his majesty belonging, or in

fications had already been introduced into these rules. As regards the exclusion of foreign ships from the plantation trade, permission was granted in 1766 to some West India colonies, to import American produce in American ships, and to re-export such articles to Great Britain.[13] Later on, Ireland was placed on the same footing as Great Britain in regard to both the import and export trade of the British plantations in America and Africa.[14] And, in 1822, permission was granted to the colonies to export their own produce, and any articles legally imported thereinto, to any place in Europe, Africa, or America, either in British ships, or in ships of the country to which the goods should be exported.[15] The rule that goods the produce of Europe should be imported into the colonies only from the United Kingdom was, from the first, subject to some exceptions, such as that salt might be taken to the fisheries from any part of Europe; that wines of Madeira and the Azores might be imported thence. Many articles of European produce were, moreover, allowed to be shipped from Gibraltar and Malta to the North American colonies, and fruit, wine, salt, &c., the produce of Europe, were also allowed to be shipped from ports in Europe, to certain ports in British North America. In 1822, however, permission was granted to import a number of articles from foreign ports in Europe or Africa into the British possessions in America, but only in British ships.[16] And, three years later, Mr. Huskisson permitted the importation

in his possession, or which may hereafter belong unto or be in the possession of his majesty, his heirs and successors, in Asia, Africa, or America, in any other ship or ships, vessel or vessels whatsoever, but in such ships or vessels as do truly without fraud belong only to the people of England or Ireland, dominion of Wales, or town of Berwick-upon-Tweed, or are of the build of or belonging to any of the said lands, islands, plantations, or territories as the proprietors and right owners thereof, and whereof the master and three-fourths of the mariners at least are English (12 Car. II. c. 18, s. 1).

No sugar, tobacco, cotton, wool, indigo, ginger, fustic, or other dyeing wood of the growth, production, or manufacture of any English plantations in America, Asia, or Africa, shall be shipped, carried, conveyed, or transported from any of the said English plantations to any land, island, territory, dominion, port, or place whatsoever, other than to such other English plantations as do belong to his majesty, his heirs and successors, or to the kingdom of England or Ireland, or principality of Wales, or town of Berwick-upon-Tweed, there to be laid on shore.

[13] 6 Geo. III. c. 49.

[14] 20 Geo. III. c. 10.

[15] 3 Geo. IV. c. 44. s. 4 and c. 45, s. 2.

[16] 3 Geo. IV. 45.

into the British plantations of all classes of goods from any country, except places within the limits of the East India Company's charter, either in British vessels or in vessels of the producing country.

In bringing forward his great measure, Mr. Huskisson said: 'I am prepared to open the commerce of our colonies to all friendly states upon the same principles (though of course with some difference in the detail of its modifications) upon which they are at liberty to trade with Jersey or with Ireland. With the exception of some articles, which it will be necessary to prohibit, such as firearms and munition of war generally, and sugar, rum, &c., in the sugar colonies, I propose to admit a free intercourse between all our colonies and other countries, either in British ships or in ships of those countries, allowing the latter to import all articles the growth, produce, or manufacture of the country to which the ship belongs, and to export from such colonies all articles whatever of their growth, produce, or manufacture, to the country from which such ship came, or to any other part of the world, the United Kingdom and all its dependencies excepted. All intercourse between the mother country and the colonies will be considered a coasting trade, to be reserved entirely and absolutely to ourselves. By this arrangement the foundation of our navigation laws will be preserved, whilst the colonies will enjoy a free trade with foreign countries, without breaking in upon the great principle of those laws in respect to foreign trade, that the cargo must be the produce of the country to which the ship belongs, leaving the national character of the ship to be determined by the rules which apply in like cases in this country. The importation of foreign goods into the colonies, I propose should be made subject to moderate duties, but such as may be found sufficient for the fair protection of our own productions of a like nature.'

Mr. Huskisson's colonial policy.

Important, however, as these relaxations were, it had already become evident that we should not be allowed to continue the restrictions of the navigation laws against foreign countries without provoking severe retaliation against ourselves. By the treaty of commerce of 1815 with the United States, the principle of reciprocity as regards ship-

Retaliatory measures of foreign powers.

ping dues was recognised between the two countries. And it now appeared that Germany, France, Holland, Russia, and other countries were not content with remaining excluded from British ports, and shut out from all commerce with Britain. On June 20, 1822, the Prussian Government issued an order, making large additions to the port dues on all ships belonging to such nations as did not admit Prussian ships on a principle of reciprocity. The British Government remonstrated against this, but Prussia naturally answered, 'You have set us the example by your port and light charges, and your discriminating duties on Prussian ships, and we have not gone beyond the limits of that example. Hitherto we have confined the measure of our port and tonnage charges to ships only; but it is the intention of my government next year to imitate you still more closely, by imposing discriminating duties on the goods imported in your ships. Our object is a just protection to our own navigation, and so long as the measure of our protection does not exceed that which is afforded in your ports to Prussian ships, we cannot see with what reason you can complain.'

Mr. Huskisson saw the justice of this answer, and he had no other alternative than to open negotiations for a reciprocity treaty with Prussia. But seeing that sooner or later the same course would have to be followed with other countries also, Mr. Huskisson brought in a measure, which passed into law, authorising her majesty, by order in council, to place the shipping of any foreign state in the ports of the United Kingdom, on a footing of equality with our shipping, provided such states would afford reciprocal privileges in their ports to the shipping of the United Kingdom.[1] And it was in defence of this policy that he delivered his famous speech on the general policy of the navigation laws, a marvel of directness and clearness. Referring to the retaliatory measures of other countries, Mr. Huskisson, on June 6, 1823, said, 'In such a state of things it is quite obvious that we must adopt one of two courses. Either we must commence a commercial conflict through the medium of protective duties and prohibitions (a

The reciprocity treaties.

[1] 4 Geo. IV. c. 77, and 5 Geo. IV. c. 1.

measure of impolicy which I believe no man will now propose), or we must admit other powers to a perfect equality and reciprocity of shipping duties. The latter appears to be the course which we are bound to adopt. Its effect, I am persuaded, will lead to a great increase of the commercial advantages of the country; while, at the same time, it will have a tendency to promote and establish a better political feeling and confidence among the maritime powers, and abate the sources of commercial jealousy. It is high time, in the improved state of the civilisation of the world, to establish more liberal principles; and show that commerce is not the end, but the means of diffusing comfort and enjoyment among the nations embarked in its pursuit. Those who have the largest trade must necessarily derive the greatest advantage from the establishment of better international regulations. Let England abandon her old principle, and the United Netherlands, and the other powers who are now prepared to retaliate, will gladly concur in the new arrangement. I am prepared to hear from the other side that the proposed alteration will be prejudicial to the British shipping interest. In such an observation I cannot concur; for I think, on the contrary, that the shipping interest of this country has nothing to apprehend from that of other nations. When the alteration in the navigation laws was first projected, similar unfavourable anticipations were made by part of the shipping interest; but these anticipations have proved in the result entirely unfounded. The shipping of great Britain is perfectly able to compete with that of other countries. It is quite time to get rid of this retaliatory principle, which, if carried to the extreme of which it is susceptible, must injure every species of trade. One sort of shipping would be carrying the trade of one country and then returning without an equivalent advantage, to make way for the countervailing regulations of another power, or else to return in ballast. What would the country think of the establishment of a waggon that should convey goods to Birmingham and afterwards return empty. The consumer would be little satisfied with such a way of regulating the conveyance of his merchandise. The consequence would be that there must necessarily be two sets of waggons to do that work which was now performed by one, and that, too, at a considerable increase of price on the raw material. We are not now able to carry on a system of restriction, labouring as we have for some time been, under many and unavoidable restrictions. Our trade and commerce, it is true, are rapidly improving, but they still require that we should adopt every measure by which either could be fostered and improved. What I propose is, that the duties and drawbacks should be imposed and allowed upon all goods equally, whether imported or exported in British or foreign vessels; giving the king in council a power to declare that such regulations should extend to all countries inclined to act upon a system of reciprocity, but reserving to the same authority the power of continuing the present restrictions with respect to those powers who should decline to do so.' The concessions thus proposed met with feeble opposition in Parliament; and, under the authority of acts passed for the purpose, reciprocity treaties were thereafter concluded with a number of countries.[18]

Depression of the silk manufacture.

But it was not only upon the subject of the navigation laws that the British commercial policy had been hitherto open to objection. Whence was it that the silk manufacture was always in a sickly and decaying state, but from excess of protection and prohibitions? Sixty years had elapsed since, in deference to the noise and loud complaints of the silk weavers of Spitalfields, Coventry, and other places, the legislature had decreed the total expulsion of foreign silks from the British market, yet smuggling was largely practised, and no effort was of any avail in stopping it. In spite of every attempt to prevent it, French silks came into general use. The Spitalfields weavers had, hitherto, their own way as regards wages. On their representation, an act was passed in 1773[19] giving to the

[18] Austria, Dec. 21, 1829; America, U.S., Aug. 6, 1827; Brazil, Aug. 17, 1827; Buenos Ayres, Feb. 2, 1825; Columbia, April 18, 1825; Denmark, June 16, 1821; France, Jan. 26, 1826; Frankfort, May 13, 1832; Hanover, May 25, 1824; Hanse Towns, Aug. 14, 1824; Bremen and Lubeck, June 30; Hamburg, Mecklenburg, June 14, 1825, order in council; Muscat, Imaum of, May 31, 1839; Netherlands, Oct. 27, 1837; Ottoman Empire, Aug. 26, 1838; Oldenburg, Oct. 10, 1831, order in council; April 30, 1844, treaty; Uruguay, Aug. 26, 1842; Peru, June 5, 1837; Prussia, April 2, 1824, or German custom house; Portugal, July 3, 1842; Russia, Jan. 11, 1843; Rio de la Plata, Feb. 2, 1825; Mexico, Dec. 26, 1826; Sardinia, Sept. 6, 1841; Sweden, May 25, 1824; Venezuela, Dec. 9, 1829.

[19] 13 Geo. III. c. 68.

magistrates of London and the justices of Middlesex power to settle the wages of journeymen silk weavers. And in 1792[30] the powers of the magistrates in this matter were extended to the manufactures of silk mixed with other materials. Yet the wages fell lower than before, and general complaints were prevalent of the distressed condition of the workmen employed in the trade. Whilst masters and men were restricted from giving or receiving more or less than was laid down in the list of prices, and the manufacturers were prohibited from employing weavers out of the district, the trade was passing away from them, and under the influence of protection and prohibition every germ of improvement was completely extinguished. For years had representations been sent to the Board of Trade to apply some remedy. In 1817 the throwsters represented that if the silk thrown in this country could be discharged from all duty imposed on the raw silk, they might export their silk for the use of other countries. The East India Company also petitioned, stating that they believed they could export thrown silk like cotton yarn. In 1819 the silk manufacturers petitioned that the demand for manufactured goods had for some time so decreased as to afford serious ground of alarm to the manufacturers, and to threaten the existence of the silk manufacture in this country. The Nottingham manufacturers said that their dependence was on an export trade, and that the trade was stopped for want of an equivalent drawback of the duty on the thrown silk; and the Dublin manufacturers made the complaint that the insufficiency of drawback of the duty on the raw material, was the cause why the British manufacturer could not compete with the French in the foreign market. Yet with all these evidences of the utter failure of the system hitherto pursued, and of the absolute need of greater freedom, Mr. Huskisson met with no encouragement whatever when he introduced the subject in the House of Commons, on the evening of March 8, 1824, a determined opposition being made by all interested in the trade. But he was not deterred from his purpose. He denied, as a general proposition, that those immediately connected with any industry are necessarily the best judges of the peculiar interests

[30] 32 Geo. III. c. 44.

which are connected with their calling. He was alive to the fact that a system of monopoly must be favourable to great capitalists. But he showed the evil effects of monopoly, and urged that the monopoly in the silk manufacture had produced, what monopoly was always sure to produce, indifference with regard to improvement; and that useful zeal which gives life to industry, which fosters ingenuity, and which, in manufactures, occasions unceasing efforts to produce the article in the most economical form, had been comparatively extinguished. In his opinion it was owing to the prohibitive system that in silk only, in the whole range of manufactures, we were left behind our neighbours, and its condition afforded the best proof of that chilling and benumbing effect which is sure to be produced when no genius is called into action, and when we are rendered indifferent to exertions by the indolent security derived from restrictive regulations. Mr. Huskisson's measures consisted in a considerable reduction of duty on foreign thrown silk, and in the removal of the prohibition of foreign silk manufactures, substituting for it a duty of 30 per cent.[11] In obedience, however, to urgent petitions of the manufacturers, a law was passed prohibiting the importation of any silks, except such as were of entirely different lengths from those commonly manufactured by the French. Mr. Huskisson's measure, as a whole, certainly fell short of what was required, and of what was passed not long after, yet it was an earnest and an excellent commencement of great and substantial commercial reforms. None, indeed, could be more strongly convinced than he was that, as a general rule, prohibitions are a premium to mediocrity, that they destroy the strongest incentives to excellence, that they check invention and improvement, condemn the community to suffer both in price and quality, all the evils of monopoly; except in as far as a remedy can be found in the baneful act of the smuggler, with the additional evil, that of exposing the consumer as well as the dealer to rapid and inconvenient fluctuations of prices. And thus we find that, not content with what he had done with the silk manufacture, Mr. Huskisson went on to propose greater and more substantial reforms in other branches of trade.

The woollen manufacture had been nursed and dandled

[11] 5 Geo. IV. c. 2.

by the legislature; a favourite child it was, which, like other favourites, had suffered rather than profited by being spoilt and petted in rearing, whilst the younger industry, that of cotton, coming into the world much later, had thriven better by being much more left to rough it and make its own way in life. The duties on foreign woollens were 50*l.* to 67*l.* 10*s.* per cent. These Mr. Huskisson proposed to reduce to 15*l.* per cent.[31] The cotton manufacture was protected by a duty on certain descriptions of goods of 75*l.* per cent., on others of 67*l.* 10*s.* per cent., and on a third class of 50*l.* per cent. These duties he wished to reduce to 10*l.* per cent. on all foreign articles manufactured wholly of cotton, whether from the East Indies or elsewhere. The duties on linen manufacture ranged from 40*l.* to 180*l.*, and Mr. Huskisson proposed to reduce them to 25*l.* per cent. Upon foreign earthenware there was a duty of 75*l.* per cent., and he proposed to reduce it to 15*l.* per cent.; and upon iron manufacture the duty was 6*l.* 10*s.* per ton, and he reduced it to 1*l.* 10*s.* The iron masters were, of course, strongly opposed to this change, and, like the silk manufacturers, made a strong protest against it; but Mr. Huskisson did not think it fitting that with an article like iron, in univeral use in all our manufactures, in all the arts and conveniences of life, in agriculture, in houses, in ships, we should suffer from scarcity. He wondered indeed that, in order to favour the British iron masters, we should have submitted to have every article on which it is used greatly increased in price as well as deteriorated perhaps in quality.[32]

Reduction of duties on manufactures.

[31] 6 Geo. IV. c. 47.

[32] The liberal character of Mr. Huskisson's tariff will best be seen by the following comparison with Mr. Pitt's tariff of 1787, and the rates of duties in force in 1819:

Manufactures	Mr. Pitt's tariff, 1787			Rates of duties, 1819			Mr. Huskisson's tariff, 1825		
	£	s.	d.	£	s.	d.	£	s.	d.
Cotton manufactures, per cent.	44	0	0	50	0	0	10	0	0
Woollen " "	prohibited			50	0	0	15	0	0
Linen " "	41	0	0	60	0	0	25	0	0
Silk " "	prohibited			prohibited			25 to 30 per cent.		
Leather " "	prohibited			75	0	0	30	0	0
Earthenware " "	45	0	0	75	0	0	15	0	0
Iron, manufactured bar, per ton	2	16	2	6	10	0	1	10	0
Olive oil, per tun	8	8	10¾	18	15	7	4	4	0
Sugar	2	5	6	4	6	8	3	3	0

Reduction of duties on raw materials for manufacture.

But if Mr. Huskisson seemed cruel towards the manufacturers, in robbing them of the protection which they so much loved and trusted in, he did something for their benefit. The manufacturer can do nothing without the raw material, and the cost of it is an important element in the value of his merchandise. Now, it is quite clear that whatever may be the difference between one country and another with respect to soil, climate, capital, wages, and machinery, the circumstance which leads to the exportation of manufactures and makes it profitable is the advantage in the smallness of the cost of producing them. And therefore every tax on materials which increases their price adds also to the cost of production, and thus lessens the means of carrying on competition with foreigners. Mr. Huskisson saw this, and he endeavoured to improve the condition of our manufacturers by reducing the taxes on raw materials. He commenced with metals. On copper there was a duty of 54*l*. per ton. The high duty prevented copper, not only in an unmanufactured, but even in an imperfectly smelted, state, from coming into this country. This metal existed in many parts of Europe and South America, and it would have been sent here in payment of British manufactures, and here it would have undergone the process of purifying, of rolling, and of being otherwise prepared for consumption, by our superior machinery. But the duty prevented this, and Mr. Huskisson proposed to reduce it by half, viz. to 27*l*. per ton. The same he proposed for zinc, the duty on which he reduced from 28*l*. to 14*l*.; and for tin, reducing the duty from 5*l*. 9*s*. 3*d*. to 2*l*. 10*s*. per cwt. As for lead, he was content to reduce the duty from 20*l*. per cwt. to 15*l*. per cwt. On other articles necessary for manufactures reductions were also made. On olive oil the duty was 15*l*. 15*s*. per tun. Mr. Huskisson reduced it to 7*l*. a tun. The duty on wool was 1*d*. per lb., he reduced it to ½*d*. And similarly with many other things. On other enumerated and non-enumerated articles he made a general reduction of from 50*l*. per cent. to 20*l*. per cent. on all manufactured articles, and from 20*l*. to 10*l*. per cent. on all unmanufactured articles. As an illustration of the operation of the tariff on non-enumerated articles, Mr. Huskisson stated that a gentleman having imported a mummy from Egypt, the officers of the customs were not a little puzzled at what rate it should be taxed. These remains of mortality, muscles and sinews, pickled and preserved ten thousand years ago, could not be deemed a raw material, and therefore, upon deliberation, it was determined to tax them as a manufactured article. The importer, anxious that his mummy should not be seized, stated its value at 400*l.* per cwt., and thus he had to pay 200*l.* duty upon it. Such was the comprehensive and beneficial scheme of reform proposed by Mr. Huskisson; and though, in consequence of earnest prayers and remonstrances from interested parties, he was compelled to alter his plans in some measure, the reforms proved of substantial benefit to the community at large.

By the time Mr. Huskisson introduced these decided changes in the fiscal system, the committees of the Houses of Lords and Commons appointed to consider the means of improving and maintaining the foreign trade of the country had presented several important reports. Their first report dealt, as we have seen, with the navigation laws, and its recommendations were speedily put in practice. But the other reports dealt with questions not yet ripe for legislation. For instance, the timber duties required reform. They had been imposed during the war, for the avowed object of favouring the growth of timber in the North American colonies in case we should be deprived of foreign timber; but the American colonists were never led to believe that such duties would be permanent. The primary object being no longer needed, the questions at issue in the reform of the timber duties were the comparative qualities of wood imported from the different ports of the North of Europe and from the North American colonies; the comparative facility and cheapness of the supply of these different species of wood; the direction which the system of duties in force since 1809 and 1813 had given to the commerce and tonnage of the country; and the probable effect of any diminution or alteration of these duties on the consumption of the country, on the trade with Europe and the colonies, and on the several interests concerned. The general impression was that the quality of wood used in this country was very inferior, and that such inferior quality was

The timber duties.

forced into consumption by the high duty on foreign wool; that the difference in the duties was too high; that such difference had a tendency to increase the price of Baltic timber; and that in effect the differential duty was a bounty paid by the consumer of the United Kingdom to the North American colonies. At the same time, fear was entertained of the danger incident to the want of competition, from the exclusion of colonial timber; and it was still urged that it was not safe to rely altogether on a foreign source, which might fail in a moment of necessity. At most, therefore, the committee recommended only a diminution of the differential duty; but the question was then not ripe for legislation, and seemed to demand further patient consideration.

Mr. Poulett Thomson's declaration of free trade.

For many years after the first inroad was made on the policy of protection, the cry of distress continued to be raised with unabated force by the manufacturers. Whatever vicissitude of trade, whatever disturbing element influenced the ebb and flow of commercial prosperity, all was put down as the evil result of Mr. Huskisson's policy. The silk manufacturers were particularly restive under their altered condition. Distress continued to exist among the weavers, and they threw blame on the recent legislation. Mr. Huskisson, however, instead of being deterred by such remonstrances, in a year or two made further reduction in the duty of thrown silk, and reduced the duty on manufactured silk from 30 per cent. to 25. Advocates were not wanting for still treating the silk industry as an exotic, requiring to be tended with exceptional care. But Mr. Poulett Thomson well answered such appeals by saying, 'I am no rash theorist; I am not desirous of carrying a favourite principle into operation at the expense of existing interests. But I assert that your only course is a gradual, progressive, but a steady approach to a free system. I maintain, without fear of contradiction, that the very essence of manufacturing and commercial industry is freedom from legislative interference and legislative protection. Attempt to resist its course by protective enactments, you arrest its progress, you destroy its vigour. Unbind the shackles in which your unwise tenderness has confined it; permit it to take unrestrained its own course; expose it to the wholesome breezes of competition, you give it new life, you restore its former vigour. Industry has been well-likened to the hardy Alpine plant; self-sown on the mountain side, exposed to the inclemency of the season, it gathers strength in its stuggle for existence, it shoots forth in vigour and in beauty. Transplant it to the rich soil of the parterre, tended by the fostering hand of the gardener, nursed in the artificial atmosphere of the forcing glass, it grows sickly and enervated, its shoots are vigourless, its flowers inodorous. In one single word lies the soul of industry—competition. The answer of the statesman and the economist to his sovereign, inquiring what he should do to assist the industry of his kingdom was, "Let it take its own course." Such is my prayer. Relieve us from the chains in which your indiscreet tenderness has shackled us. Remove your oppressive protection; give us the fair field we ask, and we demand no more. The talent, the genius, the enterprise, the capital, and the industry of this great people will do the rest. And England will not only retain, but she will take a yet more forward place in the race for competition, for wealth, and improvement, which, by the nature of things, she is destined to run amongst the nations of the world. Place us in that condition is our prayer, not by any violent change, but by slow and easy transition. Here we shall find security for our enterprise and reward for our labour.' Many times the shipping interest also pleaded hard for the restoration of the navigation laws to their pristine stringency; but Mr. Huskisson was not the man to vacillate in his duty, or to give way to complaints. He defended his policy with his accustomed precision and fulness. Every attempt to make the government hesitate whether to go onward or backward signally failed by his adroit answers. Motions for committees of inquiry were rejected again and again. Bills for removing restrictions met a favourable reception, and laws were passed, not to restrict but to extend still further the policy of commercial freedom, love for which had already taken root in the very heart of the people.

But whilst the commerce of the country was thus being developed, an important branch of foreign trade was altogether out of the hands of the mercantile community, and remained still the monopoly of a public company. Trade with the East Indies.

The charter of the East India Company had been renewed in 1813 for twenty years, when the trade with India was thrown open to individual enterprise, but the trade with China and many other branches of the Eastern trade still remained in the monopoly of the East India Company. The British shipowners petitioned for relief, and begged that they might be allowed to compete with foreigners. The London merchants expressed themselves mortified at finding that such a wide commercial field was wholly occupied by foreigners, it being in fact open to foreign and shut to British ships. The Edinburgh Chamber of Commerce petitioned in favour of opening the trade at once; and complaints were made of absolute grievances operating in many ways. As it was, the trade with the territorial possessions of the company could only be carried on by licence from the company. The trade with the other parts of Southern Asia and the islands of the Indian Ocean could only be carried on by licence from the board of control. The trade with China was prohibited to British vessels, unless in the actual employment of the East India Company. The whole trade was confined to ships of a certain amount of tonnage, or of ships of 350 tons and upwards. The trade by licence could only be carried on with the presidencies of Bombay, Madras, Calcutta, and the port of Penang. For the trade with Ceylon, Java, and the East India archipelago, a licence was wanted. And British ships could not sail from Brazil, or other places in South America, to India without first proceeding to Great Britain. These were evils too glaring to remain long untouched; yet neither the Government, nor the country, could practically do much to remedy them so long as the charter continued in force. The Government sent a communication on the subject to the East India Company, asking for certain relaxations. They asked that permission might be given for a direct trade from our settlements in India to foreign Europe; that the company should consent to the article of tea forming part of the return cargoes from India; that the company should form a depôt for the purchase of tea either at Prince of Wales' Island, or some place in the Eastern archipelago; that a reservation of China tonnage should be made for the public upon the principle adopted in

1793 with respect to the India tonnage; and that, in order to render these privileges available to the utmost extent, supercargoes should be allowed to proceed to China in the ship in which their adventure was embarked, for the purpose of superintending the sale. But the East India Company turned a deaf ear to all such representations, and no practical change could be made without their consent and concurrence.

CHAPTER III.

THE COMMERCIAL CRISIS.

1825–1826.

Favourable Prospects of Trade.—Foreign Mining and Loans.—Reaction.—Bankruptcies.—Help by the Bank of England.—Remedial Measures.—Formation of Banking Companies.—State of Foreign Trade.—Diminution of Taxes.—Savings Banks.

A HAPPY combination of events favourable to commerce and industry accompanied the introduction of Mr. Huskisson's measures. A succession of two or three good harvests in the years 1820–22, and great expectations of arrivals of gold from South America, elated the mercantile classes, and equally gratifying was the resolution of Government to allow the continuance of the circulation of notes under *5l.*, though the Bank of England was quite prepared to adhere strictly to the act of 1819, having an ample amount of bullion on hand to meet all outstanding engagements. The rate of interest was, moreover, low, and new avenues of trade were continually being opened. A slight check had been experienced in 1823, owing to somewhat scantier crops, and certain political quarrels between France and Spain, which it was feared might lead to an European war. But happily neither of these causes proved serious; and though, owing to them, prices remained depressed, as soon as they were removed trade was found to be on the whole, regular, sound, and satisfactory. We need not wonder, therefore, if, animated by such encouraging circumstances, several large companies were formed in 1824. Then it was that the St. Catherine Dock Company, the West India and the General Steam Navigation Companies were started. In the same year, the Thames Tunnel Company was constituted, and several important lines of railway for passenger traffic, such as the Liverpool and Manchester, the Birmingham and Liverpool, and the London and Birming-

Favourable prospects of trade.

ham were first proposed with great eclat.[1] It was, indeed, a memorable year, that could produce so many proposals pregnant with future success. But so prosperous was every branch of trade in 1824, that the supply of all articles fell short in proportion to the demand, and prices rose considerably. Thus, to a large extent, at least, from *bonâ fide* causes, and not from speculative mania, Bowed Georgia cotton rose from 7½*d.* to 1*s.* 6½*d.* per lb.; East India cotton, from 5*d.* to 1*s.* 1*d.*; China raw silk, from 16*s.* 6*d.* to 29*s.* 10*d.* per lb.; sugar of British plantations, from 29*s.* 11¾*d.* to 41*s.* 5*d.* per cwt.; coffee, St. Domingo, from 58*s.* to 79*s.* per cwt.[2]

During the year 1825, another source of excitement occurred in the exaggerated expectations entertained in consequence of the recognition of the South American states and the extraordinary accounts of the riches of their mines. Foreign mining and loans. If we might believe the statements put forth by parties interested in that quarter the great Potosi of days gone by had once more been discovered; and, as there are always many ready to take advantage of the least indications of success, and prepared to build for themselves castles in the air, several companies were formed to invest English capital, machinery, and skill in undertakings of all descriptions. Nor was it

[1] Mr. Francis, in his 'History of the Bank of England,' stated that the companies in existence and projected required a capital of 372,173,000*l.*, for which the amount of 17,605,000*l.* had actually been advanced.

[2] TABLE SHOWING THE FLUCTUATIONS OF PRICES FROM JULY 1824 TO JUNE 1826.

	July to November, 1824	Dec. 1824 to June, 1825	Jan. to June, 1826
Cotton: Bowed Georgia, per lb.	7½*d.* to 9*d.*	16*d.* to 18½*d.*	6½*d.* to 7½*d.*
East India	5*d.* „ 6½*d.*	10*d.* „ 13*d.*	4*d.* „ 5*d.*
Cochineal	16*s.* „ 19*s.*	31*s.* „ 24*s.*	13*s.* 6*d.* „ 15*s.* 6*d.*
Indigo: East India super.	10*s.* 4*d.* „ 12*s.* 10*d.*	12*s.* „ 16*s.*	7*s.* „ 11*s.*
Spices: Cinnamon	6*s.* 8*d.* „ 7*s.*	11*s.* 6*d.* „ 12*s.*	6*s.* „ 6*s.* 9*d.*
Mace	4*s.* 8*d.* „ 5*s.* 10*d.*	12*s.* „ 18*s.*	5*s.* 6*d.* „ 6*s.* 6*d.*
Nutmegs	2*s.* 8*d.* „ 3*s.* 8*d.*	6*s.* „ 12*s.*	3*s.* 8*d.* „ 5*s.*
Pepper	5½*d.* „ 6*d.*	8*d.* „ 8½*d.*	4½*d.* „ 5½*d.*
Tobacco: Virginia	3*d.* „ 7*d.*	8*d.* „ 9*d.*	3*d.* „ 8½*d.*
Silk: China raw	16*s.* 6*d.* „ 23*s.*	18*s.* „ 29*s.* 10*d.*	13*s.* 3*d.* „ 16*s.*
Sugar: B. Peruvian	29*s.* 11½*d.*	41*s.* 5*d.*	29*s.* 7½*d.*
White Havannah	35*s.* to 40*s.*	47*s.* to 55*s.*	30*s.* to 42*s.*
Coffee: St. Domingo	58*s.* „ 60*s.*	76*s.* „ 78*s.*	47*s.* „ 48*s.*
Saltpetre	13*s.* „ 20*s.*	24*s.* „ 36*s.*	22*s.* „ 24*s.*
Tallow	31*s.* „ 32*s.*	42*s.* „ 43*s.*	31*s.* „ 32*s.*
Iron: British, in pigs	6*l.* „ 7*l.*	11*l.* „ 12*l.*	8*l.* „ 9*l.*
Lead	23*l.*	30*l.*	22*l.*
Spelter	20*l.* 10*s.*	41*l.* 15*s.*	26*l.*

From Tooke's History of Prices, vol. ii. p. 157.

long before the excitement became a real mania. The shares in such companies as the Real del Monte, the United Mexican, and the Anglo-Mexican rose to an extraordinary value.[1] As the 'Annual Register' said, 'All the gambling propensities of human nature were constantly solicited into action, and crowds of individuals of every description, the credulous and the suspicious, the crafty and the bold, the raw and the experienced, the intelligent and the ignorant, princes, nobles, politicians, patriots, lawyers, physicians, divines, philosophers, poets, intermingled with women of all ranks and degrees, spinsters, wives, and widows, hastened to venture some portion of their property in schemes of which scarcely anything was known except the name.' Not content with foreign mining, foreign loans became also most attractive investments. No sooner was it understood that the state of Peru had consented to borrow, than the utmost anxiety prevailed to lend. The contractors, with scrip in hand, had difficulty in checking the eagerness of a crowd of applicants. Portuguese and Mexican, Greek and Brazilian, Peruvian and Buenos Ayres loans were in equal favour, purchasers little knowing, and caring less about, the financial or economic condition of the states to whom such money was lent. The loans contracted between 1821 and 1825 amounted in all to 48,000,000*l*.

State of the foreign exchanges.

Unfortunately there did not exist such an amount of available capital in the country as to justify investments so varied and heavy. The rise in prices of produce naturally encouraged imports, which had to be paid for; and as large sums had moreover to be remitted out for foreign loans and foreign mining, the balance of trade and payments became against us, and an adverse move in the exchanges was the immediate consequence. The exchange with Hamburg, which on November 22, 1825, was at 36.10, on December 20 had

[1] Mr. Francis, in his 'History of the Bank of England,' gave the following fluctuations in the prices of shares :—

		Dec. 10.	Jan. 11.
Anglo-Mexican	£10 paid	£33 prem.	£158 prem.
Brazilian	10 „	10 dis.	70 prem.
Columbian	10 „	19 prem.	82 prem.
Real de Monte	70 „	530 prem.	1350 prem.
United Mexican . . .	10 „	35 prem.	155 prem.

risen to 38.1; with Lisbon, from 51½ the rate had fallen to 50; and with Paris, at three days' sight, from 25.20 the rate rose to 25.50. With a large importation of produce a great fall in prices became inevitable. Cotton fell from 16*d.* and 18½*d.* per lb. to 6½*d.* and 7½*d.*; sugar from 41*s.* to 28*s.*; coffee from 76*s.* to 47*s.*; and as the Bank found its bullion diminishing, a diminution of discounts became a necessity.

A run on the banks.

Then companies, hitherto considered most flourishing, suddenly began winding up. Failures commenced. Money was not to be had; and though the usury laws were in force, any price would have been paid for prompt accommodation. But matters daily became worse. House after house succumbed, and the panic became intense, general, and most contagious. Suspicion rested upon everyone, and bankers too, suffering immensely from want of confidence, were compelled to resort to every scheme to allay the unwonted fear. A Cambridge bank advertised that they would afford every facility to the holders of their notes to have them exchanged for gold or Bank of England paper. An Oxford bank made a show of such a profusion of gold that everyone was satisfied, and no person thought of demanding it. At Norwich the Gurneys stopped the run by a show upon their counter of a pile of Bank notes many feet thick. But the failure of a banking house at Plymouth, and of a leading banking house in the city naturally led to a run, and as many as sixty-three country banks succumbed in the crisis. These banks sought in vain the assistance of the Bank to change their notes of 1*l.* and 2*l.* for gold. The Bank itself had no gold to spare. The merchants, too, turned their eyes imploringly to the Bank for help, and it was with great difficulty that they succeeded in getting advances to an extent of 400,000*l.* on the security of goods.

But the difficulty had become so serious for the Bank, that it

Extravagant as were the expectations entertained of the Real del Monte mine, it does not appear that they were altogether mistaken. In the report of M. Middleton to the Foreign Office, in 1860, it is stated that the original company spent nearly 1,000,000*l.* upon the mine without being able to declare any dividend; that the mines were subsequently sold to some Mexican speculators for about 27,000*l.*, that they spent on the mines other 30,000*l.* before they declared any dividend, but that now the total value of produce for the last ten years exceeded 6,000,000*l.*, and the annual profits were 1[illegible]0,000*l.*

found itself in the necessity of discovering some extraordinary means of deliverance. We have already seen that the Government had allowed the circulation of notes under 5*l.* till 1832, but that the Bank of England had ceased issuing them. Now, however, the happy thought occurred to one of the directors that a box of 1*l.* notes, which had never been issued, might opportunely be put in circulation. Permission was obtained from the Government to issue them, and this afforded some relief. Besides this, the friendly aid of the Bank of France was solicited and obtained. A credit was opened in Paris for 2,000,000*l.*, in bills drawn from London at three months' date. And thus, by degrees, a turn was given to the panic, which was gradually allayed as the increase in the rate of interest and the fall in prices caused the exchanges again to rise in favour of this country.

State of the Bank of England.

The Bank of England has been much censured for having stimulated the crisis by increasing the issue of notes at the very time when its bullion diminished. Doubtless, as compared with 1823, the amount of Bank of England notes in circulation in 1825 was larger, and, as will be seen from the appended note,[4] the disproportion between the circulation and the bullion on hand became greater and greater, especially when the circulation of country bankers is added to it. But we should remember that the increase of notes was to a

The crisis and the Bank of England.

[4] The following table is given by Lord Overstone in his evidence to the Committee on Banks of Issue, 1840, p. 217:—

	Bullion	Circulation	Lord Liverpool's estimate of country issues	Aggregate circulation
	£	£	£	£
Nov. 29, 1823 . .	13,761,000	19,400,000	4,000,000	23,400,000
Feb. 28, 1824 . .	13,782,000	19,730,000	6,000,000	25,736,000
May 29, „ . .	13,007,000	19,149,000	6,000,000	25,149,000
Aug. 28, „ . .	11,990,000	20,293,000	6,000,000	26,293,000
Nov. 27, „ . .	11,148,000	20,850,000	6,000,000	26,850,000
Feb. 26, 1825 . .	8,857,000	21,060,000	8,000,000	29,060,000
May 28, „ . .	6,456,000	19,683,000	8,000,000	27,683,000
Aug. 27 „ . .	3,012,000	17,464,000	—	—
Feb. 25 „ . .	2,309,000	21,955,000	—	—

The amount of country bank notes stamped from 1820 to 1825, estimated by the total amount which the stamps might circulate was as follows:—1820, 3,503,000*l.*; 1821, 4,138,000*l.*; 1822, 4,296,000*l.*; 1823, 4,129,000*l.*; 1824, 6,724,000*l.*; and 1825, 8,755,000*l.*

considerable extent owing to the increased trade. Bankers do not create trade; they only facilitate it by the help they are able to afford to their customers. At a time when the means of economising the circulation, such as the clearing house, the system of cheques, and extensive banking accounts, were by no means so great as they now are, any increase of transactions must of necessity have created the want of a larger circulation. It should be noted also that the principal increase in the issue took place towards the end of 1825, when the Bank of England was called to cover the deficiency caused by the sudden contraction of the country bank circulation, and not in 1824, when the mania for companies began. Soon after the crisis was over Parliament met, and the speech from the throne alluded to the circumstance in the following terms: 'The embarrassment did not arise from any political events either at home or abroad; it was not produced by any unexpected demand upon the public resources, nor by the apprehension of any interruption of the general tranquillity. Some of the causes to which the evil must be attributed lie without the reach of direct parliamentary interposition; nor can security against the recurrence of them be found unless in the experience of the sufferings which they have occasioned. But to a certain portion of this evil correctives at least, if not actual remedies, may be applied; and his majesty relies upon your wisdom to devise such measures as may tend to protect both private and public interests against the like sudden and violent fluctuations, by placing on a more firm foundation the currency and circulating credit of the country.' The Government was persuaded that the crisis had been greatly aided by the paper currency; that though speculation in trade had been the origin of the evil, and the spirit of gambling carried into every branch of trading had been the beginning, yet it could not have been so extensive if it had not been aided by the state of the currency. In the opinion of the Marquis of Lansdowne, 'the first effect of an issue of country bank paper is to create an artificial abundance of capital: the accumulation of capital causes a reduction of the rate of interest; by the reduction of the rate of interest facilities are afforded for speculation; speculation produces an effect upon prices; the alteration of prices checks the progress of mercantile exports, and that causes the precious metals to be sent out of the country; and then ensues that lamentable distress which arises from an accumulation of stock purchased at high prices being obliged to be sold at greatly reduced prices under the influence of alarm.'

The remedial measures proposed by the Government on this occasion were these: First, that the circulation of notes under five pounds, whether by the Bank of England or by country bankers, should be withdrawn. Secondly, that power should be given to the Bank of England to establish branches throughout the country, in order to supply the vacuum caused by the suspension of so many country banks; and, thirdly, that banks with any number of partners should be allowed to be formed throughout the country within sixty-five miles of London, provided such banks should not make their notes payable in London, nor draw bills on London for a less amount than 50*l*. It was certainly an anomalous fact that, for upwards of a century, the Bank of England had been the sole joint-stock bank, not only in London but throughout England, no banking institution being allowed to be formed with more than six partners, lest it should interfere with the monopoly of the Bank of England. Therefore the Government propositions met with no opposition, and were carried into effect by the passing of two acts, one for the better copartnership of certain bankers in England,[5] and another to limit, and, after a certain period, to prohibit, the issuing of promissory notes under a limited sum in England.[6] The crisis of 1825–6 stands out prominently in the history of British commerce, but, like all other crises, it was momentary and transient. It was a dark day—a stormy season; but the gloom was easily dispelled, and commerce resumed its ordinary course, the merchants issuing forth out of it hearty, hopeful, and sanguine of future success. In a very short time credit revived, the circulation was enlarged, the Bank of England was again able to reduce its rate of discount, and, under the influence of a good harvest, the prices of grain declined sensibly, and the imports and exports increased.

Remedial measures.

[5] 7 Geo. IV. c. 46.

[6] 7 Geo. IV. c. 6. The issue of notes under 5*l*. was restrained by the Act 17 Geo. III. c. 30, and the restriction was afterwards made perpetual. In 1797, however, the restriction was suspended, and by the last act it was finally reimposed.

The foreign trade of the United Kingdom during the period from 1821 to 1830 does not exhibit any material improvement. The official value of imports shows, it is true, a large increase from 30,000,000*l.* to 46,000,000*l.*, and the official value of British manufactures exported also an increase from 40,000,000*l.* to 61,000,000*l.*, but the declared value of exports remained pretty steady at about 37,000,000*l.* No development manifested itself in any branch of native industry, and the activity of trade, confined to imports, was mainly owing to a speculative demand, which sprung up from exceptional rumours respecting certain places of production. With France, trade continued unimportant, but a convention of commerce and navigation was concluded between the two countries in 1826 by Messrs. Canning and Huskisson and the Prince de Polignac, which abolished all discriminating duties of tonnage, harbour, lighthouse, pilotage, and other shipping dues. With Prussia, also, a convention of commerce was concluded in 1824, and at about that time the Prussian customs union first rose into importance. With Holland, too, a general treaty respecting territory and commerce in the East Indies was signed at London on March 17, 1824. And with the United States trade was increasing, notwithstanding the discouraging influences of a protective tariff and great disturbances of credit. Not content with the protective tariff of 1816, the United States Congress, listening to the complaints of manufacturers, imposed taxes which increased from twenty to thirty per cent. the value of all the cotton, woollen, and linen manufactures, iron and other metals, worn or used by the citizens of the United States. The duties levied under this tariff were on cotton 42½ per cent., on woollen goods 54 per cent., on bar iron 95 per cent., and on other articles of manufacture in proportion. There was, moreover, an enormous number of bankruptcies in the States. The paper currency was much depreciated, and a policy was pursued with regard to both commerce and banking which was not well calculated to encourage commercial enterprise. Several South American States were then rising to independence and importance. Venezuela constituted herself a republic in 1821, Central America became an independent republic in 1821, and Hayti was

State of foreign trade.

recognised as an independent state in 1825, just as Brazil and Mexico had been so recognised in 1810. X

Much of the improvement in the position of trade at this time in the United Kingdom was due to the diminution of the burdens of taxation, and the gradual liberation of many industries from the trammels of the excise. In 1822 the malt duties were considerably reduced, as well as the duties on hides and skins. In 1823 the salt duty was reduced from 15*s.* to 2*s.* per bushel; and in 1825 the 2*s.* duty was also abolished. In 1825 the duty on manufactured glass was repealed, and a small duty of 3*d.* per lb. imposed on the fluxed materials. In 1826 a considerable reduction was made in the duty on British spirits, and the duty on printed silks was repealed. And in 1830 all duties on hides and skins, and the duties on licenses to tanners and curriers were repealed. The stamp duties were also reduced; and the obnoxious duties on houses and windows, on carriages and horses, were repealed. Financial operations of considerable magnitude were made in connection with the national debt. In 1822, 150,000,000*l.* of 5 per cent. stock was reduced to 4 per cent. In 1824, 76,000,000*l.* of old 4 per cents. was reduced to 3½ per cent.; and in 1830, 153,000,000*l.* of 4 per cent. was converted into a 3½ per cent. stock. In every direction efforts were made to lighten the burdens of industry, and to open new outlets for trade and navigation. And then, too, savings banks, the first of which had been introduced as far back as 1804 at Tottenham, were first recognised by law. In 1817, a fund, called the fund for the banks for savings, was opened with the national debt commissioners, into which all savings banks' deposits were to be placed.[7] In 1826 and 1828, the legislature found it necessary to check the abuse of such banks, and in order to give greater security to depositors it prescribed that the rules of such banks should be submitted to a barrister appointed by the national debt commissioners, and rendered it obligatory that the money deposited in savings banks should be invested in the Bank of England in the name of the national debt commissioners.[8]

Diminution of taxes.

[7] 57 Geo III. c. 120. [8] 3 & 4 Wm. IV. c. 14.

CHAPTER IV.

RELATIONS OF MASTERS AND SERVANTS.

1824–1830.

Relations of Masters and Servants.—Laws against Workmen.—The Combination Laws.—Report of Committee on the same.—Repeal of Combination Laws.—Factory Labour.—Factory Laws.—The Truck System.—Emancipation of Slaves.

It is of the utmost importance to the community at large that the relations between masters and men, or between capital and labour, should be established on a satisfactory basis. The nation requires a continuous production of wealth, and anything which checks its progress is a public calamity. How sad when the springs of national prosperity are wilfully dried up, when factories are shut up and work rejected, whilst labourers are parading the streets begging for their daily bread. Yet such incidents have unfortunately been and are still of frequent occurrence, and the differences between employers and employed, which might be arranged amicably, are too often the cause of much animosity and national loss. Of late years, especially, there has been too great a disposition to strikes and turn-outs. Low wages, long hours of labour, incompatibility of character and temper, besides questions connected with machinery and apprenticeship, have given rise to ever so many disputes; but it is not too much to say, that ignorance of economic laws is generally at the bottom of them all.

Relations of masters and servants.

At one time the legislature erroneously conceived that we could remove all possibility of difference by making it highly penal on the artisan to offer any objection to whatever rate of wages was offered to him. The statutes of labour[1] retained a good portion of the ancient law of servitude, and imposed heavy penalties on workers in the various trades who

The combination laws.

[1] 5 Eliz. c. 4.

refused to work at a regular fixed remuneration, often below the market value. An artisan could not go abroad; for if he did he was liable to be stopped on the road. If any man ventured to depose before a magistrate that he had reason to believe that a certain artisan intended to go abroad, that magistrate might imprison the artisan until he had given good security that he would not quit the country. The combination laws also were very oppressive. In 1824 old statutes were still in force, which interfered in many ways with the liberty of the person as well as with the rights of labour. By a statute, of comparatively recent date, being dated from the year 1800,[1] all agreements between journeymen and workmen for obtaining an advance of wages for themselves or other workmen, or for lessening the hours of work, or for preventing or hindering any person from employing whomsoever he should think proper to employ, or for controlling or in any way affecting any person carrying on any manufacture in the conduct or management thereof, were made and declared to be illegal; power being given to one justice of the peace to convict summarily and impose two months' imprisonment upon workmen entering into any such agreement. A remedy for such a state of matters was urgently needed, and Mr. Joseph Hume, to whom the nation is indebted for many liberal and economic measures, on February 12, 1824, moved for a committee to inquire into the state of the law on the subject. In descanting on the general position of the artisan in this country, Mr. Hume laid down the broad principle, that every law ought to be repealed which shackled any man in the free disposition of his labour, provided that free disposition did not interfere with any vital interest, and thereby endanger the political existence of the state; he asserted that the property which every man has in his labour as it is the original foundation of all other property, so it is the most sacred and inviolable. And he complained of the conditions imposed on workmen, whilst masters were left entirely uncontrolled.

Report of committee on combination laws.

The committee instituted a full inquiry into the whole subject, and in their sixth report they gave the result of their observations, more especially on the

[1] 40 Geo. III. c. 106.

working of the existing combination laws. From evidence given before the committee it appeared, that combinations of workmen had taken place in England, Scotland, and Ireland, often to a great extent, to raise and keep up their wages, to regulate their hours of working, and to impose restrictions upon their masters respecting apprentices or others whom they might think proper to employ. At the very time when the inquiry was proceeding combinations were in existence, attended with strikes or suspension of work, whilst the laws had not hitherto been effectual to prevent such combinations. Serious breaches of the peace with strikes of the workmen, often of long duration, had taken place in consequence of and arising out of the combination of workmen, which had been attended with loss to both masters and workmen, with considerable inconvenience and injury to the community. It was proved that the masters had often combined to lower the rates of their workmen's wages, as well as to resist a demand for an increase, and to regulate their hours of working, and sometimes to discharge those workmen who would not consent to the conditions offered, which steps had been followed by suspension of work, riotous proceedings, and acts of violence. But that although prosecutions had frequently been carried on under the statute and common law against the workmen, and many of them had suffered different periods of imprisonment for combining and conspiring to raise their wages, or to resist their reductions, and to regulate their hours of working, there were but few instances of prosecutions against masters for combining to lower wages, and to regulate the hours of working, and no instance had been adduced of any master having been punished for that offence. It was quite evident that the laws had not only not been efficient to prevent combinations, either of masters or workmen, but that, on the contrary, in the opinion of many of both parties, they had a tendency to produce mutual irritation and distrust, and to give a violent character to combinations, and to render them highly dangerous to the peace of the community. In view of these circumstances the committee were of opinion that masters and workmen should be freed from restrictions regarding the rate of wages and hours of working, and left at perfect liberty to make any agreements they may mutually think proper. And they did not hesitate to recommend that the statute laws that interfered in this particular should be repealed; and that the common law, under which a peaceable meeting of masters or workmen might be prosecuted as a conspiracy, should be altered. The committee also found that societies, legally enrolled as benefit societies, had been frequently made the cloak under which funds had been raised for the support of combinations and strikes attended with acts of violence or intimidation; and without recommending any specific course, they called the attention of the House to the frequent perversion of these institutions from their avowed and legitimate objects. Finding, moreover, that the practice of settling disputes by arbitration between masters and workmen had been attended with good effect, the committee thought it desirable that the laws which direct and regulate arbitration should be consolidated, amended, and made applicable to all trades. The committee also recommended the abolition of all laws affecting the liberty of the artisan to go abroad. And they concluded their report with the important recommendation that, in repealing the combination laws, it was necessary to provide for the punishment of either workmen or masters who, by threat, intimidation, or acts of violence, should interfere with the perfect freedom which ought to be allowed to each party, of employing his labour or capital in the manner he may deem most advantageous.

The publication of this report was followed by immediate legislation, and the act of 1825, amended by that of 1826,[a] repealed the laws relative to the combination of workmen, but enacted, 'that any person who, by violence to the person or property, or by molesting, or in any way obstructing another, should force, or endeavour to force, any journeyman, manufacturer, workman, or other person hired or employed in any manufacture, trade, or business, to depart from his hiring, employment, or work, or to return his work before it is finished, or should prevent, or endeavour to prevent, any such person from hiring himself to, or from accepting work or employment, should be liable to imprisonment.

Repeal of the law against combinations.

[a] 5 Geo. IV. c. 95 and 6 Geo. IV. c. 129.

That any person who should use violence for the purpose of forcing or inducing any person to belong to any club or association, or to contribute to any common fund, or to pay any fine or penalty, or on account of his not belonging to any particular club or association, or on account of his not having contributed, or having refused to contribute, to any common fund, or to pay any fine or penalty, or on account of his not having complied, or of his refusing to comply, with any rules, orders, resolutions, or regulations made to obtain an advance or to reduce the rate of wages, or to lessen or alter the hours of working, or to decrease or alter the quantity of work, or to regulate the mode of carrying on any manufacture, trade, or business, or the management thereof, should be liable to imprisonment. And, lastly, that any person who should, by violence or molestation, force, or endeavour to force, any manufacturer, or person carrying on any trade or business, to make any alteration in his mode of regulating, managing, conducting, or carrying on such manufacture, trade, or business, or to limit the number of his apprentices, or the number or description of his journeymen, workmen, or servants, should be liable to imprisonment with or without hard labour. But that no persons should be punished who should meet together for the sole purpose of consulting upon and determining the rate of wages which they will require or demand, or the hours for which they will work; and that no persons should be punished who should enter into any agreement for the purpose of fixing the rate of wages or prices which the parties, entering into the agreement or any of them, should pay to their journeymen.' Thus the right, long acknowledged at common law, of freedom of labour and freedom of trade, received the sanction of the legislature; but, alas! the difficulties connected with combinations and strikes were not thereby removed, and they reproduced themselves again and again so as to call for the interference of the legislature. In 1867 a royal commission was appointed to inquire into and report on the organisations and rules of trade unions and other associations, whether of workmen or employers; and to inquire into and report on the effect produced by such trade unions and associations on the workmen and employers respectively, and on the relations between workmen and employers, and on the trade and industry of the country. The commissioners reported in 1869, and two acts were passed in 1871, one[4] to amend the law relating to trade unions, for the purpose of legalising trade unions even though they might act in restraint of trade, and providing for their registration; and another[5] to amend the criminal laws relating to violence, threats, and molestation. By the new act penalties are imposed upon every one who should use violence to any person or any property; threaten or intimidate any person in such manner as would justify a justice of the peace, on complaint made to him, to bind over the person so threatening or intimidating to keep the peace; molest or obstruct any person with a view to coerce such person being a master to dismiss or to cease to employ any workman, or being a workman to quit any employment or to return work before it is finished; being a master not to offer, or being a workman not to accept, any employment or work; being a master or workman to belong or not to belong to any temporary or permanent association or combination; being a master or workman to pay any fine or penalty imposed by any temporary or permanent association or combination; or, being a master, to alter the mode of carrying on his business, or the number or description of any person employed by him.' In the same year, however, in which the report of the royal commission on trade unions was issued an act was passed to establish equitable councils of conciliation, to adjust differences between masters and workmen,[6] and another act to amend the law relative to the determination of questions arising between employers and employed under contracts of service.[7]

Another question of great importance to the well-being of the labourer was one connected with labour in factories. Factory labour has long been fully established, and, economically, its advantages had been universally recognised. A system which combines the labour of numerous workmen for the production of that which previously resulted from individual employment, and one which is attended by so much order, economy, and simplicity of action, could not fail to prove most beneficial.

Factory labour.

[4] 34 & 35 Vict. c. 31.
[5] 34 & 35 Vict. c. 32.
[6] 30 & 31 Vict. c. 105.
[7] 30 & 31 Vict. c. 141.

Early in the history of factory labour, objection was made to the system of carrying on our industries by means of great assemblages of labourers, lest it should be prejudicial to small and isolated workshops. But the objection was entirely groundless. An inquiry on the subject was instituted by a committee of the House of Commons in 1766, and in an able report they said, 'Your committee have the satisfaction of seeing that the apprehensions entertained of factories are not only vicious in principle, but they are practically erroneous to such a degree, that even the opposite principle might be reasonably entertained. Nor would it prove difficult to prove, that the factories, to a certain extent at least, and in the present day, seem absolutely necessary to the well-being of the domestic system, supplying those very particulars wherein the domestic system must be acknowledged to be inherently defective; for it is obvious that the little master manufacturer cannot afford, like the man who possesses considerable capital, to try the experiments which are requisite, and incur the risk and even losses which almost always occur in inventing and perfecting new articles of manufacture, or in carrying to a state of greater perfection articles already established. He cannot learn, by personal inspection, the wants and habits, the art manufacture and improvements of foreign countries. Diligence, economy, and prudence are the requisites of his character, not invention, taste, and enterprise; nor would he be warranted in hazarding the loss of any part of his small capital. He walks in a sure road as long as he treads in the beaten track, but he must not deviate into the path of speculation. The owner of a factory, on the contrary, being commonly possessed of a large capital, and having all his workmen employed under his own immediate superintendence, may make experiments, hazard speculations, invent shorter or better modes of performing old processes, may introduce new articles, and improve and perfect old ones, thus giving the range to his taste and fancy, and, thereby, alone enabling our manufacturers to stand the competition with their commercial rivals in other countries.'

The real objections to the factory system were and are, not economical but social and moral. The evils complained of

Evils of the factory system.

were that factory labour brought together large numbers of workmen and their families, and attracted to certain centres great masses of the labouring classes; that it accommodated hundreds and thousands of persons in large buildings, often not well ventilated, and often under a heated and suffocating atmosphere, and without due regard to difference of sex; that it led to imprudent marriages; that it created a great chasm between the employer and employed; that it threw a greater task upon women and children than their constitutions allow of; and that otherwise it introduced habits of social life not at all beneficial to the morals of the people. These evils manifested themselves very early in the history of factory labour. In 1796, Drs. Aiken and Perceval, two eminent medical men, called attention to many facts then experienced in connection with factories which created considerable anxiety. And in 1802, Sir Robert Peel brought in a bill to set a limit to the hours of labour in cotton-mills, which passed into law.[4] It was then provided that, in all woollen and cotton mills and factories in the United Kingdom, in which three or more apprentices, or twenty or more other persons were employed, apprentices should have two complete suits of clothing yearly; that the hours of working should not exceed twelve hours, exclusive of meal times, for which three hours were allowed; that they should be instructed every day for the first four years of their apprenticeship in reading, writing, and arithmetic; that the apartments of males and females should be kept distinct; that two only should sleep in one bed; that the rooms should be washed with quicklime and water twice a year, and kept well aired; that at the midsummer sessions two visitors should be appointed to report on the condition of such mills and factories, and that copies of the act should be fixed up in two conspicuous parts of the building. In 1816 Sir Robert Peel again obtained a committee to inquire into the subject, and in 1819 he brought in another bill to regulate the labour of children employed in the great woollen, worsted, and flax mills of Yorkshire.[5] No further legislation, however, took place on the subject till 1832, when first

[4] 42 Geo. III. c. 73.

[5] 59 Geo. III. c. 66; 60 Geo. III. & 1 Geo. IV. c. 5.

Mr. Sadler, and afterwards Lord Ashley, now Earl of Shaftesbury, urged before the House of Commons the necessity for further restraints. In deference to their earnest appeal a royal commission was appointed on the subject, and thus circumstances were made known which demanded a prompt remedy. Evidence was produced of children kept working fourteen and fifteen hours a day; of cases of deformity, of stinted growth, relaxed muscles, and slender conformation, and of numerous other injuries directly traceable to the system, to say nothing of disgusting atrocities between masters and men, and of moral enormities which might well alarm the staunchest advocate of the *Laissez faire* policy. It was too clear, indeed, that more restrictive legislation was wanted, and, notwithstanding a strenuous opposition, an act was passed by which night work was forbidden in the case of persons under eighteen years of age; the hours of labour of such were limited to twelve in the day, including one and a half hours for meals; the employment of children under nine was prohibited, except in silk mills; and under thirteen the hours were restricted to eight a day, or ten in silk mills; certain holidays were allowed, and certificates of health were required, under certain penalties, from a surgeon or physician previous to the admission of a child into a factory. And this act was supplemented by another authorising the appointment of inspectors of factories.[10] But factory legislation did not end there. In progress of time further limitation was placed on the labour of children, and afterwards, from time to time, the provisions of the acts were extended to other descriptions of manufactures and workshops.[11] Would that the law could prohibit the employment of married women in factories! No wages they can earn are equivalent to the loss produced by their leaving their homes neglected, and their husbands and children unattended.

Another subject which required legislative interference on behalf of the workmen was the abuse of paying wages in goods or provisions instead of money. The practice had long ex-

[10] 1 & 2 Wm. IV. c. 39; 3 & 4 Wm. IV. c. 103; 7 & 8 Vict. c. 15.

[11] Factory Acts Extension Act, 1867, 30 & 31 Vict. c. 103, and Workshops Regulation Act, 1867, 30 & 31 Vict. c. 146.

isted, and many fruitless attempts had been made to abolish it by law. As early as 1464[12] an act was passed against the abuses prevalent in the cloth-making trade, by which labourers were forced to take a great part of their wages in 'pins, girdles, and other unprofitable wares.' A hundred years later, in the time of Elizabeth,[13] an act prohibited payment of wages in wares and other kinds among the drapers, cottoners, and friezers in Shrewsbury. In 1701,[14] in order to prevent the oppression of the labourers and workmen employed in the woollen, linen, fustian, cotton, and iron manufactures, it was enacted that all payments shall be paid in coin of the realm, and not by any cloth, victuals, or commodities in lieu thereof. Ten years after[15] the woollen manufacturers were forbidden to make payments in 'any sort of goods or wares,' and in 1740[16] an act was passed forbidding payments in 'victuals, goods, or commodities,' except at the workman's request, in the manufacture of gloves, breeches, boots, shoes, slippers, wares, and other goods. And the prohibition was repeated in later times as regards clothiers, lacemakers, cutlers, and colliers. But all apparently to no effect. In 1830 it was not an uncommon practice in certain trades for employers to set up large shops or stores for the sale to their workmen of all descriptions of necessaries, and instead of paying them their wages in money to give them tickets for these shops, usually kept by some relative or servant; or if money was given, it was with the tacit or express understanding that the workmen should resort to the warehouse or shop of their masters for such articles as were there kept. We might conceive the possibility that shops well provisioned by the masters with goods purchased at wholesale prices might prove of real benefit to the workmen, since these might prevent them from losing much in the purchase of small quantities from retail shops, often not the most scrupulous, and also enable the workmen to procure what they required near at hand; especially where the factories were in sequestered localities far away from villages. But the great evil and abuse of such a system was that the truck-masters used these shops as means of gain and extortion. Not

The truck system.

[12] 4 Edward IV. c. 1. s. 5. [13] 8 Eliz. c. 7. [14] 1 Anne st. ii., c. 18.
[15] 10 Anne c. 26; and see 1 Geo. I. c. 15, s. 11. [16] 12 Geo. I. c. 34.

only did they charge fifteen or twenty per cent. more for goods than they were worth, but were forcing on their workmen in payment of wages goods which were useless, or which were not required. The circulation of the current coin was thus checked and often superseded. Competition amongst shops was out of the question, and in many ways the system imposed a decided loss and inconvenience to the labouring population. A large number of petitions having been presented to the House of Commons complaining of the abuse, a bill to prohibit it was introduced by Mr. Lyttleton; and, though it met with a strong opposition, on the plea that workmen ought to be at liberty to come to what agreement they pleased respecting wages, and that no law of the kind could ever be effectual, public opinion decided in favour of the measure, and it passed into law.[17]

Abolition of slavery.

And last, though not least, as a measure for the emancipation of labour, we have the abolition of slavery in the British colonies. We have already seen how, thanks to the energetic efforts of Wilberforce, Clarkson, Granville Sharp, and Macaulay, the slave trade was declared illegal from January 1, 1808. How, by the unremitted labours of Lord Brougham and his friends, the slave trade was declared piracy in 1824, and treaties were concluded with maritime powers for the maintenance of a squadron on the African coast to suppress the trade in slaves. But it was not till 1830 that Lord Brougham moved in earnest for the abolition of slavery in the British colonies. What could be said in favour of slavery? The Bible and philosophy allow that black men or Africans have a soul, as we have. Physiology demonstrates that, whether black or white, we are members of the same human family. History finds between the owner and the owned no trace of legitimate conquest. Law could attach no value to the pretended contract of ownership where there is a

[17] 57 Geo. III. c. 115; 58 Geo. III. c. 51; 1 & 2 Wm. IV. c. 37. In 1870 a royal commission was appointed to inquire into the operation of the above act, and they found that the truck system is still largely prevalent. It appears that 136,000 persons are engaged at works where either shops are kept or poundage is charged on all advances made to the men before pay day; and the commissioners recommended the extension of weekly or quasi-weekly pays, and some alterations in the penal and prohibitory provisions.

total absence of title, where the subject-matter is illegal, where of the two parties one is not free to act and the other acts in bad faith. Ethnology places on a higher rank those races who work for themselves than those who cause others to work for them. Political economy affirms the superiority of free labour over forced labour. Politics condemn slavery because it corrupts the superior race. Religion and charity detest it, because it oppresses the inferior race. The state of the slave population in the West Indies was indeed most pitiful. Hated by all, mercilessly treated by their masters, without law or justice to protect them, the slaves were dying rapidly out, and the number would have been speedily exhausted but for the clandestine importation of slaves from Africa, which no vigilance could entirely prevent. In appealing against such an offence, Lord Brougham always rose to the highest pitch of indignation. 'Tell me not of rights,' he said; 'talk not of the property of the planter in his slaves. I deny the right. I acknowledge not the property. The principles, the feelings of our common nature rise in rebellion against it. Be the appeal made to the understanding or to the heart, the sentence is the same that rejects it. In vain you tell me of laws that sanction such a claim. There is a law above all the enactments of human codes—the same throughout the world, the same in all times—such as it was before the daring genius of Columbus pierced the night of ages, and opened to one world the source of power, wealth, and knowledge, to another all unutterable woes—such as it is at this day: it is the law written on the heart of man by the finger of his Maker, and by that law—unchangeable and eternal—while men despise fraud and loathe rapine and abhor blood, they will reject with indignation the wild and guilty phantasy that man can hold property in man.' Such was the fervid manner in which Lord Brougham urged the emancipation of slaves in the British West Indies. The agitation caused by the reform bill together with the promotion of Lord Brougham as lord chancellor to the House of Lords, removing as it did the most undaunted champion from the popular arena of the legislature, retarded for a while the settlement of the question. In 1832, Mr. Fowell Buxton made a motion on the subject, but at last Lord Stanley, afterward Earl of Derby, then minister of the colonies, introduced a measure, and on August 28, 1833, the famous act[16] was passed for the abolition of slavery throughout the British colonies from August 1, 1834, a compensation of 20,000,000*l.* being granted to the planters for the sacrifice thus imposed upon them. By the original measure all children under six years of age, or born after that date, were declared free; and all slaves above six years became apprenticed labourers, with weekly wages, till their final emancipation on August 1, 1836; but the nation had not patience to wait till that time, and by a subsequent measure all slaves and apprentices became universally and absolutely free in 1838.

[16] 3 & 4 Wm. IV. c. 73. Under this statute compensation was given for the freedom of 780,993 slaves. The value of the slaves was estimated at 45,281,738*l.*; the average value of a slave from 1822 to 1830 having been as high as 120*l.* in Honduras, and as low as 27*l.* 4*s.* in Bermuda. The 20,000,000*l.* was apportioned between the West India colonies, upwards of 6,000,000*l.* having been given to Jamaica, 4,20[illegible]009*l.* to British Guiana, and smaller sums to the other colonies.

CHAPTER V.

FINANCE AND BANKING.

1830–1834.

Influence of Taxation on National Resources.—Sir Henry Parnell's Work.—Influence of Duties on Raw Materials.—Influence of Duties on British Manufactures.—Effect of High Duties on Smuggling.—Lord Althorpe's Budget.—The Wine Duties.—The Timber Duties.—The Bank of England Charter.—Report of the Committee.—Bank of England Notes Legal Tender.—The London Joint Stock Banks.—The London and Westminster Bank.

Influence of taxation on national resources.

It would have been useless to expect that during war, when financial exigencies put the chancellor of the exchequer at his wits' end to supply the necessary funds, any special attention should be bestowed on the incidence of taxation on commerce and industry. With an expenditure ever varying and uncertain, yet always excessive, with the resources of the nation but little known and undeveloped, and with the national mind preoccupied by the one great thought of securing the safety of the country, that was not the time for studying the science of finance. When, however, peace was restored and matters returned to their normal condition, the state of the revenue, its huge proportions, and its strange anomalies, pressed themselves on the consideration of the thoughtful. By this time the revenue and expenditure were brought down to a level,[1] several important conversions had been made of the public funds, and Dr. Hamilton's book, showing the fallacy of the sinking fund, had borne fruit in the act of 1829, which provided that thenceforth the sum to be applied to the reduction of the debt should be the actual annual surplus of revenue over the expenditure.[2]

[1] In 1814 the total expenditure was 106,832,000*l*. In 1820 it was reduced to 4,157,000*l*.; in 1830 to 49,078,000*l*.

[2] During the whole period, from January 5, 1793, when the French war broke out, up to 1829, there was only one year (1817) in which money was not raised by

But other questions remained to be solved. Can industry be relieved of part, at least, of the heavy burden of taxation? Can any taxes be repealed or reduced without producing any material detriment to the revenue? Adam Smith had long before stated that, in the arithmetic of the customs, two and two instead of making four sometimes make only one. That the duties of customs might, without any loss to the public revenue and with great advantage to foreign trade, be confined to a few articles only; that high taxes, by diminishing the consumption of the taxed commodities, or by encouraging smuggling, frequently afford a smaller revenue to government than might be drawn from more moderate taxes; and that the temptation to smuggle can be diminished only by lowering a tax. Long experience had indeed proved the soundness of these principles, but no attempt had been made to put them into practice, and the field of inquiry and legislation was altogether untrodden, when Sir Henry Parnell published his excellent work on financial reform.

Sir Henry Parnell's work.

First among the defects of the existing tariff was the imposition of heavy taxes on the raw materials of industry. It was easy to see that, by increasing the cost of manufactures, such taxes would lessen the amount of production, and render our manufacturers less able to carry on a

Influence of duties on raw materials.

loan, in order to aid the sinking fund, besides what was required for war expenditure. After excluding the period from August 5, 1786, to January 5, 1793, during which 8,147,631l. was applied to redeem 10,241,100l. of 3l. per cent. stock, bearing interest of 307,233l. per annum, there remains 321,902,824l., which was applied between 1793 and 1829 to redeem 472,942,703l. capital stock carrying 14,468,368l. annual interest, the mean rate on the sum paid being almost exactly 4½l. per cent. per annum. During the same period the total sum of 702,163,078l. was raised by loans, for which 1,032,536,700l. capital stock of funded debt was created, carrying 35,301,392l. annual interest, or a mean rate of 5l. 0s. 6d. per cent. per annum. The actual result of all these sinking fund operations, therefore, was, that the total amount of 310,050,455l. was raised at 5l. 0s. 6d. per cent. to pay off debt carrying interest at 4½l. per cent. The difference between these two rates is 10s. 6d. per cent. per annum, amounting upon the total capital sum of 310,050,455l. to 1,627,765l. per annum, which may be set down as the increased annual charge of our funded debt, and a real loss to the public from this deceptive sinking fund system; without taking into account the expenses of the management of the sinking fund, and the increased amount of capital of debt, consequent upon the practice of borrowing on less advantageous terms for larger sums than were required to meet the actual public expenditure.—Accounts of Public Income and Expenditure, 366 of 1869, part ii. p. 718.

successful competition with foreign manufacturers. The duty on hemp greatly raised the prices of articles in universal demand, as well as the prices of sails and cordage. The duties on ashes and barilla added to the prices of the materials of several manufactures. The duty on raw silk raised the price not only of silk manufactures, but of silk thrown at home. The duty on timber injuriously affected industry in a great variety of ways, in consequence of its being used in shipbuilding and machinery. The duty on bricks and tiles fell heavily on industry, in consequence of the number and size of the buildings required for mills, factories, and storehouses. The duties on hides and skins not only injured a very important manufacture, but raised the price of one of the necessaries of life. The duty on coals and culm carried coastwise, affected the business of working coal-mines, and increased the cost of machinery, building ships, bleaching and dyeing, as well as of the steam power used in many processes of trade and manufacture.

Influence of duties on British manufactures.

Not less injurious in their working were the taxes on British manufactures, such as glass, paper, printed calico, soap, and many other articles then subjected to excise. The extent of the market for these manufactures, and consequently of the employment of capital and labour in producing them depending on the cheapness, it naturally followed that those duties, by increasing their prices, had the direct effect of limiting the market for them, and diminishing the employment of capital and labour. Moreover, the severe and vexatious regulations under which those duties were collected had most injurious consequences. By prescribing the processes of fabrication, manufacturers were not allowed to manage their trade in the way their skill and experience pointed out as the best, but were compelled to conform to such methods of pursuing their art as they found laid down in acts of parliament. And by checking activity and invention among our manufacturers, the consumers of those goods were made to pay prices increased to the extent, not only of the duties imposed, but of the additional expenses incurred in consequence of such vexatious regulations.

The taxes on luxuries were too high, and their effect was to diminish the revenue and to encourage smuggling. The taxes imposed for the protection of agriculture had the effect, not only of making the public pay a higher price for all articles of food, but by diminishing the value of annual imports, causing a corresponding diminution in the annual value of exports of British manufacture. Whilst the taxes for the protection of British manufacture, by preventing the importation of foreign goods, diminished the demand for the exportation of British goods, diminished the employment of shipping and foreign commerce, enhanced the prices of a number of articles, checked invention, gave encouragement to smuggling, and otherwise weakened and paralysed the energies of the nation.

Effect of over taxation.

Soon after the publication of Sir Henry Parnell's work on financial reform, it devolved on Lord Althorpe, as chancellor of the exchequer in Earl Grey's administration, to present his budget, and in it we have the first attempt at alleviating the burden of the poorer classes by reducing taxes which pressed more immediately on the productive resources of the country. The budget proposed the repeal of the taxes on coal, tallow candles, printed calico, and glass; the abolition of the duties upon a vast variety of articles which produced but a trifling amount of revenue, the reduction of the duty on tobacco, the equalisation of the wine duties, and a reform in the timber duties. And in order to make up the deficiency thereby created, the budget proposed new taxes on steamboat passengers, on *bonâ fide* sales of land and of funded property, an import duty on raw cotton, and other duties of minor importance. We cannot say that the idea of imposing one objectionable tax in order to relieve the nation of another was a very happy one, and we are not surprised that some severe criticism was indulged in at the preference shown in reducing the duty on tobacco rather than on tea. Yet, on the whole, the budget was well received, and it certainly embraced reforms of considerable importance in its bearings on international relations.

Lord Althorpe's budget.

It was certainly high time to alter the tariff on wines, especially as regards French wines, upon which legislation had been extremely capricious. For centuries after the Conquest, French wines had almost the entire mono-

The wine duties.

poly of the British market, and though for a time, owing to the extension of foreign trade, the dry wine of Spain acquired favour, French wine continued long to be largely used. But the asylum and support given by Louis XIV. to the Stuart family irritated the British Government, and led to the imposition of a higher discriminating duty on French wines, first of 8*l.* per ton, and afterwards of 33*l.* Then Oporto wine began to be introduced to take the place of the red wine of Bordeaux; and soon after, in 1703, the famous Methuen Treaty was concluded with Portugal, which, under the pretence of securing a permanent market for British woollens, robbed England of a great and natural trade with a neighbouring country, and compelled her to use an inferior and dearer article from a country which, under no circumstances, could ever become a large customer of British goods. During the war the duty on Portuguese and Spanish wines had been 9*s.* 1*d.* per gallon, and the duty on French wine 13*s.* 9*d.*; but in 1825 a considerable reduction of duty was made: Portuguese, Spanish, Madeira, Rhenish, and Sicilian wines were admitted at 4*s.* 6*d.* per gallon, and French at 7*s.* 3*d.* per gallon. Lord Althorpe proposed the equalisation of the wine duties at 5*s.* 6*d.* per gallon. And though the proposal was at first opposed, on the plea that we were bound by a treaty with Portugal to maintain for ever a discriminating duty of 30 per cent. against French wine, the equalisation of duties was recognised as expedient, and was carried into effect.

The timber duties.

The proposal as regards the timber duties was, however, less fortunate. Indefensible as was the system then in force, of imposing a very high differential duty on foreign timber, the public were not prepared to accept the small modicum of reform which Lord Althorpe proposed, viz. a reduction of 6*s.* a load on January 1, 1832, of 6*s.* more on January 1, 1833, and of 3*s.* more on January 1, 1834, making a total reduction of 15*s.* per load. The project was therefore rejected by a large majority, and, though the subject was remitted to a committee of the House of Commons in 1835, and a report presented which recommended a reduction of the differential duty, no alteration in the timber duties was made for a considerable time after.

The charter of the Bank of England.

Whilst the financial policy of the country fully engaged the attention of the chancellor of the exchequer, the approaching expiration of the charter of the Bank of England in 1833 required immediate consideration, especially after the circumstances which accompanied the commercial crisis of 1825. Soon after that memorable year the necessity was seen of encouraging the formation of joint-stock banks throughout the country, and an act was passed accordingly.[a] But the main rights and privileges of the Bank of England were left untouched, till an opportunity for considering them was afforded on the renewal of the Bank Charter. Was it expedient to continue all the monopolies which that institution enjoyed? Should the charter be renewed and the Bank still be highly favoured by the legislature? For centuries the Bank of England was the only banking company allowed to exist in England. As we have seen by the Bank Charter Act of 1708 it was enacted, that during the continuance of the corporation of the Bank of England, it should not be lawful for any body politic or corporate, other than the Bank of England, or for any person whatever united in partnership, exceeding the number of six persons, in England, to borrow, owe, or take up any sum of money on their bill or note, payable on demand, or on any less time than six months from the borrowing thereof. Time after time the charter, with all its privileges and monopolies, was renewed with remarkable ease. But lately the action of the Bank on the circulating medium had been freely canvassed. Not a few were ready to criticise the conduct of the Bank in times of great national exigencies, and it was felt that more than a formal inquiry was requisite. In the session of 1832, therefore, a secret committee was appointed to inquire, not only into the expediency of renewing the charter, but into the system on which banks of issue in England and Wales were conducted. Three points were specially examined into by the committee: first, whether the paper circulation of the metropolis should

[a] 7 Geo. IV. c. 46. In 1836 a committee of the House of Commons was appointed to inquire into the operation of this act, and it reported that the act was defective in not imposing any preliminary obligation to the formation of such banks, or any restriction upon the amount of the nominal capital, or on the number and amount of shares, or on the amount to be paid up, or on the publication of liabilities and assets, or on the traffic in shares.

be confined to the issue of one bank; or whether a competition of different banks of issue, each consisting of an unlimited number of partners, should be permitted; secondly, if it should be deemed expedient that the paper circulation of the metropolis should be confined, as at present, to the issue of one bank, how far the whole of the exclusive privileges possessed by the Bank of England were necessary to effect this object; and, thirdly, what checks could be provided to secure for the public a proper management of banks of issue, and especially whether it would be expedient and safe to compel them periodically to publish their accounts?

The committee had no time to complete their inquiry that session, and only submitted the valuable evidence they had received, without any formal report. Yet many matters of moment date from that inquiry: such as the publication of the accounts of the Bank, the publication of the amount of bullion held by the Bank, and the partial adoption of the principle of currency by which the Bank of England, as well as the country banks' circulation, should be regulated by the state of foreign exchanges. These and many other points were brought out with great fulness in the evidence before the committee; and, upon the presentation of the report, Lord Althorpe proposed that the Bank of England should continue to have the monopoly of the circulation; that no bank, with power to issue notes, with more than six partners, should be allowed to be established within sixty-five miles of London; that the charter should be renewed for twenty-one years, terminable at the end of ten years; that weekly accounts of bullion and securities, and of paper in circulation and deposits, should be presented; that Bank of England notes should be legal tender except at the Bank; that the usury laws should be so far modified as to exempt from its operation bills of exchange not having more than three months to run; that a fourth of the debt due to the Bank should be paid; that in future the Bank should deduct 120,000*l.* a year from its charge on account of the management of the public debt; that bankers should be allowed to pay a composition duty in lieu of the stamp duty; and that facilities should be given for the establishment of joint-stock banks at a certain distance from

Report of the committee on the Bank Charter.

London. These proposals of the Government had been accepted by the Bank, but the House of Commons strongly demurred to the principle of making Bank of England notes legal tender.

Why should Bank of England notes be thus exceptionally treated? Was it not introducing a species of inconvertible paper money? The reasons alleged for the proposal were, that in 1825 the danger of exhaustion did not so much occur from the demand for gold to meet the notes as from the necessity of enabling country bankers to pay their deposits. That in most of the country districts the amount of notes issued by the bankers bore but a small proportion to the amount of their deposits and engagements, for which they were obliged to provide in times of pressure; yet that it was to meet these that they applied to the Bank for bullion. It was therefore to guard against such a danger that it was thought desirable to make Bank of England notes legal tender. The measure was not intended for the benefit of the country bankers; its object was to keep in circulation as much paper as possible, and to prevent any unusual demand for gold upon the Bank of England. And upon such pleas, though very weak in themselves, after much discussion, the clause passed, as well as the main proposition, for the renewal of the Bank Charter.[4]

Proposal to make Bank of England notes a legal tender.

Yet the bill was not allowed to pass without the insertion of one more clause, which, whatever was the design of its framer, exercised considerable influence on the future monetary institutions of the country. When the bill was passing its last stages through the House, a clause was introduced, to the effect that any company or partnership might carry on the business of banking in London, or within sixty miles thereof, provided such body did not borrow or take up in England any sum of money either on bills payable on demand, or at any less time than six months from the borrowing thereof. By introducing this clause, the governors of the Bank of England believed that they would effectively prevent the

Joint-stock banking in London.

[4] 3 & 4 Wm. IV. c. 98. By this statute bills of exchange not having more than three months to run were exempt from the operation of the usury laws; and three years after, by the 7 Wm. IV. and 1 Vict., the act was extended to bills of twelve months and under.

establishment of any bank in London, and that they might thus enjoy for many years an undisputed monopoly; but they were wholly deceived. This clause proved soon after to be the open door by which joint-stock banks were permitted in the metropolis, and, on the strength of that very act, in 1834, the London and Westminster Bank commenced business.

That this unexpected event should disconcert the Bank of England we might well imagine. It was a bold attempt. For the first time since its formation the Bank had to realise the fact of a competitor in the field, and, whether from fear of possible results, or out of spite at such an intruder, the Bank decided to offer all the opposition in its power. The London and Westminster Bank requiring legal sanction to sue and be sued in the name of its officers, Mr. Clay introduced a bill on the subject in the House of Commons; but the Bank determined to oppose it in all its stages. The chancellor of the exchequer, espousing the cause of the Bank, opposed the bill, on the plea that it was a breach of the undertaking with the Bank on the renewal of the charter, yet the bill was read a second time by a majority of 141 to 25, and the third time by a majority of 137 to 16. But the Bank never relaxed its efforts to defeat it, and when the bill was presented to the Lords it was rejected by a large majority. The London and Westminster Bank, however, was not to be foiled by such manœuvres. Undismayed by the powerful opposition, it advanced towards completion, and only avoided the difficulty of suing by putting forward its trustees instead of its officers. The Bank of England then refused to keep a drawing account for the London and Westminster Bank, and soon after, in 1838, the Bank of England commenced legal proceedings to prevent the London and Westminster Bank accepting bills drawn at six months' date. For two years the suit was carried on, and it ended by the master of the rolls granting an injunction to restrain the London and Westminster Bank from accepting bills at less than six months' date. Even this, however, did not disconcert the London and Westminster Bank. Persistent in its efforts to the last, it caused its country agents to draw upon the bank in London without needing acceptance, in the same manner as the Bank of Ireland draws upon the Bank of England. And thus,

The London and Westminster and the Bank of England.

by one expedient after another, the London and Westminster Bank succeeded in neutralising the opposition, and the Bank of England became at last tired of its absurd and ill-conceived jealousy. A peculiar feature of the new bank was the establishment of branches in different parts of the metropolis. On the same day when the head office was opened in Throgmorton Street, a branch was established in Waterloo Place. In 1836 a branch was opened in Holborn and another in Whitechapel; Southwark came next, then Oxford Street, and so by degrees the London and Westminster Bank, under the able direction of its first manager, Mr. James W. Gilbart, a man distinguished for his talent, judgment, and liberality, became a bank second to none in the metropolis, and a formidable rival to the national institution, the Bank of England. Nor did it remain long alone. Soon after, other banking institutions were established in the metropolis. The London Joint Stock Bank came immediately after, in 1836; the Union Bank of London followed in 1839; after that the London and County Bank, originally the Surrey, Kent, and Sussex Bank, in 1839; and the Commercial Bank of London in 1840. Not only in the metropolis, but throughout the country, a great stimulus was given to the establishment of joint-stock banks, of which there was great need.

CHAPTER VI.

MEANS OF COMMUNICATION.

1830–1840.

Introduction of Railways.—Objections to Railway Travelling.—Opening of the Liverpool and Manchester Railway.—Death of Huskisson.—Results of Railways.—Railway Legislation.—Introduction of Steam Navigation.—The Electric Telegraph.—The Post Office.—Sir Rowland Hill and the Penny Postage.

AMONGST modern inventions the railway certainly holds a high and foremost rank, and it is of so useful a character that the wealth and advancement of any state have come to be estimated by the number of miles of railways laid down in it. The origin of railway communication must be found in the tramway long used in coal and iron mines. In 1802 Richard Trevethick first invented a self-acting steam carriage, which, being adapted for the drawing of waggons, was first introduced in 1804 on the Merthyr Tydvil Railway, and drew ten bars of iron at the rate of five miles an hour. Locomotive power was successfully applied by George Stephenson on the Killingworth Railway in 1814, and its success led to the application of the same on the Stockton and Darlington Railway in 1821. And as the machine was perfected and greater speed was attained, the idea was suggested to apply the invention to the conveyance of passengers and the transport of goods throughout the country. In 1820 Thomas Gray, of Nottingham, conceived the idea of extending railways over the kingdom. Two years later William James, of London, endeavoured to establish a railway between Liverpool and Manchester; and in 1824 Joseph Sanders, of Liverpool, issued the first prospectus for such an undertaking.

Introduction of railways.

But what was to be done as regards the locomotive? The

Opposition to railways.

company offered a premium for the best that could be constructed. Four engines competed, and Stephenson's 'Rocket' was the successful one. But great opposition was offered to this mode of conveyance. The government itself, perplexed and not knowing what to do, granted 130,000*l.* for putting the high road from London to Birmingham in a condition so perfect as to compete with any railway! All kinds of misconceptions and fears were suggested against the practicability, utility, or safety of such a mode of travelling. The formation of railways, it was said, would prevent cows grazing and hens laying; the poisoned air from the locomotives would kill birds as they flew over them; the preservation of pheasants and foxes would no longer be possible; householders adjoining the projected line would have their houses burnt up by the fire thrown from the engine chimneys, while the air around would be polluted by clouds of smoke; horses would no longer be of any use; oats and hay would prove unsaleable commodities; travelling by road would be rendered highly dangerous; country inns would be ruined; the boilers would burst; and passengers would be blown to atoms. An influential publication laughed at the absurdity of the idea. 'As to those persons who speculate on making railways generally throughout the kingdom, and superseding all the canals, all the waggons, mails, and stage-coaches, postchaises, and, in short, every other mode of conveyance by land and by water, we deem them and their visionary schemes unworthy of notice. What, for instance, can be more palpably absurd and ridiculous than the following paragraph, on which a prospect is held out of locomotive travelling twice as fast as stage-coaches? We should as soon expect the people of Woolwich to suffer themselves to be fired off from one of Congreve's ricochet rockets, as trust themselves to the mercy of such a machine going at such a rate.'

Inauguration of the Liverpool and Manchester Railway.

Yet, notwithstanding all these forebodings of evil, the Liverpool and Manchester line approached completion, and the time came for trying the great experiment. It was indeed to be a great era in the history of commerce, and a festival day for mechanical industry. For the day appointed, September 15, 1830, great preparations were made. The Duke of Wellington, Sir Robert Peel, Mr. Huskisson, and many other distinguished persons were invited to the ceremony. And at the appointed time eight locomotives, all built by Robert Stephenson, on the model of the 'Rocket,' took part in the procession. The train consisted of twenty-nine carriages; the number of passengers was about 600. At eleven o'clock the procession started from Liverpool accompanied by flags, music, and enthusiastic cheers of numberless spectators. The train passed safely Wavetry station, Olive Mount cutting, Rainhill Bridge, the Sutton incline, and the Sankey viaduct to Parkhurst. There, however, the train stopped to enable the locomotive to take in water, and there the sad accident arose which turned the great festival party into a mourning procession. To afford an opportunity to the Duke of Wellington to see the entire procession, it was arranged that all the trains should pass before him whilst his carriage was stationary. Mr. Huskisson and other gentlemen alighted from their carriage, and as he was going to shake hands with the Duke, the 'Rocket' passed rapidly and knocked him down, its wheels passing over his leg and thigh. Thus in a moment, what was the occasion of unlimited congratulation became the source of universal consternation. The journey was indeed completed, but Mr. Huskisson was conveyed to a place close by where he expired that same evening.

Death of Huskisson.

Yes! the same Huskisson who first inaugurated freedom of trade and navigation, inaugurated also by his own death one of the greatest of modern discoveries, one of the most valuable agents in modern commerce and intercourse. Honour to his memory! That we have emerged from a state of inactivity and entered on a career of boundless prosperity, we owe certainly to the initiatory measures of Huskisson. In his long and honoured career he did much to enlarge the field of British commerce, to improve our commercial code, and to promote the wellbeing of every class of society. By his able advocacy our colonies obtained that freedom of intercourse, without which they could never have attained their present importance. It was Mr. Huskisson who swept away some of the most injurious restrictions on our shipping. His speeches on the currency, on the combination laws, and on apprenticeship may be read with instruction and pleasure. Freedom was his motto, and in all the legislative acts which bear his impress, freedom is the foremost and prominent principle. Well read in the school of the economists, he was the first to bring their teaching to the test of actual practice. He was the first British minister whose whole system of commercial policy was founded on sound, liberal, and enlarged principles, and who laboured earnestly and successfully to promote the power, happiness, and glory of his own country, not by seeking to exalt her at the expense of others, but by opening her ports to the ships and goods of all countries, and making her the centre and animating principle of a vast commerce founded on the satisfaction of the reciprocal wants and desires that subsist among nations.

And what has been the result of the marvellous invention of conveying passengers and goods by railway? First of all, an immense saving of time and money. Before the railway was established between Liverpool and Manchester there were twenty-two regular and seven occasional extra coaches which, if full, would carry 688 persons. The railway carried, in eighteen months, 700,000 persons, or on an average 1,070 per day. The fare per coach was 10*s*. inside, 5*s*. outside; by railway 5*s*. inside, 3*s*. 6*d*. outside. By coach it took 4 hours to go from Liverpool to Manchester or *vice versâ*, by railway 1¾ hours. The rate of goods by canal was 15*s*. per ton, by railway 10*s*. 8*d*. By canal it took 20 hours, by railway 2 hours. But these rates of saving and travelling have all been immensely extended of late years, and we should have some stupendous figures were we to calculate the total amount saved by the millions of passengers now yearly travelling by rail all over the world, and by the immense tonnage of goods so conveyed.

Results of railways.

Much might be said on railway legislation. The genius of British enterprise certainly consists in its freedom and daring. When railway travelling was first projected the idea seemed all but chimerical, and it was most hazardous for capitalists to venture investing their capital on such works. To have fettered, therefore, the companies with any restrictions

Railway legislation.

or conditions would have been most injudicious.[1] Even after the success of the Liverpool and Manchester Railway, the consequences to society which would result from the adoption of this new means of communication were seldom correctly appreciated by men of the best understanding, and under such circumstances it is less to be wondered at, that extensive powers should have been given to railway companies, without the accompaniment of such safeguards as subsequent experience proved to be necessary for the protection of the public. At the first, railway companies were not intended to have a monopoly of their lines. On the contrary, provision was made, in all or most of the acts of incorporation, to enable all persons to use the road on payment of certain tolls to the company, under such regulations as the company might make to secure the proper and convenient use of the railway. But no sooner were railways worked on a large scale with locomotive power, than it was found impracticable for the public in general to use the lines either with carriages or locomotive engines; and the railway companies, in order to make their undertakings remunerative, were compelled, with the assistance of the persons who had been previously engaged in the carrying trade of the country, to embark in the business of common carriers on their lines of railway, and conduct the whole operations themselves. When, in 1840, a committee of the House of Commons was appointed upon the railway system, they came to the conclusion that the right secured to the public by the railway acts of running their engines and carriages on the railways, was practically a dead letter, because no provision had been made for ensuring to independent trains and engines access to stations and watering places along the lines; because the rates for toll limited by the act were almost always so high as to make it difficult for independent persons to work at a profit, and because the necessity of placing the running of all trains under the complete control of one head, interposed numerous difficulties in the way of independent traders. In 1844, Parliament again directed its attention to the increasing

[1] See the 7 Geo. IV. c. 49. An act for making and maintaining a railway from Liverpool to Manchester, with certain branches therefrom; capital 510,000*l*. in 100*l*. shares.

importance of railway communication, and a committee was appointed on the subject. It was evident, indeed, that railways had by that time acquired a complete monopoly of the means of communication, not so much in consequence of the privileges conferred on the companies, as by the superior accommodation and cheapness of travelling which they afforded. It was clear, too, that there was yet ample scope for the extension of the railway system, and that nothing should be done to induce so much as a reasonable suspicion of good faith with regard to the integrity of privileges already granted, one of the elements of encouragement to future undertakings being a just and equitable dealing with those already established. Many recommendations were made by the committee respecting the rates of tolls and other means of control, and the result of this inquiry was the passing of the act in 1844,[1] which provided that if the clear annual divisible profits should amount to 10 per cent. on the paid-up capital of any railway authorised in that or any subsequent session at the end of twenty-one years from the passing of the act sanctioning the line, the lords of the treasury might revise the tolls, fares, and charges so as to reduce the dividend to 10 per cent., such revision being, however, accompanied by a guarantee on the part of the crown that the revised rates should produce a dividend to the company of 10 per cent. for a further period of twenty-one years.

Steam navigation.

With the successful inauguration of railways for personal communication and the carriage of goods, we must associate the wonderful progress of steam navigation. As far back as the sixteenth century, an experiment was made to apply steam power to navigation, but with no practical results, and it was not till 1807 that practical attempts were made to render Watt's famous steam engine serviceable to navigation. It wanted the connecting-link, the use of revolving paddles instead of oars. In 1736 Jonathan Hull took out a patent for a tow boat to be propelled by a paddle wheel set in motion by a sort of steam engine. In 1788 Mr. Miller, of Dalswinston, made a small engine, by which he succeeded in moving a vessel at the rate of seven miles an hour. Symington came next with his patent, and in 1803 the 'Charlotte

[1] 7 & 8 Vict. c. 85.

Dundas' towed vessels on the Forth and Clyde Canal. Again, however, America came up to British achievements, and Robert Fulton, in 1807, made the first successful voyage by steam from New York to Albany. In 1812 Henry Bell started a steamboat on the Clyde, and that was soon after followed by a boat making a passage from Glasgow to London. In 1820 packets were established between Holyhead and Dublin, and in 1838 an ocean passage was accomplished by the 'Great Eastern' from Bristol, and the 'Sirius' from Cork, to New York. Thus little by little steam navigation was introduced on rivers, on the high seas, and on the Atlantic Ocean, and what was one day a rare experiment speedily became a regular means of navigation, destined henceforth to fill the highest position in the maritime intercourse of nations, and to supersede to a large extent sailing ships, both for near and distant navigation.

The electric telegraph.

A marvel even greater than the steamboat, however, is the electric telegraph. The employment of a galvanometer, lines of wire, and a battery as a means of telegraphing, was suggested by Ampère in 1820. And in 1833 Gauss and Weber, of Göttingen, united the Observatory and Physical Cabinet, distant about a mile from each other, by two wires suspended in the air. But it was only when Messrs. Cooke and Wheatstone, in 1837, patented a fine needle telegraph that the invention was first put into practical operation by the construction of a line of telegraph for general purposes, and by the application of the same to the Blackwall Railway, which, being worked by rope traction with the accommodation of intermediate stations, rendered an efficient telegraphic system necessary. By means of the telegraph a communication could be maintained between the two termini and half a dozen intermediate stations, and signals could be transmitted to and from every station at intervals of a quarter of an hour throughout the day. Other improvements were subsequently made in the telegraph by Dr. Steinheil, Professor Morse, and Mr. Davy. In 1841 Mr. Bain invented his electric telegraph with a printing apparatus for recording the results of ordinary inked types. In 1843, Mr. Cooke introduced the plan of suspending the wires on posts. And after successive inventions, by which the instrument was more and more perfected and rendered fit for general use, the Electric Telegraph Company was formed in 1846, which purchased most of the patents of Messrs. Wheatstone and Cooke and of Mr. Bain, and became for a time almost the sole means by which telegraphic communication was carried on throughout the kingdom. Nor did it end there. Not content with transmitting news by electricity upon land, the thought was soon after conceived of causing it even to cross the mighty ocean, and a submarine telegraph was laid, first from Gosport to Portsmouth, then from Dublin to Holyhead, and soon after across the Channel from Dover to Calais. It was on September 27, 1851, that the first telegraphic message reached England from the French coast. The Submarine Telegraphic Company was then formed, and they constructed other lines from Dover to Ostend, Folkestone to Boulogne. And last, though not least, came the great Atlantic telegraph, with its wonderful wire perfectly insulated amidst the mass of water in the very depth of the ocean, connecting the old world with the American continent.

But we have not yet done with the wonders and curiosities of communication, for prominent among internal reforms stands the simple contrivance known as the penny postage, which so greatly facilitated intercourse with the most distant parts, cemented the bonds of family relationship, promoted the diffusion of knowledge, strengthened the cords of national life, and so contributed to unity of political feeling throughout the country. And it was a great reform. Only a few years before the lowest general post rate was fourpence, and even when the twopenny post was adopted that rate was only for the conveyance of a single letter from any post office in Great Britain to any place not more than eighty miles off, increasing according to distance, so that a letter from London to Edinburgh was charged 13*d.* In Ireland the postage rate was somewhat different, and between Great Britain and Ireland higher rates were charged. The general average charge on all single letters conveyed by the general post was between 7*d.* and 7¼*d.* We may well imagine what a check this high rate imposed on general intercourse, how unwilling the people were to write except in cases of

The post office.

absolute necessity, and in how many ways the high postage was evaded. The franking of letters had been greatly abused, it being quite common for members of parliament to sign a large packet of covers at once and to supply them to friends in large quantities. These were sometimes sold, and often given to servants in lieu of wages. And the smuggling of letters was very prevalent. The high rate of postage not only hindered social and commercial intercourse, but greatly injured the revenue, which for many years had remained quite stationary. It was under such circumstances that Mr. (now Sir) Rowland Hill set himself to study the postal system, and soon propounded his popular scheme of a uniform penny postage. As he analysed the cost of conveying a letter through the post office, Sir Rowland Hill found it to consist, first, of the expense of receiving and preparing the letter for the journey, and taxing each letter with a distinct rate of postage; secondly, of the cost of transit from post office to post office; and thirdly, of the expense of delivering the letters; whilst the rate of postage was made to depend entirely on the distance which constituted, in reality, but a small fraction of the cost. It seemed natural to charge more for a letter from London to Edinburgh than for one from London to Bristol, but in reality the greater distance made no material difference in the cost. The great expense arose from the difficulty of weighing each letter, detecting the slightest enclosure, and receiving the charge on delivery. Diminish these and a uniform rate becomes practicable. Hence the happy idea of a uniform penny postage for all letters, on condition of the prepayment of letters by stamped labels. The suggestion was the result of careful thought and study, and experience proved that the calculation was based on solid foundations. No sooner was the project made public than it attracted great and hearty support. Petition upon petition were presented to Parliament in favour of the scheme. Lord Brougham, who at once seized on the proposal, reminded the Lords of the reception given in 1784 to the postal reforms suggested by Mr. Palmer. Pressure was exercised from all quarters on the post office authorities, for the adoption of the penny postage. They however were hostile to any experi-

Sir Rowland Hill's scheme.

ment in that direction, and again and again replied that it was inexpedient and impossible. But a reform so needful and beneficent was not allowed to be stifled by the objections advanced by the officers of the post office, and in a short time from its first promulgation Sir Rowland Hill's plan was carried into effect. By it many important organic improvements were introduced, among which a large reduction in the rate of postage; the adoption of the charge by weight abolishing the charge for mere enclosures; the prepayment of correspondence; the simplification of the mechanism and accounts of the department; the establishment of a book post; increased security of valuable letters by reducing the registration fee; great extension of the money order system; more frequent and more rapid communication between the metropolis and the larger provincial towns; a vast extension of the rural deliveries; a great extension of free deliveries; greatly increased facilities for the transmission of foreign and colonial correspondence; a more speedy despatch of letters when posted; a more prompt delivery on arrival; and the division of London and its suburbs into ten postal districts. Into the practical results of the scheme, financially as well as socially, it is needless to enter. Its success has far exceeded all anticipations. Sir Rowland Hill calculated that the number of letters would increase fivefold, that the gross revenue would continue at about the same amount, and that the net revenue would suffer a loss of about 300,000*l.* The results showed that the letters increased not five, but eight or ten fold; that the gross revenue, instead of remaining the same, increased more than a million and a half; and that the net revenue, instead of diminishing by 300,000*l.*, rose more than 400,000*l.* The plan was on every aspect a remarkable one, and not only England but the world owes a deep debt of gratitude to the great originator of the penny postage.

CHAPTER VII.

CORN LAWS.

The Corn Laws.—The Corn Law of 1801.—The new Corn Law of 1804.—The Corn Law of 1816.—Injurious Effects of the Corn Laws.—The Sliding Scale of 1828.—Mr. Villiers' Motion.—Formation of the Anti-Corn Law League.—Mr. Villiers' Motion renewed.—Object of the Anti-Corn Law League.

The Corn Laws.

THE Corn Laws had long been a bone of contention in England, but being maintained for the interest of a class who clung to them as their anchor of safety, vain had hitherto been the effort to introduce a wiser and more beneficial policy. In the opinion of their advocates protection was necessary in order to keep certain poor lands in cultivation, and to encourage the cultivation of as much land as possible in order to provide for the wants of the country. Let the cultivation of such land cease, and we shall be dependent on foreigners for a large portion of the people's food. And such dependence will be fraught with immense danger, inasmuch as, in the event of war, the supplies may be stopped or our ports may be blockaded, the result of which may be famine, disease, or civil war. According to the defenders of protection it was the advantage gained by the Corn Laws that enabled landed proprietors and their tenants to encourage manufactures and trade. Abolish the corn laws and half the country shopkeepers will be ruined, mills and factories will be stopped, large numbers of the working classes will be thrown out of work, disturbances will ensue, capital will be withdrawn, and no one dare venture to say what may be the fatal consequences.

In 1801 the price of wheat reached the high limit of 155*s.* a quarter, and we may well imagine what sufferings that price entailed among the people, at a time especially when trade and manufacture were so much paralysed by the continental war. Happily, for two or three years afterwards, a succession of good harvests changed the condition of things, and in March, 1804, the price of wheat fell to 49*s.* 6*d.* per imperial quarter. But singularly, what was anxiously desired by the people was esteemed a great disaster by the agricultural interest. They complained that with the high cost of production, in consequence of high wages, high rate of interest, and the heavy cost of implements of husbandry, they could not afford to sell at such prices. Meetings were held throughout the country to consider the case of the farmers. Mr. Western brought the state of agriculture before the House of Commons, and a committee was at once appointed on the subject. The farmers contended that at a time when all foreign supplies were shut out from our markets, and when we were more than ever depending on home production, it was the bounden duty of the legislature to pass laws which would encourage the production of grain at home, so that the nation might be as much as possible independent as regards the first necessaries of life. But what if all the measures hitherto taken for the protection of the farmers resulted only in the aggravation of the sufferings of the people. It was easy by means of prohibitions and bounties to raise the price of corn and to give an artificial stimulus to agricultural prosperity, but the people were not able to buy bread at famine prices especially at a time when taxes were so heavy. The report of the committee of the House of Commons presented the same session in 1804, was to the effect that the price of corn from 1791 to the harvest of 1803 had been very irregular, but that upon an average it had increased in a great degree in consequence of the years of scarcity, and had in general yielded a fair profit to the grower. It appeared to the committee, moreover, that high prices had had the effect of stimulating agricultural industry in bringing into cultivation large tracts of waste lands; and that this fact, combined with the abundance of the two last productive seasons, and other causes, occasioned such a depression in the value of grain as would tend to the discouragement of agriculture, unless maintained by the support of Parliament. Nor was there much difficulty

The Corn Law of 1801.

in persuading the legislature to give heed to such recommendations. Very soon after the presentation of the report, a corn law was passed,[1] which imposed a duty of 24*s.* 2*d.* per quarter on wheat, when the price of home market should be under 63*s.*; of 2*s.* 6*d.* when the price should be at or above that rate, and under 66*s.*; and of 6*d.* a quarter when it should be above that rate. After all, however, the fear entertained by the farmers and the agricultural interest was not very substantial, for again, in 1804, the harvest was deficient in quantity, and inferior in quality, and all apprehensions that bread might become too cheap were entirely out of the question. A proposal indeed was made to encourage the growth of corn in Great Britain, and yet to diminish the price thereof for the benefit of the people by exempting farmers from all direct taxes. But that would have only transferred the burden from one class to another. The time had not yet arrived for acting on the 'laissez-faire' principle. Artificial aid was sought for on all sides, and that always ended in disappointment.

The Corn Law of 1804.

At the conclusion of the French war in 1815 precisely the same state of matters arose as in 1804. By the opening of the ports, wheat, which hitherto averaged 5*l.* 10*s.* a quarter, having suddenly fallen to 3*l.* 5*s.*, immediately the farmers raised a cry of distress. Again a committee of the House of Commons was appointed to inquire into the state of the law affecting the corn trade, and once more the legislature was engaged in framing a corn law,[2] which resulted in an act prohibiting the importation of wheat when the price was under 80*s.*, and rendering it free when above 80*s.* Yet serious misgivings existed as to the ultimate effect of the restrictive legislation respecting corn in the minds of many, and in the very House of Lords, which traditionally stood in bold defence of a protective policy, protests were lodged, which indicated the existence of a more enlightened opinion on the real bearings of the whole question. Lord Grenville and his compeers protested against this new corn law, because they were adverse in principle to all new restraints in commerce, deeming it most advantageous to public prosperity to leave uncontrolled the

The Corn Law of 1816.

[1] 44 Geo. III. c. 109. [2] 55 Geo. III. c. 26.

free current of national industry. In their opinion 'the great practical rule, of leaving all commerce unfettered, applied more peculiarly, and on still stronger grounds of justice as well as of policy, to the corn trade than to any other. Irresistible, indeed, must be that necessity which could, in their judgment, authorise the legislature to tamper with the sustenance of the people, and to impede the free purchase and sale of that article, on which depends the existence of so large a portion of the community. They thought that expectations of ultimate benefit from any corn law were founded on a delusive theory. They could not persuade themselves that such a law would ever contribute to produce plenty, cheapness, or steadiness of price. So long as it operated at all, its effects must be the opposite of these. Monopoly is the parent of scarcity, dearness, and uncertainty. To cut off any of the sources of supply can only tend to lessen its abundance. To close against ourselves the cheapest market for any commodity, must enhance the price at which we purchase it. And to confine the consumer of corn to the produce of his own country, is to refuse ourselves the benefit of that provision which Providence itself has made for equalising to man the variations of climate and of seasons. But, whatever might be the future consequences of that law, at some distant and uncertain period, they were convinced that these hopes must be purchased at the expense of a great and present evil. To compel the consumer to purchase corn dearer at home than it might be imported from abroad, was the immediate practical effect of the law just passed. In this way alone could it operate. Its present protection, its promised extension of agriculture must result (if at all) from the profits which it created by keeping up the price of corn to an artificial level. These future benefits were the consequences expected, though they confidently believed erroneously expected, from giving a bounty to the grower of corn by a tax levied on its consumers.' Such were the reasons urged against the corn law of 1815, and certainly they do honour to those who recorded them in the journal of the House. But many a year was to pass ere the protests of the few did become the deliberate conviction of the entire community.

For twelve years nothing further occurred on the subject of

the corn laws, except the emission of repeated cries of distress by the agricultural classes, especially in the House of Lords, which seemed always open to any amount of unmeasured language against the dreaded free trade in corn. But the country learnt by bitter experience how direct is the relation between dear bread and bad trade, and the time again arrived when the working of the corn law was to be laid before the legislature. 'The corn laws,' said Mr. Whitmore, 'have inflicted the greatest injury upon the general trade of the world that ever perhaps was produced by injudicious legislation. They have deranged its course, stagnated its current, and caused it to flow in new and far less beneficial channels than it formerly occupied. To the corn laws he attributed the great and ruinous fluctuation of prices, which is the inevitable result of a system of restriction. The more the basis from whence your supplies are drawn is widened, the greater the steadiness of prices; the more it is narrowed, the more constant and the more fatal is their effect on the fluctuations to which you are subject. In the early times, when there was a difficulty in the conveyance of bulky commodities from one part of the country to another, arising from want of roads, when there existed a prejudice as well as a legal penalty against what was called forestalling and regrating, the fluctuations in prices were immense. And the same holds good as regards other times and other countries.' Lord Lauderdale himself, notwithstanding his fear of foreign competition, clearly showed what are the solid and what the fictitious ways to agricultural prosperity. 'I will take upon myself,' he said, 'to assert, that if there is any one proposition in political economy which may be affirmed without qualification, and which admits of no exception, it is this, that the interests of landlords properly understood are absolutely identified with the general interests of the country. Landlords have no interest in high prices; high prices raise rents nominally and in appearance; and, now and then, some temporary advantage may be obtained from them for which landlords will always pay afterwards with more than compound interest; but rents can only be raised largely, permanently, and beneficially to landlords by one of two causes, both of which are equally conducive to the prosperity of all other classes; first, by improvements in agriculture, which leave a larger surplus produce after the expenses of cultivation are defrayed; and secondly, by improved and extended markets. Now all improvements of agriculture which increase the surplus produce of the country are obviously a direct addition to the public wealth. And how are markets improved and extended? By new communication—roads, railways, canals—but principally by the continual rise and increase of large towns within our own empire, rendered rich and prosperous by thriving manufactures, and by all the improvements in skill and machinery connected with such establishments. The best job for the landlord is the prosperity of trade in all its branches, as the best job for trade is a prosperous state of agriculture. There is nothing to make the inhabitant of the town and the cultivator of the soil jealous of each other; quite the contrary, for the more each produces the more he will have to exchange for the other; and this is the foundation of the great internal trade which is worth one hundred times more than all the foreign commerce of the country put together.'

Yet, notwithstanding all these truths, the farmers clung tenaciously to protection; and it was not without a great struggle that they allowed the corn laws to be relaxed to a small extent. In the session of 1827 resolutions were passed in the House of Commons, to the effect that corn might always be imported free of duty, in order to be warehoused, and that it should be admissible for home consumption at a shilling per quarter duty when the price of wheat should be 70*s.*, and at two shillings more for every shilling that the price fell below 70*s.* per quarter. These resolutions, however, made no progress, in consequence of the change of government. In the following session, the House of Commons passed other resolutions on the subject, to the effect of imposing a sliding scale from 23*s.* per quarter when the price of wheat should be 64*s.*, and 16*s.* 8*d.* when the price should be 69*s.*, to one shilling per quarter when the price should be at and above 73*s.* per quarter. And upon these bases a new corn law was passed,[1] which, like its predecessors, did not long remain in force.

The Corn Law of 1828.

[1] 9 Geo. IV. c. 38.

It was ten years after the passing of this first sliding scale, or on March 15, 1838, that Mr. Villiers, seconded by Sir William Molesworth, first commenced his attack on the policy of the corn laws in the House of Commons, but it had very little effect. In those days political economists were simply allowed to speak and complain. Their opinions were received as mere speculative theories, their recommendations as far beyond the reach of practical statesmanship. Hence there was only one minister present when the motion was made, and as might have been expected, it was lost by an overwhelming majority. But about that time a lecture was advertised to be delivered at Bolton, the birthplace of Arkwright and Crompton, on the corn laws, by a person quite a stranger to the town. It was a new subject for a lecture, and as the public mind was directed to the question the lecture drew a fair number of hearers. But the lecturer found, only when it was too late, that it was not easy to deal with economical questions before a mixed audience, and he completely broke down. The audience, not prepared for the disappointment, then became impatient and vociferous, and a riot was impending, when a youth, a medical student, rushed to the platform, and on the spur of the moment addressed the people on the subject in a vigorous and manly manner. The people were delighted at this turn, and Mr. Paulton won for himself enthusiastic admiration. On the news of such an event travelling to the neighbouring towns, the volunteer lecturer was overwhelmed with invitations to redeliver his address, and everywhere he captivated the audience with his eloquent attacks on monopoly and monopolists.

Mr. Villiers' first motion.

Then, too, Mr. Cobden first addressed the Manchester Chamber of Commerce on the subject, urging that body to petition for the repeal of the corn laws. And as the interest in the question grew and extended, and it became evident that a special and more popular agency was wanted for the purpose, in October of the same year seven men first united themselves with a view to establish an Anti-Corn Law Association. The list of the provisional committee was afterwards increased to thirty-seven, conspicuous among them being John Bright, George Wilson, and Richard Cobden. And the object of

Formation of the Anti-Corn Law League.

the association was declared to be to form a fund in order to diffuse information, by lectures or pamphlets, on the bearing of the corn laws, to defray the expense of petitioning, and, above all, to create an organisation to bring numbers together in such force and with such energy of purpose, as to secure the great object by the complete freedom of trade, by the destruction not only of the corn monopoly but of all the other monopolies bolstered up by this monster grievance. Small was the support at first obtained by this new association. Very few then appreciated its great moral importance. 'For the first two or three years of our agitation,' said Mr. Cobden, 'it was a very hopeless matter, and there was no eclat nor applause. . . We sat in a small room, and we had a dingy red curtain drawn across the room that we might not be chilled by the paucity of our number. Two or three were all that were here (Newall's Buildings) on one occasion, and I recollect saying to my friend Prentice, "What a lucky thing it is the monopolists cannot draw aside that curtain and see how many of us there are, for, if they could, they would not be much frightened."' It was not long, however, ere the small association began to manifest its power and influence, and when, aided by the powerful support of some at least of the leading journals, its voice resounded through the length and breadth of the land. Meetings and conferences then succeeded each other. From the manufacturing districts the movement spread to the metropolis, and with a clearly defined purpose in view, and with the highest economic authorities to appeal to in support of their principles, the Anti-Corn Law agitators made everywhere a profound and lasting impression.

On March 12, 1839, Mr. Villiers again brought the subject of the corn laws before the House of Commons, now however backed by a strong party both inside and outside the House. His motion was, 'That this House resolve itself into a committee of the whole House, to take into consideration the act 9 Geo. IV., regulating the importation of foreign grain.' Mr. Villiers showed that the corn laws were not beneficial to the agricultural interest, and that neither the agricultural labourer nor the farmer reaped from them any benefit. He asserted that the community at large

Mr. Villiers' motion.

suffered an immense loss through them, equal to a poll tax of 8s. a head, or a tax of 2l. on each family in the kingdom, and he demonstrated that commerce and shipping were greatly injured by them. Mr. Villiers' motion was seconded by Sir George Strickland, and on his side spoke Mr. Poulett Thomson, Sir William Molesworth, Mr. Grote, Mr. Clay, Lord Howick, Sir Henry Parnell, Mr. Ward, Lord John Russell, Mr. Hume, Mr. Fielden, and Mr. O'Connell; whilst against him were Sir James Graham, Sir Robert Peel, and a host of conservatives. The discussion was animated and well sustained, and after five whole nights' debate the votes were taken and the motion was lost by 195 to 342. In the House of Lords, too, a discussion was commenced on the subject. On March 14 the Earl of Fitzwilliam moved, 'That the act 9 Geo. IV. c. 60, entitled "An Act to amend the law relating to the importation of corn," has failed to secure that steadiness in the price of grain which is essential to the best interest of the country;' but the motion was lost by 24 against 224. A day after Lord Brougham moved, 'That this House do immediately resolve itself into a committee of the whole House, to take into consideration the importation of foreign corn.' But the motion met a similar fate, only seven having voted for it, and sixty-one against it. Slow is the progress of any measure in the House of Commons when any substantial reform is contemplated, but slower still is its advance in the House of Lords. Coming less in contact with the mass of the people, comparatively strangers to their feelings and wants, conservative by interest and hereditary policy, the peers of the realm are necessarily the last to admit the need of change, and the last to make concessions to the altered exigencies of the times. Nevertheless there have never been wanting enlightened members in the upper house who sought the maintenance and preservation of their order from that same law of progress on which all the institutions of the realm depend, and who, far from regarding their interests as antagonistic to those of other classes of society, had the wisdom to discern that we are all subject to the same laws, influenced by the same circumstances, and alike bound to obey those laws of nature, which, more than any human contrivance, determine the progress and prosperity of states.

The result of Mr. Villiers' motion in the House of Commons was not likely to discourage the Anti-Corn Law Association. On the contrary, it imparted to it a new life and a fresh impulse. Determined to persevere till the end, the agitators saw in the strength of their opponents only an additional cause for more energetic labours. A meeting was accordingly organised in London, and the same voice which first gave strength and vivacity to the Manchester gathering, was now heard exclaiming, 'We are the representatives of three millions of people, a far greater number of constituents than the House ever could boast of. We well know that no great principle was ever indebted to Parliament for success—the victory must be gained out of doors. The great towns of Britain have extended the right hand of fellowship to each other, and their alliance will be a Hanseatic league against the feudal corn law plunderers.' The Anti-Corn Law League was never a political organisation. For years it went on lecturing, distributing tracts, and acting as a peripatetic university in instructing the people on the evil of commercial monopoly. Never did it allow itself to be tempted to other political topics. The league did not even wish to interfere with the system of taxation, further than extinguishing, at once and for ever, the principle of maintaining taxes for the benefit of a particular class. 'If it be asked,' said Mr. Cobden, 'why it is that we, professing to be free traders in everything, should restrict the title of our association to that of the "National Anti-Corn Law League," I will explain the reason. We advocate the abolition of the corn law because we believe that to be the foster-parent of all other monopolies; and if we destroy that—the parent, the monster monopoly—it will save us the trouble of devouring all the rest.'

Object of the Anti-Corn Law League.

CHAPTER VIII.

COMMERCIAL CRISES.

1836 AND 1839.

Prospects of Commerce.—Committee on Trade and Navigation.—Commercial Excitement in 1836.—Number of Joint-Stock Companies.—The Bank of England and the Circulation.—The Banks of the United States.—The Crisis.—Great Distress in Trade and Manufactures.—Causes of the Crisis.—State of Trade in 1838.—Lord Overstone on the Currency.

THOUGH banking facilities had increased, it cannot be said that trade had yet become over prosperous. After the severe crisis of 1825–26, there was some improvement, but a series of deficient harvests from 1828 to 1831, when the price of wheat averaged 60s. to 66s. a quarter, the revolution in France, and a war between Russia and Poland, checked any substantial progress. The prices of produce were so low, that many India houses succumbed; and although there was all the while a considerable development of the productive power of the country, consumption never seemed to overtake production, and complete stagnation characterised every branch of business.

Prospects of commerce.

The complaints of trade found utterance in the House of Commons, when a committee was appointed in 1833 to inquire into the state of trade, manufactures, and shipping in the United Kingdom; but the evidence given before the committee was to the effect that there was no real distress among traders; that, on the contrary, the commerce and manufacture of the country were in a remarkably sound and healthy state; that they were carried on with adequate capital and reasonable returns, and that there was a general confidence in the prospect of improving markets for all the great staples both of imports and exports. Nor was it long ere this improvement manifested itself. By degrees the great depression of prices which prevailed for several years, gave place to considerable animation. Greater confidence began to be felt, a *bonâ fide* demand sprang up both at home

Committee on trade and shipping.

and abroad, and the stock of raw materials and colonial produce, instead of accumulating, underwent a sensible reduction. An abundant harvest in 1834 considerably strengthened the general tone, and added firmness to the value of all descriptions of property. In short, the state of trade decidedly improved, though, down to 1835, there was no sign of undue excitement, and prices of commodities, although in many cases at advanced rates, were not in any striking instance under the influence of speculation.

But the success which attended the formation of joint-stock banks in the metropolis and elsewhere, and the established fact that the railways already completed had proved a most profitable speculation, soon led to many projects for new lines of railways, and for joint-stock companies of a varied character,[1] and thus by degrees the share market gathered around itself all the commercial spirit of the nation, and became infinitely more attractive than the markets for produce or manufactures. Numerous were the companies formed for railway purposes. Then it was that the Great Northern, the South Western, South Eastern, London and Brighton, Drogheda and Belfast, and other principal lines were projected. Mining became a favourite branch of investment; coal, copper, slate, lead, and silver mining, each received a large share of public attention, and companies were brought out, involving the nation in immense monetary obligations. Banking companies, too, mustered largely, and many were the projects for speculative purposes which we should scarcely

Commercial excitement of 1836.

[1] The following are the objects and capital of the joint-stock companies of 1834–36:—

	Nominal capital.
Railways	£69,626,000
Mining companies	7,003,200
Packet and Navigation companies	3,533,000
Banking companies	23,750,000
Conveyance companies	500,000
Insurance companies	7,600,000
Investment companies	1,730,000
Newspaper companies	350,000
Canal companies	3,665,000
Gas companies	800,000
Cemetery companies	425,000
Miscellaneous companies	16,104,500
	£105,248,700

imagine could meet with any sympathy. Those were the days when companies could be formed and capital subscribed for a London Steam Coach Company, a Safety Cabriolet Carriage Company, a Substitute for Indigo Company, and a Floating Club House. Many loans, too, were contracted, foreign stock rose to a fictitious value, and joint-stock bank shares became the subjects of special favour. Altogether it was estimated that between 1835 and 1837, some 300 or 400 companies were started with a subscribed capital of nearly 100,000,000*l*. Again therefore a frenzy of speculation appeared in 1835–36 just as in 1825–26, but with this important difference, that whereas in the former crisis speculation was mostly directed to foreign loans and foreign mines, on this occasion it was mainly confined to national operations, many of which proved to be eminently useful.

The Bank of England and the circulation.

It is objected that the Bank of England remained too long passive in view of this important movement; that its circulation which, in January, 1834, was 18,000,000*l*., with 9,500,000*l*. of bullion in hand, after an increase of 1,000,000*l*. from April to September, returned to 18,000,000*l*.;[1] that at that limit it remained for nearly the

[1] The following table shows the amount of circulation and bullion from 1834 to 1837, thousands omitted:—

	Bank Circulation	Country Circulation	Total Circulation	Bullion
	£	£	£	£
1834 January 1 . .	18,216	10,152	28,368	9,448
April 1 . .	19,097	10,191	29,288	9,431
July 1 . .	18,805	10,518	29,413	8,695
September 23 .	19,126	10,154	29,280	7,695
December 18 .	18,304	10,659	28,963	6,720
1835 April 7 . .	18,591	10,420	20,011	6,329
June 30 . .	18,315	10,939	29,254	6,219
September 22 .	18,240	10,429	28,669	6,261
December 16 .	17,321	11,134	28,455	6,626
1836 April 5 . .	18,063	11,447	29,510	7,801
July 1 . .	17,899	12,202	30,101	7,362
September 22 .	18,147	11,733	29,880	5,719
December 15 .	17,361	12,011	29,372	4,545
1837 April 4 . .	18,432	11,031	29,463	4,071
June 27 . .	18,202	10,872	29,072	4,750
September 19 .	18,814	10,142	28,956	6,303
December 14 .	17,998	10,870	28,868	8,172

whole of 1835 and 1836, whilst the country circulation also was almost stationary at about 11,000,000*l.*; and that this was allowed whilst the bullion on hand was diminishing, so much so that towards the end of 1836 it fell as low as 4,500,000*l.* against an aggregate circulation of Bank of England and country circulation of 29,000,000*l.*; and that it was not till July, 1836, when too late, that the Bank raised the rate of interest to 4½ per cent., and in September to 5 per cent. Certainly there is much reason for this complaint, for when the directors of the Bank of England awoke from their slumbers, and resolved to refuse all bills having an indorsement of joint-stock banks of issue, a severe crash had already taken place, and the measures of restriction had only the effect of intensifying the paralysis.

Whilst matters were in this critical condition serious accounts arrived from the United States respecting the condition of their banks. To remedy the evil caused by the many bankruptcies among bankers in 1814, a charter was given to the United States Bank for twenty years. That bank had a capital of 25,000,000 dollars; it was the central bank of the United States; and the government had so far identified itself with it, as to hold shares in it to the amount of 7,000,000 dollars. But when, in 1834 the charter had to be renewed, the government refused a new charter, demanded to be repaid a portion of their capital invested in it, withdrew the government deposits, and distributed them among a number of banks. The privilege of the central bank at an end, competition for banking increased immensely. In 1834, there were 506 joint-stock banks in the United States, with a circulation of 94,000,000 dollars. In 1836, the number of banks increased to 567, with a circulation of 141,000,000 dollars; and, by 1837, there were 677 banks, with a circulation of 187,000,000 dollars. Nor were the banks much concerned about the payment of their notes, since by law the issuers were entitled to decline paying them on demand, by offering 24 per cent. interest to the holders during the period specie was withheld from them. Can we wonder that, with such a latitude, the banks became careless of the liability they undertook? A check, however, came upon the practice from an unexpected quarter. On July 11, 1837, President Jackson issued a circular to the receivers of

The banks of the United States.

public money in the Western and South-Western States, directing them to accept no payment for land but in specie, or in notes convertible into specie. And consequently all who wanted to purchase land were compelled to provide themselves with specie. Hence coin and bullion went in great quantities from New York and other Eastern States away to the Western States. The interest of money rose enormously. The banks were compelled to restrict their circulation and reduce their loans. And with a view to secure confidence, the Bank of the United States was compelled to issue notes or post bills at twelve months, payable in London and other cities, which were given out as securities. A complete panic then seized the commercial community; and, in the first three months of 1837, as many as 250 houses failed in New York alone, while the suspension of cash payments was very general. We may imagine what distress such a catastrophe produced on the trading interests of the United States. The most worthy and enterprising men of business were suddenly arrested in their progress. Merchants were unable to pay the manufacturers, and the manufacturers could no longer proceed with their work. With no money to pay, the spindle and the loom were alike stopped.

The crisis.

The reception of such tidings in this country whilst trade was in the perilous condition we have described, could not fail to create additional trouble and distress. The commercial relations between Great Britain and America have always been most intimate, and, at that particular time, an immense amount of business was carried on between them. There was something, moreover, in the mode in which such business was carried on that greatly increased the influence of the American crisis on British interests. Formerly, it was the practice of English houses having orders from the States to draw for the amount upon the transmission of the bills of lading and invoices to their correspondents. But subsequently, the leading American houses had established agents in this country, furnished with credits on the British houses connected with America, who allowed them to draw at four months' date upon the deposit of bills of lading and invoices. Had this precaution been carefully taken, no inconvenience would have arisen from the altered practice; but, unfortunately, even this security was in practice relinquished, and the American houses were able to carry on their operations entirely on credit obtained in England. The whole business was in the hands of seven large houses, six of them in London, and one in Liverpool, and these happened to be at that time under acceptances for 15,000,000*l*., for which they had no other security than the bills drawn on America as already described. When, therefore, the news reached this country of the great crash among the American bankers, the Bank of England, alarmed about the stability of many large houses in this country connected with them, sent orders to its agents in Liverpool to refuse their paper. And this was the commencement of a severe reaction and crisis in all branches of industry. Great gloom then gathered over our commerce, a panic set in in earnest, and bankruptcies, cessation of business, depreciation of goods and securities, prostration of trade, followed each other with wonderful rapidity.

Great distress in trade and manufactures.

In June, 1837, a large meeting was held at Birmingham, to consider what measures should be adopted, calculated to relieve the appalling state of commercial distress. At Nottingham a similar meeting was held, thousands of operatives being there employed on the roads by public subscription. At Manchester there were 50,000 hands out of employment, and most of those employed were working only half time. In Scotland there were many failures, and in Ireland the state of trade was still worse. Thus matters continued for some time, till by a restricted circulation, a higher rate of discount, large advances made by the Bank to banks and other houses, and by other means, the great strain of the crisis was removed, and eventually it did not leave any serious trace of ruin and bankruptcy. Serious losses there were, but in the end the storm only tended to cleanse the commercial atmosphere from many impurities.

Causes of the crisis.

To what shall we ascribe the occurrence of this crisis in the trade of the country? Many are ready to assert that it was due to excessive speculation stimulated by an over-issue of paper, and both the Bank of England and country banks have been censured for want of prudence. Yet it cannot be that the discredit of the country banks, or of their notes, aggravated the crisis, since in Liverpool and Manchester, where the crisis was most felt, the banks were not issuing their own but Bank of England notes. Probably a timely contraction of such notes, especially as the bullion diminished, might have somewhat checked speculation, or at any rate have given a wholesome warning of the approach of danger. But when we come to trace the crisis to its source, it will be found that banking operations had but little influence in producing it in comparison with those revolutions in trade and finance which often defeat the wisest calculations. In the United States the president attributed the crisis entirely to a redundancy of credit. In his message he said: 'The history of trade in the United States for the last three or four years affords the most convincing evidence that our present condition is chiefly to be attributed to an over-action in all the departments of business, an over-action deriving perhaps its first impulse from antecedent causes, but stimulated to its destructive consequences by excessive issue of bank paper, and by other facilities for the acquisition and enlargement of credit. In view of these facts, it would seem impossible for sincere inquirers after the truth to resist the conviction that the causes of the revulsion in both countries have been substantially the same. Two nations the most commercial in the world, enjoying but recently the highest degree of apparent prosperity, are suddenly, without any great national calamity, arrested in that career, and plunged into embarrassment and distress. In both countries have we witnessed the same redundancy of paper money, and other facilities of credit, the same spirit of speculation, the same partial success, the same difficulties and reverses, and, at length, the same overwhelming catastrophe.'

The year 1838 opened prosperously, the chief, if not the only adverse, event being a late and a deficient harvest, which led to a considerable rise in the price of grain, and consequently to a large importation of corn, causing bullion to flow out of the country. But there were other sources of danger. The state of credit all over Europe was bad, large sums of Dutch and other foreign securities were negotiated in this country, and the financial condition of America was regarded with great uneasiness. In 1839

State of trade in 1838.

the harvest was again unsatisfactory, and the drain of bullion continued constant and rapid; so rapid, indeed, that in September, 1839, it was reduced to 2,816,000*l.*, and the Bank of England was under the necessity of borrowing from the Bank of France 2,000,000*l.* The method pursued in this case was singular. The borrower was the Bank of England, the lender the Bank of France. But it being neither the practice of the Bank of England to draw foreign bills, nor of the Bank of France to make advances except in discount of bills or upon government securities, it was agreed that Messrs. Baring Brothers should draw upon certain bankers appointed in Paris to accept the bills, and that the Bank of France would undertake to discount them. Messrs. Baring then sold the bills in London and paid the proceeds to the Bank of England. But what was the rate of interest under circumstances so exceptional? At the commencement of 1839 the rate was only 3½ per cent.; it increased in May to 5, in June to 5½, and in October to 6 per cent. But the pressure did not last very long. Towards the end of the year it was nearly all over, and though the number of bankruptcies was large, the injury was not nearly so extensive in 1839 as it had been in 1837.

Lord Overstone on the currency.

The action of the Bank of England and other Banks of issue in relation to the condition of trade in 1836 and 1839 was reviewed at length by the committee on joint-stock banks in 1836, and by the committee on banks of issue in 1840. But the most severe censure was pronounced by Lord Overstone, in his remarks on the management of the circulation, and on the condition and conduct of the Bank of England, and of the country issues. To his reasoning on this important question we cannot revert; but the conclusions he arrived at were, that a strong remedy was required, and that it was expedient to secure, strengthen, and if possible to extend, the monopoly of the Bank of England as regards the currency, with the view of rendering the indirect control which she can exercise over subordinate issuers more powerful: that it was desirable to make some gradual approach towards the separation of its banking unctions from its management of currency, with the view of rendering the body which undertakes the latter duty free from all conflicting interests and motives, and at the same time make her responsibility distinct and complete, and the nature of its proceedings simple and easily understood; and that it was proper, in the meanwhile, to separate the accounts of the Bank of England, of the management of the currency, from every branch of its business, to subject the superintendence of this department to a separate committee of currency, and to associate with this committee a representative of government, whose presence should always be requisite to constitute the committee for business. In 1840 the question of the conduct of the currency was reopened by the appointment of a committee of the House of Commons to inquire into the effects produced on the circulation of the country by the various banking establishments issuing notes payable on demand, but the committee did not report fully on the subject, and only presented the large amount of evidence collected. Let it not be imagined that the Bank of England was guided by no principle in the regulation of its issues. Generally, and excepting under special circumstances, the Bank considered it quite sufficient to keep on hand securities bearing interest, to the extent of two-thirds of its liabilities, the remaining third being held in bullion and gold; any reduction of the circulation, so far as it might be dependent upon the Bank, being subsequently regulated solely by the foreign exchanges, or by internal extra demand. The object of retaining a fixed amount of securities by the Bank at a period of full currency, and continuing it afterwards, so far as it was practicable, was to throw the action of the increase or decrease in the circulation upon the public, with reference to the state of the foreign exchanges on the import or export of bullion. The rule had not been adhered to in several instances, and doubts were expressed as to the soundness of its principle as applicable to the Bank of England, from its mixing up deposits and circulation. But the Bank directors conceived that this rule had received some sort of legislative sanction, and they felt themselves bound to adhere to it as closely as circumstances would permit.

CHAPTER IX.

RELATION WITH INDIA AND CHINA. THE OPIUM WAR.

1830–1840.

Early Means of communication with India.—Privileges of the East India Company.—The Case of Monopolies.—Renewal of the Charter.—Remonstrances against the Monopoly.—Repeal of the Charter.—Triumphs of the East India Company.—Monopoly of the China Trade.—The Hong Merchants.—Introduction of Tea.—The Price of Tea.—British Relations with China.—The Opium Trade.—Prohibition of the use of Opium.—Seizure and Confiscation of Opium, and the Treaty of Nanking.

Early means of communication with India.

OF all the British possessions, India is doubtless the richest and the most important. Its wide territory, its mighty population, its rich treasures, its gorgeous scenery, and its motley races, all contribute to invest India with a charm sufficient to attract many nations to its shores; whilst its staple productions, its spices and aromatics, its precious stones and wrought silks and cottons, have been held in estimation among all civilised nations. During the middle ages the Italian republics were the channel by which the produce of the East found its way to Europe. By means of caravans, and the navigation of rivers, the produce of India found its way to the shores of the Mediterranean, and from the ports of that sea it was carried by the traders of Venice and Genoa to the different countries in the North of Europe. But great was the hardship endured in the conveyance of such merchandise. Whichever route was chosen, it was equally difficult and dangerous. Some traders took the way of the Persian Gulf to cities on the Tigris and Euphrates, regions where Solomon built cities, 'Tadmor in the wilderness, and store cities in Hamath,' making Babylon and Nineveh the Manchester and Birmingham of Mesopotamia; and thence brought their goods, by means of caravans, to cities along the eastern shores of the Mediterranean, enriching in its course Antioch, Palmyra, Tyre, Sidon, and the whole of the seaports of Phœnicia and Palestine. Others went by caravans, through Beloochistan and Persia, to the cities of Syria, and along the shores of the Caspian Sea to the towns on the Euxine. Others went to the north, through China, across the deserts of Tartary, to Moscow and the cities of Central Europe; and others, again, took the way of the Red Sea to cities in Arabia, and in after time to Alexandria in Egypt. We know how extensively the Tyrians traded with India; how they brought into Palestine all sorts of rarities of blue cloths and broidered work, in chests of rich apparel, bound with gold and made of cedar. That was indeed the age of romance in commercial enterprise, but time changed all this. When Vasco di Gama doubled the Cape of Good Hope, and found a passage by sea to the land of promise, the course of trade was turned in another direction. Instead of the plodding Italians came the daring Portuguese and the industrious Dutch, and nation after nation appeared in the field, till the English arrived, who might well say with Waller—

> Ours is the harvest where the Indians mow;
> We plough the deep, and reap where others sow.

It was on December 31, 1600, that the East India Company[1] was first incorporated, for fifteen years, with the exclusive privilege of trading to all parts of Asia, Africa, and America, beyond the Cape of Good Hope eastward to the Straits of Magellan; except such countries or ports as may be in the actual possession of any Christian prince in amity with the Queen. The company was invested with great prerogatives. It had the right to make peace and war, to maintain forces by sea and by land, to make laws, to inflict penalties, to grant exemptions, and to impose customs duties. It was, moreover, allowed to export annually 30,000*l.* of the precious metals, then the principal means of exchange with India, on condition of reimporting an equal amount of the

Privileges of the East India Company.

[1] The company was constituted 'one bodie corporate and politique in deed, by the name of "The Governour and Company of Merchants of London, trading unto the East Indies."'

same within six months after the accomplishment of a voyage. The first expedition took place in 1661 with five ships under the command of Lancaster. They approached Acheen in Sumatra, and thence they sailed to Java, from which place Lancaster sent a ship to Malacca, laden with a rich cargo of spices. He loaded also other ships with other products of India, and came back to England after an absence of two years and a half. The success of the first voyage stimulated many others. But as yet they were undertaken on the personal account of the adventurers, each of whom provided the necessary funds. It was only in 1613 that a social fund of 418,000*l.* was subscribed by the company in equal shares. By that time the company had obtained important advantages from the Grand Mogul at Delhi, especially the power to establish a factory at Surat, on the coast of Malabar; and other factories had been established for trading in other localities, without the least intention, however, of constituting them forts or places of strength for territorial conquest. But the company excited the jealousy of the Dutch and Portuguese, and dissensions and wars were the consequence.

The case of monopolies.

During the civil war in England, the commerce of India was neglected, and the affairs of the company were much embarrassed; so much so, that in the interregnum, Cromwell dissolved the company, and for three years the trade was left free. But the company was soon reinstated, and, favoured by Fortune's smiles, it became possessed of the island of Bombay, which Charles II. received as a marriage portion from Catherine of Aragon. The great difficulty, however, of the company was to keep out interlopers, who tried to wrest some portion of the Indian trade from their hands, so that when the charter was renewed in 1683, they obtained power to seize any ship and merchandise of such interlopers. But the legality of such power was tried in the great cause of Captain Sandys, 'the case of monopoly,' and which ended in favour of the interloper, all monopolies being against common law. Yet the king interdicted Captain Sandys from trading in the East Indies, and so the company preserved its privileges intact. In 1698, a new company was formed styled 'The English Company Trading to the East Indies,' and, for a time, two corporations existed, both pretending an exclusive right to trade in the same country; but it was soon found that two companies belonging to the same nation could not carry on the same trade either with profit to themselves or to the benefit of the country. The London Company had besides purchased the greatest part of the shares of the English Company, and thus the whole subject having been referred to Lord Godolphin, the two companies were united in 1702. In progress of time, however, as we have already seen, in consequence of their military exploits, under the leadership of Clive, the company acquired extensive possessions in India, by which, without ceasing to be a commercial company trading in a foreign state, it became, for all intents and purposes, a state in a state. And partly in consequence of this change, and partly through the financial difficulties in which the company was involved, a board was appointed in 1780 to control all the operations which in any wise related to the civil or military government or revenue of the territories and possessions of the East India Company.

Renewal of the charter.

Ten years after this, previous to the renewal of the charter in 1793, a searching inquiry was instituted into the effect of the monopoly exercised by the company in the Indian trade; and though the charter was renewed till 1813, power was granted to private traders to export to India any article of British produce or manufacture, except military stores, ammunition, masts, spars, cordage, pitch, tar, and copper; and the company's civil servants and free merchants in India were allowed to ship on their own account and risk, all kinds of Indian goods, except calicoes, dimities, muslins, and other piece goods; such imports or exports, however, to be in the company's ships only, the company appropriating 3,000 tons of shipping for the use of private traders. But the trade continued very limited, although great were the efforts of the company and greater still the eagerness of private traders to promote it. It was indeed evident that so long as the trade was fettered by monopoly the commerce with India could never develop itself to its legitimate proportions.

Thus matters continued till 1813, when, as we have already narrated, the charter, being about to expire, considerable efforts were made to abolish the monopoly. The merchants of London, Liverpool, Manchester, Glasgow, Paisley, Greenock, Birmingham, petitioned both Houses of Parliament against the renewal of the charter and the maintenance of the monopoly. They asked that free trade be proclaimed in the whole trade with India and China; they represented the need of opening new markets since European commerce was at an end; they appealed to the distress in the country through want of trade; they showed what large fields of commerce were still uncultivated, and how scanty were the fruits from the trading of the East India Company. But the government was prevailed upon to renew the charter for twenty years longer, and a bill was introduced by Lord Castlereagh for the purpose. There was a great discussion. The first clause for the renewal of the charter passed without a division. The second clause for continuing to the company the exclusive privilege of trade with China for the twenty years was met by an amendment by Mr. Canning, limiting the privilege to ten years; but the amendment was lost by a majority of sixty to twenty-nine. The clause granting to the company the exclusive trade in India was opposed and rejected, and, thus far curtailed, the monopoly of the East India Company was confirmed, so far as China was concerned, till 1831.[1]

Remonstrances against the monopoly.

But the time came, when this most successful of all commercial companies, this most powerful of all commercial monopolies, this company which for a century had ruled nearly the whole of the Indian continent, and exercised, moreover, unlimited control over the trade of China, Japan, Siam, and other countries in Asia, containing nearly one-third of the human race, was called upon to renounce for ever its commercial character, and to become, for a time at least, only an instrument for governing the vast territory of British India. The time came when that mercantile career, which had been the source of all other triumphs, and the cause of its abundant wealth, had at last to be entirely extinguished; when that monopoly, which had received such universal condemnation, could no longer be sustained, and when the action of the company was thenceforth

Repeal of the charter.

[1] 53 Geo. III. c. 155.

to become exclusively of a political character.[1] It is needless to advert to the shortcomings of the company now that it is virtually defunct. Apart from the evil inherent in commercial restrictions and monopolies of any kind, apart from the doubtful policy pursued by the company towards native rulers, it is impossible to withhold a tribute of admiration to a corporation of merchants who, with less eclat and fewer privileges than were conceded to their rival companies in France, Holland, and Portugal, succeeded, by dint of great energy and much practical wisdom, in overcoming all obstacles, and not only in acquiring the most princely fortunes, but actually in securing for Britain an empire the most splendid and sumptuous which human ambition could ever aspire to possess.

Triumphs of the East India Company.

In graphic and eloquent language did Macaulay depict the triumphs of the East India Company, when the great question was discussed in the House of Commons on 'July, 10, 1833.' 'In what state did we find India, and what have we made of India? We found society throughout that vast country in a state to which history scarcely furnishes a parallel. The nearest parallel would perhaps be the state of Europe during the fifth century. The Mogul empire in the time of the successors of Aurungzebe, like the Roman empire in the time of the successors of Theodosius, was sinking under the vices of its internal administration, and under the assaults of barbarous invaders. At Delhi, as at Ravenna, there was a mock sovereign or mere pageant, immured in a gorgeous state prison. He was suffered to indulge in every sensual pleasure. He was adored with servile prostration. He assumed and bestowed the most magnificent titles. But, in fact, he was a mere puppet in the hands of some ambitious

[1] 3 & 4 Wm. IV. c. 85. The progress of the trade with India and China during the last twenty years of the monopoly of the East India Company was considerable. In 1814 the declared value of British produce and manufactures exported from the United Kingdom to India and China conjointly was 2,113,000l. In 1831 the value exported to India alone was 2,576,000l. and to China 815,000l. From India to China the value of produce and manufacture exported in 1813–14 was 1,324,000l., and in 1833–34 3,559,000l. In 1814 there were imported from India and China conjointly 2,850,000 lbs. cotton, 26,000,000 lbs. tea, and 1,116,000 lbs. silk. In 1831 there were imported from India alone 33,000,000 lbs. cotton, and from China 32,000,000 lbs. tea, and 682,000 lbs. silk. The total exports of the three Indian Presidencies in 1831 amounted to 9,671,000l.

subject; while the Honori and Augustuli of the East, surrounded by their fawning eunuchs, revelled and dozed without knowing or caring what might pass beyond the walls of their palace gardens. The provinces had ceased to respect a government which could neither punish nor protect them. Society was a chaos. Its restless and shifting elements formed themselves every moment into some new combinations, which the next moment dissolved. In the course of a single generation, a hundred dynasties grew up, flourished, decayed, were extinguished, were forgotten. Every adventurer who could muster a troop of horses might aspire to a throne. Every palace was every year the scene of conspiracies, treasons, revolutions, parricides. Meanwhile, a rapid succession of Alarics and Attilas passed over the defenceless empire. A Persian invader penetrated to Delhi, and carried back in triumph the most precious treasures of the house of Tamerlane. The Affghan soon followed, by the same track, to glean whatever the Persian had spared. The Jauts established themselves on the Jumna. The Sikhs devastated Lahore. Every part of India, from Tanjore to the Himalayas, was laid under contribution by the Mahrattas. The people were ground down to the dust by the oppressor without and the oppressor within, by the robber from whom the nabob was unable to protect them, by the nabob who took whatever the robber had left to them. All the evils of despotism and all the evils of anarchy passed at once on that miserable race. They knew nothing of government but its exactions. Desolation was in their imperial cities, and famine all along the banks of their broad and redundant rivers. It seemed that a few more years would suffice to efface all traces of the opulence and civilisation of an earlier age. Such was the state of India when the company began to take part in the disputes of its ephemeral sovereigns. About eighty years have elapsed since we appeared as auxiliaries in a contest between two rival families for the sovereignty of a small corner of the peninsula. From that moment commenced a great and stupendous process, the reconstruction of a decomposed society. Two generations have passed away, and the process is complete. The scattered fragments of the empire of Aurungzebe have been united in an empire stronger and more closely knit together than that which Aurungzebe ruled. The power of the new sovereign penetrates their dominions more completely, and is far more completely obeyed than was that of the proudest princes of the Mogul dynasty.'

Great, however, as were the results of the cessation of the mercantile character of the East India Company upon our relations of trade with India herself, greater still, and even more striking, were the consequences which flowed from the abolition of their exclusive trading with China.

Monopoly of the company in the trade of China.

From the day when Marco Polo first visited the kingdom of Kathay many were the embassies, and many the overtures, addressed to the Chinese government for the inauguration of direct relations with Britain and other European states, but all to no effect. But the utmost that could be obtained was a kind of clandestine trade through the East India Company.[1] Was it proper, was it well, that a chartered company should have the sole right to carry on a trade of such vast dimensions? Can monopoly be beneficial at any time? A justification for it was offered, based on the exclusive and peculiar character of the Chinese. It was alleged that a people which had learned to dwell alone for so many centuries, and which was proud of its own civilisation and industry, would have extreme difficulties in first coming into contact with the foreign traders of the West, especially had they acted without any control or supervision. The East India Company, in support of its pretensions to maintain the long coveted monopoly, asserted that it might have proved a hard problem for the Chinese government to solve how to deal with the casual and unconnected adventurers who first traded to China—entire strangers to the habits, customs, and languages of the natives, as well as irreconcilably differing from them in respect of national characteristics. And it was assumed that, under such circumstances, the action of a well-regulated

[1] The trade of the United Kingdom and of British subjects with China was by law vested in the East India Company, until April 1831. The Russians were excluded from Canton in consequence of the privilege they enjoyed of trading with China overland. The French, the Dutch, the Swedes, and the Danes, resorted to Canton, but their trade was very insignificant. The American trade with China increased since 1814, and was popular there in consequence of the large importation of dollars.

company, acting with honour and prudence, calculated to inspire confidence and encourage intimacy of relations, was of great benefit. But such allegations did not agree with the evidence that the Chinese have always been keen to engage in trade; whilst, as to the advantage of a well-regulated company over private traders, it was greatly neutralised by the fact that the company had ceased practically to be a purely commercial company, and had acquired all the character of a military power.

As it was, the relations between the East India Company and China continued for a long time trammelled and restricted. The Chinese government made fitting regulations for the management of trade with foreigners, so as to prevent any evil which might result from their presence. Their permanent residence in China was forbidden. Care was taken that their ships should be disarmed upon their arrival in Chinese waters. And, instead of allowing them to trade with the natives generally, the whole of the foreign trade was specially limited to certain Chinese or 'Hong' merchants, who were required by their license to become jointly and severally responsible to the government, not only for the duties and charges on their trade with foreigners, but for their orderly behaviour and good conduct. By degrees, and by constant contact, the jealousy of the Chinese towards the East India Company gave way; but the strange combination of the mercantile and warlike character which the company presented was not likely to allay their fear and to remove their prejudices. Canton was the place where the Hong merchants and the East India Company carried on their dealings. The Canton factory of the company consisted of twelve supercargoes and eight writers, a surgeon, an assistant, a tea inspector and his deputy; and, for a long time, the practice was to barter British manufactures for tea.

The Hong merchants.

Tea was quite a new article to this country, though the tea plant had been cultivated in China, and even in India from very remote antiquity. It is not mentioned in the Bible, but an account of it was given by some Arabian travellers who visited China about the year 850 of the present era. When the first Russian ambassador to China was about to

Introduction of tea.

depart from the court of the Mogul in 1630, he was offered a quantity of tea as a present to the czar, but the ambassador declined to receive it, as it would only encumber him with a commodity for which he had no use. The Dutch East India Company were the first to introduce it into Europe, and a small quantity came to England from Holland in 1666. The East India Company thereafter ordered their agent at Bantam to send home small quantities, which they wished to distribute as presents, but its price was 60s. per lb., and it was little thought of. Twenty years elapsed before the company first decided on importing tea, but by degrees it came into general use. In 1712 the imports of tea were only 156,000 lbs.; in 1750, they reached 2,300,000 lbs.; in 1800, 24,000,000 lbs.; in 1830 30,500,000 lbs., and in 1870 141,000,000 lbs.

The price of tea.

We paid dearly for our tea under the company's monopoly. Without any competition to furnish any check, and with no knowledge whatever of the Chinese trade and products, we scarcely knew in this country whether tea was sold at a fair price, or whether the company was making extortionate gains. Yet a comparison could be made between the prices ruling in England and those on the Continent. Comparing the price of tea sold by the company in 1828–29 with the prices of the same qualities sold in Hamburg, it was found that we paid an excess of not less than 1,800,000*l*. There were consumed in this country 20,000,000 lbs. of Congou, which were sold by the company at 2*s*. 4*d*. per lb., whilst the same quality was sold at Hamburg at 1*s*. 2½*d*. per lb., being an excess in charge of 1*s*. 1½*d*. per lb. or 50 per cent.[4] How was this? What justification was there for such an excess? Did not the law furnish any protection to the public? The act of 1784 prescribed that there should be at least four sales a year, at which there should be put up such quantities of tea as were

[4] The import duty on tea was reduced by Mr. Pitt in 1784 to 12½ per cent. But the financial exigencies of the war caused a return to the heavy duty of 90 per cent. *ad valorem*, at which rate it remained till 1819, when it was raised to 100 per cent. on all tea worth above 2*s*. per lb. at the company's sales. In 1834 the duties were changed to 1*s*. 6*d*., 2*s*. 2*d*., and 3*s*., according to quality. In 1836 the duty was made uniform at 2*s*. 1*d*., to which 5 per cent. was added in 1840, and at that rate it remained till 1850, when Mr. Gladstone reduced it first to 1*s*. 10*d*. and then to 1*s*. 6*d*.

judged equal to the demand, and that the tea so put up should be sold to the highest bidder offering 1*d.* per lb. beyond the putting up price, which should include the prime cost thereof, freight and charges of importation, interest, and insurance. The company acted to the letter of this act. But what was the first cost? Not the price at which they purchased the tea from the Hong merchants, but the price of the manufactures which they gave for it, including the cost of all the machinery for conducting the trade, the expense of the Canton factory, and of all the paraphernalia of that concern, with the addition of an extraordinary charge by way of estimating the tael of silver at 6*s.* 4*d.*, while the proper value was only 5*s.* 3*d.* This is what the British nation paid for the company's monopoly of the China trade, a monopoly not limited to the trade between England and China, but extending also to the trade between India and China; no private merchant being able to send a ship from Calcutta or Bombay to Canton without a license from the company.

As soon as the monopoly of the East India Company of the trade with China ended, the British government sought to open direct communication with the Chinese government, and for that purpose Lord Napier was appointed to proceed to China as chief commissioner. On his arrival, first at Macao and then at Canton, in July, 1834, Lord Napier, according to instructions, addressed himself to the viceroy announcing his arrival. Instead, however, of receiving a cordial reception, he only met with a contemptuous refusal on the part of the Chinese celestials to recognise either his character or his mission. Might not such a reception be ascribed to the fact that, instead of sending a civilian, we sent a military officer, backed by marines and men-of-war? Whatever be the reason, Lord Napier, indignant at the Chinese government, forthwith requested the superior officer to proceed with the 'Imogene' and 'Andromache' to the anchorage of the trade at Whampoa; but, as the frigates passed the batteries off the Boca Tigris, fire was opened upon them, and thus in an instant we passed from peace to war. Notwithstanding this encounter, the local government of Canton agreed that trade should be reopened, provided the chief commissioner would retire from Whampoa to Macao; and

British relations with China.

two edicts were published, calling on the English merchants to elect a taepan, or a commercial chief, to control the English shipping, and to prevent smuggling; but no notice was taken of such edicts. Meanwhile, Lord Napier died at Macao, and Mr. Davis, who had long been resident in China, succeeded him. In 1835, Mr. Davis embarked for England, leaving Sir George Robinson as his successor, and for a couple of years nothing occurred to disturb the amicable relations between Britain and China.

The opium trade.

A cause, however, of great annoyance and difficulty between the two countries, was the smuggling of opium in open violation of the imperial laws of China. So far as the Indian government was concerned the opium monopoly was from the first a simple question of revenue. The poppy had been cultivated in India for centuries, and under the Mogul dynasty a considerable revenue was derived from opium. When the subject first attracted the attention of the Bengal government in 1786 Lord Cornwallis decided that the best method of raising a revenue from opium was by a system of monopoly from the ryots or native cultivators; and, in order to secure the most effectual supervision and control, the cultivation of the poppy was confined to the provinces of Behar and Benares. China had long been an open market for opium; but the Turkey opium and Malva opium sent from Central India threatened to destroy the revenue of the Indian government, and therefore in self-preservation it entered into treaties with many independent states for the purpose of controlling the cultivation of the poppy by payment of stipulated sums to the rulers of such states. These treaties lasted till 1830, and after that the government ceased to interfere with the culture of the poppy, and for a specified sum granted a pass which secured a free transit to a chest of opium from Malacca to Bombay. What, however, the Indian government had not attempted, viz. the smuggling of opium into China, the English merchant had vigorously pursued. The first small adventure of the kind was attempted in 1733. In 1780 an opium depôt was established in Lark's Bay, and soon after a direct shipment was made to Canton, which produced considerable profit. As yet, however, the importation of opium into China was permitted at a fixed duty, and the transaction was therefore only an evasion of the revenue law.

But in 1796, in consequence of the injurious effects of the drug on the health and morals of the people, the emperor issued a proclamation prohibiting the use of opium, as well as the importation of the same. And finding, that the prohibition was constantly set at nought by smugglers, in 1816 an edict was issued imposing penalties upon all foreign vessels which brought opium into the Canton river, and holding the Hong merchants responsible both for the discovery whether any vessel had opium on board and for the due exaction of the penalties. But it made no difference. The opium remained on board the vessel at Whampoa, and thence the smugglers took it in long boats pulling twenty to thirty muffled oars, fully armed and equipped, in defiance of the Mandarin boats placed to watch them. Foiled in his endeavours, the Chinese government resolved to compel opium ships to retire from Whampoa, but the smugglers retired into the outer waters, where none of the existing laws could take effect upon them, and resorted in the first instance to the anchorage about Macao. Thither, however, the viceroy followed their movements, and they then retired to Lintin, which became the place of constant resort and permanent anchorage of the foreign vessels connected with the opium traffic. Again, on November 3, 1834, an imperial edict was issued, imposing penalties on those who might take the opium from the ships, on the officers who might be negligent in keeping guard, on those who should take fees for conniving at the breach of the law, and on those who should melt or prepare opium. And the edict threatened a complete stoppage of trade should this smuggling be persisted in; but all was to no effect. On September 9, 1836, another imperial decree was issued, formally prohibiting the opium traffic; and the viceroy of Canton also issued an order against the continuance of receiving ships in the outer water. But the foreign merchants paid no regard to the edict, and their ships continued at Lintin. The Hong merchants having reported this to the viceroy, orders were given to expel such ships; yet they remained in the offing as before, and smuggling continued as ever, though the seizures increased both in the river and on board the foreign boats.

Prohibition of the use of opium.

In 1838, however, the boats resisted the search, and, in defiance of all laws, a British merchant was concerned in bringing some opium up to Canton, which was discovered and seized. The Hong merchants interfered, as they were responsible for such infractions of the law; and matters were about to become critical, when, on July 12, 1838, Captain Elliot, the British superintendent of the trade of British subjects in China, accompanied by two ships of war, proceeded to Canton to seek a reception, and forwarded an open letter for transmission to the governor. But no reception was granted, and a British boat having passed the Boca Tigris was fired upon.

Confiscation of opium. Treaty of Nanking.

A proclamation was then issued to foreigners announcing the arrival of an imperial commissioner to put a stop to the opium traffic, and forthwith an edict was issued, demanding the instant delivery of every particle of opium, under threat of immediate forfeiture. The edict was executed to the letter, and Captain Elliot having required of the merchants the surrender into his hands of all the opium, he gave up the whole of it to the Chinese officials, and thus upwards of 20,000 chests of the noxious narcotic were abandoned and lost. But no sooner did one trouble end than another began. In August an affray took place at Macao, between English sailors and Chinese villagers, in which a Chinese was killed. Commissioner Lin demanded that the murderer should be given up, but Captain Elliot refused. And in retaliation the commissioner prohibited any provision or other articles to be supplied to the British at Macao; in consequence of which the superintendent left Macao and invited all who wished to quit the place to follow him. Further complications afterwards arose, and in the end a war arose, which was concluded by the treaty of Nanking on August 29, 1842, by which British subjects were allowed to trade at Canton, Amoy, Foochowfoo, Ningpo, and Shanghai, Hong Kong was ceded to Britain, the value of the opium confiscated, six million dollars, was repaid, the monopoly of the Hong merchants abolished, and three million dollars due by them repaid, and an indemnity of twelve million dollars agreed to be paid between 1843 and 1845.

CHAPTER X.

THE COLONIAL TRADE.

Colonial Legislation.—Custom Duties in the Colonies.—The Sugar Duties.—Differential Duties.—Free and Slave Labour.—Consumption of Slave-grown Produce.

THERE remained much to be done as regards colonial legislation. Although Mr. Huskisson intended that there should be an open trade between the colonies and foreign countries, he did not enact this by positive legislation. He only gave power to the crown to adopt open trade with any country willing to meet us on equitable terms; and, in consequence of this measure, the crown entered into treaties with foreign powers with respect to the navigation laws. But this reciprocity principle was after all of limited application. Many countries had no advantages to offer us in exchange. Many were shut up in their own mistaken views of commercial policy; and, with all these, the commerce of the colonies was hermetically shut. Was it wise to cripple our own trade, or the trade of our colonies, because foreign countries chose to cripple theirs? There was an obvious fallacy in the reciprocity principle. It seemed indeed plausible, and even reasonable, but it did not stand the test of scrutiny. Its advocates said: 'We are friends to free trade; we grant all the benefit which you tell us will arise from an unrestricted interchange of commodities between different nations; we agree to all your reasoning; but, in order that there should be a free interchange, it is necessary that the removal of our restricted regulations should be met by corresponding measures on the part of other nations. If this be not the case, we are giving away the advantage we possess of supplying at least ourselves with our own productions; we throw open our ports to receive

Colonial legislation.

the produce of the industry of foreign countries, whilst they shut their gates to ours, and we destroy our national industry in those articles in the production of which foreigners excel us without their becoming in their turn customers of ours.' But as Mr. Poulett Thompson observed, 'The fallacy of this reasoning lies in this: these gentlemen misunderstand the nature of trade. In order to buy we must also sell. We may open our ports to the silks and wines of France, to the corn of Germany and Russia, to the drugs of Asia and of India; but we can get no pound's worth of any commodity without giving in return a pound's worth of our own productions. Our manufacturers will give away nothing; they will not send their goods to foreign ports without getting an equivalent in return; and I will venture to say that the producers of foreign commodities of French silks, of German cloth, with which, according to these gentlemen, this country has been and will be overwhelmed, are as little likely to make a present to the British consumer of their hard worked produce without taking in return the staple articles of this country.' Unfortunately, whilst we were discussing the point the colonies were suffering. But there was another colonial grievance which also demanded correction.

Custom duties in the colonies.

Some of our British colonies, especially the West Indies and Canada, had a customs legislation framed exclusively for the interest of the mother country. No article was more important to the West Indies for ordinary consumption than fish, yet no fish was allowed to be imported except the produce of our fisheries. Lumber, staves, and other articles necessary for manufactures, as well as flour and provisions, were charged the immoderate rates of 30 to 40 per cent., and foreign manufactures had to pay a duty of from 20 to 30 per cent. Not only, therefore, were many colonies precluded from having direct relations with foreign countries, but they had to pay for such goods as they received a high and heavy tax to benefit the manufacturers of Great Britain. Nor was there any uniformity in the levying of such duties. Whilst the West Indies and Canada charged from 30 to 40 per cent., the Cape of Good Hope and New South Wales charged only from 3 to 10 per cent. It was reserved for Mr. Labouchere, in 1841, to effect a great reform by doing away with all prohibitions, and reducing the duties to very moderate amounts. In introducing his measure Mr. Labouchere justly said, 'We have to legislate for a great empire, whose interests are deeply affected by the trade regulations which we lay down; and it is important that the empire should know that the spirit in which we legislate for it is not a feeling of narrow jealousy, watching only the peculiar interests of those whom we represent, but a wide and comprehensive desire to confer equal benefit on all parts of the empire, and on all the various classes of its multifarious people. I cannot forget that it is by perseverance in a system of monopoly and exclusion that other great colonial empires have fallen to pieces. A great colonial empire is indeed glorious, but it is at least uncertain; and the only way in which colonial possessions are to be kept together is by acting towards them all in a spirit of equal and impartial justice, treating them all with parental kindness, not allowing any favourite in the family, and considering their greatness and their prosperity and happiness our prosperity and happiness.' The proposals of the government did not meet with much opposition, and thus another great advance was made in the adoption of a just policy towards the colonies.[1]

Another important measure connected with the colonies was the equalisation of the sugar duties. In 1836 the duties on East and West India sugar were already equalised, but not so the duties on colonial and foreign sugar. It was only during the reign of King James that sugar was specially mentioned in our tariff, and for a long time the importation was unimportant. At the commencement of the present century the quantity imported was 4,000,000 cwt., and during the whole period of the war, from 1801 to 1814, the average consumption in the United Kingdom was only 18 lbs. 7 oz. for each individual, the average rate of duty being 26*s.* 2*d.* per cwt. After the war, the social condition of the people being far from satisfactory, the consumption somewhat lessened, whilst our policy of excluding all foreign grown sugar, and especially slave-grown sugar,

The sugar duties.

[1] 1 & 2 Vict. c. 113.

by a prohibitory duty of 3*l.* 3*s.* per cwt., rendered any chance of improvement morally impossible. A differential duty was also imposed upon Mauritius and East India sugar, which continued till 1825 as regards Mauritius, and till 1836 as regards the East India. In 1840, Mr. Ewart moved that all British sugar should be charged a duty of 24*s.*, and all foreign sugar a duty of 34*s.* per cwt., but the motion was lost by 27 to 122. On May 7, 1841, Lord John Russell described the condition of the British West Indies after the abolition of slavery, and showed how, after a momentary state of suspense, those colonies had already returned to a state of prosperity. He described the distress which existed in the manufacturing districts; a considerable portion of the working population of the country being unable to enjoy the ordinary necessaries and comforts of life. The revenue was, moreover, declining. The taxes were not producing as much as was required; and he moved that, 'Considering that it is practicable to supply the present inadequacy of the revenue to meet the expenditure of the country by a judicious alteration of protective and differential duties without any material increase in the public burdens, such a course will, in the opinion of the House, promote the interests of trade, afford relief to the industrious classes, and is best calculated to provide for the maintenance of public faith and the general welfare of the people.' But a strenuous opposition was made to the proposal, not only by the advocates of a restrictive policy, but by those who had been the earnest advocates of the abolition of slavery. Sir Robert Peel and Mr. Gladstone led the opposition; and Lord Sandon proposed the amendment, 'That, considering the efforts and sacrifices which Parliament and the country have made for the abolition of the slave trade and slavery, with the earnest hope that their exertions and example might lead to the mitigation and final extinction of those evils in other countries, this House is not prepared, especially with the present prospect of the supply of sugar from British possessions, to adopt the measure proposed by Her Majesty's Government for the reduction of duty on foreign sugar.' For eight nights did the Commons debate this important question, and the issue was the defeat of Lord John Russell's motion by 281 to 317. Immediately after,

Sir Robert Peel moved a vote of want of confidence in the ministry, and, after another five nights' struggle, it was carried by 312 to 311, the majority of 1 thus ousting the liberal cabinet.

Defeated by so slight a majority, the effort for the equalisation of the sugar duties was renewed speedily after. In 1842 Mr. Labouchere moved that colonial sugar be charged 20s., and foreign sugar 30s., and the motion was lost by 164 to 245. In 1843 Mr. Hawes proposed a differential duty of 10s., and he lost his motion by 122 to 203. In March, 1844, the member for Taunton proposed the admission of Brazilian sugar at the same duty as colonial, and he again lost the motion by 132 to 205. And, in June, 1844, Lord John Russell's motion for a duty of 24s. on British sugar, and 34s. on foreign, was lost by a majority of 69. In that year, however, the first inroad was made on the exclusion of foreign sugar by discriminating between sugar the growth of China, Java, or Manilla, or of any other foreign countries which her majesty in council shall have declared to be admissible as not being the produce of slave labour and other foreign sugar, Lord John Russell insisting upon making no such distinction, but placing the produce of all countries on an equal footing.

Differential duties.

In 1845 Sir Robert Peel introduced his measure on the sugar duty, proposing to reduce the duty on British West India, Mauritius, and East India sugar from 1*l.* 5*s.* to 16*s.* and 14*s.* per cwt. according to quality, foreign free labour from 3*l.* 3*s.* to 1*l.* 8*s.* and 1*l.* 3*s.* 4*d.*, and other foreign sugar from 3*l.* 6*s.* 1½*d.* to 3*l.* 3*s.* And again Lord John Russell moved as an amendment, 'That it is the opinion of this House that the plan proposed by Her Majesty's government in reference to the sugar duties professes to keep up a distinction between foreign free labour and foreign slave labour sugar, which is impracticable and illusory; and, without adequate benefit to the consumer, tends so greatly to impair the revenue as to render the removal of the income and property tax at the end of three years extremely uncertain and improbable.' The amendment, however, was lost by 94 to 236. Again in July, 1845, Viscount Palmerston moved for an address to the

Free and slave labour.

crown, praying that 'Spanish subjects be permitted to import into the United Kingdom all the productions of the territories of the Spanish crown, paying thereupon no higher duty or customs than those which are paid by the subjects or citizens of the most favoured nations on the production of like articles being the productions of the territories or possessions of such nations;' and he lost the motion by 87 to 175. And so the differential duty continued till in August, 1846, Lord John Russell reduced the duty on slave labour sugar from 3*l.* 3*s.* to 2*l.* 2*s.*, and in 1848 finally equalised the duties on all free and slave labour sugars. The results of these reforms in the sugar duties will hereafter appear in an immense increase in the consumption of sugar, in a great expansion of the revenue, and more especially in an increased trade with all producing countries. A great change indeed took place in this branch of industry; and another proof was afforded of the soundness of the doctrine that high duties are injurious rather than beneficial to the revenue, by checking the consumption and restricting the commerce of the country.

An interesting moral problem was before the legislature in this discussion on the sugar duties. Slavery was a great wrong, a crying evil, and the nation cheerfully paid twenty millions to get rid of it in all the colonies. Treaties had been concluded with foreign countries for the extinction of the slave trade, and a fleet of vessels was maintained at great expense, to prevent the carrying of slaves. Should we, in the face of all this, open the British market to the slave produce of Cuba and Brazil, and thus undo with one hand what we did with the other? No, said the West India planter, interested in his monopoly. Certainly not, said the philanthropic abolitionist. But there was no evidence to show that the prohibition of the importation of foreign sugar into the United Kingdom had operated to the discouragement of slavery in the sugar producing colonies. We were moreover receiving thankfully any quantity of cotton, and had no objection to the importation of tobacco, from the United States of America, which were also the produce of slave labour. And all the while we were narrowing the supply of one of the necessaries of life to the masses of the people, which they could ill spare.

Consumption of slave-grown sugar.

This was indeed demanding a sacrifice too great for an object of doubtful utility, and the differential duties had eventually to be abandoned.[1] Years had to pass before slavery was abolished by Spain and Portugal, and before the smuggling of slaves from Africa was effectually suppressed. But a higher restraint than prohibitions or high duties was the verdict of the world against the institution of slavery. Whatever be the interest at stake, no civilised nation can with impunity act in opposition to the moral sense of mankind, or the dictates of religion and humanity.

[1] The sugar duties have been subjected to great changes. After the equalisation of duties on slave labour and free labour sugar, a distinction was introduced in 1845 between sugar equal to white clayed and not equal to white clayed, the rates varying also according to the countries whence sugar was imported. In 1854, this farther distinction was abolished, and after other changes, from May 2, 1870, the duties have been established at 6s. 8d. for unrefined first class; 5s. 3d. for second class; 4s. 9d. for third class; 4s. per cwt. for fourth class, including juice; 1s. 9d. for molasses; and 6s. per cwt. for sugar refined and candy.

PART IV.

1842–1857.

FROM SIR ROBERT PEEL'S ADMINISTRATION

TO

THE COMMERCIAL CRISIS OF 1857.

SUMMARY.

1842–1857.

We have now arrived at a period in our commercial survey richer in events and more memorable for improvements than any of the preceding ones. A tentative and experimental commercial policy gave place to a bold and independent action on the part of her Majesty's government. Sir Robert Peel, urged by the Anti-Corn Law League, and stimulated by the distress in Ireland, openly adopted the maxims of free trade, and, under his guidance, the corn laws were abolished, the tariff was remodelled, and the principle of protection abandoned. The increase of trade which followed largely developed the wealth of the country. The banking laws, which gave rise to so much conflict of opinion, were systematised. An extensive railway system was established; and, though more than one crisis tried severely the public and private credit of the nation, trade and industry made steady progress. The universal exhibitions also exercised a most beneficial influence. And the discovery of rich mines of gold in California and Australia supplied a welcome addition to the metallic currency of the world. Unhappily, Sir Robert Peel was cut off by a sad accident in the midst of his illustrious career; but his mantle could not have fallen into worthier hands than in Mr. Gladstone's, a financier and economist of the highest order, who still more largely secured for the nation a free access to the produce and manufactures of the world.

CHAPTER I.

SIR ROBERT PEEL'S COMMERCIAL REFORMS.

1841-1850.

Accession of Sir Robert Peel.—Inauguration of Economic Reforms.—The Corn Laws.—State of the Revenue and Expenditure—The British Tariff.—The Income Tax.—More Commercial Reforms.—Reciprocity of Foreign Countries.—Export of Machinery.

THE day had arrived when the government of the country had to be confided to the great Conservative party in the House. For some time past the administration of Lord Melbourne had shown unmistakable signs of inherent weakness, and its opponents, counting among them such men as Sir Robert Peel, Lord Stanley, Mr. Gladstone, and Disraeli, were decidedly gaining strength and influence. The Conservative party is supposed to regard with suspicion if not with dislike the liberal tendencies of the nation, and they certainly resisted the passing of the Reform Bill, the repeal of the Test and Corporation Acts, and the emancipation of Roman Catholics. Yet a memorable Conservative administration is before us, which inaugurated an era of great prosperity, and one which, under the presiding genius of Sir Robert Peel, has ever since been held in grateful remembrance for the practical wisdom which it displayed, and the bold and vigorous commercial and financial policy it carried into effect. Sir Robert Peel had already gained for himself a high reputation as a statesman. As a member of the Bullion Committee of 1810, as under-secretary for the colonies during the most trying years of the continental war, as secretary for Ireland, in all these capacities, he proved himself an able minister and an economist of much practical wisdom; and it was a good omen for the country when, in September 1841, at a time of much financial anxiety, Sir Robert Peel was called to take the helm of the state.

Sir Robert Peel's administration.

There was something novel and encouraging in the speech from the throne which opened the labours of the new adminis-

Inaugura-tion of economic reforms.

tration. 'Her Majesty is anxious that this object, viz. the increase of the public revenue, should be effected in the manner least burdensome to her people; and it has appeared to Her Majesty, after full deliberation, that you may at this juncture properly direct your attention to the revision of duties affecting the productions of foreign countries. It will be for you to consider, whether some of the duties are not so trifling in amount as to be unproductive to the revenue, while they are vexatious to commerce. You may further examine whether the principle of prohibition, in which others of these duties are founded, be not carried to an extent injurious alike to the income of the state and the interest of the people. Her Majesty is desirous that you should consider the laws which regulate the trade in corn. It will be for you to determine whether those laws do not aggravate the natural fluctuation of supply, whether they do not embarrass trade, derange currency, and by their operation diminish the comfort and increase the privations of the great body of the community.' Surely this was a programme more liberal than could have been expected from a Conservative ministry; but the temper of the people and the exigencies of the time demanded that and a great deal more. Gloom and discontent prevailed extensively throughout the manufacturing districts. The Anti-Corn-Law League had by this time become formidable. The demand was loud and imperious for cheap food, and the total repeal of the corn laws. And on the day fixed for the announcement of the ministerial measure some five hundred deputies from the Anti-Corn-Law Associations in the metropolis and provinces went in procession to the House of Commons, but were refused admittance. Yet with all this the government was not disconcerted, and with imperturbable gravity Sir Robert Peel exposed the policy of the cabinet on the corn laws.

The corn laws.

At first Sir Robert Peel did not attach much weight to the influence of these laws. In his speech in the House, he said that to his mind the question was not so much what was the price of food, as what was the command which the labouring classes of the population had of all that constituted the enjoyments of life. His belief and the belief of his colleagues was, that it was important for the country to take care that the main source of the supply of corn should be derived from domestic agriculture. And he contended that a certain amount of protection was absolutely required for that industry. But he made a most important avowal, one which no Protectionist ministry had ever made, that protection should not be retained for the special benefit of any particular class, but only for the advantage of the nation at large, and in so far only as was consistent with the general welfare of all classes of society. Sir Robert Peel then entered on the extent of such protection, and having taken 54*s.* to 58*s.* per quarter, as the price at which corn should range for a fair remuneration to the agriculturist, he asked—Shall the corn laws be based on a sliding scale, or on a fixed duty? A sliding scale was introduced in France in 1819, one had been adopted in Belgium, the Netherlands, and other countries, and it seemed to have the advantage of adapting itself to every circumstance. But experience did not confirm the hopes entertained of its working. It did not hinder prices falling lower than was wanted in years of abundance, or rising higher than was desirable in years of scarcity; and it had the same prejudicial effect as every corn law of causing the cultivation of land to be regulated, not by its inherent capacity, but by the amount of forced stimulus given to it by the legislature. Besides these radical defects, the objections urged against the sliding scale were, that the reduction of duty was so rapid as to hold out temptation to fraud; that it operated as an inducement to retain corn, or combine for the purpose of influencing the averages; that the rapid decline of the duty was injurious to the consumer, the producer, the revenue, and the commerce of the country; that it was injurious to the consumer because, when corn was at a high price, say between 66*s.* and 70*s.*, and just when it would be for the public advantage that corn should be liberated for the purpose of consumption, the joint operation of increased price and diminished duty induced the holders to keep it back, in the hope of realising the price of upwards of 70*s.* and so paying only 1*s.* duty; that it operated injuriously to the agricultural interest because it held out a temptation to keep back corn until it could be suddenly entered for consumption at the lowest amount of duty, when agriculture lost the protection which the law intended it should possess; that it was injurious to the revenue because, instead of corn being entered for home consumption when it arrived, it was retained until it could be introduced at 1*s.*, the revenue losing the difference between 1*s.* and the amount of duty which would otherwise have been levied; that it was injurious to commerce because, when corn was grown at a distance, in America for instance, the grower was subject to the disadvantage, that before his cargo arrived in this country the sudden entries of wheat at 1*s.* duty from countries nearer England might have so diminished the price and increased the duty, as to cause his speculation to prove not only a failure but ruinous. These were formidable objections to any sliding scale, but between a gradual and a fixed rate of duty there was not a material difference. A fixed duty of 8*s.* per quarter was too low as a protection in time of abundance, and was in effect a prohibitory duty in time of scarcity. Nor was it possible to maintain more than a nominal duty when prices began to rise. It was indeed difficult to strike the balance of advantage and inconvenience between the sliding scale and the fixed duty, and, on the whole, Sir Robert Peel favoured the principle of the sliding scale, that is, of making the duty upon corn vary inversely with the price in the home market, taking the average of the market prices from returns collected by excise officers. Having fixed 20*s.* duty when the average price of wheat was 50*s.* and 51*s.* per quarter, he made that duty fall by a reduction of 1*s.* a quarter as the average price rose 1*s.* with some slight modifications, so that the duty should be only 1*s.* per quarter, when the price of wheat rose to 73*s.* a quarter and upwards, and a Bill so framed he presented to the House of Commons. The House was not prepared at the time for a very liberal measure. Lord John Russell's motion for a fixed duty was not more popular; and therefore, notwithstanding a few expressions of dissatisfaction, the government proposal was well received. Lord John Russell's amendment was lost by 226 to 349, and Sir Robert Peel's bill passed into law.[1] But the country was not satisfied. Meetings continued to be held in the manufacturing districts, and Mr. Villiers, stimulated by

[1] 5 & 6 Vict. c. 14.

the representations and efforts of the Anti-Corn-Law League, again brought forward his motion for the total repeal of the corn laws, which was again lost by the enormous majority of 90 to 393. The battle of the corn laws had by this time become violent both in and out of parliament, and Mr. Villiers was not likely to be dispirited by the result of this division.

State of the revenue and expenditure.

It is not, however, by the vain attempt to render a corn law acceptable that the commercial administration of Sir Robert Peel will be remembered. That was at best a temporary and transitory measure. It is when we consider his financial policy, or the plan which he devised for improving the state of the finances, and imparting new life to commerce and industry, that we recognise the breadth of view, the sound wisdom, and practical knowledge which Sir Robert Peel possessed. For years past the finances of the country had been allowed to get into complete disorder. An annual deficiency of one or two millions had become a chronic evil, and no means of escape presented itself.[1] With a disaffected people, and frequent riots in the manufacturing districts, with a paralysed trade, and wages reduced to the minimum, any idea of imposing new taxes, or making those existing, heavier, was out of the question. A temporary and casual deficiency might have been met by an issue of exchequer bills; but what would have been the use of thus providing against the difficulty when there was no ground whatever for expecting any improvement? On the other hand, to resort to loans in times of peace in order to balance the revenue and expenditure was equally inadmissible; and it would have been an expedient unworthy of such a nation as England. What then was to be done? Sir Robert Peel was alive to the fact, that a timely and moderate reduction of taxes is favourable rather than injurious to the revenue. He knew that, though for the moment such a reduction might show a loss, the revenue would soon recover itself, and probably exceed the amount previously produced. But, unfortunately, the few precedents he had for such an operation, attempted in times not very prosperous, were not encouraging. In 1825, the revenue from

[1] The deficiency in the year ended April 5, 1841, was 1,157,601*l.*; in the year ended April 5, 1842, 117,627*l.*; and 1843, 2,701,510*l.*

wine amounted to 2,153,000*l*. The duty was then reduced from 9*s*. 1½*d*. to 4*s*. 2¾*d*. per gallon: what was the result? The year after, the revenue was 1,400,000*l*.; it afterwards increased to 1,700,000*l*., but it fell again to 1,400,000*l*. The duty on tobacco had been reduced from 4*s*. to 3*s*. per lb. Before the reduction the revenue was 3,378,000*l*; immediately after it fell to 2,600,000*l*.; and, though it rose somewhat from that point, had not reached the previous amount. Of course, wine and tobacco being articles of luxury, the consumption could not be so affected by a reduction of duty as it would be in the case of tea, sugar, and other necessaries of life. And, moreover, the resources of the country were at that time comparatively undeveloped. Still, such experience did not warrant the expectation that a reduction of taxes would have the effect of filling the exchequer.

The British tariff.

But the circumstances of trade required instant relief, and the tariff needed a thorough reform and simplification. Two years before, in 1840, on the motion of Mr. Hume, a committee of the House of Commons was appointed to inquire into the duties levied on imports, and to determine how far they were imposed for purposes of revenue; and in their report the committee said, 'The tariff of the United Kingdom presents neither congruity nor unity of purpose: no general principles seem to have been applied. The tariff often aims at incompatible ends; the duties are sometimes meant to be both productive of revenue and for protection, objects which are frequently inconsistent with each other. Hence they sometimes operate to the complete exclusion of foreign produce, and in so far no revenue can of course be received; and sometimes, when the duty is inordinately high, the amount of revenue is in consequence trifling. They do not make the receipt of revenue the main consideration, but allow that primary object of fiscal regulations to be thwarted by the attempt to protect a great variety of particular interests at the expense of revenue, and of the commercial intercourse with other countries. Whilst the tariff has been made subordinate to many small-producing interests at home by the sacrifice of revenue, in order to support their interest, the same principle of interference is largely applied, by the various discriminating duties, to the produce of our colonies, by which exclusive advantages are given to the colonial interests at the expense of the mother country.' Such were the general features of the tariff, the result of years of careless legislation on the subject. The fact was indeed too evident that it was necessary to prune the overburdened tariff, and to liberate a large variety of articles from the needless trammels of legislation.

The income tax.

But how to accomplish this without a handsome surplus revenue? Fortunately Sir Robert Peel was not deterred by the state of the revenue, and determined to do what was necessary for trade. And he acted wisely. Untrammel industry from the bonds of legal restrictions, open the avenue to wealth and prosperity, and there is no fear but the revenue will set itself speedily right. He proposed, therefore, to reduce considerably all the duties on the raw materials of manufacture, all duties on goods partially or wholly manufactured, as well as the duties on timber, and all export duties, together producing 1,500,000*l.*; and to make up this loss, as well as the original deficit in the revenue, amounting to 2,570,000*l.*, by an income and property tax of 7*d.* in the pound, which he expected would produce 3,700,000*l.*;[1] by the equalisation of the stamp and spirit duties, which would give 400,000*l.*; and by a small tax on the exportation of coals, which would give 200,000*l.*, making in all 4,340,000*l.* It was a very simple plan, yet there was profound wisdom in Sir Robert Peel's budget. The real value of the reductions proposed could scarcely be estimated by the amount of relief in taxation they each and collectively afforded. The great evil attending the heavy taxes on raw materials was that they put our manufactures in a disadvantageous position in the markets of the world, and restricted the field for the employment of capital and labour. As was said in the discussion on the budget, suppose 50,000 head of cattle were to be annually imported in consequence of such remissions, such importation would produce

[1] The amount of duty assessed in 1843 was 5,608,316*l.* The amount of property assessed was: Schedule A, 95,284,497*l.*; Schedule B, 46,769,915*l.*; Schedule C, 27,909,793*l.*; Schedule D, 71,330,344*l.*; Schedule E, 9,718,454*l.* Total, 251,013,003*l.*

but a small effect on the price of meat, but it would create an import trade to the amount of half a million of money, a trade which in its nature would tend to produce an export trade in return of an equal amount. Our export trade is measured and limited by our import trade. If an individual merchant cannot afford to send his goods to other countries without obtaining any return, neither can all merchants collectively, and the country as a whole, afford to export commodities to foreign countries if in some shape or other imports are not received from those countries in return. Reduce the duties on imports, and you thereby promote the export of our produce and manufactures. Remove those taxes which burden our manufactures, and you promote the importation of those articles which are necessary to the comfort and welfare of the nation. The income tax might be odious, 'inquisitorial, intolerable,' yet it was at that time the only means by which reforms in the tariff could be attempted. And the nation, having balanced the evil and the good of the proposal, and being convinced that the advantages preponderated, cheerfully accepted the government proposal, and the budget passed triumphantly.

More commercial reforms.

The commercial policy thus inaugurated by Sir Robert Peel being in perfect accord with sound economic principles, could not fail to be successful. From 1841 to 1843, as we have seen, there was a yearly deficit in the budget. In the year ending April 5, 1844, Sir Robert Peel found himself in possession of a handsome surplus of 2,600,000*l.*, which was exceeded in the following year, and continued at a high point for four consecutive years. The exports of British produce, which in 1842 had fallen to 47,000,000*l.*, increased to 52,000,000*l.* in 1843, to 58,000,000*l.* in 1844, and 60,000,000*l.* in 1845. The shipping entered and cleared increased from 9,000,000 tons in 1842 to 12,000,000 tons in 1845. In every way, financially and commercially, the results fully realized the anticipations formed, and Sir Robert was encouraged to advance still further in the same direction. Nothing important was attempted in the budget of 1843, but in 1844 the duty on wool was abolished; the duties on currants and coffee were reduced, and a great change was made on the duties on marine insurance. And then the first inroad was made on the exclusion of foreign sugar, by distinguishing sugar, the growth of China, Java, or Manilla, or of any other countries which her majesty in council shall have declared to be admissible, as not being the produce of slave labour, from other foreign sugar. In 1845, another still more important series of reform was introduced. The duty on cotton wool, which, however slight and inappreciable on the coarser material, pressed rather heavily on the finer muslin, was abolished. The export duty on coals, which had been found vexatious and injurious, was removed. The timber duties were further reduced. The duty on glass was removed from the tariff, and so the duties on 430 articles which produced little or no revenue, including fibrous materials, such as silk, hemp, and flax, furniture, woods, cabinet maker's materials, animal and vegetable oil, ores and minerals, &c. In 1846 the liberal policy was further extended. Hitherto our manufacturers had been benefited by the free access granted to the raw materials. It was right to ask of them to relinquish some at least of the protecting duties still in existence. And the duties on linen, woollen, and cotton manufactures were reduced from 20 to 10 per cent. The silk duties, then at 30 per cent., were also reduced to 15 per cent. A reduction was made on the duties on stained paper, on manufactures of metals, on earthenware, on carriages, and on manufactures of leather; and the duties on butter, cheese, and hops, were further reduced.[1]

But was it right to effect all these reforms without asking for reciprocity on the part of foreign countries? For years past it was known that Her Majesty's government had used every effort to enter into treaties with several states, such as Brazil, Portugal, Spain, and France, with a view to enter into a system of mutual concessions. In 1843 and 1844 Mr. Ricardo brought the subject before the House of Commons, and moved for an address to Her Majesty praying that Her Majesty be pleased to give directions to her servants not to enter into any negotiations with foreign

Reciprocity of foreign countries.

[1] In 1842 there were 1,090 articles and subdivisions of articles charged with distinct rates of import duty in the Customs tariff. In 1846 the number was reduced to 424.

powers which would make any contemplated alterations of the tariff of the United Kingdom contingent on the alterations of the tariff of other countries; and expressing to Her Majesty the opinion of the House, that the great object of relieving the commercial intercourse between this country and foreign nations from all injurious restrictions would be best promoted by regulating our own customs duties, as might be most suitable to the financial and commercial interests of this country, without reference to the amount of duties which foreign powers might think it expedient for their own interest to levy on British goods. But in those cases the government opposed the motion, and Mr. Ricardo was defeated. Mr. Gladstone especially defended the policy of endeavouring to obtain such treaties. Mr. Gladstone said that he did not wish to be trammelled by an abstract proposition; and that unless Mr. Ricardo could show that there were no possible circumstances in which a commercial treaty could be aught other than evil, he had no right to call upon the House to affirm his resolution. The government, however, now practically acted on the policy advocated by Mr. Ricardo, and Sir Robert Peel avowed it frankly.

'I have no guarantee,' he said, 'to give you that other countries will immediately follow our example. I give you that advantage in the argument. Wearied with our long and unavailing efforts to enter into satisfactory commercial treaties with other nations, we have resolved at length to consult our own interests, and not to punish other countries for the wrong they do us, in continuing their high duties upon the importation of our products and manufactures, by continuing high duties ourselves, encouraging unlawful trade. We have had no communication with any foreign government upon the subject of these reductions. We cannot promise that France will immediately make a corresponding reduction in her tariff. I cannot promise that Russia will prove her gratitude to us for our reduction of duty on her tallow by any diminution of her duties. You may therefore say, in opposition to the present plan, "What is this superfluous liberality, that you are going to do away with all these duties, and yet you expect nothing in return?" I may, perhaps, be told that many foreign countries, since the former relaxation of duties on our part—

and that would be perfectly consistent with the fact—foreign countries, which have benefited by our relaxations, have not followed our example; nay, have not only not followed our example, but have actually applied to the importation of British goods higher rates of duties than formerly. I quite admit it. I give you all the benefit of that argument. I rely upon that fact as conclusive proof of the policy of the course we are pursuing. It is a fact that other countries have not followed our example, and have levied higher duties in some cases upon our goods. But what has been the result upon the amount of your exports? You have defied the regulations of these countries. Your export trade is greatly increased. Now, why is that so? Partly because of your acting without wishing to avail yourselves of their assistance, partly because of the smuggler not engaged by you in so many continental countries whom the strict regulations and the triple duties which are to prevent the ingress of foreign goods have raised up, and partly, perhaps, because these very precautions against the ingress of your commodities are a burden, and the taxation increasing the cost of production, disqualify the foreigner from competing with you. But your exports, whatever be the tariff of other countries, or however apparent the ingratitude with which they have treated you, your export trade has been constantly increasing. By the remission of your duties upon the raw material, by inciting your skill and industry, by competition with foreign goods, you have defied your competitors in foreign markets, and you have been enabled to exclude them. Notwithstanding their hostile tariffs the declared value of British exports has increased above 10,000,000*l.* during the period which has elapsed since the relaxation of duties on your part. I say, therefore, to you that these hostile tariffs, so far from being an objection to continuing your policy, are an argument in its favour. But, depend upon it, your example will ultimately prevail. When your example could be quoted in favour of restriction, it was quoted largely. When your example can be quoted in favour of relaxation as conducive to your interest, it may perhaps excite at first in foreign governments, in foreign boards of trade, but little interest or feeling: but the sense of the people of the great body of consumers will prevail; and in spite of the desire of government and boards of trade to raise revenue by restrictive duties, reason and common sense will induce relaxation of high duties. That is my firm belief.'

Another evidence of the liberal views held by Sir Robert Peel's cabinet at this important period was the abolition of the prohibition to export machinery. There is scarcely anything for which Britain is more distinguished than for her power to mould and subdue the hardest metal, and to convert the shapeless and roughest mass of inert matter into the most useful mechanical instrument. No country in the world possesses factories for machinery as extensive as Manchester and its immediate neighbourhood. And when we consider that it is by this superiority in mechanical contrivances that England maintained her manufacturing industry, and rendered foreign nations in a manner tributaries to her power and skill, we may almost sympathise with those who entertained grave apprehensions from our allowing these very machines, these wonders of art, to be sent to rival nations. They thought it rather hard to hasten or actively promote the successful manufacturing rivalry of foreign competitors by supplying the Continent with English machinery of the best description. And they reasoned respecting the exportation of machinery in the same manner as they did as regards prohibiting our artisans to emigrate, or allowing the exportation of coals. If we happen to possess any special aptitude or privilege, why should we throw it away? Why build the fortune of others with our own hands? Yet experience has proved that it is in vain to attempt to keep for ourselves any advantage we may chance to possess. Our superiority to other nations must be maintained by the constant exercise of skill and energy which set us from the first at the head of other countries. We cannot rely upon fictitious expedients for keeping other nations behind us. At the very time when we prohibited the exportation of our machinery other nations, especially Belgium, France, Germany, and Switzerland, were making considerable progress in them. Our position had become untenable. The prohibition to export machinery applied by law to several articles specified by a schedule attached to the Customs' Regu-

Exportation of machinery.

lation Act of 1825; but a discretionary power was vested in the board of trade, to permit the export when the machinery was of great bulk and contained a great quantity of raw material, and to restrain it when the machinery was of modern improvement, and depended mainly upon the ingenuity and excellence of the mechanism, and also when the raw material used was but trifling. It is easy to see how difficult it must have been for the board of trade to use this discretion aright. In practice, whilst the most ingenious pieces of mechanism found their way through the customs, tools, which are as important as machinery, were not allowed to be exported. But machines of all kinds were smuggled continually. Passengers not only took drawings and plans, but secreted machinery in their luggage. Sometimes a piece of machinery was sent to the quay and the remainder to the docks. Sometimes machinery was secreted in bales of goods which custom-house officers could not readily unpack. In many ways the law was evaded. The prohibition of exportation positively injured manufacturers of machinery. A machine maker in England discovering some new mechanical combination, or inventing a new machine, might secure a protection for the invention on the Continent in the same manner as in this country; but when the patent applied to a machine, the export of which was prohibited, he was obliged either to establish a manufacture on the Continent, which was inconvenient and almost impracticable if he was not present to superintend, or to throw himself into the hands of foreigners, and thus derive only a portion of the return, all of which he would have got had his invention remained in his own hands. If the latter method was adopted it became necessary to supply such foreigners with the knowledge requisite for the construction of the machine, to furnish drawings and specifications, possibly to send a model machine, which, being made in this country, could be sent to the Continent only in a surreptitious manner. Thus instead of calling into activity the works connected with our own coal and tin mines and the labour and industry of a large body of our industrious artisans, the manufacturer was compelled to call all those advantages into operation in foreign countries. We have already seen that the committee on the combination laws, appointed in

1825, was to have inquired into the operation of the law respecting the exportation of tools and machinery, but had no time to complete their inquiry on the subject. In 1843, the inquiry was resumed, and, after having examined a large number of witnesses, the Committee reported that, considering that machinery was the only product of British industry upon the exportation of which restraints were placed, they recommended that the law prohibiting the exportation of such should be repealed, and that the trade of machinery should be placed upon the same footing as other departments of British industry. The government acted upon this report. A bill on the subject was introduced, and the exportation of machinery was set free.[1]

[1] 6 & 7 Vict. c. 84.

CHAPTER II.

THE BANK CHARTER ACT.

1844—1845.

Conflicting Opinions on Monetary Legislation.—Committee of 1819.—Committee of 1826.—Committee of 1831.—Committee of 1836.—Committee of 1840.—Committee of 1841.—Theory of Lord Overstone, Colonel Torrens, and Sir Robert Peel.—Theory of Mr. Tooke and Mr. Fullarton.—Sir Robert Peel's Motion.—Currency Laws for Scotland and Ireland.—Law of Joint Stock Companies.—Practice of the Board of Trade on granting Charters.—Committee on Joint Stock Companies.

The Bank Charter Act of 1844 has been subjected to considerable criticism. Dealing as it did with the monetary organisation of a great commercial nation, legislating in accordance with a special theory of currency and banking, interfering with established customs and in some cases even with private rights, the bank act has by one class been held up as the masterpiece of Sir Robert Peel's administration, and by another as only a piece of blundering and meddling legislation, useless in times of ease and prosperity, and most injurious in times of anxiety and panic. As we have already seen, certain phenomena of exchange were very variously accounted for. In the difference for example between the market and the mint price of gold, or between the value of banknotes and coin, one party saw evidence of an excess of currency, another the simple effect of the export of bullion to the Continent. In the main conclusions of the bullion committee there was a universal concurrence. The act of 1819 was accepted by most parties as a just and necessary measure, since the restriction of cash payments could be considered only as an exceptional measure which extreme circumstances alone could justify. Yet on the occasion of the crises in 1826, 1836, and 1839, conflicting views have been expressed respecting the relative influence of the causes immediately connected with the

Conflicting opinions on monetary legislation.

currency and causes special to the times of a political or economic character. Sir Robert Peel, however, who since 1829 had become a decided convert to the bullionist theory, was not at a loss to account for them, and saw in all these circumstances a clear and decided reason for checking by law any excess of issue which endangered the maintenance of a metallic currency. Taking advantage, therefore, of the expiration of the time for which the privileges of the Bank of England had been granted, Sir Robert Peel, on May 6, 1844, propounded his new scheme for controlling and regulating the issue of notes. Much had been done already in the way of clearing the ground for further legislation on the currency, and at the cost of some repetition it is well to refer to the different inquiries instituted on the subject, at least since the famous bullion committee.

The first document in date and importance are the two reports of committees of the Houses of Lords and Commons in

Committees of 1819.

1819, on the expediency of the resumption of cash payments by the Bank of England. Before those committees, appeared Samuel Thornton, Thomas Tooke, David Ricardo, Alexander Baring, and many other financial authorities; and their reports, besides dealing with the immediate subject before the committees, dwelt also on the point how far, during the restriction, the circulation was the cause of the unfavourable state of the foreign exchanges. Some of the witnesses attributed it to an excess in the circulating medium of the country; others to the effect of the Mint regulations respecting the silver coinage; others to the operation of foreign loans, to the investment of capital in foreign funds and speculations, and to the large purchases of corn abroad. The Lords committee reported that many of those who maintained that it is at all times in the power of the Bank to exercise a complete control over the rise and fall of the exchanges, and over the price of gold, nevertheless thought that the great loans contracted by foreign states since the peace, the investments made by persons in this country in foreign securities, the pressure which took place in the money market at Paris and other commercial towns on the Continent and in America, and the great importation of corn during the year 1818, all concurred in lowering the exchanges. On the other hand, many of those who attributed the high price of gold and the unfavourable state of the exchanges chiefly to such operations, and who denied or doubted the fact that the issue of the notes of the Bank of England had been excessive, nevertheless thought that an excessive increase or diminution of their issue was capable of affecting the exchanges.

In 1826 a committee of the House of Commons was appointed to enquire into the state of the circulation of promissory notes under the value of five pounds in Scotland and Ireland. As regards Scotland it appeared that notes of not less than twenty shillings had been at all times permitted by law, and upon this the committee's report was decidedly unfavourable. 'The presumption on general principles appears to your committee to be in favour of an extension to other parts of the United Kingdom of the rule which it has been determined to apply to England. Provision would thus be made for equally apportioning among all parts of the empire that charge which is inseparable in the first instance from the substitution of a metallic in the room of a paper currency. The wider the field over which a metallic circulation is spread the greater will be the security against its disturbance from the operation of internal or external causes, and the lighter on any particular part will be the pressure incidental to a sudden contraction of currency.' Yet the witnesses from Scotland were adverse to any change in the laws which regulated the issue of promissory notes in that country, and the committee could not advise the passing of a law prohibiting the future issue in Scotland of notes below five pounds. In Ireland the same practice prevailed as in Scotland, but the committee had not sufficient information to enable them to pronounce a decisive opinion upon the general measures which it might be fitting to adopt with respect to the paper currency of Ireland. The House of Lords committee in the same year reported to the same effect.

Committee of 1826.

Six years after, in 1832, a committee was appointed to inquire into the expediency of renewing the charter of the Bank of England, and into the system on which banks of issue in England and Wales were conducted. The

Committee of 1832.

committee inquired whether the paper circulation of the metropolis should be confined to the issue of one bank and that a commercial company, or whether a competition of different banks of issue, each consisting of an unlimited number of partners, should be permitted; and also what checks might be provided to secure for the public a proper management of banks of issue, and especially whether it would be expedient and safe to compel them periodically to publish their accounts. Among the witnesses were John Horsley Palmer, Samuel Jones Loyd (Lord Overstone), Thomas Tooke, George Grote, and many others equally eminent. The committee made no complete report, but the evidence was full of information as to the principle on which the Bank was guided in the regulation of its issue and on the management and privileges of the Bank.

Committee of 1836.

Again, in 1836, a committee was appointed to inquire into the operation of the Act of 7 Geo. IV. c. 46, permitting the establishment of joint stock banks, and whether it was expedient to make any alteration in the provisions of that Act. The committee did not fully report in that year, but stated that the Act had stimulated both credit and circulation. The committee was reappointed in 1837 and in 1838, and important evidence was given on the operation of the country branches of the Bank of England established in 1826, after the crisis, for the purpose of affording greater facilities to the commercial world and of improving the circulating medium. It was clear, however, that some further legislation was required on joint stock banks, since the law imposed no obligation on the formation of such beyond the payment of a licence duty, required no deed of settlement, and made no restriction as to capital, shares, or declaration of dividends.

Committee of 1840.

In 1840 another committee sat on the effects produced on the circulation by the various banking establishments issuing notes payable on demand, which made no formal report. The witnesses on that occasion included Mr. J. B. Smith and Mr. Richard Cobden representing Manchester, besides representatives of the Bank of England, and others. In evidence before the committee on the Bank charter in 1832 Mr. Horsley Palmer stated that the plan on which the Bank acted in ordinary circumstances in the regulation of its issue was to retain an investment, in securities bearing interest, to the extent of two-thirds of its liabilities, the remaining one-third being held in bullion and coin, and that any reduction of the note circulation was, so far as was dependent upon the Bank, subsequently affected by the foreign exchanges or by internal extra demand. It seemed, however, that in several instances this rule had not been adhered to, and doubts had been expressed as to the soundness of its principle as applicable to the Bank of England. Conceiving that this rule had received some sort of legislative sanction, the Bank directors felt themselves bound to adhere to it as nearly as circumstances would permit, and on a particular occasion they thought themselves fettered by this impression. Without entering into the question either of the soundness of the rule or of the degree of sanction which it might be supposed to have received from the legislature, the committee were of opinion that such an impression on the part of the directors of the Bank of England ought not to prevent them from acting on any other principle of management which, after their further experience, and upon mature consideration, they might consider to be better adapted to attaining the primary object in view, that of preserving under all circumstances the convertibility of their notes.

Committee of 1841.

In 1841 the same committee was reappointed, and made two reports, which recommended a more frequent publication than was then required of the Bank notes in circulation in England and Wales, and of the bullion in the Bank of England, and that a similar publication should be made of the Bank notes in circulation in Scotland and Ireland. This report is specially valuable for the evidence of the country bankers and of Mr. James William Gilbart, the manager of the London and Westminster Bank, who considered at some length the laws which regulate the circulation of bank notes in different parts of the kingdom. Summing up certain observations on a table of the circulation, he said: 'The general conclusion I would draw is, that the Bank of England is governed by certain laws which do not apply to the country circulation; that the country circulation of England is also governed by laws peculiar to itself; that the circulation of Ireland is also governed by laws peculiar to itself; that the circulation of Scotland is also governed by laws peculiar to itself; that those respective circulations are all governed by uniform laws, as is shown by their arriving at nearly the same point at the same period of the year; and therefore that you cannot introduce any system by which all those various circulations, governed by different laws, can be amalgamated into one system; that such a system would be at variance with itself, and would tend to destroy that beautiful system of country banking which now exists, a system which has tended very much to the prosperity of this country, which by receiving the surplus capital of different districts and giving out the capital for the encouragement of trade, calls forth all the natural resources of the country, and puts into motion the industry of the nation, and at the same time supplies a circulation which expands and contracts in each district according as it is required by the trade or agriculture of the district.'

Besides these public inquiries much had been written on the subject of banking and currency, and the conflicting theories had on one side as their champions Mr. Jones Loyd (afterwards Lord Overstone), Colonel Torrens, and Sir Robert Peel, and on the other Mr. Tooke and Mr. Fullarton. And from their writings Mr. Danson deduced the following propositions given in a paper on the accounts of the Bank of England under the operation of the Acts read before the Statistical Society.[1]

Messrs. Jones Loyd, Colonel Torrens, and Sir Robert Peel held—

Theory of Lord Overstone, Colonel Torrens, and Sir Robert Peel.

'1. That the amount of the circulating medium in the hands of the public may be greater or less than is properly required for the transaction of the current business of the community; and that when greater it tends, by the excess, to make the use of the circulating medium too cheap. 2. That as the value of all other commodities is measured by that of the circulating medium, prices, or the nominal expressions of their value, are at such periods enhanced. 3. That such enhancement, by reducing exports and stimulating imports, turns the foreign exchanges against us, and leads to a drain of bullion. 4. That if, on the other hand, the amount

[1] Journal of the Statistical Society, vol. x. p. 132.

of the circulating medium be reduced below that properly required for the time, a contrary effect will ensue, producing favourable exchanges, and an influx of bullion. 5. That one principal cause, and that which has heretofore been the most common in this country, of an undue expansion of the circulating medium, is the putting or keeping in circulation by their issuers of too large an amount of bank notes payable on demand. 6. That the issuers of such notes can regulate at will the amount of them in circulation. And, 7. That if the bank notes in circulation be kept in strict proportion to the bullion in the hands of their issuers, the amount of the circulating medium will be prevented from becoming greater than it should be, and the mischief held to arise from its becoming so will be averted.'

Mr. Tooke and Mr. Fullarton held—

Theory of Mr. Tooke and Mr. Fullarton.

'1. That no greater amount of the circulating medium, whether in coins or notes, is ever in actual use, or therefore in circulation, than is required by the current transactions of the community; for that so much of it as there is no present use for, goes either into hoards or into bankers' deposits. That if hoarded, it ceases to have any effect as circulating medium; and that if deposited with bankers, it can only pass again into use at interest, which interest will only be paid by those who have a profitable use for it. 2. That while a large portion of the circulating medium is dependent solely upon the credit of its issuers, its extension can, in fact, only be limited by the state of that credit on the one hand, and by the aggregate demand of those who are willing to pay for its use, on the other. 3. That while there is a large fund of deposits in every part of the country payable on demand, an issuing banker cannot affect the aggregate amount of the circulating medium by issuing or withdrawing his notes. 4. That the amount of bank notes in circulation, representing only one portion of the addition made by the operation of bankers to the amount of the circulating medium, through the agency of their credit with the public, a restriction upon the amount of the addition so made must be ineffectual, unless it be accompanied by a like restriction on such of their other operations as have the same or a similar effect; and that, therefore, the omission of any regard to deposits and their effect in supplying readily and extensively the place of a portion of the circulating medium of this country, must render the restriction now placed upon the bank notes in circulation ineffectual to limit the amount of the circulating medium, whenever it shall become practically inconvenient either to bankers or to the public. 5. That the true measure of the voluntary addition made by a banker to the amount of the circulating medium is found, not in the amount of his notes in circulation, but in the terms upon which he makes advances, or, in other words, upon the price he charges for the use of so much of the circulating medium as he happens to command, either by the actual possession of money, or by his credit; and 6. That any attempt to control the issuing banker by law in the management of this branch of his business would be in fact an attempt to fix the price of the use of money, or of credit held sufficient to represent money, which, like all other prices, is, and must continue to be, governed by influences wholly beyond the control of the legislature.'

Thus far, then, the question of banking and currency had already been amply debated when Sir Robert Peel, on May 6, 1844, brought forward his motion on the Bank charter. Commencing with an inquiry into the foundation of our currency, Sir Robert Peel startled his audience with his attempt to bring into a concrete form the idea embraced in the word 'pound.' What is the signification of that word, a 'pound,' with which we are all familiar? What is the engagement to pay a 'pound'? If a 'pound' is a mere visionary abstraction, a something which does not exist, either in law or in practice, in that case one class of measures relating to paper currency may be adopted; but if the word 'pound,' the common denominator of value, signifies something more than a mere fiction: if a 'pound' means a quantity of the precious metal of certain weight and certain fineness, if that be the definition of a 'pound,' in that case another class of measures relating to paper currency will be requisite. 'Now,' he said, 'the whole foundation of the proposal I am about to make rests upon the assumption that, according to practice, according to law, according to the ancient monetary policy of this

Sir Robert Peel's motion.

country, that which is implied by the word "pound" is a certain definite quantity of gold with a mark upon it to determine its weight and fineness, and that the engagement to pay a "pound" means nothing and can mean nothing else than the promise to pay to the holder, when he demands it, that definite quantity of gold.' Having thus established what is the real measure of value, and shown the advantage of adhering to a gold standard, Sir Robert Peel proceeded to urge the necessity of securing a certain relation between the paper currency and bullion, and of framing laws for maintaining a strict adherence to that relation. 'It appears to me,' he said, 'that we have from reasoning, from experience, from the admissions made by the issuers of paper money, abundant ground for the conclusion that, under a system of unlimited competition, although it be controlled by convertibility into coin, there is not an adequate security against the excessive issue of promissory notes. We should infer, certainly from reasoning, that free competition in the supply of any given article will probably ensure us the most abundant supply of that article at the cheapest rate. But we do not want an abundant supply of cheap promissory paper. We want only a certain quantity of paper, not, indeed, fixed and definite in nominal amount, but just such a quantity of paper, and that only, as shall be equivalent in point of value to the coin which it represents. If the paper be cheaper than the coin, it is an evil and not an advantage. That system, therefore, which provides a constant supply of paper equal in value to coin, and so varying in amount as to ensure at all times immediate convertibility into coin, together with perfect confidence in the solvency of the issuers of paper, is the system which ought to be preferred. Now, unless the issuers of paper money conform to certain principles, unless they vigilantly observe the causes which influence the influx or efflux of coin, and regulate their issues of paper accordingly, there is danger that the value of the paper will not correspond with the value of the coin. The difference may not be immediately perceived, nay, the first effect of undue issue by increasing prices may be to encourage further issues; and as each issuer, where there is an unlimited competition, feels the inutility of individual efforts of contraction, the evil proceeds, until the disparity between gold and paper becomes manifest, confidence in the paper is shaken, and it becomes necessary to restore its value by sudden and violent reductions in the amount, spreading ruin among the issuers of paper, and deranging the whole monetary transactions of the country. If we admit the principle of a metallic standard, and admit that the paper currency ought to be regulated by immediate reference to the foreign exchanges—that there ought to be early contractions of paper on the efflux of gold—we might, I think from reasoning, without the aid of experience, argue that an unlimited competition in respect to issue, will not afford a security for the proper regulation of the paper currency.' Here we have the whole of the premises upon which the scheme was founded. It should be observed that Sir Robert Peel designated as money both the coin of the realm and promissory notes payable on demand, and that by the word paper currency he meant promissory notes only, not including bills of exchange, drafts on bankers, and other forms of credit. But there is a material difference between money and paper currency. As Mr. Huskisson said, the one possesses intrinsic value, the other has none intrinsically, and represents value in so far only as it is an undertaking to pay in money the sum for which it is issued. Lord Liverpool nowhere sanctioned the definition of money as including banknotes. Nor does Mr. Tooke. It is true that Bank of England notes are legal tender, but that is only an exception which does not affect promissory notes of other bankers not so privileged. Sir Robert made no such distinction; he dealt with the whole in the same scheme of legislation, and after much explanation he summed up as follows:—'It is proposed that the Bank of England shall continue in possession of its present privileges—that it shall retain the exclusive right of issue within a district of which sixty-five miles from London as a centre is the radius. The private banks within that district which now actually issue notes will of course be permitted to continue their issues to the amount of the average of the last two years.[1]

[1] The private bankers asked for the average of the previous five years; the joint stock banks asked for the maximum of the previous two years; but Sir Robert Peel ultimately determined to take the average of the previous twelve weeks.

'Two departments of the Bank will be constituted, one for the issue of notes, the other for the transaction of the ordinary business of banking. The bullion now in the possession of the Bank will be transferred to the issue department. The issue of notes will be restricted to an issue of 14,000,000*l.* upon securities, the remainder being issued upon bullion and governed in amount by the fluctuations in the stock of bullion. If there be, under certain defined circumstances, an increase in the issue of securities, it can only take place with the knowledge and the consent of the government, and the profit derivable from such issues will belong to the public. Bankers now actually enjoying the privilege of issue will be allowed to continue their issues, provided the maximum in the case of each bank does not exceed the average of a certain prescribed period. A weekly publication of issue will be required from every bank of issue; the names of shareholders and partners will be published. No new bank of issue can be formed, and no joint stock company for banking purposes can be established except after application to the government and compliance with various regulations which will be hereafter published to the consideration of parliament.' Such is the outline of the measure as sketched to Parliament by the great statesman. It is much to be regretted that, notwithstanding the immense importance of the measure, it failed at the time to excite any great interest. Few were ready to follow Sir Robert Peel in the difficult and intricate inquiries which he broached, or to discuss with him the basis of monetary science. Mr. Hawes made an ineffectual attempt to open up a discussion by moving as an amendment, 'That no sufficient evidence has been laid before the House to justify the proposed interference with the banks of issue in the management of their circulation;' but the amendment was lost by 30 to 185, and although the bankers made strong representations on the subject, the measure went through the House with the greatest ease, and the Bank Charter Act passed into law.[1]

Nor did legislation terminate then. The year after, a similar measure was introduced for the banks in Scotland and Ireland

[1] 7 & 8 Vict. c. 32.

with slight variations, as that they might continue their issues of notes under 5*l*., and that, whilst country bankers in England were not allowed in any case to issue notes beyond their average issue for the previous thirteen weeks, the banks in Scotland and Ireland were allowed to exceed that amount, provided they kept the excess in gold. Again Sir Robert Peel found a most compliant House. His doctrines were accepted with the greatest readiness, and having met some slight objections, and explained some points to the apparent satisfaction of the House, he succeeded in gaining a complete triumph, and this other section of the banking legislation was duly registered in the statute book.[1] We shall not attempt any formal criticism on Sir Robert Peel's measures, but to our mind the question is a simple one. It is not the function of the government to demand security for the payment of common debts, or to guarantee the right working of the foreign exchanges. The making of Bank of England notes legal tender in 1832, a measure which expediency alone had prompted, strengthened the erroneous assumption that banknotes are money. It would have been better to have retraced that step, and to have left the question of securing the convertibility of banknotes into cash just as the bullion committee left it in 1810, on the responsibility of the issuers themselves. This was the only safe and intelligible position for the legislature to take. As to any attempt to regulate the circulation by law, it must be practically useless, for we are not agreed on what the circulation consists of; and certainly it is useless to deal with one species of credit, such as banknotes, whilst others, such as deposits, cheques, and bills, which are of much greater magnitude, remain untouched. To fix the amount of the uncovered issue of the Bank of England at the sum which perchance happened to be due by government to the Bank was altogether arbitrary and unphilosophical. To fix the amount of the uncovered issue of country banks, or of the Scotch and Irish banks, at the sum which happened to have been issued on a certain number of weeks in 1844, was likewise based on no solid foundation. Having once dismissed the idea of having

Currency laws for Scotland and Ireland.

[1] 8 & 9 Vict. cc. 37 & 38.

only one bank of issue throughout the country as impracticable, there was no reason why the Bank of England should have had the sole privilege of issue in London. It would have been far better to have abolished the privileges and monopoly of the Bank of England, to have paid the debt due to the Bank, and to have placed the Bank of England on the same footing as any other bank. In the long run, it will be found that free banking will prove quite as beneficial as free trading.

Closely allied with the question of banking and currency is the state of the law of joint stock companies, on which a measure was rendered most urgent after the revelations of 1825 and 1835. Properly to understand the real state of the question, let us briefly review the changes previously made in the law of partnership and joint stock companies. For trading and public enterprise, the association of capital and labour, and the accumulation of small investments into great reservoirs, which are involved in the principles of companies, are absolutely necessary. Those gigantic undertakings which have been conceived and perfected with so much skill, and which have exercised so powerful an influence in promoting progress and civilisation, have mostly all been ushered into existence by the agency of public companies. At first the business pursued in distant countries was carried on by private adventurers, each risking his own property and each trading separately. They formed companies, and obtained charters of incorporation with monopolies and privileges, but they had no joint stock. Their union was suggested rather by their want of strength to militate against the difficulties of new and perilous adventures, than by any wish to accumulate the subscriptions of many into one common fund. It was long after such companies had ceased to have for their scope the mutual defence of the adventurers, that they were established for the purpose of combining large and small sums of capital for undertakings of a permanent character. Then it was that it became necessary to devise means for allowing persons to embark in or withdraw their funds from a concern, and thus arose the practice of the issue and transfer of shares, which was soon found to be open to great abuse. The transfer of shares became itself a trade, and companies were formed seemingly for the sole purpose of creating shares upon which

Law of joint stock companies.

speculative transactions might be carried on. The possible results of an undertaking were in many cases but a secondary consideration; care was taken to get up the prices of shares to an exorbitant height, and then they were thrown on the market, leaving the unfortunate last purchasers to bear heavy losses. This kind of dealing was carried on for a considerable time, but it reached its climax with the South Sea bubble. And then a stop was put to it by the legislature, by the passing of an act rendering illegal and void the acting or presuming to act as a corporate body, the raising or pretending to raise transferable stock, and the transferring or pretending to transfer or assign shares in such stock without legal authority.[5] In other words no company was thenceforth allowed to be formed with the ordinary powers or rights of acting in a corporate or semi-corporate capacity except by royal charter. A complete obstacle was, however, thus interposed to the formation of trading companies which was injurious to commerce, and greatly hindered the investment of unemployed capital. So that after having remained a dead letter in the statute book for a long time, the act had to be repealed.[6] Yet practically, considerable hinderance continued to be interposed to the formation of companies from the fact that no power existed allowing any number of persons to act in a corporate capacity and to sue and be sued by an officer of the company. How could a company composed of some hundreds of persons exercise its rights at all if in every case the names of all the shareholders had to be used? To prevent this evil, no other means existed but to get an act of Parliament. This method of course was troublesome and expensive, and it then became necessary to pass an act[7] enabling the crown by letters patent to grant to any trading company any of the privileges of suing and being sued in the name of an officer upon such terms and conditions as his majesty should think fit. But this statute did not remove the evil. It only mitigated it by throwing on the crown the responsibility of according the rights and privileges to whomsoever it pleased.

The concession of the right of trading with limited liability,

[5] 6 Geo. I. c. 18. [6] 6 Geo. IV. c. 91. [7] 4 & 5 Wm. IV. c. 94.

also connected with the granting of a charter, was particularly difficult and invidious. The circumstances which the treasury esteemed sufficient justification for granting letters patent with such privilege were the following:—1. Where the object for which the association is formed is one of a hazardous character, in which many individuals may be disposed to risk moderate sums, the aggregate of which may constitute a large sum sufficient for the undertaking, but in which a single capitalist, or two or three under an ordinary partnership, would be unable or unwilling to engage. The working of mines was an example of this species of adventure. 2. Where the capital required is of so large an amount that no single partnership could be expected to supply it, as in the case of railways, canals, docks, and works of that description. 3. Where no great advance of capital, but extended responsibility, is desirable, as in the case of assurance companies; and, 4. Where the object sought can only be effected by a numerous association of individuals, such as the formation of literary societies, charitable institutions, and similar bodies. In 1837 the president of the board of trade instructed Mr. Bellenden Ker to inquire into the state of the law of partnership, more especially as regards the difficulties which existed in suing and being sued when partners are numerous, and to consider whether it would be expedient to introduce a law, authorising persons to become partners in trade, with a limited responsibility similar to the French law of partnership *en commandite*. But the report was unfavourable to such an innovation. Mr. Ker himself deemed it inexpedient to adopt such a system, and among those whose opinions were quoted, Mr. Samuel Jones Loyd, Mr. Thomas Tooke, Mr. Larpent, Mr. Horsley Palmer, Mr. Kirkman Finlay, and Mr. John Gladstone, pronounced themselves decidedly against limited liability; whilst Lord Ashburton, Mr. G. W. Norman, and the Hon. Francis Baring, expressed an opinion in its favour.

Practice of the Board of Trade in granting charters.

Thus matters continued till 1844, when the necessity of introducing some check to the frauds and equivocations practised in connection with joint-stock companies, appeared to require some effective remedy. On February 16, a committee of the House of Commons was appointed

Committee on joint-stock companies.

to inquire into the state of the law respecting joint-stock companies other than banking, with a view to the greater security of the public; and the evidence brought before them was of a startling character. There were companies in existence faulty in their nature, inasmuch as they were founded on unsound calculations, and which could not by any possibility succeed. There were companies so ill constituted that miscarriages or failures incident to mismanagement would be sure to attend them. And there were companies both faulty and fraudulent in their object, being started for no other purpose than to create shares for the purpose of jobbing in them; or to create, under the pretence of carrying on a legitimate business, the opportunity and means of raising funds to be shared by the adventurers who started the company. These companies adopted, as far as possible, the outward characteristics common to those of the best kind; exhibited an array of directors and officers, announced a large capital, adopted the style and title of a company; issued plausible statements intimating excellent purposes; used some conspicuous place of business in a respectable situation, and employed throughout the country respectable agents and bankers; but many of these characteristics were fictitious. The directors had either not sanctioned the use of their names, or they were not the persons supposed to be. In many cases there was neither capital, subscribers, or deed of settlement. The style of the company might be unobjectionable, because any company might adopt any style; but its purposes, though plausible, were often founded on calculations which did not admit of success, and it ought not only not to have received the sanction of authority of parliament or of the crown, but the very statutes which were cited as conferring its authority might be found to have a very different object. Such being the state of the law on joint-stock companies, and such the defects in many of those in existence, the committee recommended a plan of registration of such companies; and thereupon the act was passed which provided for such registration, and gave power to all registered companies to sue and be sued in the name of their officers.[*] The act applied to every joint-stock company, formed for any commercial purpose,

[*] 7 & 8 Vict. c. 110.

or for any purpose of profit, or for the purpose of assurance; but it excepted banking companies, for which a special act [1] was passed, prescribing similar conditions as to registration, but adding that the capital of the company should in no case be less than 100,000*l.* and the shares 100*l.* each. Here we have another instance of over legislation. Can ever registration be a sufficient guarantee against fraud? Allowing that it is an evidence for the time being of the existence of a compact between a certain number of persons, what security does it afford that the terms of such compact are not rescinded the moment after? or that the capital promised is either not brought in or withdrawn? or that the registered shareholders do not transfer their shares? And moreover, unless the registrar be invested with a judicial character and with authority to investigate the accuracy of the matters registered, what certainty does it afford of the reliable character of the particulars registered? Valuable as registration is, it can never be relied upon as a sufficient security against fraud, and there is always danger lest the semi-official character given by it to a company may have the effect of creating a spirit of confidence where none should exist.

[1] 7 & 8 Vict. c. 113.

CHAPTER III.

REPEAL OF THE CORN AND NAVIGATION LAWS.

1846—1849.

The Anti-Corn Law League.—Sir Robert Peel's policy.—A new Cabinet.—The Recall, and the Abolition of the Corn Laws.—State of Ireland and the Potato Crop.—The Potato Disease.—Price of Wheat.—Emigration.—Repeal of the Navigation Law.

The Anti-Corn Law League.

THE Anti-Corn Law agitation was one of those movements which, being founded on right principles, and in harmony with the interest of the masses, was sure to gather fresh strength by any event affecting the supply of food. It was popular to attempt to reverse a policy which aimed almost exclusively to benefit one class of society. It was well known that the League wanted to outset an economic fallacy, and that they wished to relieve the people from a great burden. And as time elapsed and the soundness of the principles propounded by the League at their public meetings was more and more appreciated, their triumph became certain, and Her Majesty's government itself began to see that it was no longer possible to treat the agitation either by a silent passiveness, or by expressed contempt. The economic theorists had the mass of the people with them. Their gatherings were becoming more and more enthusiastic. And even amidst conservative landowners there were not a few enlightened and liberal minds who had already, silently at least, espoused the new ideas. No change certainly could be expected so long as bread was cheap and labour abundant. But when a deficient harvest and a blight in the potato crop crippled the resources of the people and raised grain to famine prices, the voice of the League acquired greater power and influence. Hitherto they had received hundreds of pounds. Now, thousands were sent in to support the agitation. A quarter of a million was readily contributed. Nor were the contributors Lancashire mill owners exclusively. Among them were merchants and bankers, men of heart and men of mind, the poor labourer, and the peer of the realm. The fervid oratory of Bright, the demonstrative and argumentative reasoning of Cobden, the more popular appeals of Fox, Rawlins, and other platform speakers, filled the newspaper press and were eagerly read. And when parliament dissolved in August 1845, even Sir Robert Peel showed some slight symptoms of a conviction that the days of the corn laws were numbered. Every day, in truth, brought home to his mind a stronger need for action, and as the ravages of the potato disease progressed, he saw that all further resistance would be absolutely dangerous.

A cabinet council was held on October 31 to consult as to what was to be done, and at an adjourned meeting on November 5 Sir Robert Peel intimated his intention to issue an order in council remitting the duty on grain in bond to one shilling, and opening the ports for the admission of all species of grain at a smaller rate of duty until a day to be named in the order; to call parliament together on the 27th inst. to ask for an indemnity, and a sanction of the order by law; and to submit to parliament immediately after the recess a modification of the existing law, including the admission at a nominal duty of Indian corn and of British colonial corn. A serious difference of opinion, however, was found to exist in the cabinet on the question brought before them, the only ministers supporting such measures being the Earl of Aberdeen, Sir James Graham, and Mr. Sidney Herbert. Nor was it easy to induce the other members to listen to reason. And though at a subsequent meeting, held on November 28, Sir Robert Peel so far secured a majority, it was evident that the cabinet was too divided to justify him in bringing forward his measures. And he decided upon resigning office.

Sir Robert Peel's policy.

This resolution having been communicated to the Queen, Her Majesty summoned Lord John Russell to form a cabinet, and, to smooth his path, Sir Robert Peel, with characteristic frankness, sent a memorandum to Her Majesty embodying a promise to give him his support. But Lord John Russell failed in his efforts, and the Queen had no alternative but to recall Sir Robert Peel, and give him full power to

A new cabinet.

carry out his measures. It was under such circumstances that parliament was called for January 22, 1846, and on January 27 the government plan was propounded before a crowded house. It was not an immediate repeal of the corn laws that Sir Robert Peel recommended. He proposed a temporary protection for three years, till February 1, 1849, imposing a scale during that time ranging from 4s. when the price of wheat should be 50s. per quarter and upward, and 10s. when the price should be under 48s. per quarter, and that after that period all grain should be admitted at the uniform duty of 1s. per quarter. The measure, as might have been expected, was received in a very different manner by the political parties in both Houses of Parliament. There was treason in the conservative camp, and keen and bitter was the opposition they offered to their chief. For twelve nights speaker after speaker indulged in personal recriminations. They recalled to Sir Robert Peel's memory the speeches he had made in defence of the corn laws. And as to his assertion that he had changed his mind, they denied his right to do so. Mr. Colquhoun 'wondered that Sir Robert could say, "I have changed my opinion, and there is an end of it." But there was not an end of it. His right hon. friend must not forget the laws by which the words of men of genius—whether orators or poets—are bound with them. His right hon. friend's words could not thus pass away. They were winged shafts that pierced many minds. They remained after the occasion which produced them passed away. His right hon. friend must remember that the words which he had used adhered to the memory, moulded men's sentiments, guided public opinion. He must recollect that the armour of proof which he had laid aside, and the lance which he had wielded, and with which he had pierced many an encumbered opponent, remained weighty and entire. Greatly did he wish that his right hon. friend were again on this side to wield them—that he were here to lead their ranks and guide them by his prowess. But if not, they retained at least his arms, these lay at their feet, strewed all around them, an arsenal of power.' Petulant remonstrances like these were of course of little avail. Sir Robert Peel and Mr. Cobden were ready to meet every challenge and to refute every argument with their unanswerable logic of facts. And when the opposition endeavoured to throw all the responsibility of a measure of such a character on the prime minister, Mr. Cobden besought them to turn from the will of one individual to those laws economic and divine which seemed to impose the duty of laying wide open the door for the importation of food. 'Oh, then, divest the future prime minister of this country of that odious task of having to reconcile rival interests; divest the office, if ever you would have a sagacious man in power as prime minister, divest it of the responsibility of having to find food for the people! May you never find a prime minister again to undertake that awful responsibility! That responsibility belongs to the law of Nature; as Burke said, it belongs to God alone to regulate the supply of the food of nations. . . . We have set an example to the world in all ages; we have given them the representative system. The very rules and regulations of this House have been taken as the model for every representative assembly throughout the whole civilised world; and having besides given them the example of a free press and civil and religious freedom, and every institution that belongs to freedom and civilisation, we are now about giving a still greater example; we are going to set the example of making industry free—to set the example of giving the whole world every advantage of clime and latitude and situation, relying ourselves on the freedom of our industry. Yes, we are going to teach the world that other lesson. Don't think there is anything selfish in this, or anything at all discordant with Christian principles. I can prove that we advocate nothing but what is agreeable to the highest behests of Christianity. To buy in the cheapest market and sell in the dearest. What is the meaning of the maxim? It means that you take the article which you have in the greatest abundance, and with it obtain from others that of which they have the most to spare, so giving to mankind the means of enjoying the fullest abundance of earth's goods, and in doing so carrying out to the fullest extent the Christian doctrine of "Do ye to all men as ye would they should do unto you."' The passing of the measure was, however, more than certain, and after a debate of twelve nights' duration on Mr. Miles' amendment, the government obtained a majority of 97, 337 having voted for the motion and 240 against it. And from that evening the corn law may be said to have expired.[1] Not a day too soon, certainly, when we consider the straitened resources of the country as regards the first article of food caused not only by the bad crop of grain but by the serious loss of the potato crop, especially in Ireland.

Ireland and the potato crop.

Ireland has often grievously suffered from social and political wrongs, from absenteeism and repeal cries, from Protestant and Roman Catholic bigotry, from orangeism and ribbonism, from threatening notices and mid-day assassinations, but seldom has her cup of adversity been so brimfull as in 1845 and 1846 from the failure of the potato crop. Though comparatively of recent importation, the first potato root having been imported by Sir Walter Raleigh in 1610, potatoes had for years constituted a large proportion of the food of the people of Ireland. A considerable acreage of land was devoted to that culture, and an acre of potatoes would feed more than double the number of individuals that can be fed from an acre of wheat. Such cultivation was, moreover, very attractive to small holders of land. It cost little labour. It entailed scarcely any expense, and little or no care was bestowed on it, since the people were quite satisfied with the coarsest and most prolific kind, called lumpers or horse potatoes. Nor was it the food of the people only in Ireland. Pigs and poultry shared the potatoes with the peasant's family, and often became the inmates of his cabin also. One great evil connected with potato culture is, that whilst the crop is precarious and uncertain, it cannot be stored up. The surplus of one abundant year is quite unfit to use in the next, and owing to its great bulk it cannot even be transported from place to place. Moreover, once used to a description of food so extremely cheap no retrenchment is possible, and when blight comes and the crop is destroyed the people seem doomed to absolute starvation. This unfortunately was the case in 1822 and 1831. In those years public subscriptions were got up, king's letters issued, balls and bazaars held, and public money granted. But in 1845 and 1846 the calamity was greater than any previously experienced.

[1] 9 & 10 Vict. c. 22, suspended by 10 & 11 Vict. c. 1.

The potato disease.

The potato disease first manifested itself in 1845. The early crop, dug in September and October, which consists of one-sixth of the whole, nearly escaped; but the whole of the late crop, the people's crop, dug in December and January, was tainted before arriving at maturity. In that year there was a full average crop of wheat. Oats and barley were abundant, and turnips, carrots, and greens, including hay, were sufficient. Yet on the continent the rye crop failed, and the potato disease appeared in Belgium, Holland, France, and the West of Germany. On the whole the supply of grain was fair during the year 1845, and prices ruled moderately high. In 1846, however, blight attacked the potatoes with even greater fury and suddenness in the month of July, and it attacked both the early crop and the people's crop, at the same time that the wheat crop proved under an average. Barley and oats were also deficient, and the rye crop again failed on the continent. In the previous year some counties escaped the potato disease, but this year the whole country suffered alike. The loss was indeed very great. Probably 13,000,000*l.* was a low estimate, and from 4,000,000 to 5,000,000 quarters of grain at least would be required to replace it. As might be expected, the news of such a disaster had a fearful effect throughout the country, and the utter helplessness of many millions of our fellow-subjects became a subject of the greatest anxiety.

Government commission on the potato disease. Means of relief.

As soon as the potato disease appeared in 1845 government took the step of appointing Professors Kane, Lindley, and Playfair, to inquire into the nature of the disease, and to suggest means for preserving the stock, but this was of little avail. Urged now by necessity, the government even stepped out of its province, and sent orders to the United States for the purchase of 100,000*l.* worth of Indian corn, established depôts in different parts, and formed relief committees. But this was nothing compared with what became necessary to be done in 1846. Public works were then commenced on a large scale, giving employment to some five hundred thousand persons. The poor law acted with unparalleled vigour, to the extent that in July 1847 as many as three millions of persons were actually receiving separate rations. A loan of 8,000,000*l.* was made by government expressly to supply such wants, and every step was taken by two successive administrations, Sir Robert Peel's and Lord John Russell's, to alleviate the sufferings of the people. Nor was private benevolence lacking. The Society of Friends, always ready in acts of charity and love, was foremost in the good work. A British association was formed for the relief of Ireland, including Jones Loyd (Lord Overstone), Thomas Baring, and Baron Rothschild. A Queen's letter was issued. A day of general fast and humiliation was held, and subscriptions were received from almost every quarter of the world. The Queen's letter alone produced 171,533*l.* The British association collected 263,000*l.*; the Society of Friends 43,000*l.*; and 168,000*l.* more were entrusted to the Dublin Society of Friends. The sultan of Turkey sent 1,000*l.* The Queen gave 2,000*l.*, and 500*l.* more to the British ladies' clothing fund. Prince Albert gave 500*l.* The National Club collected 17,930*l.* America sent two ships of war, the 'Jamestown' and 'Macedonian,' full of provisions; and the Irish residents in the United States sent upwards of 200,000*l.* to their relatives to allow them to emigrate. But with all this, the people passed through a most eventful catastrophe. One-third of the people at least was reduced to destitution. A large number died by fever and pestilence. Such as could raise the requisite funds emigrated to America. Crowds of emaciated and famished people flocked by every available means to English ports. The rest were kept alive by employment on public works, by private local charity, by local subscriptions, by contributions from all parts of the world, and by the most extensive system of gratuitous distribution of food which history affords any record of.

The price of wheat and other grain did not rise much at first. Indeed, for a lengthened time but faint conception was entertained of any want of foreign grain. The potato failure was comparatively a new thing, and few imagined that it would act powerfully on the consumption of grain. In 1845 the average price of wheat was no more than 50*s.* 11*d.* per imperial quarter, it having risen from a minimum of 45*s.* 3*d.* in March to 58*s.* 10*d.* in November; whilst the

Price of wheat.

average price of barley was 31*s.* 8*d.*, and of oats 22*s.* 6*d.* In 1846 also the average price of wheat was 54*s.* 8*d.*, the price having ruled first 55*s.* 6*d.*, falling to 46*s.* 3*d.* in August, and rising to 60*s.* 7*d.* in November, whilst the average price of barley was 32*s.* 8*d.*, and of oats 23*s.* 8*d.* But in 1847 a sudden great rise took place. The price of wheat rose from an average of 69*s.* 11*d.* in January to an average of 92*s.* 10*d.* in June; the price of barley was 50*s.* 2*d.* in January, 53*s.* 5*d.* in February, and 52*s.* 11*d.* in May and June; and oats, commencing at 29*s.* 6*d.* in January, rose to 34*s.* 2*d.* in June. In July, however, a sudden change took place by the concurrent action of large importations and excellent prospects of the approaching harvest, so that prices fell at a rapid pace. From June to December wheat fell from 92*s.* 10*d.* to 52*s.* 3*d.*, barley from 52*s.* 11*d.* to 30*s.* 9*d.*, and oats from 34*s.* 2*d.* to 21*s.* 10*d.* per imperial quarter. The importation of grain had never been so large as in this year. In former years 1,000,000 or 2,000,000 quarters was the maximum, but in 1846 we imported 4,752,174 quarters of grain and meal, and in 1847 as much as 11,912,864 quarters, the greatest increase having taken place from Russia and America. Then indeed we realised that the corn laws could not be maintained any longer. Our dependence on foreign grain became very great, and thankful indeed we were, that by the wisdom and foresight of our legislators even the last corn law and the navigation law were suspended and our ports opened to the supply of food from any quarter of the globe.

Another important consequence of the potato disease was an enormous stimulus to emigration. Great is the change in the state of public opinion and law as respects emigration. In olden, yet not very remote times an absolute prohibition existed against the departure of artisans from this country, and we would have regarded as a dire misfortune the departure of hundreds and thousands of families from our shores in quest of happier homes and more fruitful sources of industry. Now, we see whole fleets of emigrant ships carrying away many of the ablest and most industrious of our working population without a murmur of complaint or a feeling of sorrow. And why? Because we feel that they only obey the

Increase of emigration.

law of nature which is always foreseeing and beneficent. Even savages are impelled by their economical condition to be always moving in quest of food, and when civilisation created new wants, a still greater impulse was given to migrations from place to place. Sometimes the centres of industry became grand points of attraction. Sometimes religious and political dissensions have been the causes of great emigration. But motion is a law of human society, and endless processions are always moving, now from south to north, and anon from north to south; at one time from west to east, and at another from east to west. As for this country, the constant alternation of times of prosperity and distress in commerce and manufactures renders it the more necessary for our working people to have other outlets for their industries than are afforded within these circumscribed islands, and it is fortunate that the colonies are ever open for the employment of any number of labourers. As early as 1826 and 1827, the subject of emigration engaged the attention of the House of Commons, and their recommendation was that the emigrants should be settled upon land granted by the state, and that whatever fund be advanced for their benefit should be subject to repayment. In 1831, a royal commission inquired into the subject, and whilst it did not approve of any direct grant of money for emigration to Canada and other North American colonies, it recommended that as respects New South Wales and Van Diemen's Land the proceeds of public land sold should be devoted, as loans of 20*l.* and upwards, towards the passage money of families of mechanics and agricultural labourers, and as bounties of, and towards the conveyance of, young unmarried females. This recommendation was subsequently adopted, and carried out by the colonial office, and then a loan for the Australian emigrants was converted into a free gift and increased to 30*l.*, the bounty to single females being also increased to 30*l.* But notwithstanding these encouragements, the emigration from the United Kingdom continued very limited for a long time. For sixteen years, from 1815 to 1830, the average number of emigrants was only 23,000 per annum, most of whom went to the North American colonies and the United States of America. From 1831 to 1840, the average number of emigrants increased to

70,000 per annum, Australia then commencing to attract great attention, and from 1841 to 1846 the average still further increased to 100,000. But in 1847 and subsequent years, the stream of emigration flowed in a most rapid manner. Ireland sent forth the greater part of her labouring population, and in the decennium from 1847 to 1856 the number of emigrants actually increased to 280,000 per annum. It was a pitiful sight to see those crowds of worn-out Irish embarking in rags and penniless for a foreign shore. But they went away from a place of sorrow and suffering to a country which seemed to open a boundless field for the exercise of honest industry. Nor was the benefit of emigration limited to the emigrants themselves. The advantage was quite as great to the mother country. Here, they added nothing to national wealth. They constituted the mortified part of the social system which needed amputation. There, not only they ceased to trench upon the labour of others, but, after providing food for themselves, they became large customers for our produce and manufactures.

Ere we pass from the repeal of the corn law and its consequences reference must be made to an achievement certainly not less important in relation to the economic policy of the country, the repeal of the navigation law. In 1845 these laws were consolidated, and it seemed as if they were to continue for many a year in existence, but the necessity for suspending their operation in 1846 and 1847, and the progress of public opinion in matters of free trade, suggested an inquiry into the operation and policy of such laws in 1847. Of that committee Mr. Milner Gibson was chairman, and during the year they published five reports on the subject, containing valuable evidence tending to show the objections to such laws and the injury which they caused, notwithstanding their restricted operation, a large portion of the trade being no longer protected by them. Evidence was given to the effect that, looking to the geographical position of this country, and to the peculiar energy of her people, the extent of her trade, her great capital, and her success in maritime enterprise, there need be no limit to the prosperity of her shipping were it not for the restrictions and unnecessary charges imposed on it by

Repeal of the navigation law.

the navigation act, the registry act, and several other acts. It was urged, that if we could reduce the cost of ships, and consequently of freights, we should increase trade to an enormous extent; that the immense traffic which railways occasioned in this country was the strongest proof that cheap conveyance on the sea would be attended with similar results, and that we should not only obtain a much larger quantity of goods than have hitherto come to market, but that we should find new exchangeable commodities which did not then come here; that we should bring the timber of India or Australia at half its present cost; and that we should carry on the fisheries to a much greater extent, and be enabled to increase every branch of industry in this and other countries to a very large extent. Shipowners certainly prognosticated all manner of evil likely to arise from the repeal of the navigation laws. They warned the nation that such laws had raised it to the station it held, and that without them it would as rapidly go down as it had risen. They were certain that the repeal of such laws would reduce shipping property fully 30 per cent. in value, and introduce the cheap navigation of other countries in competition with the costly navigation of this country, and that, despairing of success, the British shipowner must retire from the contest. Really, however, the advocates of the navigation laws had little to say in their favour based on substantial facts. The committee made no report in 1847, but the general impression was that the repeal of such laws would benefit trade, and that the necessity for action had become imminent.

Reciprocity and the navigation laws.

Accordingly in 1848, as soon as public attention could be given to the subject, Mr. Labouchere, in committee of the whole house, moved a resolution to the effect: 'That it is expedient to remove the restrictions which prevent the carriage of goods by sea to and from the United Kingdom and the British possessions abroad, and to amend the laws regulating the coasting trade of the United Kingdom, subject, nevertheless, to such control as may be necessary, and also to amend the laws for the registration of ships and seamen.' But a concerted opposition was made to such proposition, and Mr. Herries moved a counter resolution: 'That it is essential to the national interest of the country to maintain the fundamental principles of the navigation laws, subject to such modifications as may be best calculated to obviate any proved inconvenience to the commerce of the United Kingdom and its dependencies, and without danger to our national strength.' The discussion was long and animated, and the two opposing views were fully enforced and illustrated, but it ended, as might have been expected, in the defeat of Mr. Harries's amendment by a majority of 294 against 177. But the session was lost, and the subject had to be deferred to another year. Again, however, in 1849 Mr. Labouchere proposed the same resolution, only adding that provision should be made giving power to the Queen in council to re-enact these laws, wholly or in part, with regard to any countries as to which the government might think fit that they should be preserved. Power was given to him to bring in a bill, and it was read a second time by a majority of 266 to 210. As originally proposed the bill was intended to throw open the coasting trade as well as the foreign trade, but the government of the United States having notified their refusal to reciprocate this concession, and some objection having been raised by the department of customs because of the difficulty of enforcing effectual regulations to guard the revenue from danger, the clauses relating to the coasting trade were withdrawn, and the bill passed into law.[1] But even this restriction was ultimately relinquished, and both the navigation on the coast of the United kingdom and the manning of British ships were left entirely free.[2]

[1] 12 & 13 Vict. c. 29. [2] 16 & 17 Vict. c. 107, and 17 & 18 Vict. c. 120.

CHAPTER IV.

A COMMERCIAL CRISIS.

1847.

Increase of Capital.—Means of Transport.—Commercial Crises.—The Bank of England and the Bank Charter Act.—Reaction.—Petition for Relief.—The Government Letter.—Parliamentary Enquiry.—Report of the House of Commons Committee.—Report of Committee of the House of Lords.—Vote in the House of Commons.—Bad Harvests in France.—The Bank of France and the Revolution.

Increase of capital.

ONE of the important objects contemplated by the restriction imposed on the issue of notes being the checking of speculation and the preventing as far as possible of great monetary crises, we might have expected that for some years at least trade would be safe, slow, and progressive. But it was not long ere a great revolution manifested itself in trade and finance, which completely disappointed even the well-wishers of the new monetary legislation. It was estimated by the late Mr. Wilson, in his work on 'Capital, Currency, and Banking,' that the annual accumulation of property in the United Kingdom between 1840 and 1845 could not be less than sixty millions sterling. And though a large portion of such saving was required in the numerous branches of industry for their own improvement and extension, there must always be a large surplus in quest of any promising employment. In truth, capital in England increases more rapidly than the means of profitably and safely employing it, and consequently from time to time a fierce competition arises between the owners of capital for the means of investing their surplus stock. Ever since the reforms introduced by Sir Robert Peel the country had been very prosperous, the labouring classes were fully employed, and capital had been steadily growing in the country. The amount of bullion in the Bank of England had never been so large. Consols were at par. The rate of interest for short periods on the best securities did not exceed 2½ per cent. There was in fact a great want of means of investment, and when it was found that one or two great lines of railway proved most successful, and other lines unusually inviting, the people readily rushed into railway speculation. Nor was this either unreasonable or inexpedient.

The railway was working a moral reformation in the country. At the close of the last century the internal transport of goods was so very slow and expensive as to prevent the transport of all goods except manufactured articles or goods of light weight, which could bear a high rate of transport. Not many articles could well stand a charge of 40s. a ton from Liverpool to Manchester, and 13*l*. a ton from London to Leeds. Heavy goods and minerals were transported by sea only, and many of the richest districts of the country remained unproductive, awaiting the tardy advancement of the art of transport. When the railway was introduced, all this was changed. By the facility afforded for passenger traffic, and by the certainty and rapidity of conveyance of goods, however burthensome and heavy, the resources of the country were being developed in an extraordinary manner. Districts hitherto secluded and unknown were found to possess advantages for commerce and industry which the inhabitants themselves had never dreamt of. An immense economy of capital and labour was the necessary attendant of such a change in locomotion. A man could do more in one day than he could have done formerly in three or four. The merchant could look for his returns in much less time than he had been in the habit of receiving them. Altogether the nation saw that the railway system was a wonderful engine of material progress, and it became evident that every town of any importance, and every district possessing either agricultural or mineral wealth, must sooner or later have its railway. From 1821 to 1826 railway acts were passed authorising the raising of a capital of 1,263,000*l*. From 1826 to 1843 the capital authorised to be raised was 57,387,000*l*. by shares, and 21,658,000*l*. by loans. Total 79,045,000*l*. In 1844 railway acts were passed involving an expenditure of about 15,000,000*l*. In 1845 the rage for railway speculation reached an extraordinary height. The prices of shares both of railways in operation and of merely projected lines rose immensely. The Leeds and Thirsk Rail-

Means of transport.

way 50*l*. shares, with 2*l*. 10*s*. paid, were selling in March at 3*l*. 10*s*., and in September at 23*l*. 15*s*. The Bolton, Wigan, and Liverpool 40*l*. shares, with 4*l*. paid, were worth in January 4*l*. 10*s*., in September 42*l*. 15*s*. The Great Western shares were quoted at 156*l*. in January, and in September 228*l*. The Midland which in January was at 114*l*., in September rose to 188*l*. It is easy to see how princely fortunes were created or lost, and how wild the people were with a market so excited. But what rigging of the market, what abortive schemes, and what frauds! How could a frenzy like this fail to bring about its own retribution?

Commercial crises and panics seem to follow a given law. Trade seems to run in cycles of 7 or 10 years. We had panics as near as possible in 1797, 1807, 1817, 1826, 1837, 1847, 1857, the number seven, the golden number, being a fatal year apparently. But we need not be surprised. Times of prosperity are often succeeded by times of adversity. Under the influence of steady success, years glide on, and we are flushed with prosperity. A crisis comes, and we must retract our steps. Experience, then, teaches caution, and under its wise guidance courage revives, but we speedily return to a state of indiscretion, and a fall is certain to succeed. This alternation of ups and downs has, however, been too frequent and too regular not to engage the most earnest attention, and many are the theories that have been suggested regarding them, though they are the consequences of natural causes, which no legislation can foresee and prevent, nor the action of any bank effectually control. According to some the Bank of England is the cause of all mischief. Whoever follows the majority of the speeches and opinions expressed with reference to currency, cannot fail to see that the directors of the Bank of England were generally supposed to enjoy the great privilege of acting as conservators of the currency and regulators of the money market. According to them it is the Bank that capriciously regulates the rate of interest; the Bank that makes money scarce or abundant; the Bank that applies the screw; the Bank that loosens it. Yet such a notion is absolutely erroneous. Very limited, indeed, is the power of the Bank. It is not the Bank that makes money scarce or abundant. It is

Commercial crises.

not in the power of the Bank to keep any amount of issue in circulation for any time. It is not the Bank that creates speculation; it is not the Bank that can arrest it. The economic laws which regulate the issues of notes are more powerful than any caprice of Bank directors, and prove in reality of much more salutary control than any legislative restriction.

Nothing could have been more carefully devised than the Bank Charter Acts of 1844 and 1845. It was clearly the intention of Sir Robert Peel that they should prevent the panics and pressures which so often spread alarm and confusion in the mercantile world. And yet how fruitless have they proved, at least for that purpose. Scarcely two years elapsed after the passing of the acts when another panic took place, exceeding in intensity and duration any yet experienced. When the Bank Charter Act passed in 1844 capital was abundant, so much so that in September 1844 the rate of interest fell from 4 per cent. to 2½ per cent. for bills at short, and 3 per cent. for bills at long dates, and in 1845 the rate fell to 2½ per cent. for bills and notes. Consequently there was considerable speculation in railway and much animation in every branch of business. Still the amount of bullion in the Bank was on the increase, and in the week ending August 29, 1846, it reached the enormous sum of 16,000,000*l.* By that time, however, the failure of the potato crop, and the consequent need of a large importation of corn, manifested itself and an extraordinary excitement prevailed in the share market, which produced a rise in the rate of interest to 3 per cent. It would have been better had the Bank raised the rate of discount still higher. But it did not do so till January 1847, when the rate was raised first to 3½ per cent., and soon after to 4 per cent., by which time the bullion and reserve had considerably diminished. Considerable alarm then commenced to be felt, and on April 8 the Bank increased the rate of discount to 5 per cent., without naming that it applied to bills of the term of 95 days, so that although the minimum rate was charged for bills having no more than sixty days to run, much higher rates were charged for long dated paper.

The Bank of England and the Bank Charter Act.

What was the effect of this increased tightness of the money market on speculation may well be imagined. As it became more and more difficult to provide funds to meet the heavy calls for railway purposes, the value of shares fell fearfully, causing heavy losses to all who held them. Gradually the alarm and anxiety spread to the various branches of trade. The cotton trade, which had been for a year or two in a feverish condition, owing to the shortness of the American crop, suffered immensely. Considerable speculation had taken place in pig-iron, makers selling large quantities of pig-iron for future delivery; and prices went down from 5*l.* to 3*l.* per ton. The corn merchants, who for some time had great difficulty in obtaining advances upon cargoes in consequence of the high rate of discount, lost immense sums from the great fall in prices which took place, owing to the prospect of an abundant harvest. And the result of this was the failure of many houses in the corn trade which became the signal for heavy bankruptcies. Several banks succumbed, and credit was severely shaken. It being impossible for the London bankers and discount brokers to meet the demand of their customers, they were obliged to resort to the Bank of England. Money was hoarded to a considerable extent. Consols fell to 85, and everything seemed to indicate an approaching national bankruptcy.[1]

Reaction.

In July 1847 the merchants and bankers of the City of London petitioned for an immediate remedy. They complained that they were suffering under a monetary pressure without precedent, that there was a complete suspension of the ordinary facilities for business, that they could no longer discount legitimate commercial bills, and that all monetary accommodation was withheld. They stated that the panic was not caused either by any undue extension of commerce, or by a spirit of speculation. But that whereas in former times the Bank of England had the power of continuing facilities to commerce until trade was restored, then the Bank of England, in consequence of the Bank Charter Act,

Petition for relief.

[1] In the evidence given before the committee on the Bank Acts in 1858 it was stated that in 1847 the majority of the houses that failed were of old standing, originally most legitimate and respectable, but that at a later period of their existence they got into a vicious system of credit.

could give no facilities whatever. In conclusion, the London merchants petitioned the house that a relaxing power should be lodged with the exchequer, and that the Bank should have power to issue notes on silver bullion without restriction. No step was, however, taken in parliament, and matters grew worse and worse. Under such circumstances, a deputation of Liverpool merchants waited on Her Majesty's ministers, and presented a memorial warning the government that unless some relief was afforded many merchants of undoubted respectability and absolutely wealthy would be compelled to suspend payment. Still the government refused to move. At last a deputation of London merchants waited on the government, on Saturday, October 23, and made a statement which convinced the prime minister that the time had arrived when the restrictions of the Bank Charter Act must be removed. A promise was then and there given that relief would be afforded, and the deputation retired, convinced that on that very day greater accommodation would be granted to the public.

A cabinet council was thereupon held at Lord John Russell's house, on the Sunday following, and on the 25th, the following letter was issued: The government letter.

Downing Street, October 25, 1847.

Gentlemen,—Her Majesty's Government have seen with the deepest regret the pressure which has existed for some weeks upon the commercial interests of the country, and that this pressure has been aggravated by a want of that confidence which is necessary for carrying on the ordinary dealings of trade.

They have been in hope that the check given to transactions of a speculative character, the transfer of capital from other countries, the influx of bullion, and the feeling which a knowledge of these circumstances might have been expected to produce, would have removed the prevailing distrust.

They were encouraged in this expectation by the speedy cessation of a similar state of feeling in the month of April last.

These hopes have, however, been disappointed, and Her Majesty's Government have come to the conclusion that the time has arrived when they ought to attempt, by some extraordinary and temporary measure, to restore confidence to the mercantile and manufacturing community.

For this purpose they recommend to the directors of the Bank of England, in the present emergency, to enlarge the amount of their discounts and advances upon approved security; but that, in order to retain this operation within reasonable limits, a high rate of interest should be charged.

In present circumstances they would suggest that the rate of interest should not be less than 8 per cent.

If this course should lead to any infringement of the existing law Her Majesty's Government will be prepared to propose to parliament, on its meeting, a bill of indemnity. They will rely upon the discretion of the directors to reduce, as soon as possible, the amount of their notes, if any extraordinary issue should take place, within the limits prescribed by law.

Her Majesty's Government are of opinion that any extra profit derived from this measure should be carried to the account of the public, but the precise mode of doing so must be left to future arrangement.

Her Majesty's Government are not insensible of the evil of any departure from the law which has placed the currency of this country upon a sound basis; but they feel confident that in the present circumstances the measure which they have proposed may be safely adopted, and at the same time the main provisions of that law, and the vital principle of preserving the convertibility of the bank note, be firmly maintained. We have, &c.

(Signed) J. RUSSELL,
CHARLES WOOD.

The Governor and Deputy-Governor of the Bank of England.

By the issue of this letter a better spirit was imparted to trade, and the panic was at an end. The improvement was produced, however, not so much by any immediate issue of notes, as by the assurance thereby afforded, that accommodation might now be obtained. This, as Mr. Glyn stated, 'produced the same effect as if the Bank of England had made an issue, because it brought out the hoards of notes and they went into circulation.' Thus the letter practically added to the circulation of the country, and removed the cause of the panic. And it is singular that although the treasury letter authorised a departure from the limits imposed by law, no extra issue ever took place.

Parliamentary inquiry. Report of the House of Commons committee.

In November parliament was called together, and the first question discussed was the position of the Bank of England, and the appointment of committees of both houses to enquire into the causes of the recent commercial distress, and how far it has been affected by the laws for regulating the issue of bank notes payable on demand.

The discussion itself was not of great importance, except as eliciting the opinion of Sir Robert Peel as to the effect of his measure on the crisis, and certainly his speech throws great light on the relation of the Act of 1844 to that of 1819. The committee of the House of Commons consisted of the Chancellor of the Exchequer, Sir Robert Peel, Mr. Cobden, Mr. Herries, Mr. Cayley, Mr. Labouchere, Mr. Disraeli, Mr. Glyn, Mr. Home Drummond, Sir James Graham, Mr. Thomas Baring, Lord George Bentinck, Mr. Beckett, Mr. Alderman Thompson, Mr. Hudson, Mr. J. L. Ricardo, Mr. James Wilson, Mr. F. T. Baring, Lord John Russell, Mr. Spooner, Mr. Goulburn, Mr. Cardwell, Mr. Hume, Mr. Thornley, Sir William Clay, and Mr. Tennent, and, after a searching enquiry, it reported that there was a concurrence of opinion amongst the witnesses that the primary cause of the distress was the deficient harvest, especially of the potato crop in 1846, and the necessity for providing the means of payment in 1847 for the unprecedented importation of various descriptions of food which took place in that year.[2] Among other causes, the deficient supply of cotton,[3] the diversion of capital from its ordinary employment in commercial transactions to the construction of railroads,[4] the undue extension of credit, especially in our transactions with the East, and exaggerated expectations of extended trade were stated as having contributed to the same result. The committee commented on the conduct of the Bank of England, and concluded by stating that they had under their consideration, whether it was advisable that powers should be conferred by law upon the government to enable them to meet the advent of circumstances which might call for extraordinary interference, but that they came to the conclusion that, looking to the impossibility of foreseeing what the precise character of the circumstances might be, it was more expedient to leave to those with whom the responsibility of the government might rest at the

[2] In 1847 there were imported 11,500,000 cwt. wheat, 2,750,000 cwt. barley, 4,690,000 cwt. oats, 15,461,000 cwt. maize, and 6,329,000 cwt. flour of wheat.

[3] The imports of cotton, which in 1845 were 6,400,000 cwt., decreased in 1846 and 1847 to 4,200,000 cwt.

[4] The capital paid up in shares and loans for railway purposes was in 1845 88,481,000*l.*; in 1846, 126,296,000*l.*, in 1847, 167,321,000*l.*, and in 1868, 200,173,000*l.*

time, to adopt such measures as might appear to them best suited for the emergency. The committee, therefore, after a careful review of all the evidence, were of opinion that it was not expedient to make any alteration in the Bank Act of 1844. But this resolution was arrived at by a very slender majority. Mr. Hume moved, 'That, in the opinion of this committee, the laws for regulating the issue of bank notes payable on demand have aggravated the commercial distress in England in the year 1847,' and the motion was lost by eleven members voting in the affirmative and thirteen in the negative. Nearly every paragraph of the report originally prepared by the chancellor of the exchequer met with strong opposition, and was the subject of a division.

The committee of the House of Lords in their report entered at much greater length into the operation of the Bank Charter Act. After examining into the causes and extent of the distress of 1847, and the effects of the treasury letter of October 25, the report went on to show that the principle of the Bank Act requiring that the efficiency of the circulation should be identical with its money amount is erroneous, because it depends on many other circumstances, such as the rapidity of circulation, the number of exchanges performed in a given time, as well as upon its numerical amount; and that, moreover, such a rule is inapplicable to periods of favourable and of adverse foreign exchange. The committee dwelt on the increased fluctuations in the rate of discount since the passing of the act of 1844; criticised the limitation of the amount of silver by the act of 1844, an alteration of which would not involve any alteration in the standard; and then entered into the remedial measures recommended by the witnesses giving their opinion in favour of the introduction of a discretionary relaxing power, to be vested in the Bank of England alone, rather than in the Government, or the Government and the Bank conjointly. Generally, the opinion of the committee was decidedly adverse to the operation of the bank acts. 'To those who may have expected that the 7 & 8 Vict. c. 32 would effectually prevent a recurrence of cycles of commercial excitement and depression, the contrast between the years 1845 and 1847 must produce a grievous dis-

Report of committee of the House of Lords.

appointment. To those who anticipated that the act would put a check on improvident speculation the disappointment cannot be less, if reliance is to be placed (as the committee are confident it may) on the statement of the governor of the Bank, and of other witnesses, that speculations were never carried to such an enormous extent as in 1846 and the beginning of 1847. If the act were relied on as a security against violent fluctuations in the value of money, the fallaciousness of such anticipation is conclusively proved by the fact, that whilst the difference between the highest and lowest rate of discount was in the calamitous years 1837 and 1839 but 2½ to 2¾ per cent., the difference in 1847 rose to 6¾. If it was contemplated that the number and the extent of commercial failures would have been lessened, the deplorable narrative of the governor of the Bank, recording the failure of thirty-three houses comparatively in large business, in London alone, to the amount of 8,129,000*l.*, is a conclusive reply. If the enormous extent to which railroad speculation has been carried be considered as an evil to which no sound system of banking could have applied a corrective, such a corrective has not been found in an act, since the passing of which, during a period of three years, an increased railway capital of upwards of 221,000,000*l.* has been authorised to be raised by parliament, and when the enormous sum of 76,390,000*l.* is stated, on high financial authority to have been actually expended on railways in two years and a half. If the power of obtaining banking accommodation on moderate terms were considered to be promoted by the act of 1844, it cannot be said that this important object has been attained, since it appears in evidence that in 1847, in addition to an interest of 9 or 10 per cent., a commission was also frequently paid, raising the charge to 10, 20, or 30 per cent., according to the time which bills had to run. The committee are fully aware that alternations of periods of commercial excitement, and of discredit, of speculation, and of collapse are likely to arise under all systems of currency: it would be visionary to imagine that they could be averted altogether, even if the circulation were exclusively metallic. But it is on this account that great care should be taken to avoid increasing an evil, perhaps inevitable, by any arbitrary and artificial enactments.'

Before the presentation of these reports a discussion took place on the subject in the House of Commons, when Mr. Herries moved, 'That, looking to the state of distress which has for some time prevailed among the commercial classes, and to the general feeling of distrust and alarm by which the embarrassments of trade have been aggravated, it is the opinion of this house that Her Majesty's ministers were justified during the recess of parliament, in recommending to the Bank of England, for the purpose of restoring confidence, a course of proceeding at variance with the restrictions imposed by the Act of the 7 & 8 Vict. c. 32, and that this house will resolve itself into a committee upon the said act.' Mr. Herries further declared his opinion that should the house assent to that proposition, he would propose, 'That it is expedient that the limitations imposed by the Act 7 & 8 Vict. c. 32 upon the Bank of England, and the Act 8 & 9, c. 36 & 37, in relation to the issue of notes payable on demand, be suspended, subject to such conditions as may be provided by any act to be passed for that purpose.' The first motion was, however, lost by 122 to 163, and thus the discussion ended. In August 1848, again Mr. Herries brought the subject before the house, and moved 'That this house will, early in the next session of parliament, take into its serious consideration the reports from the committee of this house and from the committee of the House of Lords, communicated to this house, appointed to inquire into the causes of the recent commercial distress, and how far it has been affected by the laws for regulating the issue of bank notes payable on demand.' But the motion was negatived without a division.

Vote of the House of Commons on the Bank Acts.

Some circumstances which had considerable influence on the trade of England at this period have not yet been mentioned. They are the bad harvest, and the unsettled condition of France in 1847. In that year the price of wheat, which usually ranged at 40s. to 50s. per quarter, rose to 67s. 4d., and instead of exporting, France had to import large quantities of grain, for which she had to make heavy payments. The commerce of France had not prospered during the reign of Louis-Philippe. The imports for home consumption were checked by a prohibitory tariff, the exports were not

Bad harvests in France.

increasing, and the people were not able to bear the losses and sacrifices which a bad harvest always entails. Were matters closely scrutinised, it would be found, that it was more from economic evils than from political instability, that France entered into that revolution which seemed to shake from the very centre not only France but every throne in Europe.

The Bank of France and the French Revolution.

The revolution of 1848 had a considerable influence not only on trade and industry,[6] but on banking and finance. On the Bank of France the revolution produced a great change. In 1815 the capital of the bank had been reduced to 62,900,000 fr., its two branches at Rouen and Lyons were closed, and its operations were limited to the metropolis. After the revolution of 1830, the want of banking accommodation being great, departmental banks were opened at Lyons, Marseilles, Lille, Orleans, Havre, and Toulouse, and the amount of their discounts rose from 352,000,000 fr. in 1838 to 851,000,000 fr. in 1847. The Bank of France, however, became jealous of their progress, and on the occasion of the renewal of its charter sought and obtained a stipulation prohibiting the formation of any new departmental bank. But when, in 1848, the provisional government made enormous demands on the resources of the bank, and a suspension of cash payments became necessary, a further step was taken towards the unification of banking, and by an arbitrary measure all the departmental banks were suddenly converted into branches of the Bank of France. The year of 1848 was a trying one for France and for all countries. Commerce and industry can never make progress whilst revolution and uncertainty weaken the institutions of the state.

[6] The imports and exports of France were greatly affected by the revolution. In 1847 the value of imports was 53,713,000*l*., and of exports 50,828,000*l*. Total, 104,541,000*l*. In 1848 the imports were 34,475,000*l*., the exports 46,120,000*l*., total 80,595,000*l*., a decline of 23 per cent. The declared value of British manufactures exported to France in 1847 was 2,551,000*l*., and in 1848 1,025,000*l*.

CHAPTER V.

INTERNATIONAL EXHIBITIONS.

1851—1867.

The Lord Mayor's Banquet.—Prince Albert's and Sir Robert Peel's Speeches.—History of Industrial Exhibitions.—Results of the Exhibition of 1851.—Comparative state of Industry.—Progress of International Exhibitions.

The Lord Mayor's banquet.

ON the evening of March 21, 1850, a banquet was given by the Lord Mayor of London to inaugurate a great event in the history of modern civilisation—the International Exhibition of 1851. The banquet took place in the Egyptian Hall, which was tastefully decorated for the occasion. On the rows of the lofty Corinthian columns which range along each side of the hall were suspended shields of the arms of the several counties, cities, and towns of the kingdom, the mayors and other authorities of which were invited, and these insignia were intermixed with trophies formed of the chief articles of productive industry for which the several localities were celebrated, and of the implements used in the different districts. Thus, on the column dedicated to the counties of Gloucester and Wilts, was a trophy in which were combined a sickle, sheaves of corn, a flitch of bacon, and a cheese. On another column, associated with the shields of Northumberland, Derbyshire, and Staffordshire, were specimens of lead ore, miners' implements, coal, and pottery ware. In the spaces between the columns were suspended banners and streamers of various colours with the arms of the Aldermen of London; whilst other portions of the hall were richly decorated with armorial devices, including the national arms and emblems of England, Scotland, Ireland, and Wales. In the great window were introduced pictorial designs and scenic representations referring to the forthcoming exhibition. The upper portion of the window at the eastern end was filled in with two colossal figures representing Peace and Plenty encircling with a wreath of laurel an immense globe of the world. Beneath this group was a large picture representing the Port of London filled with ships, from every quarter of the earth, disembarking the produce of the several countries. The western window was decorated with a colossal allegorical figure of Britannia, who held in her hand a ground plan of a building for the approaching exhibition.

Better, however, than any gaudy ornaments were the noble words spoken on the occasion by the royal guest, the Prince Consort, who from the first made the undertaking altogether his own. 'Gentlemen,' he said, 'the exhibition of 1851 is to give us a true test and a living picture of the point of development at which the whole of mankind has arrived in this great task, and a new starting-point from which all nations will be able to direct their further exertions. I confidently hope that the first impression which the view of this vast collection will produce upon the spectator will be that of deep thankfulness to the Almighty for the blessings which He has bestowed upon us already here below; and the second the conviction that they can only be realised in proportion to the help which we are prepared to render each other, therefore, only by peace, love, and ready assistance, not only between individuals but between the nations of the earth.' Others spoke on the occasion: Lord John Russell, the Earl of Derby, the Earl of Carlisle, the French Ambassador, each gave utterance to thoughts suited to the occasion, and Sir Robert Peel said, 'It is a noble undertaking to bring together into one spot, and within the view of the world, those valuable productions which an allwise and beneficent Creator has distributed among the different climes and various regions—to stimulate the ingenuity and exercise the mental faculties of man, and through their exertion to enable His creatures to provide for the physical comforts, the intellectual improvement, the social happiness of mankind. It is a noble object to test by actual experiment to what extent the ingenuity and skill of the nations of the earth has corresponded to the intentions of their Creator, and to improve the advantages

Prince Albert's and Sir Robert Peel's speeches.

which each country can offer the other in supplying the wants and adding to the happiness of mankind. In other countries and in other climes splendid spectacles have been provided for the gratification of the people. There still remain the ruins of ancient edifices, almost uninjured by time, where for the gratification of the people showy and costly spectacles were provided. On a Roman holiday hecatombs of wild beasts were slain and sanguinary conflicts took place of man against man. We propose to gratify the people by other agencies more in harmony with our civilisation and our Christianity—to teach them gratitude to the Almighty Creator, by exhibiting the wonderful contrivances of nature for the happiness of man, and to draw closer the bonds of amity and general intercourse by the honest rivalry of industry and skill.'

Of industrial exhibitions there had been many at different times. As early as in 1757 the first attempt was made in France to collect works of art. In 1761 an exhibition of machinery was held in the rooms of the Society of Arts in England. In 1798, whilst France was in the midst of anarchy and revolution, an industrial exhibition was held, in which sixteen departments took part. Only one hundred and ten exhibitors appeared, but they comprised men of great distinction, who afterwards achieved for themselves considerable celebrity. Some idea of the character of the times may be gathered from the fact that intimation was given, that at the next exhibition a medal would be awarded to the person who should inflict the greatest blow on English industry. In 1801 there was another exhibition at the Louvre, when two hundred and twenty exhibitors appeared, and it was then decided to hold such exhibitions annually, which was so far carried out by holding another in 1802. But then there was a break till 1806, and a long blank occurred till 1819, from which date Exhibitions were held in Paris every five years. Other countries also followed. Italy, Prussia, Switzerland, Spain, and Sweden each got up such exhibitions. In England, in 1828, there was an exhibition of specimens of new and improved productions of artizans and manufacturers. In 1829 there was one in Dublin of specimens of native industry. And in 1845 there was a great exhibition of manufactures at the free trade bazaar, in

History of exhibitions.

Covent Garden theatre, besides other local exhibitions in Manchester, Birmingham, Leeds, and Liverpool. In 1849, however, M. Buffet, minister of commerce of France, proposed to the French chambers of commerce that at the next exhibition foreign products should be admitted in competition. But the protectionist party refused to entertain the proposal, and it was left to the Society of Arts, animated by its illustrious president, to put forth the idea of a universal exhibition.

Results of the Exhibition of 1851.

Accordingly at the appointed time, in a palace constructed chiefly of glass and iron, of an area extending over a million square feet, by the illustrious Paxton, the products of all nations were magnificently exhibited. The half of the area was occupied by Great Britain and the colonies and the other half by foreign states. And though France and Germany had the largest share of the foreign half, every state in the four quarters of the globe was represented. Six millions of visitors inspected the wonderful treasures of art and industry. There were in all 13,937 exhibitors; and a jury, composed of British and foreign members, appointed to determine the relative merits of the articles exhibited, awarded to 117 exhibitors the council medal, to 2,954 the prize medal, and to 2,123 honourable mention.

State of industry in different countries.

And what was the state of industry thus represented? The exhibition consisted of four distinct classes of subjects: viz. raw materials, machinery, manufactures, and the fine arts, divided into thirty branches. The mineral industry of different countries was but imperfectly represented, but it was evident that in all parts of the world in Europe, as well as in America, the mineral everywhere followed the development of other industries, and above all that Great Britain was by far the most favoured country in the world for the development of mineral industry. Although the chemical manufacture had attained more subdivision in England than abroad, the great variety of products from a single manufactory was often very striking in the foreign, particularly the German, collections; a variety without inferiority of quality, which bore testimony to the excellent chemical education and varied resources of the exhibitors. Large was the collection of substances used as food, and most extensive the number of articles comprised under animal and vegetable substances chiefly used in manufactures; the vegetable comprising the gum and resin series, starches, oils, dyes, and colours, cotton, fibrous materials, and woods, and the animals, including wool, hair, wax, horns, ivory, tortoise shells, pearls, sponges, gelatine, and isinglass. The East was then, as now, the home of gums, Africa of palm oil, Turkey of madder, Mexico of logwood, and the United States of cotton. England was far ahead in machinery. In agricultural implements she was almost unrivalled, and equally so in cotton goods, but for woollen, France, Belgium, and Saxony exhibited great capacity. France fully sustained her reputation as the chief seat of the silk manufacture. She produced largely and was peculiarly successful in the finer and richer descriptions, where delicacy of design and colour is most favourably applied. Austria had made great progress; her materials were excellent, and she presented them at low prices. Prussia and the States of the Zollverein exhibited much ability in copying the productions of France and England. Belgium appeared to prefer attracting purchasers by cheapness and excellence of manufacture, rather than by superior attractiveness or novelty. In the leather manufacture France was in advance of England. The machine-made lace is a purely English invention, though for hand-made lace France and Belgium were pre-eminent. In hosiery Nottingham was far in advance. For cutlery, England had special facilities in the close proximity of coal and iron, but her superiority consisted chiefly in articles intended to supply the everyday wants and conveniences of life, and not in articles of a higher order, which involve the application of tasteful design and ornamentation. In jewellery, which affords ample scope for the display of taste, France and Germany could borrow from England whatever was worthy of imitation in her manufacture of plate for useful purposes, and England might derive instruction from the gold and silversmiths of the Continent with reference to objects of the ornament cast or *repoussé* and finely chased. In the ceramic art the Staffordshire potteries exhibited the greatest advance. It was evident, indeed, at a glance that different nations had reached different stages of progress in the several branches of human industry, and that in that aspect we had before us, the infancy of nations, their youth, their middle age, and their maturity. It was just as if a photographer had brought within his field of view the surface of the globe, with all the workshops and markets, and yet it was not a picture, it was a reality. From every part of the world were the articles themselves, and whilst roaming amidst the wonders of that crystal structure we were able to travel as it were from country to country, and to inspect their productions in art and manufacture. The exhibition was indeed a school, a museum, and a gallery. Nay, more, it was a spring, from whose waters labourers would derive fresh vigour and zeal.

Progress of international exhibitions.

Since then several other exhibitions have been held of an international character. Paris had one in 1855, which was visited by 4,500,000 persons, and London had another in 1862, which attracted 6,200,000 visitors, and Paris one in 1867 which excelled them all for extent and variety. Each of them enjoyed an unbounded popularity, each contributed its quota to the advancement of industry and art, to the stimulus of invention, and we may add to the extension of friendly feelings among the different nations of the earth. They have been indeed high festivals of industry and great tournaments of industrial nations, of which we may well be proud, and if a check had to be put to their immense development, if a time came when, instead of exhibiting the whole realm of human industry, it became necessary to be content with one or more classes of subjects at a time, the principle itself of international exhibitions is sound, the competition they engender highly beneficial, and they may yet subserve high and lofty purposes in the great economy of the world's progress.

CHAPTER VI.

THE GOLD DISCOVERIES IN CALIFORNIA AND AUSTRALIA.

1847–1851.

Want of metallic currencies.—Discovery of silver mines in Peru.—Discovery of Gold in California.—Discovery of Gold in Australia.—Effect of Gold discoveries upon the Value of Gold.—Buoyancy of Trade.—Progress of California and Australia.

Two important and joyful events marked the entrance of the second half of the nineteenth century. They were the International Exhibition of 1851 and the discoveries of gold in California and Australia. Important, indeed, they were, when we consider how many interests were thereby affected, and how vast and how permanent have been the influence which they exercised. It was needful, certainly, to replenish the coffers of the bankers of Europe. The immense development of trade seemed especially to require a corresponding increase of currencies. The coinage in many countries was reduced to very small proportions. Everywhere, either paper or mixed metals were taking the place of the precious metals, whilst the large emigration which had set in required a great abstraction of currency from Europe. On every account the discovery of more gold could not fail to exercise a most wholesome influence.

Want of metallic currencies.

It was three hundred years and more since Europe was startled with the news of the discovery of silver mines in the mountain of Potocchi, or Potosi, in Peru. An Indian pursuing some deer was climbing a steep rock. Laying hold of a bush, its roots loosened from the earth, and brought to view the existence of silver. Time after time he resorted to it, and long he kept the source of his altered fortunes involved in the deepest mystery. At last, however, he

Discovery of silver mines in Peru.

communicated the result to a friend. They quarrelled, and the news spread like wild-fire in the neighbourhood. A crowd of miners was attracted by the report, and the issue was the foundation of the largest town in all Peru, and what is more, a vein of wealth was opened which for centuries replenished the treasuries of the civilised world. How far the large importations of gold produced a depreciation of the value of precious metals relatively to other products it is by no means easy to distinguish. At first the natural effect was counteracted by the fact that whilst the overflow of gold was not so rapid or sudden as was apprehended, the discovery of the route to India by the Cape of Good Hope caused a considerable decline of prices. A long time, in fact, elapsed before the effect of these discoveries was felt in distant quarters. Adam Smith considered that it took sixty or seventy years before any sensible difference was shown in England. In France, it is said, it took fifty years before the change was complete; and when it came it did not last very long. The great enlargement of the field of industry, the augmented cost of producing silver, the altered state of society, increased wealth, and the accession of large states to the European family, speedily caused the demand to increase faster than the supply. After the great discovery of American mines no fact of any importance occurred in relation to gold and silver till 1774, when the gold regions of the Oural Mountains were discovered, and it was not till 1810 that their riches were fully developed, nor did they prove very productive.[1]

[1] Several calculations have been made of the quantity of gold and silver supposed to have passed from America to Europe from the discovery of the former country to the present time. Baron Humboldt gave some account of the production of gold and silver in America in his political essay on the kingdom of New Spain. M. Rainal, in his work on the East and West Indies, hazarded some calculations on the subject. M. St. Clair Dupont published a work 'De la production des Metaux précieux au Mexico' in 1843. There are some consular reports on the subject in 1830 and 1843. Mr. J. T. Danson gave a general statement in the Journal of the Statistical Society, vol. xiv. p. 11, and recently the 'Economist' had some voluminous estimates. According to Mr. Danson, the quantity of gold and silver probably sent to Europe, in the period from 1492 to the end of 1803, was 1,122,997,475*l*., and from 1804 to 1848, 360,597,515*l*.: total, 1,483,577,020*l*. According to the later account in the 'Economist,' there were at the time of Christ 2,245,362 kilos of gold and 62,030,123 kilos of silver, value 865,600,000*l*. From that time to the year 1492 there were extracted in Asia, Africa, and Europe, 6,123,711 kilos of gold and 13,682,107 kilos of silver, value 935,350,000*l*. From

A more important discovery, however, than of either the Mexican or the Russian mines was made only twenty years ago. In 1847 a Captain Sutter, who had long been settled in California, contracted with a Mr. Marshall for the erection of a saw-mill on the Americanos, a few miles from his fort. The tail-race being too narrow for the water to run off freely the mill wheel was taken out, so that the whole body of water in the dam might rush through and widen the race, to save the trouble of digging it out. A great body of earth was thus carried away by the torrent, and the next morning, whilst Mr. Marshall was surveying the works, he observed some shining yellow spangles or spots where the water had laid bare the bank. At first he would not take the trouble to stoop for them, but his eye being caught by a particle of superior magnitude he pocketed it up, and found that it had all the appearance of pure gold. He then collected some twenty or thirty pieces, and imagining these might be fragments of some treasures buried by the Indians, he examined the neighbouring soil and found it more or less auriferous. In joyful excitement he hurried off to Captain Sutter, and having commenced a search together, they satisfied themselves that the soil was teeming with gold. For a time they prosecuted their search quite secretly, but a Kentuckian employed in the mill guessed the causes of their unusual movements. He followed their steps and imitated their action, and though the captain tried to convince the Kentuckian and other workmen that what they took for gold was some worthless mineral, the general cry of 'Oro, oro,' was raised, and the Californian mines were fully discovered.

Discovery of Gold in California.

Discovery of Gold in Australia.

Turn now to another far corner of the earth, the colony of Australia. Long before the discovery of gold was publicly announced in Victoria pieces of the metal

1492 to 1810, including for the first time the produce of the American mines, the quantity was 3,856,487 kilos of gold, and 137,096,830 kilos of silver, value 1,625,925,000*l*. From 1810 to 1848 the quantity obtained was 1,133,704 kilos of gold and 21,963,337 kilos of silver, value 355,409,000*l*. From 1848 to 1851, California included, the quantity extracted was 389,835 kilos of gold and 3,063,411 kilos of silver, value 92,123,000*l*.; and from 1851 to 1865, which included both California and Australia, the quantity given was 1,615,654 kilos of gold and 4,051,362 kilos of silver, value 254,861,000*l*., making a total up to 1865 of 2,035,293,000*l*. of gold and 2,072,101,000*l*. of silver. Total, 4,017,379,000*l*.

had been found by shepherds and others,[1] to say nothing of Sir Roderick Murchison's clear prognostications that gold would be found there. Licenses to dig were first issued on September 1, 1851, and forthwith the half of the population of the colony gave up their pursuits for the race after gold. Lawyers forsook the courts, merchants their counting-houses, clerks their desks; and artisans and labourers fled precipitately from houses but half built and foundations but partly dug. Even clergymen were drawn to the exciting scene, and not in every case did they confine themselves to their calling. The wages of labour under such circumstances increased enormously. Provisions of all kinds rose to unprecedented prices, and altogether a state of matters arose of quite an unprecedented character. Let us endeavour to realise some facts connected with these great discoveries. Comparing 1846 with 1852, a period before and after the first discoveries, the production of gold and silver stands thus:—

	1846		1852	
	Gold	Silver	Gold	Silver
	£	£	£	£
N. and S. America .	1,300,000	5,250,000	13,300,000	7,250,000
Russia	3,500,000	1,250,000	3,500,000	—
Europe	—	—	—	1,250,000
Austria, Borneo, Africa, &c. . . .	1,200,000	—	1,200,000	—
Australia . . .	—	—	12,000,000	—
Total . .	£6,000,000	£6,500,000	£30,000,000	£8,500,000

Here is a gigantic increase, first in the total amount, from 12,500,000*l.* to 38,500,000*l.*, and more especially in gold alone from 6,000,000*l.* to 30,000,000*l.* And how different is the proportion between gold and silver. In the seventeenth century gold stood to silver as 1 to 60. In the eighteenth century the relation was 1 lb. of gold to 30 lb. of silver. At the commencement of the nineteenth century this proportion was

[1] The first discovery of gold in Australia was really made by Count Strzelecky in 1839, he having mentioned it at the time to some friends and to the governor of the colony. It was again discovered by the Rev. B. Clarke in 1841. But public attention was not attracted to the subject until the existence of extensive gold fields throughout Australia was announced by Mr. E. H. Hargreaves in 1851.

1 to 45. But since the Californian and Australian mines were discovered the production was as 1 to 5.[3]

Effect of gold discoveries. And what effect was produced by such an immense addition to the stock of the precious metals? Frightened, and not without reason, at the possible consequences, some countries, heretofore anxious to attract and retain gold in circulation, even at great sacrifices, showed a feverish anxiety to banish it altogether. In July 1850, Holland demonetised the gold ten florin piece and the Guillaume. Portugal prohibited any gold from having a current value except English sovereigns. Belgium demonetised its gold circulation. Russia prohibited the export of silver, and France, alarmed but less hasty, issued a commission to inquire into the question. A decided change seemed to have taken place in the current value of gold and silver coins. Whilst for years past, gold had always borne a small premium, now, for the first time, silver acquired the ascendancy. But with all this England did not move. The rate of interest,

[3] The relative value of gold and silver has, of course, varied in proportion to the altered production. During the reign of Ferdinand and Isabella, viz. from 1474 to 1516, the relative value between gold and silver in Spain was as 1 to $10\frac{47}{617}$; in the year 1537, and during the reign of Charles V., the relative value was fixed at 1 to $10\frac{271}{614}$; during the reign of Philip II. it was established as 1 to $12\frac{112}{1831}$; during the reign of Philip III., as 1 to $13\frac{1}{3}$: during the reign of Charles II. as 1 to $15\frac{374}{4123}$; and finally, on July 17, 1779, the relative value of the two metals was fixed as 1 to 16. In the year 1641 Louis XIII. of France issued an edict which regulated the proportion between gold and silver at the French mints, and this proportion was established at 1 to $13\frac{1}{2}$, with the view to conform in this respect to the regulations of French countries, where the proportions were as follows: in Germany as 1 to 12, in England as 1 to $13\frac{1}{3}$, in the Netherlands as 1 to $12\frac{1}{2}$, and in Spain as 1 to $13\frac{1}{3}$. These regulations lasted about a century, when it became again necessary to alter them, and accordingly in the year 1724 an edict was issued by which the proportion between gold and silver at the French mint was fixed as 1 to $14\frac{1}{2}$. At the time of this last edict the mint regulations of England established the proportions between gold and silver as 1 to about $15\frac{1}{5}$, and they remained at the same footing till the new coinage. In 1780 the relative value between gold and silver was at Amsterdam as 1 to 14·885; in France as 1 to 14·581; in Spain as 1 to 15·636; at Venice as 1 to 14·779; at Genoa as 1 to 14·915; at Leghorn as 1 to 14·510; in England as 1 to 15·169 and at Hamburg as 1 to 14·171. In the standard of British coinage at the present time 1 part of gold is worth $14\frac{2}{7}$ of silver; in the French, 1 part of gold is equal to $15\frac{1}{2}$ of silver; and in the countries where the silver standard prevails, the proportion varies from 1 to $15\frac{1}{4}$ to $15\frac{3}{4}$. (See Lords' Committee on the resumption of cash payments (1819), and Seyd, 'Bullion and Foreign Exchanges,' p. 162 (1868).

it is true, fell to the lowest possible limit, but no legislative step was taken. Nor was it needed, for it was not long before the plethora of gold entirely vanished. An immense expansion of trade all over the world, the Russian war, the Indian mutinies, the Chinese war, railways and public works, soon absorbed all the supplies, the rate of interest rose higher than ever, and we heard no more of gold losing its ancient supremacy.[1]

Progress of California and Australia.

As might be imagined, California and Australia increased immensely upon the discovery of their great treasures, and, as by magic, desert and savage places were converted into populous and thriving cities. In 1850, the population of California was 92,000, and in a very short time, shoals of immigrants from Europe, Asia, and America, swelled it into 340,000. A few years ago, California was not even named among the states of the great Republic; in 1870, it exported 11,000,000*l.* of bullion and other merchandise. And so it was with Victoria. In 1850, her population was 76,000; in 1861, it was 541,000. Her navigation suddenly swelled to enormous proportions. In 1851, the shipping entered and cleared was 195,000 tons; in 1853, it was 1,386,000 tons; and her exports, which in 1850 amounted to 744,000*l.*, in 1855 were valued at 15,489,000*l.* Large fortunes have been realized by the early settlers in both California and Australia, but now trade has settled down in a normal condition.

[1] From 1851 to 1869 there was exported from Victoria 37,000,000 oz. of gold, which at 4*l.* per oz. gave a value of 148,000,000*l.* During the same years the exports of gold and silver coin and bullion from the United States, America, amounted to 964,000,000 dollars, equivalent to nearly 200,000,000*l.* From 1851 to 1870 the amount of gold coined in the United Kingdom was 108,569,000*l.*

CHAPTER VII.

COMMERCIAL LAWS.

1851-1860.

Chambers of Commerce.—International Commercial Law.—Assimilation of Mercantile Laws.—Royal Commission on the Mercantile Laws of the United Kingdom.—Investments of the Middle and Working Classes.—The Law of Partnership.—Limitation of Liability.—Objections to Limited Liability.—The Limited Liability Acts.—State of the Patent Law.—Principles of the Patent Law.—Objections to the Patent Law.—Patent Laws in Foreign Countries.—The Law of Copyright.—Mr. Justice Talfourd's Bill.—Copyright in Foreign Countries.—Copyright in Design.—Law of Trade Marks.—Position of Aliens.—The Bankruptcy Laws.—Law on Weights and Measures.—Establishment of New Standards.—Usury Laws.—Other Law Reforms.

SETTING aside for the present the many economic questions suggested by the gold discoveries, let us turn our attention to a series of legal reforms passed from time to time which removed many hindrances to commerce and industry and imparted greater security to trade and better encouragement to the investment of capital. There may be much to amend in our system of legislation; our laws may be defective in enunciation, altogether wanting in method, and remarkable for cumbrousness of language, yet it will be admitted that the evil has been greatly remedied, and that whatever injury may result from these defects, it is greatly modified by the invaluable advantage which we possess, especially in a commercial country, of a scrupulous and impartial administration of justice.

For some of the best reforms in our commercial laws we are indebted to the chambers of commerce which are ever ready to expose the evils and inconveniences under which trade may be labouring in this and other countries. The chamber of commerce is an old institution. One existed at Marseilles as far back as the fifteenth century. One was established at Dunkerque in 1700, and when more recently a council-general of commerce was formed in Paris, composed of

Chambers of Commerce.

six councillors of state and twelve merchants or traders delegated by the principal commercial towns in the kingdom, several chambers of commerce were established which placed themselves in direct relation with the central council. In 1852 the chambers of commerce in France received a formal organisation, and their principal functions now are to give to the government advice and information on industrial and commercial subjects, to suggest the means of increasing the industry and commerce of their respective districts, or of improving commercial legislation; and to suggest the execution of works which may be required for the public service, or which may tend to the increase of trade or commerce, such as the construction of harbours, the deepening of rivers, the formation of railways, and the like.

The Liverpool Chamber of Commerce.

In Great Britain, also, there have been for a considerable time several important chambers of commerce. Glasgow had one with royal charter dated 1783; Edinburgh one since 1785: and the Manchester chamber was established in 1820. Even Hull has had a chamber of commerce since 1837; yet Liverpool, one of the largest ports in the kingdom, had no such chamber. Twelve or more separate bodies, as the Shipowners' Association, the African, the West Indian, the East Indian and China, the Mexican and South American, the Mediterranean, and the Levant Associations, existed, but they were guided by party feelings, and, whilst they were contending for the advocacy of discordant views of commercial policy, they were not able to do much for the public good. A chamber of commerce embracing and representing all the different branches of trade was first proposed in a pamphlet on the subject, by the author of this work, in 1850;[1] and after much labour the institution was established.

International commercial laws.

But the foundation of the Liverpool chamber of commerce is the more interesting from the fact that it became the parent of a great effort for the assimilation and consolidation of the Mercantile Law of the United Kingdom, and as far as possible of foreign countries also. When writing his work on the commercial laws in force in different

[1] 'Chambers and Tribunals of Commerce, and proposed General Chamber of Commerce in Liverpool.' London, 1849.

states, and exhibited the same in parallel columns,[1] the author was impressed with the striking uniformity in many of the dictates of one and all of them. There are in truth in the codes and laws of commerce of all nations many fundamental principles which neither time, nor space, nor climate can obliterate. They constitute those great maxims of right and wrong which are eternal in their origin and universal in their application. But diversity of language and phraseology has so disfigured this universal uniformity, and laws have been so largely amassed, that it has become almost impossible to distinguish what is uniform from what is dissimilar in all states. Nor is this a matter of slight importance. Commerce, it must be remembered, is essentially international. Whenever a merchant forms a partnership; purchases, sells, or ships goods; effects an insurance, or becomes a bankrupt; in either case he may find himself affected by the mercantile law of other countries. Let such laws be dissimilar, let what is lawful in one country be illegal in another, let the procedure of the courts fail to afford the same protection, let the instruments used in one country be not equally recognised in another, and the results are extreme inconvenience, loss, and, in any case, endless confusion.

Conference on the assimilation of commercial laws.

The remedy for this great anomaly was suggested by the author, in his work on international commercial law. His Royal Highness the Prince Consort, to whom the suggestion was first communicated, at once recognised its utility. The chambers of commerce gave to the proposal their full concurrence. The Law Amendment Society cheerfully co-operated with a view to its realisation, and on November 15, 1852, a conference was held in London, presided over by Lord Brougham and the Earl of Harrowby, when it was resolved, 'That the mercantile laws of England, Ireland, and Scotland are scattered and disconnected, and in many instances dissimilar and even antagonistic, a state of things tending greatly to restrict and embarrass commerce by producing

[1] 'Commercial Law, its Principles and Administrations, or the Mercantile Law of Great Britain compared with the Codes and Laws of Commerce of Foreign Countries.' London, 1850. 'International Commercial Law,' or second edition of the above. Stev and Co., London, 1862.

uncertainty, perplexity, and delay. That it is desirable that a well digested and well arranged body of mercantile law should be framed and established for the whole of the three kingdoms. That, dismissing all local and even national prejudices, the assimilation and improvement of the mercantile laws of the three kingdoms, and the improvement, and, where requisite, the assimilation of the procedure should be effected by selecting those principles and rules, wherever they may be found, which shall be deemed the best and most beneficial to the commercial classes and to the community at large, and that to this end it is necessary carefully to examine the mercantile laws and to have recourse to the experience of other countries. That it is desirable that this assimilation and improvement should be brought about by a general revision, amendment, and consolidation of the different branches of the mercantile law successively; but that while these larger measures are proceeding, much immediate relief might be afforded by a series of single acts addressed to the more pressing and grievous evils; which acts, by proper arrangements, might be made subservient to the ultimate object. That, while this work is going forward, it is important that no new measures of mercantile law should be introduced into Parliament, but such as may apply generally to the three kingdoms, or serve as steps towards a general assimilation. That a commission consisting of members of both Houses of Parliament and members of the legal and commercial professions appears the most effective means of obtaining the desired result.'

Royal commission on the mercantile laws of England, Scotland, and Ireland.

A committee having thereafter been formed to represent the views of the conference to Her Majesty's Government, a deputation proceeded to the Earl of Derby, then the first lord of the treasury, on the subject, and, in compliance with its request, a royal commission was soon after appointed to inquire and ascertain how far the mercantile laws in the different parts of the United Kingdom of Great Britain and Ireland may be advantageously assimilated. And on its reports two acts[a] were passed which introduced uniformity of principle and practice on several points. But, what was still more important, a tendency was given to uniformity of legislation, which has ever since been maintained to

[a] 19 & 20 Vict. c. 97, and 19 & 20 Vict. c. 60.

the manifest advantage of the commercial community. Would that the original design could be further realised. In the words of Mr. Justice Story, 'What a magnificent spectacle will it be to witness the establishment of such a beautiful system of juridical ethics, to realise not the oppressive schemes of "holy alliances" in a general conspiracy against the rights of mankind, but the universal empire of juridical reason, mingling with the concerns of commerce throughout the world, and imparting its beneficial light to the dark regions of the poles and the soft and luxurious climates of the tropics. Then indeed would be realised the splendid visions of Cicero, dreaming over the majestic fragments of his perfect republic, and Hooker's personification of the law would stand forth as embodied truth, for 'all things in heaven and earth would do her homage, the very least as feeling her care, and the greatest as not exempted from her power.' But we must pass to other subjects.

Investments of the middle and working classes.

With the commencement of the second half of the present century a conviction gained ground that, with the growing wealth, those who occupy a middle station in society were progressively increasing in number and in the proportion which they bore relatively to the population of the kingdom. There was a large increase in the number of depositors and amount of deposits in the savings banks; there was a large addition to the number of persons receiving under five pounds at each payment of dividends of the public debt. There was a much larger income between 150*l.* and 500*l.* assessed to income tax. But there was a decided want of increasing facilities for the safe investments for the savings of the middle and working classes. A committee of the House of Commons was therefore moved on the subject by Mr. Slaney, and they made a useful report. They found that investments in land or landed securities were much desired by the middle and working classes, but that the uncertainty and complexity of titles, and the length and expense of conveyances, together with the cost of stamps, placed this species of investments, generally, beyond the reach of those parties; and that mortgages on land were liable to the same sort of difficulties, and often proved insecure investments. They found that the crown was empowered by act of parliament in certain cases, by charter, to limit the liability of partners, but that this power was seldom exercised, did not seem guided by any clear rule, and involved expense greater even than that of obtaining an act of parliament.

Another subject of complaint was the law of partnership, which placed obstacles in the way of any body of workmen who desired to combine their money and labour in industrial undertakings. In some cases several industrious men worked together under regulations of their own, with a small capital; they were directed by managers whom they chose, the goods produced were sold for their common benefit, and the profits were divided among the contributors of capital and labour in certain proportions agreed on. But the law afforded no effectual remedy against the fraud of any one dishonest contributor or partner and no summary mode of enforcing the rules agreed to for mutual government. The committee expressed their strong opinion of the pressing necessity of the subject being attended to by the legislature. The rapid increase in population, and in wealth of the middle and industrious classes within the last half century, rendered this of great consequence. The great change in the social position of multitudes, from the growth of large towns and crowded districts, rendered it more necessary that corresponding reforms in the law should take place both to improve their condition and contentment, and to give additional facilities to investments of the capital which their industry and enterprise were constantly creating and augmenting. And it was the conviction of that committee that if such measures were carried into effect, a stimulus would be given to the industry of the country, likely to cause additional employment and contentment, without injury to any class, and with added security to the welfare of all.

The law of partnership.

Following this, Mr. Slaney, on the following session in 1851, obtained another committee of the House of Commons to consider the law of partnership and the expediency of facilitating the limitation of liability with a view to encourage useful enterprise and the additional employment of labour. The committee consisted of some eminent members, and examined witnesses of great authority, and the result of their labour was a recommendation that greater facilities should exist in granting charters, under rules published and enforced

Limitation of liability.

by the proper authorities, and that an easier mode of borrowing additional capital should be allowed, without risk, to the lender, beyond the amount of the sum advanced. The committee corroborated the general impression of great increase of personal property of late years. The population returns showed an increase of the population of almost all our largest towns, chiefly inhabited by persons dependent on personal property, at the rate of nearly 30 per cent. in every decennial period since the beginning of the century, whilst the rural inhabitants had augmented only at about one-third the same proportion. It appeared further, that in thirty-three years since the peace, whilst lands in Great Britain had increased in value to 1848 only 8,500,000*l.* (from 39,405,000*l.* in 1814–15 to 47,081,000*l.* in 1848), or a little more than five per cent., messuages, chiefly houses and manufactures and warehouses in and near towns and inhabited by persons depending greatly on trade and commerce, had augmented above 26,000,000*l.* (from 16,259,000*l.* in 1815–16 to 42,314,000*l.* in 1845) in annual value, or about 130 per cent. in the same period; whilst the value of railways, gas works, and other property, chiefly held in shares as personal property, had increased above twelvefold in the same period. The same result, showing the increase of personal property since the peace, was evident from the fact that the legacy duty was derived from a capital of 24,000,000*l.* in 1816 and 45,000,000*l.* in 1845. The course of modern legislation had been gradually to remove restrictions on the power which everyone has in the disposal of his property and to remove those fetters on commercial freedom which long prevailed in this country. The usury laws and various laws against combinations had been modified or repealed. General acts to facilitate the formation of joint-stock associations and building societies had been passed. The committee therefore thought it proper to offer suggestions of a like nature in reference to the laws of partnership, and especially as regards the unlimited liability of partners as it existed in this country. And they recommended the appointment of a commission of adequate legal and commercial knowledge to consider and prepare a consolidation of the existing laws, and also to suggest such changes in the law as the altered condition of the country might require, especial attention being paid to the establishment of improved tribunals to decide claims by and against partners in all partnership disputes, and also to the important and much controverted question of limited and unlimited liability of partners.

On the following year, in 1852, the royal commission, of which we have spoken, was appointed to inquire into the state of the mercantile law of Great Britain and Ireland, and in 1853 it was committed to them to inquire whether any or what alterations and amendments should be made in the law of partnership as regards the question of the limited or unlimited responsibility of partners. But in 1854 the commissioners reported, by a majority of five to three, against any change in that direction. Their report, embodying the reasons urged in opposition, deserves to be referred to at some length. In the opinion of the commissioners, the first question of paramount importance was, whether the proposed alteration of the law would operate beneficially on the general trading interests of the country, and they arrived at the conclusion that it would not. They were not able to discover any evidence of the want of a sufficient amount of capital for the requirements of trade. The annually increasing wealth of the country and the difficulty of finding profitable investments for it seemed to them sufficient guarantee that an adequate amount would always be devoted to any mercantile enterprise that held out a reasonable prospect of gain without any forced action upon capital to determine it in that direction; while any such forced action would have a great tendency to induce men to embark in speculative adventures to an extent that would be dangerous to the interests of the general commerce of the country. The commissioners found no reason to suppose that the reputation of the British merchants, either at home or abroad, would be raised by the establishment of firms trading with limited liability, but the contrary. They thought that the benefit supposed to accrue to men of probity and talent, by enabling them to obtain capital and establish themselves in business by the aid of partners, incurring limited liability only, was greatly overrated. Doubtless many useful enterprises calculated to produce benefit to the public and profit to those

Objections to limited liability.

who engage in them are of such magnitude that no private partnership can be expected to provide the funds necessary to carry them into effect, or to have the means of superintending or managing them, of which docks, railways, and extensive shipping companies might be taken as examples. And there were others of a more limited character, from which benefit to the humbler classes of society might be expected to accrue, such as baths and washhouses, lodging-houses and reading-rooms, to the establishment of which by large capitalists there was little inducement. These two classes of undertakings it might be desirable to encourage by limiting the liability of those who embark in them. But with regard to both, the commissioners thought they should be subjected to some previous inquiry as to the means of carrying them into effect, and the prospect of benefit to the promoters and the public. With regard to those undertakings, the execution of which involved an interference with the rights of property, the sanction of parliament always had been and still ought to be required; with regard to others the privilege of having a limited liability might be granted by charter; and for the purpose of regulating the granting of charters the commissioners recommended that a board should be established to decide upon all applications for them, that board requiring in all cases compliance with certain fixed regulations. Into the views of the minority it is needless to enter. It is sufficient to state that Mr. James Anderson, Q.C., Mr. (afterwards Baron) Bramwell, and Mr. Kirkman Daniel Hodgson dissented from the report, grounding their dissent on the following reasons: 1st. The general principle of the advisability of allowing perfect freedom in the making of contracts between man and man, only guarding against wilful deception; 2nd. The experience of other countries; 3rd. The deficiencies of the present system in providing by loans for such purposes as this change of law would effect; 4th. The little chance of such a change encouraging and increasing the abuse of credits, its tendency being rather the reverse; 5th. The inconvenience that existed from our law being different from that of all other commercial countries; and 6th. From a strong conviction that the benefits of the measure proposed were great and manifold, while the objections urged against it were not warranted by experience, and in great part imaginary.

In the same year when this report was presented, Mr. (now Sir) Robert P. Collier moved a resolution in the House of Commons, 'That the law of partnership, which renders every person who, though not an ostensible partner, shares the profits of a trading concern, liable to the whole of its debts, is unsatisfactory, and should be so far modified as to permit persons to contribute to the capital of such concerns on terms of sharing their profits without incurring liability beyond a limited amount.' The resolution, seconded by Viscount Goderich, was well supported by the house, and at the end of the discussion Mr. Collier withdrew it, on the understanding that the subject would receive the serious consideration of Her Majesty's Government.

Sir R. P. Collier's resolution.

Accordingly, in 1855, two bills were introduced by Mr. Fitzroy, Mr. Bouverie, and Viscount Palmerston; one for limiting the liability of members of certain joint-stock companies and the other to amend the law of partnership, to the effect that a person lending money to a partnership on condition of receiving a portion of profits, varying with the amount of the same, should not thereby be considered a partner. The first of these bills passed into law;[3] the second was withdrawn, but from that year the principle was admitted and the acts passed in 1856,[4] 1857,[5] 1858,[6] gradually removed the exceptions originally made affecting insurance and banking. Finally, in 1862,[7] a new act for the regulation of companies was passed, by which any seven or more persons associated for any lawful purpose, by subscribing a memorandum of association, might constitute themselves a company with limited or unlimited liability; and also an act to regulate the formation of industrial societies.[8] To the former, which is now the principal act, we must add the act of 1867,[9] with provisions allowing limited companies to be formed with directors having an unlimited liability, as well as the reduction of the capital and shares. And by the Partnership Amendment Act of 1865 the advance of money on contract to receive a share of profit, or the remuneration of an agent by a share of the profits, was made no longer to constitute the lender or the agent a partner.

The limited liability acts.

[3] 18 & 19 Vict. c. 133.
[4] 19 & 20 Vict. c. 47.
[5] 20 & 21 Vict. c. 78.
[6] 22 Vict. c. 91.
[7] 25 & 26 Vict. c. 89.
[8] 25 & 26 Vict. c. 87.
[9] 30 & 31 Vict. c. 131.

The stimulus given to art and invention by the International Exhibition led, of necessity, to the consideration of the law of patents, which had long been extremely obstructive and inconvenient. The law, then administered, was founded on the statute of monopolies[10] passed during the reign of James I., which declared all monopolies to be null and void 'except as to letters patent and grants of privilege, for the term of fourteen years or under, for the sole working or making of any manner of new manufactures, within the realm to the true and first inventor or inventors of such manufactures which others at the time of making such letters patent and inventions shall not use.' But upon this statute a complete system of law and jurisprudence had been built, and a great number of formalities had been imposed on the process of obtaining a patent, which caused considerable delay. A patent was required for each kingdom separately, the cost for the three kingdoms being from 300*l.* to 350*l.* The system of caveat was most objectionable. There was a want of protection until the patent was sealed, there was a want of access to specifications, and there were many abuses consequent on vague or general titles. Many, in fact, were the defects in the patent law which needed a prompt remedy, and for that purpose a bill was introduced early in 1851. The bill, however, was remitted to a select committee, and nothing was done that session.

State of the patent law.

Though the report of the committee dealt mainly with the principal defects of the law as it stood, the evidence of Ricardo, Brunel, and others started objections to the very principle of the patent law, which, though not sufficiently mature to arrest legislation, indicated a further stage of change and progress for which even now we are not quite prepared. In the opinion of the advocates of the patent law, he who introduces a new trade into the realm, or an invention tending to the furtherance of a trade, should have the right of the sole use of the same for a reasonable time, till the public learn the same. In their views a patent is the best mode of remunerating the person for introducing such an improvement or manufacture. The grant of a patent is based on a bargain between the inventor and the public. The inventor is not obliged to declare his discovery or invention—he may work it in secret. But the public wish to

Principle of patent laws.

[10] 21 Jac. I, c. 3.

have his invention. They desire not only to have the result of his invention but to know how the invention has been produced, in order that they may record the knowledge for future use. And how can they obtain it except from the inventor himself? Surely the knowledge of the facts connected with such discovery is the property of the inventor, which no legislation whatever can touch, and it must rest absolutely with him whether he will make known such facts to the public or not. To secure his consent, therefore, the public say to him, Tell us your secret and we will assure you against any unfair use of your discovery; and legislation steps in and says, There being two facts, the right of the inventor to keep his own discovery to himself, which is indefeasible, and the wish of the public to get it and use that discovery and to know all about it, the two desires must be made mutual and a bargain settled between the public and the inventor.

Objections to the patent law.

The opponents of the patent law, on the other hand, allege that such laws are really prejudicial to inventors themselves; that in the present state of things, when all branches, whether in manufacture or art, are in such an advanced state, and when every process in production consists of a combination of the results of the improvements effected at different times, a good invention is rarely a new idea, suddenly propounded or coming as by inspiration into the mind of man, but is simply some sensible improvement upon what has been done; that in most cases it is some small modification, which may produce very important results; that to produce a good thing one must be well acquainted with all that has been done in any particular branch; that anything so done is in a vast majority of cases dependent entirely upon the success of previous steps, which already exclusively belong to individuals by patents or otherwise; and that many of the most important inventions, such as that of paper, oil painting, glass painting, &c., were made without patents. Such objections, however, were not pressed with any weight upon the committee's attention, and on the following session the bill passed into law.[11] A supplementary act [12] being passed providing that all letters patent for inventions shall be made subject to the condition,

[11] 15 & 16 Vict. c. 83. [12] 16 & 17 Vict. c. 115.

that the same shall be void at the expiration of three years and seven years respectively from the date thereof, unless, there be paid 50*l.* at the end of the third year and 100*l.* at the end of the seventh year. These fees are certainly smaller than were charged under the old system, but surely they are large enough to be a burden on inventors, yet not sufficiently large to prevent many trivial and even useless inventions being made the subjects of patent monopoly.[19]

Patent laws in foreign countries.

The question of the policy or impolicy of the patent law is not yet settled. In 1865 a royal commission was appointed to inquire into the working of the law relating to letters patent for inventions, on which occasion much evidence was received on the defect of the patent law; and in 1870 a committee of the House of Commons was appointed, with full power to inquire into and report on every point of the important question. Many objections may be urged against the patent law, yet it is doubtful indeed whether any other method of remuneration can be devised which shall bear any proportion to the utility of the invention; and as for the total abolition of the patent law, it would be well to consider whether manufactures and industry might not suffer were the rights of the inventor ignored or insufficiently recognised. A patent law exists in almost every country, though the duration of the privilege is different. In Prussia it is for five years; in Russia for ten; in the United States for seven years; in France, Holland, Austria, Bavaria, Sweden, Spain, Portugal, Italy, for fifteen years; in Belgium for twenty-one years. The law of the United States dates from 1793; of France from 1791, modified by that of 1844; of Russia from 1812; of Prussia from 1815; of Holland and Belgium from 1817; of Austria from 1820; and of Spain from 1820. Nearly everywhere the patent law seems to be contemporaneous with the emancipation of labour.

The law of copyright.

Of a kindred character to the law of patent is the law of copyright. By common law the author of an original work had for ever the right of multiplying copies of the same, and when the copyright was purchased

[19] In the year 1870 the number of applications for letters patent recorded was 3,405, and the number of patents passed thereon was 2,180. About 72 per cent. of the patents ordinarily granted become void at the end of the third year, and about 90 per cent. at the end of the seventh year. In 1870 the stamp duties amounted to 114,228*l.*

from an author it was understood to continue in force without any limitation of time. It was in the reign of Queen Anne [14] that the right was first limited. Then, and then only, it was enacted that the authors' right—the sole right of printing and reprinting their works—should last for fourteen years, and if they should be living at the close of that period, for another fourteen years. But the act remained practically a dead letter, and in defiance of that measure the Court of Chancery gave frequent injunctions to restrain the piracy of books, as in the case of the 'Whole Duty of Man,' 'Miscellanies of Pope and Swift,' and Milton's 'Paradise Lost.' In 1766 an action was instituted [15] for printing Thomson's 'Seasons,' and judgment was given in favour of the existing copyright, the opinion being that copyright was perpetual at common law, and that it was not limited by statute, except as to penalties. When, however, the case came before the House of Lords, it decided by a small majority that the statute of Anne had substituted a short term of copyright for an estate in fee. The limitation of the right being once established the extent of that limitation became the subject of discussion, and in 1814 it was enacted [16] that an author should have a copyright of his works for twenty-eight years, and if he should survive that period that it should continue during the remainder of his life.

Mr. Justice Talfourd's bill.

Thus stood the law, when, in 1837, Mr. Talfourd in a speech full of eloquence introduced his bill in the House of Commons to extend the limit still further. 'When the opponents of literary property,' he said, 'speak of glory as the reward of genius, they make an ungenerous use of the very nobleness of its impulses, and show how little they have profited by its high example. When Milton, in poverty and in blindness, fed the flame of his divine enthusiasm by the assurance of a duration coequal with his language, I believe, with Lord Camden, that no thought crossed him of the wealth which might be amassed by the sale of his poem; but surely some shadow would have been cast upon "the clear dream and solemn vision" of his future glories, had he foreseen that, whilst booksellers were striving to rival each other in the magnificence of their editions, his only surviving descendant,

[14] 8 Anne, c. 19 (1709).

[15] Millar v. Taylor, 4 Burr. 2303 & 2408.

[16] 54 Geo. III. c. 156.

a woman, should be rescued from abject want only by the charity of Garrick, who at the solicitation of Dr. Johnson gave her a benefit at the theatre which had appropriated to itself all that could be represented of "Comus." The liberality of genius is surely ill urged for our ungrateful denial of its rights. The late Mr. Coleridge gave an example, not only of its liberality, but of its profuseness, while he thought not even to appropriate to his fame the vast intellectual treasures which he had derived from boundless research, and coloured by a glorious imagination; while he scattered abroad the seeds of beauty and of wisdom to take root in congenial minds, and was content to witness their fruits in the production of those who heard him. But ought we therefore the less to deplore, now when the music of his divine philosophy is for ever hushed, that the earlier portion of those works on which he stamped his own impress, all which he desired of the world that it should recognise as his, are published for the gain of others than his children, that his death is illustrated by the forfeiture of their birthright? What justice is there in this? Do we reward our heroes so? Did we tell our Marlboroughs, our Nelsons, our Wellingtons, that glory was their reward—that they fought for posterity, and that posterity would pay them? We leave them to no such cold and uncertain requital. We do not even leave them merely to enjoy the spoils of their victories which we deny to the author. We concentrate a nation's honest feeling of gratitude and pride into the form of an endowment, and teach other ages what we thought, and what they ought to think, of their deeds by the substantial memorial of our praise. Were our Shakespeare and Milton less the ornaments of their country, less the benefactors of mankind? Would the example be less inspiring, if we permitted them to enjoy the spoils of their peaceful victories, if we allowed to their descendants, not the tax assessed by present gratitude and charged on the future, but the mere amount which that future would be delighted to pay, extending as the circle of their glory expands, and rendered only by those who individually reap the benefits, and are contented at once to enjoy and to reward its author? It is in truth the greatness of the blessing which the world inherits from genius that dazzles the mind on this question, and the habit of repaying its bounty by words, that confuses us and indisposes us to justice. It is because the spoils of time are freely and irrevocably ours, because the forms of antique beauty wear for us the bloom of imperishable youth, because the elder literature of our own country is a free mine of wealth to the bookseller, and of delight to ourselves, that we are unable to understand the claim of our contemporaries to a beneficial interest in their works. Because genius of necessity communicates so much, we cannot conceive it as retaining anything for its possessor. There is a sense indeed in which the poets "on earth have made us heirs of truth and pure delight in heavenly lays," and it is because of this very boon; because their thoughts become our thoughts, and their phrases unconsciously enrich our daily language, because their works, harmonious by the law of their own nature, suggest to us the rules of composition by which their imitators should be guided, because to them we can resort; and "in our golden urns draw light," that we cannot fancy them apart from ourselves, or admit that they have any property except in our praise.' It was not, however, till 1842 [17] that the new copyright law was passed, which confirmed this right in the author during his lifetime, and conferred it on his heir in the event of the author's dying before the expiry of forty-two years after the publication of his writings to the extent of that period.

In nearly all countries the right of authors is now likewise secured during his or her life-time, and even for a limited number of years after death. In France, the law of 1793 declared that the right should extend during life only; the law of 1810 guaranteed the same right to the widow and to the children for twenty years, and the law of 1854 extended the period to thirty years. In the United States the term of copyright is twenty-eight years from the date of recording, but it is capable of being extended for fourteen years longer. In Germany the time fixed by the law of 1845 is for the life of the author and for thirty years after his death. An international copyright [18] exists between the United Kingdom

Copyright in foreign countries.

[17] 5 & 6 Vict. c. 100.

[18] By an act of 1838, the 1 & 2 Vict. c. 19, the crown was empowered by an order in council to give to books, prints, music, and similar articles from foreign

and Germany, Belgium, France, and Italy, and though the United States have refused to enter into any international copyright with Great Britain, there is, we trust, sufficient good faith and sense of honour among the principal publishers in both countries to render the rights of authors practically protected on both sides of the Atlantic. The trade of publishing and bookselling forms an important staple of national industry. It requires the investment of a considerable amount of capital, and gives employment to a large number of persons. And thankful we should be that the reputation of British literature for variety and solidity, as well as for freedom from licence, and high tone of morals, is unexcelled by the literature of any other country. Of course if it be proper that the authors' rights should be protected, so should the rights of artists, and accordingly a copyright also exists in every original painting, drawing, and photograph made by any British subject resident within the dominion of the crown,[19] and also a copyright in designs for ornamenting articles of manufacture,[20] the latter applying to every design, whether the application thereof take place within the United Kingdom or elsewhere, and whether the inventor or proprietor of such design be or be not a subject of Her Majesty.

Trade marks.

Quite recently another description of copyright has been created. It has been long the custom of manufacturers to stamp the articles which they produce with their names or to apply to such articles certain marks as a guarantee that the article is of their own make and of the description represented, and great is the confidence generally accorded to such marks in foreign markets. Unfortunately, however, in consequence of frequent piracies of such marks by the counterfeiting of them, or the application of similar marks to inferior articles, all security for the proper correspondence between the article and the mark ceased to exist, and the manufacturers found themselves supplanted by inferior goods. The law was clear enough that no man has a right to dress himself in colours or adopt and bear symbols to which he has

countries the same privileges of copyright as were enjoyed in this country, provided those countries conceded reciprocal privileges. By an act passed in 1824, the 7 Vict. c. 12, these powers were extended to sculpture and other works of art.

[19] 25 & 26 Vict. c. 68.

[20] 5 & 6 Vict. c. 100, and 24 & 25 Vict. c. 73.

no peculiar or exclusive right, thereby to personate another person, for the purpose of inducing the people to suppose either that he is that other person, or that he is connected with him and selling the manufacture of such other person while he is really selling his own. And whenever it was found that a fraudulent attempt was made to pirate another person's name or label, the courts of equity granted a remedy by an injunction to restrain such party from using the name or label of another. By a statute of George II. persons affixing stamps to foreign linens in imitation of the stamps affixed to those of Scotland and Ireland forfeited 5*l.* for each offence, and persons exposing for sale or packing up any foreign linens as the manufactures of Great Britain and Ireland, forfeited the same and 5*l.* for each piece of linen so exposed for sale or packed up. So the legislature empowered the Goldsmiths' Company to call upon the manufacturers to bring all the articles they made to their hall for the purpose of being assayed and stamped with their hall marks. And the Cutlers' Company of Sheffield were empowered to grant marks to any persons carrying on any of the incorporated trades, with power of summary jurisdiction before two magistrates to enforce such regulations. Apart, however, from these special laws the general remedy afforded against the counterfeiting of trade marks was by suit in equity, which was in many cases insufficient. In the United States, by a statute of New York of 1850, forgery of trade marks with intent to deceive or defraud the purchaser or manufacturer was made a misdemeanor. The law of France gave protection to trade marks, and Germany has laws somewhat similar. Consequently in 1862, an act[11] passed, by which every person who, with intent to defraud or to enable another to defraud any person, should forge or counterfeit any trade mark, or apply such forged or counterfeit mark to other goods than the same is intended to represent, was made guilty of a misdemeanor. And it was a wise legislation. The principle thus legally sanctioned will prove a check, we trust, to practices unworthy of any honourable manufacturer. It is only right that a fraud of this nature, which is really a theft of a man's reputation, should be made penal in every country, and it is

[11] 25 & 26 Vict. c. 78.

satisfactory to find that by treaties concluded with different states protection against such fraud has been secured to foreign as well as to native subjects. This leads us to the reforms made in this country in the law relating to the naturalisation of aliens.

For the promotion of commerce we cannot open our doors too wide to the merchants of all countries. It would be an interesting inquiry to ascertain how many of those industries which now thrive so prosperously in this country were originally introduced by foreigners. We owe banking to the Lombards, the silk industry to the French and Italians, the sugar refinery to the Germans. And it is the same with other countries. France is largely indebted to the Italians, Holland to the French, and America to English, Irish, and German immigrants. We almost imagine that without the foreign element engrafted upon it, a country would soon lose its energy and suffer in its best interests. In this country, public policy was early in favour of foreign merchants, and Magna Charta expressly excepted merchant strangers from all restrictions against aliens, the advantage of inducing foreigners to come having been fully recognised by the first princes of the House of Plantagenet, and especially by Edward III. But from Richard II. to the Revolution, except perhaps during the reign of Elizabeth, a different policy prevailed, and foreigners were regarded with feelings of jealousy and aversion, and even subjected to odious restraints. They were prohibited from selling by retail; they were obliged to sell their merchandise within a certain time after their coming into this country, and to invest the proceeds of them in British produce. Sir Josiah Child, Algernon Sydney, Sir William Petty, and Sir William Temple endeavoured to disabuse the public mind respecting the bad influence of foreign settlers. But considerations of a political character stood for a considerable time in the way of any radical reform. After the Reformation, when the policy of excluding Roman Catholics from the realm became a question of state, a further difficulty was interposed to the denization of foreigners by the enactment that no one should be naturalised unless he had received the Sacrament of the Lord's Supper, and unless he had taken an oath of supremacy and

Legal position of aliens in England.

allegiance. This state of things was confirmed and firmly established by the Act of Limitation of William III. and it was then enacted that no person born out of the United Kingdom, and of the colonies, even though naturalised or denizens, unless born of English parents, could not become a member of the Privy Council or of either house of parliament, nor fill any office trust, civil or military, nor receive from the crown any grant of land, &c. In progress of time, however, the constant influx of refugees from France in consequence of the revocation of the Edict of Nantes opened the mind of the nation to the great utility of giving ample facilities to such migration, and a statute was passed allowing such aliens to acquire the rights of natural born subjects by their taking the oath of allegiance. Still it was not till the sixth year of George IV. that aliens were relieved from the necessity of taking the sacrament in case of naturalisation; and with a few modifications, introduced at different times, the law continued to impose many disabilities on aliens whether friends or enemies. When Mr. Hutt introduced his bill in 1843, aliens were debarred from the possession of real property, and certain descriptions of personal property; they could not take houses on lease for a term of years without danger of forfeiture; nor hold British registered shipping nor any share therein; they could not claim any commercial benefits by virtue of treaties with other states, and were absolutely excluded from all places of trust. By obtaining from the crown letters patent of denisation, foreigners were relieved from these disabilities so far that they could hold and transmit all kinds of real and personal property, but they could only transmit real property to such of their children as might have been born subsequent to their denisation. They were also permitted, when otherwise qualified, to vote at elections of members of parliament. But it was only by obtaining from parliament an act of naturalisation, that foreigners acquired all the privileges of denisation and a slight addition to them. Foreigners might inherit real property and transmit it to any of their children without distinction as to the time of their birth; and when they had resided in this country seven years from the period of their naturalisation, without having quitted it for more than two months at any one time, they became entitled to the benefit of British treaties in their commercial relations with foreign states. But to either of these methods the great objection was the expense and delay attending them whilst the whole law required to be ascertained and consolidated. To remedy this state of things, an act[88] was passed which provided that alien friends might take and hold by purchase, gift, bequest, &c., any species of personal property as effectually and with the same rights and remedies as if they were natural born subjects, and that they might grant lease, devise, bequest, &c., and hold land or houses for any number of years not exceeding twenty-one. But that upon taking the prescribed oath aliens might become naturalised by obtaining a certificate from the secretary of state for the home department by which they could enjoy all the rights and capacities which a natural born subject of the United Kingdom can enjoy or transmit, except the right of becoming a member of Her Majesty's Privy Council, or of either house of parliament. Since then, however, the law relating to aliens has again been greatly altered. By the Naturalisation Act of 1870,[89] an alien may now hold real and personal property of every description in all respects as a natural born British subject, and by acquiring a certificate of naturalisation, he becomes entitled to all political and other rights, powers, and privileges, in the same measure as a natural born British subject.

Another important reform was the amendment and consolidation of the bankruptcy law. In a country so eminently commercial as Great Britain, misfortunes, miscalculations, and disasters, must needs go hand in hand with success and prosperity. Sometimes the result of grave error or misconduct, sometimes the consequence of accidents and misfortunes, and at other times the effect of a combination of events altogether beyond control, whatever may be the cause, bankruptcy and insolvency are of no unusual occurrence in this country. Yet when we consider the large number of traders and the amount of business carried on between the merchants of the United Kingdom and with every part of the world, we may well wonder that the losses are not much greater, and that the number of traders who are annually wrecked is

The bankruptcy law.

[88] 7 & 8 Vict. c. 49.
[89] 33 Vict. c. 14.

not considerably larger. Think of the immensity of the transactions, the risk run, the time for which the risks are pending, the distance of the parties carrying on mutual trading, and the multitudinous circumstances, social, political, and economical, which influence trade. Think of the liberality with which credit is granted, the amount of confidence exhibited, and the extreme facility with which commercial transactions of enormous magnitude are daily concluded. And what could England do without credit? Credit is the life of commerce. In a country where private credit is accessible to all useful enterprises, a person active and intelligent may undertake commercial or industrial operations with comparatively small resources. Where, on the contrary, there is no credit, commerce languishes and becomes the exclusive domain of rich capitalists and so producing a want of competition and comparative dearness of every article of consumption. It is by credit that the whole capital of the country is rendered productive. It is by credit that the great machinery of human transactions is supported and speeded. Although not of itself a productive power, credit is a great purchasing power: it is a moving power, which at the command of the merchant creates commodities. A loss sustained through the misuse of credit is practically the same as a loss sustained by the absolute diminution of capital. And where such is the case need we wonder that the state provided specific laws for the preservation of credit? The laws regulating the rights of debtor and creditor have partaken very much of the characteristic of the countries and ages in which they were enacted. Among the Greeks, and prior to the era of Solon, the insolvent debtor became, together with all his family, the slave of his creditor, and as such he might be sold into foreign parts to pay a debt. Among the Romans the debtor was at first treated with unusual severity, but under Julius Cæsar with great leniency. Among the Jews the creditor had a right to seize the person of his debtor, of his wife and children, except that once in every seven years the debt was cancelled. In progress of time, however, laws of such a nature were abandoned for a more humane system. In England the necessity of taking the jurisdiction in matters of bankruptcy out of the hands of the common law, arose very early with the extension of trade. A statute passed during the reign of Henry VIII.[34] empowered certain commissioners to proceed against 'such as do make bankrupt,' and to take the bodies of the offenders, and with their lands, goods, and chattels, for payment of all the creditors rateably according to the quality of their debts. During the reign of Elizabeth[35] the same power was given to other commissioners, the law being framed exclusively in favour of the creditor. The statute of Anne,[36] however, for the first time made the innovation, that when the debtor had surrendered the whole of his effects, and conformed to the law of bankruptcy, he should be entitled to his discharge from all further liability for debts previously contracted. These statutes were amended and consolidated by 6 Geo. IV. c. 16, but that again was repealed in 1849 by the 12 & 13 Vict. c. 106. Inasmuch, however, as the bankrupt acts were expressly confined to traders, other laws were passed for the relief of insolvent debtors, which constituted a separate system of procedure, and this continued until the bankrupt and insolvent laws were amalgamated in 1861.[37]

Law of weights and measures.

The utility and desirability of a uniform system of weights and measures have long been recognised in the United Kingdom with a view to the saving of time, the prevention of mistakes, and the avoidance of litigation; and the establishment of such uniformity has been sought by a vast number of legal enactments, determining the standards, prescribing the manner of using weights and measures, charging certain persons with the control of the same, and establishing penalties and punishments. And yet but little progress has been made towards the attainment of the object, partly because it is impossible to control the despotic influence of custom, and more especially in consequence of the want of principles and adaptation which characterise the weights and measures in use. There was, to say the least, a great want of precision in the definition that 'an English penny, called a sterling, round and without clipping, shall weigh thirty-two wheat corns in the midst of the ear,' or that 'three barley-corns, round and dry, make an inch.' We need not wonder that, starting from such a basis, everything was involved in great confusion.

[34] 34 & 35 Henry VIII. c. 4. [35] 13 Eliz. c. 7. [36] 4 Anne, c. 17.
[37] 24 & 25 Vict. c. 134.

To remedy this state of things, a committee of the House of Commons was appointed in 1758 to inquire into the standards of weights and measures; and, upon their report, a yard measure constructed by Bird was declared to be the 'standard yard,' and a new Troy pound, constructed under the direction of the committee, was declared to be the legal standard of weights. But such arrangement does not appear to have satisfied the demands of science, and an absolute necessity existed for remedying the grievous defects of the weights and measures in use. Hence, in 1814, a committee of the House of Commons was appointed to inquire into the original standards of weights and measures, and their report was, that a pendulum vibrating in a given time and place was the best standard of measure; that the unit of weight should be ascertained from that of a number of cubic inches of distilled water at a given temperature; and that the unit of capacity should be a vessel containing a given weight of distilled water. Having once fixed on the vibrations of the pendulum as the best standard of measure, the next question was how to measure such vibrations. Accordingly, on March 15, 1816, an address was moved in the House of Commons to the Prince Regent desiring him to give directions for ascertaining the length of the pendulum vibrating seconds in time, in the latitude of London, as compared with the standard measure in possession of the house. The Prince Regent complied with the wishes of the house, and the work was entrusted to the Astronomer Royal, with the assistance of the Royal Society. Experiments were then instituted for the purpose, and a report was given in; but, though a bill founded upon it was introduced in the House of Commons, no progress was made with it.

Establishment of new standards.

In 1819 a royal commission was appointed to consider how far it might be practicable and advisable to establish within His Majesty's dominions a more uniform system of weights and measures, but again the result was very unsatisfactory, the commissioners having shrunk from the difficulty of either proposing a purely scientific basis, or of imposing absolute uniformity. They saw no practical advantage in having a quantity commensurable with any original quantity

Royal commission on the standards.

existing, or which may be imagined to exist, in nature, except as affording some little encouragement to its common adoption by neighbouring nations. They thought it scarcely possible that the departure from a standard, once universally established in a great country, should not produce much more labour and inconvenience in its internal relations than it could ever be expected to save in the operations of foreign commerce and correspondence, which always are, and always must be, conducted by persons to whom the difficulty of calculation is comparatively inconsiderable, and who are also remunerated for their trouble either by the profits of their commercial concerns or by the credit of their scientific acquirements. And they were of opinion that the duodecimal scale of division was much preferable to the decimal scale. Their report was therefore strictly conservative in its general character. They recommended for the legal determination of the standard yard that which was employed by General Roy in the measurement of a base on Hounslow Heath, as a foundation for the trigonometrical operations carried on by the ordnance throughout the country. And they proposed, upon the authority of the experiments made by the committee of the Royal Society, that it should be declared, for the purpose of identifying or recovering the length of this standard, in case that it should ever be lost or impaired, that the length of a pendulum vibrating seconds of mean solar time in London, on the level of the sea, and in a vacuum, is 39·1372 inches of this scale; and that the length of the mètre employed in France, as the ten-millionth part of the quadrantal arc of the meridian, has been found equal to 39·3707 inches. The measures of capacity the commissioners recommended to be calculated by the weight of the water these are capable of containing; and they proposed the adoption of a new standard gallon, containing ten pounds avoirdupois of distilled water, at 62° of Fahrenheit. As for the general principles of uniformity, whilst the commissioners fully acknowledged that it is desirable in every commercial country, in order to the saving of time, the prevention of mistakes, and the avoidance of litigation, they expressed their opinion that such uniformity cannot consistently with logical accuracy, with natural justice, and with the liberty of the subject, be very precisely defined, or very peremptorily and arbitrarily enjoined on every occasion. Another committee of the House of Commons was afterwards appointed on the same subject, and the result was the passing of an act, in 1824,[28] fixing the standards of weights and measures, and otherwise making regulations for establishing uniformity in the same. By that act, for the first time a formal definition was given to the unit of measure, by declaring that the straight line or distance between the centre of the two points in the gold studs in the brass rods, now in the custody of the clerk of the House of Commons, whereon the words and figures 'Standard Yard, 1760,' are engraved, shall be, and the same is hereby declared to be, the original and genuine standard of that measure of length or lineal extension called a yard; and that the straight line, or distance between the centres of the two points in the said gold studs in the said brass rod, the brass being at the temperature of 62° of Fahrenheit's thermometer, shall be, and is hereby denominated, the *Imperial Standard Yard*, and shall be, and is hereby declared to be, the unit or only standard measure of extension.

Usury laws.

The abolition of the usury laws was another important reform. At one time strong opinions were entertained respecting the immorality and even illegality of lending money at interest. By a statute of Henry VIII.[29] the maximum allowable rate of interest was 5 per cent., but any legalisation of the rate was objected to and under Edward VI.[30] a statute was passed prohibiting the taking of any interest, and rendering the money lent and the interest subject to forfeiture, and the offender liable to fine and imprisonment. An act of Elizabeth[31] confirmed the statute of Henry VIII., and ordained that all brokers should be guilty of a præmunire that contracted for more than five per cent., and that the securities themselves should be void. Under James I.[32] the rate of interest was fixed at 8 per cent.; under Charles II.[33] at 6 per cent.; and under Queen Anne[34] at 5 per cent., the latter act providing that all contracts and agreements, whereupon or whereby there shall be received or taken directly or indirectly any higher rate of

[28] 5 Geo. IV. c. 74. [29] 37 Henry VIII. c. 9. [30] 5 & 6 Edw. VI. c. 20.
[31] 13 Eliz. c. 8. [32] 21 Jac. I. c. 17. [33] 12 Car. II. c. 13.
[34] 12 Anne c. 16.

interest shall be utterly void, and that the mere act of taking a higher rate of interest than the one mentioned, even though the original contract should be perfectly valid, shall render the offender liable to forfeit treble the value of the money lent by him. But all such acts proved barren of real results, and they had to be relinquished, though not without considerable misgivings. In 1818 a committee of the House of Commons was appointed to consider the effect of the laws that regulate or restrain the interest of money, which examined amongst others, Mr. David Ricardo, Sir Samuel Romilly, Mr. Edward Sugden (afterwards Lord Chancellor St. Leonards), Mr. John Thornton, and Mr. Nathan Rothschild. After much inquiry, the committee reported that the laws regulating or restraining interest had been extensively evaded, and had failed of the effect of imposing a maximum on such rate; that of late years, from a constant excess of the market rate of interest above the limit permitted by law, they have added to the expense incurred by borrowers on real security, and that such borrowers were compelled to resort to the mode of granting annuities on lives, a mode which was made a cover for obtaining higher interest than the legal rate, and further subjected the borrowers to enormous charges, or forced them to make very disadvantageous sales of their estates. In the opinion of the committee, the construction of such laws as are applicable to the transactions of commerce, as then carried on, was attended with much uncertainty as to the legality of many transactions of frequent occurrence, and consequently was productive of much embarrassment and litigation. And that that period, when the market rate of interest was below the legal rate, afforded an opportunity peculiarly suitable for the repeal of the said laws. But, notwithstanding such a decided report, no steps were taken either to abolish or to lessen the inconvenience of the usury laws. Public opinion was not yet ripe for the change. During the crisis of 1826, however, it was felt that the prohibition to charge more than 5 per cent. when the value of money was much higher practically prevented borrowers from obtaining accommodation, and rendered the crisis still more calamitous. When, therefore, the Bank Charter Act had to be renewed, the committee of 1832 decided that it would be expedient to repeal the usury laws as far as regarded bills of exchange of three months and under. And accordingly an act to that effect was passed in 1833.[25] In 1836, upon the occurrence of another panic, the evil of the usury laws was still more felt; and in 1837 an act passed to extend the law of 1837 to bills of exchange of twelve months and under.[26] In 1839,[27] the law was again relaxed by rendering it lawful to stipulate for any rate of interest upon which the parties might agree as to all personal contracts, but made an exception as to real securities. The question was again raised by Lord Lansdowne in 1841, upon which occasion Lord Ashburton said that the relaxation had conferred great benefit on the lender, but not on the borrower. A committee of the House of Lords was then appointed to inquire into the effect of the alteration made in the laws regulating the interest on money, but that committee made no report, and only published the evidence. And thus the law remained till 1854, when a bill was introduced to abolish all the usury laws. Hitherto all the steps taken had been of a tentative character, because, in ignorance of the economic principles which regulate money as a medium of exchange, people could not be brought to believe that money was as much a commodity as any ordinary article of produce, that its value must be regulated like the value of any other commodity, by the ordinary principles of demand and supply, and that it was as impossible to fix the rate of interest at which it should be lent as to fix the price at which corn and butter should be sold. This prejudice, however, gradually disappeared, and it became easy to extend the same principle with respect to interest on money lent on land and other property as on bills of exchange. As a matter of fact, people were not deterred from raising money upon such securities at a higher rate of interest than 5 per cent. by the state of the law, only they had recourse to collusive practices and fraudulent proceedings in order to evade its operation, the result of which was that a much higher rate was paid than if money could have been obtained at the market value. The usury laws produced immense inconvenience; they affected

[25] 3 & 4 Will. IV. c. 98. [26] 7 Will. IV. & 1 Vict. c. 80. [27] 2 & 3 Vict. c. 37.

to do what all the powers of the legislature could not do, to apply a different principle to one description of commodity, from that which was applied to every other, and they interfered with the principle of supply and demand. And so they were altogether abolished.[38]

These are some only of the statutes of importance passed in recent years having immediate reference to trade and navigation; but we should not forget that the common law also has made immense progress, and that ever since Lord Mansfield we have had a succession of judges who made commercial law the subject of special study. Certain leading cases have, moreover, established important principles of mercantile jurisprudence. The case of Devayne *v.* Noble (Clayton's case) governs the doctrine of appropriation of payments. The 'Gratitude' settled that a master may hypothecate her cargo or freight for repairs in a foreign port. The law of general average, of implied warranties, of time policy, and of return premium on insurance, was decided, and many other points have from time to time come under the consideration of our tribunals. Then we should notice the establishment of the County Courts in 1846,[39] for the purpose of affording a cheap and speedy mode of recovering small debts; the County Courts Admiralty Jurisdiction Act,[40] introducing nautical or mercantile assessors to the assistance of the judge in the settlement of mercantile disputes; the registration of bills of sale, as a prevention of frauds upon creditors,[41] the act to facilitate the more speedy arrest of absconding debtors,[42] and many other measures calculated to give the best guarantee for the fulfilment of mercantile obligations. We have not a code as other nations possess, yet we have in our body of jurisprudence the basis of a beautiful and systematic fabric, whose depths and proportions will ever secure to Britain the gratitude and admiration of the civilised world, an edifice which expands with the growth of mercantile intercourse, strengthens with the refinement of public morals and intelligence, and is supported by those pillars of judicial acumen which adorn our temples of justice.

Other reforms.

[38] 17 & 18 Vict. c. 90. [39] 9 & 10 Vict. c. 95. [40] 31 & 32 Vict. c. 71.
[41] 17 & 18 Vict. c. 36. [42] 14 & 15 Vict. c. 52.

CHAPTER VIII.

MR. GLADSTONE'S BUDGET.

1852.

The Chancellor of the Exchequer.—Mr. Gladstone.—Previous reforms in the Excise, Customs, and Inland Revenue.—The Income Tax.—The Soap Duty.—The Tea Duty.—The Customs Tariff.—The New 2*l.* 10*s.* Stock.—Duties on Receipts and Bills of Exchange.—The Expenses of War.

IN Mr. Gladstone England has had a minister of finance of the highest order. Of business habits and with mercantile sympathies, a scholar and a statesman, a man of wide observation and comprehensive views, grave in speech and earnest in character, Mr. Gladstone is the very personation of a minister dealing with the finances of a state. The chancellor of the exchequer in the British cabinet has duties scarcely inferior to those of the prime minister. Properly to regulate the wants of the nation and to estimate its resources, to anticipate with any exactitude the produce of taxation and to balance the burdens on different classes of society—these, though only the elementary principles of the science of finance, are matters fraught with enormous difficulties. It seemed wonderful that Mr. Pitt could so well provide for the extraordinary exigencies of a protracted war. It was almost by a *coup de main* that Sir Robert Peel converted a bankrupt exchequer into an exchequer at once provident and affluent. But what seems magic or a *coup de main* is only the evolution of wisdom, the foresight of the minister, and in these qualities Mr. Gladstone rivalled, and perhaps excelled, his eminent predecessors.

The duties of the chancellor of the exchequer.

Mr. Gladstone was in the twenty-third year of his age when he entered the House of Commons in the conservative interest as the nominee of the Duke of Newcastle for the borough of Newark, and in a few years he was called to take part in the government of the country as lord of the treasury and under secretary of state for the colonies. In 1841 he was

Mr. Gladstone.

vice-president of the board of trade and master of the mint, and in 1843 he succeeded the Earl of Ripon as president of the board, under Sir Robert Peel's administration, in which capacity Mr. Gladstone gave invaluable aid to Sir Robert in the simplification of the tariff. But Sir Robert Peel's ministry fell, and Mr. Gladstone, freed from the burden of the state, paid a visit to Italy, a visit memorable for the influence it exercised on the government of the late King of Naples, by the exposition of the abuses of the prison discipline, and their effect on the distinguished patriot Poerio. In 1847 Mr. Gladstone was elected member for the University of Oxford, but, though still in the ranks of the conservative party, he refused to join the Earl of Derby's ministry in 1852. A year after, however, the coalition cabinet was formed, and Mr. Gladstone assumed in it the conspicuous place of chancellor of the exchequer.

Previous reforms in the excise, customs, and inland revenue.

Great reforms had already been made in the finances of the country when Mr. Gladstone became chancellor of the exchequer. In the excise the duties had been repealed on plate glass,[1] hides and skins,[2] salt,[3] printed

[1] The duty on plate glass was reduced from 4*l*. 18*s*. to 3*l*. per cwt. in 1819. In 1825 the duty on the manufactured article was repealed, and a duty of 3*d*. per lb. imposed on the fluxed materials. This duty was reduced from 3*d*. to 2½*d*. per lb., whilst 6*d*. per lb. was imposed on the manufactured article in 1832. Again this 6*d*. was reduced to 2*d*. per lb. in 1835. In 1841 the duty was reduced to ½*d*. per lb., and in 1845 both duty and license were repealed.

[2] In 1822 the various rates on hide and skin were reduced to one-half, and in 1830 they were repealed. A duty of 1½*d*. per lb. on tawed and lamb skins, and of 1*s*. per dozen on kid skins repealed.

[3] The salt duty in England was reduced from 15*s*. to 2*s*. per bushel in 1823, and the remaining duty was repealed in 1825. One of the earliest benefits derived from the cessation of the war and the reduction of the national expenditure was the abolition of the salt duty. It pressed hard upon the people. No article is more indispensable in the household of the rich and the poor than salt. It gives relish to our food; it promotes cleanliness and health; it is used for a hundred purposes, and, being one of the necessaries of life, it was good to render it as speedily as possible free of duty. Yet many nations have taken salt as a fit subject for duty. In ancient Rome salt was heavily taxed. In modern countries it forms the subject of a government monopoly. And in India salt, like opium, has long been monopolised by the state and heavily taxed. The clamour for the repeal of such a duty, when it was at the rate of 15*s*. per bushel, or thirty times the value of the salt, must have been very great, but the legislature was not soon prepared to abandon 1,500,000*l*. of revenue from this article. Happily salt is as abundant as it is useful and necessary. Every country in the world seems to produce it. Both kingdoms of nature, the organised and the inorganised, supply it. While whole

silk,[4] printed cottons,[5] candles,[6] tiles,[7] soap,[8] stone bottles,[9] starch,[10] stained paper,[11] and bricks.[12] In the customs the im-

strata of the earth are covered with rock salt, salt springs, salt lakes, salt marshes, the whole ocean may be said to be a rich mine of salt. A wonderful provision this of nature which is ever bountiful of the most coveted articles, and is always giving liberally of those things which are most useful and wholesome. But the great value of salt is not confined to its dietary purposes. The chemist has analysed its constituent elements and has revealed to us properties and capacities which few had ever imagined it did possess. But it is just the evil connected with customs or excise duties not the least that they prevent our becoming acquainted with the uses and value of many articles. The constituent parts of salt water are—chloride of sodium 71·9, chloride of magnesium 9·4, sulphate of magnesia 6·4, sulphate of lime 4·4, chloride of potassium 1; and some quantities of bromide of magnesium, carbonate of lime, silicic acid, and ammonia. For a considerable time France was obtaining soda from Spain, and Marseilles was the chief entrepôt for it. But at the commencement of the present century, Leblanc discovered the method of manufacturing carbonate of sodium from common salt, the process consisting in first converting the chloride of sodium into a sulphate of soda by means of sulphuric acid, and decomposing the latter by means of coal and carbonate of lime upon the floor of the reverberatory furnace. This was a most useful discovery, which endowed the world with cheap glass, soda, and many other advantages, and it is to be regretted that Leblanc himself never received any reward for his admirable discovery, and lived in poverty and despair. In this country Leblanc's process was first introduced in 1814, on a limited scale, for the preparation of soda crystals, which were then sold at 60*l.* per ton; but it was not till 1823 that common salt, having been relieved from taxation, Mr. Muspratt's works at Liverpool were erected, laying the foundation of a manufacture of chemical products which has since become the largest in the world. At first, so great was the benefit derived from the simple conversion of the chloride of sodium into soda, that the muriatic salt produced by it was not collected. It was soon, however, found that it was a compound of chlorine which possessed great bleaching properties. It became then an object of moment to separate the chlorine from the muriatic acid, and this was attained by mixing it with peroxide of manganese and sulphuric acid as a dense suffocating yellow gas. And as it was inconvenient to transport it either as liquid muriatic acid or as gaseous chlorine, it was combined with lime, thus forming a hypochlorite of that substance known as chloride of lime, or bleaching powder, used for purposes of disinfection, bleaching linen and cotton goods, rags for the manufacture of paper, &c. Thus by a variety of agencies, and by the concurrence of many varied circumstances, the utility of salt has been immensely increased. In a valuable paper on the subject in the 'Journal of the Society of Arts,' vol. i. p. 425, by Mr. Owen Huskisson, the processes involved in the manufacture of salt were minutely described, and its uses summed up as follows: 'It is used in the arts as a coarse glaze for pottery; gives hardness to soap; improves the whiteness and clearness of glass. In dyeing it is used as a mordant, and for improving certain colours; it preserves melting metals from oxidation, by defending their surface from the air; it is employed with advantage in some assays, and enters into many other important processes. To the chemist it is valuable, as a source of soda and chlorine and their compounds, from which he obtains the chloric acid, and combines

For Notes [4], [5], [6], [7], [8], [9], [10], [11], [12], see next page.

port duties were removed on most of the raw materials, and on coals imported coastwise, as well as all export duties on British goods and on coals. In the inland revenue also reforms had been made in the stamp duties, on life and marine insurance, bills of lading, pamphlets, advertisements, and newspapers. Yet with all this much remained to be done to free industry from unnecessary burdens. Unfortunately, however, a pamphlet by Prince de Joinville, a letter by the Duke of Wellington, a volume by Sir Francis Head, excited considerable apprehensions regarding the state of the army and navy. The coup d'état of Napoleon III. in 1852 was regarded as the

with potash to form chlorate of potash so largely used in the manufacture of lucifers. To the agriculturist salt is useful as a manure and dressing to certain lands. It is used at the table as a flavouring or seasoning agent, being a necessary article of food essential for the preservation of health and the maintenance of life. It is also largely used in the preservation and curing of alimentary substances. In medicine it is used as a vomit, purgative, to restore the saline constituents of the blood, alterative, astringent, dentifrice; as an external application to sprains and bruises; its tonic power proves useful in dyspepsia, and promotes digestion, and in correcting the weakened state of the intestines which favours the propagation of worms. Dissolved in water, it forms a stimulating bath, and is a chemical antidote against poisoning by nitrate of silver.' The manufacture of alkaline products is itself a most important industry in Newcastle, and the Tyne, and Lancashire. The economist or the student who wishes to find illustrations of the opposing influences of taxation and science on industrial process, will find a mine of information in the reports of the juries for the International Exhibitions of 1851 and 1862, and more especially in the report on chemical products and processes at the latter exhibition by Dr. Hoffman. Truly the resources which nature offers to our use are inexhaustible, and are still but imperfectly fathomed. How much do we owe to those illustrious few who, wonderfully rich in their power of analysis and depth of intellect, are fortunate enough in laying bare those mysteries which have so long defied the keenest and most patient investigations.

[4] A duty of 6*d*. per yard on printed silks was repealed in 1826.

[5] The duty of 3½*d*. per square yard on printed cottons was repealed in 1831. The licence to calico printers of 20*l*. was also repealed.

[6] In 1832 the duties of 1*d*. per lb. on tallow candles and 3½*d*. on wax and spermaceti candles were repealed, and the license duty to candle makers of 2*l*. and 5*l*. was also repealed.

[7] The duties on tiles were repealed in 1833.

[8] In 1833 the soap duties were reduced to one-half the former rates, viz. hard to 1½*d*. per lb., and soft to 1*d*. per lb. In 1853 they were repealed.

[9] The duty of 5*s*. per cwt. on stone bottles was repealed in 1834.

[10] The duty on starch of 3½*d*. per lb. repealed in 1834.

[11] In 1836 the duty of 1¾*d*. per square yard on stained paper was repealed. The licence to stained paper makers, 4*l*., repealed, and the paper duty reduced to one uniform rate of 1½*d*. per lb.

[12] In 1839 the duties on bricks were reduced, and in 1850 repealed.

first step in a career of conquest, and the result was a large increase on the expenditure always fatal to financial reforms.

It was under these untoward circumstances that Mr. Gladstone succeeded to the management of the finances of the country; yet in that very year he made the first of those financial statements which, like those of Sir Robert Peel, rendered the delivery of the budget an occasion of absorbing interest to the community. The condition of the revenue was indeed better than Mr. Disraeli had anticipated; but a large sum was required, and the first question for him to solve was, Shall the income tax be reimposed? The tax had been in operation from 1799 to 1802, from 1806 to 1815, and from 1842 to 1852. In a time of great difficulty, it enabled the government to raise the income of the country above its expenditure. At another time it had been the instrument by which the government were enabled to introduce most useful reforms. Why should the government not return to it once more, in order to perfect the reforms which were still needed in the commercial and fiscal system? And this was Mr. Gladstone's resolve, though he had serious objections to that method of taxation. 'The general views of Her Majesty's Government with respect to the income tax,' concluded Mr. Gladstone, 'are, that it is an engine of gigantic power for great national purposes; but at the same time, that there are circumstances attending its operation which make it difficult, perhaps impossible, at any rate in our opinion not desirable, to maintain it as a portion of the permanent and ordinary finances of the country. The public feeling of its inequality is a fact most important in itself. The inquisition it entails is a most serious disadvantage, and the frauds to which it leads are an evil which it is not possible to characterise in terms too strong.' Having thus decided upon the renewal of the income tax, and upon extending the probate duty over both real and personal property, Mr. Gladstone discussed the proposed remission of taxation.

The income tax.

The first item in his budget under this head was the excise duty on soap, a tax most injurious to the comfort and health of the people, and a burden on manufacturing industry, soap being extensively employed in many processes of

The soap duty.

manufacture. The excise had established many stringent regulations in order to arrest the surreptitious production of soap, which whilst powerless to prevent the making of soap secretly without taking out any licence, effectively prevented improvements in the processes, so that the quality of soap made in foreign countries, where no such regulations were imposed, was invariably superior to that of English soap. A duty, moreover, was imposed on one of the chief ingredients, used in manufactures, and the duties were so regulated that our manufacturers were chiefly restricted to the employment of a material which was not calculated to produce soap of the finest quality. The duty down to 1833 was at the rate of 3*d.* per lb. on hard soap, and 1½*d.* per lb. on soft soap, besides the taxes on the raw materials used in its manufacture, such as tallow, barilla, and turpentine or resin, the direct and indirect taxes together forming 120 to 130 per cent. *ad valorem.* In 1833 the duty was reduced 50 per cent., or to 1½*d.* per lb. on hard and 1*d.* per lb. on soft soap, and so it remained till 1853, when, though the amount of revenue produced by it was upwards of 1,000,000*l.*, the duty was entirely abolished.

The tea duty.

The next important reform was on the tea duty, which was then at the high rate of 2*s.* 2½*d.* per lb. When tea was first used in this country a duty of 8*d.* a gallon was charged on the decoction made from the leaves, but soon after it was changed into a duty of 5*s.* per lb. on the tea itself. With such a high duty, however, as this, smuggling was easy and profitable, and the revenue suffered considerably. In 1745 the necessity of checking this illegitimate traffic having become indispensable, on the recommendation of a committee of the House of Commons, the duty was reduced at least 50 per cent., and the measure succeeded admirably, both commercially and financially. But the legislature did not understand the economic laws which regulate the consumption of such articles, and in 1759 it again increased the duty from 65 to 120 per cent. Again, however, smuggling became general. The honest dealer was beaten out of the market by the unfair competition of the smuggler, and much temptation to adulteration was thereby afforded. Once more, therefore, the legislature tried to remedy this evil, and following the precedents of

1745, in 1784 the duty was reduced from 119 per cent. to 12½ per cent. For some time this policy was persisted in with great success, but the exigencies of the war in 1795 threw all economic considerations out of view. The duty was first increased from 12½ to 25 per cent.; then by successive augmentations it was raised to 96 per cent. *ad valorem*, at which rate it continued till 1819, when the duty was raised to 100 per cent. on all tea worth more than 2*s*. per lb. at the company's sales. In 1824 the duties were somewhat modified, and in 1830 a uniform duty of 2*s*. 1*d*. per lb. was imposed, to which 5 per cent. was added in 1840. At that rate it continued till in 1853 Mr. Gladstone reduced the duty to 1*s*. 10*d*. per lb. with prospective further reductions to 1*s*. per lb., which, however, the Russian war arrested for some time.

Still more important among Mr. Gladstone's reforms was the improvement of the tariff. The principle which he adopted was, first to abolish altogether the duties which were unproductive, except in cases where there might be some special reasons for retaining them on account of their relation to other articles; and in the next place to abolish, as far as considerations of revenue would permit, duties on articles of manufacture except those which were in the last stage as finished articles, and were commonly connected with hand labour—for in regard to these cases he thought it more prudent and proper to proceed in the mode, not of abolition, but of reduction. As a general rule such duties were not to be higher than 10 per cent.; but he allowed the silk duties to remain at 15 per cent. out of consideration to a certain class of operatives. He substituted rated duties for duties *ad valorem*; abolished the 5 per cent. addition to customs duties made in 1840; put an end to all differential duties by lowering those on the foreign article to the level of those on the colonial; lowered the duties on many articles of food, and set altogether free 123 articles which produced but a small amount of revenue. Mr. Gladstone anticipated that such remissions would act not only upon the consumers of particular articles enabling them to increase their particular consumption of the various articles, but that they would act upon consumers generally, and that they would operate powerfully in the extension and

The customs tariff.

invigoration of the trade of the country. 'These,' he said, 'are the proposals of the government. They may be approved or they may be condemned, but I have at least this full and undoubting confidence, that it will on all hands be admitted that we have not sought to evade the difficulties of our position; that we have not concealed those difficulties either from ourselves or from others; that we have not attempted to counteract them by narrow or flimsy expedients; that we have proposed plans which, if you will adopt them, will go some way towards closing up many vexed questions—questions, such as, if not now settled, may be attended with public inconvenience, and even with public danger, in future years.'

Another financial operation was proposed by Mr. Gladstone in connection with the budget of 1852, but it was not equally successful. He wished to create a 2*l*. 10*s*. stock, and he offered to the holders of 3 per cent. either to change it for a new 3½ per cent. stock, guaranteed against redemption for forty years, at 82*l*. 10*s*. of the new for every 100*l*. of the old stock; or a new 2½ per cent., also guaranteed against redemption for forty years, at the rate of 110*l*. of the new for every 100*l*. of the old, or for exchequer bonds at par. The plan was favourably received at first, but no one seemed to act upon it, and eventually only about 3,000,000*l*. of 2½ per cent. stock was taken. In truth, the strength of Mr. Gladstone's operation was the expectation of great changes in the value of money from the discoveries of gold, and as these were not realised no disposition existed to relinquish the 3 per cent. stock which amounted to 500,000,000*l*.

The new 2*l*. 10*s*. stock.

The operation of Mr. Gladstone's financial reforms was to some extent arrested by the war with Russia; yet in 1853 the great reform was made in the tax on receipts, by reducing the duties from various rates to one uniform rate of 1*d*.; and in 1854 the stamp duties on bills of exchange were greatly reduced. Besides this, in that year the method of paying customs duties by cheques was first introduced, which relieved the trader from all risks in the transmission of notes and coin, the customs department of much needless labour, and bankers of the necessity of keeping

The duties on receipts and bills of exchange.

a large amount of notes on hand to meet the demands of their customers. In this way a considerable economy in the use of bank notes and coin was effected, and the payment of customs duties was reduced to a system of transfer of credits in the books of private bankers and those of the Bank of England.

The expenses of war.

Nor must we omit to notice that when the Russian war brought a large increase of the expenditure, and a great temptation to resort to loans as in former days, Mr. Gladstone was the first to protest against throwing the burden of present calamities on a future generation. It was desirable, he thought, to make the nation feel the evils of a war expenditure by allowing it to encroach on their comforts. 'The expenses of a war,' said Mr. Gladstone, 'are the moral check which it has pleased the Almighty to impose upon the ambition and the lust of conquest that are inherent in so many nations. There is pomp and circumstance, there is glory and excitement about war, which, notwithstanding the miseries it entails, invests it with charms in the eyes of the community, and tends to blind men to those evils to a fearful and dangerous degree. The necessity of meeting from year to year the expenditure which it entails is a salutary and wholesome check, making them feel what they are about, and making them measure the cost of the benefit which they may calculate.'

CHAPTER IX.

THE RUSSIAN WAR.

1854—1856.

Dispute of the Holy Places.—Interest of England in Turkey.—Aggression of Russia.—Declaration of War.—Trade with Russia.—Effect of Blockade.—International Law.—Prussia and the Blockade.—Effect of War on Fibrous materials.—Production of Fibres in India.—Number of Captures.—The Declaration on Maritime Law.

SCARCELY had the fear of a French invasion subsided, when a cloud rose from the east, which was ere long to introduce war and discord all over Europe. For a considerable time Russia had asserted a right to assume a kind of protectorate over her coreligionists in Turkey which England regarded with great suspicion. A singular dispute, however, brought into great prominence the aims and extent of Russian policy in Turkey. The holy places in Jerusalem consisted of certain churches built on the spots connected with the life of Christ, some held in possession by Roman Catholic and some by other Christian communities in Jerusalem, including the Greek, the Armenian, Syrian, Coptic, and Abyssinian; the right of possession being exercised by putting a carpet and lighting a candle on the altar. But this joint possession of churches, with distinct rights to certain altars, was a source of frequent dispute between the Latin and Greek. At one time a fire having broken out in the chapel of the Armenians and destroyed their principal sanctuary and other portions belonging to the Greeks, the Catholics charged the Greeks with having expressly caused the fire in order to claim compensation, but the Greeks retorted the charge against the Armenians. Again, in 1847, a quarrel arose owing to the sudden disappearance of a silver star from the church of Bethlehem just at the time when the Greeks were worshipping in the sanctuary,

Dispute of the holy places.

and the Latins charged the Greeks with the robbery. At last France intervened with a view to settle these constant quarrels, and succeeded in inducing the Porte to form a mixed commission to inquire into the question. But whilst the commission were prosecuting these inquiries, the Emperor of Russia wrote an autograph letter to the Sultan demanding the integral preservation of the religious privileges of the Greeks at Jerusalem. The tone of the letter alarmed the Sultan, and the commission was reconstructed, composed exclusively of Ottoman functionaries. The commission thereafter made their report recommending the maintenance of the *status quo*, and the report was confirmed by the Porte, and accepted by France under protest. Russia, however, made capital of the matter, and caused a firman to be published with due solemnity in accordance with the report.

Declaration of war.

Other difficulties afterwards arose, by whom excited it is difficult to say, but in February, 1853, Prince Menschikoff arrived at Constantinople as ambassador extraordinary from Russia to make a formal demand to the Porte to reduce into a treaty the rights, privileges, and immunities in favour of the Greek Church, and to assign a convenient locality in the city of Jerusalem, or its neighbourhood, for the building of a church for the Russian co-religionists, and a hospice for poor or sick pilgrims, such foundations to be put under the protectorate of Russia. This ultimatum, being considered derogatory to the power and destructive of the independence of the Porte, was refused, and thereupon the Russian government caused the invasion by Russian troops of the principalities of Moldavia and Wallachia, which were under the sovereignty of the Porte, though under the protection of Russia. A declaration of war on the part of Turkey was the immediate consequence of this step. Hostilities commenced, and France and England, interested in the preservation of the independence of the Ottoman Empire, caused their fleets to enter the Bosphorus; and on March 28, 1854, England declared war against Russia. Though the independence of Turkey was the apparent cause of the war, jealousy of Russian influence in Europe and Asia was the real motive. In the east especially, Russia and England seemed likely to confront each other, both having great rival Asiatic empires, Russia in the north, England in the south, the one extending towards China and Affghanistan, the other through Persia and Bokhara. It was this rivalry which rendered the war popular in high circles in England, and it was the desire of checking a power adverse to democratic institutions that rendered the war acceptable even to liberals, except, indeed, men of sterner temper than the multitude, men like Cobden and Bright. Setting aside, however, the political object of the war, we are interested in seeing what effects it had on trade and finance.

Trade with Russia.

To Russia we had not hitherto exported much British manufacture and produce, the value of our exports having been on an average under 2,000,000*l.* per annum, on a total of 60,000,000*l.* to 70,000,000*l.*; but our imports thence were of the greatest importance in grain, tallow, seed, hemp, flax, wool, and timber. There was, moreover, a circumstance connected with such imports which greatly affected British traders. The produce exported to England came from distant provinces in the interior of Russia, and was brought to the shipping ports in the height of winter, when snow was on the ground, transit being most easy at that time, with a view to its being ready for shipment when the shipping season came, which was from May to November. But to get that produce forwarded in time, the London houses were under the necessity of making large advances in cash to native dealers, so as to enable them to proceed into the interior some thousands of miles with the means of purchasing produce, and fulfilling their contract. These advances were made in cash in St. Petersburg, and were provided on the spot either by remittances from London, or by drafts from St. Petersburg by the English agents there of the London houses. Some 7,000,000*l.* of capital and many British ships were thus engaged in the Russian trade when the relations between the two countries became hostile, and certainly, had not the actual break out of war been put off by negotiation till the produce was ready for shipment, considerable losses must have been sustained.

Declaration of neutral trading.

War was, however, at last proclaimed, and with the declaration of Her Majesty's Government granting reprisals against the ships, vessels, and goods of the Emperor of Russia, and of his subjects, or others inhabiting any of his countries, came the important statement that in order to preserve the commerce of neutrals from unnecessary obstructions, Her Majesty was willing for the present to waive a part of the belligerent rights appertaining to her by the law of nations. That it was impossible for Her Majesty to forego the exercise of her right of seizing articles contraband of war, and of preventing neutrals from bearing the enemy's despatches, and she must maintain the right of a belligerent to prevent neutrals from breaking any effective blockade which might be established with an adequate force against the enemy's forts, harbours, or coasts; but that Her Majesty would waive the right of seizing enemy's property on board a neutral vessel unless it were contraband of war. It was not Her Majesty's intention to claim the confiscation of neutral property, not being contraband of war, found on board enemy's ships; and Her Majesty further declared that, being anxious to lessen as much as possible the evils of war, and to restrict its operations to the regularly organized forces of the country, it was not her present intention to issue letters of marque for the commissioning of privateers.

Prohibition of exportation of arms.

Previous to the declaration of war, a royal proclamation had been issued on February 21, prohibiting the exportation of warlike stores, including all arms, ammunition, and gunpowder, as well as naval stores and marine engines, and what pertains thereto. This general prohibition, however, having been found inconvenient to the traders and manufacturers of arms, permission was granted by an order in council, dated April 11, 1854, to export such articles to any place other than Russian territories, upon taking a bond from the person exporting such prohibited articles that they shall be landed at the port of destination. But even this order was found to be too indefinite and ineffectual, and on April 24 another order in council was issued ordering that the officers of customs should not prevent the export of any articles except only gunpowder, saltpetre, and brimstone, arms and ammunition, marine engines and boilers, and the component parts thereof, the latter to be prohibited only when destined for any place in Europe north of Dunkirk, or to any place in the Mediterranean Sea east of Malta.

As might be expected under such circumstances, all articles of Russian produce rose enormously in value. Tallow, usually at 36s. to 38s., rose to 64s. per cwt.; hemp from 30*l.* rose to 47*l.*; linseed from 44s. rose to 54s. per quarter. A pressing demand for Russian produce gave rise to extraordinary high prices; nor did the large imports from other countries help materially to reduce them. The price of consols was also seriously affected. In April 1853, whilst still under the influence of the gold discoveries, consols reached 101. On March 30, 1854, on the declaration of war, they fell to 85*l.* 2*s.* 6*d.*, and with this fall railway and other property had a similar downward tendency. After a little, however, the absence of Russia from the markets of the country became less and less felt. Russian produce itself came to this country from Prussia and Holland. India sent us large quantities of fibrous materials; America supplied grain; and, with the rest of the world open, it mattered little that a few Russian ports on the Baltic and the Black Sea continued in a state of blockade. But to Russia the war must have produced a considerable loss of trade. The 'Petersburg Gazette,' writing in September 1854, made it appear as if the war would produce but little loss of trade. It said: 'It is known that an enormous quantity of tallow is being prepared in the nine melting-houses. This article used to find its principal vent in our Baltic ports, from which it was, for the most part, sent abroad. For the want of the naval service this year 453,000 poods of tallow had been prepared worth nearly a million of roubles. While the tallow was being melted and refined, the end of the winter came, and at the same time the complete rupture between Russia and England. Our merchants took the alarm on the supposition that tallow this year would not be in demand from abroad. Navigation opened, and they sent, nevertheless, their goods by the Volga to Rybinsk. In the spring our trade found another outlet. It is true tallow was not sent to the Baltic ports, but it went by land to Prussia. From Rybinsk they sent it by small steamers to Iver and beyond, down the Volga. Thence it was taken on by carriage to the frontier; the carriage cost 31 silver copecks per pood. In this way our merchants got rid of

Effects of war on British and Russian trade.

all their tallow, not without profit, and political events had no influence on the movements of commerce. Our tallow will reach England, but by another route.' Eventually, however, such expectations were not realised. In 1853 the exports from European Russia amounted to 22,000,000*l.*; in 1854 they were only 8,776,000*l.*, and in 1855 they fell to 4,618,000*l.* And the imports into European Russia, which in 1853 amounted to 14,295,000*l.*, fell in 1854 to 8,669,000*l.* Nor could it be otherwise. Previous to the war Russia exported her principal Baltic produce chiefly to England. The blockade stopped that altogether, and though some produce found its way out of the country by land, the difficulties and consequent expense of transport rendered the losses very heavy to Russian producers and exporters. How far the blockade answered the political object we shall not inquire, but it is evident that at whatever expense, Russia continued to receive sufficient provisions from other parts of Europe, and she was not altogether precluded from continuing her foreign trade. During the war 206 vessels were captured and brought before the high court of admiralty, and of these 78 were Russian. Of the total number captured, 160 were condemned, 30 restored, and 16 were captured only in part or not adjudicated on.

Declaration of maritime law.

The Russian war practically ended with the taking of Sebastopol and the complete invasion of the Crimea in September 1855. But the general treaty of peace was concluded on March 30, 1856, which neutralised the Black Sea and threw its waters and its ports open to the mercantile marine of every nation; extended the application of the free navigation of rivers, established by the Congress of Vienna, to the Danube and its mouths, and provided for the admission of consuls into the ports situated upon the coast of the Black Sea. Still more remarkable, however, amongst the acts of that congress, was the Declaration respecting maritime law, signed on April 16, to the following effect: 'Considering that maritime law, in time of war, has long been the subject of deplorable disputes, that the uncertainty of the law and of the duties in such a matter give rise to differences of opinion between neutrals and belligerents, which may occasion serious difficulties and even conflicts, that it would be consequently advantageous to establish a uniform doctrine on so important a point: that the plenipotentiaries assembled in congress at Paris cannot better respond to the intentions by which their governments are animated than by seeking to introduce into international relations fixed principles in this respect: the plenipotentiaries, being duly authorised, resolved to concert among themselves as to the means of attaining this object; and having come to an agreement have adopted the following solemn Declaration:

'1. Privateering is, and remains, abolished;

'2. The neutral flag covers enemy's goods, with the exception of contraband of war;

'3. Neutral goods, with the exception of contraband of war, are not liable to capture under enemy's flag;[1]

'4. Blockades, in order to be binding, must be effective, that is to say, maintained by a force sufficient really to prevent access to the coast of the enemy.'

The Declaration was signed by the plenipotentiaries of Great Britain, Austria, France, Prussia, Russia, Sardinia, and Turkey. And their respective governments having engaged to bring the Declaration to the knowledge of the states which did not take part in the congress of Paris, and to invite them

[1] The first English treaty which contained the principle 'free ship, free goods' was that of Westminster in the year 1654, concluded between John IV., King of Portugal, and Cromwell. That treaty, confirmed by that of Whitehall in 1661, and re-confirmed by that of Lisbon of 1703, continued unaltered till 1810, when in the 26th article of the treaty of Rio de Janeiro, 'the power of carrying in the ships of either country goods and merchandise the property of the enemies of the other country was renounced and abrogated. In 1655 the Lord Protector concluded a treaty with Louis XIV, containing the same principle, but it was not inserted in the treaty of Breda in 1667. In 1677, however, the treaty of St. Germain-en-Laye contained an article declaring 'that goods of the enemy of the most Christian King should not be taken or confiscated if found on board ships appertaining to the subjects of Great Britain except contraband of war.' In subsequent treaties the same clause was inserted. In the treaty of Madrid of 1665, and in all other treaties with Spain till 1796 the same stipulation was made, and the treaty of 1814, which ratified the treaties existing in 1796, renewed the principle. The treaty of Breda with the United Provinces in 1667 contained it, and so the treaty of the Hague of 1780. All the treaties between France and Spain; between Spain and the United Provinces; between the United States and the South American States, and between France and the South American States, have the same stipulation.—See Sir William Molesworth's Speech, July 4, 1854, and Sir Travers Twiss's 'Law of Nations,' vol. ii. p. 156.

to accede to it, in a short time the Declaration was acceded to by Baden, Bavaria, Belgium, Denmark, Bremen, Brazil, Brunswick, Chili, the Argentine Confederation, the German Confederation, Equador, Hesse, Lubeck, Haiti, Hamburg, Hanover, the Two Sicilies, the Roman States, Greece, Guatemala, Mechlenburg, Nassau, the Netherlands, Oldenburg, Parma, Peru, Portugal, Saxony, Sweden, Switzerland, Tuscany, and Wurtemburg. Spain, however, objected to the first article relating to privateering and accepted the three others. Mexico did the same. And the United States of America offered to accept the declaration on condition that private property at sea be declared free from capture.

The question of international maritime law has been often discussed since this important Declaration was signed, but the policy thereby traced has been adhered to generally, notwithstanding frequent attacks made on its policy. Nor can it be considered sufficiently advantageous to the interests of commerce. Mr. Cobden advocated the further extension of the principle of lessening the impediments to commerce during war, and warmly did he commend the exemption of private property from capture at sea, during war, by armed vessels of every kind; the limitation of blockades to naval arsenals, and to towns besieged at the same time on land, and the inviolability of merchant ships of neutrals on the high seas to the visitation of alien government vessels in time of war, as in time of peace.[1] Let us hope, however, that international arbitration will ere long be substituted for the barbarous custom of war.

Reforms of international maritime law.

[1] See a paper on 'International Maritime Law,' by Henry Ashworth, Esq.: Social Science Association, 1864.

CHAPTER X.

TRADE WITH THE EAST.

1855—1857.

Relations with China.—Entrance into Canton.—The Case of the 'Arrow.'—Mission of the Earl of Elgin.—Treaty of Tien-tsin.—Hostilities at Takoo.—Trade with Chinese Ports.—Mission to Japan.—Treaty with Japan.—The Coinage of Japan.—British and American Traders.—Issue of a new Coinage.—Sir John Bowring's mission to Siam.—Treaty with Siam.—Consular Jurisdiction in the East.—Mutinies in the East Indies.—Transfer of Government of British India to Her Majesty.—Economic Reforms in India.—Trade of India.—Commerce with Central Asia.—Communication with India.

THE war with Russia ended, information reached this country that the relations with China had once more been disturbed.

Relations with China.

The treaty of Nanking of 1842 had stipulated that British subjects with their families and establishments should be allowed to reside for the purpose of carrying on their mercantile pursuits without molestation or restraint at the cities and towns of Canton, Amoy, Foochow-foo, Ningpo, and Shanghai. And it was only in view of the danger or difficulty of allowing foreigners to enter the city of Canton, that the treaty signed at Bocca-Tigris provided that, *in the meantime*, British subjects should enjoy full liberty and protection in the neighbourhood on the outside of the city of Canton. But time passed without any progress being made in providing for free access to the city of Canton, and all the negotiations for the purpose had proved of no effect. In a despatch on the subject Viscount Palmerston said: 'These engagements, thus solemnly recorded, the Chinese government has now declined to fulfil. But the faithful performance of treaty engagements by sovereigns is the security for peace between nations. The Queen of England has fulfilled her treaty engagements to the Emperor of China. The Emperor of China has not fulfilled his treaty engagements to the Queen of England. Why has the Emperor broken his word? Is it because he is unwilling to keep his engagements, or because he is unable to do so? If he is unwilling to keep his engagement, how can the British government trust to the Emperor's word, and how can there be lasting peace between the two governments? If the Emperor is unable to keep his promise, because his word and his orders are not respected by his subjects, how can he expect that foreign governments should show him more respect than his own subjects are willing to show; and will not foreign governments be obliged to inflict on the Chinese people, in order to repress their violence, those punishments which the Emperor is too weak to be able to award?'

Thus matters stood, when, in 1852, Dr.—now Sir John—Bowring was appointed superintendent of the trade of British subjects in China, his instructions being 'to insist upon the performance by the Chinese authorities of the engagements which existed between the two countries, but not to resort to measures of force without previous reference home, unless in the extreme case of such measures being required to repel aggression or to protect the lives and property of British subjects.' From the first, however, Sir John Bowring was not disposed to remain passive on the subject. Soon after his arrival, he communicated to the Earl of Clarendon his conviction that the entrance into the city of Canton might be effected without serious difficulty, and that no better or more appropriate period could be found for peremptorily urging upon the Chinese authorities that the engagement entered into by the Chinese government as to the entrance into the city of Canton should be fulfilled without further delay. Still Her Majesty's Government urged upon Sir John Bowring not to pursue the correspondence and not to press for personal intercourse. On February 13, 1854, the Earl of Clarendon sent a note to Sir John Bowring to the effect that there were points which it was desirable to secure, and to which England had even a right by treaty, and among those were free and unrestricted intercourse with the Chinese authorities and free admission into some of the cities of China, especially Canton. But that the treatment of these questions required much

Entrance into Canton.

caution, for if we should press them in menacing language, and yet fail in carrying them, our national honour would require us to have recourse to force, and in order to obtain results the practical advantage of which was not clearly demonstrated, we might place in peril the vast commercial interests which have already grown up in China, and which with good and temperate management would daily acquire greater magnitude.

Thus cautioned by Her Majesty's Government, Sir John Bowring continued his correspondence with commissioner Yeh respecting the entry into Canton, and his official reception and his efforts were still unavailing, when, on October 8, 1856, Consul Parker informed him that the 'Arrow,' a lorcha sailing under British colours, had been suddenly boarded by a force of Chinese officers in a war boat of large size and heavy armament, and that they had pinioned and carried away nearly the whole of the crew, leaving only two out of the fourteen men on board, adding to this act of violence the significant insult of hauling down the national ensign. The 'Arrow' was a Chinese ship belonging to a Chinese trader, sailing under a colonial certificate of registry renewable annually, bearing date Hong Kong, September 27, 1855, and therefore, at the time, no longer under its protection. But it was urged that the Chinese had no knowledge of the expiration of the certificate, and Consul Parker affirmed that the inviolability of the British flag might be satisfactorily and easily vindicated by reprisals on one or more of the war boats of the Chinese force by which the violence was committed. Accordingly, an apology was demanded from commissioner Yeh, and immediately on the receipt of a very unsatisfactory answer, an imperial junk was seized in Canton. Taking advantage of this opportunity, Sir John Bowring wrote to Admiral Sir M. Seymour that the circumstances were auspicious for requiring the fulfilment of treaty obligations as regards the city of Canton, and for arranging an official meeting with the imperial commissioners within the city wall. A more peremptory demand was thereupon made to that effect, and having been met by more evasions, steps were being taken for blockading the Canton river, when, in view of the imminence of another war, the Earl of Elgin arrived as High Commissioner and

Act of violence on the 'Arrow.'

plenipotentiary for the settlement of various important matters between Her Majesty and the Emperor of China.

Instructions to the Earl of Elgin.

The demands which the Earl of Elgin was instructed to make were reparation of injuries to British subjects, complete execution at Canton, as well as at the other ports, of the stipulations of the several treaties, compensation for losses incurred in consequence of the late disturbances, the assent of the Chinese government to the residence at Pekin of a British minister, a revision of the treaties with China, with a view to obtaining increased facilities for commerce, such as access to cities on the great rivers, as well as to Chapoo and other ports on the coast, and also permission for Chinese vessels to resort to Hong Kong for purposes of trade from all ports of the Chinese empire without distinction. The latter demand was considered of great importance, for although since the conclusion of the treaty of Nankin, the trade of foreign nations with China had been greatly extended, yet it fell far short of what might reasonably be expected under an improved system of intercommunication with the Chinese people. As yet the trade was confined to free ports, to which alone foreigners were entitled to resort, and from which alone Chinese vessels could proceed for purposes of trade to the island of Hong Kong. And it was one of the main objects of Lord Elgin's mission to endeavour to liberate the trade with China from these restrictions, and to induce the Chinese government to consent to throw open the ports of China generally to foreign commerce, and to allow the subjects of foreign powers freely to communicate with the great cities in the interior, but more especially with those which are situated on the large rivers, and those lying immediately within the seaboard of the north-eastern coast.

Preliminary negotiations and treaty of Tien-tsin.

On his arrival at Hong Kong the Earl of Elgin placed himself in agreement with the ministers of France and the United States, and sought for information from the principal merchants and chambers of commerce respecting the wants of trade and the operation of the Chinese tariff. This done, he made his demand on the Chinese commissioner and waited for an answer; but again the answer having been long and evasive, the Earl of Elgin saw no other way but a forced entry into the city, which he was not long in effecting. From Canton, the Earl of Elgin sent a despatch to the prime minister of the Emperor of China, referring to the negotiations which had been opened with Commissioner Yeh prior to the occupation of the place, and to the disregard of the demand then made, and declaring that it was the intention of Great Britain and France to continue to occupy the city of Canton till all the differences between the two countries were settled. Again, however, all attempts at conciliation proved unsuccessful, and the British and French ministers resolved to move up the river towards Tien-tsin.[1] The contest was short though sharp, and on June 26 a treaty of peace, friendship, and commerce was concluded, by which every demand was acceded to on the part of China. The treaty provided for the residence of a British ambassador at Pekin and the establishment of consuls in the dominions of the Emperor of China. It permitted the profession and teaching of Christianity, authorised British subjects to travel to all parts of the interior, permitted British merchant ships to trade upon the great river (Yang-tse) and, as soon as peace was restored, at such ports as far as Han-Kow, not exceeding three in number, as should be determined upon. In addition to the cities and towns of Canton, Amoy, Fuchow, Ningpo, and Shanghai opened by the treaty of Nanking, the Tien-tsin treaty permitted British subjects to frequent the cities and ports of New-Chwang,[2] Tang-Chow, Tai-Wau (Formosa), Chau-Chow (Swatow), and Kiung-Chow (Hainan), and settled many other points including the question of the transit duties which had given rise to much difficulty, besides the payment of two millions of taels on account of the losses sustained by British subjects through the miscon-

[1] The city of Tien-tsin is situated at the junction of the Grand Canal and the Peiho, and is about 62 miles from the mouth of the river, near which are the adjacent villages of Tung-ku and Hoi-ku, which together constitute the town of Taku. Tien-tsin is the port for the two provinces Chih-li and Shan-si: Chih-li on the east is 58,949 square miles, and had a population of 14,000,000; Shan-si on the west is 55,268 square miles, and had a population of 27,000,000. Tien-tsin is moreover the nearest port to the central and western parts of that vast tract of Asia belonging to the Chinese empire which passes under the name of Mancharia in the east, and Mongulia in the centre and west.

[2] The port on the Sua-muren, which has taken the place of New-Chwang is known as Ying-tsu, and was opened to foreigners in May 1861.

duct of the Chinese authorities at Canton, and two millions more on account of the military expenses of the expedition.

With the conclusion of peace the mission of the Earl of Elgin ended, and Mr. Bruce was appointed Her Majesty's minister in China. But the Chinese government once more interposed obstacles to the reception and permanent residence of the British minister at Pekin, and as he proceeded up the Peiho, on his way to the capital, an attack was made against Her Majesty's ship at Takoo. Again, therefore, England and China came into collision. France joined in demanding an apology, and hostilities having once more commenced they were prosecuted till by another convention, dated October 24, 1860, a further indemnity of 4,000,000 dollars was obtained, the allies taking military possession of Chusan until the whole indemnity was paid. Since then a British minister has resided at Pekin, consuls have been appointed to the principal ports of China,[*] and trade has proceeded without hindrances, though efforts have been made to procure further facilities than those accorded by the treaty of Tien-tsin. Regarded in a moral aspect, we can scarcely congratulate ourselves on the extension of trade by the exercise of force. The right of trading, it is true, is a natural right, but it is only an imperfect right, inasmuch as each nation is the sole judge of what is advantageous or disadvantageous to herself, and whether or not it be convenient for her to cultivate any branch of trade or to open trading intercourse with any one country. Therefore no nation has a right to compel another nation to enter into trading intercourse with herself, or to pass laws for the benefit of trading and traders. By the two wars against China an enormous market has been opened to British industry; but we may well doubt whether the policy thus pursued and adhered to would not stand condemned if judged by the principles of ethics and

Hostilities at Takoo.

[*] The diplomatic and consular service in China consists of an envoy extraordinary and minister plenipotentiary at Pekin, and consuls and vice consuls at Amoy, Canton, Whampoa, Foo-chow-foo, Hankow, Kiu-kiang, New-Chwang, Ningpo, Pagoda Island, Shanghai, Swatow, Taiwan, Tsinsing, Tangchow, Tien-tsin, Taku, Shanghai, Swatow, Taiwan, Tamsuy, Chinkiang, Chefoo, Ningpo, and Pagoda Anchorage. In 1868 the value of the trade of all the ports, as centres of consuming and producing districts, was 61,265,000*l*. Shanghai and Tien-tsin were the most important for imports, and Shanghai, Foo-chow, Hankow, and Canton for exports.

international law. The objection offered to the admission of opium into China can never be allowed to be a justifiable cause of the war of 1842. The seizure of criminals from a Chinese ship, whose license to hoist the British flag had expired, was no lawful justification for the second war of 1857. And whilst there was reason to complain that the jealousy and animosity of a class stood in the way of peaceful trade with a whole nation, we could scarcely expect that such jealousy would be overcome by measures of force and repression, only certain to make the feud deeper and more lasting. But British energy and industry have overcome many more obstacles than those which hindered our intercourse with China.

In 1840, before the opium war, our exports to China amounted to half a million only. Canton was formally opened by an imperial edict in July 1842, and Shanghai in 1844, and our exports forthwith increased to about one million. On the conclusion of the treaty of Tien-tsin, in 1858, our exports amounted to 3,000,000*l.*; in 1870 they were 6,000,000*l.*; and besides this the trade between India and China, mainly in British hands, has also trebled in a few years. And it will continue to increase probably in even a greater ratio. Some fear was lately entertained that the foreign trade of China would gradually pass into Chinese hands. The opinion of the British consuls, however, is to the contrary, and in a memorandum on the subject, prepared at the foreign office, the conclusion arrived at seems to be that the direct import trade, as well as the export trade, in articles of European consumption remains, and is likely to remain, in foreign hands; that should the indirect or distributing trade be undertaken entirely by Chinese instead of by foreign commission agents, as seems probable, except perhaps as regards opium, the result may be expected to be beneficial to British trade and shipping, as it will be followed by an increased demand for foreign goods, and by the extended employment of foreign vessels; and that this indirect or distributing trade, on which the general trade depends, has been created and is maintained by the opening to foreign commerce of the several provincial districts of China by means of the consular treaty ports as ports of entry.

Increasing trade with China.

Counting on the influence which the chastisement inflicted on China might have on other eastern nations, the Earl of Elgin took advantage of the interval between the signing of the treaty and the discussion of the Chinese tariff, for proceeding to Japan, with a view to procuring the opening up of communication with the government of that country. Arrived at the bay of Yeddo, Lord Elgin made known to the foreign minister of the emperor, his arrival and his instructions to deliver a steam yacht, which Her Majesty the Queen of Great Britain had sent as a proof of her esteem and regard to His Majesty; and added that he possessed full powers to adjust and conclude such treaties, agreements, and conventions as might be conducive to the extension and improvement of the relations of commerce and amity between Great Britain and Japan. For full two centuries had Japan eschewed all contact with the outer world, and a decree had been issued dated 1637, making it a capital offence for the natives of Yeddo to travel into other countries. At the commencement of the seventeenth century the East India Company obtained some footing in Japan, and a commercial treaty was concluded in 1613 by which authority was given to the company to enter into all the ports of Japan, and to abide, buy, sell, and barter as they pleased; but the company was not successful in its transactions, and withdrew from the trade. Since then, however, the prohibition of trade had been issued, and acted upon especially against the Portuguese. And when, in 1673, English ships arrived at Japan and wished to resume the right of trading, the Japanese, who had ascertained, probably from the Dutch, that the King of England, Charles II., had married a daughter of the King of Portugal, refused compliance with the request, and extended to the English also the prohibition.

Mission to Japan.

In 1854 the United States sent a mission to Japan for the purpose of obtaining facilities in those waters for providing provisions and coals, and negotiations commenced, which resulted in a treaty, signed at Kanagawa on March 31, stipulating for the immediate opening of the port of Hakodadi, as well as for authority to the United States government to establish consuls in the two ports. In the same year, Admiral Sterling, then commanding in those seas, entered

Relations with Japan.

into a convention with the government of Japan with regard to the opening of Nagasaki and Hakodadi to British ships, and obtained the privilege of access to the country for British merchants. But little result had been obtained from that treaty when the Earl of Elgin opened negotiations on the subject. Happily the overtures of the British minister were well received; and, contrary to all previous experience, commissioners were at once appointed by the Tycoon, and a treaty of peace, friendship, and commerce was signed in the English, Japanese, and Dutch languages at Yeddo, August 26, 1858, and ratified July 11, 1859.

Treaty with Japan.

The treaty empowered the Queen of the United Kingdom to appoint a diplomatic agent to reside at Jeddo, and consuls at the open ports;[4] granted ample recognition of consular jurisdiction, and the immunities of exterritoriality; opened to British subjects, at specified periods, several of the most important ports and cities of Japan, viz. Hakodadi, Kanagawa, and Nagasaki, Ne-e-gata, or other convenient port on the coast of Neppo and Hiogo; gave power to land and store supplies for the use of the British navy at Kanagawa, Hakodadi, and Nagasaki, without payment of duty; and power to British subjects to buy from and sell to Japanese subjects directly, without the intervention of the Japanese authorities; provided that foreign coin should pass for corresponding weight of Japanese coin of the same description; authorised British and Japanese subjects freely to use foreign or Japanese coin in making payments to each other; and gave a right to British subjects for one year to demand of the Japanese government Japanese coin in exchange for theirs, equal weights being given; and power to export all description of gold and silver, coined and uncoined. The treaty further established the abolition of tonnage and transit dues, and reduction of duties on exports from 35 per cent. to a general rate of 5 per cent. *ad valorem*; and concluded with a general clause that the British government and its subjects should be allowed free and equal participation in all privileges, immu-

[4] The British diplomatic and consular service in Japan consisted in 1870 of an envoy extraordinary at Yeddo, and consuls at Hakodadi, Kanagawa, Ne-e-gata, Nagasaki, Hiogo, and Osaka.

nities, and advantages that may have been or may be hereafter granted by his majesty the tycoon of Japan to the government or subjects of any other nation.

The coinage of Japan.

Thus far matters proceeded in a most satisfactory manner. Unfortunately, however, the treaty itself contained the seed of imminent discord in the clauses respecting the currency,[5] and it was not long before the newly-formed intimacy between the two countries was seriously endangered. When the American squadron visited Japan, in 1853, there were current in Japan a small round coin, with a square hole, called cash; a similar larger coin, weighing less than two of the former, but bearing a fourfold value—the two kas piece; a large lozenge-shaped bronze coin, called a tempo, of the nominal value of 96 or 100 kas; an oblong silver coin, called an ichibu or bu, and valued at 16 tempos or 1,600 kas; and a smaller gold and silver coin, half ichibu.[6] The silver was over-

[5] Gold appears to have even been more abundant than silver in Japan. Marco Polo, writing in 1298, said 'The inhabitants of Zipangu have gold in the greatest abundance, its sources being inexhaustible.' An old Spanish writer of the seventeenth century stated that the palaces at Yeddo were covered with plates of gold. Kämpfer wrote in the eighteenth century that the riches of Japan consisted in all sorts of minerals and metals, particularly in gold, silver, and copper. Ralph Fitch in 1588 wrote that the Portuguese had a great carac which went thither every year and brought from thence every year 600,000 crusados (more than 500,000 dollars). In 1637 six Portuguese galliots visited Japan with cargoes of silk, and carried away in exchange 3,000,000 dollars. The Dutch in 1640 exported 1,400 chests of silver, each of 1,000 taels, that is, nearly 2,000,000 dollars. According to a Japanese pamphlet written in 1708, from 1611 to 1706, there were exported from Japan silver 112,268,700 taels (34,000,000*l.*), gold 6,192,600 kobang (11,000,000*l.*). In 1672 the exportation of silver was prohibited, and the nominal value of gold was raised in the proportion of 1·7 to 15. In 1696 its fineness was for the same object reduced from 20 carats 10 grains, to 13 carats 7 grains. In 1710 the weight was reduced from 4·7 momme (237·7 grains troy) to 2·5 momme (145·6 grains troy). According to Sir Stamford Raffles in the two hundred years from 1540 to 1740, Japan must have been drained of bullion to the value of 200,000,000 dollars.—Mr. Alcock's report, 1866, p. 617.

[6] The coins in circulation in 1866 were the rio or kobang, a thin oval gold coin, weighing ·88 momme (51·25 grains troy). The bu or ichibu (from 'ichi,' one, and 'bu,' a portion), an oblong silver coin weighing 2·3 momme (133·95 grains troy). The nibu or two bu piece, a yellow oblong coin of gold and silver mixed, weighing 1·6 momme (93·184 grains). The nishu, a small oblong silver coin, half a momme (29·12 grains). The nishu or two bu piece, a silver-gilt coin. The senior mongseng, an iron coin, 1,700th of an ichibu. The hachi-mongseng or eight mongseng piece, a mixed iron and copper circular coin, with a square hole in the centre. The tempo, called also hiyaku-mongseng, or 100 mongseng piece, a large oval coin with a hole in the middle.—Mr. Alcock's report, p. 631.

valued as compared with the copper and gold coins, so that the silver ichibu passed for three times its value, and was in reality only a token coin. Since, however, by the British treaty with Japan, and by one precisely similar concluded between the United States and Japan, the Japanese government bound themselves for one year to give Japanese coin in exchange for British or American, weight for weight, and they became bound to supply ichibus against dollars, it became a practice for the foreign merchant to take 100 dollars to the customs house and to obtain for them token coins weight for weight, viz. 311 ichibus. But with this money the foreign merchant could go to the market and obtain gold kobang worth two to three times the intrinsic value of his dollars. He had, in fact, only to send kobang to Shanghai and have them converted into dollars to recommence the operation.

Abuses committed by British and American traders.

The British and American traders, alive to their opportunity, sought to take advantage of it to the full, and made demands on the treasury for fabulous sums of Japanese silver coin, in the names of fictitious persons, till the kobangs actually came to an end.[7] The Japanese government then found out the folly of the clause in the treaty, and the impossibility of carrying it into effect. To meet the want of sufficient currency, in July 1859 a new silver coin was put into circulation at the open ports by the British representatives of the value of a half ichibu, containing as much silver as an ichibu and a half of the old currency, so that two of these coins were about equal in weight to a Mexican dollar; and as the kobang still passed as 4 ichibus, the foreigner, instead of obtaining the kobang for about 1⅓ dollars, had to pay nearly 4 dollars for it, which was about the true value. A circular was promulgated announcing the issue

[7] Some idea of the unscrupulous manner in which such demands were made upon the Japanese customs may be formed from the fact that one applicant alone required ichibus for one sextillion, two hundred quintillions, six hundred and sixty-six quadrillions, seven hundred and seventy-seven trillions, eight hundred and eighty-eight billions, nine hundred and ninety-nine millions, two hundred and twenty-two thousand, three hundred and twenty-one. Not only were the sums in their preposterous amount an insult to the Japanese government, to whose officers these requisitions were presented, but they were documents essentially false and dishonest, as purporting to be the names of individuals having a real existence, and entitled to demand facilities for trade, whereas mere words were used as names, and made to convey gross and offensive comments.

of the new coin, but the measure was resisted as an infringement of the spirit, if not of the letter, of the treaty. How could a coin struck exclusively for foreign use be termed Japanese coin? So long as the old coinage was not recalled, this could only be considered as a tax on the foreign trade of 200 per cent., and therefore the new half ichibu was recalled. In 1860 a new plan was adopted. Of the five kobangs that existed the nominal value of two was changed from 4 to 13½ ichibus, and before the close of the year a new gold kobang was brought out less than one-third of the value, both intrinsic and nominal. On July 1, 1860, the year expired in which the Japanese government was by treaty compelled to exchange its own money for foreign coin, weight for weight, and the rate of exchange fell, so that in September only 200 ichibus were given to the 100 dollars. Since, however, the difficulty would reappear as the clause of the treaty came into operation with the opening of the several ports, a convention was concluded on June 25, 1866, by the sixth article of which the Imperial Government undertook to enlarge the Japanese mint, so as to admit of the Japanese government exchanging into native coin of the same intrinsic value, less only the cost of coinage, at the places named for the purpose, all foreign gold or bullion in gold or silver that should at any time be tendered to them by foreigners or Japanese. But, inasmuch as the execution of this measure depended on the consent of the various powers with whom Japan concluded treaties to modify the stipulations in those treaties relating to the currency, the Japanese government proposed to those powers the adoption of the necessary modifications in the said stipulations, and on receiving their concurrence was prepared from January 1, 1868, to carry the above measure into effect. The rates to be charged as the cost of coinage were to be determined thereafter by the common consent of the contracting parties.*

* In 1871 a new currency was established in Japan, consisting (1) of gold coins of 20, 10, 5, and 1 *yen*, the latter to be the unit and legal tender in all payments to any amount; (2) of silver *yens*, as subsidiary coins, to be legal tenders for sums not exceeding ten *yens*, and of copper coins of one and a half, and 1-10th *sen* to be legal tender for sums not exceeding one *sen*.

By a happy concurrence of events, the trade in the east seemed to open itself out most wonderfully. In the spring of 1855, Sir John Bowring, being in China, proceeded on a special mission to Siam to see if that country, also, could be brought to break down the wall of separation which isolated her from the rest of the world, and he was successful. There was a time when Bangkok was the third among the commercial cities east of the Cape of Good Hope, and there, as in Japan, the Portuguese were first in the field. But neither they nor the Dutch nor the French succeeded in establishing permanent relations of trade. The East India Company also tried to do so in vain. In 1822 Mr. John Crauford went on a mission to Siam, deputed by the governor-general of India to the courts of Siam and Cochin China. In 1826 Captain Burney was sent from India for the express purpose of obtaining the co-operation of the Siamese in the contest in which the Indian government was engaged with the Birmese, and a treaty was concluded on the subject. But no practical good resulted from these efforts, and it was not till Sir John Bowring undertook this mission, that permanent relations were established between England and Siam.

Sir John Bowring's mission to Siam.

The treaty of friendship and commerce concluded on April 18, 1855, and ratified on April 5, 1856, declared that all British subjects arriving at Siam should receive from the Siamese government full protection and assistance to enable them to reside in Siam in all security and to trade with every facility, free from oppression or injury on the part of the Siamese, and that the interests of all British subjects at Siam should be placed under the regulation and control of a consul, who would be appointed to reside at Bangkok. The Siamese government reserved to themselves the right in case of scarcity to prohibit the exportation of rice, salt, and fish. And after making other provisions, the treaty declared that the British Government and its subjects should be allowed free and equal participation in any privileges that might have been or hereafter might be granted by the Siamese government to the government or subjects of any other nation.

Treaty with Siam.

A large extension of trade followed the establishment of intercourse with these Asiatic countries, and for its protection,

Consular jurisdiction in the east.

both under the custom relating to Europeans in the east and under special treaties concluded with China, Japan, and Siam, British traders are placed in those countries under the immediate jurisdiction of the British consuls. This consular jurisdiction is very old. The Levant Company had jurisdiction in civil cases and exercised a certain jurisdiction in criminal cases. When the Levant Company ceased to exist, Her Majesty's Government came into its place. But doubts having been raised as to the legality of such jurisdiction, the foreign Jurisdiction Act[9] was passed, by which the crown was enabled by order in council to exercise any jurisdiction which it acquired in foreign countries either by grant, capitulation, treaty, usage, or sufferance in the same manner as the crown exercises such jurisdiction in a conquered or ceded colony. And an order in council was accordingly issued empowering the consuls to act in the manner in which they had been in the habit of acting both in civil and criminal cases. In the following year an order in council was passed for the administration of criminal justice in the Levant. And in 1856, upon the report of a commission of inquiry, a supreme judge was appointed at Constantinople for the disposal of civil and criminal cases. In China and Japan, the consular courts are regulated by an order in council of 1865.[10]

The East Indian Mutiny. Transfer of the government of India to Her Majesty.

Besides, however, the increasing interest created in these foreign countries by the opening of new trades attention was directed to India, the most important of all British dependencies, in 1857, in consequence of the breaking out of a serious insurrection. An utterly groundless report that the grease used in the arsenal for preparing the cartridges for the Enfield rifles was composed of the fat of pigs and cows, and that it was intentionally used for the purpose of forcing the Hindoos to embrace the Christian

[9] 6 & 7 Vict. c. 94.

[10] In 1870 an international commission assembled at Cairo to examine the reforms proposed by the Egyptian Government in the administration of justice in Egypt. The Egyptian Government, being desirous that the consular jurisdiction should cease, offered certain guarantees; but the international commission could not decide upon them until the Government presented the Penal Code, and the Code of Criminal Investigation, which it promised to do in a short time.

faith, quite revolutionised the government of India. The insurrection, indeed, was easily quelled, and British supremacy was speedily re-established, but the outbreak and the circumstances attending it, showed an absolute necessity carefully to reform the institutions of that vast empire, and accordingly on August 2, 1858, an act was passed for the better government of India,[11] whereby the government of the territories in the possession or under the government of the East India Company and all powers in relation to such government vested in the company in trust for Her Majesty ceased to be vested in the same, and were vested in Her Majesty to be exercised in her name. In the same year, also, a committee of the House of Commons was appointed 'to inquire into the progress and prospects, and the best means to be adopted for the promotion of European colonisation and settlement in India, especially in the hill districts and healthier climates of that country, as well as for the extension of commerce with central Asia.' The report of that committee was of the utmost importance, and if it did not give much encouragement to emigration and colonisation, it pointed out the immense resources of India and the means by which these might be still more developed.

Financial reforms in India.

For many years the government of India had encouraged in every possible manner the growth of commerce and the extension of industry, but from the year of the mutiny dates a continuous course of economic progress almost unparalleled in magnitude. The abolition of inland duties was effected in Bengal in 1836, in Bombay in 1838, and in Madras in 1844, and by that measure the transit of produce for home consumption was made altogether free, and considerable impetus was given to the internal trade of the country. The export of sugar to British ports was rendered free of duty in 1836, and cotton was exempted from export duty in 1847, so that Indian sugar and cotton were enabled to compete in foreign markets with like productions of other countries. Contrary to all sound policy, export duties are still levied in India, on cotton goods, grain, hides, indigo, lac oils, seeds, shawls and spices; in Ceylon, on cinnamon, coffee, sugar,

[11] 21 & 22 Vict. c. cvi.

and other articles; in Mauritius, on sugar; in New South Wales, on gold; in Canada, on oak, and other logs; in Jamaica, on coffee, rum, sugar, and woods; and in other West India colonies, on a large number of articles. The navigation laws as well as all impediments to the coasting trade were abolished in 1848, and considerable remissions of customs duties were made in successive years. Add to this the great expenditure incurred for public works, such as the grand trunk road extending from Calcutta to Peshawur, a distance of 1,423 miles, the improvement of navigable rivers, the establishment of railways[19] and telegraphs, and we need not be surprised if the trade of India increased from a little over 14,000,000*l*. in 1834–35 to upwards of 123,000,000*l*. in 1865–66, or at the rate of about 3½ millions annually during the entire period, the increase in the last eleven years of that period having been at the rate of 8,000,000*l*. per annum.

One peculiar feature of the commerce of India is the large excess of exports over imports and the important part which treasure has in that trade. During twenty-nine years, from 1841 to 1869 inclusive, the exports of India amounted to 876,729,000*l*. and the imports to 770,390,000*l*., but of this amount of imports, 489,390,000*l*. were of merchandise and 281,000,000*l*. of treasure, viz. gold and silver. The exports of India are large, consisting of cotton, opium, rice, indigo, jute, silk, and wool; and though the imports are also increasing, the exports are greatly in excess. Therefore, whereas from 1841 to 1850 the proportion of treasure to merchandise imported was 20 per cent., from 1851 to 1869 the proportion was 38 per cent. India has been for years draining Europe of her bullion, and from England and France all the available silver is constantly finding its way to the coffers of India, there to be either hoarded or converted into ornaments. Between India and England the trade has largely increased of late years. In 1833, when the monopoly of the East India Company expired, the whole amount of exports of British produce and manufacture was under 3,000,000*l*.; in 1870 it was

The trade of India.

[19] In 1870, there were open for traffic in India, 4,581 miles of railways. The number of passengers carried was 18,146,000, and the capital invested in railways was 89,458,000*l*.

19,300,000*l.* The real value of imports from India, which in 1855 amounted to less than 13,000,000*l.*, in 1870 was 25,000,000*l.* The commerce of India with central Asia is large, though on the other side of the Himalaya and Sulymani range are the Russians and the Chinese. Russia has steamers on the sea of Aral and on the most extensive of its tributaries, the Amoo Darea, the ancient Oxus. From Asterabadon the south-east of the Caspian, the key of central Asia, the Russian ports extend almost all the way to China, and whilst Russia has in Kiachta a place of ingress to China, Tibet is supplied by China.

Communication with India.

How effectively to open India to British enterprise has been a problem of immense difficulty. The extent of the country, the number of races inhabiting it, the many provinces into which it is divided, the difference of languages and religions; these and many other circumstances have always made India far more inaccessible to British industry than even more distant countries on the Atlantic and Pacific. From the very beginning the great object in view has been to bring India nearer to Europe. It is not a question now between the sea passage by the Cape of Good Hope, and the land transport by caravans. It is a question between different lines of railways, and between the best mode of telegraphic communication. Even for postal purposes the problem has been one extremely important to solve. Till quite recently 35 days were occupied between London and Calcutta, *viâ* Marseilles, and 24 days between London and Bombay. But as railway extended greater speed has been attained. Telegraph communication also exists by two distinct lines, by the Turkish and Russian. The Turkish route line goes from London to Turin and Brindisi, thence by the submarine cable across the lower Adriatic to Constantinople; from Constantinople to Bagdad, and thence by the Persian Gulf line to Kurrachee. The Russian line proceeds *viâ* the Hague to Berlin, thence crosses the Russian frontier, passing through Mysolowitz and Tiflis to Julpha on the Arras, and from that place over the Persian system to Bushire and Kurrachee. The question of railway communication between the Mediterranean, the Black Sea, and the Persian Gulf, is still under consideration, especially the route intended to connect Constantinople with the Persian Gulf, starting from Scutari to Aleppo, then down the valley of the Euphrates to Bagdad and Bussorah, and thence to the head of the gulf, a distance of 1,700 miles. The two latest and greatest achievements, however, in the means of communication between Europe and India have been the opening of the Suez Canal and the tunnelling of Mont Cenis. The former has immensely shortened the distance, and expedited the conveyance of goods traffic, the latter has revolutionised the passenger traffic. The distance between the United Kingdom and China by the usual sailing route round the Cape was 11,650 geographical miles, and by the canal 6,515, showing a difference of 5,135 miles.[16] The Mont Cenis Tunnel has levelled the mighty Alps, and once more placed Italy, as she was in her best days in the middle ages, in the very centre of trade.

[16] In 1872 the transit from London to Calcutta may be estimated to take the following time: goods, *via* Suez Canal, 35 to 40 days; a passenger, by railways, 21 days; and a telegram, 12 to 18 hours.

CHAPTER XI.

COMMERCIAL CRISIS.

1857.

Effect of Gold Discoveries.—Crisis in the United States.—Alarm and Crisis in England.—State of the Bank of England.—Failures in Scotland.—The Treasury Letter.—Excess of Circulation.—Fall of Prices.—The Crisis in the North of Europe.—Parliamentary Inquiry.—John Stuart Mill on the Bank Acts.

Effect of gold discoveries on trade.

FOR many years after the discovery of gold in California and Australia, the trade of the country was in a most prosperous condition. An extensive demand for the United States, for France, and for Australia had imparted a wonderful buoyancy to business. The agricultural interest was prosperous from excellent harvests; the prices of bread, meat, and provisions were highly remunerative. Money was at a low rate, and so abundant was it that Mr. Gladstone was induced to bring forward his plan for the reduction of the national debt by the issue of Exchequer bonds at 2½ per cent., whilst the Bank of England saw in its coffers, in July 1852, the largest sum ever on hand, 22,000,000*l.* in amount. But little by little a great and perceptible change took place in the economic condition of the country. If the import of bullion had increased enormously of late years, so did the export, principally of silver to India and China,[1] increase in a high ratio. Whilst an increase of the European stock of bullion was estimated to have taken place of 79,000,000*l.* between 1851 and 1856, the Bank of England saw its own stock decreasing sensibly; the causes of the export to the east being

[1] The exports of gold and silver bullion and specie were as follows: 1852, 10,295,000*l.*; 1853, 18,906,000*l.*; 1854, 22,586,000*l.*; 1855, 18,528,000*l.*; 1856, 21,852,000*l.*; and 1857, 33,567,000*l.*

a large expenditure in railways, and heavy payments to be made for silk and other articles imported. The war in the Crimea also necessitated large remittances of money for the payment of the troops, and there was moreover a considerable amount of uncertainty and anxiety as to the future, always unfavourable to confidence in trade and finance. The rate of interest reflected this altered state of matters. For a considerable time since 1849 the minimum rate charged by the Bank of England was 2½ per cent.; and even 2 per cent.; but on the third week of 1853 there was a rise to 3 per cent.; and by the end of the year it rose to 5 per cent.; rising to 5½ per cent. in 1854. In 1855 the rate fluctuated between 4 and 5 per cent.; and in 1856 it touched 7 per cent.

Crisis in the United States.

About this time, however, a new source of disturbance was manifested in a crisis in the United States, which commenced with a great depreciation of railway securities, and was followed by the failure of a very important corporation called the Ohio Life and Trust Company. Before October 8, 1857, the tidings from America had become very serious. News came that the banks in Philadelphia and Baltimore had suspended cash payments; that cotton bills were reduced to par, and bankers' drafts to 105; that railway securities were depreciated from 10 to 20 per cent.; that the artisans were thrown out of employment; that discounts ranged from 10 to 20 per cent.; that in New York 62 out of its 63 banks suspended cash payments; and that in Boston, Philadelphia, and Baltimore the banks, generally, did the same. At a time when the transactions between America and England were so numerous and so large, when the declared value of British and Irish produce exported to the United States was nearly 22,000,000*l.*, and the amount of securities held by English capitalists in America was estimated at 80,000,000*l.* —the state of commercial disorder in that country could not fail to produce great alarm. The effect of the American calamity fell with the greatest weight upon those engaged in trade with that country, and Liverpool, Glasgow, and London naturally exhibited the first evidences of pressure. On October 27 the Borough Bank of Liverpool closed its doors; and on November 7 the great commercial house of Dennistoun and Company suspended payment. The Western Bank of Scotland failed on November 9, and on the 11th the City of Glasgow Bank suspended. The Northumberland and Durham District Bank failed on the 26th, and on the 17th the Wolverhampton Bank for a time stopped payment.

Alarm and crisis in England.

Great alarm naturally prevailed in London, the centre of all the monetary transactions of the world, in consequence of such occurrences, and there was reason to apprehend that serious evils would result from them. It must be remembered that the vast sums deposited with the joint-stock banks, at interest, are chiefly held at call; and that the bill brokers who carry on their enormous transactions without any cash reserve, rely on the payment of their bills falling due, or, in extremity, on the power of obtaining advances from the Bank of England on the security of bills under discount. What if the deposits were withdrawn, and the banks should be unable to accommodate the bill brokers? Yet it is indispensable that at a time of commercial pressure and alarm the banks who are liable to return all the money so held should limit their discounts almost exclusively to their own customers, and add to their reserves, both in their own tills and at the Bank of England. It is known, also, that a periodical disturbance in the reserve of notes at the Bank of England regularly occurs at the time when the dividends upon the national debt are paid. And though as yet the deposits seemed to be in a satisfactory state, it was evident at that particular juncture that the deposits at the Bank of England were increasing at the expense of those of other establishments; so that bill brokers were compelled to resort to that establishment for assistance. To so great an extent did this take place, that the principal discounting house went to the Bank to ask whether they could obtain advances to an indefinite amount, and in fact received on one day, the day on which the treasury letter was issued, no less a sum than 700,000*l*. Eventually two discount houses failed, and the position of the Bank began to be very critical. On November 11 the bullion had fallen to 6,524,000*l*., and the reserve to 581,000*l*., whilst the discounts and advances amounted to 18,064,000*l*. A rise of the rate of interest to 0 per cent. failed to check the demand. A state of discredit set in which threatened the most serious results, until at last the necessity for government interposition became apparent, and, after correspondence on the subject, a government letter was issued, dated November 12, in which, in consideration of the discredit and distrust which existed from the withdrawal of the large amount of paper circulation, the directors of the Bank were authorised in the existing emergency to meet the demand for discounts and advances, upon approved securities, even in excess of the limits to their circulation prescribed by the act of 1844. As on a former occasion, in 1847, the letter calmed the public mind, and so far tended to mitigate the severity of the pressure, but it did not immediately diminish the demand for discount and advances. This continued to increase till November 21, on which day the Bank had advanced in discounts 21,000,000*l.*, a sum exceeding the whole amount of their deposits both public and private; a sum nearly three-fold the amount of their advances in July, when the rate was reduced to 5½ per cent. and more than double what they had advanced on October 27 when the first bank failed. Half of these loans was made to the bill brokers, and partly upon securities, which under other circumstances the Bank would have been unwilling to accept. They were made for the purpose of sustaining commercial credit in a period of extreme pressure.

But at this point we cannot do better than take the statement prepared by the directors of the Bank, with respect to the monetary condition of the country, previous to the issue of the government letter. On October 24 the bullion in the issue department was 8,771,000*l.*; the reserve 4,079,000*l.*; the notes in the hands of the public 19,766,000*l.*; the discounts and advances 10,262,000*l.*; and the deposits 16,126,000*l.*; the rate of discount at the Bank being 8 per cent. for bills having not more than 95 days to run. In the following week a great shock to credit, and a consequent demand on the Bank of England for discount, arose from the failure of the Liverpool Borough Bank, whose re-discounted bills were largely held by the bill brokers and others in London. The effects of this and other failures, however, up to this time, had not occasioned any alarming pressure on the resources of

State of the Bank of England.

the Bank or great disquietude in commercial affairs in London. On November 5 the reserve was 2,944,000*l.*; the bullion in the issue department 7,919,000*l.*; and the deposits 17,265,000*l.* The rate of discount was advanced to 9 per cent., and on November 10 to 10 per cent. The continental drain for gold had ceased, the American demand had become unimportant, and there was at that time little apprehension that the Bank issue would be inadequate to meet the necessities of commerce within the legalised sphere of their circulation.

Upon this state of things, however, supervened the failure of the Western Bank of Scotland and the City of Glasgow Bank, and a renewed discredit in Ireland, causing an increased action upon the English circulation, by the abstraction in four weeks of upwards of two millions of gold to supply the wants of Scotland and Ireland; of which amounts more than one million was sent to Scotland, and 280,000*l.* to Ireland, between November 5 and 12. This drain was in its nature sudden and irresistible, and acted necessarily in diminution of the reserve, which on the 11th had decreased to 1,462,000*l.*, and the bullion to 6,666,000*l.* The public became alarmed, large deposits accumulated in the Bank of England, money-dealers having vast sums lent to them upon call were themselves obliged to resort to the Bank of England for increased supplies, and for some days nearly the whole of the requirements of commerce were thrown on the Bank. Thus, on the 12th, it discounted and advanced to the amount of 2,373,000*l.*, which still left a reserve of 581,000*l.*

Failures in Scotland.

The Treasury letter.

Such was the state of the Bank of England accounts on the 12th—the day of the publication of the following letter from the Treasury:

Downing Street, November 12, 1857.

Gentlemen,—Her Majesty's Government have observed with great concern the serious consequences which have ensued from the recent failure of certain joint-stock banks in England and Scotland, as well as of certain large mercantile firms, chiefly concerned with the American trade. The discredit and distrust which have resulted from these events, and the withdrawal of a large amount of the paper circulation authorized by the existing Bank Acts, appear to Her Majesty's Government to render it necessary for them to inform the directors of the

Bank of England, that if they should be unable, in the present emergency, to meet the demands for discounts and advances upon approved securities without exceeding the limits of the circulation prescribed by the Act of 1844, the government will be prepared to propose to Parliament, upon its meeting, a bill of indemnity for any excess so issued. In order to prevent this temporary relaxation of the law being extended beyond the actual necessities of the occasion, Her Majesty's Government are of opinion that the Bank terms of discount should not be reduced below their present rate. Her Majesty's Government reserve for future consideration the appropriation of any profit which may arise upon issues in excess of the statutory amount. Her Majesty's Government are fully impressed with the importance of maintaining the letter of the law, even in a time of considerable mercantile difficulty; but they believe that, for the removal of apprehensions which have checked the course of monetary transactions, such a measure as is now contemplated has become necessary, and they rely upon the discretion and prudence of the directors for confining the operation within the strict limits of the exigencies of the case. We have, &c.,

(Signed) PALMERSTON.

G. C. LEWIS.

'Although the letter produced a considerable effect in allaying the extraordinary fear and alarm, the demand for discount and advances continued to increase till November 21, when they reached their maximum of 21,616,000*l*. The public also required a much larger quantity of notes than usual at that season, the amount in their hands having risen on the 21st to 21,554,000*l*. Under the authority of the letter from the Treasury the Bank issued 2,000,000*l*. of notes in excess of the limits of the circulation prescribed by the Act of 1844, and passed securities to the issue department to that amount. That, however, is not the measure of the amount actually parted with by the Bank, which did not exceed 928,000*l*., the remainder of the 2,000,000*l*. having been retained as a reserve of notes in the banking department, which, at the same time, also held 407,420*l*. in coin. In discounts and advances, the sum supplied to the public between November 12 and December 1 amounted in the aggregate to 12,645,000*l*.'

Excess of circulation.

The losses produced by this crisis were very heavy, especially from the fall in the prices of merchandise. In July 1857, Bengal silk was quoted 15*s.* to 33*s.* 6*d.* per lb.; in January 1858, 11*s.* to 24*s.*; fall 28 per cent.: China silk, July 1857, 10*s.* to 29*s.*; January 1858, 6*s.* to 7*s.*; fall 66 per cent.: tallow fell from 60*s.* to 50*s.*, sugar from 55*s.* to 35*s.* per cwt.; cotton from 7*d.* to 6*d.*; tin from 135*s.* to 122*s.* per cwt.; tea, Congou, from 1*s.* 3*d.* to 1*s.* per lb. Taken generally the prices of commodities fell from 20 to 30 per cent. Yet with all this, the chief failures in 1857–58 did not arise so much from the panic as from the effect of a system of acceptances and open credits, or from trading on fictitious credit, then largely prevalent. Upon a review of the circumstances connected with the chief failures, the committee of the House of Commons stated, 'It is impossible for your committee to attribute the failure of such establishments to any other cause than to their inherent unsoundness, the natural the inevitable result of their own misconduct. Thus we have traced a system under which extensive fictitious credits have been created by means of accommodation bills, and open credits, great facilities for which have been offered by the practice of joint-stock country banks discounting such bills, and rediscounting them with the bill brokers in the London market, upon the credit of the Bank alone, without reference to the quality of the bills otherwise.'

Fall of prices.

The crisis of 1857 was not limited to England and America. The suspension of several London houses connected with the Swedish trade, a large amount of whose bills were indorsed by Hamburg firms, coupled with the effect of over-speculation and an undue expansion of credit, caused great excitement and alarm in Hamburg; and so great was the excitement that the senate obtained a silver loan of 10,000,000 marks banco from Austria, to be employed in discounting good mercantile bills. In Norway and Denmark, the commercial community was in great straits; and the Norwegian and Danish Government came to the assistance of traders by contracting a public loan for the very purpose. In Sweden a crisis as severe took place, and to meet it the National Bank was authorised to borrow abroad 12,000,000 of ris dollars, to be apportioned according to the wants of the different towns. In Prussia a law was passed on November 27 abolishing the legal rate of

The crisis in the north of Europe.

interest for money advanced on securities for a period of three months, so that the commercial crisis was but partially felt. But Holland passed through the difficult times without any reverses, and so did Belgium. Truly there is a close bond of interest between the great centres of monetary transactions.. Observers of meteorological phenomena are able to trace the advance of a storm from its first rise and all along its course as it sweeps over the ocean, and so may we in commercial and monetary crises trace their progress as they advance to London and Paris, and see them gathering strength till they finally fill all Europe with alarm and distress.

On the assembling of parliament, a bill to indemnify the governor and company of the Bank of England, in respect of certain issues of their notes, and to confirm such issues, and to authorize further issues, for a time to be limited, was presented by Mr. Fitzroy, the chancellor of the exchequer, and Viscount Palmerston, and passed into law. And a committee of the House was moved to inquire into the operation of the Bank Acts of 1844 (7 & 8 Vict. c. 32) and of the Bank Acts for Ireland and Scotland of 1845 (8 & 9 Vict. c. 37 & 38); and into the causes of the recent commercial distress, and to investigate how far it has been affected by the laws for regulating the issue of bank notes payable on demand.

Parliamentary inquiry.

Before that committee many witnesses appeared, among whom were the governor and deputy-governor of the Bank of England, Mr. William Newmarch, F.R.S., Mr. John Stuart Mill, Mr. Hubbard, Mr. Norman, and Lord Overstone, each of whom expressed distinct opinions on the working of the Bank Act. Mr. John Stuart Mill was against any restriction by law of the issue of notes, except that of convertibility. He thought the separation of the two departments of the Bank of England most prejudicial, and productive of violent and frequent fluctuations in the rate of discount, though in some cases, as at the commencement of a revulsion from a state of over speculation, it might be useful. He was in favour of removing the present restrictions both from the Bank of England and from all other banks. And in his opinion the convertibility of the note would be quite as safe without the Act of 1844 as with it. But other witnesses expressed a con-

John Stuart Mill on the Bank Acts.

trary opinion, and after two years' labour, the committee reported that no mischief would result from a temporary continuance of the present state of things, under which the Bank of England held the powers given by the Act of 1844, subject to a notice of twelve months which may at any time be given by the House of Commons through the Speaker. Draft reports were also proposed by Mr. Spooner and Mr. Cayley, but on the motion that the report prepared by the chancellor of the exchequer be read a second time, nineteen members of the committee voted in the affirmative, and two only in the negative, viz. Mr. Spooner and Mr. Cayley. The Bank Charter Acts have thus been allowed to remain undisturbed in the Statute Book of the realm; and though a few years after, Her Majesty's Government was once more under the necessity of suspending their operation, the different questions connected with that legislation have not been reopened.

PART V.

1860–1870.

FROM THE CONCLUSION OF THE TREATY OF COMMERCE WITH FRANCE

TO

THE STATE OF COMMERCE IN 1870.

SUMMARY.

1860—1870.

The conclusion of the Treaty of Commerce with France opened a new era in International trading. Hitherto we were content to wait for liberal concessions in the admission of British produce and manufactures, till the evidence of our own success and the inherent advantage of a free trade policy should secure the spontaneous adoption of a liberal legislation in foreign countries. Now, for the purpose of enlarging our commercial relations with France we consented to render a further step in economic reform the basis of a reciprocal agreement. Whatever importance, however, attaches to that treaty, and beneficial as it was, especially at a time when the trade with the United States of America was paralysed by their civil war, its effects on British commerce were not so great, as the opening of larger markets in the East, and the wonderful development of many other branches of trade. Commerce was advancing at an unprecedented rate for many years when another crisis greatly agitated our monetary circles, but even that was of short duration, and when another Universal Exhibition was held in Paris, Britain was able to exhibit her enormous achievements in productive industry. Since then circumstances have concurred in rendering British commerce more supreme than ever it was. Whilst other nations have been spending their energies in destructive wars, Britain has been enjoying a continuous course of prosperity. And we close the period embraced by our history, with British commerce expanded to a wonderful extent, with wealth largely increased, and with every prospect that England advancing at greater and still more gigantic strides will maintain her position as the greatest commercial nation in the World.

CHAPTER I.

TREATIES OF COMMERCE.

The Budget of 1860.—Economic policy of France.—The Emperor's Letter.—Negotiations for a Treaty of Commerce.—Conclusion of the Treaty.—Reception of the Treaty in England.—Reception of the Treaty in France.—More Treaties of Commerce.—Commercial Treaties with Belgium, the Zollverein, Italy and Austria.—Negotiations with Spain and Portugal.—Results of the Treaties of Commerce.—Reduction of Tariffs.—Progress of Free Trade.—Effect of Free Trade on Shipping.—Local Charges on Shipping.—Tax on Shipping passing Elsinore.—Effect of the Sound Dues.—The Stade Dues.—Discriminating Dues.

The budget of 1860.

THE budget of 1860 was a remarkable one. It abolished the paper duty, so long the object of popular animadversion; it swept away the duties on manufactured articles, silk manufacture included—the last anchor of protection; it removed from the customs tariff many hundred articles;[1] it reduced the wine duties; it reimposed the income tax; and, above all, it inaugurated a new treaty of commerce with France. Hitherto our trade with France was comparatively small, and France consumed only small quantities of British produce and manufactures. Railways, steam packets, and telegraphs, brought us closer to one another. The universal exhibition had shown how varied were our respective productions, and how useful we might be to each other, yet a custom barrier kept us asunder. Any remission made in this country of duties on French produce, met with little or no response from our neighbours. While we opened our ports, and left our manufacturers and producers exposed to an unlimited competition, while we repealed every restriction in our navigation laws, and threw open to foreign vessels our direct and indirect trade,

[1] In the British Customs tariff in 1844 there were 1,098 articles, and subdivision of articles, charged with distinct rates. In 1869 there were only 65, yet these 65 produced a revenue of 22,435,000*l*. while the 1,298 in 1844 produced 22,647,000*l*.

our colonial, and even our coasting trade, France persisted in a policy of prohibitions; she adhered to the old principles of protection; she excluded from her markets our chief manufactures; and, at the very time when she was reaping the fruits of a policy of freedom, which she did not understand, her parliament and her press were casting upon us the severest invectives and the most wanton abuse.

Economic policy of France.

The economic policy of France had long been of a most erroneous character. Her manufacturers and her miners entrenched themselves behind a wall of protection and prohibitions. Colbert, wise reformer though we acknowledge him to have been, was compelled to leave the tariff nearly as entangled as he found it. Turgot, who abolished the exclusive rights of corporations and established internal free trade in corn, was not sufficiently long in power to effect any substantial and permanent reform in the commercial policy of the country. And when, after the close of the American war, Lord Auckland and M. de Rayneval concluded the famous treaty of commerce and navigation, which so distinguished the ministry of Mr. Pitt, the French manufacturers rose up in arms, and the common cry of 'Treason' echoed from every manufacturing district. By the war which followed the French Revolution, all treaties were, of course, cancelled. Other principles governed the counsels of the constituent assembly and of the convention than goodwill towards England or sound commercial legislation for France herself; and though at the restoration an attempt was made to remove some prohibitions, the manufacturers offered a successful resistance to all reforms, and nothing could be done. Their pretensions were very high. It was not as a concession but as a right that they claimed to have an exclusive control of the markets in France; and with a weak government they had no difficulty in obtaining the tariff of 1826, by which the crowning point of the protective system was reached. The revolution of 1830 had no effect on the economic policy of the country, notwithstanding some slender efforts in that direction made by Thiers and Duchâtel: and for nearly thirty years France was allowed to continue undisturbed under the soothing but destructive policy of protection.

Excepting some isolated reforms, it was not till 1856 that

the first announcement appeared in the 'Moniteur' that the moment had arrived when the customs prohibitions might safely be replaced by protective duties, and when a serious inquiry should be instituted into the whole question. This was followed by the lowering of the duties on machinery, the withdrawal of prohibitions from many articles of import, and the imposition of duties in their stead. In 1857 the greater portion of the export duties was abolished. On January 15, 1860, however, a letter was published from the Emperor Napoleon, addressed to the minister of state, which foreshadowed the adoption of a more liberal commercial legislation. 'For a long time past,' said his majesty, 'the truth has been established that we must multiply the means of exchange to render commerce prosperous; that without competition industry remains stationary, and prices remain too high to stimulate consumption; and that without a prosperous industry, which increases capital, agriculture itself remains in its infancy.' And what was to be done? 'Abolish the duties on cotton and wool, reduce the duties on sugar and coffee, improve the means of communication, diminish the duties on canal, and thus lighten the means of transport, grant loans for agriculture and industry, do away with all prohibitions, and enter into treaties of commerce.' This was the Emperor's programme; and since, with an absolute government as his was at that time, to will was to do, he applied himself immediately to carry his policy into effect.

Policy of the Emperor of the French.

On December 2, 1859, Earl Cowley, the British ambassador in Paris, communicated to Lord John Russell that confidential correspondence had been going on for some time between Mr. Cobden and M. Rouher, with a view to the suppression of the prohibitive system of commerce which had so long prevailed in France with respect to certain articles of British industry; a modification of the tariff respecting certain other articles; and the admission into the United Kingdom of various articles of French manufacture free of duty; that Mr. Cobden had expressed an opinion that Her Majesty's Government might not be unwilling to conclude a commercial treaty with the French government; that informal negotiations had already been initiated by the Em-

Negotiations for a treaty of commerce.

peror, but that, before submitting any proposal to the council of ministers, he desired to know the views of Her Majesty's Government. In answer to this communication Lord John Russell wrote to Earl Cowley that Mr. Cobden and himself were formally appointed plenipotentiaries to negotiate such a treaty. And in doing so, Lord John Russell stated that Her Majesty's Government were of opinion that although the activity of trade and the constant demand for labour in this country were such as to leave no pressing necessity for opportunities of extension, yet the enlargement of commercial relations, always in itself desirable, ought to be more peculiarly an object of desire in the case of two countries prepared for such intercourse, like France and Great Britain, by local proximity, combined with considerable diversities of climate, productions, and industry; that, over and above these considerations, Her Majesty's Government attached a high social and political value to the conclusion of a commercial treaty with France; that its general tendency would be to lay broad and deep foundations in common interests, and in friendly intercourse, for the confirmation of the amicable relations that so happily existed between the two countries; and that while thus making a provision for the future, which would progressively become more and more solid and efficacious, its significance at a time when the condition of some parts of the Continent was critical would be at once understood, and would powerfully reassure the public mind in the various countries of Europe.

In a very short time the treaty was concluded, and on January 23, 1860, it was signed by Earl Cowley and Richard Cobden for England, and by MM. V. Baroche and F. Rouher for France. The principal conditions of the treaty were that France should remove all prohibitions from her tariff, and reduce the duties on a number of articles of British produce and manufacture imported into France to a maximum rate of 30 per cent. *ad valorem* at once, and of 25 per cent. by October 1, 1864, such duties to be converted into specific duties by a supplementary convention. That England should abolish the duty on a number of articles the production and manufacture of France, and should reduce the duties on wine and foreign spirits, and that both parties should

Conclusion of the treaty.

engage not to prohibit the exportation of coals. The treaty was to last for ten years from the date of the ratification, February 4, 1860.

Reception of the treaty in England.

To the conclusion of such a treaty grave objections were urged. Many there were in this country who doubted the expediency of entering into any treaty on matters affecting internal legislation. When Sir Robert Peel brought forward his measures of commercial reform he acted independently and sought for no equivalent from any country. And why should France demand concessions from us now for the minimum of freedom she was about to introduce into her tariff? What, moreover, if for financial or other causes England or France might see reason in a few years to alter the customs duties? The condition, too, of binding oneself not to prohibit the exportation of coal was harsh though there might not be the slightest probability of this country ever again resorting to such a policy. On the other hand, it was admitted that it was an immense advantage to this country to procure by any means the opening of the French market to British produce and manufacture. If the reduction of duties contemplated by the treaty was not so great as might have been wished, there was reason to hope that if France fairly entered into a free-trade policy she would see it her interest to proceed further and further in the way of freedom.

Reception of the treaty in France.

To France the treaty opened a future full of promise, and we need not wonder if the reporters on the same to the emperor gave utterance to the brightest anticipations.[1] Nor must we limit the effect of the French treaty to the relations of France and England. Whatever advantage was granted by France to England, other countries

[1] À nos yeux, et les modifications du tarif anglais, et la réforme de notre législation douanière, convergent au même but, préparent à un égal degré de nouveaux éléments de prospérité publique pour les deux pays. Cette lutte pacifique n'amènera ni victoires ni défaites, mais produira de louables émulations, des enseignements mutuels, des perfectionnements réciproques. Inspirées par les sentiments de justice et de bienveillance mutuelle qui animent les Gouvernements respectifs, ces conventions assureront le règlement équitable et le développement des relations entre les deux États et consolideront l'alliance des deux peuples.

Le commerce, qui selon le langage de Mothen 'tend à faire des productions de chaque partie du globe une propriété commune à tous les peuples, qui a fait de l'Europe une grande famille, et qui, à côté des passions qui divisent les princes, a

were sure to participate under the usual clauses of the ordinary treaties of commerce enabling them to be placed in the position of the most favoured nations. Besides this, treaties were concluded between France and the principal countries of Europe, especially with Belgium on May 1, 1861, with the Zollverein on August 2, 1862, with Italy in 1863, with Switzerland in 1864; so that the tariffs of most states were lowered in terms of the original treaty. And it was something to have established that treaties of commerce are no longer to be negotiated with a view to secure any special advantage for ourselves to the injury of any other states, but to provide for the extension of commercial freedom all over the world.

More treaties of commerce.

The treaty of commerce with France doubtless inaugurated a new era in the commercial policy of many Continental states, and with great felicity of language Mr. Gladstone expatiated on its advantages when he said: 'There were times, now long gone by, when sovereigns made progress through the land, and when at the proclamation of their heralds they caused to be scattered heaps of coin among the people

placé le contre-poids des besoins mutuels et des intérêts réciproques,' poursuivra, libre d'entraves surannées, son œuvre de développement et de fécondation de la richesse des deux nations.

L'industrie devra sans doute renouveler sur quelques points un outillage arriéré remplacer les mécanismes incomplets et rechercher par de sérieux efforts la possibilité de produire économiquement; mais le succès récompensera largement de tels sacrifices, et la production française sortira plus vigoureuse et plus florissante de ces épreuves salutaires.

Toutes ces prospérités profiteront directement à ces populations nombreuses dont Votre Majesté a étudié avec tant d'ardeur les intérêts et les besoins, et qu'elle environne de ses constantes sollicitudes. Elles se traduiront pour l'ouvrier en allégement dans les fatigues de sa tâche, en régularité sinon en élévation de son salaire en diminution de prix pour tous les objets qu'il consumme et que son travail doit procurer à sa famille.

La constitution économique du pays, grâce au développement des forces inanimées, sera moins troublée que dans le passé par cette sorte de déclassement de population que l'industrie opère au préjudice de l'agriculture, et l'équilibre violemment rompu depuis quelques années tendra à se rétablir.

En même temps Votre Majesté fera exécuter les travaux nécessaires à la force et à la prospérité d'un grand État, et avant peu ses témoignages de reconnaissance, qui de tous nos grands ports de mer, de nos provinces vinicoles, du sein des industries de Lyon, de Saint-Étienne et d'autres grandes cités manufacturières, sont arrivés au pied du trône, ne rencontreront dans le pays éclairé sur ses véritables intérêts, parmi les chefs d'industrie résolus à la lutte, ni résistance, ni refus d'adhésion.

who thronged upon their steps. That may have been a goodly spectacle, but it is also a goodly spectacle, and one adapted to the altered spirit and circumstances of our times, when our sovereign is enabled through the wisdom of her great council assembled in parliament around her again to scatter blessings among her subjects by means of wise and prudent laws, of laws which do not sap in any respect the foundations of duty or of manhood, but which strike away the shackles from the arms of industry, which give new incentives and new rewards to toil, and which win more and more for the throne and for the institutions of the country the gratitude, the confidence, and the love of a united people.'

Soon after the conclusion of the French Treaty negotiations were opened with other countries to the same effect. Belgium was for a considerable time the very stronghold of protection, and in 1844 a tariff was established there, which imposed a complicated scale of differential duties, varying according to the origin and mode of transport of each article. And to make the confusion still greater, she concluded commercial treaties with several nations, establishing differential duties of the most complicated character. In 1849 the first reform was introduced in the tariff by repealing the greater number of export duties, and establishing freedom of transit. In 1850 moderate fixed duties were substituted for the sliding scale on corn. In 1852 certain preferential duties were abolished, and in 1853 all the remaining export duties were repealed. A project of tariff reform was brought in by the Government in 1854, but it was lost in consequence of a change of ministry. In 1856 all the differential duties were abolished, and in 1857 the raw materials were allowed to be imported duty free. Since, however, by the treaty of commerce concluded in 1861 between Belgium and France, considerable reductions were made in the Belgian tariff in favour of France, Her Majesty's Government found it necessary, in 1862, to conclude a similar treaty, by which the regulations established for goods imported from France into Belgium were applied to similar goods imported from Great Britain and its possessions; each of the two powers engaged to extend to the other any favour or privilege, or reduction in the tariff

Commercial treaty with Belgium.

of duties of importation or exportation, on articles mentioned or not mentioned in the treaty, which either of them might grant to any third power, and agreed that neither should establish against the other any duty or prohibition of importation or exportation, which should not, at the same time, be applicable to all other nations. This treaty was to continue in force for ten years, dating the tenth day after the exchange of ratifications.

With the Zollverein a treaty of commerce was concluded on May 30, 1865, by which among other things it was stipulated that any favour, privilege, or reduction in the tariff of duties of importation or exportation which either of the contracting parties may concede to any third power, should be extended immediately and unconditionally to the other; and that no prohibition of importation or exportation should be established by either of them against the other which should not at the same time be applicable to all other nations, and the contracting parties further engaged not to prohibit the exportation of coal, and to levy no duty upon such exportation.

Commercial treaty with the Zollverein.

With Italy a treaty of commerce was concluded on August 6, 1863, ratified October 29, containing similar conditions of reciprocity.

Commercial treaty with Italy.

And with Austria a treaty was concluded on December 16, 1865, providing that the Austrian customs tariff should be so regulated that the duty to be levied upon articles, the produce or manufacture of the dominions of her Britannic Majesty, upon their importation into the Austrian States, should, from January 1, 1867, not exceed 25 per cent. of the value, with the addition of the cost of transport, insurance, and commission, necessary for the importation into Austria as far as the Austrian customs frontiers. And that from and after January 1, 1870, the maximum of these duties should not exceed 20 per cent. of the value with the additions above defined. On December 30, 1869, another convention of commerce was concluded with Austria by which she engaged that during the continuance of the convention British produce and manufactures should be admitted into Austria at the rates specified in the tariff annexed to the treaty.

Commercial treaty with Austria.

Negotiations were also opened with Spain and Portugal for

the conclusion of similar treaties of commerce with them, and it was the more needful to procure thereby a revision of their tariffs, since these countries were, in consequence of their treaties of commerce with France, practically charging differential duties on British goods. But they consented to lower their duties on British goods only on condition of Her Majesty's Government consenting to lower the duty on Spanish and Portuguese wine above 26 degrees of strength to one shilling per gallon. This Her Majesty's Government refused to do lest it should injure the revenue in spirits, and consequently further negotiations were suspended.

Negotiations with Spain and Portugal.

Ought the policy initiated by the treaty of commerce with France be adhered to, or should we now return to a policy of inaction trusting that sooner or later every enlightened country will adopt a liberal policy? This is a question of grave importance, which remains yet to be solved by Her Majesty's Government. By the treaties of commerce it should be observed Great Britain has not swerved one iota from the principles of commercial freedom. On our side we abandoned for ever certain duties. On the foreign side there was nothing but relaxations. Only we have no other equivalents to offer unless we are disposed to relinquish all customs and excise duties which would enable us to obtain concessions from Spain and Portugal in return for the abolition of the wine duties, from Prussia for the abolition of spirit duties, and from the United States for the abolition of the tobacco duties. Whatever may be yet reserved for the future, there is reason to be thankful for the large expansion of trade with France, especially at a time when the insurrection in the United States of America inflicted so much injury on British commerce. Nor can a better proof be given of the benefit of a free commercial intercourse with our nearest neighbour than the fact that our total trade with France increased from 26,432,000*l.* in 1859 to 59,590,000*l.* in 1870, being at the rate of 125 per cent. in eleven years.

Results of the treaties of commerce.

But the best recommendation of the French treaty is the stimulus it has afforded to the improvement of the tariff in the principal countries, as may well be seen from the following examples as regards cotton, woollen, and worsted manufactures:

Reductions of Tariffs.

Cotton Manufactures, Piece Goods.

Countries	Lowest and Highest Rates of Import Duties per cwt.				Percentage of Decrease
	1840		1870		
	£ s. d.	£ s. d.	£ s. d.	£ s. d.	per cent.
Russia .	7 11 9	—	5 10 4	—	27 to 22
Zollverein	7 12 6	—	1 10 8 to	4 11 5	80 40
Belgium .	3 8 4 to	7 18 6	0 1 4	0 7 3	11 76
Spain .	6 2 6	37 1 11	5 9 3	9 3 5	11 76
Italy .	1 15 2	3 10 5	1 0 4	2 7 0	42 83
Austria .	4 5 4	10 13 4	1 12 6	4 11 5	62 57
Woollen and Worsted.					
Russia .	8 13 5	24 13 7	5 18 3	28 3 6	81 19
Zollverein	5 0 11	7 12 5	1 10 6	3 16 4	60 50
Belgium .	3 18 0	9 2 11	ten per cent. *ad valorem* or 5.58 per cent.		35 increase to 42 decrease.
Spain .	2 18 5	22 17 4	8 1 0	17 16 2	4 increase to 23 decrease.
Italy .	2 6 9	7 0 3	1 12 6	8 5 0	80 to 60 decr.
Austria .	5 8 8	10 13 4	1 18 7	5 1 7	65 to 62 decr.

Whatever objections, therefore, might have been urged against obtaining concessions by treaties, it cannot be denied that the results of them have been highly satisfactory. Compare the tariffs of most states of Europe in the years immediately preceding the reforms introduced by Sir Robert Peel with those in force at present, and we realize the force of the observation that at no former period has any system of policy been so generally and speedily adopted as the system of free trade. 'A century has not elapsed since it was first thought, or rather hinted at as an abstract theory. Fifty years have not elapsed since it was first seriously and generally discussed as a question of practical policy; twenty years have not elapsed since the necessity of framing our whole commercial policy on it was recognised, and already it has become more or less acknowledged as the only policy of the whole civilized world. It is pretty clear, therefore, that its roots are implanted in human nature and in the natural laws of society; and from it there can be no retrograde movement to protection and prohibition without ruin and destruction. Wise statesmen should study not only how they can most easily and most speedily carry out completely the principles of this policy, and they ought carefully to eschew every act contrary to them.'

Progress of free trade.

In connection with the treaties of commerce, we may advantageously advert to the removal of other restrictions to trade and navigation which became the subject of diplomatic negotiation and settlement. The abolition of the navigation laws and the opening of the coasting trade to the unrestricted competition of all nations rendered British shipowners more than ever interested in the removal of many burdens which were pressing on shipping property both at home and abroad. The provisions of the Passengers Act, the liabilities imposed by the Merchant Shipping Act, the burden of passing tolls, and the unequal and onerous charges for lighthouses and pilotage in various parts of the kingdom, accompanied by the want of reciprocity on the part of foreign countries in imposing differential duties, and shutting up their colonial and coasting trade, placed British shipowners in a position of disadvantage in relation to shipowners of foreign countries, and they reasonably demanded a full and impartial inquiry.

Effect of free trade on shipping.

The local charges on shipping were of a very varied character and were levied in the ports and harbours of the whole kingdom. In many cases the right to levy these charges either depended on local acts, or if claimed originally on a common law title, that title had been confirmed by local act, but in very many cases the title depended on common law entirely. The charges consisted of petty customs, or charges levied in respect of anchorage, keelage, or charges levied on goods in the nature of cranage, lastage, wharfage, or other kindred dues. In some cases these vexatious imports were especially oppressive, since, whilst British ships were exposed to all the annoyance, foreign ships were in many cases exempt under the Reciprocity Treaty clauses.[2] An inquiry having been instituted on the subject by a Royal commission in 1854 the report recommended that a single body of conservators be constituted for each public harbour, that all dues both on ships and on goods levied within its limits be transferred to such conservators, that the tariffs be revised, that all exclusive privileges within public harbours be abolished, that the passing tolls be abolished, and that all payments from the public funds under the Reciprocity Treaties should cease.

Local charges on shipping.

[2] 59 Geo. III. c. 54; 1 & 2 Vict. c. 113; and 14 & 15 Vict. c. 47.

And accordingly an act[4] was passed which abolished such passing tolls and liberated British ships from many of the most oppressive charges, especially those in return for which no benefit was received.

Burdens, however, of a similar character existed abroad which demanded the intervention of diplomacy. For many centuries the crown of Denmark assumed the right to levy tolls on ships and merchandise passing between the German Ocean and the Baltic Sea, and duties equivalent to the same on goods passing overland between the North Sea and the Baltic. When and how this right originated it is not easy to find out; but, whether by the law of might or of right, the Danes, who were proprietors of both sides of the channel, did levy such duties, and ships passing the Sound had no choice but to pay. The first treaty in which the right of Denmark to levy these dues was assumed or acknowledged was the treaty of Spire, concluded with Holland in 1544, in which a distinction was introduced between privileged and unprivileged nations. Unprivileged nations, such as England, France, Portugal, and Russia, had to pay dues amounting to about one per cent. *ad valorem.* Privileged nations had to pay only nominal duties. Other treaties followed, and in 1814 the Sound dues were recognised throughout Europe. The congress of Vienna did not interfere with them, and in 1841 England concluded a treaty with Denmark, which established a regular tariff on the subject, based on that of Christianople of 1645.

Imposts on ships passing between the North Sea and the Baltic.

But, whether politically recognised or not, such dues were a great burden on navigation and a heavy charge on British shipping. The detention of vessels at Elsinore was a fertile source of mischief. No one could see, as far as the cargoes were concerned, what good it did to anyone. And the obstruction was ill consented to by the states interested in the navigation of the Sound. Such being the case, the United States, though unwilling to recognise the right of Denmark, were the first to make a proposition to pay to Denmark a fair indemnity for the abolition of the dues,

Injurious effects of the Sound dues.

[4] 24 & 25 Vict. c. 47.

upon the supposition that they had been levied for lights and other purposes essential to navigation. And under these circumstances a committee of the House of Commons was appointed on the subject. Denmark, having meanwhile offered to accept, at once, a sum representing the capital value of the payments annually made on account of Sound dues, the committee reported that such proposal should become the foundation of a final and satisfactory settlement of the question. And accordingly, negotiations were opened, which resulted in the conclusion of a treaty, dated March 14, 1857, the principal stipulations of which were as follows: 1. That no more duties should be imposed, nor any charge whatever made, either in regard to vessel or cargo, upon ships sailing from the North Sea to the Baltic, or *vice versâ*, in passing through the Belts or the Sound; 2. That Denmark should preserve and maintain in the best style all the lights and lighthouses actually existing, either at the entrance or into the approaches to the harbour, roads, rivers, or canals, or along her coasts, as well as the buoys, beacons, and sea-marks actually existing, and serving to facilitate navigation in the Kattegat, the Sound, and the Belts; superintend the service of pilotage; permit, without any restriction, any private individual, Dane or foreigner, to establish and to station in the Sound or in the Belts freely, and on the same conditions, tugs serving exclusively for the towing of vessels; extend to all the roads or canals which connect the North Sea and the Elbe with the Baltic the exemption from dues which was accorded in some of those lines of communication to the national or foreign goods; reduce the duties on all the said roads or canals to a uniform rate; and 3. That the different powers interested should pay to the King of Denmark, as compensation for the sacrifices imposed upon him, the sum of 30,476,000 rigsdollars, of which 16,126,855 rigsdollars, equivalent to 1,125,206*l.* fell upon Great Britain.

Of a similar character to the Sound dues were the Stade dues, levied by Hanover on merchandise and shipping ascending the river Elbe. About 40 miles from the mouth of the Elbe and 23 miles from Hamburg, just at the confluence of the river and the smaller stream of the Schwinge,

The Stade dues.

is the little town of Stade, and at this point every ship of every country, with the exception of those of Hamburg and Hanover, was called upon to interrupt her voyage, and was compelled to exhibit her papers to the Hanoverian functionary. On her arrival at Hamburg a Hanoverian commissioner made his appearance and proceeded to charge duty on the goods forming the cargo, and not until all demands were satisfied was the ship permitted to break bulk, and the cargo allowed to be discharged. The history of this toll is an interesting one. The toll seems to have originated in 1308 in a grant by Conrad II., German emperor, to the then archbishop of Hamburg and Bremen, to ensure the safety of his soul; the archbishop being permitted to levy telonium, or custom, in a market place called Stade. At first it was but a market toll, but afterwards it was converted into a passage duty. The archbishopric of Bremen having been secularised, the toll was transferred to Sweden at the peace of Westphalia, in satisfaction for all her expenses in connection with the Thirty Years' War. Subsequently, Denmark conquered the duchies of Bremen and Wieden from Sweden, and she levied the tolls. In 1715, George I. purchased the toll for 300,000 dollars, and in 1819 he formally ceded the same to Hanover. Whatever right, therefore, the King of Sweden had legally acquired over the Stade dues, was legally transferred to the King of Great Britain as Elector of Brunswick Luneburg. And thus it stood when, at the Congress of Vienna in 1815, it was decided that the navigation of all navigable rivers should be free.[*] But Hanover asserted that this was a maritime and not a river tax, and so it escaped. In 1842 a committee

[*] Les Puissances dont les États sont séparés ou traversés par une même rivière navigable s'engagent à régler d'un commun accord tout ce qui a rapport à la navigation de cette rivière. Elles nommeront à cet effet des commissaires qui se réuniront au plus tard six mois après la fin du congrès, et qui prendront pour bases de leurs travaux les principes.

109. La navigation dans tout le cours des rivières indiquées dans l'article précédent, du point où chacune d'elles devient navigable jusqu'à son embouchure, sera entièrement libre et ne pourra sous le rapport de commerce être interdite à personne, bien entendu que l'on se conformera aux règlements relatifs à la police de cette navigation, lesquels seront conçus d'une manière uniforme pour tous et aussi favorables que possible au commerce de toutes les nations.

110. Le système qui sera établi tant pour la perception des droits que pour le maintain de la police, autant que faire se pourra, sera le même pour tout le cours de

of mediation was proposed between Hanover on the one side, and Hamburg and Denmark on the other; and in 1844 a treaty was concluded by which the dues were recognised by England, at least for a limited period. Nothing was done after that till 1858, when a committee of the House of Commons was appointed to inquire into the subject, and upon the report of that committee to the effect that it was expedient to give notice to terminate the treaty of 1844 negotiations were opened for the redemption of the tolls, and this was effected by the payment on the part of England of 155,000*l.* as her share.

Discriminating duties imposed by foreign countries.

Of far greater range than even any of the dues we have yet mentioned were the restrictions on navigation, and the discriminating duties imposed by foreign countries against British ships long after we abolished all restrictions against theirs. When the navigation law repeal bill was first introduced by Mr. Labouchere, it proposed also the opening of the coasting trade, but objections were urged to that, and the clauses were withdrawn. In 1854, however, the restriction was abandoned, with the reserve only that, 'if it shall be made to appear to Her Majesty that British vessels are subject in any foreign country to any prohibitions or restrictions as to the voyages in which they may engage, or as to the articles which they may import into or export from such country, it shall be lawful for Her Majesty (if she think fit), by order in council, to impose such prohibitions or restrictions upon the ships of such foreign country, either as to the voyages in which they may engage, or as to the articles which they may import into or export from any part of the United Kingdom or of any British possession in any part of the world, as Her Majesty may think fit, so as to place the ships of such country on as nearly as possible the same footing in British ports as that on which British ships are placed in the ports of such country.'[1] But this clause was never acted upon. And though many countries, especially Spain, France, Portugal,

la rivière, et s'étendra aussi, à moins que des circonstances particulières ne s'y opposent, sur ceux de ses embranchements et confluents qui dans leur cours navigable séparent ou traversent différents États.

[1] 12 & 13 Vict. c. 29; 16 & 17 Vict. c. 107.

Holland, Belgium, Sweden, and the United States of America, maintained for some time their restrictions on British navigation, no step whatever was taken by England against them. There appeared, certainly, a marked injustice in the fact that whilst American ships could freely trade on the coast of the United Kingdom, and even on the coasts of British India, Ceylon, and Victoria, the United States of America not only shut out British vessels from the carrying of goods in the vast coasting trade of their Atlantic and Pacific seaboards, but denied to British ships running between New York and Aspinwall, and between Panama and San Francisco, the privileges enjoyed by the American national flag. But after all, the loss produced by these illiberal measures on the part of foreign countries on British shipping was not to be compared to the loss which thereby resulted to themselves. Whilst British shipping prospered and increased, American shipping suffered and declined.

CHAPTER II.

CIVIL WAR IN THE UNITED STATES.

1861—1864.

Relations with the United States.—Difference between the Northern and Southern States on the Tariff.—The Slavery Question.—Election of Abraham Lincoln.—Hostilities between the North and South.—Blockade of Southern Ports.—Granting of Belligerent Rights.—The Efficiency of the Blockade.—Trade with Confederate States.—The 'Alabama' Dispute.—The Finances of the United States.

THOUGH separated from us by the wide ocean, so great is the interdependence between America and England, and so intimate are the relations between the old and the new world, that a serious insurrection which threatened to sever into distinct portions the great republic of the west could not fail to have an enormous influence on British commerce and industry. For some time past a marked division was apparent between the industrial and the agricultural states of the Union both on the question of free trade *versus* protection, and on the limitation or extension of slavery supremacy in the Republic being eagerly contested for both by the free labour and by the slave labour states.

Relations with the United States.

When the constitution was first framed, all the states being purely agricultural, they were all in equally need of foreign manufactures, and the duties levied were exceedingly moderate. But the war with England altered the industrial position of the respective states. The Northern States then took to manufactures, and the Southern gave themselves to agriculture. The Southern States did not offer any strong objection to the raising of import duties, not because they had faith themselves in the benefit of protection, but because they held that any special disadvantage which might fall on the Southern States, was counterbalanced by the benefit they enjoyed of sharing in the national prosperity. But the Northern went too far, when, not content

Difference between the Northern and Southern States on the tariff.

with a fair amount of protection, they wished to establish a monopoly. When, therefore, in 1823, a large increase was proposed on many of the existing duties, the Southern States refused to submit to it, especially as the measure had been carried by the small majorities of 107 to 102, in the House of Representatives and by 25 to 21 in the Senate. In 1832 a more formidable difference occurred on the same subject. There was then no excuse for imposing a high tariff on the ground of revenue, and therefore South Carolina, which had always been opposed to the exercise of power by the federal government, took the lead in a movement of direct opposition to it. At first, the delegates contemplated resigning their seat in congress, but they were content to secure the formation of a committee to inquire into the powers of the federal government with respect to the subjects then agitated. The committee having been duly appointed, and the inquiry gone through, they published a report, to the effect 'that the federal constitution was a compact originally formed, not between the people of the different States, as distinct and independent sovereignties, and that when any violation of the letter or the spirit of that compact took place, it is not only the right of the people, but of the state legislature, to remonstrate against it; that the federal government was responsible to the people, whenever it abused or injudiciously exercised powers intrusted to it, and that it was responsible to the state legislature, whenever it assumed powers not conferred to it.' The committee reported also, 'that all legislation for the protection of domestic manufactures, was unconstitutional, as being in favour of a local interest, and that congress had no power to legislate, except upon subjects of general interest.' Upon the reception of this report, the State of Carolina passed a resolution, 'That the Tariff Acts were not authorised by the constitution of the United States, and violated the true meaning and interest thereof, and were null and void.' And eventually the different states decided upon boldly throwing down the gauntlet to the union. President Jackson, alarmed at the agitation, lost no time in issuing a proclamation, appealing to Carolina and other states to remember the toil and blood which American liberty cost, the sacredness of the constitution, and the importance of the union. But the legislature of South Carolina, then in session, authorised the governor to issue a counter proclamation. General orders were issued to raise volunteers, and a rapture was at hand, when, Virginia having appealed to the patriotism and magnanimity of South Carolina, a compromise was effected, by which Congress reduced all the duties which exceeded 20 per cent. and declared that, after 1844, customs duties should be levied only for the purpose of raising such revenues as may be necessary to an economical administration of government. But the compact was not adhered to. The tariff of 1843 exhibited no improvement on the former tariff, and that of 1846 established much higher rates. Some slight reductions were afterwards made in 1857, but Mr. Morrell's tariff, in 1861, made matters worse.

The slavery question was even more complex than that of customs duties. In 1787, when the constitution was settled, slavery existed in every state of the Union except Massachusetts, though soon after, the other Northern States took steps for its abolition. Early in fact in the history of the Union, as Mr. Maddison said, the States were divided into different parties, the result not of difference of size but of other circumstances, the most material of which were connected partly with climate and principally with their having or not having slaves. Still, even then slavery was regarded as an evil to be deplored and if possible to be got rid of. But the evil increased. So long as indigo and rice formed the staple of the planting States the increase of slaves was not very material. But when the cotton gin was invented and the value of the cotton crop became more and more important new Slave States were added, and the slave population was increasing faster than the free. In 1818 a contest began as to the limits of the slave territory, when the Missouri compromise was entered into, whereby the South and the North each gained two states. Subsequently the Southern purchased Florida. Then Arkansas was admitted as a Southern State, while Michigan entered as a free state. Subsequently came California and afterwards New Mexico. So that, in 1861, slavery existed in 15 out of the 31 states, sent 30 senators and 88 representatives to congress, and more than once the president himself owed his election to the influence of the Slave States.

The slavery question.

Thus matters stood when, in November 1860, Abraham

Election of Abraham Lincoln.

Lincoln, the Republican candidate, was elected by a large majority as President of the United States. In this election North and South were openly arrayed against each other, and the result, fatal to Southern influence, became the signal of a great change. Not a month had elapsed after the election took place when a state convention was held in South Carolina, which declared the Union subsisting between South Carolina and other states under the name of the United States dissolved. Other states followed in adopting a similar resolution. Mississippi did so on January 8, 1861, Florida on the 10th, Alabama on the 11th, Georgia on the 19th. Louisiana and Texas came next, and they were succeeded by North Carolina, Virginia, Tennessee, and Arkansas. All the slave states thus made common cause against the free states, and on February 4, 1861, they constituted a provisional government for themselves under the title of the Confederate States of America. Events after this advanced very rapidly.

Hostilities between Northern and Southern States.

On April 12 hostilities were commenced between the Federal and Confederate States. Fort Sumpter was attacked, a large army was set in motion, and on the 19th the President declared the blockade of the ports of seven states, and announced to foreign ministers that he would break off relations with any country which should recognise the Southern Confederacy. Grave difficulties, however, immediately arose out of this step. A blockade, it must be remembered, is essentially a war right, affecting in a most direct manner the rights and relations of neutral states. But for a state of war, the United States had no right whatever to stop a single British ship upon the high seas, nor had they any right to blockade so large a coast, and thereby to acquire the right of search, detention, and capture. When, therefore, the United States asked and demanded to exercise the right of blockade they admitted the existence of a state of belligerency, and the British Government acted accordingly and recognised the Confederate States as belligerents. But the American Government remonstrated against this, maintaining that the act of recognition by Her Majesty's Government of insurgents as belligerents on the high seas before they had a single vessel afloat was precipitate and unprecedented; and that the insurgents never bore the appearance of belligerents on the ocean excepting in the shape of British vessels manned and armed in British ports. In truth there was much incongruity in the position assumed by the United States. Whilst, on the one hand, asserting that the Union was not and could not be broken, and that it was called upon to check an internal revolution, the American Government was acting as a belligerent, precluding friendly nations and neutral states from carrying on a large portion of their accustomed trade. 'A civil war,' said Vattel, 'produces in a nation two independent parties who consider each other as enemies. These two parties must be considered as thenceforward constituting at least for a time two separate bodies, two distinct societies, and to stand in precisely the same perdicament as two nations who engage in a contest and being unable to come to an agreement have recourse to arms.' Her Majesty's Government recognised the existence of two independent parties for the time being, but by so doing it never meant to prejudge the question of final recognition.

Other difficulties arose out of this blockade. The Conference of Paris of 1856 specifically stated that a blockade in order to be binding must be effective; that is to say, maintained by a force sufficient really to prevent access to the coast of the enemy. It was evident, however, that in this case it was almost impossible to blockade so extensive a coastage. The blockade was maintained in a very ineffective manner, the vessels were too few in number and not suitable in class for the purpose of preventing access to the various harbours and inlets indenting it. And, consequently, there were many evasions. Numerous steamers were ready to run into the blockaded ports by night, by day, whenever and howsoever they might evade the blockading squadron. And this was another ground of complaint on the part of the United States.

Disputes concerning the efficiency of blockade.

Nor were the blockade runners content to remain on the high seas on the alert for an entrance: they made Metamoros and Nassau the starting-points of their operations, just as Heligoland was the chief place for contraband during the French war, and Metamoros and Nassau

Disputes concerning trade with Confederate States.

rose on a sudden to a state of opulence. Yet it could not be said that the British Government should have stopped that trade. It was carried on from New York as it was from London and Liverpool, and the fact that some goods were afterwards transported across the frontiers to Texas did not vitiate the legitimate character of that trade. Nor was it possible to say beforehand that certain goods would be consumed in Mexico, and certain other goods would be carried into the so-called Confederate States. The American Government wished to impose all manner of restrictions on the exports from New York to the Bahamas lest they should go to the insurgents. But British subjects as neutrals had a perfect right to sell goods to anyone. And it is not a violation of neutrality to carry on active trade with a belligerent state.

The 'Trent' dispute was a case, where, regardless of all observance of international law, an American ship arrested a British mail steamer, and having made a forcible passage on board, American officers seized Messrs. Mason and Slidell and their secretaries, supposed ambassadors from the Confederate States, and let her go; a system of high-hand practice altogether indefensible.

The 'Trent' dispute.

But a greater difficulty arose from the alleged evasion of the foreign belligerent act in the building and despatch of men-of-war from British ports to the Confederate States. As soon as hostilities commenced, the Confederate States, finding themselves without ships and harbours, sent orders to Liverpool for the building of ships of war, and first a gunboat, called the 'Oreta,' then the 'Georgia' and the 'Florida,' were made ready for the conflict. On June 23, 1862, however, Mr. Adams, the American ambassador in London, made known to the British Government that a vessel known as 'No. 290' or the 'Alabama' was building in Liverpool, and on the 30th he requested Earl Russell to cause the ship to be detained. Earl Russell referred the matter to the customs authorities, under whose supervision the registry of ships and other matters connected with navigation are placed, but owing to the particular structure of the ship and to the want of evidence of any fitting out or arming as a war vessel the commissioners of customs did not feel themselves justified in arresting the vessel;

The 'Alabama' dispute.

and they reported on July 1 that there was no attempt on the part of the builders to disguise what was apparent, that she was intended for a vessel of war, that she had several powder canisters on board, but that as yet she had neither guns nor carriages. The report received from the customs was sent to Mr. Adams on July 4, with a suggestion that the United States consul at Liverpool should procure further proof of equipment. Mr. Adams acted on the suggestion, and on the 22nd and 24th sent further depositions, together with an opinion of Mr. now Sir R. P. Collier in favour of a seizure. On the 29th the law officers reported that she should be seized, but on that same morning the ship had sailed from the Mersey under pretext of a trial trip. A copy of the law officers' report was then sent to the Bahamas in case the 'Alabama' should go there; she, however, proceeded to Angoa Bay in the Azores where she met the 'Baham' and 'Agrippina' with her armament, her commander Captain Semmes and 42 men, and then she hoisted the Confederate flag and sailed for Port Royal, Martinique. So provided, she went to Blanco Island where she was coated, and having destroyed the United States ship 'Hatteras' off Galveston, she sailed afterwards to Jamaica, where she was received and recognised as a regularly commissioned ship of war. And from that time she continued her depredations at the Cape of Good Hope and elsewhere until she was finally sunk by the United States ship 'Kearsage' off Cherbourg on July 19, 1864. How far the United Kingdom was responsible for the escape of the 'Alabama' is the question to be decided by the arbitrators appointed under the Washington treaty.

Persisting in its measures of intimidation and warfare against the insurgents, President Lincoln, in July, 1862, sanctioned a bill for the confiscation of property and emancipation of slaves and of all persons who did not deposit their arms in sixty days. In September another proclamation was issued declaring all slaves of the states in revolt on January 1, 1863, free from that day, and accordingly on that day all slaves found in Texas, Arkansas, Mississippi, Alabama, Florida, Georgia, North Carolina, South Carolina, Louisiana, and Virginia, in a state of rebellion, were declared to be free. But the insurrection was speedily quelled, and after the un-

Abolition of slavery.

happy tragedy of the assassination of Lincoln, subsequent to his re-election, the blockade was raised and peace was restored. Into the further questions concerning the restoration of peace and the abolition of slavery we shall not enter. There are, however, other economic questions of grave moment which had a direct influence on the finances and trade of the United Kingdom which must engage our attention.

The finances of the United States now almost for the first time acquired an extraordinary magnitude. In 1861 the expenditure of the United States amounted only to 18,000,000*l.*; in 1862 it suddenly rose to 119,000,000*l.*; in 1863 to 187,000,000*l.*; in 1864 to 270,000,000*l.*; and in 1865 to 395,000,000*l.*[1] Very soon after the rupture with the South in 1862 the New York banks suspended cash payments and began to issue inconvertible notes. The United States Government followed the example, and it also began to issue inconvertible notes. On February 20, 1862, an Act of Congress was passed authorising the treasury to issue on the credit of the United States $150,000,000 United States notes. And from that time large annual issues took place, which led to a considerable depreciation of the currency when compared with the value of gold in the first six months to the extent of only 3 per cent. but subsequently of as much as 155 per cent. The currency being so depreciated the exchanges between New York and London suffered in the same proportion. And the prices of produce calculated in paper currency rose in an equal ratio.[2]

The finances of the United States.

Still more important were the effects of the war on the commerce between the United States and England. In 1860 our imports from the United States amounted to 44,727,000*l.*, a large portion of which consisted of cotton. Suddenly, however, with the closing of the Southern ports a large portion of the American trade ceased, and the amount of our imports thence was reduced by more than half. In 1860 we imported altogether 1,391,000,000 lbs. of cotton, of

Effect of the insurrection on trade and cotton supply.

[1] The public debt of the United States in 1864 was 13,493,000*l.*, and in 1869, 518,542,000*l.* The public expenditure in 1869 was 121,829,000*l.*

[2] The rate of exchange New York to London on January 5, 1861, was 103; on January 11, 1862, 111; on January 3, 1863, 146; on January 2, 1864, 165; on January 7, 1865, 213½; on January 6, 1866, 152½; and on January 5, 1867, 100¼.

which 1,115,890,000 lbs., or 75 per cent., were from the United States. In 1862 the imports of American cotton amounted only to 6,394,000 lbs. And, consequently, the average price of middling Orleans cotton, which in 1860 was 6$\frac{3}{16}$d. per lb., rose in 1864, to 27¾d.[*] Perplexed how to obtain the necessary quantity of cotton, India was put in motion to produce more largely than she had hitherto done. And though for manufacturing purposes Surat cotton is inferior to American cotton, gradually the manufacturers learnt how to use it mixed with other descriptions, and the importation of Indian cotton, which in 1860 was 204,000,000 lbs., rose in 1866 to 615,000,000 lbs. But the imports have since receded, and in 1870 were only 341,000,000 lbs. Much, certainly, has been done in India to improve the cultivation of cotton by the selection of indigenous seed, by the introduction of exotic seed, by a better cultivation of the soil, by the improvement of pressing bales, by the improvement of roads, and by the construction of railways. Nevertheless, it is the price that regulates the extent of cotton cultivation in India as elsewhere; and whether or not India will ever be able to compete permanently with America is doubtful. The cotton requirements of the world are estimated at nearly 3,000,000,000 lbs., the half of which is for Great Britain alone, and the other half for Europe, America, and India. It is much to be desired that every facility should be accorded to the cultivation of the article in every country in which it may be advantageously grown. To the United States the insurrection has been most injurious. Their finances have been disorganised; their commerce and navigation considerably reduced; their whole economic policy has been reversed. Would that a better counsel prevailed in the United States as to the manner of remedying their shattered fortunes!

[*] The following quotations of extreme prices of cotton from Messrs. George Holt & Co.'s circular may be useful.

	1830	1840	1850	1860	1864	1870
Upland . .	11½ to 22½	7 to 7¾	7½ to 8¾	7¼ to 8	31 to 32½	8¾ to 12
New Orleans	16½ „ 23½	8 „ 9	9 „ 10	8½ „ 9	25 „ 33	9 „ 12¾
Sea Island .	26 „ 33	18 „ 20	20 „ 20	26 „ 26	60 „ 74	45 „ 48
Surat . . .	12½ „ 19	5½ „ 6	5¼ „ 6¾	5¼ „ 5¾	16¼ „ 27¾	7¾ „ 11½

CHAPTER III.

COMMERCIAL CRISIS.

1866.

The Société de Crédit Mobilier.—Limited Liability Companies.—Finance Companies.—Finance Securities.—Large Companies and their Results.—Overend, Gurney, & Co. Limited.—Great Expansion of Trade.—Drain of Bullion to the East.—Fall of Money in London and other Places.—Component Parts of the Rate of Interest.—The Supply of Capital in England.—The Demand for Capital in England.—A uniform Rate of Interest.—Policy of the Bank of England.—The Crisis of 1866.—Suspension of the Bank Charter Act.—Comparison of the Crisis of 1866 with former Crises.—Effect of the Government Letter on Credit at Home and Abroad.—Mr. Watkins' Motion for a Royal Commission negatived.

The Société de Crédit Mobilier.

ONE of the first objects which the Emperor Napoleon had at heart, after he strengthened his position, by the restoration of the empire, in 1852, was the revival of industry and commerce in France, which had long been languid and depressed, and for that purpose he greatly encouraged the formation of railways, and the incorporation of trading companies. Many were therefore the enterprises thereafter started, and great was the activity thereby introduced. Prominent, however, among the companies then formed was the '*Société de Crédit Mobilier*,' the objects of which were to subscribe and acquire stock and shares in industrial enterprises, especially railways, canals, &c.; to issue obligations of the society to the extent at least of the amount invested by the companies formed for such purposes; to sell or give on security for advances the shares acquired by the society; to undertake loans, to lend on public securities, to open credits; to pay interest and dividends; in short, to do for itself all that could be done by a number of companies, and to become immediately interested in and almost responsible for the success of enterprises undertaken by any other company whose shares they acquired. The capital of the Société de Crédit Mobilier was fixed at 2,400,000*l.* and its issue of circulating paper at ten times that amount. The Société went vigorously to work. Many companies which would never otherwise have seen the light came into existence under its auspices. And for several years its profits were so very large, its deposits so considerable and its annual reports so enticing that it did seem as if France had discovered a new branch of business in the shape of finance companies well worthy of imitation in this country.[1]

As we have seen, the principle of limited liability, long advocated as a means for encouraging the investment of capital in commercial adventures, was for the first time admitted by the English law in 1855; and certainly if we can test the success of legislation by the readiness with which it is adopted and acted upon by the community here is a case where the reform seemed to meet a decided want. Before 1856 almost every company formed was on the principle of unlimited liability. From that date scarcely any company was constituted but with limited liability. An immense stimulus was given to joint-stock enterprises by the very fact that the losses could never exceed the amount which the investors at the time intended to risk. From 1856 to 1868 there were formed 7,056 companies, involving in the aggregate the nominal investment of 893,000,000*l.* And of these 6,960 with a capital of 883,000,000*l.* were with limited liability, and 96 with a capital of 10,000,000*l.* were with unlimited liability. Many a private partnership was then formed into a limited company, and many companies with unlimited liability were converted into companies with limited liability.

Limited liability companies.

Many of these companies, styled as the 'International Financial,' the 'London Financial,' the Imperial Mercantile Credit,' the 'Crédit Foncier et Mobilier,' the 'Joint-Stock Discount,' and others, were founded for purposes similar to those of the 'Société de Crédit Mobilier' of Paris, and adopted not a few of its objectionable features. Before this new agency came into existence no public works could be un-

Finance companies.

[1] See an able article 'On the Recent History of the Crédit Mobilier' by Mr. Newmarch, F.R.S., *Journal of the Statistical Society*, Vol. XXI., p. 444.

dertaken until shares were actually sold and sufficient capital was obtained for the purpose. But by the intervention of the finance companies the projectors of public works no longer needed to wait until the savings of the people were gathered. No sooner was a project started involving investments of millions, at home or abroad, than the finance companies agreed to indorse the bills of such companies, and debentures, bonds, stock, and preference shares were created and circulated as if the company had been actually in operation and the works were already in progress. The understanding of course was that the bills would be renewed from time to time; but what if by a sudden collapse of credit such bills could not be discounted?

And on what were such bills founded? They represented no real value. As the 'Economist' stated: 'Such securities were a pure speculation on the future, and a speculation subject to one principal and many smaller casualties. Take the case of a railway; the line must be finished and placed in actual working before the obligations representing its cost can have any ascertained value at all. An unfinished railway or dock has no value whatever. In the second place the line must not only be finished and actually worked, but in order to impart value to the bonds and shares there must be a positive profit surplus. The difference between securities such as these, wholly dependent on future and uncertain events, to happen at distant and irregular dates and liable to become worthless by the premature stoppage of the undertaking, and the class of securities which long experience has shown to be best suited to the requirements of bankers and money dealers is not marked in its character, but so wide and glaring as to prepare any prudent person to expect mischief.'

Fictitious securities.

The magnitude of the projects afloat was moreover sufficient to create alarm. From 1856 to 1868 as many as 300 companies were formed in the United Kingdom with a nominal capital of 1,000,000*l.* and upwards each, or an aggregate of 504,000,000*l.* But what became of them? Many existed only in the imagination; a fifth of them were abandoned before starting, and 87 more were speedily wound up. In a short time, out of 300 companies as many as 178 ceased

Large companies, and their results.

to exist and 122 remained. And out of 504,000,000*l.* supposed to have been invested by these large companies more than two-thirds disappeared, some through bankruptcy, some through winding up, and some by a sudden disappearance from the market. Nor was the condition of the smaller companies more satisfactory. Many of the insurance companies and amalgamations were of a most unsatisfactory character, and considerable doubt was entertained respecting a variety of undertakings stimulated by the facility of issuing shares provided by limited liability companies.

Of all companies, however, that which created the greatest interest was the 'Overend, Gurney, & Co. Limited.' For many years the house of Gurney had been held in the highest estimation in the city of London, both on account of its reputed wealth and for its well-known business capacity. As a billbroker and a great discount house, the firm exercised an enormous influence in the financial transactions of the country, and certainly for upwards of sixty years it was in a position to afford facilities second only to those within reach of the Bank of England. Its profits were enormous. So late as 1860 the partners divided among themselves an annual sum of 190,000*l.* Unfortunately, however, the two pillars of the house were by this time removed: the head of the house, Samuel Gurney, died in 1856, and David Barclay Chapman retired in 1857, and their successors made considerable advances of a very doubtful character, which placed them in a position of difficulty. Finding themselves therefore in the possession of a well-established business, the good will of which was valued at half a million, yet wanting fresh capital, the representatives of the house resolved to convert the business into a limited liability, and having communicated the state of affairs to a select number of friends they jointly brought out a prospectus, and issued shares of 50*l.* each towards a capital of 5,000,000*l.* The public, altogether unacquainted with the condition of the house, and having no doubt whatever respecting its wealth, eagerly accepted the offer, and without difficulty 'Overend, Gurney, & Co. Limited' took its place among the banking and financial companies of London.

Overend, Gurney, & Co. limited.

Side by side with the formation of these numerous companies there was a large development of every branch of commerce and industry in the United Kingdom. In 1856 the total value of imports was 172,000,000*l.* In 1860 it increased to 210,000,000*l.* and in 1866 to 295,000,000*l.* The exports, which in 1856 amounted to 139,000,000*l.*, rose in 1860 to 164,000,000*l.* and in 1866 to 239,000,000*l.* The trade of the country was large and profitable. And besides this, numerous bills passed through parliament authorising the construction of public works, requiring a capital in 1865 of 126,000,000*l.* and in 1866 of 175,000,000*l.* There seemed no end indeed of the demand for capital at home and abroad.

Great expansion of trade.

But another circumstance must be taken into account as exercising considerable influence on the financial condition of the country, and that is the drain of precious metals to the East. The balance of trade between India and the United Kingdom, or still more accurately between the East and West, has been for years in favour of the East; the imports of produce and manufactures into India and China being far less in amount than their exports. In 1841 the value of merchandise imported into India was 8,400,000*l.* and its exports 13,500,000*l.* In 1851 the imports were valued at 11,500,000*l.* and the exports at 18,000,000*l.* In 1861 the imports of merchandise into India amounted to 23,500,000*l.* and the exports to 33,000,000*l.* When, however, a sudden and extraordinary impetus was given to the growth of cotton for export, to supply the void created by the American insurrection, the disproportion increased enormously; so that whilst in 1865 the imports of merchandise into India amounted to 28,000,000*l.* her exports were valued at 68,000,000*l.* And no other means existed for balancing this great indebtedness than the transmission of treasure, which in the case of India was always in the shape of silver. What became of the silver in India, why they prefer silver to gold, how far the adoption of a gold currency would modify the demand for silver, are important questions. But in whatever metal it be paid, an extraordinary withdrawal of bullion is continually taking place to pay the balance, and the metal seems to remain sunk in India, hoarded, buried, or converted into ornaments, never again to circulate through Europe and America.

Drain of treasure to the East.

Value of money in London and other places.

Given, then, a large number of joint-stock companies for banking, financial, assurance, and other purposes, involving the nation in liabilities at home and abroad for enormous sums, a flourishing trade increasing yearly at a rapid pace, a constant drain of bullion to the East, and a considerable amount of speculation, and we cannot wonder if the value of money increased considerably and the financial condition of the country became in every way very critical. The first result of all this activity was a considerable increase in the rate of interest. It is a singular fact that, although in London there is always the largest amount of disposable capital, the rate of interest has for many years been higher there than in Hamburg, Francfort, Amsterdam, and Berlin. From 1855 to 1864, whilst the average rate in London was 4·57 per cent., in Hamburg it was 3·05, in Francfort 3·51, in Amsterdam 3·74, in Berlin 4·41 per cent. And the rate of interest has been increasing since the discoveries of gold in California and Australia. Divide the twenty years from 1844 to 1864 into four periods of five years each, and we have in the first period the average rate of 3*l.* 11*s.* 7*d.*; in the second 3*l.* 6*s.* 11*d.*; in the third 4*l.* 11*s.* 8*d.*; and in the fourth 4*l.* 15*s.* 3*d.* per cent.

Component parts of the rate of interest.

The rate of interest, it should be remembered, is composed of three distinct elements. First, there is the interest proper, that is the natural produce, rent, or increment of capital; second, the insurance for risk; and, third, the expenses of management. The first depends in the same manner, as in the case of any other commodity, on supply or demand. The second varies with the state of credit and the class of securities. The third is great or small as the lender deals on a large or on a small scale, as the capital is dealt out from a great receptacle, like the Bank of England, or by such as the smallest money dealer. The most important of these three, however, is the relation of supply and demand. Let it not be imagined that the supply of capital is indefinite, and that a banker has nothing to do but to issue paper currency to put into circulation any amount of capital. Capital is that portion of wealth already acquired which is appropriated to reproductive employment. When a bank lends notes to its customer it lends capital which it borrows from the community. In whatever form the loan may take place it always represents so much capital.

In our highly developed system of banking most of the reserve fund of the country finds its way to the banks. Instead of each individual investing his spare money in a private and direct manner, the bankers become the intermediate agents between a numerous class of lenders and a numerous class of borrowers, and the funds held by them on deposit may be said to constitute by far the greater part of the available resources of our merchants. The amount of such deposits has increased enormously in recent years. Those at the London joint-stock banks have grown from 180,000*l.* in 1836 to 12,000,000*l.* in 1850, 41,500,000*l.* in 1857, and from 70,000,000*l.* to 80,000,000*l.* in 1865.[1] The country and private banks may have some 20,000,000*l.* more, and the Bank of England has a very large amount of public and private deposits, especially of bullion always on hand. And this may be said to be the loanable or available capital for investment in the United Kingdom. Besides this there are, of course, the vast stock of goods, the large amount of railway property, and the foreign securities; but these are not available as a loan fund. Present liabilities cannot be discharged with them. That which regulates the rate of discount in England is the aggregate of the deposits and bullion on hand. This is what constitutes the supply of capital.

The supply of capital in England.

And what is the demand? First of all there is the large amount drawn for home and foreign trade. In a state of quietness and prosperity, even without any positive speculation there is a great deal of buying and selling. In expectation of higher prices the stock of merchandise is enlarged, and credit and currency are in proportionally increasing demand. Secondly, whenever large public works are undertaken they require the conversion of a considerable part of the floating into fixed capital, and consequently leave so much less for the general wants of trade. The formation of public com-

The demand of capital in England.

[1] In 1834 the London and Westminster Bank was the only Joint Stock Bank in London, and had deposits of 180,000*l.* In 1872 that Bank had deposits to the amount of 25,205,000*l.*

panies for enterprises abroad has the effect of collecting large proportions of the savings of the people for investments in fixed property in different countries, and foreign loans have the same effect. In this manner, there are occasions when the demand made upon the floating loan fund is excessive, when enterprises are undertaken demanding capital far beyond the power of the country, and when therefore a strait takes place which is indicated by a very high rate of interest.

Bearing in mind these important economic facts which must regulate the value of capital, of which money is merely the symbol or representative, let us see what has been the policy pursued on the subject. So long of course as the usury laws were in force, the current rate of interest gave no indication whatever of the value of money. From 1704 to 1837 the rate charged by the Bank of England seemed extremely steady, so as never to be higher than 5 per cent., nor lower than 4, but that was not what needy borrowers paid, nor was it any evidence of stagnation of business. It was only when this incubus was removed that the rate began to represent the real value of capital. During the pressure of 1839 the Bank raised the rate to 6 per cent., at which rate it remained for several months. At one time an erroneous opinion obtained that the rate of interest might be kept pretty equal at the pleasure of the Bank of England. But the futility of the attempt was seen, and in 1844 a new era was inaugurated. It being vain to think of a uniform rate on the face of the constantly varying nature of money, the Bank of England then resolved to charge for its accommodation a rate of interest in direct relation to the supply and demand of money, taking the state of the reserves, which to a certain extent is the index of the amount of unemployed capital, as its guide. It was objected that constant fluctuations are of great injury to trade, that an even rate of interest was a great desideratum, and that in any case for reasons of general policy and as a matter of prudence the Bank should never lower its rate below 4 per cent. But how can these fluctuations be avoided? Money as a commodity must necessarily be subject to perpetual change of value, and no restriction can make that value immovable.

A uniform rate of interest.

Policy of the Bank of England.

On the passing of the Bank Act the country was in a state of great prosperity; capital had largely accumulated and the reserve was large. It amounted to 9,032,000*l.* against 13,305,000*l.* deposits, or to 67 per cent. Consequently the rate of discount fell from 2½ to 3 per cent. This gave great stimulus to speculation, and the mania for railways followed, which required large investments. Unfortunately the potato failure thereafter succeeded, which caused the necessity for a large importation of grain; and the result was, that on October 16, 1847, the reserves diminished to 3,071,000*l.* against liabilities on deposits of 15,072,000*l.*, being only 20 per cent., which rendered it necessary for the Bank to raise the rate to 8 per cent. From 1848 to 1852 the rate kept very low, in consequence of the discoveries of gold in California and Australia; and, on May 1, 1852, there were 12,069,000*l.* reserve against 18,774,000*l.* liabilities, being in the proportion of 64 per cent. Again, however, from that time under the operation of free trade, and in consequence of the opening of new markets, commerce largely expanded and investments increased. The Russian war demanded large sums for the Crimea. The East became more than ever entitled to large remittances for fibrous materials. The mutinies in India followed, and another crisis set in, when it was found that the reserve had diminished to 4,400,000*l.* against liabilities of 21,860,000*l.*, or to only 20 per cent. And, consequently, the directors of the Bank increased their rate to 10 per cent. After this the rate declined, but it did not fall very low. For a short time only in 1859 the rate was 2½ per cent., but it soon increased to an average of 5 per cent. in 1860, and to 6 per cent. in 1861. From 1862 till towards the end of 1863, the rate remained at from 3 to 4 per cent. When, however, in the week ending December 3, 1863, it was found that there remained only 6,400,000*l.* bullion and notes in reserve to meet a liability in deposits public and private and seven days bills, of 19,670,000*l.*, the rate was raised to 8 per cent. But matters did not seem to mend by such a step; the deposits, public and private, were increasing, the reserves still diminishing; and, in September, 1864, the Bank was constrained to go higher than at any previous time, by fixing 9 per cent. as a minimum charge for accommodation: and that had the desired effect, at least for a time. But the excessive demand of capital never ceased. Many of the joint stock companies continued to work upon the credulous. The finance companies had a large amount of 'finance' paper on hand. The house of Overend, Gurney & Co. was established; and the day came when those who counted on the continuance of prosperity for maintaining their schemes afloat, found the usual channels of accommodation effectively and suddenly obstructed.

The air had long, indeed, been overcharged by an electric heat which portended a violent storm and thunder and that burst out in a crisis both sudden and severe. One day financial affairs seemed at the very height of prosperity, on the other they were at the lowest depth of discredit and declension. Friday, May 11, 1866, will long be remembered in the city of London. 'About midday, yesterday,' said the 'Times,' 'the tumult became a rout. The doors of the most respectable bankinghouses were besieged, more perhaps by a mob actuated by the strong sympathy which makes and keeps a mob together, than by creditors of the bank, and throngs, heaving and tumbling about Lombard Street, made that narrow thoroughfare impassable.' On the same day, a meeting of the committee of joint stock banks was held, and a deputation waited on the Chancellor of the Exchequer with a request, that he should authorise the Bank of England to issue interest-bearing post-bills at 7 days or at 30 days, to any extent that might be deemed prudent. And, for the third time, the Bank of England had to be entrusted by Government with powers to exceed the limits in their issue imposed by the Bank Charter Act. In the letter to the Chancellor of the Exchequer dated May 11, the governor and deputy governor of the Bank stated that they had advanced that day upwards of 4,000,000*l.* to bankers, bill-brokers, and merchants in London; that they commenced that morning with a reserve of 5,727,000*l.*, but they could not calculate upon having as much as 3,000,000*l.* in the evening; that they had not refused any legitimate application for assistance; and that, unless the money taken from the Bank was entirely withdrawn from circulation, there was no reason to suppose that that reserve was insufficient.

The crisis of 1866.

On the same day on which the letter was written, Earl

Suspension of the Bank Charter Act. Russell and Mr. Gladstone sent the following communication to the Bank, authorising, if need be, the departure from the Bank Act, and forthwith the following Treasury letter was issued :—

Downing Street, May 11, 1866.

Gentlemen,—We have the honour to acknowledge the receipt of your letter of this day to the Chancellor of the Exchequer, in which you state the course of action at the Bank of England under the circumstances of sudden anxiety which have arisen since the stoppage of Messrs. Overend, Gurney, and Co. (Limited) yesterday.

We learn with regret that the Bank reserve, which stood so recently as last night at a sum of about five millions and three-quarters, has been reduced in a single day, by the liberal answer of the Bank to the demands of commerce during the hours of business, and by its just anxiety to avert disaster, to little more than one-half of that amount, or a sum (actual for London, and estimated for the branches) not greatly exceeding three millions. The accounts and representations which have reached Her Majesty's Government during the day exhibit the state of things in the City as one of extraordinary distress and apprehension. Indeed, deputations composed of persons of the greatest weight and influence, and representing alike the Private and Joint Stock Banks of London, have presented themselves in Downing Street and have urged with unanimity and with earnestness the necessity of some intervention on the part of the State to allay the anxiety which prevails, and which appears to have amounted, through great part of the day, to absolute panic.

There are some important points in which the present crisis differs from those of 1847 and 1857. Those periods were periods of mercantile distress, but the vital consideration of banking credit does not appear to have been involved in them as it is in the present crisis. Again, the course of affairs was then comparatively slow and measured, whereas the shock has in this instance arrived with an intense rapidity, and the opportunity for deliberation is narrowed in proportion. Lastly, the reserve of the Bank of England has suffered a diminution without precedent relatively to the time in which it has been brought about, and, in view especially of this circumstance, Her Majesty's Government cannot doubt that it is their duty to adopt without delay the measures which seem to them best calculated to compose the public mind, and to avert the calamities which may threaten trade and industry.

If, then, the directors of the Bank of England, proceeding upon the prudent rules of action by which their administration is usually governed, shall find that, in order to meet the wants of legitimate commerce, it is requisite to extend their discounts and advances upon approved securities, so as to require issues of notes beyond the limit fixed by law, Her Majesty's Government recommend that this necessity should be met immediately upon its occurrence, and in that event they will not fail to make application to Parliament for its sanction.

No such discount or advance, however, should be granted at a rate of interest less than 10 per cent., and Her Majesty's Government reserve it to themselves to recommend, if they should see fit, the imposition of a higher rate.

After deduction, by the Bank, of whatever it may consider to be a fair charge for its risk, expense, and trouble, the profits of these advances will accrue to the public.

We have the honour to be, Gentlemen,
Your obedient Servants,
RUSSELL.
W. E. GLADSTONE.

To the Governor and Deputy-Governor
of the Bank of England.

Doubtless 10 per cent. as a minimum charge for accommodation by the Bank of England had a most pernicious influence on business generally; but it was the only way by which an effectual check could be placed on speculative investments, and, so far, it was a wholesome restriction. So sharp, indeed, was its operation, that the Bank did not require after all to infringe the provisions of the Bank Act.

The operation of the different crises on the circulation and reserve of the Bank of England has always been rapid and important. In 1847 the rate of interest rose from 5½ per cent. on October 2 to 8 per cent. on the 23rd; at which rate it remained till November 20, when it fell to 7 per cent. In 1857 the rate rose from 5½ per cent. on October 3; again to 8 per cent. on the 24th; and then to 9 and 10 per cent. on November 7 and 14. But in 1866 the rate rose from 6 to 10 per cent. in three weeks, from April 25 to May 16. In 1856 the notes in circulation varied from 19,577,000*l.* on October 2 to 21,764,000*l.* on the 30th. In 1857 the circulation varied from 20,824,000*l.* on October 3 to 22,235,000*l.* on November 21. In 1866 it varied from 22,588,000*l.* on April 25 to 26,650,000*l.* on April 16. And the reserve of notes in 1847 was reduced to 1,176,000*l.*, in 1857 to 957,000*l.*, and in 1866 to 730,000*l.* As on other occasions, the value of securities

Comparison between the crisis of 1866 and former crises.

in 1866 fell very considerably; yet it is to be remarked, that whereas, in former cases, the greatest depreciation took place in the value of commodities, some of which had reached speculative prices, in 1866 the greatest fall was in the value of shares in banking and other public companies.[1]

Effect of the Government letter on credit at home and abroad.

Moreover, whilst the panic was more sudden and rapid, the restoration of credit was very much slower in returning than after any former crisis. The high rate of 10 per cent. was maintained for upwards of three months, so long indeed that it began to be feared that it would itself operate as a discouragement to business and as an undue indication of fear and alarm. Not only at home, but even abroad, the bankruptcy of Overend and Gurney, the issue of the Government letter, and the maintenance of this high rate of discount, had a prejudicial influence. Foreigners could not

1	PRICES		
	1865	Jan. 1, 1866	May 12, 1866
BANKS:			
Agra and Masterman . .	56 pm.	32 pm.	1 dis.
Alliance	10½ "	4½ "	10 "
Barnards'	—	Par	15 "
Bank of London . . .	22 "	13 pm.	5½ pm.
Chartered, of India . . .	15 "	4½ "	2 dis.
Chartered Mercantile, of India .	50 "	22 "	9 pm.
City	15 "	12 "	5½ "
Commercial, of India . .	7 "	5 "	No price
Hindustan	6 "	6 "	16 dis.
Imperial	14½ "	9½ "	2 pm.
Imperial Ottoman . . .	7 "	8½ "	1½ dis.
London and County . . .	65 "	59 "	47½ pm.
London Joint Stock . . .	41 "	36 "	27 "
London and Westminster . .	80 "	77 "	70 "
Merchant Bank . . .	7 "	2½ "	6 dis.
Union of London . . .	3 "	39 "	32 pm.
MISCELLANEOUS:			
Contract Corporation . .	1 dis.	9 dis.	No price
Credit Foncier . . .	3½ pm.	3½ pm.	3½ dis.
Discount Corporation . .	3 dis.	3 dis.	13 "
Financial Corporation . .	½ "	No price	No price
General Credit	3½ pm.	2½ pm.	2 dis.
Imperial Mercantile Credit .	3½ "	2½ "	10 "
International Financial . .	2½ "	1 "	2½ "
London Financial . . .	9 "	1 "	19½ "
Joint Stock Discount . .	½ dis.	1 "	Winding up
Oriental Financial . . .	4 "	8 "	9 dis.
Ottoman Financial . . .	3 "	5 "	15 "
Smith, Knight, and Co. . .	1½ "	14 dis.	15 "

understand the meaning of such a course. A vague rumour spread that the Bank of England was in danger, and a national bankruptcy almost imminent. So spread was it, that the Earl of Clarendon felt it incumbent on him to send a circular to the British embassies and legations throughout Europe accounting for the panic, and stating that 'Her Majesty's Government have no reason to apprehend that there is any general want of soundness in the ordinary trade of this country which can give reasonable ground for anxiety or alarm either in this country or abroad; they are satisfied, on the contrary, that the present crisis, peculiar and unprecedented as it is, is one of a character essentially more favourable than others which have been successfully passed through; and that all that is required is, that all classes should co-operate with the Government in endeavouring to allay needless alarm, and in acting with prudence and forbearance while so much agitation prevails. It appears to Her Majesty's Government to be of great importance, that the commercial interests abroad should be reassured in regard to what is passing in this country.' The losses produced by the crisis were enormous; the depreciation of prices and shares was very great, and the difficulty of disposing of securities almost insurmountable. But it ended at last, and matters returned to their ordinary course.

Mr. Watkins' motion for a Royal Commission negatived.

On July 31 Mr. Watkins moved in the House of Commons, 'that a humble address be presented to Her Majesty, praying that she will be graciously pleased to issue a Royal Commission directed to the investigation of the causes which have led to the late severe and protracted pressure in the money market, and to the continuance for a long period of a minimum rate of discount of 10 per cent. at the Bank of England; and also to investigate the laws affecting currency and banking in the United Kingdom.' The motion was seconded by Mr. Ackroyd, but the Government declined to accede, and after a night's discussion the question was not further resumed. There was, indeed, nothing to do in the matter. The principle of the Bank Charter Act had been inquired into over and over again. The different schools of economists and financiers had met together, and had failed to come to any agreement. The causes of the late panic were on the surface; the relief afforded had the desired effect; and nothing more could be done. Sir Stafford Northcote, as President of the Board of Trade, said, 'Admitting, as I do, that there are inconveniences in the law as it stands, and that it is desirable, if you can do it, to alter the law so far as to get rid of those inconveniences, I think those inconveniences are as nothing compared with the disaster which would result from its being held out to the world, and the commercial public, that it is possible, by any remodelling of those portions of our law, to obviate the consequences of the imprudent and unsound trading of which, unfortunately, we must admit there has been too much. If we are to go upon the principle of softening, as far as possible, the consequences of men's imprudence to themselves and others, we must beware that we do not encourage that imprudence and over-speculation which we have so much reason to lament. In the great success of our commercial enterprises there is something that is fascinating to us, and we are easily carried away by the great power we have of making our large capital do the work of a much larger capital; and therefore it is particularly necessary we should impress upon the people of England now, that if we were everywhere to unshackle the limits of enterprise, there is too much danger of enterprise rapidly growing into insane speculation. If the Government were indifferent to the sufferings of the commerce of this country, no doubt they would be greatly to blame. If they were unwilling to investigate the possible application of remedies so far as these sufferings were occasioned or aggravated by legislation, no doubt they would be greatly to be blamed. In my opinion, they would be still more to blame, if they were, by any action or language of theirs, to encourage the mischievous belief that it is possible to avert the consequences of reckless, imprudent, and unsound speculation by any measure tampering with our banking or our currency laws.'

CHAPTER IV.

BRITISH INDUSTRY AT THE PARIS UNIVERSAL EXHIBITION AND ITS RESULTS.

1867.

Industrial Progress of the United Kingdom.—Invention in the United Kingdom.—Coal, Iron, and Steel.—Products of Coal.—Gas.—Colours.—Paraffin.—Hardware.—Electro-plating.—Papier Maché.—Machinery.—Chemical Manufacture.—Cotton and Woollen Manufactures.—Industrial Competition.—Industrial Progress of Foreign Countries.—Relation of Industrial Population to Industrial Progress.—Need of extended Commercial Education.

Industrial progress of the United Kingdom.

THE holding of another International Exhibition in Paris in 1867 afforded an opportunity of comparing the latest achievements in productive industry. It was another glorious festival. It provoked great emulation. It brought forth marvels of skill; and if it cannot be said that England stood pre-eminent over all nations in many distinct classes, she was certainly second to none in the variety and extent of her products and manufactures. Truly it is well to exhibit our power on such occasions, since, as a matter of fact, we are probably the greatest of all producers. Yes, Britain is a perfect beehive of human labour. Taking space and population into account, possibly there is no other country in the world where there is so large a proportion of labourers, where harder work is gone through all the year round, and where the reward of labour is more liberal than in the United Kingdom. No industrial census has ever yet been taken, and we have but little information of the geographical allocation of the different industries; but they are fairly spread over the country. Lancashire is the seat of the cotton manufacture; the West Riding of Yorkshire, of the woollen and worsted;

Birmingham of the metal manufacture; and Newcastle and Sunderland of the great coal mines of the country. But the best evidence of the increase of industry is the large increase of the urban population. In 1801 the town population of England was in the proportion of twenty-four per cent. of the whole. In 1871 it was in the proportion of fifty-six per cent. Within the last seventy years the population of the metropolis increased 23 per cent.; that of Manchester 406 per cent.; that of Leeds, 416; that of Glasgow, 518; and of Bradford, 998 per cent.

Inventions in the United Kingdom.

But it is not enough to say that Britain is a great productive country. She is more. By her genius and inventions she has been foremost in discovering and applying many of those powers and machinery which now facilitate production all the world over.[1] With much skill and appropriateness, therefore, the British executive of the commission for the Paris Exhibition designed several of such inventions on the blinds in the windows of the Machinery Gallery. In one of them was 'Steam Machinery;' 'Watt's first Sun and Planet engine M.DCC.LXXXVIII., by which rectilinear was converted into rotary motion for the purpose of driving machinery.' In another, 'Locomotives;' 'Puffing Billy, made by William Hedley M.DCCC.XIII., to work the Wylam collieries—the first locomotive engine with smooth wheels.' In another, 'Locomotives;' the 'Rocket, made by George Stephenson M.DCCC.XXIX., gained the prize of 500*l.* in the Liverpool and Manchester railway competition.' And in another, 'Spinning Machinery;' 'first Spinning Machine, made and worked by Richard Arkwright M.DCC.LXIX.' The space allotted to British exhibitors at the Paris Universal Exhibition was only 70,000 superficial feet, the demand being for four times that amount; yet there was sufficient to indicate where the real strength of British in-

[1] The last one hundred years have been very prolific in inventions. From 1617, when patents were first registered, to 1763, there were granted in the United Kingdom only 1,245 patents. From 1763 to 1870 the number of patents has been 58,982; of which 22,230 from 1763 to 1852, and 36,752 from 1852 to 1870. From 1858 to 1868 the number of patents granted in France was 89,973; in the United States, 1852–59, 95,849; in Belgium, 1854–69, 26,836; in Austria, 1852–69, 10,418; in Italy, 1855–68, 3,284; in Prussia, 1854–69, 1,111; in Saxony, 1854–69, 2,143; in Wurtemburg, 1854–68, 1,073; in Sweden and Norway, 1854–68, 1,395.

dustry rests. Let us see what the United Kingdom can show of real achievements especially within the last fifty years.

Britain is rich in her mines. Coal and iron will always hold the very first rank in her industries, not only for their intrinsic value as sources of wealth, but for their special advantages as motive powers in all other industries. One hundred years ago there was produced in Great Britain about 6,000,000 tons of coals per annum. Since then, by improvements in the knowledge of the structure of the earth, by the general introduction of edge rails, of iron and horse-power and engine planes for the traction of trains of waggons, by the working of larger areas from the same shafts, by improved ventilation, and by other discoveries, the production of coal has increased to upwards of 100,000,000 tons a year; and, lest any fear should be entertained, that, at this rate, the coal mines might soon be exhausted, we are assured by the royal commissioners, who recently investigated on the probable quantity of coal contained in the coalfield, that there is coal enough already formed to last not less than 1,233 years longer. A most important result this, since coal is the only agent employed in the production of heat; and it has been ascertained that one pound of pure coal yields, in combining with oxygen, in combustion theoretically an energy equal to the power of lifting 10,180,000 lbs. one foot high, though the highest practical value realised is 1,200,000 lbs., or less than one-eighth of the theoretical value. In the production of coals, Great Britain is far in advance of all other countries. According to the latest accounts, whilst Great Britain produces 100,000,000 tons a year, the Zollverein produces 26,000,000 tons, the United States, 14,000,000 tons, France 12,000,000 tons, Belgium 10,000,000 tons, and Austria 5,000,000 tons. The development of the anthracite coal trade of Pennsylvania has been very marked. In 1820 the whole yield of the four great divisions of the anthracite region was 365 tons; in 1870 it was 15,849,000 tons.

Coal.

Closely attached to our collieries are the iron mines. In 1788 the iron make of Great Britain was only 68,000 tons per annum. But here, too, immense improvements have been introduced. By opening new localities, by reducing the expense of fuel, by employing the cheapest material,

Iron and Steel.

by utilising the gases and waste heat of the blast and puddling furnaces, by modifying the character of the furnaces, by economising the wasteful processes of refining, and, above all, by substituting mechanical for human labour, the production of iron has increased enormously, and has now reached 4,700,000 tons per annum of pig iron, representing a value of 12,000,000*l*., whilst, if we take the manufactured iron in bar, sheet, and rails, the value would be double or treble that amount. Within the last thirty years Prussia, France, Belgium, and the United States have made considerable progress in the manufacture of iron; yet, at this moment, Great Britain produces four times as much as either of them, and a quantity greater than that produced by all the other countries of the world put together. One of the greatest inventions of modern times is Mr. Bessemer's process of making steel. In 1851 the entire production of steel in Great Britain was 51,000 tons. In 1870 the production of Bessemer's steel alone, independently of the quantity produced by the old method, amounted to 300,000 tons, the reduction in price having been 20*l*. to 30*l*. per ton.

Products of coal gas.

Coal and iron are moreover the parents of many other industries. From coal we get two most useful products, light and colour. About one hundred and fifty years ago the attention of men of science was directed to the stream of inflammable air issuing from wells and mines in the coal districts; and several communications on the subject were presented to the Royal Society. In 1738 the Rev. Dr. Clayton gave an account of certain experiments by which he distilled gas from coal. And, in 1792, Mr. William Murdoch constructed an apparatus by which he lighted with gas his own house and office at Redruth in Cornwall. Subsequently, part of the factory of Boulton and Watt was lighted in this manner; and, in 1807, gas was first seen in its full brilliancy in the Colonnade and front of Carlton House; whence, in a few years, it spread all over the kingdom, and we may say all over the world.

Colours.

The extraction of colours from coal is still more recent. In 1825 Faraday, in an examination of the oily products separated in the compressed oil gas-holders, first obtained benzol. Several years after it was found that benzol, distilled with an excess of caustic lime, yielded a colourless volatile liquid identical with the substance previously prepared by Faraday. In 1845 Dr. Hoffman established experimentally the presence of benzol in coal-tar oil; and, in 1848, Charles Mansfield, in an experimental inquiry, carried on in Dr. Hoffman's laboratory, showed that an inexhaustible supply of this substance might be obtained from coal-tar. Benzol was then transformed into nitro-bensol and thence came aniline. The colorific tendency of aniline had long been known; but it was Mr. W. H. Perkins who first detected the industrial value, and took a patent for it in 1856. The first colour prepared by him was aniline-violet, better known as 'mauve.' In 1859 'Magenta' was obtained. Subsequently the same colour was obtained by the action of tetrachloride of tin on aniline red; a magenta dye was formed from it, and also a new product called rosaniline. Further discoveries procured additional colours, such as a beautiful crimson dye, Magdala, from naphthalin and alizarine; the tone of the colouring matter of the madder root from anthracene. Wonderful results these, when we consider how our manufacturing industry had hitherto depended on the importation of dyeing woods.

Paraffin.

Not less important is the manufacture of paraffin from coal and kindred mineral substances. In 1781 Lord Dundonald obtained a patent for a method of extracting or making tar, pitch, essential oil, volatile alkali, mineral acid from coal; and, in 1812, an oil, identical with that of petroleum, was obtained from the asphalt limestone. In 1829 Reschenbach, the proprietor of chemical works in Moravia, discovered paraffin, a wax-like substance which seemed to have no affinity for other bodies. In 1833 and 1834 Dr. Bley obtained a quantity of volatile oil and some ammoniacal products by distilling from coals; but it was not until 1847 that a petroleum spring was found in Derbyshire, and, soon after, the manufacture of paraffin from coal attained a high degree of excellence. Recently, ozokerit or mineral wax, has been discovered in a coal mine, and from it candles have been manufactured of a very luminous character.

From iron, and by means of iron, we have a hundred industries passing by the general title of hardware. The Soho factory, planted by Matthew Boulton in 1796, produced a vast variety of articles, from steam engines to buckles; but many of the most interesting branches are of very modern dates. The steel pen was known in 1809 and 1810, but was only developed as an article of industry in 1829. At the first meeting of the British Association in Birmingham in 1839 steel pens were almost unknown. Now they have almost superseded the quill. The electro-plating industry is quite new. It was the famous electrician Volta who first gave out that, when a pair, or a series, of different metals are brought into contact with a suitable liquid, a current of electricity is generated. Dr. Henry of Manchester found, that where a current of electricity passed through a conducting liquid it decomposed the ingredients of that liquid and caused their elements to be set free at the two immersed electric poles. In 1801 Dr. Wollaston wrote a paper in the 'Philosophical Transactions of the Royal Society,' where he stated that if a piece of silver in connection with a more positive metal be put into a solution of copper, the silver is coated over with the copper, which coating will stand the operation of burnishing. And, in 1805, a letter appeared in the 'Philosophical Magazine,' from Brugnatelli to Van Mons, announcing that he gilt in a complete manner two large silver medals, by bringing them into communication by means of a steel wire with the negative pole of a voltaic pile, and keeping them one after the other immersed in ammoniuret of gold newly made, well saturated. In 1834 Mr. Henry Bessemer applied copper on lead casting, so as to produce antique heads in relief for mantlepiece ornaments; and, in 1836, Messrs. Elkington took out a patent for coating copper and brass with zinc by means of an electric current generated by a piece of zinc attached to the articles by a wire, and immersed in the metallic solution with them. At the Exhibition of 1851 electro-plating was still treated as a new and untried discovery. Now, however, it is most extensively used.

Hardware electro-plating.

But the most important among metallic industries is the production of machinery, those prime movers which so contribute to the development of power, those wonderful workers so precise in their various changes and movements, remarkable alike for the embodiment of scientific principles

Machinery.

and the introduction of rigorous exactitude in their mechanical contrivances. What has machinery done for industry was well said by the able reporter on machines and tools at the International Exhibition in 1862. 'The discovery of the steam engine, capable of setting in motion an enormous quantity of manufacturing machines, and to carry their products by land or sea to every part of the world, led to a large and constant demand of mechanical constructions. The constructors were thus stimulated in their energies and ingenuity to find out new means, and the result was the large adaptation and improvement of lathes and drills, and the invention of the steam hammer, forging press, punching and shearing, planing, shaping, slotting, and other machine tools with which are now constructed our steam engines fixed or locomotive. The civil engineer, within our own recollection, compelled to build his bridges by employing the manual labour of workmen to drive the piles with hand monkeys, to pump out the water slowly with the Archimedean screw, and raise the superstructure by the aid of masons and carpenters, now drives the piles by steam power, and uses large steam pumping engines, or sinks cast-iron cylinders, and raises, by powerful cranes, the blocks of stone, or even an entire span, constructed at some iron works. The shipwright, who formerly was accustomed to shape his timbers by the tedious labour of adzes, and put them successively together, month after month, now gives the curve to his angle-iron ribs, bending them with few strokes, prepares all his iron plates by machinery, and rivets them in an expeditious manner. The roadmaker who, in past times, was entrusted with the establishment of the means of communication from town to town is now superseded by the railway engineer, who, disregarding hills, valleys, and rivers, and piercing the very mountains by machines, traces his lines from one end of the country to the other, in order to place his iron rails, upon which trains driven by engines travel at the rate of sixty miles an hour.'

In other departments of industry the change and progress have been as rapid. Quite a new industry has been introduced on the Tyne within the last forty years, in the manufacture of chemical products and processes, embracing carbonate of sodium, sulphuric acid, hydrochloric acid, and

Chemical manufacture.

bleaching powder. In 1840 the exports of alkali were only 85,200 cwt.; in 1870 they amounted to 3,857,000 cwt. It was only in 1814 that Leblanc's invention was introduced into this country, but by the skill of Mr. Charles Tennant of Glasgow, the energy of Mr. James Muspratt of Liverpool,[1] and the application of capital and industry, the chemical industry has acquired immense importance, and gives employment to a large number of people.

Cotton and woollen manufactures.

Nor have the older industries been standing still. In the cotton manufacture there has been an immense improvement. In 1790 a spinner could only produce a hank per spindle per day; in 1812 he could produce two hanks per day; and, in 1830, 2·75. The self-acting mule is a wonder of precision. The manufacture of calico is a wonder of perfection. Muslins are made superior far to the Indian muslin. The lace manufacture and the whole of the hosiery industry have been created, we may say, since 1815. In the woollen machinery the improvement has been very great. The worsted has made gigantic progress. The first spinning machinery was erected in Bradford in 1790, when a few frames were set up in a private house. Now the machinery used in Bradford is nearly as perfect as that used in Manchester. In 1834 manufactures of worsted weft and cotton warp were first introduced. In 1836 the alpaca wool was introduced, and soon after mohair, or goat's wool, from Asia Minor. The increase in every branch of the textile industry has been rapid and great, causing an immense consumption of the raw materials, and a corresponding development in the number of factories for spinning and weaving. In 1870 there were 6,158 factories, and the total value of cotton, woollen, silk, and linen merchandise and yarn exported reached 112,000,000*l.*

Industrial competition.

With an advance so marked in these and almost every branch of human industry, it was reasonably thought that England could well meet universal competition; and, had proper efforts been made to secure a full and satisfactory exhibition of such development at Paris, the position of England at the

[1] The value of the production of the Lancashire and Tyne branches of the Alkali manufacture was in 1866 4,000,000*l.*, and the quantity of salt decomposed for the purpose 351,000 tons.

Universal Exhibition there would have been undoubtedly unsurpassed. But the apathy of some of our leading manufacturers, and the difficulty of transport, interfered materially with the exhibition of some of the leading articles of British industry, and consequently it did seem as if other countries were in some cases on a higher level than England. It was on the other hand as evident, from the richness and variety of the exhibitions of other countries, that they are no longer labouring under any great difficulty in developing their resources; that with an open sea, with railways, and river and canal communication, they possess ample means for the conveyance of coals, goods, and produce, at a comparatively insignificant cost; that, under the energising influence of free trade, though as yet scarcely understood and very imperfectly adopted, continental nations have become eager for improvement; and that with them, as with us, the first effect of open competition has been an increasing attention to the economic laws of production. Their manufacturers, seeing how vain it is to linger any longer on the delusive hopes of a protective legislation, give themselves in a manly manner to master their altered positions by the exercise of augmented energy, greater economy of power and of time, and an increasing use of machinery. Capital is not only increasing everywhere, but is largely invested in commerce and manufacture, as more attractive and profitable than agriculture; keenness for trade and devotion to mercantile enterprises are being widely spread, and the love of comfort and material wealth has produced a much greater appreciation of the substantial benefits of labour and industry than has ever before existed. Nor is it possible to witness the wonderful display of machinery without perceiving that, even in that primary element of strength, Britain is no longer without formidable competitors; and that those wonderful inventions which have made this country illustrious have ceased to be her exclusive property, and have to the fullest extent become the property of the world.

Industrial progress of foreign countries.

With these facts before us we need not be surprised if, at the close of the Paris Exhibition, representations were made by the British jurors that the competition had become very keen, and that, in many cases, Britain had been excelled by other countries. Dr. Lyon Playfair wrote to Lord Taunton: 'I am sorry to say that, with very few exceptions, a singular accordance of opinion prevailed, that our country had shown little inventiveness, and made little progress in the peaceful arts of industry since 1862.' Mr. Edward Huth stated: 'Having closely examined the woollen textile fabrics during the Exhibition in 1851, and having acted as juror for these fabrics in the Exhibition of 1862, as well as at the present one in Paris, I had opportunity of comparing the progress that has been made by various countries in this important branch of industry, and I am sorry to say that, although we may still be unsurpassed in many of our productions, we no longer hold that pre-eminence which was accorded to us in the Exhibition of 1851.' Professor Frankland reported: 'As a juror in class 44 of the present Paris Exhibition, I was not only forcibly struck by the want of evidence of progress in the different branches of chemical manufactures carried on in Great Britain, but still more so at the great advance made by other nations, but more especially by Germany, France, and Switzerland, in respect of such manufactures since the year 1862, when, as a juror in the corresponding class, I had also an opportunity of comparing the chemical manufactures of different nations.' The testimony thus borne by such high authorities was the more important and useful, since it was accompanied by the expression of the opinion that the leading cause of British backwardness and want of progress was a decided defectiveness in industrial or technical education, and that the best remedy that could be applied was the introduction of extended scientific education.

Inquiries on the relation of industrial education to industrial progress.

Soon after the publication of these reports, Mr. Bernard Samuelson, M.P., wrote a letter to the Vice-President of the Committee of Council on Education, concerning technical education in various countries abroad, in which he affirmed, 'That the rapid progress of many trades abroad has been greatly facilitated by the superior technical knowledge of the directors of works everywhere, and by the comparatively advanced elementary instruction of the workers in some departments of industry.' The author of this work made a report to the Privy Council on technical, industrial, and professional instruction in Italy and other countries. The chambers of commerce reported on the trades injured by the want of a technical education; and a committee of the House of Commons was appointed for the purpose of inquiring into the provisions for giving instruction in theoretical and applied science to the industrial classes. The committee was appointed on March 24, 1868, and in July it agreed upon a report which detailed the state of scientific instruction of the foremen and workmen engaged in manufactures, the smaller manufacturers and managers, and the proprietors and managers-in-chief of larger industrial undertakings; as well as the relation of industrial education to industrial progress. 'The industrial system of the present age,' said the committee, 'is based on the substitution of mechanical for animal power; its development is due in this country to its stores of coals and of metallic ores, to our geographical position and temperate climate, and to the unrivalled energy of our population.' 'The acquisition of scientific knowledge was shown by the witnesses to be only one of the elements of an industrial education and of industrial progress. And although the pressure of foreign competition, where it existed, was considered by some witnesses to be partly owing to the superior scientific attainments of foreign manufacturers, yet the general result of the evidence proved that it was to be attributed mainly to their artistic taste, to fashion, to lower wages, and to the absence of trade disputes abroad, and the greater readiness with which handicraftsmen abroad in some trades adapted themselves to new requirements. Nearly every witness spoke of the extraordinarily rapid progress of continental nations in manufactures, and they attributed that rapidity not to the model workshops which are met with in some foreign countries, and were but an indifferent substitute for our own great factories and for those which are rising in every part of the continent, but besides other causes, to the scientific training of the proprietors and managers in France, Switzerland, Belgium, and Germany, and to the elementary instruction which is universal amongst the working population of Germany and Switzerland. All the witnesses concurred in desiring similar advantages of education for this country and were satisfied that nothing more was required and that nothing less would suffice in order that we may retain the position which England held in the van of all industrial nations.' The committee then made several recommendations with a view to the extension of scientific teaching into secondary schools, and the establishment of superior colleges of science, and schools for special scientific instruction, in the different centres of industry. And in furtherance of these recommendations the Committee of Council on Education offered additional grants to schools for science classes. Mr. Whitworth, with princely liberality, founded thirty scholarships of the annual value of 100*l*. each, to be applied for the further instruction of young men, natives of the United Kingdom, selected by open competition for their intelligence and proficiency in the theory and practice of mechanics and cognate sciences, with a view to the promotion of engineering and mechanical industry in the country. And a royal commission has been appointed to make inquiry with regard to scientific instruction and the advancement of science.

Need of extended commercial education.

But nothing has as yet been done to advance the theoretical and practical knowledge of commerce in the United Kingdom after the example of the superior institute of commerce at Antwerp, the superior school of commerce at Paris, the technical schools of commerce in Italy, and the commercial colleges in the United States of America. There is but one professorship of the principles of commerce in the whole of the United Kingdom (in King's College, London), and with it there is no endowment and no scholarship whatever. We much need some other princely benefactor or benefactors to aid the diffusion of commercial education. It is to be regretted that England, the very centre of the commerce of the world, should be so deficient in the means of elevating the character and enlarging the understanding of those engaged in trade; that our mercantile classes should alone be left to acquire, often at the cost of dearly-bought experience, the knowledge of even the first principles which govern mercantile intercourse; that the important economic phenomena exhibited in the state of the money market and foreign exchanges should to the large majority appear but enigmatic problems and be so seldom apprehended in their nature and bearing; that the instruments of commerce, such as bills of exchange, bills of lading and policies of insurance, should be mechanically handled with little or no knowledge of the signification of their different clauses; and that the laws affecting mercantile relations, such as partnership, agency, sale, shipping, and insurance, should be altogether unknown to the large majority. Manchester has her Owen College, for which sumptuous provision has been made by her intelligent and public-spirited manufacturers; Newcastle has her College of Science; and the Merchant Company has recently endowed a Chair of Commercial and Public Economy and Mercantile Law in the University of Edinburgh. It is much to be desired that in connection with the effort to promote technical instruction for industrial pursuits our public companies and our merchant princes should provide for the encouragement of technical instruction for commerce and banking.

CHAPTER V.

INTERNATIONAL WEIGHTS, MEASURES, AND COINS.

Need of Uniformity in Weights, Measures, and Coins.—Memorial of the Society of Arts for a Uniform System.—Decimalisation of the Coinage.—Formation of the International Decimal Association.—Introduction of the Metric System of Weights and Measures.—International Coinage.—Practical Achievements.

Need of uniformity in weights, measures, and coins.

BESIDES imparting a stimulus to industrial education, the international exhibitions have from the first directed attention to the importance of securing uniformity in the weights, measures, and coins of all countries. For purposes of commerce it would be decidedly convenient were one common system established. In ancient times the Latin tongue was the universal language of science. Amidst the jargon of the many hordes of barbarians who invaded Europe on the destruction of the Roman empire, men of science could speak to one another in a language common to them all. And when we endeavoured to solve the problems of the industrial and scientific discoveries with which these great exhibitions abounded, the want came home to all of us of some ready means for mastering those instruments of calculation which enter so closely into the conception and execution of the works of art in every country. The evil arising from the great confusion in the weights, measures, and coins in use in all states had long been experienced. Men of science of all countries most liberally deposit fruitful seeds of thought and discovery in their memoirs and transactions that they may become the heritage of mankind, yet though reduced to the certainty of numbers they often fail to become fully available from the discordant method pursued in their exposition. With the great facility of communication by land and sea, with thought flashing through the air and penetrating the very depths of the ocean, and with a liberal commercial policy largely promoting the interchange of produce and manufacture between different countries, we must regret that we have a want of agreement in the instruments of exchange, which must arrest progress and in many cases absolutely prevent the increase of trade.

Memorial of the Society of Arts for a uniform system.

Happily the Society of Arts, whilst still fresh in the recollection of the glorious exhibition of 1851, seized the moment when public attention was given in this country to the decimalisation of the coinage for generalising a question which had hitherto been apprehended solely from a national aspect, and from that moment the attainment of universal uniformity in such instruments of exchange ceased to be theoretical and utopian, and received the countenance of thoughtful and wise men of all countries. In their memorial to the Lords Commissioners of her Majesty's Treasury in the year 1853 the Society of Arts, after urging the importance of a system of decimal coins, weights, and measures in advancing the arts, manufactures, and commerce of the country, pointed out how the growing intelligence and education of every people were sweeping away those feelings of personal antipathy which formerly existed, and how much the beneficent result would be increased by facilitating international relations; that a uniformity in weights, measures, and coins would be of the utmost importance to commerce, and in weights and measures specially would greatly facilitate scientific research. They submitted, as a matter of grave consideration, whether, in introducing a change to a decimal system of coins, weights, and measures, some arrangements might not be made with neighbouring nations for the adoption of a uniform system throughout the world; that sooner or later such a system would be loudly called for by different nations, and the inconvenience of a second change might be obviated by a little judicious forethought; that it was worthy of the country which had inaugurated unrestricted commerce and unrestricted navigation, and which exerted by its exhibitions and its policy the most unrestricted competition, to make the first advances towards such a glorious result; and that there was nothing incapable of realization in the idea, since several nations on the continent of Europe have already a common coinage, and the metric system of weights and measures is still more widely adopted.

Decimalisation of the coinage.

The decimalisation of the coinage had for a considerable time been the subject of discussion. The commissioners for the restoration of the standards of weights and measures in 1840 summed up the advantages of it as follows: 'In our opinion the scale of binary subdivision is well adapted to the small retail transactions which seldom become the subject of written accounts, and which constitute a large part of the daily transactions in every country. The decimal scale, however, appears to us to be by far the most convenient for all transactions which become the subject of written accounts, and for all transactions of whatever kind in which great numbers of weights and measures are combined by addition or multiplication.' In 1847 Sir John Bowring moved for an address to the Crown in favour of the issue of silver pieces of the value respectively of one-tenth and one-hundredth part of a pound as a step to the complete introduction of the decimal system. And consequently the florin or two-shillings piece was soon after put into circulation. In 1853, on the motion of Mr. William Brown, a committee of the House of Commons was appointed to take into consideration the practicability and advantages or otherwise that would arise from adopting the decimal system of coinage. And the committee reported that there was a concurrent testimony to the effect that the adoption of a decimal system would lead to greater accuracy, that it would simplify accounts, would diminish the labour of calculations to the extent of one-half and in some cases four-fifths; and by facilitating the comparison between the coinage of this country and other countries that have adopted the decimal system would tend to the convenience of all those who are engaged in exchange operations of travellers and others. The committee then recommended the retention of the pound as the unit, but the division of the same into ten florins, ten cents, and ten mils. The country, however, was not prepared for this measure and no step was taken on the subject till 1855, when Mr. William Brown moved resolutions expressing satisfaction at the issue of the florin and recommending the issue of silver coins to represent the value of one-hundredth part of a pound, and copper coins to represent the one-thousandth part of a pound, to be called cents and mils respectively. But the resolution in favour of the florin was only carried by a majority of 135 to 56, and that which advocated further progress in that direction had to be withdrawn. The next step was the appointment of a royal commission, three in number, to consider how far it might be practicable and advisable to introduce the principle of decimal divisions into the coinage of the United Kingdom, but no good result came from the commission. The commissioners disagreed: one (Lord Monteaglo) withdrew from it, and the conclusions of Lord Overstone and Mr. Hubbard were unfavourable to any further advance.

Formation of the International Decimal Association.

In 1855 an International Association was established for the promotion of one uniform decimal system of weights, measures, and coins in all countries. And this association, after studying the comparative claims of the different systems of weights and measures in use throughout the world, resolved in favour of the metric on account of its scientific and international character. In 1862 a committee of the House of Commons was appointed on the motion of the late Mr. William Ewart to consider the practicability of adopting a single and uniform system of weights and measures, with a view not only to the benefit of our international trade but to facilitate our trade and intercourse with foreign countries. And the labours of this committee are memorable. With Richard Cobden among its members, animated by the general influence of the international exhibition, and aided by witnesses of the highest eminence from different countries, an international character was imparted to the whole of its proceedings, which could not fail to influence the final report. Accordingly the Committee recommended that the use of the metric system should be rendered legal in the United Kingdom, that the government should sanction its use in the levying of customs duties and in public contract, and that the gram should be used as a weight for foreign letters and books at the post office. And an act[1] was passed

[1] 27 & 28 Vict. c. 117.

providing that, notwithstanding anything contained in any act of parliament to the contrary, no contract or dealing should be deemed to be invalid or open to objection on the ground that the weights or measures expressed or referred to in such contract or dealing are weights or measures of the metric system, or on the ground that decimal subdivisions of legal weights and measures, whether metric or otherwise, are used in such contract or dealing. A permissive measure is doubtless insufficient, but sooner or later we may anticipate the entire substitution of the metric system for the present practice. Considerable progress has, also been made regarding international coinage. On December 23, 1865, a monetary treaty was concluded between France, Belgium, Italy, and Switzerland, whereby their respective coinage, which was already in the main uniform, was rendered legal in all the states so agreeing. And in 1867, on the occasion of the Universal Exhibition in Paris, two congresses were held for the extension of the principles of such a convention, one at the Palais de l'Industrie and the other at the ministry for foreign affairs. Both these conferences agreed upon the general adoption of one standard of coinage, and that gold, on the same fineness of nine-tenths fine, on the decimal division, and on the adoption of such a system of coinage having direct analogy to the monetary system of the convention. But when the question came to be considered in England, and the proposal of reducing the pound sterling from 113·001 grains to an equivalent of a 25 franc piece or 112·008, was discussed in all its bearings, the difficulty appeared insurmountable, and a royal commission appointed for the purpose reported against the change.

International coinage.

Whatever difficulty may yet exist to the full realization of a uniform system of weights, measures, and coins, it must be allowed that much has already been accomplished in that direction. The metric system of weights and measures is in compulsory use in countries with an aggregate population of 186,000,000, comprising France, Holland, Belgium, Greece, Spain, Cuba, Porto Rico, Portugal and her colonies, Italy, Roumania, Switzerland, Chili, Ecuador, Uruguay, Brazil, Mexico, the Argentine Confederation, New Granada, and Peru. And in addition other countries with about 200,000,000 more people

Practical achievements.

have partially or in a permissive manner, including the whole of our possessions in India and in the United States of America, and the United Kingdom, adopted the same system. In respect to the coinage also considerable advance has been made towards unification. Whilst France, Belgium, Italy, and Switzerland, have by the monetary convention of 1865 agreed upon one uniform system, Austria, Spain, and Portugal are making arrangements for adapting their coinage to that of the convention. It is no exaggeration to say that at this moment 400,000,000 persons have come to an agreement upon one system of weights and measures and 100,000,000 as to one system of coinage also. Viewed from the light of social and commercial requirements we may lament the slow progress of these economic reforms, yet when we compare periods sufficiently distant there is reason to be thankful that so much has been achieved, and that the barbarism of so many conflicting customs is gradually giving place to a scientific and uniform system.

CHAPTER VI.

COMPARATIVE PROGRESS OF COMMERCIAL NATIONS.

Causes of relative Progress.—Progress in the Century.—France.—Belgium.—Holland.—Russia.—The Hanse Towns.—Prussia and the Zollverein.—Austria.—Spain.—Portugal.—Italy.—Switzerland.—Greece.—Turkey.—Morocco.—Persia.—China.—Siam.—Japan.—United States.—Brazil and other South American States.—British Exports.—The future of International Trade.

A COMPARISON of the relative progress of nations in commerce and industry will show that it is not any one element alone that will place a state in a position of decided superiority. Causes of relative progress. The possession of valuable resources, whether mineral or agricultural, a favourable geographical situation, easy means of communication, energy of character, and even the strength of race, have considerable influence in determining the commercial position of different states. England has iron and coal, France has considerable agricultural wealth, Italy is wonderfully well situated, Germany has all the strength of the Anglo-Saxon race. Nevertheless, whilst England exports produce and manufactures at the rate of 6*l*. 3*s*. 2*d*. per head, France exports at the rate of 2*l*. 18*s*. 8*d*. and Italy at the rate of 1*l*. 4*s*. 8*d*. per head. In truth, the possession of material advantages is not nearly so important as the ability of rendering them subservient to our purposes. Coal and iron were long known to exist in certain localities in England, but it was only when Watt's steam power facilitated mining operations that these minerals became really available. It was northern energy and activity that awakened into life the dormant races of Asia and Africa. Nations are often capable of great exploits. Holland wrested from the sea the soil on which her cities are built. Italian skill perforated Mont Cenis. French enterprise constructed the Suez Canal. Yet in a long and keen competition Britain excelled all nations in trade and navigation.

We have seen what the state of trade was in different countries one hundred years ago. Since then, Australia and New Zealand have been discovered, extensive territories in America have been peopled and cultivated, many new states have been created, valuable powers of nature have been discovered and utilised, many new products have acquired a commercial value, science and art have made wonderful strides, and international exchange has been immensely promoted. What nation has benefited most by these changes? Alas that what a bountiful Providence has bestowed with no sparing hand should have been so often wasted and abused! How much more extensive would the traffic of the world be at this moment but for the obstructions wantonly thrown in the way by war, ignorance, and a most erroneous commercial policy. Nearly every nation has had a share in these sad shortcomings. Only whilst many of them have remained behind helpless and prostrate, Britain most successfully triumphed over all difficulties.

Progress in the century.

France is not an apt scholar in the school of experience. At the commencement of our history we found her in 1763 humiliated and vanquished, closing a wretched war by the cession of some of her valued possessions. Sullen and discontented, she gave herself to industry and trade; but soon after an opportunity offered for retrieving her political fortune, and in 1776 we saw her taking side with the American colonies, and creating another general war. The peace of Versailles of 1783 placed her in a somewhat better condition, but scarcely half a dozen years elapsed when in 1789 she was in a ferment of revolution. From that moment to the conclusion of the Treaty of Vienna in 1815, a period exceeding a quarter of a century, France was fearfully distracted at home, and abroad in actual war with nearly every state. The restoration of the Bourbons brought to her no prosperity, and their reign was suddenly arrested by the revolution of 1830. Louis-Philippe was for a time prosperous, but again the revolution of 1848 stopped progress. Then came the short period of the republic, with its anomalies and its *coupe d'état*, which opened the way for another empire in 1852, during which it seemed as if France was tired of the vain pursuit of glory, and that, taking

France.

the happy motto *L'empire c'est la paix* as her guide, she was disposed to give herself in earnest to recover what she had lost. But jealousy of the aggrandisement of neighbouring states corroded her very heart, and in 1870, despite all entreaties and against the judgment of the civilised world, she once more unsheathed the sword against Germany, to retire from the contest shattered, defeated, and impoverished. How could commerce and industry advance under conditions so unfavourable? In 1815 the exports of France were not more than in 1787. Up to 1830 the trade of France continued in a very depressed state, nor did it improve much whilst labouring under a most restrictive tariff. In 1855 Napoleon began to relax somewhat the French commercial policy, and from that moment the progress of France became rapid, so that in the ten years from 1858 to 1868 the exports of France increased from 75,000,000*l.* to 132,000,000*l.* or at the rate of 7½ per cent. per annum. France is an extensive country placed in the very centre of Europe, bordering on the ocean and the Mediterranean, and surrounded by the most civilised and advancing nations of the world. She has a rich soil, a people skilful and fertile in resources, and she possesses many industries which are peculiarly her own, and in which she has scarcely any rival. She has about 14,000 miles of railway, and she has a considerable river and canal navigation. What she requires is peace and a sound commercial legislation. Let her have this blessing and she will speedily regain all she has lost. Let her be for ever turbulent or at war, or let her once more adopt a system of protection and restrictions, and her decadence is certain and irremediable.[1]

Belgium.

Belgium was not an independent state in 1763. It was only in 1831 that her separation from the Netherlands was effected, and in 1839 that her neutrality was guaranteed; but her progress ever since has been steady and extensive, and her institutions have granted sufficient encouragement to labour and industry. The British Consul at Antwerp reported that public opinion in Belgium was favourable to the principles

[1] It does not augur well for the future of France that on February 2, 1872, the National Assembly passed a resolution authorising the government to give notice of withdrawal in convenient time from the treaties with England and Belgium.

of free trade; that in 1861 the Antwerp chamber of commerce put forth views of a most advanced character, and passed a vote in favour of the entire abolition of customs duties; that in 1864 the Conseil supérieur de l'Industrie et du Commerce, composed of delegates from all the chambers of commerce in the country, resolved, 'That the laws relating to customs and excise should always be in harmony with each other, but inasmuch as the absolute suppression of customs duties would exercise a more energetic action upon the development of public wealth than any measure of mere reform, however liberal, it is desirable that the government should constantly tend towards the attainment of that object;' and also that the Customs Reform Association was gaining favour in the country. Between 1858 and 1868 the exports of Belgian produce increased from 15,000,000*l.* to 26,000,000*l.*, or at the rate of 7½ per cent. per annum. France, Britain, Holland, and the Zollverein are the countries with which Belgium has the largest trade. Belgium has about 1700 miles of railway; her mineral resources are considerable and her textile industries of great value.

Holland has always preserved her character for prudence and caution. Whilst other countries have been disturbed by strikes, she has been allowed to work out steadily her own problems of internal reforms and colonial management. At home her trade is prosperous, but in Java and Surinam it has long remained in a most unsatisfactory condition, arising principally from the monopoly of the Nederlandsche Handel Maatschappij, or Dutch trading company. On this subject the Rotterdam chamber of commerce, in May 1868, petitioned that in its judgment 'it was high time for the state to cease to be the principal house directly engaged in trade, and for the trade itself to undertake the import of colonial wares.' Of all colonial systems, the Dutch, which monopolises for the state the commercial resources of the colony, is by far the most objectionable. And what has been the result? Java and Surinam have remained stationary whilst all the world has been progressing. From 1857 to 1867 the export of Dutch produce from Holland increased from 19,000,000*l.* to 28,000,000*l.* or at the rate of 4¾ per cent. per

Holland.

annum. One fourth of the imports and exports of Holland are from and to Great Britain. The imports and exports of Java, Madura, and Sumatra are valued in all at 10,000,000*l.* The causes of the prosperity of Holland in olden times have been the subject of many inquiries. In an able paper on the statistics of that kingdom Mr. Samuel Brown said: 'As the earliest champions of civil and religious freedom, and affording a home from intolerance and oppression, when the rest of Europe was nowhere safe from religious persecution, the Hollanders always had our cordial sympathy and aid. Having won their land from the ocean, they have only been able to maintain it against returning destruction by the most incessant patience, vigilance, and skill; and yet on several occasions have given proofs of the greatest unselfishness and most devoted patriotism, by voluntarily sacrificing the results of years of labour and expense and again submerged large portions of the soil rather than allow the invader a footing thereon. By their industry, honesty, and enterprise they carried on a commerce with distant lands unrivalled at the time, and had their ships and traders on every sea. They still hold populations with colonies nearly six times their own in number, with a large and increasing trade; and having so many points in common with this nation, and so many claims on our good will, we cannot but be gratified to notice the visible signs of prosperity and progress which these brief statistical notices record.'

Russia is an empire of enormous area, and has an extensive productive power; what she wants are better means of communication, and freedom of intercourse with other countries. The former she is endeavouring to supply by the construction of many lines of railways, the latter she must obtain by the introduction of a more liberal commercial policy. Moscow, not St. Petersburg, is the centre of the Russian railway *réseau.* From Moscow two great lines will proceed west and north-west to the Gulf of Finland and the Baltic; two other lines north and north-east to the Volga and Siberia; and other lines southward to Astrachan on the Caspian Sea, and to Tsaritsyn on the Don. The length of these new lines with those already open will be about 10,000 miles, and there is every prospect that the works will prove most remunerative, from the immen-

Russia.

sity of the internal traffic. The customs tariff of Russia is in course of constant improvement. The tariffs of 1850, 1857, and the more recent changes, have been liberal and progressive. The statistics of the Russian trade give us the amount of imports and exports by sea only. Besides these, however, large transactions are carried on by land, mainly with China, by barter, with which she has several treaties. The emancipation of the serfs was a reform of the greatest importance, and will yet go far to vivify Russian life, and to render the place of Russia in Europe and Asia more and more conspicuous. Meanwhile, the progress of Russian commerce is considerable. Between 1857 and 1867 the exports have increased from 27,000,000*l.* to 39,000,000*l.*, or at the rate of 4½ per cent. per annum. The commerce of Asiatic Russia bears a small proportion to that of European Russia, the proportion being as 4 to 35. Among the European nations with which Russia carries on foreign trade, Prussia and Britain hold the first rank; and among the Asiatic, Bokhara and China.

Norway, Sweden, and Denmark.

The three Scandinavian States, Norway, Sweden, and Denmark, have not an extensive trade. The principal productions of Norway are fish and iron; of Sweden, oats and timber; of Denmark, grain, hides, and oil cake. Their imports and exports were valued, in 1867, at 9,000,000*l.* for Norway, and at 14,000,000*l.* for Sweden; Denmark giving no valuation for her trade. Norway has a large tonnage of merchant ships; from about 300,000 tons in 1850, her tonnage increased to upwards of 1,000,000 tons in 1870, and her annual receipts from freights is considerable.

The Hanse Towns.

The Hanse Towns are no more. They have been incorporated with the North German Confederation. Nevertheless, Hamburg, Bremen, and Lubeck will ever be important outposts for the continent of Europe, and their traffic continues undiminished. In 1858 the value of imports to Hamburg was 30,000,000*l.*, in 1867 it reached 54,000,000*l.*, the increase being at the rate of 8 per cent. per annum. The Marine Insurance Association has largely increased its transactions, which amounted in 1868 to 615,000,000MB. The Bank of Hamburg or the North German Bank, and the Union Bank, transact an enormous business. And with the abolition of guilds and her accession to the Zollverein, Hamburg bids fair to increase still more in commercial importance. In 1867 Hamburg and Bremen had a commercial marine of 475,000 tons.

Of other parts of the German Union, or Zollverein, the commercial information is very imperfect, since no definite data can be gathered either from the quantities of produce imported or exported, or from the amount of customs revenue. The Prussian ports have considerable navigation, but the land traffic is even more important than the maritime, and of that the accounts are very imperfect. The German Union had in 1868 an aggregate customs revenue of 3,500,000*l.*

Prussia and the Zollverein.

Few countries have passed through so many vicissitudes as Austria, and few have suffered more from the privileges of the nobles, the system of guilds, the extended monopolies and the restrictive tariff. And it is only recently that she has inaugurated a more liberal commercial policy which found expression in the treaties she concluded with the United Kingdom, Prussia, France, Holland, Belgium, and Switzerland. As we have seen, a treaty of commerce was concluded with Austria on December 16, 1865, by which Britain conceded to Austria the same advantages which were conceded to French subjects by the French treaty, and to the Zollverein by the treaty of 1865, and Austria bound herself to regulate her tariff in such a way that the duties to be levied on British produce should not exceed 25 per cent. from January 1, 1867, and 20 per cent. from January 1, 1870. The progress of Austrian commerce of late years has been considerable. Between 1858 and 1868 the increase in the exports was from 26,000,000*l.* to 43,000,000*l.*, being at the rate of 6½ per cent. per annum. In 1868 Austria had 3,900 miles of railways, and her resources are considerable, but with a more certain political position she will afford an excellent field for the investment of capital.[1]

Austria.

Spain has undergone many changes in her government and institutions, and within the last few years she has entered on

[1] It is much to be regretted that by the compulsory conversion of the English issue of bonds into internal bonds and the imposition of income tax upon them, Austria has forfeited her credit in the London Stock Exchange, and Austrian securities are excluded from the official list.

a career of progress and prosperity. Her policy is no longer of a paternal government. The programme of her new administration was well expounded by Señor Figuerola in 1868, in these words: 'The creation and maintenance of industry must not be based on privileges which, containing the leaven of injustice, recoil in the long run on their possessors; nor yet upon aid from the state, at the bottom of which there is always a marked principle of communism. They must appeal to other and wider spheres of activity, and if they are in harmony with the financial laws governing human society, it is there, and there alone, that reliance must be placed by those who apply their activity to the production of wealth. This, then, must be the work of the revolution if it is to produce lasting results instead of evaporating in vain boasts and barren declamations: to compel individuals to cast off the yoke of state protection and exercise their own strength and intelligence, relying on the study of natural phenomena and the utilisation of natural conditions for success in enterprise. Government must, step by step, reduce the sphere of action, enlarging that of the individual, who must be taught to respect his labour and himself.' Down to 1866 there was but little increase in the commerce of Spain. From 1856 to 1866 the exports increased from 10,000,000*l.* to 12,000,000*l.*, being at the rate of 2 per cent. per annum.

Spain.

Portugal has made some progress towards a sound system of commercial legislation; and, after many years' efforts, she has freed the Douro wine trade from the incubus of a pernicious monopoly. Portugal as well as Spain would go further in the way of reducing their tariff, on condition that Britain would admit their wines at a uniform duty of 1*s.* per gallon. But the British government could not endanger the large revenue derived from spirits by the introduction of wines of from 30 to 40 degrees of strength at so low a duty, and the negotiation failed. There is no account of the whole exports of Portugal; but those of Lisbon, in 1868, amounted to about 2,000,000*l.*, having somewhat declined since 1865.

Portugal.

Italy has large resources. She has an extensive coastage and many excellent harbours on the Mediterranean and the Adriatic. Her liberal policy has invigorated every institution, and given new life to Italian commerce and manu-

Italy.

factures; and though as yet the rate of progress has not been considerable, there is a good prospect of a constant and increasing development. 'We have full faith,' said Count Cavour, in the pages of the *Risorgimento*, 'in Italian industry, not only on account of the beneficent reforms already introduced, not only on account of those reforms in the customs laws which tend to the improvement of our internal and external relations, but principally because we trust to see reawakening in our people—animated by a generous and united spirit, and called to new political life—that skill which made their illustrious ancestors powerful and rich in the middle ages, when the Florentine and Lombard manufactures, and the ships of Genoa and Venice had no rivals in Europe. Yes, we have faith in the skill, the energy, the enlightened power of the Italians, much more likely to increase commerce and industry than any legislative protection or unjust privileges.' In 1868 the exports of Italian produce amounted to 31,500,000*l.*, and the navigation of Italian ports was 7,200,000 tons, besides a coasting trade amounting to 11,000,000 tons. The commercial relations of Italy will probably benefit largely from her having once more become the point of contact between the East and West and the channel for the conveyance of the rich products of India and China to the Mediterranean and Adriatic states.

Switzerland has a considerable trade. Up to the end of last Switzerland. century her foreign trade was confined to dealings, on a very limited scale, with some neighbouring countries. Now she trades with all the world. Without ports, hemmed in by powerful states and shut up by mountains, she is still making a wonderful progress. By the introduction of commercial and political freedom, by habits of thrift and perseverance, by taking advantage of the inexhaustible water power always at her disposal, and by the introduction of railways, she has overcome all difficulties, and she has been able to give great stimulus to her industries. The special trade of Switzerland has been estimated at 35,000,000*l.*, but no official account is given of the value of her imports and exports.

The commerce of Greece in 1865 did not exceed 3,200,000*l.* of imports, and 1,500,000*l.* of exports of domestic Greece. produce.

Turkey is an agglomeration of states and pashaliks, with not many elements of cohesion among themselves. Scarcely any country possesses a position so favourable and productions so varied and valuable for trade as these provinces; but their government is weak, their resources are undeveloped, their administration is inimical to the progress of trade. Our traders are protected by the exceptional method of a consular jurisdiction, but that only marks the insufficiency and untrustworthiness of the Turkish administration of justice. Of the trade of the Turkish empire there is no collective account. At Constantinople the navigation is large. In 1864 the tonnage entered and cleared exceeded 7,000,000 tons, and many lines of steam vessels traded to that port. Smyrna has imports and exports reaching to 6,000,000*l.* The trade of Erzeroum is valued at 2,000,000*l.*, besides a considerable transit trade with the Caucasian provinces and Persia. Aleppo has imports and exports valued at 2,600,000*l.* Salonica has a trade of nearly equal importance. Then there are Bagdad, Bussorah, and Trebizond; besides Roumelia, Epirus, Rhodes, the Sporades Islands, including the celebrated Patmos; above all, the Moldo-Wallachian kingdom, whose trade is valued at upwards of 10,000,000*l.*; and Egypt, whose imports alone are valued at 9,000,000*l.* That Turkey may soon become progressive, commercial, and civilised, must be the desire of all Europe. Turkey.

Morocco has many natural advantages—a hardy, patient, and industrious population, a climate healthy and temperate, and a most fruitful soil. Tangiers has a trade amounting to nearly 2,000,000*l.* Dar-el-Baida, Laraiche, Mazagar, Mogador, Rabat, Taffee, and Tetuan have each many branches of industry, and their exports consist of beans, canary seed, linseed, Indian corn, and fruit; yet the total value of them is not very considerable. Morocco.

The external trade of Persia is given at about 4,000,000*l.* Her exports to Astrachan and Georgia consist in fruits, furs, and caviare. A considerable quantity of opium is produced in Persia, and she also exports raw silk. The British consul reports that, rich in minerals, capable of producing grain, cotton, silk, and wool to any extent, and possessing Persia.

immense forests whence the finest timber might readily be obtained, what Persia requires is internal security and a good currency.

China. China is largely increasing in commercial importance. In 1848, there were only Canton, Amoy, and Shanghae open as treaty ports. In 1868, besides these ports, Foo-chow-foo, Ningpo, Takow, Tamsui, Kui-Kiang, Hankow, Che-foo, Tien-tsin, and New Chang have been opened for traffic. In 1868, the imports of the treaty ports amounted to 22,000,000*l*., and their exports to about 21,000,000*l*.

Siam. The exports of Siam are considerable. The value of the cargoes entered at Bangkok in 1869 was 752,000*l*., and of cargoes cleared, 1,000,000*l*.

Japan. The trade of Japan is fast developing. The junk trade is extensive. Osaka and Hiogo have been recently opened to foreign trade, and Yokohama, Nagara, Ki, and Hakodate are becoming of great commercial value. With silk and tea for their outward freights, with new and extensive markets for their imports, and with a supply of coal at hand for their steamers, there appears to be no reason why the foreign settlements at Osaka and Hiogo should not become as large and thriving as those in any other part of Japan.

United States. The United States have made a rapid and wonderful progress. In 1800 the population of the United States was 5,300,000; in 1830 it was 12,866,000; and in 1870 it reached 38,000,000. The annual value of manufactures in 1820 was 12,553,000*l*.; in 1860 it was estimated at 400,000,000*l*. The tonnage of shipping belonging to the United States in 1800 was 972,000 tons; in 1830, 1,191,000 tons; in 1860, 5,354,000 tons; and in 1869 the tonnage amounted to 4,144,000 tons. The imports into the United States in 1800 amounted to 18,250,000*l*.; in 1830 to 14,125,000*l*.; in 1860 to 72,432,000*l*.; and in 1869 to 86,980,000*l*. The exports from the United States in 1800 were 14,194,000*l*.; in 1830 14,769,000*l*.; in 1860, 80,024,000*l*.; and in 1869, 59,573,000*l*. The value of real and personal property in 1810 was estimated at 376,000,000*l*.; in 1830 at 752,800,000*l*.; in 1860 at 2,825,000,000*l*. The abolition of slavery and the insurrection of the Southern States are great landmarks in the recent history of the United States, and if the high tariff, the enormous financial indebtedness, the reverses in banking and currency which became necessary consequences of so great a revolution, have checked for a time the development of their unbounded riches, we can well trust the shrewdness, common sense, and soundness of mind of the American people for a speedy return to that state of enviable freedom from burdens and unclogged industry under which they made their first and lasting great leap into commercial prosperity.

Brazil and other South American States.

Among the States of South America Brazil holds the chief rank, her imports in 1869 amounting to 19,000,000*l.* and her exports to 23,000,000*l.* Bahia is a most important commercial port, and so is Para. The navigation of the river Amazon is now free to all nations. The Argentine Republic has a trade amounting to 10,000,000*l.*, the exports of Buenos Ayres consisting principally in wool and hides. The port of Monte Video in Uruguay has a trade of about 10,000,000*l.* Guatemala, San Salvador, Guayaquil, and New Granada have each considerable traffic. The Isthmus of Panama is of great commercial value as the connecting link between the Atlantic and the Pacific Ocean. Mexico has not much trade, but her mining resources are considerable.

British exports.

If we now add to these countries the trade of the British Colonies, including chiefly the North American and the West Indies, Australia and British India, whose aggregate exports amount to upwards of 100,000,000*l.*, and, above all, the exports of the United Kingdom, which in 1870 amounted to 199,000,000*l.*, we find that the total exports of all nations amount to an aggregate of upwards of 850,000,000*l.*, more than one-third of which is exported by British traders from the United Kingdom and British India.[1]

[1] The progress of the British colonies other than India has been considerable, but by no means uniform. The North American group, comprising Ontario and Quebec, New Brunswick, Nova Scotia, Prince Edward Island, Newfoundland, British Columbia, and Vancouver's Island, with an area of 632,000 square miles, and a population in 1869 of 4,100,000, had in 1827–31 average annual imports and exports of the value of 7,000,000*l.*, and in 1869 of 29,800,000*l.*, showing an annual increase of 27½ per cent. The West India group, with an area of 12,681 square miles, and a population in 1861 of 934,000, had in 1832–36 imports and exports averaging 12,000,000*l.* per annum, and in 1869 9,000,000*l.*, showing an annual decrease of about 1 per cent. The African group, consisting of Natal, Cape

Large, however, as is the present amount of international exchange, we cannot say that it has in any manner reached its ultimate extent. *The future of international trade.* Assuming the population of the world to be considerably over one thousand million human beings, that at the very minimum they will require food and clothing to the value of ten pounds per annum each, and that not more than half that amount is produced in the same countries in which the consumption takes place, the aggregate exports would need to be above five thousand millions worth of produce and goods, whereas at present they are considerably under one thousand millions. If the productive power of the world is great, the consuming power is still greater. The field of international commerce present and future is very vast, and what we see of its progress gives but a very imperfect idea of its probable expansion. There is one great hindrance to the progress of international commerce—it is the maintenance of customs duties as part of the public revenue. In the United Kingdom the customs in 1870 contributed about 20,000,000*l.* to a revenue of 70,000,000*l.*, or about 28 per cent. within the largest proportion contributed in any country in Europe previous, at least, to the late Franco-German war. In Russia the customs contributed 6 per cent.; in Holland 4 per cent.; in Belgium 7 per cent.; in Spain 8 per cent.; in Austria 5 per cent. It is for the United Kingdom to take the lead in the great movement of abolishing for ever this financial obstacle to the commerce of the world, and her example will give a fresh stimulus to the extension of a liberal commercial policy.

of Good Hope, Gold Coast, Sierra Leone, and Gambia, of 223,000 square miles, and a population of about 900,000, had in 1827–31 an average trade of 900,000*l.*, and in 1869 of 6,150,000*l.*, showing an increase at the rate of 14 per cent. per annum. And the Australian group, comprising New South Wales, Victoria, South Australia, Western Australia, Tasmania, New Zealand and Queensland, with a united area of 2,542,000 square miles, and a population in 1869 of 1,817,000, had in 1827–31 an average annual trade of about 1,000,000*l.*, and in 1869 of 63,000,000*l.*, showing the wonderful increase of 150 per cent. per annum. Including the Straits Settlements, Ceylon, Mauritius, Labuan, Hong Kong, Bermuda, Honduras, British Guiana, Gibraltar, Malta, the British colonies have a total area of 3,571,000 square miles, and a population of 9,600,000, whilst British India alone has 963,929 square miles, and a population of 151,000,000.

CHAPTER VII.

STATE OF BRITISH COMMERCE.

1870.

Triumphs of Commerce.—Progress of British Commerce.—British Imports.—British Exports.—Direction of Exports.—Navigation, Banking, and Currency.—Insurance.—The Home Trade.—Increase of Property.—Use of Wealth in the promotion of Science and Art.—Use of Wealth in works of Benevolence.—True Source of British Prosperity.—Influence of Commerce on the Peace of the World.

Triumphs of commerce.

WE have now concluded our view of the various circumstances which have had a direct or indirect influence on British commerce, from the advent of the great mechanical inventions in the cotton manufacture to the present time, a period of about one hundred years of incessant activity, and of almost superhuman effort in the promotion of material progress. What has commerce done for England—ay, for the world—during this century? It has stimulated the active powers of man, and developed to an almost unlimited extent the resources of nature; it has promoted enterprise, discovery, and inventions; it has advanced agriculture, mining, and fisheries; it has made the sea the highway of nations, and rendered rivers, canals, roads, railways, and telegraphs instruments of intercourse between the most distant states. Ignorance, prejudice, and wars have thwarted its progress, yet, with its enlightening, diffusive, and pervasive power commerce stretched its action and influence over all regions. From being the humble vocation of the few it succeeded in attracting the attention of whole communities, and where once it was held in contempt as a sordid and mean occupation, the time has come when commerce has become itself a power which exercises a mighty influence on the politics of nations, and in a great measure controls the conduct of states.

The increase of commerce in the United Kingdom during the last one hundred years is something wonderful. In 1763 the population probably was 10,000,000. In 1870 it was 31,000,000, showing an increase of 326 per cent. But if the population has increased three times, the imports increased thirty times, from 10,000,000*l.* to 303,000,000*l.*; the exports nearly twenty times, from 13,000,000*l.* to 244,000,000*l.*; the navigation of ports fifteen times, from 1,500,000 tons to 36,000,000 tons; and the shipping belonging to the kingdom fourteen times, namely, from 550,000 tons to 7,100,000 tons. The whole trade of the kingdom actually doubled itself during the last fifteen years, from 260,000,000*l.* in 1855 to 547,000,000*l.* in 1870. This is the rate at which British commerce has been increasing; but large figures give an imperfect idea of their meaning. A trade amounting to about 550,000,000*l.* a year in a population of 31,000,000, means immense activity, large increase of comforts, and great accumulation of wealth.

Progress of British commerce.

The fifteen millions of tons of shipping which entered at ports in the United Kingdom laden with precious produce from all parts of the world, estimated in value at 303,000,000*l.*, brought large quantities of raw materials for our manufactures, of articles of food for the masses of the people, and of foreign merchandise to satisfy the increasing wants of the community. Of raw materials our manufacturers stand in absolute need. Whatever shortens the supply of such articles as cotton, silk, and even wool, limits the power of production. A bad crop of cotton in the far distant regions beyond the ocean, a disease in the cocoon, or any other calamity which increases the price of these articles, is so much actual loss to whole communities in Lancashire and Yorkshire, and through them to the whole kingdom. In 1840 there were entered for home consumption in the United Kingdom 4,545,000 cwt. cotton, 48,421,000 lbs. wool, and 1,896,000 lbs. flax and hemp. In 1870 the consumption was 9,836,000 cwt. cotton, 171,000,000 lbs. wool, and 5,300,000 lbs. flax, hemp, and jute. The world, we are thankful to say, has ample stores of produce to supply us with food, and, thanks to free trade, our people can get it whenever wanted. A large portion, indeed, of our population now

British imports.

depends on foreign corn,[1] and we could not well do without the oxen and bulls, sheep and lambs, bacon and beef, butter and cheese, sugar and coffee, fish and eggs, which come in so great quantities. Ever since 1840 the increase in the consumption of foreign articles of food has been very large. The consumption of butter has increased from 1·05 lbs. to 4·15 lbs. per head; of cheese, from ·92 lbs. to 3·67 lbs. per head; of corn, from 42·47 lbs. to 124·39 lbs. per head; of tea, from 1·22 lbs. to 3·81 lbs. per head; of sugar, from 15·20 lbs. to 41·93 lbs. per head. What folly, what crime, was it by law to hinder the people from getting what will sustain life. And our people are well pleased to use foreign clocks and watches, foreign gloves and silks, and other articles of finery, which our neighbours near or far can produce cheaper or better than we can. The interest of the largest number should always be the first consideration in any sound legislation. Of the 303,000,000*l.* of imports nearly 140,000,000*l.* consisted of raw materials, 100,000,000*l.* of articles of food, 30,000,000*l.* of manufactured articles, and the remainder of other products and merchandise.

British exports.

Of course, if we import largely we also export extensively. A great part of our imports represents what is actually due to Britain in profits, in freights, in interest of money invested abroad, and for other purposes; the remainder we pay for in goods and produce, or it may be in bullion. What gives an open market to British merchandise all over the world is its universal adaptation to the wants of man wherever situated. Luxuries are useless to the great mass of the people; but calico, iron, hardwares, are so useful and so cheap that they readily find purchasers even among the most uncivilised. Machinery gives to British producers immense facility; but our labourers are really good workers,

[1] In an able paper on the home produce, imports, and consumption of wheat, by J. B. Lawes, F.R.S. and Dr. Gilbert, it was shown that from 1852-3 to 1868-9 the average area under crop in wheat was 3,922,586 acres, the average yield 28¼ bushels per acre, and the total produce 13,810,013 quarters, from which deducting 2¼ bushels per acre for seed, left available consumption 12,706,785 quarters. To these there was added an average annual importation of 6,375,272 quarters, making in all 19,082,057 quarters available for consumption. The average annual population of the United Kingdom having been 28,816,816, there were available for consumption per head 3·5 bushels from home produce, 1·8 bushels from imports; total, 5·3 bushels per head.

and, even although wages are higher here than elsewhere, the labour performed is cheaper, from its greater effectiveness, and from the saving of unnecessary supervision. Cotton comes to us from America, a distance of thousands of miles; yet our ability to manufacture it is so great that we can pay the freight and profits, and send it back again in a manufactured state, cheaper than the Americans can manufacture it for themselves. The exports of British produce and manufactures quadrupled since 1840, the increase having been from 51,406,000*l.* in 1840, to 199,640,000*l.* in 1870. During the last fifty years there has been some change in the distribution of our exports. A somewhat less proportion goes now to Europe and to America, but a larger proportion to Asia, Africa, and Australia. Between 1840 and 1870 the exports to Europe decreased from 51 per cent. of the whole, to 41 per cent., and to America from 37 to 29 per cent. But the exports to Asia increased from 10 to 18 per cent.; to Africa from 2 to 7 per cent.; and to Australia from almost nothing to 5 per cent. If we divide our exports as between foreign countries and British colonies and possessions, we find that in 1840 one-third of our exports was sent to the colonies, and two-thirds to foreign countries; and in 1870 three-fourths went to foreign countries, and one-fourth to British colonies, notwithstanding the immense increase of our trade with India and Australia.

But it is worth while to dwell a little longer on the peculiar direction of our exports. In 1840 our largest customers in Europe were, in their order, the Hanse Towns, Holland, France, Italy, and Russia. In 1870 they were the Hanse Towns, France, Holland, Russia, and Italy. In the table in the Appendix we have placed Turkey in Europe, but to a large extent it is an Asiatic state. The trade with Asia shows a great increase with China and Japan, besides British India, the Straits Settlements, and Hong Kong. In Africa we have large transactions with Egypt, as well as with the Cape of Good Hope. As regards America, the half of our exports is to the United States, and the other half between the British colonies and the South American States. And Australia has become one of our largest outlets. Comparing the amount of our exports of British produce and manufactures

Direction of exports.

with the population of these countries, we find that Belgium takes them in the proportion of 18*s*. 5*d*. per head; the United States of America in the proportion of 14*s*. 5*d*.; France at the rate of 6*s*. 1*d*.; Italy of 4*s*. 1*d*.; and Russia at the rate of 2*s*. 5*d*. per head. It is not so much the competition between native and British produce that checks the extent of the markets for our goods, as the inability of the people to purchase our manufactures. To our exports of British produce and manufactures we should add the export of foreign and colonial merchandise, which, in 1870, amounted to 44,000,000*l*. England has long been a great entrepôt for the produce of all countries, and large profits are derived from the freight, storage, insurance, labour, wages, and interest of capital employed in this branch of foreign trade. And there is no reason why gold and silver bullion and specie should not be incorporated with our trade accounts. Are they not merchandise? In 1870 the imports of them amounted to 29,455,000*l*., and the exports to 18,920,000*l*.

Navigation.

As we have seen, a considerable amount of tonnage is now employed in the foreign and coasting trade of the United Kingdom, and notwithstanding the great competition, the British flag floats on every sea. When Mr. Huskisson dared to invade the sacred domain of our protectionists, the navigation laws, and Mr. Labouchere, twenty years later, abolished for ever the monopoly which they secured, all manner of evil forebodings were urged by our shipowners. What have been the results of that policy? Have British ships retired from the contest? Are they less employed? Is the business less profitable? In 1849, the year when the navigation laws were abolished, the shipping entered and cleared was in the proportion of 70·9 per cent. British, and 29·1 foreign. In 1870 the proportion was 70·3 British and 29·7 foreign. A few foreign seamen are now employed, but never was there a larger number of British seamen employed, and freights have increased instead of diminishing. Since 1849, whilst British ships increased at the rate of 74 per cent., United States ships increased at the rate of 30 per cent., French ships at the rate of 55 per cent. The efficiency of our shipping has likewise considerably increased. In 1849 with a tonnage of

3,096,000 tons of British ships employed in the home and foreign trade entered and cleared, there were 9,670,000 tons of British ships, being at the rate of about 3 tons trade to each ton of shipping. In 1870, with a tonnage of 5,559,000 tons, the British tonnage entered and cleared was 25,072,000 tons, being at the rate of 4·51 tons trade to each ton of shipping.[1] The abolition of the navigation laws has been a source of strength, not of weakness, to British shipping, and the amount of freight now earned far exceeds what was received in former years.

What better evidence of the activity of business in the United Kingdom at the present moment than the Post Office? Post Office. In 1839 the estimated number of letters delivered in the United Kingdom was 76,000,000, or scarcely 3 letters per head of the population. In 1870 the number of letters delivered was 863,000,000, or more than 27 letters per head, showing an increase of 800 per cent., to say nothing of the 130,000,000 book packets, newspapers, and pattern packets, and 19,000,000*l.* money orders issued by the Post Office. Some idea of the relative importance of the principal towns in the kingdom may be formed by the number of letters delivered from their respective post offices. In one week, ending March 31, 1870, London sent out 126 letters per 100 of the population, Manchester 159, Liverpool 100, Leeds 71, Bradford 67, Glasgow 81.

To facilitate the enormous transactions of commerce the intervention of bankers is of the greatest utility. The functions Banking and currency. of a bank in the commercial body have been compared to those of the heart in the human body. It attracts to itself capital, the life-blood of commerce, from every direction in the minutest rills, and having accumulated it in a great reservoir propels it through all the arteries and channels of commerce, vivifying and nourishing it, and spreading vigour and health through the whole commercial body. At the end of December 1870 the Bank of England had a capital of 14,553,000*l.*, a note circulation of 24,539,000*l.*, and deposits public and private to the extent of 24,000,000*l.* The London

[1] The increase of steam ships has materially aided the increase of navigation. In 1840 the United Kingdom had only 771 steamers, 87,000 tons. In 1970 she had 3,178 steam vessels, 1,112,000 tons.

joint-stock banks had collectively a capital amounting to nearly 9,000,000*l*., and deposits which reached 84,000,000*l*. The Scotch banks had a capital of 9,000,000*l*., and deposits and current accounts amounting to 63,000,000*l*. The Irish banks also had a considerable amount. The supply of a sufficient amount of currency attracted great attention not many years ago, and the Bank Charter Act, which restricted the amount of one species only of the same, the bank notes, was the subject of great and acrimonious discussion. But the bank note circulation bears a much smaller relation now to the commerce of the country than ever it did. In 1840 there were notes in circulation, including notes of the Bank of England, country banks, Scotch and Irish banks, to the extent of 13*s*. 8*d*. in the pound of the exports of British merchandise.[3] In 1870 that form of circulation was reduced to 4*s*. 5*d*. in the pound of the exports. But other forms of circulation are now in operation. The number of stamps sold for inland bills of exchange increased from 4,780,000 in 1859 to 6,400,000 in 1869. The number of banking cheques impressed with the 1*d*. stamp in the United Kingdom in the year ending March 31, 1861, was 31,000,000, and in the year ending March 31, 1871, about 52,000,000. The clearing house economises the currency to an enormous extent. Mr. Babbage estimated that in 1839 the daily average amount cleared was 3,000,000*l*. In 1869 the daily average was 10,400,000*l*. There is considerable difference also in the rapidity of the circulation. In 1844 a five pound note remained in circulation for 105 days; in 1871 it remained in circulation only 79 days.[4] At one time a considerable amount of currency was required to pay customs duties; in 1855, the system was introduced of paying them by drafts.

For the security of trade there are institutions of great

[3] A table in the Appendix shows that the circulation of the Bank of England notes, which in 1792 amounted to 11,417,000*l*., in 1870 was 24,410,000*l*.

[4] The life of a bank note may be taken to have been as follows:—

	5*l*.	10*l*.	20*l*. to 100*l*.	200*l*. to 500*l*.	1000*l*.
	Days	Days	Days	Days	Days
1844	105	87	38	14	12
1871	79	61	26	8	9

value which give rise to transactions of considerable importance, and prominent among these is the business of insurance against fire and marine risks, and life insurance with its invaluable application for the security of debts. In 1763 the sum insured against fire in England and Wales was 173,000,000l. In 1867 the amount insured in the United Kingdom was 1,365,000,000l. The amount of marine insurance must be large if we include the operations at Lloyd's and those of the public companies.[5] And so it is also with life insurance, for which the offices are liable to the extent of upwards of 330,000,000l., the premium income being 9,750,000l., and the accumulated fund of the companies, 86,000,000l.[6]

Insurance.

Of the home trade of the country we have no certain data. There is the railway traffic, the receipts of which in 1869 amounted to 41,000,000l. There is the whole traffic in agricultural produce, and in articles of clothing and other necessaries produced at home. There is the enormous business in home and foreign securities carried on at the Stock Exchange,[7] and there are the transactions in shares in the numerous companies for commercial, banking, and financial purposes. The payment of wages alone, amounting probably to

The home trade.

[5] In the years 1861–70 it was found that 5,231 vessels wrecked were insured for 11,285,000l., and 1,485 cargoes for 2,340,000l. The average tonnage of British ships being 215 tons, it would follow that the ships were insured at the rate of 6l. per ton, and the cargoes at 8l. per ton. The British and foreign vessels entered and cleared at ports in cargoes and in ballast in 1870 were of 36,640,000 tons. At 6l. per ton they represent 220,000,000l. The vessels with cargoes only were 31,620,000 tons, and at 8l. per ton they represent 253,000,000l., making a total of 473,000,000l. Some proportion of this value may be insured abroad, but the insurances made at Lloyd's on foreign ships engaged in the foreign trade must be considerable, so that the amount of marine insurance may be estimated at 400,000,000l. to 450,000,000l.

[6] See the British Life Insurance Chart, by William White, Esq., F.S.S.

[7] The amount of transactions at the Stock Exchange may be estimated by the amount of clearances at the clearing houses. In ordinary days the clearing amounts to 10,000,000l. On settling days 24,000,000l. Assuming the 14,000,000l. to arise from Stock Exchange transactions, these, twice in the month, would represent business amounting to 336,000,000l. On Consols settling days also a large amount of business takes place, and even allowing for the double drawing of cheques in many cases, the amount of transactions on the Stock Exchange must greatly exceed 800,000,000l. a year. It is estimated that foreign funds are held in this country to the extent of 800,000,000l.

some 300,000,000*l.* in money, entails operations of vast extent. It is indeed morally impossible to form any correct idea of the magnitude of such operations.

One thing, however, is certain. The result of all this traffic is an immense increase of wealth, which is accumulating by gigantic strides. In 1843 the total annual value of property and profits assessed to income tax in Great Britain only was 251,000,000*l.* In 1870 the total value of property and profits assessed in Great Britain was 409,000,000*l.* The amount assessed under Schedule D for gains arising from any profession or trade in Great Britain in 1843 was 71,000,000*l.*, and in 1870 165,000,000*l.* In 1843 the amount invested in railways was 65,000,000*l.*; in 1870, 530,000,000*l.* And it is gratifying to know that wealth is spreading among a much larger number of persons than it was at one time. In 1830 the number of depositors in the savings banks was 412,217, and the amount of deposits at their credit was 13,507,000*l.* In 1870 the number of depositors, including the post office savings banks, was 2,568,000, and the amount of deposits 53,000,000*l.* In 1830 the amount of such deposits per head of the population was 12*s.* 8*d.*; in 1870 it was 1*l.* 14*s.* 2*d.* The income tax returns show that the number of persons assessed for incomes under 300*l.* increased from 1854 to 1870 at the rate of 47 per cent., the number assessed for incomes from 300*l.* to 1000*l.* increased at the rate of 61 per cent., and the number assessed for incomes from 1000*l.* and upwards at the rate of 63 per cent. The increase is very considerable in every direction.

Increase of wealth.

The rate of progress, however, will be found still more striking and we may better realize how much commerce and manufactures tend to the increase of national wealth, if we divide the agricultural from the industrial and other counties. Comparing the increase of property assessed under Schedules A and D in 1814–15 with 1869–70, we find that in the agricultural counties the total amount increased at the rate of 83 per cent.; in the industrial counties at the rate of 215 per cent.; in the textile counties at the rate of 362 per cent.; and in the metropolitan at the rate of 238 per cent. And if we take the increase of population into

Increase of wealth in agricultural and industrial counties.

account, we find the increase per cent. in the period to have been at the rate of 12 per cent. in the agricultural, 29 per cent. in the industrial, 69 per cent. in the textile, and 25 per cent. in the metropolitan counties. In England the increase of property was at the rate of 201 per cent., and in relation to population at the rate of 20 per cent. In Wales, the increase of property was at the rate of 208 per cent., and in relation to population 51 per cent. And in Scotland the increase of property was at the rate of 228 per cent., and in relation to population (the increase of such having been smaller than in England and Wales) at the rate of 80 per cent. Taken altogether, the people of Great Britain may be stated to be 41 per cent. richer in 1870 than 1810 in the assessable value of fixed property, income and profits. But the proportion would be considerably larger were all descriptions of property capable of being so calculated, and, above all, if the power of the people over commodities and comforts were taken into account.

Revenue and expenditure.

The collection of the public revenue has been easy and regular. From 1844, when free trade measures had begun to produce good result, to this time, there had been twenty-eight budgets, and in twenty-two of them the revenue produced more than the amount estimated by the budgets. The amount of capital of unredeemed funded debt, which on January 5, 1841, was 766,371,000*l.*, was reduced on March 31, 1871, to 731,309,000*l.* Unfortunately, the annual expenditure, especially for the forces, is large, and the excess available for the reduction of the national debt from year to year has been comparatively insignificant. In 1840 the revenue was 47,433,000*l.*, and the expenditure 49,285,000*l.* In 1870 the revenue was 69,945,000*l.*, and the expenditure 69,548,000*l.*

Uses of wealth in the promotion of science and art.

And thankful we are that good use is often made of wealth to promote learning and to mitigate the sufferings of mankind. What country in the world possesses so many scientific societies, all free and self-supporting, the spontaneous creation of men of science, as Britain? And each and all of them have a high economic value. The Royal and Mathematical Societies are labouring to evolve the principles of those sciences which govern alike the phenomena of the material universe and the practical problem of the law of probabilities. The Statistical Society subjects the real worth of economic doctrines to the close test of numbers, to the great correctives of experience and facts, using the inductive rather than the deductive method for the guidance of the philosopher and statesman. The Astronomical Society is expanding our knowledge of the meteorology and magnetism of the universe, as well as of the laws which govern the motion of the stars, to the immense benefit of navigation. The Chemical Society is ever analysing matter, finding new products, and enriching us with an extended knowledge of their wonderful capabilities. The Geographical is exploring for us unknown regions, and makes us acquainted with the habits and wants of distant races. The Geological maps out for us the very strata of the earth. And the British Association for the Advancement of Science and the National Association for the Promotion of Social Science propagate scientific truths all over the kingdom, and bring to light the latent powers of every corner of the state. The 50,000 men devoted to scientific pursuits in the United Kingdom are not only the ornaments but the very strength of the British empire. The arts also are cultivated and appreciated. The wealth contained in our private and public galleries is enormous, as was shown in the magnificent Exhibition of Art Treasures at Manchester; and the Science and Art Department as well as the Royal Commissioners of the National Gallery are not sparing in their efforts to acquire for the nation any *chef d'œuvre* within their reach.

Literature of commerce.

The literature of commerce comprises works of great practical value. For its general principles, the student will necessarily turn to the most celebrated works on political economy, especially those of Adam Smith and John Stuart Mill, Ricardo, M'Culloch, and Thorold Rogers. On banking, Gilbart's Principles and Practice, and M'Leod's History are valuable. For general information on trade and navigation there is no work so full as M'Culloch's Dictionary, and for general facts and data relating to prices and currency, there is Tooke and Newmarch's History. Of special treatises there are many, such as Goschen on the Foreign Exchanges, Lord Overstone's Tracts, Francis's History of the Bank of England, and

Laing's Theory of Business. For information relating to the different commercial crises, and the operation of the Banking Laws, the student must consult the reports of committees of both Houses of Parliament in 1832, 1840, 1848, and 1857. Porter's Progress of the Nations shows the influence of commerce on the increase of wealth, and the Statistical Abstract of the United Kingdom and of the Colonies will keep the student *au courant* with the present condition of commerce. And if Cobden is gone,[8] his Speeches, published by the Cobden Club, will always furnish the most unanswerable arguments in favour of the great principle of freedom of trade and industry.

Use of wealth in works of benevolence.

Many of our merchant princes are conspicuous for their benevolence. And brilliant examples have been given of a cosmopolitan charity, ever ready to answer to the call of humanity from whatever quarter it may come. Witness the effort made in 1847 to mitigate the sufferings and privations caused by the failure of the potato crop in Ireland; the sumptuous contribution given to the sufferers from the inundations in France in 1853; the patriotic fund of 1856; the large sum collected for Indian relief; the munificent sum granted by Mr. William Brown, of Liverpool, for a free library; the sumptuous gift of Mr. Peabody; the princely benefactions of the Baroness Coutts; the rich endow-

[8] Richard Cobden died on April 2, 1865, when 61 years of age, and on the 3rd, in expressing the sentiments of the House of Commons at such a loss, Viscount Palmerston said: 'Sir,—It is many years ago since Adam Smith elaborately and conclusively, as far as argument could go, advocated as the fundamental principles of the wealth of nations, freedom of industry and unrestricted exchange of the objects which are the results of industry. These doctrines were inculcated by learned men—by Dugald Stewart and others. They were taken up in process of time by leading statesmen, such as Mr. Huskisson, and those who agreed with him. But the barriers which long-established prejudice—honest and conscientious prejudice—had raised against the practical application of those doctrines, prevented for a long series of years their coming into use as instruments of progress in the country. To Mr. Cobden it was reserved by his untiring industry, his indefatigable personal activity, the indomitable energy of his mind, and by, I will say, that forcible Demosthenic eloquence with which he treated all the subjects which he took in hand—it was reserved to Mr. Cobden, aided, no doubt, by a phalanx of worthy associates—by my right hon. friend, the President of the Poor Law Board (Mr. Villiers), and by Sir Robert Peel, whose memory will ever be associated with that of Mr. Cobden, by exertions, which never were surpassed, to carry into practical application those abstract principles, with the truth of which he was so deeply impressed, and which at last gained the assent of all reasonable men in the country.'

ments of Sir David Baxter; the most liberal foundation of scholarships of Sir William Whitworth; and the recent splendid exhibition of goodwill towards the Parisians in the time of their calamity. It is from wealth drawn from commerce that churches, schools, and hospitals are scattered with profusion all over our cities, and most of our noblest institutions for the benefit of the poor and the relief of suffering derive constant sustenance. And it is from the same prolific source that the pioneer of civilization, and the self-denying missionary—men such as Moffatt and Williams, and Duff and Livingstone—are sent forth to the very ends of the earth to break the fallow ground, and to open a highway for the renovating influences of religion and charity.

True source of British prosperity.

Into the distant future we cannot penetrate. What revolutions may yet come to pass, what may be the course of trade as new communications open, what new marts of merchandise may yet flourish, whether some race may yet come to the surface, possessing greater force of character, greater energy and skill than the Anglo-Saxon, we cannot say. Babylon, Thebes, Carthage, Athens, and Rome were probably as great and even as populous as London now is, and yet they are gone. And so it may be of Britain should she ever be enervated by luxury and degraded in her morals, should virtue hide her face and rectitude depart from her streets. But we trust otherwise. We have faith in the moral influences at work. We have confidence in the strength of will, sober judgment, and untiring energy of the Saxon race; and happy will it be if, realising the true source of her strength and success, Britain knows how to use her wealth, power, and influence towards the maintenance and the promotion of 'the true, the good, and the beautiful.'

Influence of commerce on the peace of the world.

Commerce has done much for Britain, and we trust it will do still more for all nations—for the world. In the words of John Stuart Mill, 'commerce first taught nations to see with goodwill the wealth and prosperity of one another. Before, the patriot, unless sufficiently advanced in culture to feel the world his country, wished all countries weak, poor, and ill-governed but his own; he now sees in their wealth and progress a direct source of wealth and progress to his own country. It is Commerce which is rapidly rendering war obsolete, by strengthening and multiplying the personal interests which are in natural opposition to it. And it may be said, without exaggeration, that the great extent and rapid increase of international trade, in being the principal guarantee of the peace of the world, is the great permanent security for the uninterrupted progress of the ideas, the institutions, and the character of the human race.'

APPENDIX.

APPENDIX.

FOREIGN TRADE OF THE UNITED KINGDOM.

Trade of England with Foreign Parts.

Thousands omitted.

Years	Imports	Exports	Years	Imports	Exports
	official value £	official value £		official value £	official value £
1763	10,429	13,027	1771	11,441	14,629
1764	9,614	14,627	1772	12,056	14,096
1765	9,910	12,806	1773	10,164	12,874
1766	10,359	12,162	1774	11,809	13,810
1767	10,971	11,987	1775	11,908	13,033
1768	10,053	12,872	1776	10,180	11,651
1769	10,844	11,473	1777	10,839	10,722
1770	11,002	12,142	1778	8,923	10,080

Trade of Great Britain.

Thousands omitted.

Years	Imports	Exports	Years	Imports	Exports
	official value £	official value £		official value £	official value £
1779	9,868	11,894	1790	16,390	17,636
1780	9,956	11,364	1791	17,190	20,016
1781	11,094	9,258	1792	17,037	22,095
1782	8,216	10,422	1793	16,972	17,734
1783	11,510	12,618	1794	19,539	22,633
1784	13,493	13,167	1795	20,100	22,231
1785	14,267	13,656	1796	20,422	25,130
1786	13,615	14,317	1797	17,900	23,881
1787	15,582	14,317	1798	25,122	27,317
1788	15,842	14,817	1799	21,067	29,567
1789	15,416	16,815	1800	28,258	34,382

Trade of the United Kingdom.

Thousands omitted.

Years	Imports	Exports: Produce and Manufactures of the U. Kingdom	Exports: Foreign and Colonial Merchandise	Total Exports	Produce and Manufactures of the U. Kingdom
	official value £	official value £	official value £	official value £	real value £
1801	31,786	24,928	10,438	35,365	Records not complete for these years.
1802	29,826	25,632	12,776	38,409	
1803	26,623	20,468	8,074	28,541	
1804	27,820	22,687	8,989	31,676	
1805	28,561	23,377	7,088	31,061	38,077
1806	26,900	25,862	7,782	33,614	40,875
1807	26,731	23,391	7,674	31,065	37,246
1808	26,796	24,611	5,838	30,419	37,275
1809	31,751	33,542	12,835	46,377	47,371
1810	39,302	34,062	9,507	43,569	48,439
1811	26,510	22,681	6,223	28,904	32,891
1812	26,163	29,509	9,718	39,226	41,717
1813	Records destroyed by fire.				
1814	37,755	34,207	19,366	53,573	46,491
1815	32,987	42,880	11,749	58,629	51,610
1816	27,132	35,715	25,481	49,195	41,651
1817	30,831	40,111	10,292	50,403	41,818
1818	36,885	42,702	10,860	53,562	46,471
1819	30,777	33,534	9,905	43,438	35,211
1820	32,472	38,394	10,056	48,949	36,424
1821	30,838	40,832	10,630	51,462	36,655
1822	30,531	40,213	9,228	53,170	36,965
1823	35,798	43,827	8,601	52,430	35,357
1824	37,468	48,730	10,205	58,935	38,423
1825	44,209	47,151	9,169	56,320	38,871
1826	37,814	40,966	10,076	51,012	31,537
1827	44,908	52,222	9,831	62,053	37,181
1828	45,167	52,788	9,917	62,735	36,813
1829	43,995	56,218	10,620	66,838	35,813
1830	46,300	61,152	8,518	69,701	38,272
1831	49,728	60,686	10,745	71,431	37,164
1832	46,611	65,025	11,045	76,070	36,451
1833	45,944	69,987	9,834	79,821	39,667
1834	49,365	73,835	11,562	85,397	41,649
1835	49,029	78,360	12,798	91,157	47,372
1836	57,296	85,220	12,392	97,512	53,291
1837	54,762	72,540	13,235	85,779	42,069
1838	61,268	92,454	12,712	105,165	50,062
1839	62,048	97,395	12,796	110,191	53,234
1840	67,493	102,707	13,774	116,481	51,406
1841	64,444	102,179	14,723	116,903	51,634
1842	65,253	100,256	13,586	113,842	47,381
1843	70,216	117,877	13,956	131,833	52,279
1844	75,297	131,538	14,398	145,956	58,584
1845	85,298	134,599	16,279	150,876	60,111
1846	75,934	132,318	16,308	148,615	57,787
1847	90,922	126,310	20,041	146,172	58,842
1848	93,517	132,619	18,377	150,996	52,849
1849	105,884	164,528	25,559	190,087	63,596
1850	100,469	175,137	21,874	197,311	71,368
1851	110,485	190,668	23,720	214,388	74,449
1852	109,331	197,177	23,328	219,505	78,077
1853	123,009	214,327	27,745	242,072	98,934

Trade of the United Kingdom—*continued.*

Thousands omitted.

Years	Imports	Exports: Produce and Manufactures of the United Kingdom	Exports: Foreign and Colonial Merchandise	Exports: Total Exports
	real value £	real value £	real value £	real value £
1851	152,692	97,165	18,840	97,184
1855	123,660	95,688	21,003	116,701
1856	172,511	115,827	23,393	139,220
1857	187,844	122,066	24,108	146,174
1858	164,581	116,609	23,174	139,782
1859	179,182	130,412	25,281	155,693
1860	210,531	135,891	28,630	164,521
1861	217,485	125,103	34,529	159,632
1862	225,717	123,992	42,176	166,168
1863	248,919	146,602	50,300	196,902
1864	274,952	160,449	52,170	212,620
1865	271,072	165,836	52,995	218,832
1866	295,290	188,917	49,988	238,906
1867	275,183	180,962	44,840	225,803
1868	295,460	179,677	48,101	227,778
1869	295,460	189,953	47,061	237,106
1870	303,296	199,641	44,494	244,134

Declared Real Value of British and Irish Produce exported from the United Kingdom to various Foreign Countries and British Possessions.

Thousands omitted.

Places	1840	1850	1860	1870	Percentage increase 1840–1870
EUROPE.					
Foreign Countries.	£	£	£	£	
Russia	1,003	1,155	3,268	6,903	336
Sweden and Norway . .	197	363	1,015	2,015	922
Denmark and Iceland . .	201	451	781	2,024	906
Prussia	219	424	1,884	2,930	1,242
Hanover	71	232	1,107	405	514
Hanse Towns	5,266	6,756	10,864	16,899	219
Holland	3,416	3,512	6,115	11,292	228
Belgium	880	1,136	1,610	4,476	409
France	2,378	2,401	5,250	11,616	393
Portugal	1,188	1,118	1,847	2,101	77
Spain	404	865	2,471	2,514	522
Italy	2,102	2,791	4,513	5,267	143
Austrian Territories: Illyria, Croatia, Dalmatia, and Venetia till 1861 .	497	607	993	1,714	244
Greece	—	202	343	948	—
Turkey, Wallachia, Moldavia	1,164	2,811	4,582	6,460	461
British Possessions.					
Channel Islands . . .	259	506	559	759	193
Gibraltar	1,111	388	1,159	770	39
Malta	166	314	704	1,001	504
Ionian Islands . . .	89	136	345	ceded to Greece	
	21,294	26,500	45,967	80,150	276

Declared Real Value of British and Irish Produce, &c.—continued.

Thousands omitted.

Places	1840	1850	1860	1870	Percentage Increase 1840–1870
Asia.					
Foreign Countries.	£	£	£	£	
China	521	976	2,872	6,138	1,071
Java and Sumatra . .	349	507	1,414	897	157
Japan	—	—	—	1,615	—
Syria and Palestine . .	223	303	655	1,186	432
British Possessions.					
Hong Kong	—	496	2,446	8,407	—
British India	5,213	7,212	16,965	19,309	270
Singapore and Straits Settlements	687	562	1,671	2,232	239
Ceylon	123	218	671	907	637
	7,119	10,406	26,691	35,793	402
Africa.					
Foreign Countries.					
Egypt	79	649	2,481	8,752	10,977
Morocco	14	32	171	229	1,535
French Possessions . .	52	19	45	127	131
Spanish „ . .	908	1,152	2,354	3,564	181
Western Coast, Africa . .	260	434	951	904	247
British Possessions.					
Mauritius	326	369	538	483	48
Cape of Good Hope and Natal	417	797	2,065	1,867	317
Possessions on River Gambia	93	41	28	40	56
Sierra Leone	—	70	315	217	—
Possessions on Gold Coast .	137	88	97	401	192
Other Possessions . .	10	45	109	127	—
	2,296	3,700	9,054	16,701	627
America.					
Foreign Countries.					
United States and California	5,283	14,892	21,667	28,335	436
Mexico	465	452	463	911	96
Central America . . .	2	251	182	360	—
Haiti and San Domingo .	252	276	418	395	56
New Granada . . .	—	331	811	2,135	—
Venezuela	360	301	324	144	60
Ecuador	—	83	74	57	—
Brazil	2,625	2,545	4,447	5,353	104
Uruguay (Monte Video), Argentine Confederation .	614	909	2,705	3,162	414
Chili	1,335	1,136	1,703	2,686	101
Peru	800	846	1,381	1,766	120
Danish West Indies . .	324	592	658	761	134
British Possessions.					
North American Colonies:					
Hudson's Bay Settlement .	77	102	80	45	—
Newfoundland . . .	281	343	460	524	86
Canada	1,563	1,998	2,138	4,376	179
New Brunswick . . .	502	411	403	529	5
Prince Edward Island } Nova Scotia } .	424 {	57	74	125	—
		328	529	1,127	195
W. Indian Is. and Guiana	3,177	2,030	3,417	3,362	5
British Honduras . .	398	183	142	160	59
British Columbia . .	—	—	37	73	—
	18,483	28,030	41,114	56,387	205

Declared Real Value of British and Irish Produce, &c.—continued.

Thousands omitted.

Places	1840	1850	1860	1870	Percentage increase 1840–1870
AUSTRALIA	£ 2,044	£ 2,590	£ 9,707	£ 9,825	380
OTHER COUNTRIES . .	72	130	334	707	881
Total to Foreign Countries and British Possessions .	51,308	71,367	135,891	199,640	289

Decennial Percentage Increase.

	1840–1850	1850–1860	1860–1870
Europe . . .	21	84	63
Asia . . .	45	156	34
Africa . . .	61	114	84
America . .	61	46	37
Australia . .	26	274	1
All countries . .	39	90	46

Relative Position of the Different Parts in the Whole Trade of the Kingdom.

	1840	1850	1860	1870
Europe . .	41	37	36	40
Asia . . .	13	15	19	18
Africa . . .	5	5	7	8
America . .	37	40	30	29
Australia . .	4	3	8	5
	100	100	100	100

IMPORTS AND EXPORTS CLASSIFIED, 1870.

Imports.

Thousands omitted.

PRINCIPAL ARTICLES OF FOOD.	Declared real value £	RAW MATERIALS—*continued.*	Declared real value £
Corn	34,169	Oil	6,586
Sugar	17,596	Hides	4,609
Tea	10,098	Copper, ore and unwrought	4,081
Butter	6,794	Guano	3,476
Animals living, bacon, beef, meat	6,582	Tallow	3,292
Wine	4,817	Indigo	2,721
Coffee	4,942	Spelter	2,071
Spirits	3,216	Caoutchouc	1,698
Fruit	3,052	MANUFACTURES.	
Rice	2,310	Silk	15,245
Eggs	1,102	Woollen	4,997
Spices	847	Cotton	1,624
Cocoa	371	Leather	1,381
Chicory	150	Iron	1,376
		Glass	919
RAW MATERIALS.		Paper	712
		Clocks and Watches	630
Cotton	53,469	Lace	512
Wool	15,812	Candles	285
Wood	13,550	Musical instruments	201
Flax and Hemp	10,368	Linen	173
Silk	9,295	Jewellery	155
Seed	8,371	Corks	140

Exports.

Thousands omitted.

TEXTILES.	Declared real value £	MANUFACTURES.	Declared real value £
Cotton Manufactures and Yarn	71,416	Machinery	5,293
Woollen "	26,812	Haberdashery	4,813
Linen and Jute "	11,372	Hardware	4,468
Silk "	2,604	Leather	2,623
		Telegraphic Wires	2,522
MINERALS.		Apparel	2,205
Iron	21,075	Arms and Ammunition	1,887
Coals and Coke	5,514	Beer and Ale	1,682
Tin	2,999	Earthenware	1,693
Copper	2,817	Alkali Soda	1,186
Lead	1,280	Sugar, refined	934
Zinc	141	Glass	832

Quantities of Principal Imported and Exciseable Articles retained for Consumption per head of the total Population of the United Kingdom.

Articles		1840	1850	1860	1870
Bacon and Ham	lbs.	0·01	1·41	1·27	1·98
Butter	"	1·05	1·30	2·26	4·15
Cheese	"	0·92	1·38	2·24	3·67
Cocoa	"	0·08	0·11	0·11	0·20
Coffee	"	1·08	1·13	1·23	0·98
Corn, wheat, and flour	"	42·47	81·76	118·86	124·39
Eggs	No.	362	384	583	13·95
Potatoes	lbs.	0·01	5·48	2·18	2·80
Rice	"	0·90	1·63	1·41	6·74
Sugar, raw	"	15·20	21·79	33·11	41·93
Sugar, refined	bushels			1·03	5·83
Spirits	galls.	0·14	0·17	0·19	0·27
Spirits, British	"	0·83	0.87	0·74	0·74
Malt	bushels	1·59	1·47	1·45	1·84
Wine	galls.	0·25	0·23	0·23	0·49
Tea	lbs.	1·22	1·8[illegible]	[illegible]·67	3·81
Tobacco	"	0·86	1·0[illegible]	1·22	1·34
Currants	bushels	1·15	2·58	3·59	4·08

Custom Tariffs on Principal Articles of Consumption.

Articles	1820	1840	1850	1860	1870
Corn wheat, per qr.	9s. 3d. average	4s. 11d. average	1s.	1s.	—
Tea . . . per lb.	96 to 100 per cent. ad valorem	2s. 1d.	2s. 2¼d.	1s. 5d.	6d.
Sugar . per cwt. unrefined	27s. to 63s.	24s. to 63s.	12s. to 17s.	12s. 8d. to 16s.	4s. 8d. to 5s. 8d.
Coffee . . per lb.	6d. to 1s. 3d.	6d. to 1s. 3d.	1½d. to 3¼d.	3d. to 4d.	3d. to 4d.
Wine . . per gal.	2s. 5d. to 7s. 6d.	2s. 9d. to 5s. 6d.	2s. 10¾d. to 5s. 9¼d.	3s. 10¾d. to 8s.	1s. to 2s. 6d.
Spirits . . per gal. foreign	22s. 6d.	22s. 6d.	15s.	8s. 2d. to 8s. 6d.	10s. 2d. to 10s. 5d.

TRADE WITH THE PRINCIPAL COUNTRIES.

Total Trade of the United Kingdom in 1870, Classified in order of Amount with the Principal Foreign Countries and Colonies.

Places	Imports	Exports	Total
	£	£	£
1. United States	49,805	31,306	81,111
2. France	37,607	21,983	59,590
3. India	25,090	20,094	45,184
4. Hanse Towns	9,174	22,781	31,955
5. Holland	14,315	17,304	31,619
6. Russia	20,561	10,070	30,631
7. Australia	14,075	10,735	24,810
8. Egypt	14,117	8,829	22,946
9. Belgium	11,248	8,949	20,147
10. British North America	8,515	7,584	16,099
11. China	9,481	6,363	15,844
12. Turkey	6,462	6,184	12,646
13. Brazil	6,127	5,544	11,672
14. Italy	3,819	6,282	10,101
15. Prussia	4,888	4,655	9,543
16. Spain	6,067	3,113	9,180
17. Sweden	6,399	1,930	8,329
18. British West Indies	4,469	2,658	7,128
19. Peru	4,881	1,853	6,734
20. Chili	3,828	2,767	6,596
21. Denmark	3,005	2,316	5,321
22. Portugal	3,022	2,253	5,275
23. Straits Settlements	2,517	2,407	4,954
24. Ceylon	3,450	941	4,391
25. Cape of Good Hope	2,434	1,625	4,059
26. Argentine Confederation	1,486	2,428	3,914
27. Norway	2,191	1,237	3,428
Other Countries	25,194	28,909	54,181
Total	303,257	244,080	547,337

Annual Average Prices of Grain in England and Wales.

Years	Wheat	Barley	Oats	Years	Wheat	Barley	Oats
	s. d.	s. d.	s. d.		s. d.	s. d.	s. d.
1763	*36 1¼			1817	96 11	49 4	32 5
1764	*41 6¾			1818	86 3	53 10	32 5
1765	*48 0			1819	74 6	45 9	28 2
1766	*43 1½			1820	67 10	33 10	24 2
1767	*57 4			1821	56 1	26 0	19 6
1768	*53 9¾			1822	44 7	21 10	18 1
1769	*40 8			1823	53 4	31 6	22 11
1770	*43 6¾			1824	63 11	36 4	24 10
1771	48 7	26 5	12 2	1825	68 6	40 0	25 8
1772	52 3	26 1	16 8	1826	58 8	34 4	20 8
1773	52 7	29 2	17 8	1827	58 6	37 7	28 2
1774	54 3	29 4	18 4	1828	60 5	32 10	22 6
1775	49 10	26 9	17 0	1829	66 3	32 6	22 9
1776	39 4	20 9	15 5	1830	64 3	32 7	24 5
1777	46 11	21 1	16 1	1831	66 4	38 0	25 4
1778	43 3	23 4	15 7	1832	58 8	33 1	20 5
1779	34 8	20 1	14 5	1833	52 11	27 6	18 5
1780	36 9	17 6	13 2	1834	46 2	29 0	20 11
1781	46 0	17 8	11 1	1835	39 4	29 11	22 6
1782	49 3	23 2	15 7	1836	48 6	32 10	23 1
1783	54 3	31 3	20 5	1837	55 10	30 4	23 1
1784	50 4	28 8	18 10	1838	64 7	31 5	22 5
1785	43 1	24 9	17 6	1839	70 8	39 6	25 11
1786	40 0	25 1	18 6	1840	66 4	36 5	25 8
1787	42 5	23 4	17 2	1841	64 4	32 10	22 6
1788	46 4	22 8	16 1	1842	57 3	27 6	19 3
1789	52 9	23 6	16 6	1843	50 1	[illegible] 6	18 4
1790	54 9	20 3	19 5	1844	51 3	[illegible] 8	20 7
1791	48 7	26 10	18 1	1845	50 10	[illegible] 8	22 6
1792	43 0	—	16 9	1846	54 8	[illegible] 8	23 8
1793	49 3	31 1	20 6	1847	69 9	44 2	28 8
1794	52 3	31 9	21 8	1848	50 6	31 6	20 6
1795	75 2	37 5	24 5	1849	44 3	27 9	17 6
1796	78 7	35 4	21 10	1850	40 3	23 5	16 5
1797	53 9	27 2	16 3	1851	38 6	24 9	18 7
1798	51 10	29 6	19 5	1852	40 9	28 6	19 1
1799	69 0	36 2	27 6	1853	53 3	33 2	21 0
1800	113 0	59 10	39 4	1854	72 5	36 0	27 11
1801	119 6	68 6	37 6	1855	74 8	34 9	27 5
1802	69 10	33 1	20 1	1856	69 2	41 1	25 2
1803	58 10	25 1	21 6	1857	56 4	42 1	25 0
1804	62 3	31 0	21 3	1858	44 2	34 8	24 6
1805	89 9	44 6	28 4	1859	43 9	33 6	23 2
1806	79 1	38 8	27 7	1860	53 3	36 7	24 5
1807	75 4	39 4	28 4	1861	55 4	36 1	23 9
1808	81 4	—	33 1	1862	55 5	35 1	22 7
1809	97 4	47 0	31 5	1863	44 9	33 11	21 2
1810	106 5	48 1	28 7	1864	40 2	29 11	20 1
1811	95 3	42 3	27 7	1865	41 10	29 9	21 10
1812	126 6	66 9	44 6	1866	49 11	37 5	24 7
1813	109 9	58 6	38 6	1867	64 5	40 0	26 0
1814	74 4	37 4	25 8	1868	63 9	43 0	28 1
1815	65 7	30 3	23 7	1869	48 2	39 5	26 0
1816	78 6	33 11	27 2	1870	46 10	34 7	22 11

* Those marked with an asterisk are prices from the register kept in the Audit Book of Eton College, per Winchester Quarter.

NAVIGATION.

Shipping Entered and Cleared to and from Great Britain.

Thousands omitted.

Years	Entered inwards			Entered outwards			Total entered and cleared
	British	Foreign	Total	British	Foreign	Total	
1772	758	136	894	924	73	996	1,896
1773	796	115	911	874	57	932	1,843
1774	821	135	956	809	69	878	1,834
1775	913	135	1,078	888	68	966	2,044
1776	765	191	957	872	74	946	1,903
1777	815	252	1,067	830	102	932	1,999
1778	702	199	901	732	94	826	1,727
1779	581	210	824	643	149	792	1,616
1780	575	228	803	731	154	885	1,688
1781	504	262	766	608	71	679	1,445
1782	496	280	777	625	226	851	1,628
1783	813	313	1,136	870	169	1,039	2,175
1784	1,003	212	1,216	932	118	1,050	2,266
1785	1,075	167	1,242	1,115	121	1,182	2,424
1786	1,077	187	1,264	1,115	121	1,236	2,500
1787	1,058	258	1,316	1,211	138	1,349	2,665
1788	1,328	230	1,558	1,411	129	1,541	3,099
1789	1,397	190	1,587	1,499	103	1,602	3,189
1790	1,428	277	1,705	1,399	140	1,542	3,247
1791	1,452	321	1,773	1,511	185	1,696	3,469
1792	1,5[illegible]	204	1,791	1,507	171	1,678	3,469
1793	1,3[illegible]	332	1,672	1,240	187	1,427	3,099
1794	1,4[illegible]	334	1,786	1,382	219	1,601	3,387
1795	1,242	390	1,632	1,145	382	1,527	3,159
1796	1,384	519	1,903	1,154	477	1,631	3,534
1797	1,150	556	1,706	1,104	396	1,500	3,206
1798	1,289	420	1,709	1,318	366	1,684	3,393
1799	1,375	446	1,821	1,302	414	1,716	3,537
1800	1,379	763	2,142	1,444	734	2,178	4,320
To and from the United Kingdom.							
1801	922	780	1,702	1,346	805	2,151	3,853
1802	1,333	480	1,813	1,777	457	2,234	4,047
1803	1,116	638	1,754	951	574	1,525	3,279
1804	905	607	1,512	906	585	1,491	3,003
1805	953	692	1,645	971	606	1,577	3,222
1806	904	613	1,517	899	568	1,467	2,984
1807 } 1808 }	lost						
1809	939	759	1,698	950	699	1,649	4,347
1810	896	1,176	2,072	861	1,138	1,999	3,771
1811 } 1812 } 1813 }	lost						
1814	1,847	566	2,413	1,876	571	2,447	4,860
1815	1,993	656	2,649	2,105	672	2,777	5,427
1816	1,967	318	2,284	1,988	330	2,318	4,602
1817	2,241	402	2,642	2,219	396	2,615	5,258
1818	2,458	704	3,162	2,401	671	3,072	6,235
1819	2,413	478	2,891	2,264	491	2,755	5,646
1820	2,270	408	2,678	2,208	391	2,599	5,276

Shipping Entered and Cleared to and from the U. Kingdom—continued.

Thousands omitted.

Years	Entered inwards			Entered outwards			Total entered and cleared
	British	Foreign	Total	British	Foreign	Total	
1821	2,204	366	2,630	2,224	351	2,575	5,205
1822	1,604	409	2,133	1,530	457	1,986	4,129
1823	1,741	583	2,324	1,547	563	2,110	4,434
1824	1,797	759	2,567	1,657	740	2,401	4,971
1825	2,144	958	3,102	1,794	906	2,700	5,802
1826	1,951	694	2,645	1,737	692	2,430	5,074
1827	2,087	752	2,839	1,888	768	2,656	5,495
1828	2,094	634	2,728	2,006	608	2,614	5,342
1829	2,184	710	2,894	2,063	730	2,793	5,688
1830	2,180	758	2,938	2,102	758	2,860	5,798
1831	2,367	875	3,242	2,301	896	3,197	6,439
1832	2,186	640	2,826	2,229	651	2,880	5,706
1833	2,184	762	2,946	2,244	758	3,002	5,948
1834	2,298	834	3,132	2,296	853	3,149	6,281
1835	2,442	867	3,309	2,420	905	3,325	66,35
1836	2,505	989	3,494	2,532	1,035	3,567	7,061
1837	2,617	1,006	3,623	2,517	1,037	3,584	7,207
1838	2,785	1,211	3,997	2,875	1,223	4,099	8,096
1839	3,111	1,331	4,442	3,096	1,399	4,495	8,928
1840	3,197	1,460	4,657	3,293	1,489	4,782	9,439
1841	3,361	1,291	4,652	3,429	1,337	4,766	9,418
1842	3,295	1,205	4,500	3,375	1,252	4,627	9,127
1843	3,545	1,302	4,847	3,636	1,341	4,977	9,824
1844	3,647	1,402	5,049	3,853	1,444	5,297	10,347
1845	4,311	1,375	5,686	4,235	1,796	6,031	11,717
1846	4,295	1,806	6,101	4,393	1,921	6,314	12,415
1847	4,942	2,254	7,196	4,770	2,313	7,083	14,279
1848	4,565	1,961	6,526	4,724	2,056	6,780	13,306
1849	4,884	2,035	6,919	4,785	2,299	7,084	14,003
1850	4,700	2,400	7,100	4,742	2,662	7,404	14,505
1851	4,938	2,934	7,872	4,882	3,225	8,108	15,980
1852	4,934	2,952	7,887	5,051	3,191	8,243	16,130
1853	5,055	3,888	8,943	5,213	4,234	9,447	18,390
1854	5,374	3,787	9,161	5,370	4,137	9,507	18,668
1855	5,271	3,680	8,951	5,647	3,889	9,538	18,489
1856	6,391	4,162	10,553	6,556	4,480	11,036	21,589
1857	6,854	4,621	11,475	6,840	4,863	11,703	23,179
1858	6,430	4,532	10,962	6,452	4,896	11,348	22,310
1859	6,585	4,637	11,222	6,727	4,955	11,682	22,904
1860	6,889	5,284	12,173	7,026	5,490	12,516	24,689
1861	7,721	5,458	13,179	7,699	5,716	13,416	26,595
1862	7,856	5,231	13,091	8,090	5,354	13,444	26,535
1863	8,430	4,826	13,256	8,589	4,893	13,483	26,739
1864	9,028	4,487	13,515	9,173	4,516	13,689	27,204
1865	9,623	4,694	14,316	9,735	4,844	14,579	28,897
1866	10,692	4,920	15,612	10,464	5,086	15,550	31,162
1867	11,198	5,141	16,339	11,172	5,245	16,417	32,756
1868	11,226	5,397	16,622	11,434	5,624	17,058	33,681
1869	11,721	5,476	17,198	12,067	5,644	17,712	34,910
1870	12,380	5,733	18,112	12,692	5,835	18,527	36,640

Tonnage of Ships belonging to the British Empire.

Thousands omitted.

Years	Great Britain	Colonies		Years	United Kingdom	Colonies	British Empire
	tons	tons	tons		tons	tons	tons
1763	556	—	556	1816	2,504	280	2,784
1764	590	—	590	1817	2,421	264	2,685
1765	618	—	618	1818	2,452	222	2,674
1766	635	—	635	1819	2,451	215	2,666
1767	641	—	641	1820	2,439	209	2,648
1768	635	—	635	1821	2,355	204	2,560
1769	655	—	654	1822	2,315	204	2,519
1770	683	—	683	1823	2,303	204	2,507
1771	666	—	666	1824	2,348	211	2,559
1772	674	—	674	1825	2,329	225	2,554
1773	673	—	673	1826	2,411	224	2,636
1774	682	—	682	1827	2,181	279	2,460
1775	697	—	697	1828	2,193	323	2,516
1776	695	—	695	1829	2,200	317	2,517
1777	699	—	699	1830	2,201	330	2,532
1778	701	—	701	1831	2,224	358	2,582
1779	663	—	663	1832	2,262	356	2,618
1780	619	—	610	1833	2,271	363	2,634
1781	626	—	626	1834	2,312	404	2,716
1782	615	—	615	1835	2,360	423	2,783
1783	670	—	670	1836	2,350	443	2,792
1784	793	—	793	1837	2,333	457	2,791
1785	860	—	860	1838	2,421	470	2,891
1786	932	—	932	1839	2,401	498	2,899
1787	1,088	—	1,088	1840	2,584	543	3,128
	United Kingdom		British Empire	1841	2,935	577	3,512
				1842	3,041	578	3,620
1788	1,275	81	1,360	1843	3,007	581	3,588
1789	1,303	87	1,391	1844	3,044	593	3,637
1790	1,376	90	1,461	1845	3,123	591	3,714
1791	1,415	96	1,511	1846	3,200	617	3,817
1792	1,437	103	1,540	1847	3,306	645	3,952
1793	1,453	111	1,564	1848	3,401	651	4,052
1794	1,456	133	1,590	1849	3,485	658	4,144
1795	1,426	119	1,574	1850	3,565	668	4,232
1796	1,460	159	1,619	1851	3,662	670	4,332
1797	1,454	161	1,615	1852	3,759	665	4,424
1798	1,494	172	1,666	1853	4,030	734	4,764
1799	1,551	202	1,753	1854	4,249	794	5,043
1800	1,698	157	1,856	1855	4,349	901	5,250
1801	1,786	202	2,038	1856	4,367	945	5,312
1802	1,901	227	2,128	1857	4,559	973	5,531
1803	1,986	182	2,168	1858	4,658	952	5,610
1804	2,077	191	2,268	1859	4,663	997	5,660
1805	2,093	191	2,284	1860	4,659	1,052	5,711
1806	2,080	184	2,264	1861	4,807	1,088	5,895
1807	2,097	184	2,281	1862	4,934	1,108	6,041
1808	2,130	194	2,324	1863	5,328	1,296	6,624
1809	2,167	201	2,368	1864	5,627	1,476	7,103
1810	2,211	215	2,426	1865	5,760	1,562	7,322
1811	2,247	227	2,474	1866	5,779	1,518	7,298
1812	2,263	216	2,479	1867	5,754	1,479	7,233
1813	2,349	165	2,514	1868	5,780	1,455	7,236
1814	2,414	203	2,617	1869	5,714	1,456	7,170
1815	2,478	203	2,681	1870	5,691	1,458	7,149

RAILWAYS.

Railways in the United Kingdom.

Years	Number of Miles open in the United Kingdom at the end of each Year	Total Capital, Paid up Shares, Loans, &c. (Thousands omitted)	Number of Passengers (Thousands omitted)
		£	
Ending June 30			
1845	2,441	88,481	33,791
1846	3,036	126,296	43,791
1847	3,945	167,322	51,352
1848	5,127	200,173	57,965
1849	6,031	229,748	63,842
1850	6,621	240,271	72,854
1851	6,890	248,211	85,391
Ending December 31			
1852	7,336	264,165	89,136
1853	7,686	273,324	102,287
1854	8,054	286,069	111,207
1855	8,280	297,585	118,595
1856	8,707	307,595	129,347
1857	9,094	315,375	139,009
1858	9,542	325,375	139,194
1859	10,002	334,364	149,807
1860	10,433	348,130	163,483
1861	10,869	362,327	173,773
1862	11,551	385,218	180,486
1863	12,229	404,215	204,699
1864	12,789	425,719	229,349
1865	13,289	455,478	251,959
1866	13,854	481,872	274,404
1867	14,247	502,263	287,808
1868	13,803	511,681	301,136
1869	15,145	518,779	305,761
1870	15,537	529,909	330,004

RATE OF INTEREST.

Rates of Discount for First Class Bills in the London Money Market, from the Second Report of Committee on Commercial Distress, p. 37.

Years	Months	Per cent.
1824	January	3½
1825	June	4
	November	4½
1826	January	5
	June	4½
	August	4
1827	February	3½
	June	3
1828	December	3½
1829	January	4
	February	3½
	April	4
	May	3½
	August	3
1830	March	2¾
	May	2½
	October	2¾
	November	3
	December	4
1831	January	3¼
	February	3
	March	3½
	May	4
	August	3½
	October	4
1832	February	3½
	March	3¼
	July	3
	October	2⅝
1833	January	2¾
	February	2½
	March	2¼
	May	2½
	September	3
	November	3¼
1834	February	3
	March	2¾
	April	3
	May	3¼
1834	September	4
	October	3¾
1835	February	3¼
	March	3½
	April	3¾
	June	4
	August	3½
	September	3¾
1836	March	3½
	April	3½
	June	4
	August	4½
	September	5
	November	5½
1837	May	4½
	August	4
	September	3½
	November	3¼
	December	3½
1838	February	3
	April	2¾
	May	2½
	June	2¾
	July	3
	August	2¾
	September	3
	November	3½
	December	3½
1839	January	3¾
	May	4
	June	5
	July	5½
	August	6
	September	6½
1840	January	5
	February	4¾
	May	4½
	June	4¾
	July	4½
1840	September	4¾
	October	5
	November	6
	December	5¾
1841	January	5½
	February	5
	April	4½
	June	5
	July	4½
	September	4¾
	October	5
	November	5½
	December	5
1842	January	4¾
	February	4¼
	March	3¾
	May	3¼
	June	3½
	July	3½
	August	3
	September	2½
	October	2¾
	November	2½
1843	January	2½
	February	2¼
	March	2
	June	2½
	August	3
	October	2¼
	November	2
	December	2½
1844	January	2½
	February	2
	May	1¾
	June	2
	August	1¾
	September	2
	October	2¼
	November	2¾

Minimum Rates of Interest charged by the Bank of England, with the Dates when such Minimum Rates were fixed; from the Passing of the Bank Charter Act, 1844.

Years	Months	Per cent.	Years	Months	Per cent.	Years	Months	Per cent.
1844	Before the pass-		1856	4 December	6½	1862	9 January	2½
	ing of the Act	4		18 December	6		22 May	3
	5 September	2½	1857	2 April	6½		10 July	2½
1845	16 October	3		18 June	6		24 July	2
1846	6 November	3½		16 July	5½		30 October	3
	27 August	3		8 October	6	1863	15 January	4
1847	14 January	3½		12 October	7		28 January	5
	21 January	4		19 October	8		19 February	4
	8 April	5		5 November	9		23 April	3½
	5 August	5½		9 November	10		30 April	3
	25 October	8		24 December	8		16 May	3½
	22 November	7	1858	7 January	6		21 May	4
	2 December	6		14 January	5		2 November	5
	23 December	5		28 January	4		5 November	6
1848	27 January	4		4 February	3½		2 December	7
	15 June	3½		11 February	3		3 December	8
	2 November	3		9 December	2½		24 December	7
1849	22 November	2½	1859	28 April	3½	1864	20 January	8
1850	26 December	3		5 May	4½		11 February	7
1851	—	3		2 June	3½		25 February	6
1852	1 January	2½		9 June	3		16 April	7
	22 April	2		14 July	2½		2 May	8
1853	6 January	2½	1860	19 January	3		5 May	9
	20 January	3		31 January	4		19 May	8
	2 June	3½		29 March	4½		26 May	7
	1 September	4		12 April	5		16 June	6
	15 September	4½		10 May	4½		25 July	7
	29 September	5		24 May	4		4 August	8
1854	11 May	5½		8 November	4½		8 September	9
	3 August	5		13 November	5		10 November	8
1855	5 April	4½		15 November	6		24 November	7
	3 May	4		29 November	5		15 December	6
	14 June	3½		31 December	6	1865	12 January	5½
	6 September	4	1861	7 January	7		26 January	5
	13 September	4½		14 February	8		2 March	4½
	27 September	5		21 March	7		30 March	4
	4 October	5½		4 April	6		4 May	4½
	18 October	6 & 7		11 April	5		25 May	4
1856	22 May	6		16 May	6		1 June	3½
	29 May	5		1 August	5		15 June	3
	26 June	4½		15 August	4½		27 July	3½
	1 October	5		29 August	4		3 August	4
	6 October	6 & 7		19 September	3½		28 September	4½
	13 November	7		7 November	3		2 October	5½

Minimum Rates of Interest charged by the Bank of England—continued.

Years	Months	Per cent.	Years	Months	Per cent.	Years	Months	Per cent.
1865	5 October	6	1866	6 September	5	1869	15 July	3
	7 October	7		27 September	4½		10 August	2½
	23 November	6		8 November	4		4 November	3
	28 December	7		20 December	3½	1870	21 July	3½
1866	4 January	8	1867	7 February	3		23 July	4
	22 February	7		30 May	2½		28 July	5
	15 March	6		25 July	2		4 August	6
	3 May	7	1868	19 November	2½		11 August	5½
	8 May	8		3 December	3		18 August	4½
	11 May	9	1869	1 April	4		25 August	4
	12 May	10		6 May	4½		1 September	3½
	16 August	8		10 June	4		15 September	3
	23 August	7		24 June	3½		29 September	2½
	30 August	6						

CIRCULATION.

Average Annual Circulation of Bank of England Notes, 1792–1871.

Years	Number	Years	Number	Years	Number
	£		£		£
1792	11,407	1819	17,915	1846	20,286
1793	11,589	1820	17,223	1847	19,155
1794	11,833	1821	17,429	1848	18,085
1795	11,483	1822	16,825	1849	18,403
1796	11,221	1823	18,034	1850	19,398
1797*	10,990	1824	19,677	1851	19,473
1798*	12,568	1825	19,880	1852	21,856
1799*	13,471	1826	21,068	1853	22,633
1800*	15,150	1827	21,217	1854	20,709
1801*	15,809	1828	20,616	1855	19,793
1802*	16,579	1829	19,399	1856	19,648
1803*	16,465	1830	20,174	1857	19,467
1804*	17,407	1831	18,008	1858	20,222
1805	15,518	1832	18,201	1859	21,318
1806	12,493	1833	19,102	1860	21,270
1807	12,540	1834	18,800	1861	20,019
1808	13,009	1835	18,057	1862	20,844
1809	14,026	1836	17,846	1863	20,675
1810	15,918	1837	18,334	1864	20,587
1811	15,875	1838	18,976	1865	21,096
1812	15,689	1839	17,628	1866	23,197
1813	16,069	1840	16,793	1867	23,465
1814	17,903	1841	16,895	1868	23,924
1815	17,660	1842	17,561	1869	23,455
1816	17,583	1843	19,559	1870	23,312
1817	20,558	1844	20,251	1871	24,410
1818	19,737	1845	20,722		

* Include Bank notes under 5*l.*

WEALTH.

Amount of Gains arising from any Profession or Trade Assessed to Income Tax.

Thousands omitted.

Years	England	Scotland	Great Britain	Ireland	United Kingdom
	£	£	£	£	£
1843	63,022	8,308	71,330		
1844	56,627	8,401	65,029		
1845	55,506	9,589	65,095		
1846	60,888	9,104	70,292		
1847	60,867	9,709	70,576		
1848	60,068	10,123	70,192		
1849	56,702	10,352	67,061		
1850	51,977	9,956	64,931		
1851	55,587	10,130	65,717		
1852	58,451	10,627	69,078		
1853	59,863	10,175	70,038		
1854	76,216	12,186	88,402		
1855	74,610	11,890	86,500	4,780	91,280
1856	72,579	11,003	83,582	4,019	88,201
1857	78,512	11,109	81,621	4,578	89,199
1858	77,503	8,548	86,051	4,788	90,839
1859	77,412	8,071	85,513	4,852	90,365
1860	81,931	8,626	90,517	4,892	95,439
1861	81,531	8,373	89,904	4,836	91,740
1862	85,209	9,306	91,515	4,859	99,373
1863	88,810	9,464	98,274	4,816	103,121
1864	96,083	10,309	107,292	4,919	112,210
1865	106,898	11,901	118,799	5,276	124,075
1866	115,602	12,901	127,797	5,932	134,439
1867	147,679	17,677	160,856	5,733	173,089*
1868	147,576	16,562	164,138	7,710	171,848
1869	149,451	16,075	165,526	7,527	173,064

* The assessments on quarries, mines, ironworks, canals, railways, gasworks, etc., were transferred from Schedule A to Schedule D, from April 6, 1866.

Progress of Great Britain in Population and Wealth.

(Deduced from the Census Reports and from Returns of the House of Commons, 511 of 1868, and 454 of 1870.)

Thousands omitted.

England	Population 1811	Population 1871	Population Per Cent Increase	Assessed Income to Income and Property Tax under Schedule A. 1814–15	Schedule A. 1869–70	Schedule A. Per Cent. Increase	Assessed Income to Income and Property Tax under Schedule D. 1814–15	Schedule D. 1869–70	Schedule D. Per Cent. Increase	Income per Head under Schedules A and D 1814–15	Income per Head 1869–70	Percentage Increase or decrease in 60 years
Agricultural Counties:				£	£		£	£		£ s. d.	£ s. d.	
Bedford . . .	70	146	108	365	786	115	98	381	288	6 12 3	7 19 10	21
Berks . . .	119	196	64	721	1,193	65	300	730	143	8 11 7	9 16 2	14
Bucks . . .	118	176	19	664	1,112	67	223	427	91	7 10 4	9 0 0	20
Cambridge . . .	101	186	84	703	1,380	96	234	663	183	9 8 6	10 19 9	18
Cumberland . . .	134	220	64	736	1,078	46	180	917	426	6 16 9	9 4 1	31
Devon . . .	383	601	57	1,925	3,029	57	697	1,811	159	6 16 11	8 11 0	24
Dorset . . .	125	198	58	724	1,123	55	242	424	75	7 14 6	7 19 8	3
Essex . . .	252	466	85	1,581	2,682	69	601	1,161	93	8 13 2	8 4 11	−9
Hereford . . .	91	125	32	630	918	50	62	229	253	7 7 3	9 8 8	27
Hertford . . .	111	193	73	584	1,154	97	262	683	161	7 12 5	9 5 2	21
Huntingdon . . .	42	64	52	326	470	44	108	187	73	10 6 8	10 5 4	—
Lincoln . . .	238	437	41	2,093	3,528	68	374	1,120	199	10 7 3	9 18 6	15
Norfolk . . .	292	439	50	1,572	2,923	86	523	1,116	216	8 19 4	9 0 10	30
Northampton . . .	141	244	73	918	1,581	67	185	604	226	7 12 1	8 19 0	−15
Oxford . . .	120	178	48	791	1,191	50	309	570	84	9 3 4	9 17 10	8
Rutland . . .	16	22	37	138	192	39	31	56	80	10 11 3	11 5 5	6
Salop . . .	165	218	34	1,085	1,514	42	279	749	168	7 7 5	5 4 7	−29
Somerset . . .	303	463	52	2,397	3,229	40	1,283	2,089	112	11 13 0	13 9 7	15
Suffolk . . .	231	348	48	1,148	2,089	81	444	858	93	6 16 1	8 8 9	24
Southampton . . .	245	544	122	1,237	2,518	103	919	1,889	84	8 16 5	7 14 8	12
Westmoreland . . .	46	65	41	299	385	28	52	187	240	7 12 7	8 16 0	−18
Wilts . . .	192	257	33	1,206	1,654	37	380	740	96	8 5 8	9 6 9	12
	3,561	5,814	63	21,712	35,692	64	7,736	19,367	187	8 8 0	9 5 2	12

Industrial and Mining Counties:												
Gloucester . . .	286	534	90	1,319	1,929	46	357	1,131	211	5 17 2	5 14 8	−2
Stafford . . .	295	857	190	1,198	3,139	161	517	3,915	661	5 18 3	8 5 4	42
Northumberland .	183	387	106	1,368	1,839	34	411	2,306	400	9 16 7	9 19 9	1
Durham . . .	165	685	315	805	1,782	121	219	3,266	1,211	6 7 7	7 13 6	12
Derby . . .	185	381	105	883	1,656	88	210	3,051	1,851	5 12 9	12 7 2	130
Cornwall . . .	221	362	63	921	1,295	40	234	910	288	5 4 9	5 19 10	15
Monmouth . . .	62	195	214	303	617	103	111	749	574	6 10 4	7 3 2	10
Warwick . . .	229	634	172	1,270	3,168	149	666	3,972	496	6 9 0	11 5 2	33
Worcester . . .	169	339	100	819	1,712	109	274	1,300	374	6 9 4	8 17 9	37
	1,795	4,374	143	8,889	17,165	93	3,059	20,536	571	6 13 1	8 12 4	29
Textile Counties:												
Lancashire . . .	838	2,819	240	3,129	12,099	285	2,288	24,462	971	6 10 11	12 19 8	97
Yorkshire . . .	985	2,135	145	4,761	11,036	131	1,717	14,875	766	6 11 5	10 12 10	63
Chester . . .	227	561	147	1,115	2,671	139	287	1,778	219	6 3 6	7 18 7	28
Leicester . . .	150	269	79	982	1,576	60	320	932	168	8 9 7	9 9 6	8
Nottingham . . .	163	820	96	747	1,600	114	314	1,288	310	6 10 2	9 0 6	38
	2,363	6,404	171	10,714	28,982	169	4,921	43,335	779	6 12 8	11 5 10	69
Metropolitan Counties:												
Middlesex . . .	953	2,539	166	5,666	18,052	218	14,687	52,375	256	21 15 3	37 14 9	27
Kent . . .	372	847	127	1,690	4,776	182	1,622	3,024	86	8 18 1	9 4 2	3
Surrey . . .	321	1,090	236	1,577	5,717	263	1,582	7,060	345	9 15 0	11 14 5	20
Sussex . . .	190	417	119	920	2,605	183	366	1,609	339	8 15 4	10 3 1	49
	1,839	4,893	167	9,853	31,150	216	18,258	60,068	250	15 5 9	19 11 10	25

Progress of Great Britain in Population and Wealth—continued.

Thousands omitted.

	Population.			Assessed Income to Income and Property Tax under Schedule A			Assessed Income to Income and Property Tax under Schedule D			Property per Head.		Increase Per Cent.
	1811	1871	Increase Per Cent.	1814-15	1869-70	Increase Per Cent.	1814-15	1869-70	Increase Per Cent.	1814-15	1869-70	
ENGLAND:				£	£		£	£		£ s. d.	£ s. d.	
Agricultural counties	3,561	5,814	63	21,712	35,692	61	7,786	18,367	137	8 3 0	9 5 11	12
Industrial and mining counties	1,795	4,374	142	8,889	17,165	93	3,059	20,536	571	6 13 1	8 12 4	29
Textile counties . .	2,358	6,401	171	16,714	28,983	169	4,927	43,344	779	6 12 8	11 5 10	69
Metropolitan counties	1,889	4,896	167	9,866	31,153	216	18,258	64,068	250	15 5 9	19 4 10	26
ENGLAND	9,553	21,488	125	51,171	112,992	120	33,980	186,318	330	9 19 1	12 1 4	20
WALES	611	1,216	98	2,824	4,560	96	807	8,554	1,057	4 6 1	6 15 1	51
SCOTLAND	1,806	3,359	96	6,611	14,272	115	2,771	16,624	490	5 4 3	9 4 0	80
GREAT BRITAIN . . .	11,969	26,063	118	60,189	181,814	119	37,058	166,493	349	8 2 5	11 9 1	41

TREATIES OF COMMERCE.

Treaties of Commerce and Navigation between the United Kingdom and Foreign Countries.

Those marked with asterisks have the 'Most favoured clause,' viz. that any favour, privilege, or reduction in the tariff of duties of importation or exportation, which either of the contracting parties may concede to any third power, shall be extended immediately and unconditionally to the other.

EUROPE.

AUSTRIA.

3 October	1813	16 December	1865*
5 November	1815	30 April	1868
3 July	1838	30 December	1869

BELGIUM.

27 October	1851	1 May	1861
8 April	1852	23 July	1862*

DENMARK.

11 July	1770	16 June	1824*
14 January	1814		

FRANCE.

23 August	1814	23 January	1860*
30 May	1814	27 June	1860
20 November	1815	12 October	1860
26 January	1826*	16 November	1860
8 February	1826		

GERMANY.

Reuss Greitz, Reuss Schleiz, Saxony, Schwarzburg, Thuringian Union			2 March	1841*
Baden			10 May	1847*
Bremen	29 September	1825	3 August	1841
Frankfort	13 May	1832	29 December	1835
Hanover	22 July	1844	22 June	1861
Hanse Towns	20 September	1825	3 August	1841
Lubeck			29 September	1825
Luxembourg			3 August	1841
Mecklenburg Schwerin, Mecklenburg Strelitz			1 May	1844*
Nassau			2 May	1841
Oldenburg			4 April	1844
Prussia	5 November	1815	2 April	1824
	20 May	1827	2 March	1841*

EUROPE—*continued.*

Anhalt, Baden, Bavaria, Brunswick, Frankfort, Hanover, Lippe, Luxemburg, Mecklenburg Schwerin, Mecklenburg Strelitz, Nassau, Oldenburg, Prussia, Reuss Greitz, Reuss Schleitz, Saxony, Schwarzburg, Thuringia, Saxe Altenby, Coburg Gotha, Meiningen and Weimar, and Waldeck . . . . . . 30 May 1866*

ITALY.

6 August	1863*	26 November	1867

PORTUGAL.

29 January	1642	27 December	1703
10 July	1654	22 July	1835
23 June	1661	18 January	1836
16 May	1703	3 July	1842*

SPAIN.

13 May	1667	5 October	1750
23 May	1667	10 February	1763
18 July	1670	3 September	1786
12 September	1700	14 July	1786
2 July	1713	28 October	1790
13 July	1713	14 January	1809
28 November	1713	5 July	1814
7 December	1713	28 August	1814
3 December	1715	9 February	1824
14 December	1718	3 January	1852
4 November	1729	7 July	1857

SWEDEN.

11 April	1654	18 July	1812
9 May	1654	3 March	1813
17 July	1656	24 April	1824
21 October	1661	18 March	1826*
5 February	1766		

SWITZERLAND.

6 September	1855*

NETHERLANDS.

13 August	1814	27 October	1837*
12 August	1815	8 August	1850
17 March	1824*	27 March	1851*
21 December	1815		

RUSSIA IN EUROPE AND ASIA.

18 July	1812	30 March	1856
11 January	1843	12 January	1859*

TURKEY IN EUROPE AND ASIA.

5 January	1809	19 August	1858
16 August	1838	29 April	1861*

EUROPE—*continued.*

GERMANY.

Wurtemburg	2 March	1841	30 May	1865*
Zollverein	2 March	1841	30 May	1865*
Minor States	2 March	1841	30 May	1865*

GREECE.

4 October	1837	29 March	1864

ASIA.

AVA.

24 February	1826
23 November	1826

BORNEO.

27 May	1847*

CHINA.

29 August	1842
8 October	1843*
4 April	1846
6 April	1847
26 June	1858*
24 October	1860

PERSIA.

January	1801
25 November	1814
28 October	1841
4 March	1857*

SIAM.

20 June	1826*
18 April	1855*
13 May	1856*

JAPAN.

14 October	1854
26 August	1858*
22 October	1864
26 June	1866
1 January	1868

AFRICA.

ABYSSINIA.

2 November	1849*

ADEN.

2 November	1839

ALGIERS.

16 April	1682
28 August	1816

EGYPT.

16 August	1838
15 July	1840

COMORO.

3 June	1850

JOHANNA.

3 June	1850

LIBERIA.

21 November	1848*

MOROCCO.

23 January	1721
1 February	1751
28 July	1760

MOROCCO—*continued.*

8 April	1791
14 June	1801
9 December	1856*

TRIPOLI.

18 October	1662
5 March	1675
1 May	1676
11 October	1694
19 July	1716
19 September	1750
22 July	1762
10 May	1812
29 April	1816

TUNIS.

5 October	1662
30 August	1716
19 October	1751
22 June	1762
2 May	1812
17 April	1816
9 September	1825

Sandwich Islands.

31 July 1843
14 February 1844
26 March 1846

Madagascar.

27 June 1865

AMERICA.

Argentine Confederation.

2 February . . . 1825*

Bolivia.

5 June 1837
29 September . . . 1840*

Brazil.

19 February . . . 1810
17 August 1827 (expired 1844)

Chili.

10 May 1852
4 October . . . 1854*

Costa Rica.

27 November . . . 1849*

Columbia.

18 April 1825*

Dominica.

6 May 1850*

Equator.

16 April 1825
3 May 1851*

Honduras.

27 August 1856

Mexico.

14 July 1786
26 December . . . 1826*

New Grenada.

18 April 1825
28 January . . . 1850
11 February . . . 1860

Paraguay.

4 March 1853

Peru.

5 June 1837
10 April 1850*

Parana, Uruguay, Argentine Confederation.

10 July 1853

Salvador.

24 October . . . 1862*

Texas.

13 November . . . 1840

United States.

24 December . . . 1814
3 July 1815*
20 October . . . 1818*
6 August 1827*
19 April 1850

Uruguay.

5 June 1854
26 August 1842

Venezuela.

26 August 1842
18 April 1825*
29 October . . . 1834

INDEX.

www.ingramcontent.com/pod-product-compliance
Lightning Source LLC
Chambersburg PA
CBHW031946290426
44108CB00011B/700